W9-CHT-798

The Financial System and the Economy

The Financial System and the Economy

Maureen Burton

California State Polytechnic University Pomona

Ray Lombra

Pennsylvania State University

WEST PUBLISHING COMPANY

Minneapolis/St. Paul • New York • Los Angeles • San Francisco

WEST'S COMMITMENT TO THE ENVIRONMENT

In 1906, West Publishing Company began recycling materials left over from the production of books. This began a tradition of efficient and responsible use of resources. Today, 100% of our legal bound volumes are printed on acid-free, recycled paper consisting of 50% new paper pulp and 50% paper that has undergone a de-inking process. We also use vegetable-based inks to print all of our books. West recycles nearly 27,700,000 pounds of scrap paper annually—the equivalent of 229,300 trees. Since the 1960s, West has devised ways to capture and recycle waste inks, solvents, oils, and vapors created in the printing process. We also recycle plastics of all kinds, wood, glass, corrugated cardboard, and batteries, and have eliminated the use of polystyrene book packaging. We at West are proud of the longevity and the scope of our commitment to the environment.

West Pocket parts and advance sheets are printed on recyclable paper and can be collected and recycled with newspapers. Staples do not have to be removed. Bound volumes can be recycled after removing the cover.

Production, Prepress, Printing and Binding by West Publishing Company.

British Library Cataloguing-in-Publication Data. A catalogue record for this book is available from the British Library.

Cover Images: Comstock, Superstock and Tony Stone Images
Indexer: Terry Casey
Text Designer: Merry Obrecht Sawdey
Copyediting: Cheryl Wilms
Art: Patricia Isaacs, Parrot Graphics
Composition: Parkwood Composition Services, Inc.

Photo credits follow index.

COPYRIGHT ©1997   By WEST PUBLISHING COMPANY
                    610 Opperman Drive
                    P.O. Box 64526
                    St. Paul, MN 55164-0526

All rights reserved

Printed in the United States of America

04 03 02 01 00 99 98 97   8 7 6 5 4 3 2 1 0

Library of Congress Cataloging-in-Publication Data

Burton, Maureen.
    The financial system and the economy / Maureen Burton, Ray Lombra.
        p.   cm.
    Includes bibliographical references and index.
    ISBN 0-314-09503-9 (alk. paper)
    1. Finance. 2. Money 3. Banks and banking. 4. Financial
institutions. 5. Financial services industry. 6. Monetary policy.
I. Lombra, Raymond E. II. Title.
HG173.B87   1997   96-26925
332.1-dc20   CIP

*To my husband, Al Gagnon
and my children Susie and David
With special appreciation to George Galbreath*
—Maureen Burton

To my mom and dad, Elsie and Gene Lombra
—Ray Lombra

About the Authors

Maureen Burton

Maureen Burton received a BA from the University of Missouri at Columbia in 1971, an MA from California State University, Fullerton, in 1979, and a Ph.D. from the University of California at Riverside in 1986. All were in economics. She taught at Chaffey College from 1984 to 1987 and at Cal Poly Pomona since 1987 where she is a full professor, has been Coordinator of the Graduate Program, and is currently chair of the Economics Department. In addition to other publications, she co-authored an introductory text *Economics* (Harper Collins, 1987) with S. Craig Justice. Her main areas of research include monetary theory and financial markets.

Ray Lombra

Born in Hamden, Connecticut, Ray Lombra received a BA in Economics from Providence College in 1967 and an MA and Ph.D. from Penn State University in 1971. He served as a senior staff economist at the Board of Governors of the Federal Reserve System from 1971–1977 and specialized in financial markets analysis and the formulation and implementation of monetary policy. He joined the faculty of Penn State University in 1977, and has taught money and banking at the undergraduate level and monetary theory and policy at the graduate level for 20 years. He is a winner of the College distinguished teaching award for innovations and instruction and is the author and editor of 5 books and over 80 scholarly publications. Articles on monetary policy, the determination of interest rates, stock prices, and exchange rates, financial innovation, globalization, and expectations formation have appeared in leading journals, including the *Quarterly Journal of Economics,* the *Journal of Money, Credit and Banking,* the *Journal of Monetary Economics,* and the *Review of Economics and Statistics.*

Brief Table of Contents

Table of Contents

Preface

Financial markets and institutions have undergone significant changes in recent years. Transformations have been driven by technology, innovation, deregulation, competition, and financial crises. The growth of international trade and flexible exchange rates has escalated the development of international currency markets. Financial institutions have entered nontraditional venues on both the liabilities and assets sides of their balance sheets. Laws forbidding interstate banking have been overturned. Market participants have developed creative ways to hedge risks. Controversy continues over monetary policy and the increasing need for international coordination. In the late 1980s, taxpayers and regulators struggled to deal with financial instability brought on by the savings and loan debacle and problems within other intermediaries. All of these anomalies are taking place in a world with competing views regarding the linkages between the real and financial sectors and the formulation and execution of monetary policy.

The Financial System and the Economy covers the traditional material found in a money and banking text and incorporates many of the recent changes and controversies within the financial services industry.

The strength of the text is its clear and engaging writing style and strong intuitive approach. It avoids the encyclopedia approach and seeks a balance between policy, theory, and institutions. Students find it easy to understand and enjoyable to read. The text makes use of many examples and analogies to illustrate how financial innovation, technological and structural changes, and globalization affect the financial environment. Much attention is paid to how and why institutions evolve. Graphs are used sparingly and equations are used even more sparingly.

Each chapter contains many exhibits with case studies and examples that make the material more interesting for students. Exhibit topics include the Lincoln Savings and Loan Scandal, the failure of Continental Illinois, the collapse of Barings Bank and Orange County, California, paying bills over the phone, the current Federal Reserve Board, the use of intermediate targets since 1970, stock index futures and the crash of 1987, a field guide to open market operations, the secondary market in mortgages, the Phillips Curve, and how price expectations are formed.

The text is designed to be used in an introductory undergraduate course in money and banking or financial markets analysis taught in either an economics or finance department. It may also be suitable for use in a financial markets course in an MBA Program.

The Financial System and the Economy contains five parts:

◆ Part I consists of a five-chapter introduction. The student is introduced to the economy, money and credit, financial intermediaries, the circular flow, and the Federal Reserve System.

◆ Part II (five chapters) covers markets for financial instruments, derivatives and foreign exchange, and how relevant prices including interest rates, derivative prices, and exchange rates are determined.

◆ Part III (five chapters) focuses on financial institutions and the forces that shape them. The roles of technology, competition, globalization, and regulations are emphasized in discussing how institutions evolve.

◆ Part IV (five chapters) covers monetary theory including the money supply process, the demand and supply of money and credit, and the financial aspects of the behavior of households, firms, government, and the foreign sector. The aggregate demand and supply model is presented and integrated with a complementary model of macro-equilibrium based on the flow of funds between sectors.

◆ Part V (four chapters) analyzes monetary policy in an increasingly globalized environment and focuses on the formulation of monetary policy by the Fed Open Market Committee and subsequent execution of the policy directive by the Trading Desk of the New York Fed. The role of the Fed watcher and the growing need for international coordination are also analyzed.

The text is designed to be flexible. After completing Part I, the instructor can emphasize financial markets and prices (Part II), financial institutions (Part III), monetary theory (Part IV), or monetary policy (Part V) depending on the focus of the class. In parts that are not being emphasized, chapters may be skipped.

Special Features

Several other features of *The Financial System and the Economy* deserve mention.

First, Chapters 18 and 19 present unique coverage about the financial aspects of the behavior of households, firms, government, and the foreign sector. Sources and uses of funds statements from the flow of funds accounts for each sector are presented.

Chapter 20 uses the aggregate demand and aggregate supply model, developed without the use of the IS-LM framework, to explain macroeconomic equilibrium. Chapter 20 also presents a model of macroeconomic equilibrium from a flow of funds framework, stressing that the macroeconomy is in equilibrium when the desired net financial investment of surplus sectors is equal to the desired net financial deficits of deficit sectors. The sources and uses of funds for each sector developed in the previous two chapters are integrated into the complete model. Chapter 21 makes the analysis more dynamic by looking at various macroeconomic disturbances and the adjustments over time.

International aspects of financial markets and institutions are mixed throughout the body of the text and in international boxes. In addition, two chapters are devoted to international coverage. Chapter 9 analyzes exchange rate determination and Chapter 24 looks at monetary policy under either fixed or flexible exchange rate systems in an increasingly globalized environment.

In addition to the traditional material covered in the policy section, the text looks in detail at how the Fed Open Market Committee makes decisions and how those decisions are implemented by the New York Fed.

The text contains annotated suggested readings that give the student some idea about how the readings relate to the material in the chapter. In addition, the suggested readings sections contain internet and world wide web addresses that pertain to financial markets and institutions.

An appendix includes descriptions of materials found on internet and world-wide web addresses relating to financial markets. Students with access to the internet and the world-wide web will be able to obtain information that pertains to the financial sector.

Some chapters have review and analytical questions and problems that direct the student to go to a world-wide web or internet address to locate and analyze financial market data.

Pedagogical Tools

In addition to presenting the material in a clear and concise manner, we have incorporated the following pedagogical tools to enhance the student's understanding.

1. **Learning Objectives** at the beginning of each chapter tell the student where the chapter is heading and what questions will be answered.
2. Three to five **RECAP** sections are dispersed throughout each chapter summarizing analytical material the student should know before moving forward.
3. Twenty-one boxed sections called **Looking Out, Looking Back,** or **Looking Forward** contain historical and international material as well as projections about the future.
4. Sections called **Cracking the Code** teach students how to read the financial pages of daily newspapers including futures and options prices, and stock, bond, and Treasury bill quotes.
5. **Key Terms** are bold-faced in the text where they are defined, listed at the end of each chapter, and appear as **Margin Definitions.**
6. **Chapter Summaries** are clear and well written.
7. A **Glossary** at the end of the text defines all of the key terms in the text.
8. Annotated **Suggested Readings** direct the student to related materials and include information available on the internet.
9. **Review and Analytical Questions** appear at the end of each chapter. In addition, chapters contain optional questions that instruct the student to obtain information from an internet site.
10. An **Appendix on Internet and World-Wide Web Sites, prepared by Meenakshi Rishi of Ohio Northern University,** contains information about financial markets and institutions. The student is given the type of material included along with the internet address. Many of these internet sites are also mentioned in the Suggested Readings and used in the Review and Analytical Questions.
11. **Answers to Odd-Numbered Review and Analytical Questions** appear at the end of the text.

Supplementary Materials

◆ **Study Guide:** Written by Reynold Nesiba of Augustana College in South Dakota, this supplement provides chapter outlines and review questions to reinforce each chapter of the text.

- ◆ **Instructor's Manual:** Prepared by Angel Perez, the manual includes chapter outlines, chapter summaries, key terms, solution to all chapter questions, solutions to internet problems, and additional questions for classroom discussion.
- ◆ **Test Bank:** Developed by Melanie Paiste, it contains approximately seventy multiple-choice items per chapter, many of which have been classroom tested by the text authors.
- ◆ **Transparencies:** There are 175 four-color transparencies selected by the author which include key exhibits and chapter objectives.

Acknowledgments

Many people made important contributions to this text. Special thanks go to Bob Horan, the editor at West who was always supportive, creative, and helpful. Without his persistence and dedication, this text would not be published. Others at West also deserve recognition. Sandi Dooling and Janine Wilson, competent professionals, were a pleasure to work with. The text's production editor, Stephanie Syata, did a first rate job. All of them provided immediate answers and assistance and went the extra nine yards to help with this project. We are glad for the opportunity to work with such a fine group of people.

Another person also deserves special recognition. Professor Emeritus George Galbreath spent 40 years teaching money and banking in the California State University System. For this reward, George has hundreds of students who are better people and scholars for having studied under him. He is the epitome of a great university professor. With regards to this text, George read every word of the manuscript and gave invaluable suggestions.

Four other colleagues also gave invaluable help. Drs. Mohammad Safarzadeh and Hamid Falootoom of Cal Poly Pomona gave indispensable computer assistance, Professor James Sutton of Cal Poly Ponoma gave research support and Dr. Bryan Taylor gave access to his extensive data base at Global Financial Data in Alhambra, California.

A note of appreciation goes to students, who over the past three years have taken an interest in this text, especially Michael Rowe, Carrie Meile, and Trisha Durk. In addition, I am indebted to Angel Perez, Debbie Bannister, Gabriel Watson, Sebastian Sohn, Bunchon Songsamphant, and Tim Miller for their research assistance. We would also like to thank the following outside reviewers whose comments were greatly appreciated.

Burton and Lombra reviewers

William L. Beaty
Tarleton State University

Gene Boni
County College of Morris

David W. Brasfield
Murray State University

James R. Bruehler
University of Illinois at Urbana—Champaign

Catherine Carey
Western Kentucky University

John E. Charalambakis
Asbury College

Maureen E. Dunne
Framingham State College

Frank Falero
California State University, Bakersfield

James R. Frederick
Pembroke State University

Harry Greenbaum
South Dakota State University

Nell S. Gullett
University of Tennessee at Martin

Bassam E. Harik
Western Michigan University

John J. Hatem
Georgia Southern University

Paul A. Heise
Lebanon Valley College of Pennsylvania

Colleen F. Johnson
Eastern Oregon State College

Richard H. Keehn
University of Wisconsin—Parkside

Robert J. Korbach
University of North Dakota

James W. Lynch
Robert Morris College

Jessica J. McCraw
The University of Texas at Arlington

Michael S. Miller
DePaul University

Athanasios G. Noulas
Seton Hall University

Clifford Nowell
Weber State University

James E. Payne
Eastern Kentucky University

Ronnie J. Phillips
Colorado State University

Meenakshi Rishi
Ohio Northern University

Carol Rowey
Community College of Rhode Island

William C. Schaniel
West Georgia College

M. Scott Shepherd
Southern Illinois University at Edwardsville

Richard M. Simon
Ohio Northern University

K. P. Sridharan
Delta State University

Stacey L. Suydam
Montana State University—Billings

John A. Swiger
Our Lady of the Lake University

Paul M. Taube
The University of Texas—Pan American

Daniel Teferra
Ferris State University

Duncan R. Tye
Western Carolina University

Roy Van Til
University of Maine at Farmington

Samuel C. Webb
Wichita State University

Pamela Whalley
Western Washington University

Laura Wolff
Southern Illinois University at Edwardsville

PART ONE

Introduction

1

Introduction and Overview

> *Well begun is half done.*
> —Aristotle—

Learning Objectives

After reading this chapter, you should know:

- ◆ The subject matter of economics and finance
- ◆ The general role of the financial system in a modern economy
- ◆ The major functions of financial markets and financial intermediaries
- ◆ What saving is and its uses
- ◆ How the financial system channels funds from lenders to borrowers
- ◆ The role of the Federal Reserve and its regulatory and monetary policy responsibilities

What This Book Is About

Why do home buyers now have a choice among many types of fixed and variable interest rate mortgage loans? Why has it been difficult for government policymakers to produce both low inflation and low unemployment? Why have financial regulations changed so dramatically in the last 15 years? Why does the international value of the dollar fluctuate so much? Why is the chronic federal government budget deficit such a political and economic issue? Why do banks and others pay so much attention to what the Federal Reserve is doing?

We could go on, but you get the idea. The list of questions represents only a sample of the issues that motivate the discussions of theory, institutions, and policy found throughout the text. As the previous questions indicate, these matters affect many aspects of our lives every day.

This chapter begins your study of money and the financial system. It is designed to introduce the subject matter and provide an overview of the key concepts and relationships. Most of the details are ignored and most terms are not rigorously defined and examined; this is an introduction! However, don't underestimate the importance of a good beginning.

Economic and Financial Analysis of an Ever-Changing System

In the course of our study we will examine issues and utilize modes of analysis that are part of the subject matter and methodology of modern economics and finance. Generally speaking, **economics** is the study of how a society decides what gets produced, how it gets produced, and who gets what. More specifically, given unlimited wants on the part of society, economics is concerned with the following processes:

Economics The study of how society decides what gets produced, how it gets produced, and who gets what.

1. How scarce resources (labor, capital, and natural resources) are allocated in the production process among competing uses.[1]
2. How income generated in the production and sale of goods and services is distributed among members of society.
3. How people allocate their income through spending, saving, borrowing, and lending decisions.

For methodological convenience, economics is traditionally divided into a study of the causes and consequences of individual decision-making units such as households and business firms in a particular market, and a study of the causes and the effects resulting from the sum of decisions made by all firms or households in many markets. The former type of analysis is called **microeconomics;** the latter, more aggregative analysis, is called **macroeconomics.**

Microeconomics The branch of economics that studies the behavior of individual decision-making units such as households and business firms.
Macroeconomics The branch of economics that studies the aggregate or total behavior of all households and firms.

---

[1]When capital is used in this context, economists mean machinery and equipment that is utilized to produce other goods and services. For example, a sewing machine that produces shirts is capital.

Finance is, broadly speaking, the study of the financial or monetary aspects of the production, spending, borrowing, and lending decisions already mentioned. More to the point, finance deals with the raising and using of money by individuals, firms, governments, and foreign investors. We are familiar with our decisions to spend, borrow, lend, or save. Our everyday language includes familiarity with such terms as interest rates, checking accounts, debit cards, banks, and credit cards. Finance in this context deals with how individuals, to quote Webster's Dictionary, "manage money."

At a more aggregative, macro level, finance is concerned with how the financial system coordinates and channels the flow of funds from lenders to borrowers and vice versa, and how new funds may be created by financial intermediaries in the borrowing process. The channeling and coordination process and its effects on the cost and availability of funds in the economy link developments in the financial system to developments in the rest of the economy. This aspect of financial analysis is emphasized in this text.

As you will soon learn, the production and sale of goods and services within the economic system are intimately related to the deposits, stocks and bonds, and so forth, which are bought and sold in the financial system. Put more dramatically, what happens on Wall Street can have a profound effect on what happens on Main Street, and vice versa.

Because the financial system is vital to a healthy economy, the government regulates and supervises its operation. Such regulatory policy is aimed at promoting a smooth-running, efficient financial system. By establishing and enforcing operating regulations for financial markets and institutions, regulators seek to promote competition and efficiency while preserving the safety and soundness of the system.

Complicating our analysis of the interaction between the financial system and the economy is the fact that the financial system is not stagnant. It continually evolves and changes, sometimes at a faster pace than at other times. For various reasons to be discussed in later chapters, the past two decades have seen rapid change, including increased globalization of financial markets. The system is different from what it was 20 years ago, and it will be different 20 years hence. The major forces producing these changes are changes in government regulations, and innovations in the ways people spend, save, and borrow funds.

In recent decades, firms and individuals developed new ways to raise and use money through financial innovation. Today, many manifestations of the financial innovation of recent decades are all around us. For example, most checking accounts now earn interest and 24-hour automatic teller machines (ATMs) are common. Debit cards are widely accepted at grocery stores, gas stations, and department stores. Home equity lines of credit allow homeowners to borrow against the equity in their homes by writing checks as the need arises. None of these innovations were prominent 15 years ago. Brokerage firms, such as Merrill Lynch, have merged with real estate companies, insurance companies, credit card companies, and retail firms, creating new types of financial institutions. These developments have had an impact on spending, saving, borrowing and lending decisions. Not surprisingly then, we shall closely examine the causes and consequences of these changes in the financial system.

Because of financial innovation and other factors, Congress and the regulatory authorities such as the Federal Reserve have had to reconsider the costs and benefits associated with certain regulations. From the early 1970s until the late 1980s, the resulting changes in regulation had mostly been in

Finance The study of how the financial system coordinates and channels the flow of funds from lenders to borrowers—and vice versa—and how new funds are created by financial intermediaries in the borrowing process.

Deregulation The removing or phasing out of existing regulations.

the direction of **deregulation,** which is the removing or phasing out of some existing regulations. Regulations were changed because many people felt that they had become increasingly ineffective; firms and households had found ways to get around them through financial innovation. At times, they had come to inhibit competition and weaken rather than strengthen the financial system. Financial crises, sometimes requiring taxpayer bailouts in various financial markets, produced fresh attempts at "re-regulation" during the late 1980s and early 1990s. New ways of regulating would be analyzed and tested. However, the goals of ensuring the safety and soundness of the financial system while fostering efficiency and competition would remain the same.

 ## Finance in Our Daily Lives

Money Something acceptable and generally used as payment for goods and services.

Simply put, an individual's financial objective is to make payments when due and to manage funds efficiently until needed. To make payments we need **money**—that is, something that is acceptable in payment, whether it's for a cup of coffee or rent on a beach house.[2] Throughout this book keep in mind that only money can be generally used for payments.

In our daily lives, we receive income periodically (weekly, monthly, etc.), and our expenditures are more or less continuous, depending, of course, on our lifestyles. Given this lack of synchronization between the receipt of income and expenditures, we need to manage our money over, say, a month so that funds will be available when purchases of goods and services—called consumption spending—are made. Income that is not spent on consumption is

Saving Income not spent on consumption.

called **saving.** Part of household saving may be spent directly on investment goods, such as new houses.[3] With the remainder of saving, individuals will acquire financial assets, since these funds also have to be managed.

How might these funds not used for consumption or investment in such things as houses be managed? We could take currency (paper money), put it in an empty coffee can, and bury it in the backyard. We also could put the funds into a savings or money market account to earn some interest. Other alternatives include buying corporate bonds, shares of common stock, Treasury bills, and so on. Which we buy depends on how we wish to balance the key financial characteristics of concern to savers. These include the expected return (gain) and the risk of loss associated with acquiring and holding a particular asset. Some assets, like Treasury bills, are relatively riskless; you can be pretty sure the government will pay the interest and principal you are due if you own such bills. Other assets, such as bonds issued by new corporations not yet earning significant profits may offer a much higher return, but they also carry the risk that the firm will declare bankruptcy and you will get nothing! Moreover, if an unexpected need arises and you need to get back the funds you originally lent, you want your funds to be invested in liquid assets that can be converted quickly to cash without substantial loss. Balancing such

---

[2] Credit cards are not money. When an individual uses a credit card, he or she is taking out a loan by authorizing the institution that issued the credit card to make a payment with money on his or her behalf. Ultimately, the individual must pay credit card balances with money.

[3] As used here, investment in houses is expenditures for new residential construction, which renders a service over a period of time.

considerations is the essence of the managing of a portfolio—that is, a collection of financial assets—be it by an individual or by a financial institution.

What has just been described should not be foreign to any student, but to facilitate clarity and effective communication, the terminology employed in this text must be distinguished from colloquial use. *Income* is the flow of revenue (receipts) we receive over time for our services. With this income we can buy and consume goods. If we have funds left over after consumption, we are saving and we have to decide how to allocate those funds among the various types of financial assets available or to invest them in real assets such as new houses. If, however, we spend more than we earn, we have a deficit and have to decide how to finance it. When we spend less on consumption and investment goods than our current income, we are called **surplus spending units (SSUs).** If the opposite is true, we would have a deficit and we are called **deficit spending units (DSUs).** Exhibit 1-1 portrays SSUs and DSUs.

So far we have restricted our analysis to individuals and households. However, business firms may also spend more or less than their income. In as much as business firms do not spend on consumption, all of business income is saving except income distributed as dividends to the owners of the firms. With their saving, business firms make investment expenditures in capital and inventories or acquire financial assets. The investment expenditures of firms often exceed their available funds.[4] Exhibit 1-2 shows the uses of saving for business firms and households.

The fact that some people or business firms are in deficit positions while others are in surplus positions, creates an opportunity or a need for a way to

Surplus Spending Units (SSUs) Spending units such as households and firms with income that exceeds spending. Deficit Spending Units (DSUs) Spending units such as households and firms where spending exceeds income.

---

[4] As we shall see in Chapter 18, firms also make investment expenditures to replace worn-out capital.

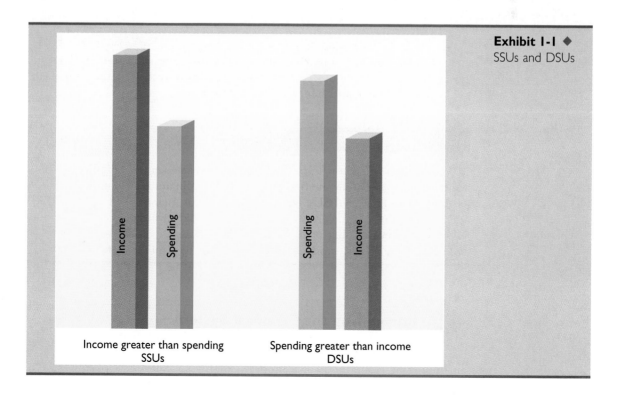

Exhibit 1-1 ◆
SSUs and DSUs

Income   Spending   Spending   Income

Income greater than spending
SSUs

Spending greater than income
DSUs

Exhibit I-2 ◆
The Uses of Saving

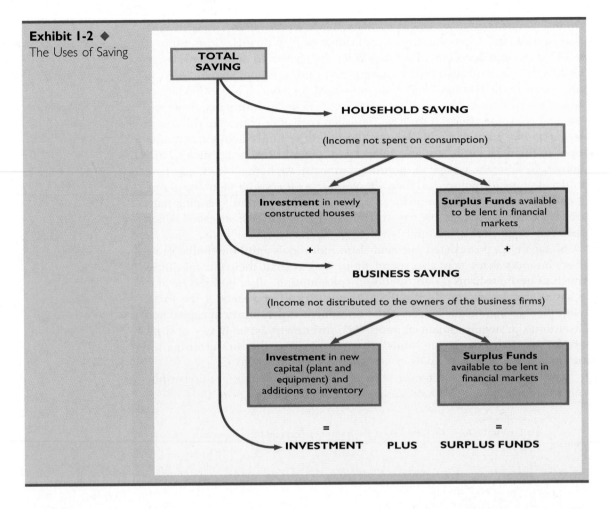

match them up. The financial system links up these SSUs and DSUs. The government and foreign sectors may also spend more or less than their current available funds and hence be SSUs or DSUs.

RECAP

Economics studies how scarce resources are allocated among conflicting wants. Finance studies how the financial system coordinates and channels the flows of funds from SSUs to DSUs. SSUs spend less than their current income. DSUs spend more than their current income. Household saving may be used for investment in new housing or to acquire financial assets. Business saving may be used for investment in capital and inventories or to acquire financial assets.

 ## Introducing the Financial System

A well-organized, efficient, smoothly functioning financial system is an important component of a modern, highly specialized economy. The financial system provides a mechanism whereby an individual unit (firm or household) that is an SSU may conveniently make funds available to DSUs who intend to spend more than their current income. The key word here is "conveniently."

The financial system has two major components. One is **financial markets** where the SSUs can lend their funds directly to the DSUs. An example would be the market for corporate bonds. General Motors can sell bonds, say, to finance the construction of a new plant in Mexico, and Emma from Kansas can purchase some of the bonds with the income she does not spend on goods and services. This is called **direct finance.** Purchasing stocks is another example of direct finance.

The other major component of the financial system is made up of the **financial intermediaries**—various institutions such as banks, savings and loan associations, and credit unions—that serve as go-betweens to link up SSUs and DSUs. Here the linkage between saver and borrower is indirect. For example, a household might deposit some surplus funds in a savings account at a bank, and the bank, in turn, might make a loan to a DSU. This is called **indirect finance.** Even though the ultimate lender is the SSU, the DSU owes repayment of the loan to the financial intermediary, and the financial intermediary owes repayment of the deposit to the SSU.

Exhibit 1-3 pulls together the discussion on this point. SSUs can lend funds either directly in the financial market or indirectly through financial inter-

Financial Markets Markets in which spending units trade financial claims.

Direct Finance When SSUs lend their funds directly to DSUs.

Financial Intermediaries Financial institutions that borrow from SSUs for the purpose of lending to DSUs.

Indirect Finance When DSUs borrow from financial intermediaries that have acquired the funds to lend from SSUs.

Exhibit 1-3 ◆
The Financial System

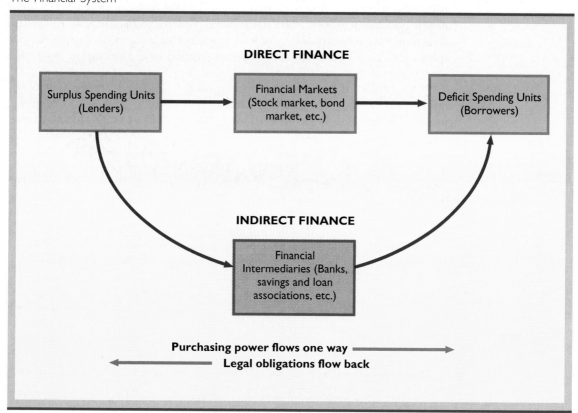

mediaries. If they lend funds in the financial markets they acquire direct or primary financial claims against the income of the borrower. The DSUs borrow funds by issuing these financial claims in the market. The claims are assets owned by the holder/purchaser; they are liabilities owed by the issuer. A perfect example would be the General Motors bonds mentioned above; they are assets to Emma and liabilities to General Motors.

If the SSUs lend funds through financial intermediaries, they acquire indirect or secondary financial claims from those intermediaries who, in turn, acquire direct claims on DSUs. Putting funds into a savings account would be a classic example of acquiring a secondary claim on a financial institution. The institution would, in turn, make loans directly to a DSU. In the lending activities of some financial intermediaries, new funds (money) may also be created, which meet the needs of a growing economy. In either case, when funds flow directly from SSUs or indirectly from intermediaries, credit is extended.

More on Financial Intermediaries

One might ask, "Why do we need financial intermediaries? Why don't savers lend directly to borrowers?" To answer this, let us begin with the initial choices and decisions that would face us as a household. If we are working, we have a steady flow of income. If we spend only part of our income on consumption and investment goods, then we are a surplus household or SSU. If we spend more than our income, then we must borrow, making us a deficit household or DSU. Since it is more pleasant to decide what to do with a surplus than to worry about how to finance a deficit, let us assume that we spend only part of our income on consumption and investment. Now what should we do with our surplus?

A SSU basically has two decisions to make. The first choice is between holding the surplus in the form of cash (paper currency and coin) or lending it out.[5] Because cash does not earn interest, we would probably decide to lend out at least a portion of our surplus funds to earn some interest income. This leads us to the second decision the surplus household must make: How and where is the surplus to be lent? We could go directly to the financial markets and purchase a new bond being issued by a corporation. Presumably we would not pick a bond at random. For example, we might consider selecting a bond issued by a reputable credit-worthy borrower who will be likely to pay the promised interest on schedule and also to repay the principal, or the original amount of the loan, when the bond matures in, say, ten years. In short, we would have to be able to appraise the risk or probability of **default,** which is the failure of the borrower to pay interest, to repay principal, or both.

Default When a borrower fails to repay a financial claim.

To minimize the risk of our surplus being wiped out by the default of a particular borrower, we might want to spread our risks out and diversify. This can be accomplished by spreading our surplus over a number of DSUs.[6] In

---

[5] There is another option. If we owe back debts, we could employ surplus funds to pay off those debts.

[6] If we have only a small amount of surplus funds available, it may be extremely difficult to diversify to a significant extent.

nontechnical terms, we would want to avoid putting all our eggs into one basket.

All of this would, of course, take time and effort. Moreover, most SSUs are not experts in appraising and diversifying risk. As a result, many would prefer to rely on others, such as financial intermediaries, for such expertise. Financial intermediaries acquire the funds of SSUs by offering claims on themselves. What this means is that the SSU has really made a loan to the financial intermediary and therefore has a financial claim on the intermediary in the amount of the surplus funds. To determine its profit, the financial intermediary subtracts what it pays to SSUs for the use of the funds from what it earns on the loans and other investments it makes with those funds. A savings and loan association is one type of financial intermediary. Like claims on other intermediaries, claims on savings and loans are called indirect or secondary claims.

The financial intermediaries pool the funds they acquire from many individual SSUs and then use the funds to make loans to businesses and households, to purchase bonds, and so forth. The intermediaries are actually lending out the surpluses they accept from individual SSUs while also appraising and diversifying the risk associated with lending directly to the DSUs. Because they specialize in this kind of work, it is reasonable to presume that they know what they are doing, and, on average, do a better job than individual SSUs could do. Put a bit more formally, financial intermediaries minimize the costs—called **transactions costs**—associated with borrowing and lending.

> **Transactions Costs** The costs associated with borrowing and lending or making other exchanges.

An additional factor that helps explain why SSUs often entrust their funds to financial intermediaries is that the secondary (indirect) claims offered by intermediaries are often more attractive to many surplus units than the primary (direct) claims available in financial markets. One reason is that, in many cases, the secondary claims of intermediaries are insured by an agency of the federal government such as the FDIC.[7] Therefore, less risk of default is often associated with holding a secondary claim rather than a primary claim.

Another reason for the attractiveness of secondary claims is that their liquidity is often greater than that associated with primary claims. **Liquidity** refers to the ease of exchanging a financial claim for cash without loss of value. Different types of claims possess varying degrees of liquidity. A claim easily exchanged for cash, such as a savings deposit, is highly liquid; a less liquid claim involves more significant time, cost, and/or inconvenience in the exchange. A rare oil painting is an example of a less liquid asset.

> **Liquidity** The ease with which a financial claim can be converted to cash without loss of value.

Suppose you loaned funds directly to a small, obscure corporation and the loan's term of maturity (the time from when you gave them the funds until they must pay back the principal) was two years. You have their financial claim in the form of a loan contract and they have your surplus funds. What would happen if, after one year, you suddenly wanted the funds back for some emergency expenditure? One possibility would be to ask the corporation to pay you back at once, before the due date of the loan. If this option is closed because the borrower is unwilling or unable to pay off the loan immediately,

---

[7] The Federal Deposit Insurance Corporation (FDIC) enables the public to feel confident that funds deposited in a bank or savings and loan, up to a limit (currently $100,000), are safe. If the institution fails, the FDIC will step in and pay off the depositors. When financial institutions were failing daily during the early years of the Great Depression in the 1930s, the government became convinced of the pressing need for such an agency.

you might try to sell the claim on the borrower to someone else who is willing to hold the claim until maturity. While organized markets do exist for the buying and selling of certain types of existing financial claims, such markets do not exist for all types of claims. The hassle associated with unloading the loan contract in a time of crisis should be obvious. To avoid such inconvenience, many SSUs would prefer to hold claims on financial intermediaries and let the "experts" worry about any problems.

Depository Institutions and Other Types of Intermediaries

Depository Institutions
Financial intermediaries that issue checkable deposits.

Checkable Deposits Deposits that are subject to withdrawal by writing a check.

The most familiar type and the largest group of financial intermediaries are **depository institutions** consisting of commercial banks, savings and loan associations, credit unions, and mutual savings banks. Not surprisingly, their principal source of funds is the deposits of individuals, business firms, and governments, both domestic and foreign. The depository institutions are particularly popular with SSUs because the secondary claims purchased by SSUs from depository institutions—that is, the deposits—are often insured, and therefore relatively safe. **Checkable deposits,** which as the name implies are subject to withdrawal by writing a check, are now offered by all depository institutions. Such deposits are money per se since they can be used in their present form as a means of payment. Other claims on depository institutions, such as savings deposits, are also quite liquid.

Other types of intermediaries offer specialized secondary claims. For example, insurance companies offer financial protection against early death (life companies) or property losses (casualty companies), while pension plans provide financial resources for one's old age. All of these specialized intermediaries collect savings in the form of premium payments or contributions from those who participate in the plans. Each intermediary then uses the funds acquired to purchase a variety of primary claims from DSUs. Investment-type intermediaries, such as mutual funds and money market funds, offer the small saver greater opportunities to diversify than would otherwise be realized by pooling the surplus funds of many small savers and investing them in financial markets. Exhibit 1-4 highlights the various types of intermediaries.

Although our analysis covers intermediation in general, we are particularly interested in the role of depository institutions. There are many important reasons for the special attention given to depository institutions. They are by far the largest type of intermediary. They also are a central part of the process determining the nation's money supply. Since one of our main objectives is to understand the nature and role of money in our economy, we will focus on the behavior of depository institutions and the process of intermediation in which they engage. By examining how money is provided, what it costs to obtain money when we need it, and what we can earn when we have enough of it to lend out, we will learn much about how money and the financial system affect the economic well-being of our economy.

RECAP

When SSUs lend directly to DSUs, direct finance occurs. When SSUs put their funds in financial intermediaries, which then lend to DSUs, indirect finance occurs. Financial intermediaries acquire the funds of SSUs by

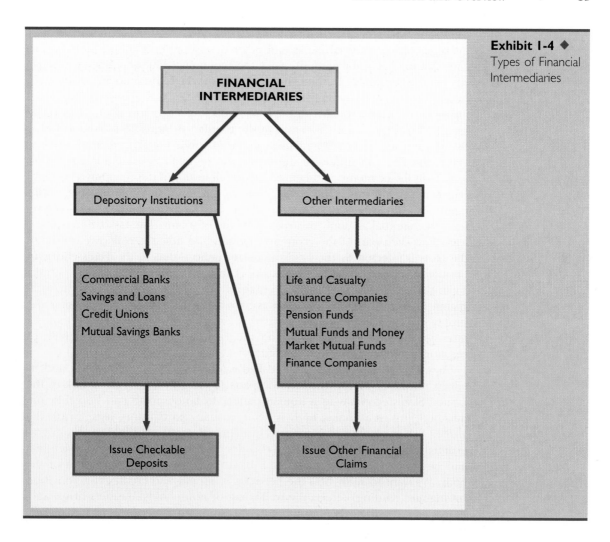

Exhibit 1-4 ◆
Types of Financial
Intermediaries

issuing claims on themselves. They use the funds to purchase the financial claims of DSUs. The most important financial intermediaries are depository institutions that issue checkable deposits.

 The Federal Reserve System

The way in which depositories serve as intermediaries and affect the money supply is greatly influenced by the **Federal Reserve.** The Federal Reserve is a quasi-independent government agency that serves as our nation's central bank. The Fed, as it is often called, has a profound influence on the behavior of banks through its regulatory policy and its ability to affect interest rates and the total volume of funds available for borrowing and lending. In recent years, depository institutions have experienced a declining share of the funds available for lending from SSUs to DSUs, while other financial institutions and nonfinan-

Federal Reserve (Fed)
The central bank of the
United States that regu-
lates the banking system
and determines monetary
policy.

cial institutions received an increasing share.[8] Because the Fed has the greatest influence on commercial banks and other depository institutions, there is concern that the Fed's ability to influence the economy through traditional avenues has actually declined. Despite this concern, the Fed continues to maintain a leading role in determining the overall health of the U.S. economy. The Fed's influence on banks spreads through a number of channels to other financial intermediaries, and more generally to the transfer of funds from SSUs to DSUs. By affecting interest rates and the volume of funds transferred from SSUs to DSUs, the Fed can influence the aggregate, or total, demand for goods and services in the economy, and hence, the overall health of the economy. A general representation of this relationship is shown in Exhibit 1-5. The middle of this figure—the financial system and economic behavior of spending units—represents the essential anatomy or structure of the economy. The task before us is to learn how each part of the economy operates and how the collective activity of the parts is affected by the Fed's **monetary policy**—that is, the Fed's efforts to promote the overall health and stability of the economy.

In terms of Exhibit 1-3, the Fed monitors the performance of the financial system and the economy with an eye towards augmenting or reducing the supply of funds flowing from SSUs through financial markets and financial intermediaries to DSUs. Any action the Fed undertakes sets off a chain of reactions as depicted in Exhibit 1-5.

As we begin to think about the Fed's conduct of monetary policy and its effects on the economy, the following analogy might be helpful: Think of the United States economy as a human patient to be observed and hopefully understood. Just as a human body is made of many parts (arms, legs, torso), the United States economy is composed of many sectors (household, business, government, and foreign). Money and the acts of spending and saving and lending and borrowing are analogous to the blood and the circulatory system of the body. We want to study how the behavior of money and credit extension (borrowing and lending) affects the well-being of households, business firms, and, more generally, the overall economy. By focusing on the borrowing and lending

Monetary Policy The Fed's efforts to promote the overall health and stability of the economy.

---

[8] Examples of very large nonfinancial institutions that have entered the lending business include General Electric (GE), American Telegraph and Telephone (AT&T), and General Motors (GM), all of which now issue credit cards.

Exhibit 1-5 ◆
The Influence of the Fed's Monetary Policy

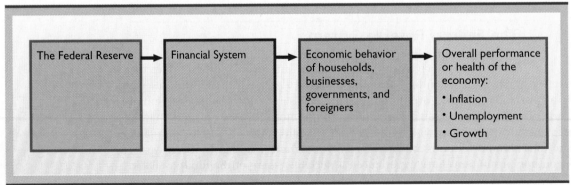

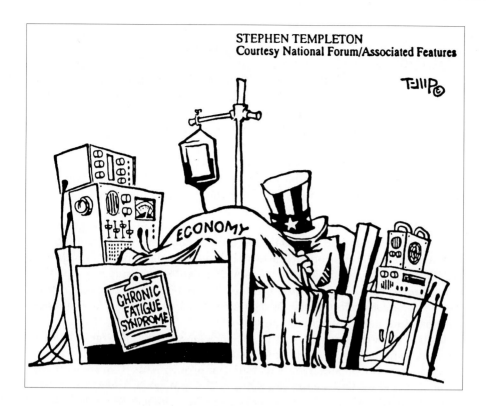

STEPHEN TEMPLETON
Courtesy National Forum/Associated Features

of money and spending and saving, we shall see how the major sectors of the economy interact to produce goods and services and to generate income.

The health of the U.S. economy varies over time. At times it appears to be well and functioning normally; at other times, it appears listless and depressed; and at still other times, it seems hyperactive—characterized by erratic, unstable behavior. By studying how all the key parts of the economy fit together, we should be able to learn something about the illnesses that can strike this patient. What causes a particular type of illness (say, inflation or unemployment)? How is the illness diagnosed? What medicines or cures can be prescribed? If more than one treatment is possible, which will work best? Are any undesirable side effects associated with particular medications? Are the doctors who diagnose the problems and administer the treatment (the policymakers) ever guilty of malpractice?

Answers to all these questions will depend in part on "what makes the patient tick" and how we define "good health." A human patient's health is determined by the deviations, if any, from a well-established set of precise criteria involving temperature, reflexes, blood chemistry, appetite, and so forth. For the economy, however, no well-established, precise criteria allow us to judge its health. Rather, loosely defined goals or objectives such as "full" employment, "low" inflation, and so on are used. If everyone agrees on these goals, including how to define and measure them, and the economy seems to be operating in the neighborhood of the goals, then we might say the economy is in good health. If we are heading toward the goals then the economy's health would be improving. On the other hand, if the economy seems to be deviating from the agreed-upon goals or objectives, then the economy is not in good health and prescriptive measures may be necessary to improve matters.

The Role of Policy: Changing Views

Good health for the economy, as with humans, has both short- and long-run dimensions. Over the long run, we and policymakers would like to have the economy grow such that the quality of life and standard of living for an increasing population can improve. In the short run, we would like to minimize the fluctuations or deviations from the long-run growth path. In economics these short-run fluctuations of the economy are part of what is appropriately called the **business cycle.** Exhibit 1-6 defines the various stages of the business cycle and illustrates their relationship with the longer-run growth of the economy.

The economy, like most of us, has its ups and downs. During a recovery or **expansion,** economic activity, as measured by the total quantity of goods and services being bought and sold, increases and unemployment falls. During a **recession** or contraction, economic activity falls and unemployment rises. Just before the peak, all is bright and the economy/patient seems truly healthy. When at the trough, all is bleak and the economy/patient appears quite ill. Over the longer run, a calculation of the average growth rate (trend) that smoothes out the expansions and contractions can be made.

The key question is whether policymakers can, in fact, "manage" the economy successfully. Can they use monetary policy to minimize the short-run fluctuations of the economy over its long-run growth path? Can they use government spending and taxing decisions **(fiscal policy)** to speed up or slow economic activity as needed? Can they, over time, change the growth rate of output? Since a look at the historical record does not provide an encouraging answer to this question, many have wondered about the appropriate role of policy in a modern, complex economy.

Business Cycle Short-run fluctuations in the level of economic activity as measured by the output of goods and services in the economy.

Expansion The phase of the business cycle during which economic activity increases and unemployment falls.

Recession The phase of the business cycle during which economic activity falls and unemployment rises.

Fiscal Policy Government spending and taxing decisions to speed up or slow down the level of economy activity.

Exhibit 1-6 ◆
Long-Run Economic Growth and the Business Cycle

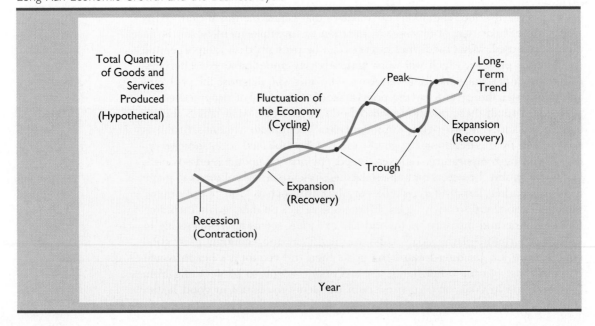

In the medical profession, before you can diagnose and deal with an ailment, considerable study and knowledge of causes and possible treatments is required. Despite the best efforts of eminent researchers, there are many things we do not know about various diseases. So too in economics; cures for all the economic ills we may encounter are not known.

Why are the goals that policymakers are trying to achieve on behalf of society so elusive? The complex answers fall into three possible areas.[9] First, the diagnosticians might fail to understand all the causes of the problems. What this really means is that we do not understand enough about how the economy functions. Second, the policymakers may be reluctant to use the currently known medicines to treat the patient because of undesirable side effects associated with particular remedies. They may, in fact, see the side effects as being worse than the disease. Third, the cure for the problem may not yet be known, so that more research will be needed to find a useful therapeutic approach. Thus far we have assumed that the illness can only be cured by the doctors and their medicines. But could the patient get better by itself?

Prior to the Great Depression of the 1930s, many economists tended to see the economy as inherently stable, having strong self-correcting tendencies. The prevailing belief was that the economy would never drift away from full-employment equilibrium for long; any disturbance or shock that pushed the economy away from full employment would automatically set in motion forces tending to move the economy back to full-employment equilibrium.[10] Thus, before the Depression, many economists felt that there was no need for corrective government action when the economy was disturbed—that any movement away from equilibrium would be temporary and self-correcting. This view of the economy provided an economic rationale for the government to pursue a **laissez-faire,** hands-off policy.

Laissez-Faire The view that government should pursue a hands-off policy with regard to the economy.

The Great Depression altered this view of the economy's internal dynamics. Between 1929 and 1933, the unemployment rate increased from about 3 percent to about 25 percent. The downturn was experienced worldwide and persisted until the start of World War II. Few could argue, in the face of such evidence, that the problem was correcting itself. The work of John Maynard Keynes and others suggested that once the economy's full-employment equilibrium was disturbed, its self-correcting powers were likely to be overwhelmed by other forces. The net result would be that the economy could operate below full employment for some time.

This new perspective gave the government an economic rationale for attempting to stabilize overall economic activity. A consensus formed that a highly developed market economy, if left to itself, would be unstable. As a result, "activist" stabilization policy has been practiced by both Democratic and Republican administrations since the mid-1930s. Until recently, there has been relatively little debate about whether the government should intervene. Rather, the debate has been about when, how, and to what degree the

---

[9] The complex answers are tackled in Part V of this text.

[10] Equilibrium is a concept used by economists to help analyze the economy. It refers to a state of the economy from which there is no tendency to deviate—a state of rest. Of course, in reality, the economy is constantly being bombarded with disturbances and is hardly ever "at rest." The concept of equilibrium, then, is an analytical device that helps us sort out the influences of many different factors which, in the real world, are often all changing at the same time.

government should use its policies to help reestablish a full-employment, low-inflation equilibrium.

The economy's performance in the 1970s and the early 1980s gave rise to doubts about the government's ability to stabilize the economy. As summarized in Exhibit 1-7, the growth trend of the economy was below that achieved in the 1960s and the fluctuations around the trend were quite large. The unemployment and inflation rates were both higher in the later decades. This raised many questions. Does the government know how to proceed in trying to restore the patient's health? If it proceeds without adequate knowledge, can policy make things worse rather than better? Many came to revert back to the view that the proper role of policy in the economy was the pre-Depression "less government intervention is better" perspective. But reducing the role of government may be elusive, with attempts in the 1980s resulting in larger government deficits and not less government.

Although the economy experienced healthy growth from about 1983 until the late 1980s, many believed that this growth was produced by large government deficits and increases in military spending. Chronic trade deficits, problem loans to less-developed countries, troubles within the savings and loan industry, and collapse of the junk bond market were of concern to many.

The recession of the early 1990s caused anxiety, not because of how deep or how long it was, but rather because of the sluggish manner in which the recovery took place. Growth remained lethargic well into the first half of 1993, and in some regions beyond that. The clear perception was that the economy was broken and needed to be fixed. The election of Bill Clinton to the presidency in 1992 focused on one issue: getting the economy back on track.

By early 1994, economic growth had accelerated and even though inflation rates remained subdued, the Fed became concerned that the high economic growth rate could precipitate inflation. Beginning in February 1994, the Fed attempted to slow the growth rate of the economy. Over the course of the next year, the Fed took actions to increase interest rates seven times. In July, 1995, the Fed reversed courses and took action that led to a small decrease in interest rates. Further actions to reduce rates were taken in December, 1995, and January, 1996. Also during 1994, what appeared to be a frustrated electorate gave the Republican Party the largest Congressional mid-term victory in history. The new Congress was committed to reducing the size and scope of government.

Exhibit 1-7 ◆
Average Inflation, Unemployment, and Growth During Recent Decades

	Inflation	Unemployment	Growth (Output)
1960s	2.4%	4.75%	4.35%
1970s	7.0	6.25	3.18
1980s	5.5*	8.25	2.77
1990–1995	3.5	6.35	1.68**

*Actually, if 1980 and 1981 are not considered, inflation averaged just under 4 percent for the remainder of the 1980s.
**Figured through 3rd quarter 1995 only.

SOURCE: *Economic Report of the President*, February, 1996.

Whether such a change in leadership will produce different and better policies and thus better performance of the economy over time remains to be seen. One thing is clear; monetary policymakers and those affected by changes in the financial environment—each one of us—will make better decisions if we understand as best we can money and credit extension and their roles in the economy.

Summary of Major Points

1. Economics is concerned with how, given people's unlimited wants, scarce resources are allocated among competing uses, how income is distributed, and how people allocate their incomes through spending, saving, borrowing, and lending decisions.

2. Finance focuses on the financial side of these decisions—that is, the raising and using of funds by households, firms, and governments.

3. The financial system coordinates and channels the flow of funds from lenders to borrowers and creates new liquidity for an expanding economy. The characteristics of this process have changed over time as innovation and changes in regulations have occurred.

4. Spending units that spend less than their current income on consumption and investment are called surplus spending units (SSUs); they are the ultimate lenders in society. Spending units that spend more than their current income are called deficit spending units (DSUs); they are the ultimate borrowers in society.

5. In allocating funds among the various types of financial assets available, SSUs are concerned about the expected return, the risk of loss, and the liquidity associated with acquiring and holding a particular asset.

6. Direct finance involves lending directly to DSUs. Indirect finance involves lending to a financial intermediary, which in turn lends to DSUs. The lenders receive financial claims and the borrowers receive funds from the financial intermediaries.

7. Financial intermediaries exist because they help to minimize the transactions costs associated with borrowing and lending. The financial services provided include appraising and diversifying risk, offering a menu of financial claims that are relatively safe and liquid, and pooling funds from individual SSUs.

8. The most important types of financial intermediaries are the depository institutions: commercial banks, savings and loan associations, mutual savings banks, and credit unions. These institutions are central to the process of determining the nation's money supply.

9. The Federal Reserve is a quasi-independent government agency that serves as our nation's central bank. Its regulatory policy is aimed at promoting a smooth-running, efficient, competitive financial system. The Fed's monetary policy, which influences interest rates and the volume of funds available for borrowing and lending (credit extension), is directed at enhancing the overall health and stability of the economy.

10. Views on the appropriate role of policy in the economy—that is, how "activist" policymakers should be in trying to manage the economy—have varied over time. Following the relatively poor performance of the economy in the 1970s, views have shifted somewhat back toward the pre-Depression perspective that "less government intervention is better."

Key Terms

Business Cycle
Checkable Deposits
Default
Deficit Spending Units (DSUs)
Depository Institutions
Deregulation
Direct Finance
Economics
Expansion
Federal Reserve
Finance
Financial Intermediaries
Financial Markets

Fiscal Policy
Indirect Finance
Laissez-Faire
Liquidity
Macroeconomics
Microeconomics
Monetary Policy
Money
Recession
Saving
Surplus Spending Units (SSUs)
Transactions Costs

Review Questions

1. Provide a short discussion or definition of the following terms: economics, finance, SSUs, DSUs, direct and indirect finance, financial intermediaries, liquidity, business cycle, depository institutions, and monetary policy.

2. Some people have money; some people need money. Explain how the financial system links these people together.

3. Dispute the statement: "Since I have high credit card limits, I have lots of money." Are credit cards money? Why or why not? (Hint: See Footnote 2.)

4. When are the surplus funds I have available to lend in financial markets equal to my saving?

5. Why do financial intermediaries exist? What services do they provide to the public?

6. What are transactions costs? Does financial intermediation increase or decrease transactions costs?

7. What is a depository institution? What is a checkable deposit? How does a depository institution differ from other intermediaries? Give three examples of depository institutions.

8. Why does the Fed monitor the economy? What actions can the Fed take to affect the overall health of the economy?

9. Why have views changed concerning the appropriate role of stabilization policies in managing the economy? Briefly discuss the historical evolution of these views.

10. What are the pros and cons of lending to my next door neighbor rather than putting my surplus funds in a bank?

11. Define laissez-faire and fiscal policy. Who determines fiscal policy? Who determines monetary policy?

Analytical Questions

12. From least to most, rank the following assets in terms of their liquidity: cash, savings deposits, gold, a house, a rare oil painting, a checkable deposit. Explain your rank order.

13. Are the following examples of direct or indirect financing?
    a. John purchases stock from the biotech firm that employs him.
    b. Mary purchases a newly issued government security.
    c. John places $3,000 in a savings account at the local savings and loan.
    d. John receives a loan from Mary.
    e. John receives a loan from Friendly Savings Bank.

14. Bill's income is $4,000. He spends $3,000 on consumption and $300 on an investment in a newly constructed house. He acquires $700 in financial assets. What is his saving? What is the amount of surplus funds he has available to lend?

15. A firm spends $100,000 on investment in plant and equipment. It has available funds of $30,000 and borrows the additional funds from a bank. Is the firm a DSU or a SSU? What is the amount of the surplus or deficit?

16. What are the phases of a business cycle? Draw a graph of a typical business cycle and label the various phases.

17. The *misery index* is defined as the sum of the unemployment and the inflation rates. Use Exhibit 1-7 to calculate the misery index for each decade since 1960.

The Financial System and the Economy

| Back | Forward | Home | Reload | Images | Open | Print | Find | Stop | N |

1. Access the following website: (http//stats.bls.gov:80/eag.table.htm). List some key economic variables that are tracked on this web page. What U.S. government agency is responsible for the data listed here?

Suggested Readings

If the material covered in the text is to come alive and make sense to you, we suggest you try to read *The Wall Street Journal* and *Business Week* regularly. In fact, hardly a day goes by without a report on an issue that is in some way relevant to our subject. You might also consult the *New York Times, Washington Post,* or the *Los Angeles Times;* all have good financial sections. . . . "or browse the financial sections of *USA Today* (http://www.usatoday.com) or CNN (http://www.cnnfn.com) on the world wide web."

Go to the library and thumb through the *Federal Reserve Bulletin.* A half-hour investment here will reveal the types of data collected and distributed by the Fed (contained in the second half of the *Bulletin*) and the range of issues the Fed concerns itself with (contained in the first half). . . . "A plethora of financial statistics can also be found in the Federal Reserve Bank Economic Database website (http://www.stls.frb.org/fred/)."

A wealth of information about the current state of the economy and attempts at stabilization by the government can be found in *The Economic Report of the President.* It is published annually during the month of February by the United States Government Printing Office and is available at the reference desk of most libraries. . . . "It is also available on the internet at (gopher:// UMSLVMA.UMSL.edu:70/11/library/govdocs/ERPS)."

The Statistical Abstract of the United States contains summary data on income, expenditures, wealth, prices, and banking and finance (among other things). It is published annually during December by the Bureau of the Census, Department of Commerce. The *Survey of Current Business,* published monthly by the Bureau of Economic Analysis, Department of Commerce, contains current business and income statistics. . . . "*The Statistical Abstract of the United States* is also available on the following Bureau of the Census website (http:// www.census.gov/ftp/pub/statab/www)."

2

Money: Some First Principles

> *If it waddles like a duck,*
> *and quacks like a duck,*
> *then it is a duck.*

Learning Objectives

After reading this chapter, you should know:

◆ How money is defined by its functions

◆ How to apply the definition in measuring what money is and what it is not

◆ Why the Federal Reserve publishes numerous measures of monetary aggregates including M1, M2, M3, and L

◆ The meaning of domestic nonfinancial debt (DNFD)

◆ How and why money and the payments system have evolved over time

◆ How the existence of money facilitates the development of an economy

Conceptualization: A Key Building Block

As the week ends in the dormitory dining hall, Mary, the dining hall supervisor, calls Randy, the dishwasher, over and gives him his pay envelope. It should contain $50. Finding the envelope somewhat thicker than normal, Randy opens it and discovers five $10 tickets to the university's Spring play next Saturday night. Tired, and somewhat irritated, especially since he has already seen the performance, he tells Mary he wants money, not these tickets. Mary tries to persuade Randy to accept the tickets instead, but fails and eventually produces a university check made out to Randy for $50.

A simple, and some might say, silly story. Yet it touches on most of the key issues addressed in this chapter: Why did Randy want money instead of the tickets? Why does he accept the check? Why aren't the tickets money? Why aren't they as good as money? Those of you who think the answers to such questions are obvious might be tempted to skip this chapter. Don't do it! As we shall see, the term *money* is used rather sloppily in everyday language. In this book, however, we need to be precise about the definition of what money is and how it is measured.

Defining Money

Unfortunately, students often treat definitions as something to be tolerated and memorized. No one would deny that memorization is a part of the learning process, but what is stored in our minds must be more than a collection of words. Definitions are part of a theoretical framework that facilitates our analysis and understanding. In the present context, understanding how money matters will be quite difficult unless we are clear on the definition of what money is and the measurement of what serves as money. Thus, defining money, the subject of this section, is of considerable importance.

A good definition enables us to separate the thing being defined from all other things. Economists define money in terms of its specific functions within the financial system; that is, by what it does. By specifying precisely what it does, we can distinguish money from everything else we observe in the financial system, even those things that at first glance appear quite similar. Of particular interest is what makes money unique; what does it do that other things do not?

The primary function of **money,** and the function that distinguishes it from all else in the financial system, is that it serves as a generally acceptable **means of payment,** or **medium of exchange.** As Chapter 1 stated, money is what we generally use to make payments, and hence, what is generally accepted as payment. The importance of money's function as a means of payment is so obvious that it is often overlooked.

Imagine a world without money where all goods were exchanged or traded by **barter**—that is, by trading goods for goods. If you worked in a computer factory, you might be paid in keyboards, which would not only be difficult to exchange for other goods and services but also rather cumbersome to carry around. To buy groceries, for example, you would have to persuade the grocer to accept your keyboards for payment. There would be no reason for the grocer to do so, unless she had a use for additional keyboards or knew some-

Money Anything that functions as a means of payment (medium of exchange), unit of account, and store of value.

Means of Payment (Medium of Exchange) Something that is generally acceptable to make payments.

Barter Trading goods for goods.

one else who did. Finding such a **double coincidence of wants,** in which the grocer has what you want (groceries) and you have what she wants (keyboards), would often be extremely difficult. Thus, exchange under a barter system would be costly in terms of search time—that is, in terms of the time spent looking for someone who has groceries and wants computer keyboards. In general, the considerable time and effort associated with barter makes it a cumbersome and inefficient way to conduct transactions. It raises transactions costs, which are all the costs involved with making exchanges. In turn, higher transactions costs hold down the volume of exchange in the economy. This is why barter economies tended to be mostly agricultural. With the volume of trade relatively low and costly, one could never be sure of finding a double coincidence of wants. The result was that almost everyone produced the food and other things they needed to survive, making very few exchanges necessary. If some individuals did decide to specialize and trade, they would have an incentive to produce goods that were easy to trade, rather than the goods that they were good at producing. For efficiency to occur, people should specialize in what they can most efficiently produce, which is exactly what "money" in an economy encourages.

Double Coincidence of Wants In barter, when each person involved in a potential exchange has what the other person wants.

Fortunately, all this process is not necessary in a modern economy since we do have something that serves as a generally acceptable means of payment, money. As a result, people can exchange goods and services for money and vice versa. To illustrate, Randy, the dishwasher, planned to exchange a week's labor for $50 and the $50 for groceries. However, if Randy had accepted the tickets—a type of barter transaction—he could not have eaten until he found a grocer who wanted tickets to the play. If he failed to do so by curtain time on Saturday, he would find that the tickets had become worthless and hence he would go hungry for the next week. A monetary exchange facilitates trade by reducing the transactions costs involved by eliminating the need for a double coincidence. That said, now is a good time to read over Exhibit 2-1.

Something that becomes generally acceptable as a means of payment in exchange for goods and services will necessarily also function as a **store of value.** To be acceptable, something must store value or, more specifically, purchasing power because people receive money and spend it at different points in time. In other words, there is a difference between the time pattern of people's receipts of money and the time pattern of their expenditures. If, today, you are paid for your labor services and do not need to purchase anything until tomorrow, you would presumably be unwilling to accept anything in payment that is likely to decline in value before you spend it. (Could Randy have sold the tickets for $50 the next day, given that the play had been the night before?) Conversely, people will accept something as a means of payment in exchange for goods and services when they believe that they can easily exchange it for something else of like value in the near future.

Store of Value Something that retains its value over time.

We now know that money functions as a means of payment and store of value and what these functions mean. However, for monetary exchange to proceed in an orderly fashion, there must be some method of specifying the quantity of money required to pay for a given quantity of a particular good. In other words, there is a need for an accounting unit, commonly referred to as a **unit of account.** Because all domestic prices and financial records including debts are expressed in dollars, the dollar serves as the monetary unit of account—that is, the standard measure of value. To appreciate why it is convenient to have a standardized unit of account, imagine the poor grocer

Unit of Account A standardized accounting unit such as the dollar that is the consistent measure of value.

Exhibit 2-1 ◆
Money, Exchange,
and Economic
Development

The body of the text describes (1) how the high transactions costs associated with barter tend to hold down the volume of exchange, and (2) how the low volume of exchange tends to "keep people on the farm." Most of us take for granted the existence of money; we have never experienced a barter system. How and why economies evolved from a primitive barter system to an advanced monetary system is a long story. The short, somewhat allegorical version is that the high costs of barter exchange provided an economic incentive for people to devise a better system. Important in the early evolution of the system were the merchants who established trading posts or so-called general stores. They purchased goods from farmers, often paying for them with a receipt that could later be used by the farmer to purchase other goods at the store. The other goods in turn had been acquired by the merchant from other farmers. The receipts were an early form of money, as were the gold and silver nuggets, which also came to be exchanged for goods and services at the trading posts and elsewhere. Eventually, as governments developed and the benefits of standardizing the money within an economy became apparent, governments came to produce and certify coins and paper notes (currency) as money.

By eliminating the need for a double coincidence of wants, the existence of money dramatically reduces the costs of conducting trade, thereby encouraging a larger volume of exchange. More opportunities for exchange, and less time and effort involved in the process, mean that not all of an economy's participants need to individually produce the same goods to survive and prosper; labor time is not wasted in the trading process. Each person can now more easily specialize in the production of goods to which they are relatively best suited, trade these goods for money, and use the money to purchase goods produced by others. The development of the financial system, and the resulting division of labor (and other resources) into the production of an increasing variety of goods, is a key ingredient in the process of economic development. The accompanying schematic diagram ties these several thoughts together.

Transaction costs associated with barter

encourage

Development of money

facilitates

Exchange (trading)

facilitates

Specialization and division of labor

facilitates

Economic development

and the grocer's customers who, in the absence of money and a unit of account, would have to remember that one computer keyboard equals four quarts of milk, one crate of oranges equals three pounds of cheese, and so forth.[1] A unit of account makes it possible to compare the relative values of different goods and services and to keep records about prices and debts, thus facilitating actual transactions throughout the economy.

---

[1] Each exchange value, such as one computer keyboard equals four quarts of milk, is one relative price (the price of a keyboard in terms of milk). If the grocer trades in n goods, the general formula to determine the number of relative prices she would have to remember is $[n \times (n-1)]/2$ relative prices. For example, if she traded ten goods, she would have to remember 45 relative prices $(10 \times 9)/2$. If she traded in 100 goods, she would have to remember 4,950 relative prices $(100 \times 99)/2 = 4,950$. In our world with hundreds of thousands of items, imagine how many relative prices there would be.

In sum, money is whatever circulates in a modern economy as a generally acceptable means of payment. By necessity money will also function as a store of value, and its unit of measurement will naturally become the unit of account and measure of value. The functions of money are portrayed in Exhibit 2-2.

The Monetary Aggregates and Domestic Nonfinancial Debt

Given our definition, measuring the quantity or stock of money in an economy should be straightforward: add together those things functioning as a means of payment. In reality, as usual, measurement is not quite so simple. There are at least two difficulties. First, what functions as a means of payment in an economy will change over time and need to be revised as an economy's financial system evolves. For example, once gold and silver coins were money. Now they are gone, having been replaced by paper currency, coins made out of nonprecious metals, and checkable deposits. Second, some things may be difficult to classify; that is, some financial claims are on the borderline between being and not being a means of payment. For example, **money market deposit accounts (MMDAs)** have limited check-writing privileges—up to three checks

Money Market Deposit Accounts (MMDAs) Financial claims, with limited check-writing privileges, offered by banks since 1982, which earn higher interest than fully checkable deposits and require a higher minimum balance.

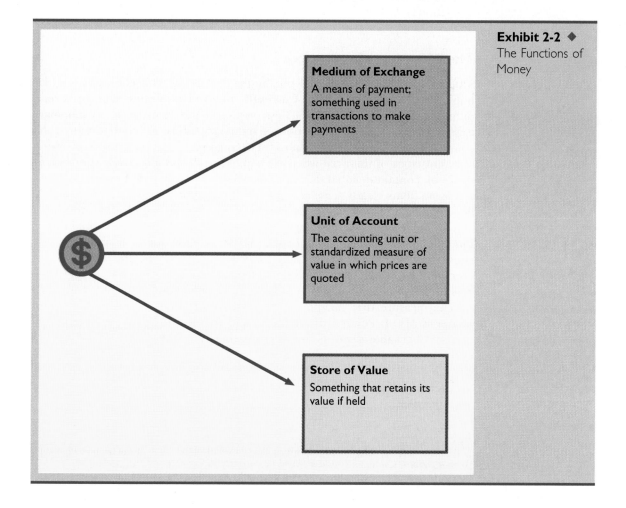

Exhibit 2-2 ◆
The Functions of Money

Medium of Exchange
A means of payment; something used in transactions to make payments

Unit of Account
The accounting unit or standardized measure of value in which prices are quoted

Store of Value
Something that retains its value if held

per month. First offered by banks in 1982, they earn higher interest than most checking accounts and generally require a high minimum balance. Because of the limited check-writing privileges, money market deposit accounts have some characteristics of checking accounts, and hence, are a borderline case.

Classification is not merely an esoteric or semantic issue. As we shall see in the next chapter, the Fed has often guided its policy actions in part by what is happening to the money supply. Therefore, at any point in time, the Fed must have as accurate a measurement of the quantity of money as possible. Given the existence of several financial claims that are close to being full-fledged means of payment and some controversy within the economics profession over the adequacy and narrowness of the means of payment definition, it should come as no surprise to learn that the following points apply:

1. Rather than relying on only one measure, the Fed hedges its bets by collecting, publishing, and monitoring data on several monetary measures.
2. The items included in the various measures have changed over time as the financial system and new means of payment evolve, and as the Fed strives to improve its monetary measures.
3. The Fed further "covers the bases" by monitoring and publishing a broad measure of outstanding credit that measures unpaid loans and debts, since changes in credit market activity can also be used to guide Fed policy actions.

The Monetary Aggregates

Among the many jobs carried out by the Fed is the collection and regular publication of financial data. Currently, the Fed publishes data on several different monetary measures. These measures are referred to as **monetary aggregates**—that is, the collection of monetary assets. Exhibit 2-3 shows the composition of **M1, M2, M3,** and **L.** The aggregates are comprised of several different types of financial assets. (Chapter 6 and the glossary at the back of the book contain detailed descriptions of each item included in M2, M3, and L.) Some items clearly serve as a means of payment (currency and checkable deposits), some are clearly not means of payment ("large" time deposits), and some are in between (money market deposit accounts). You should notice that M2 consists of everything in M1 plus some other highly liquid assets. M3 consists of everything in M2 plus some less-liquid assets, and L consists of everything in M3 plus some additional less-liquid assets. Thus, as the aggregate gets bigger, in general, less-liquid assets have been added.

The measure that *currently* corresponds most closely to the definition of money is M1. It consists of currency held by the public and checkable deposits.[2] **Checkable deposits** are deposits that can be withdrawn by writing a check to a third party. They consist of

◆ **Demand deposits,** which are noninterest-earning checking accounts issued by banks.

Monetary Aggregates The measures of money—including M1, M2, M3, and L—that are monitored and tracked by the Fed.
M1 Currency in the hands of the public plus checkable deposit.
M2 Everything in M1 plus other highly liquid assets.
M3 Everything in M2 plus some less liquid assets.
L Everything in M3 plus some additional less liquid assets.

Checkable Deposits Deposits that are subject to withdrawal by writing a check.
Demand Deposits Noninterest-earning checking accounts issued by banks.

---

[2] M1 also contains travelers checks, which are a relatively small fraction of the total aggregate. For our purposes here, we consider M1 to be currency in the hands of the public plus checkable deposits.

Exhibit 2-3 ◆
The Monetary Aggregates and Domestic Nonfinancial Debt as of January, 1996 (in billions of dollars)

M1

Currency in the hands of the public	$ 373.6
Demand deposits at commercial banks	393.5
Other checkable deposits (Deposits that can be withdrawn by unlimited check writing)	343.2
Travelers' checks	8.9
Total M1	**$1,119.2**

M2

M1 plus

Small savings and time deposits (<$100,000), including money market deposit accounts	$2,087.2
Individual money market mutual funds	468.6
Total M2	**$3,675.0**

M3

M2 plus

Large time deposits	$ 416.6
Term repurchase agreements and term Eurodollars	280.2
Institutional money market mutual funds	230.6
Total M3	**$4,602.4**

L

M3 plus

Nonbank public holdings of U.S. savings bonds and Short Term Treasury Securities	$ 652.7
Commercial paper	437.2
Bankers' acceptances	11.7
Total L	**$5,704.0**

DNFD

Federal: { Credit market debt of the U.S. government and state and local governments	$ 3,634.7
Nonfederal: { Corporate bonds / Mortgages / Consumer credit (including bank loans) / Other bank loans / Commercial paper / Other debt instruments	$10,265.5
Total DNFD	**$13,900.1[a]**

[a]Numbers may not sum to totals because of rounding.

SOURCE: *Federal Reserve Statistical Release H.6 (508)*, Board of Governors of the Federal Reserve, May 9, 1996.

◆ Other checkable deposits, which are interest-earning checking accounts issued by any of the depository institutions.

M1 contains the "monetary" assets that we *currently* use in transactions, and will, in general be what we have in mind throughout the text when we refer to the *money supply*. All the components of M1 are means of payment. This is not true of M2, M3, and certainly not of L; for example, large time deposits, a component of M3, cannot generally be used to buy groceries.

Negotiable Orders of Withdrawal (NOW) Accounts Interest-earning checking accounts.

Notice the word *currently* has been italicized in the last two paragraphs. The reason, hinted at in the earlier part of this section, is that as financial regulations have changed and financial practices have evolved, the Fed has on a number of occasions refined and reconstructed the various monetary measures. For example, **negotiable order of withdrawal (NOW) accounts,** essentially interest-bearing checking accounts were not even in existence in 1970. "Born" in 1972 in Massachusetts and New Hampshire by some clever financial institution executives, these accounts were initially counted as part of M2. However, when their volume grew and they became legalized nationwide, they were "promoted" to M1, having become generally acceptable means of payment. Money market deposit accounts, on the other hand, are, as of this writing, included in M2. Because of the limitations on usage (only three checks per month), the Fed has concluded that depositors do not generally use these accounts as means of payment. Hence, money market deposit accounts are included in M2—an aggregate containing M1 and other items which are so close to money that they are often referred to as **near monies.**

Near Monies Highly liquid financial assets that can easily be converted to transactions money (M1) without loss of value.

The other near monies included in M2 are small time deposits, passbook savings deposits, and individual money market mutual funds. As previously stated, these assets are defined in more detail in Chapter 6 and in the glossary. Even though they are not used to make transactions, they are all fairly liquid near monies because they can easily be converted to transactions money (checkable deposits or currency) without loss of value for the principal. Exhibit 2-4 discusses the relationship between money, near monies, and other financial claims.

The essential point to keep in mind as we end this section on measuring money is that measurement is not nearly so straightforward as one might have imagined. The difficulties and ambiguities, in turn, contribute to revisions in the various measures from time to time, and lead the Fed to hedge its bets by monitoring several measures rather than relying on only one. Such flexibility is required by a dynamic financial system that is evolving through time as rules, regulations, and payment practices change.

RECAP

Money is anything that functions as a means of payment (medium of exchange), a unit of account, and a store of value. Money is acceptable in payment for goods and services. The Fed monitors several measures of money. M1 (transactions money) is currency in the hands of the public plus checkable deposits. M2 includes everything in M1 plus other highly liquid assets. M3 includes everything in M2 plus additional highly liquid assets. L consists of everything in M3 plus some additional less liquid assets.

Domestic Nonfinancial Debt

Domestic Nonfinancial Debt (DNFD) An aggregate that is a measure of total credit market debt owed by the domestic nonfinancial government and private sectors.

Before we leave this section on money and the monetary aggregates, we need to introduce another aggregate that the Fed keeps track of along with M1, M2, M3, and L. This aggregate is **domestic nonfinancial debt (DNFD),** which is a measure of outstanding loans and debts accumulated in the present and past years. Take a look at Exhibit 2-3 again for the components of DNFD.

In Chapter 1 we saw that surplus spending units (SSUs) usually lend their surplus funds to the deficit spending units (DSUs) through the financial system (financial markets and financial intermediaries). Put another way, purchasing power is transferred from those who have it to those who need it. What is transferred, in fact, is current purchasing power in exchange for another financial asset, or a future claim on money. In effect, the SSUs "rent out" their surplus funds to DSUs for a given period of time, much as a landlord rents out an apartment. In financial markets, the SSU (lender) acquires a financial asset, which is a claim on and liability of the DSU (borrower). The claim, an asset to the holder and a liability to the issuer, is really an IOU—a promise by the borrower to repay the original amount borrowed (the principal) plus "rent" (the interest) to the lender.

Financial claims, other than money, are issued by DSUs or financial intermediaries. The intermediaries issue claims on themselves and then, in turn, lend to DSUs. There are many different types of financial claims that exist within the financial system, reflecting the wide variety of borrowers and lenders and the tendency to tailor particular types of claims to match the preferences and needs of the SSUs and DSUs. In the early 1990s, the trend among SSUs has been to bypass depository institutions and to put a large share of their surplus funds into the most rapidly growing type of intermediary, mutual funds.[a]

Since all financial claims, whether they be bank deposits, stocks, or T-bills, are claims on money, they can in some sense be compared with one another as well as with money. Traditional standards of comparison include the risk and the liquidity of various claims.

Risk refers to the possibility or probability that the value of a claim declines. One example of risk is the possibility that a borrower will default, failing to pay back all or part of the principal or the interest. This risk is similar to the risk the renter will burn down the apartment or fail to pay his rent and be difficult to evict. The higher the probability of receiving less money back than expected, the more risky the financial claim is relative to money.

The liquidity of a financial claim (or asset) is determined by how easy or difficult it is to convert the asset into money. The ease (or difficulty) is defined in terms of the cost and time associated with converting the asset into money. If the costs are high or it takes considerable time to convert a particular type of asset to money, it is usually referred to as *illiquid*. As the costs and time required to exchange a particular asset approach zero, the liquidity of an asset increases, with money representing perfect liquidity.[b]

So what does this all have to do with the monetary aggregates? Some items included in M2, such as savings deposits, are very liquid and holding them exposes the owner to little risk; hence the term *near monies*. Other items, less liquid and/or entailing more risk, are included in M3, L, or DNFD. See, there is some logic to the system!

Exhibit 2-4 ◆ Money and Other Financial Claims

[a]Mutual funds are investment pools in which a large number of shareholders purchase securities such as stocks and bonds.

[b]During the middle of the nineteenth century, coal miners' wages in Staffordshire were paid partly in beer! Commenting on this practice, Charles Fay, a historian, remarked: "This currency was very popular and highly liquid, but it was issued to excess and difficult to store" (*Life and Labour in the Nineteenth Century*, Cambridge: Cambridge University Press, 1920, p. 197).

Specifically, DNFD refers to total credit market debt owed by the domestic nonfinancial sector including the U.S. government, state and local governments, private nonfinancial firms, and households. Don't let the length of this definition confuse you. Domestic merely means U.S. entities excluding foreign entities. Nonfinancial debt excludes the debt of financial institutions—those institutions that borrow solely to re-lend. The reason for excluding the debt of financial institutions is that including such debt would be double counting.

For example, suppose Friendly Savings and Loan borrows surplus funds from small passbook savers and re-lends them to John and Mary to buy their first home.[3] If the debt of the financial institution is counted, both the mortgage debt of John and Mary and the debt of Friendly to the passbook saver would be included in the aggregate. The argument is that this is double counting, since the ultimate transaction went from the passbook saver to John and Mary with the savings and loan in between. Furthermore, the financial debt of Friendly to the passbook saver is offset by the financial claim (mortgage) they hold against John and Mary.

If all this sounds a bit confusing, think of DNFD as merely a measure of the unpaid claims lenders have against borrowers excluding the debt of financial intermediaries.[4] DNFD is probably the best measure of outstanding nonfinancial credit that we have. When credit flows increase, DNFD (the aggregate amount of debt outstanding) goes up. Likewise, when credit flows decrease, DNFD declines. Exhibit 2-5 shows the relative size of the monetary aggregates and DNFD.

---

[3] Passbook savings accounts are bank accounts that carry a stipulated rate of interest and from which funds can usually be withdrawn at any time without a penalty.

[4] Some households, businesses, or government units have financial claims against one party while owning a financial debt to another. For example, a household may have purchases of corporate bonds (claims) while at the same time owing credit card debt to a bank.

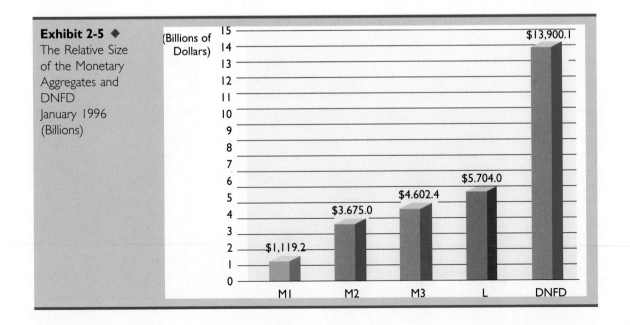

Exhibit 2-5 ◆
The Relative Size of the Monetary Aggregates and DNFD
January 1996
(Billions)

LOOKING FORWARD

United States Currency to Get New Look

In mid-March 1996, a new $100 bill was introduced—the first newly designed U.S. currency since 1928. Like the old bill, the new bill still has Ben Franklin's picture on it but the picture is enlarged and moved to the left. To its right is a watermark that also portrays Ben. Ink that seems to change from green to black at certain angles is used in the numeral in the lower right corner and security threads that glow red when exposed to ultra-violet light are woven vertically through each bill.

All these changes make the $100 bill more difficult to counterfeit. At the present time, officials claim that counterfeiting is a relatively minor problem with only nine bills in every million found to be counterfeit.* Still, technological advances in photocopiers, printers, etc. in recent years have prompted officials to make the currency more difficult to counterfeit before the problem escalates. Old $100 bills will not be recalled but rather replaced as banks return worn-out bills in the regular course of business.

To facilitate the transition to the new bill, the Treasury Department and the Fed have engaged in a public relations campaign to inform the public of the reasons for the change. Since billions of dollars of U.S. currency circulate outside this country, the campaign goes beyond the domestic economy to foreign holders of dollars, including foreign central bankers, who may be fearful that the old bills will be recalled or worth less than their face value.

Other denominations, starting with the $50 bill will be introduced about once a year until the entire currency has been changed over in the year 2001. The last bill to be changed will be the $1 bill. Vending machine owners may have a difficult time getting their machines to accept the new $1 bills.

*"$100 Question: Will Ben's New Look Stop Counterfeits?" *The New York Times*, September 28, 1995, D19.

The Economy and the Aggregates

In the early and mid-1980s, M1 was the primary measure of money that the Fed watched. Targets were set for the growth rate of M1 and the Fed monitored these targets to provide a barometer of economic activity. If M1 growth was above the target rate, the Fed would take actions that resulted in a slowdown in the growth of M1. If M1 growth was below the target, the Fed would take actions that resulted in a speedup in the growth of M1. In either case, the goal was to nudge the economy in the desired direction.

M2 gained importance and prominence during the late 1980s in the execution of monetary policy by the Fed. It seemed that during this period, there was a more stable relationship between changes in M2 and economic activity than between changes in M1 and economic activity. This caused the Fed to watch the growth rate of M2 for signals about how well the economy was doing and to deemphasize the role of M1. In the early 1990s, the stable relationship between changes in M2 and changes in economic activity also seemed to break down. The growth rate of M2 moved in erratic and unpredictable ways. As a result, the Fed has also deemphasized the use of M2 as a policy indicator.

In the early 1990s, the Fed increasingly used changes in the growth rate of DNFD as an indicator of the direction of the economy. DNFD seemed, at least at that time, to have a quite stable relationship with changes in economic activity. If credit growth was increasing, then spending was likely to be going up. If credit extension was slowing, then the growth rate of economic activity was also likely to be slowing. Hence, we can see why the Fed was interested in monitoring changes in this broad aggregate.

For our purposes, then, it is probably best to think of M1 as a measure of transactions money, and M2 as one of several broader measures of money or other indicators (including M3, L, and DNFD), which may, at times, be closely related to economic activity, and hence closely monitored by the Fed in its execution of monetary policy. If you are baffled about why the relationships between the aggregates and economic activity change, don't be discouraged. By the time you have completed this text, we hope to have provided you with fairly good explanations of the reasons these changes occur. Don't forget that the financial system of the economy in which we live is dynamic, innovative, and evolving. Exhibit 2-6 shows how the various aggregates have grown over time.

 RECAP

In addition to the monetary aggregates, the Fed monitors DNFD, a broad measure of credit. DNFD includes public and private debt but excludes the debt of financial institutions to avoid double counting. Sometimes a given aggregate has been more highly correlated with the level of economic activity than at other times.

 The Evolution of the Payments System

Like the human race, the current financial system has evolved from a primitive state and will continue to evolve in the future. This tendency to

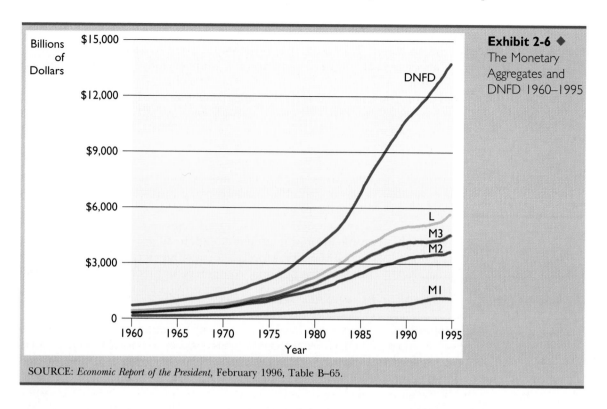

Exhibit 2-6 ◆ The Monetary Aggregates and DNFD 1960–1995

SOURCE: *Economic Report of the President*, February 1996, Table B–65.

change, discussed in the last section with regard to changes in those things functioning as a means of payment, is significantly influenced by the technology used to execute transactions. The **payments mechanism** is the means by which transactions are completed—that is, how money is transferred among transactors.

If someone now asked you what made up the U.S. money supply, we hope you would answer: "currency held by the public and checkable deposits, the primary components of M1." Checkable deposits are payable on demand to third parties. For example, if you write a check to your grocer, the first two parties are you and the depository institution; the grocer is the third party. The check in payment for goods purchased is an order for your bank to debit (subtract) a certain number of dollars from your checkable deposit account. The dollars are then credited (added) to the deposit account of the grocer, the third party. Thus, a checkable deposit is a means of payment and the check is the method used to transfer ownership of the deposit between parties to a transaction. The point is that the check itself is not money; if it were, printing presses would work around the clock! The balances in checkable deposits are money.

Ongoing technological innovations may eventually make checks much less important, or even obsolete, as a means of transferring purchasing power. All indications suggest that we are making an increasingly larger percent of payments with an **electronic funds transfer system.** Within this system, payments are made to third parties in response to electronic instructions rather than instructions written on a paper check. Note that an electronic funds transfer system does not eliminate the need for deposit accounts; it is just a more efficient way of transferring funds from one deposit account to another. To pay your grocery bill, for instance, your account is debited by the amount of

Payments Mechanism The means by which transactions are consummated; that is, how money is transferred in an exchange.

Electronic Funds Transfer System The transfer of funds to third parties in response to electronic instructions rather than instructions written on a paper check.

your bill, and the grocer's account is credited by the same amount at the time of the exchange. The whole system is computerized so that no written checks are necessary. All you need is an account number and a debit card that you present to the grocer. The grocer, in turn, enters the prices of your purchases into a computer terminal (called a **point-of-sale terminal**), and, at the end of the month, you receive a statement giving your current balance and a record of all the charges and deposits to your account. This is just like a checking account statement, but you do not have to write all those checks.

Currently, many employers, in cooperation with banks, pay salaries by automatically crediting their employees' bank accounts rather than by issuing the customary weekly or monthly check. This is a form of an electronic funds transfer system. Your depository institution most likely has **automatic teller machines (ATMs),** which permit you to make deposits and withdrawals, even late at night when the institution itself is closed. In all probability, your college has a few ATMs on campus. This too is a form of an electronic funds transfer system. As the ownership of personal computers and modems spreads, it will

Point-of-Sale Terminal
Computer terminals that use a debit card to electronically transfer funds from a deposit account to the account of a third party.

Automatic Teller Machines (ATMs) Machines that permit a depositor to make deposits and withdrawals to an account even if the financial institution is closed.

Exhibit 2-7 ◆
Forget Your Checkbook

Bobbi doesn't own a computer, but she still has not been left out of the telecommunication revolution—not as long as she has a telephone. Once a month Bobbi dials up her bank and pays all of her bills over the phone. She is hooked into an automated payments system that contains a list of the names, addresses, and account numbers of the bills she regularly pays. Each account is assigned a number, and she tells the bank, by keying in certain numbers on her push button phone, to make a payment, in a certain amount, on the due date of the bill. She never writes a check, nor pays for a stamp to mail a bill. Moreover, the amount of the bill does not come out of her account until the exact due date. Assuming that some of her bills have due dates in the middle or latter part of the month, and that she has an interest-earning checking account, this practice saves her the interest that she would have lost if she paid all of her bills on the first day of each month.

Increasingly consumers are offered opportunities to pay bills over the phone. (In some locations, the first bill consumers can pay like this is their phone bill!) Banks also offer customers the service of having monthly payments, such as house or car payments, automatically deducted from checking or savings accounts. These opportunities cut down on check writing, which despite being popular with consumers, is a relatively inefficient (high cost) way of making payments in this computer age.

Despite the advantages of electronic or automatic payments, consumers have been slow to give up checks for two reasons. First, checks leave a "paper trail," which many consumers still trust more than computers. Secondly, many consumers don't want to give up the "float." Float is the time from when a check is written to a third party until the check is actually deducted from the account. The third party first deposits the check in its bank, which then sends it to the first party's bank for payment. When payment is made, the check is then deducted from the first party's account. Float can be a few days, and many consumers like the cushion, particularly if times have been hard, and payday falls on a Monday. The consumer can safely buy groceries Friday night without the worry of bouncing a check!

be possible to conduct a large portion of one's financial transactions from home.

Basically, electronic funds transfer systems are nothing more than the application of available modern computer and telecommunication technology to the entire area of financial transactions and services. Their aim is to reduce the physical handling and labor costs associated with an ever-expanding volume of paper checks, deposit slips, and so forth, as well as to provide increased convenience and service to the public. As questions regarding the privacy of financial records, security of the system, and legal responsibilities are resolved, the adoption of new payments practices and electronic funds transfer systems will spread. The result will be an evolution in how money is used and, perhaps, changes in what functions as money. Barter to Indian beads to gold and silver coins to checkable deposits to the next innovation—the evolution of money and the payments mechanism go hand in hand as an economy develops.

Read Exhibit 2-7 to see how consumers in some parts of the country pay their bills over the telephone.

Summary of Major Points

1. The primary function of money, and the function that makes it unique, is that it serves as a generally acceptable means of payment.

2. Something that becomes a generally acceptable means of payment will, of necessity, function as a store of value.

3. The unit of account in the United States is the dollar. It serves as a common denominator or standardized unit of measure by which all prices and debts are quoted.

4. The high transactions costs associated with barter encourage the development of money. The existence of money facilitates trade which, in turn, encourages specialization and division of labor. Thus, the development of the financial system contributes importantly to an economy's growth and development.

5. Measuring money is not easy. What functions as money will change over time as an economy's financial system evolves, and some financial claims may be difficult to classify.

6. Given the importance and difficulties of measurement, the Fed monitors and publishes data on several monetary aggregates and refines and recomputes the various measures periodically.

7. M1 (currency plus checkable deposits) is the best measure of the money supply currently available for transactions purposes. In the late 1980s, M2 (everything in M1 plus other highly liquid assets) was used to guide the Fed in the execution of monetary policy. In recent years, the behavior of M2 has become a less reliable barometer of economic activity because of the less stable relationship between M2 and economic activity. The Fed has looked to other indicators, including DNFD, to aid in the execution of policy.

8. Money represents current purchasing power—a claim on goods and services. Other financial claims represent future claims on money. Financial

claims can be compared to each other and to money in terms of risk and liquidity.

9. The payments system is the means used to transfer money among transactors. Checks, for example, transfer ownership of checkable deposits such as NOW accounts. Innovations now being adopted suggest that an increasingly larger percent of payments will be made with electronic funds transfer systems. Such innovations include debit cards, point-of-sale terminals, and ATMs.

Key Terms

Automatic Teller Machines (ATMs)
Barter
Checkable Deposits
Demand Deposits
Domestic Nonfinancial Debt (DNFD)
Double Coincidence of Wants
Electronic Funds Transfer System
L
Means of Payment
Medium of Exchange
Monetary Aggregates

Money Market Deposit Accounts
Money
M1
M2
M3
Near Monies
Negotiable Orders of Withdrawal (NOW) Accounts
Payments Mechanism
Point-of-Sale Terminal
Store of Value
Unit of Account

Review Questions

1. Discuss or define briefly the following terms and concepts: means of payment, store of value, unit of account, barter, monetary aggregates, liquidity, nonfinancial debt, electronic funds transfer system, and risk.

2. What are the functions of money? Which do you think is most important?

3. Suppose we define money as that which serves as a store of value. Explain why this is a poor definition.

4. Suppose something is functioning as money within an economy. What could cause the population to lose confidence in the value of the means of payment? What do you think would happen as a result?

5. How does the Fed calculate M1, M2, M3, L, and DNFD? Are these aggregates all money? Why or why not? Which contains the most liquid assets? Which is smallest? Which is largest?

6. Why does the Fed have so many monetary measures? Which monetary aggregate is most closely associated with transactions balances? Which monetary aggregate is most commonly used in the execution of monetary policy? Why?

7. Why is the debt of financial institutions excluded from DNFD?

8. What is the payments mechanism? What changes are occurring in this mechanism? Why are they occurring?

9. Zoto is a remote island that has experienced rapid development. Zaha, on the other hand, is an island where growth has been sluggish and the level of economic activity remains low. How could the existence of money have affected these two outcomes?

10. Is it necessary for the collection of assets called money to perform all the functions given? Why or why not?

11. In what ways is money similar to other financial assets? How can money be distinguished from other financial assets?

12. Your friend took a class in money and banking two years ago and recalls that currency in the hands of the public is in M1. Explain to your friend why currency in the hands of the public is also included in M2, M3, and L.

Analytical Questions

13. Would the following assets be good "money"? Why or why not?
    a. Gold
    b. Dirt
    c. Corn
    d. Oil (often called liquid gold)

14. In which monetary aggregates are the following assets included?
    a. Small savings and time deposits (<$100,000)
    b. Money market deposit accounts
    c. Currency in the hands of the public
    d. Checkable deposits
    e. Individual money market mutual funds
    f. Institutional money market mutual funds
    g. Large time deposits
    h. Travelers' checks

The Financial System and the Economy

| Back | Forward | Home | Reload | Images | Open | Print | Find | Stop | N |

1. Use the Economic Bulletin Board to access Statistical Release H.6 published by the Fed to report on the most current measures of the money supply. You can employ the following root directory: (gopher://una.hh.lib.umich.edu:70/00/ebb/monetary/money.frb). How does the Fed differentiate between alternative measures of the money supply such as M1, M2, and M3? Which measure of the money supply is most liquid?

2. The following root director from the Economic Bulletin Board provides historical estimates of the money supply: (gopher://una.hh.lib.umich.edu:70/00/ebb/monetary/h6hist.frb). From the data, calculate and/or observe the approximate annual (seasonally adjusted) growth rates for M1 and M2 over the 1970–1994 time period. Verify that the growth rate of M1 increased from 1971 to 1985, while the growth

rate of M2 registered a downward trend over the same time period. (Hint: to calculate the approximate annual growth rates for M1 or M2 for each year, subtract the January value from the December value and then divide the result by the January value.) What are the relative growth rates of M1 and M2 in the 1990s?

Suggested Readings

John Walter provides an interesting history of the evolution of the monetary aggregates, along with additional sources of data and further readings, in an article titled "Monetary Aggregates." It can be found in *Macroeconomic Data: A User's Guide,* published by the Federal Reserve Bank of Richmond, 1990, pp. 36–44. . . . For data on the monetary and other macroeconomic variables on the internet, go to the Economic Bulletin Board at (gopher://una.hh.lib.umich.edu:70/11/ebb/).

The virtues (and vices) of home banking are discussed in the following articles: Merri Rosenberg, "Home Banking Back in the Race," *American Banker,* May 18, 1992, p. 26; Karen Gullo, "Another Shot at Banking from Home; More Banks Offer Service, But It's Rarely Profitable," *American Banker,* August 13, 1991, p. 3; and John Jaben, "Let Your Fingers Do The Banking," *Forbes,* August 19, 1991, p. 122.

E-cash, a new kind of electronic money on the Internet, is in its infant stages and may someday compete with the present system of banks, checks, and dollars. For a discussion of this ongoing innovation, see "The Future of Money," *Business Week,* June 12, 1995, pp. 66–78.

For a discussion (that may contain some surprises) about the trends in the use of cash, checkable deposits, and electronic transfers to make payments, see Michael Keeley's, "A Cashless Society," *Weekly Letter of the Federal Reserve Bank of San Francisco,* April 15, 1988, pp. 1–3.

For a short discussion of the changing role of M2, see David Ramsour's, "Nonbank Inroads Loosen Fed's Grip," *ABA Banking Journal,* September 1993, p. 20.

For subscription information, archives, and current issues of several magazines available on the internet, go to (http://www.enews.com/magazines/).

3

The Role of Money and Credit

> *Money, it turned out, was exactly like sex:*
> *you thought of nothing else if you didn't have*
> *it and thought of other things if you did.*
> —James Baldwin—
>
> *Money is like muck—not good unless you spread it.*
> —Francis Bacon—

Learning Objectives

After reading this chapter, you should know:

◆ What the interest rate is

◆ How the supply of and demand for money—and/or credit flows—influence the interest rate

◆ How, in general, changes in financial variables influence output and prices

◆ The historical relationship between changes in financial variables and changes in inflation and output growth

◆ What the CPI is

◆ Whether money and credit flows are "all that matter"

Money and Credit Matters

It is mid-February and the chairperson of the Federal Reserve is about to testify in front of the Senate Banking Committee. Financial analysts and investors anxiously await the chairperson's remarks, expecting an announcement of the Fed's monetary policy plans for the coming year, including the growth rates of the monetary aggregates and domestic nonfinancial debt (DNFD) that the Fed will seek to achieve.

It is 4:00 P.M. on Thursday. Portfolio managers, brokers and dealers in financial markets, and analysts await the Fed's weekly release of financial data, including data on the monetary aggregates and DNFD. Many eyes are glued to terminal screens as the data appear. With the Fed reporting an unexpectedly large change in the aggregates, interest rates and exchange rates could react immediately, and analysts would predict a large movement in stock prices when the stock exchanges (now closed) reopen tomorrow.

As this course unfolds, many episodes like those just depicted will occur. To understand such occurrences as completely as possible, we will have to analyze in some detail the causes and consequences of the various developments we observe. For example, what can cause the monetary aggregates or DNFD to change and what effects would such developments have on the economy's performance as measured by movements in the inflation rate and the unemployment rate?

Addressing such questions adequately requires us to develop theories, or, cause-effect statements that link together the phenomena we wish to analyze and understand. More specifically, we need to specify the cause-effect role of money and credit flows in the economy. Why does it matter if the Fed chairperson announces a planned growth rate range for M2, M3, or DNFD of 4 to 6 percent instead of 6 to 8 percent? What important things in the economy will change if the Fed engineers the lower growth rate range and why will they change? How did the Fed come to select one growth rate rather than another?

As one of the introductory chapters of this text, its general purpose is to point you in the right direction by highlighting the issues and relationships to be addressed in more detail later on. We begin with the market for money and then move to a discussion of the role of credit.

The Demand for and Supply of Money

To understand money's role in the financial system, it is helpful to view money as an asset, much as someone might view an apartment house. The rent for apartments and the quantity of apartment units produced and rented are determined by the factors affecting the supply of apartments by builders as well as the factors affecting the demand for apartments by renters.

Interest Rate The cost to borrowers of obtaining money and the return (or yield) on money to lenders.

The analysis of money proceeds in a similar fashion. The **interest rate** is the cost to borrowers of obtaining money and the return (or yield) on money to lenders. Thus, just as rent is the cost to apartment dwellers and the return to the owner, the interest rate is the rental rate when money is borrowed or loaned, and is known as the *cost of credit*.[1] By identifying and analyzing the factors affecting the supply of and demand for money, we gain considerable knowledge of the "rental rate," or interest rate, associated with borrowing or lending money and the quantity of money that is supplied and demanded. It is to this purpose that we now turn.

We begin our study by reviewing some of the specifics of demand and supply analysis as they pertain to money. First, the **quantity demanded of money** is the specific amount of money that spending units wish to hold at a specific interest rate (price). If other factors are held constant with only the interest rate allowed to vary, then there is an inverse relationship between the quantity of money demanded and the interest rate. Holding other factors constant is known as invoking the *ceteris paribus* assumption.[2] Thus, in this case, we conclude, ceteris paribus, that when the interest rate goes up, the quantity demanded of money goes down. Likewise, ceteris paribus, when the interest rate falls, the quantity demanded of money increases.

But, why is this relationship between the quantity demanded of money and the interest rate inverse? The answer is quite simple if we consider that money (even in interest-earning checking accounts) generally earns less interest than nonmonetary assets (or near monies). Consequently, as the interest rate goes up, the opportunity cost of holding money goes up, and ceteris paribus, the quantity demanded of money goes down.[3] People conserve on their holdings of money balances and substitute holdings of other financial assets that pay a higher return. Thus, when the interest rate rises, "portfolio adjustments" decrease the holdings of money whose return has not increased or has increased less than other nonmonetary assets.

Exhibit 3-1 discusses graphical analysis and is followed by Exhibit 3-2 in which we graph various interest rate–quantity demanded combinations to get a downward sloping demand curve for money.

By the **demand for money,** we mean the entire set of interest rate–quantity demanded combinations—the entire downward-sloping demand curve. The demand for money by spending units is primarily determined by spending plans and by the need to pay for purchases. Spending plans and purchases are in turn influenced by income and generally go up when incomes go up. Thus, the demand for money to hold is positively or directly related to income. When our incomes go up, we hold more money for day-to-day transactions. (Mary goes to the grocery store and takes her kids out for fast food more often after she gets a raise.) In addition to income and spending plans, in Chapter 17, we look at other factors that also affect the demand for money.

In terms of Exhibit 3-2, when the demand for money changes, the entire demand curve shifts. For example, when the demand for money decreases, say due to a decrease in incomes, the entire demand curve shifts to the left. Thus we can see that changes in factors other than the interest rate affect the demand for money and cause the downward-sloping demand curve to shift.

Quantity Demanded of Money The specific amount of money that spending units wish to hold at a specific interest rate (price).

Demand for Money The entire set of interest rate-quantity demanded combinations as represented by a downward-sloping demand curve for money.

---

[1] The market in which money is borrowed and loaned is called the *credit market*. In Chapter 4, we look in depth at interest rate determination from a credit market perspective where the interest rate is determined by the supply and demand for loanable funds.

[2] In economics, we make the ceteris paribus assumption so that we can investigate the relationship between two variables without having changes in additional variables conceal the relationship.

[3] The opportunity cost is the value of the next best alternative that is foregone.

Exhibit 3-1 ◆
Graphical Analysis

Economists tend to view graphical analysis as a powerful tool in examining a problem—a means to an end. But economics is not about graphs. Students are sometimes in danger of getting so wrapped up in the details of graphs that they lose sight of the problem. Don't let this happen.

To facilitate learning, a text should use graphs skillfully and sparingly so as to be a help rather than a hindrance to understanding. Students should strive for understanding rather than only memorization of the graphs and problems under study. In this text, descriptions have been provided for almost every exhibit, be it a graph, a schematic diagram, or a chart. After studying one of these visual devices and the discussion related to it, try covering the discussion, looking at the graph, diagram, or chart, and writing your own discussion. Once this is accomplished, then go the other way—cover the visual device, read the discussion, and try to sketch out the graph, diagram, or chart. Such an approach—looking at something with a "picture" *and* with words—is a proven aid to learning.

When the interest rate changes, we move along a single money demand curve, and there is a change in quantity demand. Be certain you are clear about the difference between a change in quantity demanded and a change in demand.

RECAP

The demand for money is the amount that will be demanded at various interest rates. The quantity demanded of money is the amount that will be demanded at a specific interest rate. The demand for money is directly related to income. Ceteris paribus, quantity demanded is inversely related to the interest rate. A change in demand is represented by a shift of the demand curve while a change in quantity demanded is a movement along a demand curve due to a change in the interest rate.

Supply of Money The stock of money (M1), which includes currency in the hands of the public plus checkable deposits.

Depository Institutions Financial intermediaries such as commercial banks, savings and loans, credit unions, and mutual savings banks, that issue checkable deposits.

Reserves Assets that are held as either vault cash or reserve deposit accounts with the Fed.

Required Reserve Ratio The fraction of deposit liabilities that depository institutions must hold as reserve assets.

The **supply of money** is a little more detailed and warrants a brief discussion. Recall from Chapter 2 that our most narrow definition of transactions money (M1) includes currency in the hands of the public plus checkable deposits. Financial intermediaries that issue checkable deposits (now often referred to as **depository institutions**) hold reserve assets equal to a certain fraction of those deposits. The **reserves** against the outstanding deposits may be held as either vault cash or for safety reasons, reserve deposit accounts with the Fed. The Fed enters the picture in two parts:

1. Depository institutions must have reserve assets equal to a certain percentage of deposit liabilities. The Fed sets the percentage of deposit liabilities that depository institutions must hold as reserve assets. This percentage is called the **required reserve ratio.** For example, if a credit union has checkable deposits in the amount of $1,000, and the Fed has set a 10 percent required reserve ratio, then the credit union must hold $100 in reserves either as cash in its vaults or as deposits with the Fed.

The quantity of money is measured on the horizontal axis while the interest rate is measured on the vertical axis. The quantity demanded of money is, ceteris paribus, inversely related to the interest rate. As the interest rate falls, quantity demanded increases. As the interest rate rises, quantity demanded falls. A shift of the money demand curve means that the demand for money has changed. A shift to the right means that the demand for money has increased while a shift to the left means that the demand for money has decreased.

Exhibit 3-2 ◆
The Demand for Money

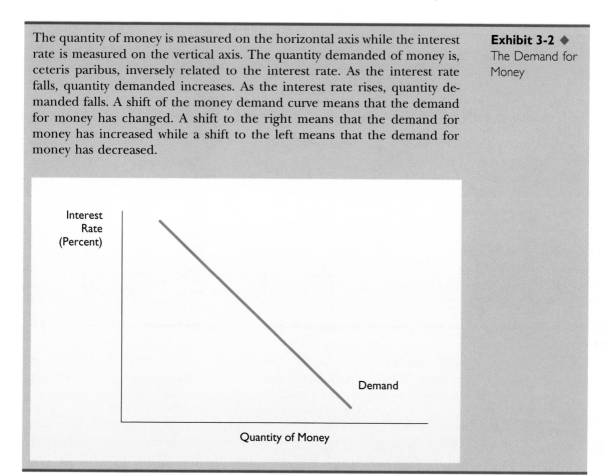

2. As we shall see in later chapters, the Fed influences the amount of cash assets outstanding and hence the amount available for reserves.[4]

Commercial banks (and other depository institutions) enter the picture by influencing the amount of checkable deposits. Banks issue checkable deposits when they receive a deposit into a checking account or when they make a loan. The borrower signs the loan papers and the intermediary (lender) credits the borrower's checking account with the amount of the loan, creating a checkable deposit or money.

Since the Fed, within some limits, controls the amount of funds available for reserves and sets the required reserve ratio, it exerts significant influence on the maximum amount of checkable deposits that depository institutions can create by making loans, and hence, significant influence on the money supply. Exhibit 3-3 depicts the relationship between the **quantity supplied of money** and the interest rate as a vertical line (supply curve). As in the case of demand, the quantity supplied of money is the specific amount that will be supplied at a specific interest rate. By the supply of money, we mean the entire

Quantity Supplied of Money The specific amount of money that will be supplied at a specific interest rate.

---

[4]From the discussion in Chapter 2, we now see that cash outside the Fed is either held by the public or deposited in a financial intermediary. If it is deposited, it serves as reserves for the financial intermediaries that issue checkable deposits, and it is considered a cash asset.

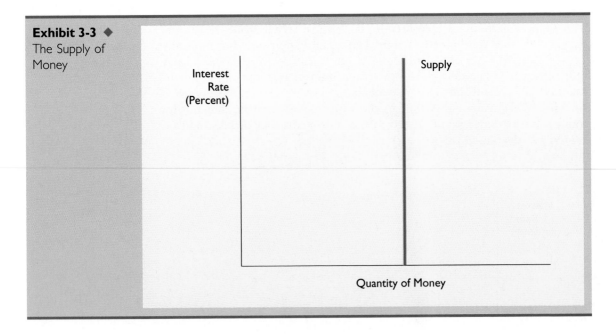

Exhibit 3-3 ◆
The Supply of
Money

Interest
Rate
(Percent)

Supply

Quantity of Money

set of interest rate–quantity demanded combinations—the entire vertical supply curve. The Fed, by changing the quantity of reserves available to the banking system or the required reserve ratio, can change the supply of money. Changes in the supply of money, initiated by the Fed, are reflected by shifts of the vertical supply curve. If the Fed speeds up the provision of reserves or reduces the required reserve ratio, the money supply curve shifts to the right, and the supply of money increases. Likewise, if the Fed slows down the provision of reserves or increases the required reserve ratio, the money supply curve shifts to the left, and the supply of money decreases.

 RECAP

Depository institutions must hold reserve assets equal to a certain fraction of deposit liabilities—called the required reserve ratio—as set by the Fed. The Fed also influences the amount of cash assets outstanding and thus the amount available for reserves. These two factors give the Fed significant influence over the money supply.

Having previewed the factors that affect demand and supply, we are now in a position to see how the interaction between the supply of and demand for money determine its availability or quantity, and its cost or the interest rate. This is done in Exhibit 3-4.[5] In this example, the market gravitates to i_e where the quantity supplied of money equals the quantity demanded. If the interest rate is above i_e, there is an excess quantity supplied of money and

---

[5]As commonly known, there are many interest rates in the economy, so speaking of "the interest rate" as if there were only one is an obvious simplification. Once the fundamentals are developed, it will be much easier to extend our analysis to take into account the many different interest rates.

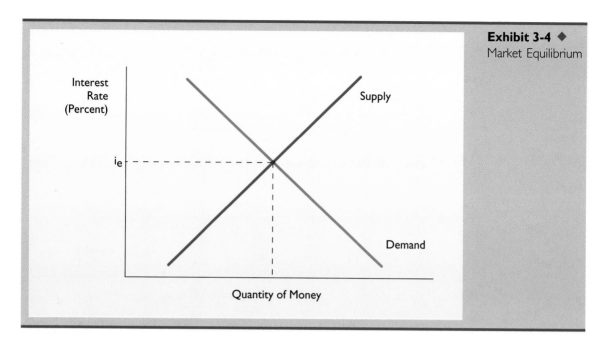

Exhibit 3-4 ◆
Market Equilibrium

hence, downward pressure on the interest rate. If the rate is below equilibrium, there is excess quantity demanded of money and market forces will cause the interest rate to rise. Once the interest rate gravitates to i_e the market will stay at the equilibrium rate until one of the curves shifts due to either a change in demand or supply.

Changes in the supply of or demand for money will affect the interest rate, just as changes in the supply of or demand for apartments will affect the rent on apartments. To illustrate the point, suppose that the Fed, through a stepped-up provision of reserves to depository institutions, succeeded in increasing the supply of money relative to the demand. In Exhibit 3-5, this corresponds to a shift of the supply curve to the right. At the original equilibrium interest rate (i_e), there is excess quantity supplied and downward pressure on the interest rate. The market gravitates to a new equilibrium at a lower interest rate (i'_e) where quantity demanded is equal to quantity supplied. Note that the analogy continues to hold: an increase in the supply of apartments, given the demand, would be expected to result in a fall in rents.

But what is the significance of changes in the demand or supply of money which, in turn, cause interest rates to change? In the preceding example, the fall in interest rates—reduction in the cost of borrowing—would probably encourage some spending units in the economy to borrow more money and use it to purchase more goods and services. Credit would increase and more specifically, the increase in the supply of money would lead to an increase in the demand for goods and services. The increased demand for goods and services, may lead to both an increase in the quantity of goods and services produced (supplied) in the future and an increase in the general level of prices.

Exhibit 3-6 depicts the importance for the economy as a whole of general relationships discussed in this section. Remember, this is just a first approximation that does not include many details; we do not expect you to understand all the specifics yet!

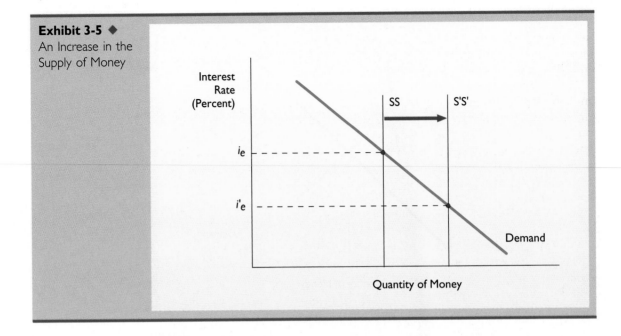

Exhibit 3-5 ◆
An Increase in the
Supply of Money

RECAP

The interest rate is determined by the supply of and demand for money. Equilibrium occurs at the interest rate where the quantity demanded of money is equal to the quantity supplied. Changes in the supply of or demand for money (shifts of the supply or demand curves) affect the interest rate. Ceteris paribus, if demand increases, the interest rate rises and vice versa. Ceteris paribus, if supply increases, the interest rate falls and vice versa.

How Credit Matters: A First Approximation

So far, we have been focusing on how the Fed influences spending via its influence on money or the monetary aggregates. This is all well and good in an economy where a large percentage of lending flows from commercial banks and other depository institutions such as savings and loans or

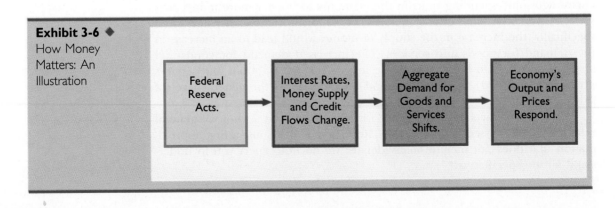

Exhibit 3-6 ◆
How Money
Matters: An
Illustration

credit unions. In such an economy, changes in the supply of money will be closely related to changes in the supply of **credit**—the flow of money from surplus spending units (SSUs) or financial intermediaries to deficit spending units (DSUs) in a given time period—and vice versa.

Credit The flow of money from SSUs or financial intermediaries to DSUs in a given time period, and vice versa.

It is fairly safe to say that this situation was typical of the U.S. economy until the late 1970s and early 1980s. Previously, when commercial banks got increases in reserves, perhaps orchestrated by the Fed, they engaged in new lending which caused both money and credit to go up. Increases in reserves, ceteris paribus, will almost invariably lead to decreases in the interest rate and increases in the supply of money and credit.

We will use DNFD as a measure of credit market debt or just "credit" outstanding and changes in DNFD to represent changes in outstanding credit.[6] Credit is borrowing power. Increases in credit cause spending (and incomes) to go up.

A word of caution is needed. Since the early 1990s, changes in money and credit flows have not been as closely related as they were in previous decades. Credit flows come from the following two sources, with the second gaining in relative importance.

1. Credit flows result from changes in credit extension by depository institutions—commercial banks, savings and loans, credit unions, and mutual savings banks. When these depository institutions make loans, they create money and extend credit.
2. Credit flows can also come from changes in lending at nondepository financial institutions and other nonfinancial institutions. For example, many nonfinancial companies now offer credit cards. This is a relatively recent phenomenon since credit cards (MasterCards and VISAs) were primarily offered by banks and other depository institutions. In addition to these inroads by nonfinancial institutions into credit extension for consumers, corporations (both medium-size and large) have developed ways to bypass banks for their working capital and finance needs. Many avenues now exist for firms to borrow directly from lenders; this borrowing and lending then spurs economic activity. Exhibit 3-7 addresses some of these dramatic changes in credit creation.

But, what does all this mean for the economy in general and the Fed specifically? Since the Fed's control over credit extension comes mainly from its influence on bank reserves and bank lending, to the extent that lending bypasses depository institutions, the linkage between money and economic activity may be weakened. The commercial banking system, the primary avenue through which the Fed works, is playing a reduced role in credit extension—undoubtedly making the job of the Fed more difficult.

 RECAP

Changes in credit extension influence changes in spending and income. Historically, the commercial banking system has been the vehicle through which credit was extended and through which the Fed exerted its influence

---

[6] Recall that DNFD is a measure of private and government debt outstanding, net of the debt of financial intermediaries. It is a good measure of the outstanding credit that has been extended over a period of time in the economy.

Exhibit 3-7 ◆
Recent Innovations
in Credit Extension

General Electric, once known only for kitchen appliances, now offers the GE Rewards MasterCard. This card gives up to a 2 percent rebate on credit card purchases and discount coupons that can be used at 24 different stores including KMart, Pier 1 Imports, Toys'R'Us, Volvo, and Waldenbooks. That's right, GE pays you to use your GE credit card! GE is not a financial intermediary, but obviously its managers are interested in getting into the credit extension business. American Express allows college students, even without income, to get American Express cards that give discount certificates to fly on Continental Airlines. AT&T and GM also offer credit cards that have special incentives. GM gives bonuses toward the purchase of its automobiles. Citibank has countered this competition with its own program that offers one advantage mile on United Airlines for every dollar in purchases on a Citibank credit card. Needless to say, banks are facing a lot of competition in this area because of all the alternatives consumers now have to obtaining credit cards from depository institutions.

In recent years, business firms have also been able to bypass banks and other financial intermediaries and go directly to SSUs to borrow money. Small and medium-size business firms that previously relied on bank loans now have access to the commercial paper market where they can borrow directly from SSUs. The result has been that commercial banks extend a declining fraction of total credit—down from almost 40 percent in the mid-1970s to 27 percent during 1995. The diminished role of banks in providing credit alters the ability of the Fed, which works primarily through the banking system, in using established methods to control the economy.

on the economy. There was a close relationship between the monetary aggregates and economic activity. By the late 1980s, commercial banks were extending a declining share of total credit (lending) in the economy. This weakened the Fed's traditional avenues of control over the economy, and the link between money and credit became broken.

Money, Credit, and the Economy: A Peek at the Data

Real Gross Domestic Product (Real GDP)
The real, or inflation-adjusted, quantity of final goods and services produced in an economy in a given time period.

Exhibit 3-8 presents data for the past 35 years on the growth rate of the money supply (M2), the growth rate of credit (DNFD), and the growth of real economic activity. The growth rate of economic activity is measured by the growth rate of **real gross domestic product (real GDP),** which is the real, inflation-adjusted quantity of final goods and services produced in an economy in a given time period, usually a year.[7] While the three measures are far from perfectly correlated—that is, they do not always move up and down together—it is fair to say that sometimes when the money supply and credit growth rates rise significantly, such as in the early 1970s, there is a general tendency for the quantity of goods and services produced and sold (real GDP)

---

[7] Real GDP is discussed further in the next chapter and at length in most principles of economics texts.

LOOKING BACK

A Brief History of Currency in the United States

Today currency in the United States is issued by the U.S. Treasury and circulated by the Fed. But this has not always been the case. During the colonial period, the British colonies were prohibited from printing or coining their own currency. Barter was commonplace and other exchanges occurred using various "monies" such as wampum (Indian beads made from sea shells), tobacco, and gold or silver coins. To help finance the Revolutionary War, the Continental Congress issued a new kind of currency called the *Continental*. Because so many Continentals had been issued, they were often not accepted in payment and the phrase "not worth a Continental" came to signify something of little worth.

The first privately owned bank in the United States, the Bank of North America, was chartered in Philadelphia in 1782. From the earliest years of banking until the Civil War, privately owned banks issued their own currency called banknotes, which were redeemable in gold and were circulated as money. Banknotes were dispersed when loans were made. However, because banks issued more notes than the amount of gold held in reserve, note holders would periodically become fearful that banks would not be able to meet commitments to redeem the notes in gold. Note holders would rush to the banks to convert their notes to gold before the banks ran out. The result was that the banknotes often circulated at a discount well below their face value and banks often failed.

Such problems (in addition to the widespread counterfeiting of banknotes) led many states by the late 1830s to require that banks post government bonds as collateral against the banknotes they issued. If a bank could not redeem its notes, the bonds would be sold with the proceeds going to the note holders. This period from the late 1830s until the Civil War, became known as the Wildcat Banking Era. Banks that were unable to redeem their notes in gold would relocate to the woods where it would be difficult for even a wildcat to find them.

During the Civil War, the government issued greenbacks to finance the war. By the end of the war, greenbacks (and closely related U.S. government notes) made up 75 percent of the money in circulation. Sundry banknotes issued by privately owned state-chartered banks made up the other 25 percent. In 1863 and 1864, Congress passed the National Banking Acts, which established a network of federally chartered national banks and created a uniform currency. The new currency was issued by the national banks and backed by government bonds. In addition, the Acts levied a 10 percent tax on the banknotes issued by state-chartered banks. Subsequently, these banknotes disappeared and the new uniform banknotes circulated at full value. The National Banking Acts were successful in providing a sound and stable national currency for the first time since the birth of the nation.

to also grow. Conversely, when the money supply growth rate drops significantly, such as in the late 1960s, real GDP growth may also tend to fall. In the late 1980s and early 1990s, it is clear that credit (DNFD) is more closely related to economic activity than M2.

Note that the shaded areas of Exhibit 3-8 depict business cycle recessions when the growth of economic activity was close to zero or actually negative. Careful examination reveals a tendency for the money supply or the flow of credit to decline around the beginning of most recessions and to increase around the beginning of most expansions (the periods beginning where the shaded areas end). Therefore, the obvious conclusion is that money and credit flows have a lot to do with fluctuations in economic activity.

To expand our look at data, Exhibit 3-9 focuses on the relationship between the growth rate of money and credit, and inflation. The exhibit utilizes data on the rate of change in the **consumer price index (CPI)** discussed in Exhibit 3-10, which also discusses the **producer price index (PPI).** The rate of change of the CPI measures the **inflation rate,** which is essentially the growth rate in the average level of prices paid by consumers in the economy. In Exhibit 3-9, these data are plotted against the same money supply and credit data used in Exhibit 3-8, with one important difference; the inflation rate data for a particular year have been plotted against the growth of the money supply and credit one year previous. In other words, the roughly 8 percent growth of the money supply and 12.7 percent growth of DNFD shown for 1980 in Exhibit 3-9, actually took place in 1979.

Why plot the data this way you ask? The rationale is quite straightforward; whenever aggregate (total) demand for goods and services increases, say as a result of a rise in the money supply or credit growth rates, there is a general tendency for output to rise fairly quickly, as shown in Exhibit 3–8, and for prices to change more gradually, as shown in Exhibit 3-9. Likewise, whenever

Consumer Price Index (CPI) A price index that measures the cost of a market basket that a typical urban consumer purchases.

Producer Price Index (PPI) A price index that measures the change in the cost of a market basket purchased by the typical producer of goods and services.

Inflation Rate The rate of change in the consumer price index that measures the growth rate of the average level of prices paid by consumers.

Exhibit 3-8 ◆

The Growth Rates of M2, DNFD, and Real GDP

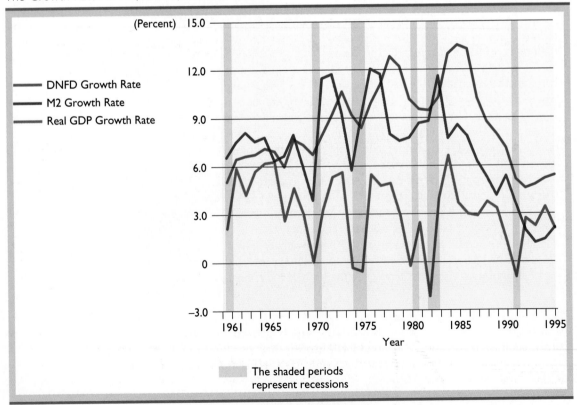

DNFD Growth Rate
M2 Growth Rate
Real GDP Growth Rate

The shaded periods represent recessions

Exhibit 3-9 ◆

The Growth Rate of the CPI (Inflation) and the Lagged Growth Rates of M2 and DNFD

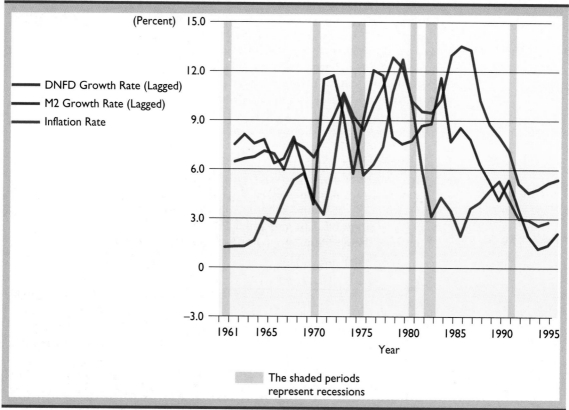

aggregate demand decreases, as a result of a fall in the money supply or credit growth rates, there is a tendency for output to fall fairly quickly, and for prices to respond with a lag. Put another way, the current inflation rate is heavily influenced by changes in money supply and credit growth that occurred some time in the past.

As was the case in Exhibit 3-8, the three data series plotted in Exhibit 3-9 are closely correlated during some time periods, but certainly far from perfectly correlated. A relationship is discernable, especially from the mid-1960s through the early 1980s; when there is a sustained and significant increase in the money supply or credit growth rates, such as occurred in the early 1970s, there is a general tendency for the inflation rate to rise one to two years later. Conversely, when the money supply and credit growth rates slow significantly, as occurred in 1981, inflation tends to subside, albeit with a time lag. During the mid 1980s through the early 1990s, the growth rates of money and credit were above inflation. Things other than changes in M2 and DNFD obviously affected the CPI during this time period.

To complete our first glimpse at the data, look at Exhibit 3-11. This exhibit shows the relationship between the growth rate of the money supply (M2), the growth rate of credit (DNFD), and the growth rate of **nominal GDP.** This

Nominal GDP The quantity of final goods and services produced in an economy during a given time period and valued at today's prices.

Exhibit 3-10 ◆
Measuring the
Inflation Rate

The major price indexes in the United States—the Consumer Price Index (CPI) and the Producer Price Index (PPI)—are computed and published monthly by the government. The CPI is designed to measure changes in the cost of a market basket of goods purchased by a typical urban consumer. The PPI measures the change in the cost of a market basket the typical producer purchases. The inflation rate is generally measured by the percentage change in one of these price indexes. For example, the CPI rose from 148.2 in 1994 to 152.4 in 1995, an increase of 2.8 percent (152.4 − 148.2 = 4.2; 4.2/148.2 = .028 = 2.8 percent). Thus, the inflation rate during 1995 was 2.8 percent.

So far, so good. But where did the index number 152.4 come from, and what does it mean? The CPI is constructed by first selecting a group of goods and services—called the *market basket* of goods and services—representative of the purchases made by a typical urban household. Then, each month, the prices of the roughly 400 items included in this same market basket are surveyed. The hypothetical example in the following table illustrates how the resulting index and inflation rate are computed.

Year	Total Cost of Market Basket	Consumer Price Index	Annual Inflation Rate
1982–84	$500	100	
1989	620	124	
1990	653.50	130.7	5.4%
1991	681	136.2	4.2
1992	701.50	140.3	2.6
1993	722.50	144.5	3.0
1994	741	148.2	2.6
1995	762	152.4	2.8

The years 1982–84 are the base period years for computing the index in the sense that prices of the market basket in future years are compared to the prices of the same market basket in 1982–84—that is, $500. More formally, the CPI in a given year is displayed in Equation 3-1.

$$(3\text{-}1) \quad CPI = \left[\frac{(\text{Cost of the market basket in the given year})}{(\text{cost of the market basket in the base period})} \right] * 100$$

Accordingly, the CPI for 1982–84 is 100, and for 1995, when the cost of the market basket rose to $762, the CPI is 152.4 [(762/500) * 100 = 152.4]. Literally, the CPI of 152.4 for 1995 means that prices were 52.4 percent higher in 1995 than in the 1982–84 time period.

exhibit differs from Exhibit 3-8 in that the growth rate of output is measured by changes in nominal GDP rather than real GDP. Nominal GDP measures the quantity of final goods and services produced in an economy during a given time period and valued at today's prices. Not surprisingly, changes in money (M2) and credit (DNFD) are more closely correlated with changes in nominal GDP than with changes in real GDP in Exhibit 3-8. This is so because the growth rate of nominal GDP encompasses changes in both real GDP and prices.[8]

As illustrated schematically in Exhibit 3-7 and graphically in Exhibits 3-8, 3-9, and 3-11, our first approximation about how money matters can be summarized by the following general proposition: A sustained and significant rise in the money supply and credit growth rates will tend to raise aggregate demand for goods and services, increase output growth and, with a lag, may at times tend to elevate the inflation rate.[9] Conversely, a sustained fall in money supply and credit growth rates will tend to lower aggregate demand, lower output growth and, after a time, reduce the inflation rate.

---

[8] In the preceding paragraph, we noticed that lagged changes in M2 and DNFD were most strongly correlated with price changes. This does not negate the fact that a weaker positive relationship exists between changes in M2 and DNFD and current price changes.

[9] This proposition assumes the economy is not starting from a position of full employment. If the economy is at full employment and there is a sustained and significant rise in the money supply and/or credit growth rates, the increase in aggregate demand will most likely lead to inflation with no increase in output.

Exhibit 3-11 ◆

The Growth Rates of M2, DNFD, and Nominal GDP

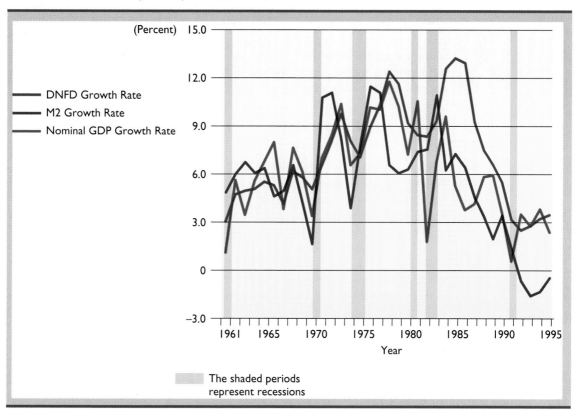

RECAP

Changes in the growth rates of money and credit are correlated with changes in nominal GDP, real GDP, and inflation. The strongest correlation is between changes in money and credit and changes in nominal GDP. Changes in inflation lag changes in money and credit. The correlations are far from perfect.

Are Money and Credit All That Matter?

The preceding discussion certainly suggests an important causal relationship that runs from changes in money and/or credit to key economic variables such as the inflation rate and real and nominal GDP growth. However, in the course of discussing the data we emphasized that the correlations among money supply growth, credit flows, and these other variables are far from perfect. In addition, the correlations do not necessarily imply causation.[10] Simply put, this lack of perfect correlation means that changes in the growth rate of the money supply and/or credit are not the only factors that influence inflation and economic activity. Other factors, such as current fiscal policy, and expectations about future monetary and fiscal policy and future inflation, can exert a powerful influence on prices and output, especially in the short run. In fact, some economists believe that the effects of movements in these other factors are as powerful, or more powerful than current and past movements in the money supply and/or credit flows, in terms of their influence on the economy. Finally, as we have seen, the relationship between the monetary aggregates and credit flows may also change over time, as commercial banks' share of total lending changes.

Money and Credit Flows: First Fiddle or Second Fiddle

Historically, money has played an important role in economic systems and economic literature—perhaps given more attention than given to the role of credit. As with most things in life, however, the historical and present roles and influence of money and/or credit in the economy are not black and white. Economists do not totally agree on what the role of money has been or is in the economy. Some economists believe that money matters more than anything else in determining the overall health of the economy; they are appropriately called **monetarists.** Other economists, as we have pointed out, now stress that it is credit flows (loans) that trigger changes in spending. Still others believe that money and/or credit flows are only two among many factors affecting the economy. Such economists carry various labels—nonmonetarist, Keynesian, neo-Keynesian, post-Keynesian, and so forth. Just as with music videos, there is often something to be gained by differentiating one's product from that of the competition!

Monetarists Economists who stress the role of money in determining the overall health of the economy.

---

[10]Events A and B are correlated if they occur together. Correlation does not mean that A caused B, or vice versa.

The controversy over the role of money and credit is somewhat like trying to determine whether the coach is the key to a team's success. Some will argue that the team won in spite of poor coaching, while others will attribute the team's triumphs to the insight and intelligence of the coach. It is difficult to resolve such debates. An important piece of evidence, however, is the team's record over a number of years. A team that continues to win year after year, even though its talent has varied noticeably, will convince even the skeptics that the coach played a key role in establishing a successful record.

Likewise, although not everyone agrees as to exactly how and to what degree money and credit matter, few dispute the contention that the weight of the historical evidence produced by economists indicates that changes in the growth rates of money and credit exert a powerful influence on spending, production, inflation, and unemployment.

Summary of Major Points

1. The interest rate is the cost to borrowers of obtaining money and the return (or yield) on money to lenders. It is the cost of credit. Ceteris paribus, the quantity demanded of money and the interest rate are inversely related.

2. The demand for money is determined by the spending plans of spending units, which are usually positively or directly related to income. The supply of money is strongly influenced by the Fed through its control over reserves and the required reserve ratio.

3. The interaction between the supply of and demand for money determines the equilibrium quantity of money and the equilibrium interest rate. In general, the initial effect of either an increase in the money supply or a decrease in money demand will be a fall in the interest rate, ceteris paribus. Conversely, the initial effect of either a decrease in the money supply or an increase in money demand will be a rise in the interest rate, ceteris paribus.

4. Credit flows (loan extensions) are also a key determinant of changes in spending and income. As depository institutions handle a declining share of credit, the relationship between the monetary aggregates and economic activity may be diminished.

5. Changes in the money supply, credit, and the interest rate will generally alter the aggregate (total) demand for goods and services in the economy. Changes in aggregate demand will, in turn, affect the overall level of output and prices. More specifically, a rise in the money supply and/or credit flows, and the accompanying fall in the interest rate will generally raise aggregate demand and lead to an expansion of output and some rise in prices.

6. Historical data suggest that a sustained and significant rise in money supply or credit growth will tend to increase output growth and, with a lag, tend at times to raise the inflation rate. Likewise, a sustained and significant fall in money supply or credit growth will tend to decrease output growth and, with a lag, tend at times to lower the inflation rate.

7. The correlations among the rate of money supply growth, credit flows, and both inflation and output growth are far from perfect; this suggests that other factors, such as current fiscal policy and expectations about future monetary and fiscal policy, also influence inflation and economic activity. Put another way, money and credit flows are not "all that matter."

8. Controversy does exist within the economics profession about the specific role of money and credit; how much do they matter and how precisely do they matter? However, few dispute the contention that the weight of the historical evidence indicates that money and credit flows exert a powerful, although changing, influence on the economy.

Key Terms

Consumer Price Index (CPI)	Producer Price Index (PPI)
Credit	Quantity Demanded of Money
Demand for Money	Quantity Supplied of Money
Depository Institutions	Real Gross Domestic Product
Inflation Rate	(Real GDP)
Interest Rate	Required Reserve Ratio
Monetarists	Reserves
Nominal GDP	Supply of Money

Review Questions

1. Briefly define the interest rate, reserves, the required reserve ratio, the inflation rate, and nominal GDP.

2. Discuss the similarities between how the price of compact disks is determined in the compact disk market and how the interest rate is determined in the market for money.

3. What is the difference between the demand for money and the quantity demanded of money?

4. What is the opportunity cost of holding money?

5. Mary and Harold Jones are a young couple with a growing income. What will happen to their demand for money over time?

6. In what form can a depository institution hold reserves? Who determines the amount of funds available for reserves? How does the Fed influence the amount of reserves a depository institution must hold?

7. What are the sources of credit? Explain the statement, "The money supply is measured at a point in time while the flow of credit is measured over time."

8. How does real GDP differ from nominal GDP?

9. Alarm clocks going off and sunrise are highly correlated. Does the noise of alarm clocks going off cause the sun to rise? Why or why not?

10. Explain the difference between money and credit. Give an example of each.

Analytical Questions

11. Show on a graph how the interest rate and the quantity demanded of money are related. Do the same for the quantity supplied of money. When is the market in equilibrium?

12. Assume the market for money is originally in equilibrium. What happens to demand, supply, quantity demanded, and/or quantity supplied, ceteris paribus, given the following events:
    a. The Fed lowers reserve requirements.
    b. Households increase their spending plans.
    c. Income falls due to a severe recession.
    d. The Fed steps up its provision of reserves to depository institutions.

13. Graph each case presented in question 12.

14. If there is an increase in the supply of money, what are the effects on interest rates, prices, and output? If there is a decrease in the supply of money, what are the effects on interest rates, prices, and output? Do these effects occur simultaneously?

15. Substituting the words "credit flows" for "supply of money," answer question 14.

16. What happens to interest rates, prices, and output if there is an increase in the demand for money? What happens to the same variables if there is a decrease in the demand for money?

17. Substituting the words "credit flows" for "demand for money," answer question 16.

18. Assume that the price of a market basket is $2,000 in the base period, $2,060 one year later, and $2,100 two years later. What is the price index in the base period? . . . after the first year? . . . the second year? What is the rate of inflation in the first year? . . . the second year?

19. Ceteris paribus, what happens to the demand for money if incomes go down? Ceteris paribus, what happens to the supply of money if reserves go up? In each case, does the interest rate change? Graph each case.

20. Use a graph to show what happens to the interest rate if the demand for money is increasing while the supply of money is decreasing?

21. Assume a price index increases from 145 to 150 to 155 over three consecutive years. Was the rate of inflation higher in the second or third year? What does it mean if a price index falls from 150 to 145?

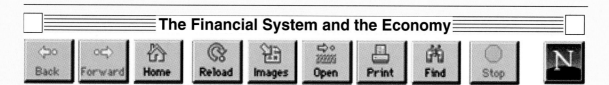

The Financial System and the Economy

1. Answer the following questions by accessing the National Income and Product Accounts at the root directory (gopher://una.hh.lib.umich.edu:70/00/ebb/nipa/gdp/gdp-tab.bea). Look up the current real GDP numbers for the U.S. economy (Table 2) and compare them to the current-dollar GDP numbers over similar time per-

iods. Why and how does the real GDP measures differ from the current-dollar GDP measure? (Note: in the body of the text, we refer to current-dollar GDP as nominal GDP.)

2. From the web sites, (ftp://stats.bls.gov/pub/news.release/cpi.txt) and (ftp://stats.bls.gov/put/news.release/ppi.txt) obtain the current estimate of inflation as gauged by the Consumer Price Index (CPI) and the Producer Price Index (PPI). The CPI for urban consumer (CPI-U) is disaggregated by expenditure category. Name the explicit expenditure categories used by the Bureau of Labor Statistics.

3. Seasonally adjusted historical data on the CPI for urban consumers (CPI-U is obtainable from the website (http://www.stls.frb.org/fred/data/cpi/cpiaucsl). From the information on the CPI "change from previous month," calculate a rough average annual inflation rate. Pay special attention to the inflation rates recorded over the mid 1970s, early 1980s and the early 1990s. Compare these rates of inflation with the annual rates of growth of M2 over the same time periods. (Use the following internet site for calculating M2 growth rates: (gopher://una.hh.lib.umich.edu:70/00/ebb/monetary/money.frb). Is there any discernible relationship between the rate of growth of the money supply and the rate of inflation?

Suggested Readings

We saw in Chapter 2 that M2 was used as a policy guide in the 1980s. A modern article by David H. Small and Richard Porter, "Understanding the Behavior of M2 and V2," *Federal Reserve Bulletin*, April 1989, pp. 244–254, provides an interesting discussion of the relationship of M2 and output.

For an interesting discussion of many of the topics in this chapter, see Fed Chairperson Alan Greenspan's "Statement to the Congress," on July 20, 1993, reprinted in the *Federal Reserve Bulletin*, September 1993, pp. 849–855.

For interesting recent discussions of the relationship among money, inflation, and economic activity in the popular press, see the following articles: W. V. Sullivan, "A Message in U.S. Monetary Data?" *Business Week*, October 17, 1994, p. 34; "Economy, Inflation Likely to Keep Growing," *ABA Banking Journal*, August 1994, pp. 21–22; Vivian Brownstein, "The Growing Threat of Inflation," *Fortune*, January 16, 1994, pp. 66–68; "Economists Agree: Inflation Won't Spike in '95 and Business Will See a Slowing Growth Rate," *Barron's*, January 2, 1995, p. 33.

4

The Financial System and the Economy: An Analytical Perspective

> *Money is always there but*
> *the pockets change; it is not in the*
> *same pockets after a change, and that*
> *is all there is to say about money.*
> —Gertrude Stein—

Learning Objectives

After reading this chapter, you should know:

♦ How the financial system channels and coordinates the flow of funds

♦ The meaning and significance of consumption, saving, and investment

♦ The role of firms and households in the output market, factor market, and financial system

♦ The role and linkages of the various markets in coordinating and balancing firm and household plans

♦ What general forces produce the activity, or motion, we observe in the economy

The Trees Versus the Forest

During a typical month, the business and financial pages of any leading newspaper might include the following reports on the economy's recent performance: industrial production rose 1 percent; retail sales rose 2 percent; the unemployment rate fell slightly; IBM issued $300 million of bonds to finance the construction of a new plant; the Consumer Price Index increased 0.1 percent; the United Auto Workers and General Motors reached agreement on a new three-year contract that will raise wages and benefits by 8 percent. The untrained eye might see little connection among these reports. The trained eye, however, sees more.

A major objective of any science—be it physics, astronomy, or economics—is to find patterns where the untrained eye sees only disorder. To discover and understand these patterns it is usually necessary to disregard inessential details. Such abstraction facilitates the identification of the fundamental and essential relationships linking the key elements of the process or phenomena being studied.

In the study of money, credit, and the financial system, you might find the details of the analysis overwhelming. Unfortunately it might obscure the broad fundamental patterns of order so important to an analytical foundation. The problem is akin to getting lost in a forest; by paying too much attention to the individual trees you can become disoriented and lose your way.

The purpose of Chapters 1–3 was to introduce the roles of money, credit, and the financial system. The general purpose of this chapter is to provide an analytical perspective on how the financial system fits into the overall economy. The circular flow analysis and accompanying diagrams should serve both as a road map through the economic "forest" and as an aerial photograph that reveals the patterns of order which link households, firms, financial markets, and financial intermediaries.

Spending, Saving, Borrowing, and Lending

In Chapter 1 we introduced and defined surplus spending units (SSUs) and deficit spending units (DSUs). To review, SSUs spend less than their current income during a particular period of time. More precisely, the surplus is the income that spending units receive but do not spend on consumer goods and services or on investments such as new houses. It is this surplus that SSUs have available to lend. The spending units that spend more than their current income during a particular period of time are DSUs. The deficit is the excess of current spending on goods and services and investments over current income.

The DSUs, such as the U.S. government or business firms, must finance their deficits. Normally, they do this by borrowing. Some DSUs accomplish this by issuing financial claims on themselves; for now we will refer to these financial claims on DSUs as **bonds.** Other types of DSUs, such as students struggling to buy books, pay their tuition, and feed themselves, may finance their deficits by taking out loans from their local banks. This too is a type of financial claim; the students agree to repay the loan principal plus interest.

Bonds Financial claims on DSUs; IOUs issued by DSUs.

Who provides the funds that the DSUs receive when they issue bonds and the funds that banks lend to students? The answer is, of course, the SSUs.[1] Rather than accumulating the surpluses in the form of cash assets in their backyards or sticking them in their mattresses, SSUs generally purchase interest-earning financial claims. For example, a household with a surplus might purchase a bond issued by the U.S. Treasury, the department that manages the government's finances, or a bond issued by a corporation. Likewise, the household might deposit the funds in a savings account at a bank, which in turn lends them to the DSUs. Thus, the SSUs are the lenders in society, and the financial system, composed of the financial markets and financial intermediaries, channels the surpluses of SSUs to the DSUs to finance their deficits.

To sum up to this point, individual spending units make two types of decisions. First, they decide whether to be a DSU or an SSU. Second, if they decide to be a DSU, they must decide how to finance their deficits; or, if they decide to be SSUs, they must decide what to do with their surpluses. Given the decisions made by individual spending units, the financial system channels and coordinates this flow of funds.

To see better the relationship among the decisions made by spending units and to integrate the financial system and the flow of funds into the economy as a whole, consider a hypothetical example involving a "typical" household and a "typical" firm. For simplicity we will ignore the foreign sector and the government sector and assume the household is an SSU and the firm is a DSU.

A Typical Household

J.P. Young holds an MBA degree and works as a middle manager at All Purpose Enterprise Incorporated, better known as APEI. Exhibit 4-1 summarizes J.P.'s receipts and expenditures during 1996. Such a summary is often referred to as an income statement or as a statement of the sources and uses of funds.

The righthand side of the table shows the total of J.P.'s receipts—called **disposable personal income**—and the various sources of this income.[2] APEI

Disposable Personal Income Income available to households to spend on consumption or to save.

---

[1] This assumption ignores the Fed and the money creation process for now.
[2] In the real world, disposable personal income is equal to income received by households—called *personal income*—minus taxes paid. Since we are ignoring the government for now, taxes are zero.

Expenditures (Uses)		Receipts (Sources)	
Consumption	$34,000	Wages and Salaries	$37,000
(spending on goods and services)		Dividends	$ 2,000
Saving	$ 7,000	Interest	$ 2,000
(acquisition of summer			
home)	$ 4,000	Rent	$ 0
(acquisition of financial		Disposable Income	$41,000
claims)	$ 3,000		
Consumption plus Saving	$41,000		

Exhibit 4-1 ◆
Financial Statement
J.P. Young (January 1, 1996 through December 31, 1996)

paid J.P. $37,000 in wages and salary over the year and an additional $4,000 was received in the form of dividends and interest on stocks and bonds that J.P. owns.

On the expenditure side of the table, we can see that J.P. spent $34,000 on goods and services; household spending on goods and services is called **consumption.** J.P. saved the remaining $7,000 of income, $4,000 of which was used by J.P. for investment in new housing and $3,000 was surplus funds that were available to be loaned in financial markets. Since disposable personal income must by definition be either consumed or saved, saving is equal to disposable personal income minus consumption. In general, such saving will take four forms. First, J.P. can make investments such as purchasing a new house. Secondly, J.P. can purchase additional stocks and bonds. These items represent financial claims on the issuer/borrower by the holder/saver. Thirdly, J.P. can place funds into a financial intermediary, such as a commercial bank or a savings and loan. Here, J.P.'s deposit represents a financial claim on the intermediary. The deposit is an asset for J.P. (it is owned) and a liability for the intermediary (it owes). Finally, J.P. can hold cash balances in the form of currency buried in the backyard or hidden under a mattress or elsewhere.[3]

So much for J.P.; what about APEI?

Consumption Household spending on goods and services.

A Typical Firm

All Purpose Enterprise Incorporated (APEI), in business since 1904, had a good year in 1996. With its profits up from the previous year and the business outlook bright, it decided to expand its scale of operations by building a new plant and acquiring additional inventories. Exhibit 4-2 summarizes APEI's financial transactions during 1996.

---

[3]Notice that the income J.P. has in excess of what J.P. spends on consumption or investment goods is identically equal to the surplus funds available to lend to others. The lending to others takes the form of direct finance such as purchasing stocks and bonds, or indirect finance (putting funds with a financial intermediary).

Exhibit 4-2 ◆
Financial Statement All Purpose Enterprise Inc. (January 1, 1996 through December 31, 1996) (in millions)

(A)	Total Expenses	**$4,400**	Total Sales	**$4,800**
	Wages and salaries	3,200		
	Interest on debt	200		
	Cost of raw materials purchased from other firms	1,000		
(B)	Net Income (Sales − Expenses)	**$400**		
	minus Dividends	200		
	equals Retained Earnings	$200		
(C)	Business Investment Spending (new capital goods—plant and equipment—and/or additions to inventories)	$500	Financing: New bonds issued Retained earnings	$300 200 $500

Part (A) of the exhibit shows the total revenue received from the sale of APEI's various products to consumers like J.P. All figures are in millions of dollars. To calculate profits, we have to subtract total expenses from the sales figure. Such expenses include the payment of wages and salaries to workers and the payment of interest to bondholders. Note that such expenses for firms are income for the recipient households. With sales totaling $4,800 million and expenses totaling $4,400 million, net income is $400 million, Part (B) of the exhibit. Given this profit performance and the outlook for future sales, APEI's managers recommend and the Board of Directors approves a dividend payment of $200 million to stockholders and a $500 million expansion project. The **investment** spending, which is the purchase of the new plant and additions to inventory, will be financed, as shown in Part (C) of the exhibit, by issuing $300 million of new bonds and utilizing the $200 million of retained earnings. Who will buy the bonds? By now we are sure you know—households like J.P. and financial intermediaries.[4]

Investment Spending by households on newly constructed houses plus spending by business firms on capital or additions to inventories.

From J.P. and APEI to the Economy as a Whole: Aggregation

Let's assume the economy is made up of 100 million households (of which J.P. is typical) and 1,000 firms (of which APEI is typical). This being the case, we can multiply the relevant values in Exhibits 4-1 and 4-2 by 100 million or 1,000, as appropriate, to determine aggregate values for income and expenditures for our hypothetical economy. Exhibit 4-3 pulls together the resulting totals for 1996.

Focusing first on the household sector, remember that J.P.'s income was $41,000. When multiplied by 100 million (the number of households), we get disposable income for the entire household sector of $4,100 billion. This is the figure shown in the exhibit. Likewise, consumption and saving for the household sector were $3,400 billion and $700 billion, respectively. Of the $7000 billion in saving, the households spent $400 billion on investment in housing and had $300 billion in surplus funds available to lend. Here again, the appropriate multiplication yields the totals shown in the exhibit.

Turning to the business sector, we multiply APEI's retained earnings ($200 million) by the number of firms (1,000) and get $200 billion, which is total retained earnings. (Note that the rest of firms' income was paid to households as dividends and has already been counted as part of household income.) In the expenditure column, the $500 billion of investment spending is equal to APEI's $500 million of investment spending multiplied by 1,000 firms. We assume that $500 million of investment spending is typical for each firm. The $300 billion excess of total investment spending over total retained earnings is the business sector's deficit; it will be financed by issuing bonds.

The relevant totals for the economy as a whole are calculated simply by adding up the relevant columns. The totals are given in the last row of Exhibit 4-3. More specifically, to calculate national income ($4,300 billion), we add household disposable income ($4,100 billion) to firms' retained earnings

---

[4]To simplify, we are ignoring that some of the capital may have been worn out in the production of output and needs replacement. We cover this extension in Chapter 18.

Exhibit 4-3 ◆
National Income
and Expenditures
for Our
Hypothetical
Economy (in
billions)

	1996		
Sector	Income	Expenditures	Receipts − Expenditures = Deficit or Surplus
Households	Disposable Personal Income $4,100	Consumption Expenditures $3,400 Investment Expenditures $400	Surplus $300
Business Firms	Retained Earnings $200	Investment Expenditures $500	Deficit −$300
Economy	National Income $4,300	Domestic Product $4,300	

($200 billion). Similarly, to calculate total expenditures on output ($4,300 billion), we add together consumption ($3,400 billion) and investment spending ($900 billion = $400 billion investment by households + $500 billion investment by businesses). Finally, we can see in the last column that the deficit in the business sector ($300 billion) is exactly offset by the surplus in the household sector; in other words, the amount of bonds sold equals the amount of bonds bought.

So what is the point of all this? Typically, households and firms meet in three separate but related market arenas. First, there is the **product market.** Firms produce and sell goods and services; they are the suppliers in the product market. Households purchase goods and services through consumption spending and investment goods such as new houses. In addition, firms purchase new capital goods and additions to inventory through investment spending. Together, households and firms are the demanders in the product market. Second, there is the **factor market** for labor, capital, and natural resources. If we focus on labor in particular, households are obviously the suppliers of labor services and firms engaged in production are the demanders. Third and finally, there is the financial system: DSUs, such as APEI, are the demanders of funds; SSUs, such as J.P. Young, are the suppliers of funds.

Our economy is populated with millions of J.P. Youngs and thousands of APEIs. Each makes spending, saving, borrowing, and lending decisions. When we add them together—that is, aggregate—we have the total demand for goods and services, the total supply of funds, the total demand for labor, and so forth. These supplies and demands produce the flow of income, expenditures, and funds depicted in our example. **National income** is the resulting earnings in each sector. The sum of expenditures in each sector equals **national expenditures** on the final output of goods and services (domestic product). And, since, in this simplified economy, whatever is spent is received by someone, national income equals national expenditures. Given these economywide relationships, the rest of the chapter shows how the various supplies and demands, and the decisions that underlie them are related.

Product Market The market for consumption spending by households and investment spending by households and firms.

Factor Market The market for inputs such as labor, capital, and natural resources.

National Income The sum of the earnings of each sector.
National Expenditures The sum of the expenditures of each sector.

The Circular Flow of Income, Expenditures, and Funds

Firms and households meet in three markets. The **circular flow diagram,** shown in Exhibit 4-4, pulls together the essential features of this simplified economy. It is designed to highlight the flow of income, expenditures, and funds, which links the various markets to the producing, spending, saving, borrowing, and lending behavior of firms and households.

In this simple circular flow diagram, real flows go in one direction while money flows go in the opposite. Households supply labor and other factors of production to businesses. Money flows from businesses to households in payment for the services of labor and the other factors of production. The payments for factor services are household income. (For simplicity, the only factor we consider is labor.) The wage rate is determined in the labor market by supply and demand.

Households purchase consumer goods and services and new houses from businesses using part of the income they have received in payment for their factor services. Money flows from households back to firms to purchase goods and services. However, usually households do not spend all of the income they receive on goods and services. Instead, they are SSUs spending less than what they receive on consumer and investment goods. The financial system links surplus households with DSUs. The DSUs are usually businesses who use the borrowed funds of the SSUs to purchase investment goods.

Funds flow from households (SSUs) to businesses (DSUs) through the financial system either directly through financial markets or indirectly through financial intermediaries. The interest rate, which equates the quantity supplied of loanable funds from SSUs with the quantity demanded of loanable funds by DSUs, is determined in the loanable funds market by supply and demand. Without highly developed financial markets, transferring the surpluses of SSUs to the DSUs would be much more difficult.

Prices in the output, labor, and loanable funds markets adjust to coordinate and balance the supplies and demands resulting from the plans of households and businesses to produce, spend, borrow, and lend. If there is a change in one market, reflecting changes in the behavior of households or firms, repercussions will be felt throughout all markets with price and quantity adjustments.

(In Chapter 3, we developed a theory of interest rate determination based on the supply and demand for money. In this chapter, we develop an alternative theory of interest rate determination based on the supply and demand for loanable funds. The appendix to this chapter reconciles the two theories.)

The roles, relationships and interdependencies that the exhibit depicts can be summarized as follows:

1. *The Roles of Firms:* They supply goods and services to the product market, demand investment goods supplied by other firms, demand factor services in the factor market, and demand funds (borrow) from the financial system.
2. *The Roles of Households:* They demand goods and services in the product market, supply factor services in the factor market, and supply funds (lend) to the financial system.

Circular Flow Diagram
A diagram that shows the real and financial flows between households and business firms.

Exhibit 4-4 ◆
The Circular Flow Diagram

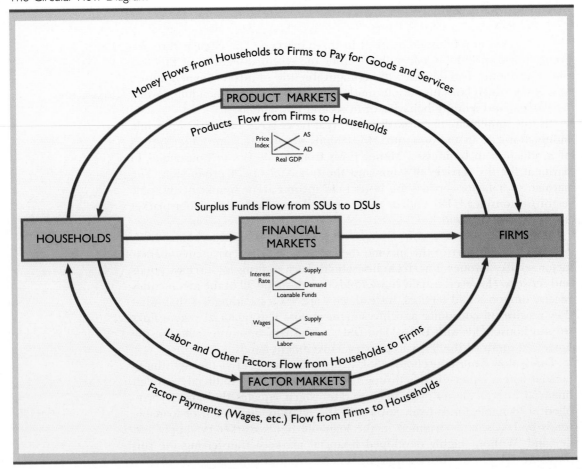

3. *The Roles of Markets:*
    ◆ The various markets coordinate and balance the supplies and de-
        mands resulting from the plans of firms and households to produce,
        spend, borrow, and lend, etc.
    ◆ A change in supply or demand in one market, reflecting changes in
        the behavior of firms or households, will have repercussions in the
        other markets. This means, of course, that the financial system can
        not be adequately analyzed in isolation from the other markets.

The last points summarize the important and somewhat subtle role of markets in the circular flow. Since significant portions of the rest of the text
emanate from and elaborate on these *fundamentals,* we will closely examine
some of the underlying concepts and analysis here.

 RECAP

The household and business sectors meet in the product market, the factor
market, and the financial market. Households demand goods and ser-

vices, supply labor and other inputs, and, in general, supply loanable funds. Businesses supply consumer goods and services, demand investment goods, demand factor inputs, and, in general, demand loanable funds. In the circular flow, real flows go in one direction while financial flows go in the opposite.

The Product Market

When we examine the market for a particular product we are primarily interested in the determination of two things—the equilibrium price the good sells for and the equilibrium quantity of the good produced and sold. The determinants of equilibrium price and quantity are the supply of the product, reflecting the decisions of the firms, and the demand for the product, reflecting the decisions of households. In general, anything that affects supply or demand alters the equilibrium price for the product prevailing in the market and the quantity of the good produced and sold.

When we look at the market for total output in the economy, the story is essentially the same. We are primarily interested in the determination of two things: (1) the overall price level—that is, the average price of goods and services produced and sold, and (2) the total quantity of goods and services produced and sold. The typical measure of the price level is a price index, as discussed in Chapter 2. The typical measure of the quantity of total output produced and sold is real gross domestic product (real GDP). As in Chapter 3, real GDP measures the real (inflation-adjusted) quantity of final goods and services produced in an economy in a given time period, say a year.

In the upper portion of Exhibit 4-4 there is a rectangle, labeled "Product Market." Exhibit 4–5 enlarges this graph so we can see more details than appear on the circular flow diagram. (Please note that many complexities are ignored in this diagram and in the two that follow. Our purpose here is to

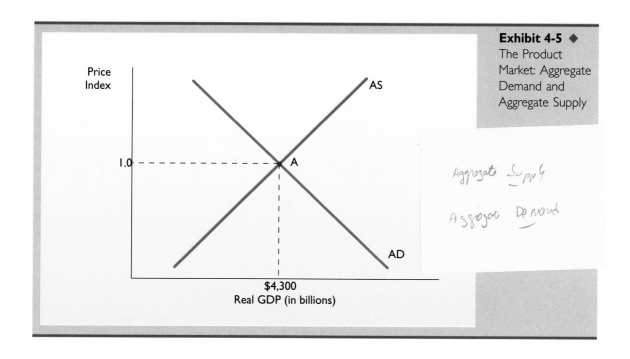

Exhibit 4-5 ◆
The Product Market: Aggregate Demand and Aggregate Supply

introduce some relevant concepts and modes of analysis. The necessary complexities will be presented once our foundation is firmly in place.) The overall price level (a price index) is measured on the vertical axis, while the quantity of real GDP is measured on the horizontal axis. These variables are determined by the **aggregate supply** of goods and services and the **aggregate demand** for goods and services.

Aggregate demand reflects the behavior of households and firms planning to engage in consumption and investment spending. The aggregate demand curve within our simplified economy shows various combinations of the price level and the quantity of real GDP that will be demanded at those prices, ceteris paribus. It is drawn with a downward or negative slope, under the reasonable presumption that as the price level rises, the purchasing power of the income or funds being used to purchase goods and services declines.[5] As a result, ceteris paribus, the quantity demanded of real GDP falls as the price level rises and vice versa.

As in all principles courses, we need to distinguish between a change in quantity demanded and a change in demand. Be sure you are clear that when the price level changes, ceteris paribus, the quantity demanded of real GDP changes and the economy moves along a given aggregate demand curve; if any variable other than the price level causes aggregate demand to change, there is a shift of the entire aggregate demand curve. For the time being, it is enough to say that if the spending plans of firms and households change, the aggregate demand curve will shift. For example, if spending plans increase, aggregate demand increases and the curve shifts rightward. Make sure you can work through a case in which spending plans decrease.

Aggregate supply reflects the behavior of firms planning to produce goods and services. The aggregate supply curve is drawn with an upward or positive slope under the reasonable presumption that, ceteris paribus, as prices go up, firms are willing to expand output (quantity supplied) in the expectation of greater profits. Again, be certain that you are clear about the difference between a change in quantity supplied and a change in aggregate supply. If the price level changes, ceteris paribus, quantity supplied changes and the economy moves along a given aggregate supply curve. A change in any variable other than the price level which alters the supply decisions of firms will cause the entire aggregate supply curve to shift and aggregate supply to change. For example, if firms decide to supply more at every price, the aggregate supply curve shifts rightward, and there is an increase in aggregate supply. Here again, you should be able to work through a case in which aggregate supply decreases.

As shown in Exhibit 4-5, the quantity demanded of real output is equal to the quantity supplied at point A. The resulting equilibrium occurs at a price level of 1.0 and a real GDP level of $4,300 billion; this is the GDP figure used in the previous numerical example. Given this starting point, anything that alters aggregate supply or aggregate demand will, in general, alter the price level and real GDP. For example, the Fed in its conduct of monetary policy can alter the spending, saving, borrowing, and lending decisions of firms and households.[6] Such actions will affect prices and output in the economy

---

Aggregate Supply The total quantity of goods and services that will be supplied at various prices. **Aggregate Demand** The total quantity of goods and services that will be demanded at various prices.

---

[5] In Chapter 20, we develop more fully the reasons why the AD curve is downward sloping.

[6] In our example, we can consider how actions of the Fed affect the circular flow even though we are ignoring the government sector. Technically, the Fed is not part of the government sector.

through their impact on aggregate demand. Striving to manage such effects so as to preserve the health and stability of the economy is what monetary policy is all about.[7] We develop the specifics of aggregate demand and aggregate supply in greater detail in Chapter 20.

RECAP

The aggregate demand curve is downward sloping and the aggregate supply curve is upward sloping. The overall price level and the level of real GDP are determined by the interaction of aggregate demand and aggregate supply. At the equilibrium price level, quantity demanded is equal to quantity supplied.

The Factor Market

The chief factor of production is labor. Accordingly, we shall focus here on the market for this particular input to the production process. As shown in Exhibit 4-4, households supply labor services and firms demand labor services. Exhibit 4-6 is an enlargement of the rectangle labeled ''Factor Market'' shown in the lower portion of Exhibit 4-4. Referring specifically to the labor segment of the factor market, the price to be determined is the wage rate, which is measured on the vertical axis. The quantity we focus on is the number of labor hours, measured on the horizontal axis.

---

[7] In an economy with a government sector, the governing body—in the United States, Congress and the president—can also alter the spending, saving, borrowing, and lending decisions of households and firms through fiscal policy (government spending and taxing decisions).

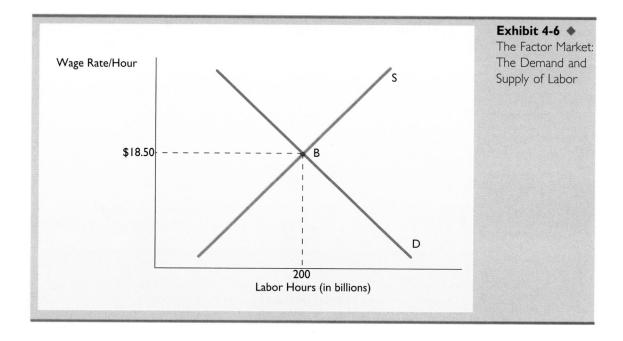

Exhibit 4-6 ◆
The Factor Market: The Demand and Supply of Labor

The demand curve for labor is downward sloping, indicating that a fall in the wage rate, ceteris paribus, will lead to an increase in the number of labor hours demanded (quantity demanded) by firms. Assuming firms have a choice of technologies, when the wage falls, labor is relatively cheaper than capital and firms substitute into the relatively cheaper factor. The supply curve for labor is upward sloping, indicating that a rise in the wage rate, ceteris paribus, will induce households to supply a larger quantity of labor services.

At the equilibrium point B the wage rate is $18.50 per hour and the number of hours workers are employed is 200 billion. These figures are also consistent with the numerical example above: we assumed 100 million households; if each supplies 40 hours of labor per week for 50 weeks a year (everyone needs at least two weeks vacation), this aggregates to 2,000 hours per worker and 200 billion hours for the economy as a whole; 2,000 hours per worker multiplied by the $18.50 hourly wage rate yields $37,000 income per year for all the J.P. Youngs in the economy.

What could change this situation? Suppose using monetary policy that the Federal Reserve was able to somehow raise the aggregate demand for goods—that is, a larger quantity of real GDP was demanded at every price level.[8] Looking back at the prevailing environment in the output market and leaving the graphs aside for a moment, what would firms observe? Initially unaware of the increase in demand engineered by the Fed, firms would probably notice their inventories of finished goods dropping as sales at retail outlets picked up. Assuming they expected the rise in demand to last for awhile, firms would in all likelihood respond by raising prices and stepping up production. But what is required to increase production? Among other things, more labor. How can firms attract more labor? If you said, "Higher wages," you are correct.

Graphically, a shift to the right in the aggregate demand curve in Exhibit 4-5 would induce a shift to the right in the labor demand curve in Exhibit 4-6. The shift of the labor demand curve corresponds to an increase in demand. The result will be higher wages and more workers employed for more hours. (We suggest that you sketch out this example graphically. Also, try one involving a drop in aggregate demand.) Again, in this example, be certain that you are clear that the demand for labor has increased, (shift of the demand curve) while the quantity supplied of labor increases as we move along the labor supply curve in response to the higher wage.

This example indicates how closely the output market and the factor market are connected.

 RECAP

The demand curve for labor is downward sloping. The supply curve of labor is upward sloping. At the equilibrium wage, the quantity demanded of labor is equal to the quantity supplied.

---

[8] The specifics of using monetary policy have not yet been discussed.

The Financial System

The financial system, consisting of financial intermediaries and financial markets, is a crucial part of the circular flow depicted in Exhibit 4-4. Viewed in a narrow sense, the role of the financial system is to facilitate the flow of funds from SSUs to DSUs, and vice versa. As pointed out in Chapter 2, however, a smoothly functioning financial system plays a much broader role. By offering a menu of alternatives to borrowers and lenders and minimizing the risks and costs of conducting transactions, such a system facilitates the efficient allocation of financial resources in an economy. Saving and investment, and thus, economic growth are in turn advanced.

The interest rate is the reward for lending and the cost of borrowing. Visualizing the financial system as one large market for funds, the focus of our attention is on the quantity of funds borrowed and lent, and the interest rate. As in the other markets, understanding supply and demand is the key to determining the interest rate (price) and quantity of loanable funds supplied and demanded.

In Exhibit 4-7, the interest rate is measured on the vertical axis and the quantity of loanable funds in billions of dollars is measured on the horizontal axis. The demand for funds, reflecting plans to borrow by DSUs (firms in our example), is downward sloping. Ceteris paribus, as the interest rate rises, the quantity of funds demanded decreases; ceteris paribus, as the interest rate falls, quantity demanded increases. This inverse relationship reflects the rational behavior of DSUs in response to changes in the cost of borrowing.

The supply of loanable funds is determined by the behavior of SSUs and the Fed. Reflecting plans to lend by SSUs (households in our example), the supply curve is drawn upward sloping. Ceteris paribus, as the interest rate increases, quantity supplied increases; ceteris paribus, as the interest rate decreases, quantity supplied decreases. This direct relationship between the

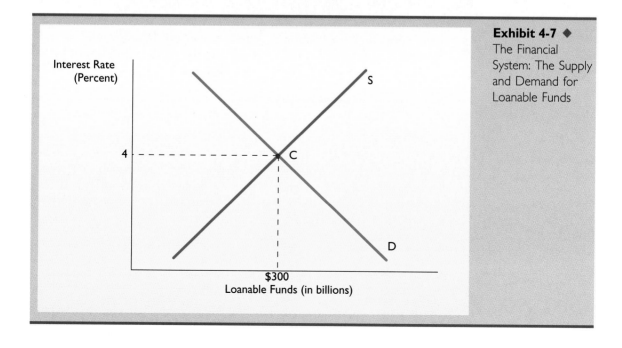

Exhibit 4-7 ◆
The Financial System: The Supply and Demand for Loanable Funds

quantity of loanable funds supplied and the interest rate reflects the rational behavior of SSUs in response to changes in the reward for lending. As for the Fed, it can in effect shift the supply curve to the right by using its tools to increase the supply of funds forthcoming from SSUs at any particular interest rate.[9] Likewise, the Fed can shift the supply curve to the left by using its tools to decrease the supply of loanable funds at any particular interest rate. Put another way, the Fed can augment or reduce the flow of funds through the financial system. (More on this in the next chapter.)

At the point the two curves intersect, the quantity of funds supplied is equal to the quantity of funds demanded ($300 billion) with a resulting equilibrium interest rate of 4 percent (point C). Here again, the situation in this market, as well as the equilibriums in the output and factor markets, is consistent with our numerical example and can be altered by a change in supply or demand. Recall our illustration in the discussion of the factor market; an increase in aggregate demand, engineered by the Fed, increased output, employment, wages, and prices. Now we can be a bit more specific. Suppose the Fed uses its tools to increase the supply of funds in a recessionary or depressed period. Utilizing standard supply and demand analysis, such a development would be expected to create an excess supply of funds in the financial system at the original equilibrium rate, resulting in a decline in the interest rate; graphically the supply curve would shift to the right in Exhibit 4-7. The drop in the interest rate, in turn, would be expected to encourage more borrowing by households and firms (movement downward along the demand for loanable funds curve) and thus, to increase consumption and investment spending.[10] It is this increase in aggregate demand in the output market, orchestrated by the Fed, that kicks off the production, employment, and price adjustments discussed above.

RECAP

The demand curve for loanable funds is downward sloping while the supply curve of loanable funds is upward sloping. At the equilibrium interest rate, the quantity demanded of loanable funds is equal to the quantity supplied.

We have covered much important ground. It's time to catch our collective breaths before proceeding. The circular flow diagram (Exhibit 4-4) and market diagrams (Exhibits 4-5 to 4-7) depict the distinctive features and important interdependencies that characterize a modern monetary economy. As our example involving an expansionary Fed action suggested, developments in one market "spill over" and affect the situations prevailing throughout the econ-

---

[9] This is analogous to the discussion of the demand and supply for money and interest rate determination in Chapter 3. When the Fed increases the supply of reserves, ceteris paribus, the money supply increases. This leads to an increase in the supply of surplus funds by SSUs and to a fall in the interest rate.

[10] According to some economists, consumption and investment would increase when the Fed increased the supply of funds regardless of whether interest rates fell.

omy. At a less analytical level, this too was the message of the schematic diagram in Exhibit 3-6.

With these fundamentals in place we are now ready to add to our analytical superstructure. More specifically, we have thus far in the chapter discussed and described the circular flows of income, expenditures, and funds through the various markets in the economy without really inquiring deeply into what makes the entire system tick. This is akin to describing the motion of the planets without developing a theory of gravity. Such a theory is essential if one hopes to understand and explain the forces producing the planetary motion we observe. In fact, the theory is what ultimately enables us to predict the motion! The next section outlines the forces producing motion—action and reaction—in the economy.

 ## Maximization: Plans, Revisions, and Actions

Each spending unit in the economy is presumed to pursue some objective or set of objectives. Understanding the goals is important for our purposes because they are what guide an economic unit's spending, saving, and financing decisions.

For households, we assume they wish to maximize **utility** or satisfaction over time. But what does this mean? If, as seems sensible, more is better than less, then people will desire to increase their holdings of goods and financial assets and, when faced with a choice, people will first select those items that provide the most utility or satisfaction. Imagine trying to choose between two identically priced goods you want—say, a new color television set and a new couch. Of course, you would prefer to have both, but if you can only have one, you will choose whichever is most useful to you now—that is, the one that yields the most utility or satisfaction.

For business firms, we assume that their decisions are guided by the desire to maximize profits. Logically, this means that firms will try to maximize the difference between their revenues from sales and their costs of production. After all, profits equal revenues minus costs. In general, firms will make production, hiring, investment, and pricing decisions by assessing the impact of alternative courses of action on costs and revenues and thus ultimately on their profits.

To sum up, each spending unit in the economy is attempting to maximize something. This maximization process is nothing more than the attempt of economic units to do the best they can, given their objectives and the circumstances they face. Such maximization plans are depicted in Exhibit 4-8.

As we all know, there are limits to what economic units can attain. The practical world does not allow us to achieve unlimited utility or unlimited profits. The fundamental economic problem is that we have infinite wants, while our means or resources are limited. Put more directly, there are constraints that limit the maximum degree of satisfaction, profits, and so on, that economic units can attain. The existence of such constraints forces economic units to choose among alternative courses of action. For example, as mentioned previously, you might prefer to purchase both a new television set and a new couch. However, if you can afford only one—if you are constrained by

Utility The satisfaction that households receive over time from consuming goods and services.

Exhibit 4-8 ◆
Goals of Various
Spending Units

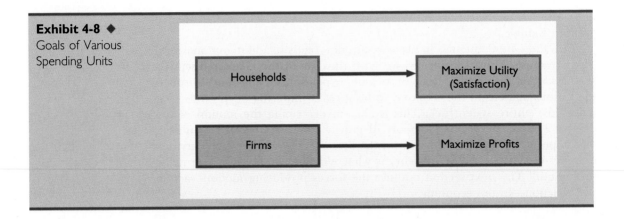

Constrained
Maximization The
course of action that
leads to the highest utility
for households or the
greatest profits for firms,
given the constraints that
each faces.

your available funds—you must make a choice between the two alternatives. Thus, every economic unit will choose the course of action that is most consistent with its objectives subject to the constraints it faces. The formal term for this process is **constrained maximization.**

But what are these constraints? It has often been said that the first rule of economics is "there is no such thing as a free lunch." All purchases of goods or financial assets must somehow be financed. More specifically, you must part with money to consummate transactions. This being the case, the constraint on an economic unit's spending can be defined in terms of its access to means of payment. In this regard, there are several financing possibilities for an individual economic unit: (1) the unit can use its existing holdings of money; (2) the unit can earn income by selling its labor (households) or its products (firms); (3) the unit can sell some of its holdings of financial or real assets accumulated from past saving; and/or (4) the unit can borrow.

What does all this have to do with the circular flow and supply and demand diagrams? We are a short step from the answer. Households will make plans to work, spend, and save. These plans will be based for the most part on their current economic and financial situations, their expectations about prices, interest rates, income, and their overall objectives. Firms will make plans to produce, hire workers, and invest. These plans will be based largely on their economic and financial situations and their expectations about prices, interest rates, and profits. Is there any reason to expect that the plans of households to work, spend, and save will mesh exactly with the plans of firms to hire, produce, and borrow? Of course, the answer is No; this would occur only by accident. So what happens if the plans don't mesh? The answer is that the plans will have to be revised. To see how and why, an example will help.

Assume we have the same simplified economy we have been using throughout this chapter, consisting of firms and households. Suppose the current interest rate is 6 percent and households in the aggregate, given the factors and objectives discussed above, plan to lend $300 billion, while firms plan to borrow $400 billion. In this case, the planned quantity demanded of funds by firms would exceed the planned quantity supplied of funds by households. This excess quantity demanded of funds would tend to raise the interest rate, and here comes the key point: as the interest rate rises we would expect households and firms to revise their plans. In particular, the rise in the interest rate to, say, 8 percent will discourage some firms from investing and thus borrow-

KIRK ANDERSON
Courtesy Madison (Wis.) Capital Times

ing. The higher cost of borrowing will make certain projects unprofitable. Given the profit-maximization objective, firms will reduce their planned investment spending. At the same time, the rise in the interest rate may well encourage our utility-maximizing households to save more.

With such actions by firms reducing the quantity demanded and such actions by households increasing the quantity supplied, the excess quantity demanded of funds shrinks. In general, the interest rate will continue to rise and plans will continue to be revised until the excess quantity demanded is eliminated. In analytical terms, an equilibrium is reached when the plans mesh; at this point the plans and resulting supplying and demanding actions of households and firms in the various markets are consistent. Such a situation is depicted by points A, B, and C in Exhibits 4-6 to 4-8; households and firms are doing the best they can do, given their objectives, the decisions of others in the economy, and the constraints they face.

By outlining the analytical basis for action by economic units, we have identified at least in a general way the forces and processes that produce the "motion" we observe in the economy. To nail down the relevant set of points, it is only necessary to see that if the economy is in equilibrium and the Fed, for example, increases the supply of funds (as discussed earlier in the chapter), the resulting fall in the interest rate will lead to a revision of plans by households and firms regarding the quantities supplied and demanded in the financial system, output market, and factor market. In effect, the size of the circular flow will grow and the "motion" of the economy will quicken.

RECAP

Given their constraints, households maximize utility and business firms maximize profits. The economy is in equilibrium when the spending plans of all economic units mesh and all markets are in equilibrium. If any factor affecting the supply and demand decisions of households or firms changes, an adjustment process will be set in motion. Prices and quantities will change until the spending plans of all economic units again mesh.

Summary of Major Points

1. Firms and households meet in three separate markets. Firms supply goods and services to the product market, demand investment goods supplied by other firms, demand factor services in the factor market, and demand funds from the financial system. Households demand goods and services in the product market, supply factor services in the factor market, and supply funds to the financial system. Taken together these supplying and demanding decisions will determine national income, the price level, real GDP, the wage rate, employment, the interest rate, and other important magnitudes.

2. Aggregate demand is the quantity of real GDP that will be demanded at various price levels. Ceteris paribus, the quantity of real output that is demanded is inversely related to the price level. Aggregate supply is the quantity of real GDP that will be supplied at various price levels. Ceteris paribus, the quantity of real GDP that will be supplied is directly related to the price level. The overall price level and the quantity of real GDP are determined by the interaction of aggregate demand and supply.

3. The quantity demanded of labor is inversely related to the wage rate, ceteris paribus. The quantity supplied of labor is directly related to the wage rate, ceteris paribus. The labor market is in equilibrium when quantity supplied is equal to quantity demanded.

4. The demand for loanable funds is determined by the borrowing plans of DSUs. The quantity demanded of loanable funds is inversely related to the interest rate, ceteris paribus. The supply of loanable funds is determined by the behavior of SSUs and the Fed. The quantity supplied of loanable funds is directly related to the interest rate, ceteris paribus. Thus, the interest rate and the quantity of loanable funds supplied and borrowed are determined by the interaction of the supply and demand for loanable funds.

5. Monetary policymakers can alter the circular flow of income, expenditures and funds, and the environment in the various markets by taking actions that will affect the supply or demand within one or more of these related markets.

6. Decisions by firms to produce, hire, invest, and borrow, and decisions by households to spend, work, save, and lend are determined by the objectives each seeks to attain and the constraints they face. We assume households attempt to maximize utility and firms attempt to maximize profits.

7. A fundamental constraint limiting the level of utility or profits attainable is that all spending must be financed with money. Typical sources of financing are existing money holdings, current income, the liquidation of other financial assets, and borrowing. Anything that changes the cost or availability of these alternatives is in effect a change in the constraints facing firms and households. They, in turn, will respond by changing their supplying and demanding plans in the various markets.

8. If the supplying and demanding plans of households and firms in the various markets do not mesh, an adjustment process will be set in motion involving changes in interest rates, prices, and other magnitudes. Such changes will, in turn, lead firms and households to revise their plans until they mesh.

Key Terms

Aggregate Demand	Flows
Aggregate Supply	Investment
Bonds	Liquidity Preference
Circular Flow Diagram	National Income
Constrained Maximization	National Expenditures
Consumption	Product Market
Disposable Personal Income	Stocks
Factor Market	Utility

Review Questions

1. Using Exhibit 4-3, explain why saving is equal to investment in our hypothetical economy with no government or foreign sector.

2. Dispute the statement: "Only households save and only business firms invest."

3. What are the two uses of saving for a spending unit? Are all spending units that save surplus spending units?

4. Define aggregate demand and aggregate supply. What are some catalysts that would cause aggregate demand to change? How are prices affected?

5. Explain the similarities and differences between product, factor, and financial markets. If a market is out of equilibrium, what will cause it to return to equilibrium?

6. Use the concept of constrained maximization to explain how the behavior of households and firms is alike.

7. Suppose the Fed uses monetary policy to decrease the supply of funds available to lend from surplus units. Explain what may happen to interest rates, prices, and real GDP.

8. Explain what may happen to wages, prices, and real GDP if there is a decrease in aggregate demand.

9. John Delaney and Rosa Moore have the same annual incomes. Use the concept of constrained maximization (and a little imagination) to show why Mr. Delaney might choose to be a DSU while Ms. Moore might choose to be an SSU.

10. Pretend that you are the teacher and today must explain to your class what will happen if the spending plans of various spending units do not mesh.

11. Households decide to save more. Will aggregate demand increase or decrease? (Hint: Consider what will happen to interest rates and investment spending.)

12. Based on information in the appendix, indicate which of the following variables are stocks and which are flows: income, investment, capital, saving, savings, consumption, GDP, and wealth.

Analytical Questions

13. Draw a simple circular flow diagram between households and firms. Explain how "real" flows go in one direction and "financial" flows go in the opposite.

14. Mary Smith earns wages of $45,000 and interest and dividends of $5,000. She spends $8,000 as a down payment on a newly constructed mountain cabin and lends $4,000 in financial markets. Assuming she spends the remainder of her income on consumption, what is her saving? Is she an SSU? What is her consumption?

15. Tech Corp had gross sales of $9 million and total expenses of $8.5 million. Assume that they want to undertake a capital investment of $1 million. What is the minimum amount of bonds they would have to issue to do so? Assume they pay out $300,000 in dividends. Now what is the minimum amount they would have to borrow?

16. Assume the economy is composed of 200,000 households of which Mary Smith from question 14 is average and 1,000 firms of which Tech Corp from question 15 is average. What is disposable income? What is investment? What is saving? Are the spending plans of the household and business sectors consistent? (Hint: Do the surplus funds, which the household sector has available to lend, equal the deficit of the business sector?)

17. Graph an aggregate demand and aggregate supply curve. What is the equilibrium price and the equilibrium quantity of real GDP? Demonstrate what happens to the equilibrium price and quantity if the Fed takes action that causes aggregate demand to fall.

18. Assume that the Fed has been successful in reducing the level of aggregate demand. Show graphically what will happen to the demand for loan-

able funds. Also show graphically what will happen to the demand for labor.

19. Assume that the Fed has been successful in increasing the supply of loanable funds. Show graphically what will happen to aggregate demand and the demand for labor.

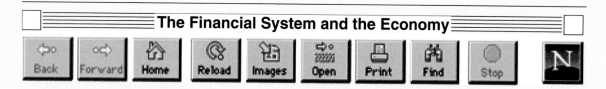

The Financial System and the Economy

1. Table 3 at the internet directory, (gopher://una.hh.lib.umich.edu:70/00/ebb/nipa/gdp/gdp-tab.bea) refers to GDP and the disposition of personal income. Access the data and answer the following questions. (The underlined terms have been explained in the chapter.)

   a. What is the most current estimate of _Personal Income_ in the United States?

   b. What is _Personal Saving_? Provide the latest estimates of personal saving and personal consumption in the United States.

   c. What is the current savings rate as a percentage of _disposable personal income_? (Hint: to calculate the current savings rate, divide personal saving by disposable personal income.)

2. From the data at the website (http://www.stls.frb.org/fred/data/business/fgdef) verify that the federal government has been running a deficit every year since 1970.

Suggested Readings

For an international perspective of some of the material in this chapter, see "Rattling the Piggy Bank," _Economist_, 335, May 6, 1995, p. 78.

"The Future of Spending" is discussed by the editors of _American Demographics_, 17, January 1995, pp. 12–19.

Maureen B. Gray and John M. Rogers discuss the relationship between the distribution of income and consumption patterns in "CE Data: Quintiles of Income Versus Quintiles of Outlays," _Monthly Labor Review_, 117, December 1994, pp. 32–37. (CE stands for consumption expenditures.)

For a discussion of possible reasons for the declining rate of saving in the United States over the past several decades, see Harold T. Gorss and Bernard L. Weinstein, "The Past and Future of U.S. Private Savings," _Challenge_, July–August 1992, pp. 42–50.

For a discussion of the standard theories of household behavior discussed in this chapter, see David Wilcox, "Household Spending and Saving: Measurement, Trends, and Analysis," *Federal Reserve Bulletin*, January 1991, pp. 1–17.

An interesting and somewhat alternative discussion of savings, investment, flow of funds, and consumption, is the article by Walter C. Neale "Who Saves? The Rich, the Penniless, and Everyone Else," *Journal of Economic Issues*, December 1991, pp. 1160–66.

APPENDIX 4-A

Interest Rates: Which Theory Is Correct? Reconciling Stocks and Flows

In Chapter 3, we developed a theory of interest rate determination based on the supply and demand for money. In this chapter, we developed a theory of interest rate determination based on the supply and demand for loanable funds. Just as there is more than one way to "get a job done," the purpose of this appendix is to convince you that there is more than one way to explain interest rates and that the two theories presented in this text are complementary and consistent.

Liquidity preference is the name given to the theory based on the demand and supply of money. It was developed by John Maynard Keynes in the 1930s. The supply of money is the stock of money and the demand for money or "preference for liquidity" is how much money spending units wish to hold. The supply and demand for money are both measured at a point in time and refer to actual **stocks.** The stock of money is partially determined by the central bank through its control over the stock of reserves and reserve requirements. Also, remember from Chapter 3 that the demand for money is based on the spending plans of spending units. Demand is positively related to income while quantity demanded is negatively or inversely related to the interest rate, ceteris paribus. The interest rate adjusts to equate the quantity supplied (stock) of money with the quantity demanded.

The loanable funds theory developed in this chapter is based on **flows** as opposed to stocks. Flows are measured through time whereas stocks are measured at a point in time. Thus, if I offer you a job for $10,000, you will want to know whether this is per week, per month, or per year. Not so for stocks. If I give you a $10,000 savings account, there is no relevant time dimension. The loanable funds theory develops the argument that the interest rate is determined by the supply and demand for loanable funds. The demand for loanable funds reflects borrowing plans by DSUs while the supply of loanable funds reflects lending plans by SSUs. Ceteris paribus, the quantity demanded of loanable funds is inversely related to the interest rate while the quantity supplied of loanable funds is directly related to the interest rate. The interest rate adjusts to equate the quantity demanded of loanable funds with the quantity supplied.

To help you see that the theories complement each other, consider what happens when the Fed increases bank reserves. When reserves increase, banks create money by incurring deposit liabilities as they acquire loans as assets. In doing so, banks have simultaneously augmented the supply of loanable funds. According to liquidity preference, an increase in the supply of money, ceteris

Liquidity Preference The theory of interest rate determination based on the supply and demand for money; it was first developed by Keynes.

Stocks Quantities that are measured at a point in time.

Flows Quantities that are measured through time.

paribus, causes the interest rate to fall, while according to the loanable funds theory, an increase in the supply of loanable funds does the same. Likewise if the Fed decreases the supply of reserves, you should be able to verify that both the stock of money and the supply of loanable funds decrease leading to a higher interest rate. Again both theories predict that the interest rate changes in the same direction.

Next consider if there is an increase in the demand for loanable funds reflecting an increased desire of people to borrow more at every interest rate. Since banks acquire loan assets when they create checkable deposits which are also money, an increase in the demand for loanable funds corresponds to an increase in the demand for money. According to both theories, an increase in the interest rate results. Likewise, a decrease in the demand for loanable funds translates to a decrease in the demand for money and a lower interest rate.

From an intuitive standpoint, we can reconcile the two theories by recognizing that when there is a change in a stock measured at different times, a flow has occurred; that is, a flow over time results in a change in a stock. For example, if I have a gallon of milk in the morning and go to the refrigerator for a glass repeatedly throughout the day and have a half gallon left at the end of the day, then I can safely say that I consumed a half gallon of milk during the day. Consumption of milk over the course of the day represents a flow, while the amount of milk in the refrigerator at a point in time is a stock. The change in the stock of milk as measured at two different points in time depicts the flow. If I save $100 per year, at the end of the year, my stock of wealth will have increased by $100 (ignoring interest payments for the time being). Correspondingly, changes in the supply (flow) of loanable funds entail changes in the stock of money as measured at two different points in time. Likewise changes in the demand (flow) of loanable funds entail changes in the demand for money. A theory stated in flows can always be reformulated in terms of stocks, and vice versa.

5

The Federal Reserve System:
An Overview of the Overseer

> *Speak softly and carry a big stick*
> —Theodore Roosevelt—

Learning Objectives

After reading this chapter, you should know:

♦ How the Fed is organized

♦ What the Fed Open Market Committee (FOMC) is

♦ The most important functions of the Fed

♦ The Fed's major policy tools

♦ What a "lender of last resort" is

♦ The controversy regarding Fed independence

Unraveling the Fed's Mystique

"Stock Market Surges Following Fed Testimony," "Interest Rates Fall in Anticipation of Easier Fed Policy," "Fed Approves Bank Merger," "Fed Actions Prevent Crisis After Bank Failure": such are the headlines one sees nearly every day in the nation's business and financial press. Yet, despite its prominent role in the financial system and the economy, the Fed and its operations are not well understood by readers of these headlines (and perhaps even the headline writers). In part, this mystique reflects the fact that the Fed's organizational structure is somewhat complex and rather different from other governmental entities and that a considerable amount of secrecy often surrounds Fed deliberations and actions.

To unravel this mystique, our study of the Fed begins with an examination of the origin, role, and organization of the Fed and its policy tools. This first look includes an analysis of the administrative (power) structure within which policy decisions are formulated and the various functions with which the Fed is charged. Many of the details regarding the formulation of policy and the precise linkages between policy actions and the economy will be examined in later chapters. For now, these are the types of questions we want to focus on: What is the Fed? Why does the Fed appear to have such great power and influence over the economy? Who does what? Why do they do it?

Organizational Structure of the System

Several years ago, a public opinion poll in one of the weekly news magazines reported that the chairperson of the Board of Governors of the Federal Reserve System was considered the second most influential person in the United States, topped only by the president. This poll reflected something about the current importance of the Federal Reserve System and monetary policy in our lives. It was not always so.

The **Federal Reserve System** was created by Congress in 1913. Experience in the United States and abroad had finally convinced lawmakers that such an institution was needed to avoid the banking crises that had periodically plagued the economy, the most recent of which had been the banking crisis of 1907. The main purpose of the **Federal Reserve Act** was simple. It created a central bank—a kind of bank for banks—that could lend funds to commercial banks during emergencies and thus provide these banks with the funds necessary to avoid insolvency and bankruptcy. An example of such an emergency is a major crop failure that results in the inability of farmers to pay off their bank loans. This concept was referred to in the 1913 legislation as providing an "elastic currency," and it is today often referred to as "the **lender of last resort**" function.

Over time, the responsibilities of the Federal Reserve have been expanded. In the midst of the Great Depression, it was clear that the limited scope and powers of the Federal Reserve System were not up to handling the nearly 8,000 bank failures that occurred during the 1930–1933 period. Additional policy tools and regulations were needed. In the **Banking Reform Acts of 1933 and 1935,** many of these tools and regulations were provided.

Federal Reserve System
The central bank of the United States that regulates the banking system and determines monetary policy and that was created in 1913.

Federal Reserve Act
The 1913 Congressional act that created the Federal Reserve System.

Lender of Last Resort
The responsibility of the Fed to provide an elastic currency by lending to commercial banks during emergencies and thus providing banks with the necessary funds to avoid insolvency.

Banking Reform Acts of 1933 and 1935 Acts passed by Congress in response to the collapse of the banking system between 1930 and 1933, which put in place many banking reforms designed to insure the safety and soundness of the system; also broadened the powers of the Fed.

The most significant change that occurred during this period involved the underlying role of the Federal Reserve—that is, the Fed's purpose and objectives. The Fed moved into a new era because of the economic crisis of the Great Depression, the changing view of the role of government policy after this collapse (discussed in Chapter 1), and the new legislation that broadened its powers. The Federal Reserve System became a full-fledged central bank. Now more than a bank for banks, it was charged with contributing to the attainment of the nation's economic and financial goals. More specifically, it was to regulate and supervise the operation of the financial system in order to (1) foster a smooth-running, efficient, competitive financial system and (2) promote the overall health and stability of the economy through its ability to influence the availability and cost of money and credit. Let us first identify the major parts of the Federal Reserve System and then discuss the Fed's functions.

Board of Governors

The core of the Federal Reserve System is the **Board of Governors,** located in Washington, D.C. The Board consists of seven members appointed by the president with the advice and consent of the U.S. Senate. Exhibit 5-1 contains brief biographical sketches of the present board members. The full term of a Board member is 14 years, and the terms are arranged so that one term expires every two years. The long tenure and staggered terms were designed to help insulate the Board from day-to-day political pressures. In theory, the President of the United States would be able to appoint only two of the seven members on the Board during a four-year term. The type of independence of judgment enjoyed by the Supreme Court would also be encouraged on the Federal Reserve Board. In actuality, deaths and early resignations of Board members have permitted recent presidents to name more than two new Board members during a four-year term. We might also note that Board members cannot be reappointed if they serve a full term and can be removed from office only under extraordinary circumstances. It has never happened.

> **Board of Governors** Seven governors of the Fed appointed by the president with Senate approval for 14-year terms.

The president appoints, with the advice and consent of the Senate, one of the seven Board members to be Chairperson for four years and one to be vice chairperson. The choice of chairperson is crucial, for experience shows that he becomes the chief spokesman for the Fed and thus a strong force in U.S. economic policy making.[1]

Federal Reserve Banks

The original Federal Reserve Act divided the nation into 12 districts. Each Federal Reserve Bank district is served by a **Reserve Bank** located in a large city in the district. Thus, as shown in Exhibit 5-2, we have the Federal Reserve Bank of Boston, the Federal Reserve Bank of New York, and so on, respectively, for Philadelphia, Richmond, Cleveland, Atlanta, Chicago, Dallas, Kansas City, St. Louis, Minneapolis, and San Francisco. The three largest, which account for more than 50 percent of Fed assets, are the Reserve Banks in New York, Chicago, and San Francisco. As we shall see in Chapter 12, all commer-

> **Reserve Bank** One of 12 Federal Reserve Banks located in a large city in the district.

---

[1] There has not yet been a female chairperson of the Board.

Exhibit 5-1 ◆
The Board of
Governors

Pictured from left to right: Lawrence Meyer, Alice Rivlin, Alan Greenspan and
President Clinton.

Laurence H. Meyer (Born 1945) Took office June, 1996; term expires January, 2002
   Background: Academic; Professor of Economics at Washington University; Economist at Federal Reserve Bank of New York, 1975–76; Ph.D. Massachusetts Institute of Technology; District: St. Louis

Vice Chairperson Alice M. Rivlin (Born 1936) Took office June, 1996; term expires January, 2010
   Background: Public Service and Academic; Deputy Director and Director of the Office of Management and Budget, 1993–1996; Brookings Institute, 1957–66 and 1969–75 and 1983–87; Founder and Director of the Congressional Budget Office, 1975–83; Professor of Public Policy at George Mason University, 1983; Member of the Council of Economic Advisers, (1993–94); Ph.D. in economics from Radcliffe College; District: Richmond

Chairperson Alan Greenspan (Born 1926) Took office August, 1987; term expires March, 2000 as chairperson and January, 2006 as a governor
   Background: Business economist; Chairman & President of Townsend-Greenspan, an economic consulting firm; Chairperson of the Council of Economic Advisers (1974–77); chaired Social Security Commission; Ph.D. in economics from New York University; District: New York

Edward W. Kelley, Jr. (Born 1932) Took office May, 1987; term expires January, 2004
   Background: Business; Chairperson of Investment Advisors and earlier Kelley Ind.; Founding director of 3 Southwest banks; M.B.A. from Harvard University; District: Dallas

Edward Kelley

Lawrence Lindsey

Lawrence B. Lindsey (Born 1954) Took office November, 1991; term expires January, 2000

Background: Academic; Assistant to President for Policy Development (1990–91); Professor at Harvard, specializing in tax policy; Ph.D. in economics from Harvard University; District: Richmond

Susan M. Phillips (Born 1944) Took office December, 1991; term expires January, 1998

Background: Academic; Professor at University of Iowa; Chairperson and Member of Commodity Futures Trading Commission (1981–87); Ph.D. in finance and economics from Louisiana State University; District: Chicago

Susan Phillips, pictured here with Deputy Treasure Secretary Lawrence Summers, presents the redesigned $100 bill.

Janet Yellen

Janet L. Yellen (Born 1946) Took office August, 1994; term expires January, 2008

Background: Academic; Professor of international business and trade at University of California, Berkeley; Economist with the Federal Reserve Bank, 1977–78; Consultant, Congressional Budget Office, 1975–76; Ph.D. in economics from Yale University; District: San Francisco

cial banks that are federally chartered national banks must join the Federal Reserve System. State-chartered banks may or may not join. The member banks within a Reserve Bank district (say, the Boston district) elect six of the nine directors of that Reserve Bank and the Board of Governors appoints the other three. These directors, in turn, appoint the president and other officials of that Reserve Bank.

The reason the original Federal Reserve Act created 12 Reserve Banks and provided for the election of directors by member commercial banks was to decentralize policy-making authority.[2] Considerable antifederalist sentiment existed in the Congress at the time. We will see later that, over time, the desire to decentralize authority has been stymied by the increased concentration of policy-making authority in Washington.

Fed Open Market Committee (FOMC)

Fed Open Market Committee (FOMC) The principal policy-making body within the Federal Reserve System; composed of the seven members of the Board of Governors and five Reserve Bank presidents.

The **Fed Open Market Committee (FOMC)** is the principal policy-making body within the Federal Reserve System. The FOMC formulates monetary pol-

---

[2] In addition, no two members of the Board of Governors may come from the same Reserve Bank district. This insures that the Board is not unduly influenced by any particular region of the country.

Exhibit 5-2 ◆

The Federal Reserve System

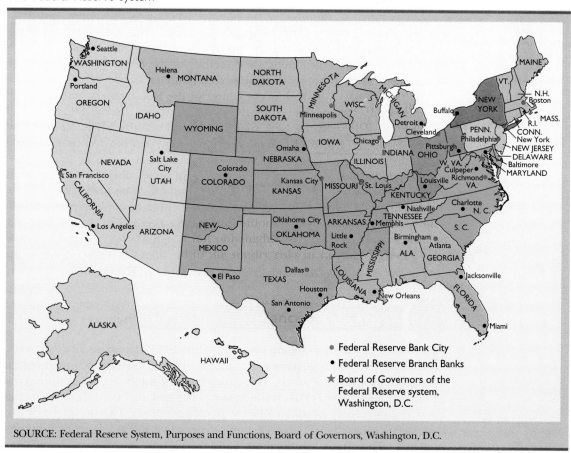

SOURCE: Federal Reserve System, Purposes and Functions, Board of Governors, Washington, D.C.

icy and oversees its implementation. The 12-person membership of the FOMC includes all seven members of the Board and five of the 12 Federal Reserve Bank presidents. The president of the New York Federal Reserve Bank always holds a seat on the FOMC and is a permanent voting member. This is so because the New York Fed, as we shall see, implements monetary policy in accord with the FOMC's instructions. The remaining four seats are filled by the other Reserve Bank presidents serving one-year terms on a rotating basis. Although only five Reserve Bank presidents have voting rights on the FOMC at any one time, all 12 presidents and their senior advisors attend FOMC meetings and participate in the discussions. By law, the FOMC determines its own internal organization. By tradition, it elects the chairperson of the Federal Reserve Board as chairperson of the FOMC and the president of the New York Federal Reserve Bank as vice chairperson of the FOMC. With the Board having seven of the 12 votes, perhaps you can see why most of the policy-making authority resides in Washington.

The FOMC meets in closed meetings in Washington eight times a year (about every six weeks or so). In early 1994, the Fed began announcing the policy decisions made at the FOMC meetings immediately following the meetings. This removed some of the secrecy previously surrounding the specific contents of the meeting. Minutes of an FOMC meeting are published shortly after the following meeting.

Policy Directive Statement of the FOMC that states its policy consensus and sets forth operating instructions regarding monetary policy.

Included in the minutes of the FOMC meeting is the **policy directive,** which is usually a two- to four-paragraph statement.[3] This statement represents a digest of the meeting, states the policy consensus of the FOMC, and sets forth the operating instructions (or directive) to the Federal Reserve Bank of New York regarding the conduct of monetary policy.

Why New York? New York is the center of the U.S. financial system. Since monetary policy affects the economy by working its way through the financial system, it is logical that the New York Fed should execute policy on behalf of the entire Fed. Since FOMC decisions affect current and future economic conditions, it is also logical that economists, financial investors, and professional portfolio managers read the minutes and policy directive carefully and monitor closely the daily operations of the Federal Reserve Bank of New York.

Now that we know something about the Fed's organizational structure, let's examine what this institution and its people are charged to do.[4] As you will see, the Fed's responsibilities are not simple in nature or scope and thus not always easily accomplished. Before moving on, however, take a look at an outline of the Fed's organizational structure found in Exhibit 5-3.

RECAP

The Federal Reserve System was created in 1913. It consists of 12 Reserve Banks. The Fed is governed by a Board of seven Governors appointed by the president to 14-year terms. The chairperson of the Board is appointed for a four-year term. The FOMC is the major policy-making board. It includes the seven Fed governors plus five Reserve Bank presidents. The president of the New York Reserve Bank is a permanent member of the FOMC and the other four slots rotate yearly among the remaining eleven Reserve Bank presidents.

The Fed's Functions

Over the 80 plus years since its inception, the Fed's powers and responsibilities have gradually expanded. In some cases, the Fed argued that it needed more powers to accomplish its existing responsibilities or that taking on additional responsibilities was a natural adjunct to what it was already doing. The Congress often responded favorably to the Fed's arguments or simply let the Fed decide on its own if it would be the best agency to handle a particular set of issues. The current list of Fed responsibilities is considerably

[3]Excerpts from a policy directive are reprinted in Chapter 23.

[4]In addition to the organizational parts of the Fed mentioned in the body of the text, three advisory councils exist—the Consumer Advisory Council, the Federal Advisory Council, and the Thrift Institutions Advisory Council. Composed of representatives from each Federal Reserve District, they meet several times a year with the Board of Governors to provide advice on issues relating to the Fed's responsibilities in the banking, consumer finance, and depository institutions areas. Federal Reserve insiders say that, as the name suggests, the advisory councils have no real power and serve mainly as a medium for public relations and the exchange of information.

Exhibit 5-3 ◆
The Organizational
Structure of the
Federal Reserve
System

Board of Governors

Seven members appointed by the president of the United States and confirmed by the Senate for 14-year terms.

One of the seven governors is appointed chairperson by the president of the United States and confirmed by the Senate for a 4-year term.

The Board of Governors appoints three of the nine directors to each Reserve Bank.

Twelve Federal Reserve Banks

Each with nine directors who appoint the Reserve Bank president and other officers of the Reserve Banks.

Federal Open Market Committee (FOMC)

Seven members of the Board of Governors plus the president of the New York Fed and presidents of four other Reserve Banks.

Nearly 5,000 Member Commercial Banks

Elect six of the nine directors to each Reserve Bank.

longer and more encompassing than even the most farsighted legislator could have imagined in 1913. Fortunately, the list can be boiled down into four functional areas, depicted in Exhibit 5-4, and outlined in the following text.

Formulation and Implementation of Monetary Policy

A primary responsibility of the Federal Reserve is the formulation and implementation of the nation's **monetary policy.** Broadly speaking, the conduct of monetary policy has two objectives: first, to ensure that sufficient money and credit are available to allow the economy to expand along its long-run potential growth trend under conditions of relatively little or no inflation; second, in the shorter run, to minimize the fluctuations—recessions or inflationary booms—around the long-term trend.

In general, the Fed takes actions to affect the cost and availability of funds in the financial system.[5] More specifically, the Fed's actions have a direct effect on the ability of depository institutions to extend credit, on the nation's money supply, and on interest rates. Leaving many of the details for a later chapter, the key point here is that what the Fed does, or fails to do, has a pervasive effect on the environment in the financial system and the overall health and performance of the economy. For example, the Fed can take

Monetary Policy The attempts by the Fed to stabilize the economy and to ensure sufficient money and credit for an expanding economy.

---

[5] The tools the Fed has available to affect the cost and availability of funds are discussed in the next section.

Exhibit 5-4 ◆

The Functions of the Fed

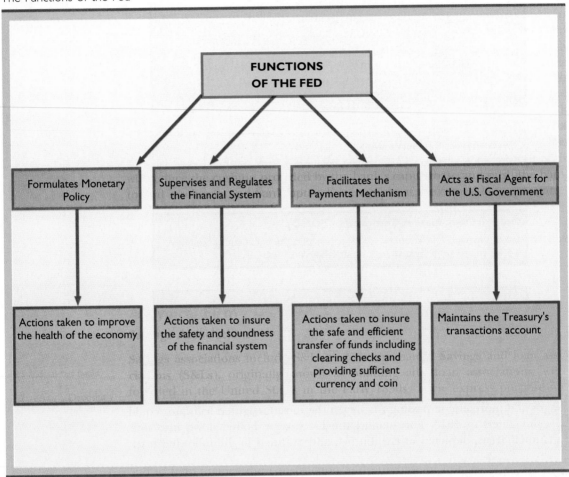

actions to increase the availability of funds that may result in an expansion of the money supply and a decline in interest rates, or it can do the reverse. Its decisions may, in turn, affect the spending, producing, borrowing, lending, pricing, and hiring decisions made in the rest of the economy.

Supervision and Regulation of the Financial System

The Fed, along with several other government agencies, is responsible for the supervision and regulation of the financial system.[6] In general, supervisory activities are directed at promoting the safety and soundness of depository institutions. From the Fed's perspective, this involves continuous oversight to

---

[6] Many of the agencies that regulate the financial system are discussed in Chapter 15. Rather than name them here, it is sufficient for you to know that the Fed has the broadest set of responsibilities, some of which overlap with the activities of other regulatory agencies.

"Interest rates gyrated wildly today, on rumors that the Federal Reserve Board would be replaced by the cast of 'Saturday Night Live'."

© 1996 Robert Mankoff from The Cartoon Bank,™ Inc.

ensure that banks are operated prudently and according to standing statutes and regulations. Operationally, this means the Fed sends out teams of bank examiners (auditors) to assess the condition of individual institutions and to check compliance with existing regulations. On a more regular basis, banks must submit reports of their financial conditions and activities.

The promulgation of regulations is, of course, an activity that complements and defines the Fed's supervisory activities. Broadly speaking, regulation involves the formulation and issuance of specific rules that govern the structure and conduct of banking. The purpose of such laws and regulations is to establish a framework for bank behavior that fosters the maintenance of a safe and sound banking system and the fair and efficient delivery of services to bank customers. Operationally, the regulations (1) define which activities are permissible and which are not, (2) require banks to submit branch and merger applications to the Fed for approval, and (3) try to ensure that consumers are treated fairly when they engage in financial transactions. In later chapters, we shall see how the rules and regulations have changed over time and the implications of these changes.

Some specifics will illustrate the scope of the Fed's responsibilities and activities. The Fed is charged with ensuring that financial institutions comply with the Truth in Lending Act, the Fair Credit Billing Act, and the Equal Credit Opportunity Act. These statutes are designed to protect the customers of financial institutions from discrimination on the basis of race, sex, or age, and from unfair or misleading lending practices. In addition, the Fed is responsible for ensuring compliance with the Community Reinvestment Act, which seeks to increase the availability of credit to economically disadvantaged areas and to insure nondiscriminatory lending practices.[7] Given these responsibilities, the Fed monitors the advertising by institutions, investigates complaints from customers, reviews standard loan contracts used by institutions, and requires the submission of numerous reports summarizing lending activity.

A more prominent example of the Fed's supervisory and regulatory activities is provided by a bank in serious difficulty and in danger of failing. The cause of the problems may be and are often related to fraudulent or misguided lending practices. Whatever the case, the Fed, along with the other relevant government agencies, tries to find an orderly solution that will preserve the public's confidence in the financial system. Often this involves finding a merger partner for the weak or failing institution, lending funds to the institution to give it time to work out its problems, and, in extreme cases, the removal of a bank's management. Perhaps you understand the quotation at the beginning of the chapter a bit better now.

Facilitation of the Payments Mechanism

Payments Mechanism
The ways in which funds are transferred to make payments.

The **payments mechanism** is at the heart of the nation's financial system. Many billions of dollars are transferred each day to pay for goods and services, to settle debts, and to acquire securities. Since any disruption of this mechanism could prove deleterious to the economy, the Fed is committed to the development and maintenance of safe and efficient means for transferring funds—that is, making payments.

The most obvious Fed activities in this area involve the provision of currency and coin, and the clearing of checks. As Exhibit 5-5 illustrates, the Fed plays a central role in transferring the funds initiated by the writing of a check.[8] The task is enormous. The Fed clears millions of checks (or similar items) each business day. Perhaps you can see why the Fed has encouraged technological advances, such as the adoption of electronic funds transfer system (EFTS), as discussed in Chapter 2, which can help to lower the cost and speed the transfer of funds.

Operation as Fiscal Agent for the Government

As chief banker for the U.S. government, the Fed furnishes banking services to the government in a manner similar to the way private banks furnish banking services to their customers. For example, the Fed maintains the Treasury's *transactions account*.[9] Government disbursements, such as the purchase of a missile, are made out of this account, and payments to the government, such as taxes, are made into this account. The Fed also clears Treasury checks, issues and redeems government securities, and provides other financial services. They act as fiscal agent of the government in financial transactions with foreign governments and foreign central banks.

---

[7]The Community Reinvestment Act is discussed in greater detail in Chapter 15.

[8]Other private institutions, known as *clearinghouses* also help "clear" a substantial proportion of the checks written in the United States.

[9]The *transactions account* of the government held at the Fed is similar to a checking account. However, the balance in the government's transactions account is not included in any monetary aggregate and therefore is not "money."

The arrows show the movement of the check through the system. The Fed plays two roles: (1) it forwards the check from the bank receiving it (Dad's) to the bank on which it is written (Mary's); (2) it transfers funds from the bank on which the check is written (drawn) to the bank receiving the deposit (Dad's). When the process is complete, Mary has less funds in her account and Dad has more funds in his.

Exhibit 5-5 ◆
The Check
Clearing System

```
┌──────────────────────┐        check        ┌──────────────────────┐
│  Mary writes check   │ ──────────────────> │  Dad receives and    │
│      to Dad          │                     │   deposits check     │
└──────────────────────┘                     └──────────────────────┘
          │                                             │
   check cancelled                              check deposited
          │                                             │
          ▼                                             ▼
┌──────────────────────┐                     ┌──────────────────────┐
│     Mary's bank      │                     │      Dad's bank       │
└──────────────────────┘                     └──────────────────────┘
          ▲                                             │
           \                                           /
            \               check forwarded           /
             \                                        ▼
          ┌──────────────────────────────────────┐
          │        Federal Reserve Bank           │
          └──────────────────────────────────────┘
```

Now that we've explained the scope of Fed activities, we can focus on the major tools the Fed has at its disposal as it attempts to encourage and maintain a sound financial system and healthy economy.

RECAP

The major responsibilities of the Fed include setting monetary policy, regulating and supervising the financial system, facilitating the payments mechanism, and acting as fiscal agent for the U.S. government.

The Fed's Major Policy Tools

When someone is suffering from a back ailment, physicians usually have several therapeutic approaches available including rest, traction, braces, muscle relaxers, surgery, and so forth. These "tools," which can be used in combination, are all designed to relieve pain and restore the patient's health. Since policymakers are similarly equipped and motivated, let's examine the Fed's major policy tools.

Open Market Operations

Open Market Operations The buying and selling of government securities by the Fed to change the reserves of depository institutions.

Open market operations are the most important monetary policy tool at the Fed's disposal. These operations, which are executed by the Federal Reserve Bank of New York under the guidance and direction of the FOMC, involve the buying or selling of U.S. government securities by the Fed. When the Fed buys securities, reserves rise, and when the Fed sells securities, reserves fall. (Details of this concept are discussed in Chapter 16.) The importance of these operations derives from the fact that they have a direct effect on the reserves that are available to depository institutions. (Recall from Chapter 3 that depository institutions are required to hold reserve assets equal to a certain proportion of outstanding deposit liabilities.) Changes in reserves, in turn, affect the ability of depository institutions to make loans and to extend credit. When banks or other depository institutions make loans, they create checkable deposits. Thus changes in reserves also affect the money supply. Subsequently, when reserves change, the money supply and credit extension also change.

The Discount Rate and Discount Rate Policy

Discount Rate The rate depository institutions are charged to borrow reserves from the Fed.

Because the Fed controls the amount of required reserve assets that depository institutions must hold, they also operate a lending facility called the discount window through which depository institutions caught short of reserves can borrow from the Fed. The **discount rate** is the interest rate the Fed charges depository institutions that borrow reserves directly from the Fed. The discount rate is a highly visible, but less important, Fed policy tool. We say that it is a "visible" policy instrument because changes in the discount rate are often well publicized, for example, on the evening news broadcast.[10]

The setting of the discount rate is the general responsibility of all 12 Reserve Banks, although it can only be changed by the Board of Governors. The process works as follows: The directors of the Reserve Banks meet together regularly and review matters relevant to administering the Reserve Banks, including the discount rate. If the directors see the need to recommend a change in the rate, they forward their recommendation to the Board of Governors, which evaluates it and either approves or disapproves the change. Thus, the ultimate authority to change the discount rate resides with the Board. In recent years, they have frequently disapproved requests for rate changes, and it is rumored that they have solicited requests for rate changes from the Reserve Banks when they wanted to change the rate and no request was in hand. Is there any doubt about who calls the shots? At any rate, the Board usually approves requests for changes in the discount rate only after the broader monetary policy stance directed by the FOMC has been decided and is in the process of being implemented. Hence, changes in the discount rate often "lag" changes in other interest rates, particularly short-term rates.

---

[10] The fact that changes in the discount rate are highly publicized makes them unlike day-to-day open market operations, which are followed closely by only a small group of experts in the financial system.

Changes in the discount rate can have several possible effects on depository institution behavior and the economy. The most obvious effect involves changes in the cost of borrowing funds (reserves) from the Fed. If a withdrawal is made from a depository, deposits go down, but the depository also loses reserves equal to the full amount of the withdrawal. Since depository institutions are required to hold reserve assets equal to a certain proportion of their deposit liabilities, the depository institution may be caught short of reserves and, as a last resort, may borrow the needed reserves from the Fed.

Increases in the discount rate raise the cost of borrowing, while decreases lower it. Holding other factors constant, we would expect an increase in the rate to lead to a drop in the volume of borrowing from the Fed. Conversely, a rise in borrowing would be expected following a decrease in the discount rate. Of course, in the real world other factors are hardly ever constant, and decisions to borrow or not borrow from the Fed will be based on several considerations.

The Fed views borrowing as a privilege accorded to depository institutions. It is not a right. Since it is a privilege, the Fed urges these institutions to borrow only when other alternatives are not available. This sentiment is spelled out in the Fed's Regulation A, which specifies the permissible size of loans, their frequency, and the reasons for which institutions may borrow. It is here that the Fed's discount policy is laid out. The rules make it clear that borrowing from the Fed is, *under normal circumstances,* to be for short periods, preferably no more than a few days or weeks. Institutions that borrow frequently, say for eight consecutive weeks or for thirty out of thirty-five weeks, can be examined by the Fed's team of auditors. The Fed views the borrowing privilege as a means for banks and other depository institutions to deal with temporary liquidity needs caused, for example, by unexpected deposit outflows or an unexpected surge in loan demands. The key word is *temporary.* If an institution borrows persistently, the Fed begins to think that the institution's management is either consciously violating the provisions of Regulation A, cannot handle the liquidity pressures, or may have a chronic problem affecting its profitability and very existence. Perhaps its solvency, which is its ability to pay off or redeem its liabilities, is questionable. At this point, the Fed will step in. If the Fed feels that the borrowing privilege is being abused, it can deny the request to borrow.

We hope you noticed that the phrase "under normal circumstances" was highlighted in the last paragraph. The purpose was to emphasize how the Fed's discount policy usually works. Occasionally, "exceptional circumstances" may affect individual institutions. Examples include a natural disaster, the shutdown of a large manufacturer in a small community, developments over which an institution's management has no control, or poor management decisions. Whatever the cause, the common thread is that the institution is experiencing severe difficulties. Borrowers may not be repaying existing loans, depositors may be withdrawing large amounts of funds, and fears over the safety and solvency of the institution may be growing.

In such circumstances, the Fed stands ready to be a *lender of last resort.* More specifically, the Fed will consider lending funds to the institution for an extended period to help facilitate the institution's adjustment to its new circumstances, to provide time for management reform, or to work out a merger or orderly closing of the institution. Whatever the case may be, the Fed's main concern is to act in a way that minimizes the risk to the public interest and the financial system. Thus the Fed's willingness to be a lender of last resort is closely related to its regulatory and supervisory responsibilities and its overall desire to preserve the public's confidence in the safety and soundness of the financial system, in general, and depository institutions, in particular.

Reserve Requirements

The major item on the liability side of depository institutions' balance sheets is, naturally enough, deposits. The Fed requires depository institutions to hold **required reserves** equal to a proportion of checkable deposit liabilities. The Fed specifies the **required reserve ratio** which is the fraction that must be held. For example, the required reserve ratio on checkable deposits is currently 10 percent.[11] This means that for each $1 in checkable deposit liabilities outstanding, a depository must hold $.10 in reserve assets.

In conjunction with its conduct of monetary policy, the Fed—the Board of Governors to be precise—may vary the required reserve ratio. To illustrate, if the Fed wanted to encourage bank lending, it could lower the required reserve ratio on checkable deposits from 10 percent to 8 percent. This would mean that depository institutions would have to hold fewer reserve assets and would have additional funds to lend or to invest in other financial assets. This seemingly small change can have a powerful effect on the supply of money and the cost and availability of credit. Despite its power, the Fed does not change the required reserve ratio very much. When it does choose to use this tool, the Fed is more likely to lower the ratio rather than to increase it. In December 1990 and again in December 1992, the required reserve ratios were lowered in an effort to stimulate the economy. As of December 1995, the ratio is 3 percent on the first $52 million of checkable deposits and 10 percent thereafter. At the present time, there are no reserve requirements on time and savings deposits even though there have often been such requirements in the past. Rather than frequently changing the required reserve ratio, open market operations have been the major instrument used to implement monetary policy.

Required Reserves The amount of reserve assets that the Fed requires depository institutions to hold against outstanding checkable deposit liabilities.

Required Reserve Ratio The fraction of deposit liabilities which must be held as reserve assets.

RECAP

The main tools of the Fed to implement monetary policy include open market operations and setting the required reserve ratio and the discount rate. Open market operations are the most widely used tool.

Who Does What Within the Fed

Having spelled out the Fed's organizational structure and functions, and having identified the major tools available to Fed policymakers, we move on to which group within the Fed has primary responsibility for each tool and

---

[11] Actually, as of December 19, 1995, the required reserve ratio is 10 percent on checkable deposits over $52 million. For checkable deposits less than $52 million, the required reserve ratio is 3 percent. The amount of checkable deposits against which the 3 percent applies is modified each year depending on the percentage change in checkable deposits. Because $52 million in deposits is a relatively small amount, we ignore the 3 percent requirement.

function. Exhibit 5-6 shows the division of responsibility within the Fed. As you can see in the diagram, the Board of Governors determines reserve requirements and the discount rate while the FOMC directs open market operations.

Clearly, the Board swings the most weight within the Federal Reserve System. The Board even exercises general supervisory and budgetary control over the 12 Reserve Banks. Remember the golden rule: "He who has the gold rules!" The Reserve Banks deal directly with depository institutions. In dealing with these institutions, the Reserve Banks administer discount policy. In addition, they are an important part of the nation's check-clearing system and play an important educational role by providing financial institutions and the public with information on Fed policy and the workings of the financial system and the economy.

We can be even more specific about where the power to make policy within the Fed lies, thanks to an economist who has had a "lifelong interest in the relationship between political processes and macroeconomic outcomes, especially in the area of monetary policy."[12] Thomas Havrilesky states that the chairperson of the Board of Governors has "power within the Fed's policy hierarchy because he molds the outcome of the meetings of the Board of Governors and the FOMC. The chairman plays a key role in shaping the FOMC policy directive. He expresses his own preferences and summarizes the sense of these meetings once deliberation and debate have been

---

[12]Thomas Havrilesky in the preface to *The Pressures on American Monetary Policy*, Boston: Kluwer Academic Publishers, 1993.

Exhibit 5-6 ◆ Division of Responsibility Within the Federal Reserve System

Board of Governors
(7 appointed members)

◆ Sets reserve requirements and approves discount rates as a part of monetary policy
◆ Supervises and regulates member banks and bank holding companies
◆ Establishes and administers protective regulations in consumer finance
◆ Oversees Federal Reserve Banks

Federal Reserve Banks (Reserve Banks)
(12 Districts)

◆ Propose discount rates
◆ Lend funds to depository institutions (discount policy)
◆ Furnish currency
◆ Collect and clear checks and transfer funds for depository institutions
◆ Handle U.S. government debt and cash balances

Federal Open Market Committee
(Board of Governors plus 5 Federal Reserve Bank presidents)

◆ Directs open market operations (buying and selling of U.S. government securities), which are the primary instrument of monetary policy

SOURCE: *The Federal Reserve System: Purposes and Functions*, Board of Governors of the Federal Reserve System, 1984, p. 5.

concluded."[13] Perhaps now you can see why this individual is such a powerful figure in U.S. policy circles.

The Federal Reserve System: An Independent Watchdog, Convenient Scapegoat, or Cunning Political Animal?

The Federal Reserve System is a quasi-government agency whose primary responsibility is to stabilize the economy. However, the Fed is just one of many agencies of the government that also tries to design policies to stabilize the economy. Others include the Council of Economic Advisers, the Department of the Treasury, and the Office of Management and Budget. Each of these agencies, unlike the Fed, is under the direct control of the executive branch of government. For example, the president can fire the chairperson of the Council, the secretary of treasury, and the budget director at any time.

The Federal Reserve was established by Congress as an independent agency to give it a certain amount of insulation from the political process. It is allegedly independent because of the way it is structured. As discussed earlier, each member of the Board is appointed to a 14-year term, so that once appointed, a member of the Board does not have to defend his or her actions to the Congress, the president, or the public. Also, the Fed does not need or get an appropriation from Congress. The Fed makes its "way" from the interest income it earns on loans to depository institutions and its holdings of government securities. Last, the Fed is exempt from many provisions of the **Freedom of Information Act** (1966) and "government in the sunshine" legislation, which call for government policy to be made in meetings open to the public. As a result, Fed policymakers usually meet in secret to formulate policy.

Nevertheless, the Fed is not completely outside the government. It is firmly embedded in our political system. In the short run, however, the Federal Reserve does not take orders from anyone in the executive or legislative branch of government. Its decisions regarding monetary policy are, in theory, not constrained by the whims of the president or Congress or by any partisan politics. We say "in the short run" because, in the long run, Congress can pass laws that the Fed must obey. It could even abolish the Fed altogether. We think it fair to say that the Fed is aware of these possibilities and behaves accordingly.

Ever since the Fed was created, politicians and academics have debated the desirability of Federal Reserve independence. The controversy has been largely focused on the degree to which the Fed should alter its policy in response to "suggestions" or directives from the Congress or the president. Evidence suggests that after 1960, "outside forces" including Congress and the executive branch became more aggressive in attempting to influence Fed actions. Obviously, the more responsive the Fed was to outside forces, the less independent it would be. The continuing debate over this issue in part reflects the frustration expressed by the president and some members of Congress in

Freedom of Information Act A 1966 law that requires more openness in government and more public access to government documents.

---

[13]Thomas Havrilesky, *The Pressures on American Monetary Policy*, Boston: Kluwer Academic Publishers, 1993, p. 4.

LOOKING OUT

Central Bank Independence and Macroeconomic Performance

Like the United States, most industrialized nations have a central bank that directs monetary policy and supervises and regulates the banking system. Unlike the United States, which is divided into 12 Federal Reserve districts, most foreign central banks (Germany excepted) are highly centralized.

Central banks also vary with regards to the degree of independence from government officials. Like the United States, almost all directors of foreign central banks are appointed by the government. However, terms are often considerably shorter than the 14-year term of Fed Governors. The shorter the term, the less independent the central bank is. In some countries, government officials are actually on the governing board as was true of the Fed in its early years when the Board of Governors was called the Federal Reserve Board. The Board included the Secretary of the Treasury and the Comptroller of the Currency. They were replaced with two appointees after the Great Depression. In some countries, central banks are mandated by law to give credit to the government. In some, it is easy for politicians to replace central bank governors. In others, it may not be so easy.

By considering the preceding factors, researchers have judged the independence of various central banks. The less independent, the more vulnerable the bank is to political pressure. Countries with the most independent central banks include Germany, Switzerland, Canada, the Netherlands, and the United States. Countries with the least independent central banks include Portugal, Greece, New Zealand, and Spain.

But what does all this have to do with macroeconomic performance? Several researchers suggest that inflation rates are lowest in countries with the most independent central banks.* Apparently the more independent the central bank, the less likely that it will expand (inflate) the economy in response to political pressure. Evidence also suggests that countries with the most independent central banks do not have higher long-run rates of unemployment. Thus, on both the inflation and unemployment fronts, an independent central bank appears to enhance macroeconomic performance.

*In addition to the Sue Bae Kim article in the Suggested Readings, see Alberto Alesina and Lawrence H. Summers, "Central Bank Independence and Macroeconomic Performance," *Journal of Money, Credit, and Banking,* 25, no. 2, May 1993, pp. 151–162.

their often unsuccessful efforts to attain our economic goals. In recent years, this frustration has led to several attempts not only to influence the Fed but also to make the Fed more responsive to the Congress. The Fed saw such moves as a serious threat to its independence and vigorously fought off overt efforts to clip its wings.

Those who support independence do so mainly on the grounds that anything less than independence will inject "politics" into monetary policy operations. This argument was put forth eloquently by Alan Greenspan, chairperson of the Board of Governors:

LOOKING BACK

Early Attempts at Establishing a Central Bank

The creation of the Fed in 1913 was not the first attempt to establish a central bank. Indeed the first effort stretches back to 1791 when the Bank of the United States was given a 20-year charter with the government providing one-fifth of the start up capital. The fledgling bank had elements of both a private and a central bank. Like other private banks, it made loans to businesses and individuals. Like a central bank, the new bank issued banknotes backed by gold, attempted to control the issuance of state banknotes, acted as fiscal agent for the government, and was responsible for the aggregate quantity of money and credit supplied in the economy. However, the bank was not without its detractors who alleged that the bank represented big city "moneyed" interests. Fear and distrust, the unpopularity of centralized power, and questions about its constitutionality all contributed to pressures to dissolve the bank. Its charter was allowed to run out in 1811.

The War of 1812 brought renewed pressures for a central bank that could oversee the financing of the war. Congress chartered the Second Bank of the United States in 1816. This bank also acted as fiscal agent for the U.S. government and issued banknotes redeemable in gold. Frictions persisted between groups who wanted a strong central bank (Federalists) and those who supported a more decentralized system (anti-Federalists). After substantially reducing its powers in the early 1830s, President Andrew Jackson vetoed the rechartering of the Second Bank of the United States and it went out of existence in 1836.

The National Banking Acts of 1863 and 1864 had been successful at establishing a uniform national currency. Despite this, the lack of a central bank meant that there was no easy way to regulate the amount of currency in circulation. Consequently, periodic shortages often developed, which led to financial crises. Such crises occurred in 1873, 1884, 1893, and 1907. However, another attempt at creating a central bank that could regulate the amount of currency in circulation would not be successful until 1913 with the establishment of the Fed.

We have to be sensitive to the appropriate degree of accountability accorded a central bank in a democratic society. If accountability is achieved by putting the conduct of monetary policy under the close influence of politicians subject to short-term election-cycle pressures, the resulting policy would likely prove disappointing over time. That is the conclusion of financial analysts, of economists, and of others who have studied the experiences of central banks around the globe, and of the legislators who built the Federal Reserve. The lure of short-run gains from gunning the economy can loom large in the context of an election cycle, but the process of reaching for such gains can have costly consequences for the nation's economic performance and standards of living over the longer term. The temptation is to step on the monetary accelerator, or at least to avoid the monetary brake, until after the next election. Giving in to such temptations is likely to impart an inflationary bias to the economy and could lead to instability, recession, and economic stagnation. Interest rates would be higher, and productivity and living standards lower, than if monetary policy were freer to approach the nation's economic goals with a longer term perspective.

The recognition that monetary policies that are in the best long-run interest of the nation may not always be popular in the short run has led not only the United States but also most other developed nations to limit the degree of immediate control that legislatures and administrations have over their central banks. More and more countries have been taking actions to increase the amount of separation between monetary policy and the political sphere.[14]

Thus, proponents of continuing the Fed's independence argue that politicians are interested in getting elected and reelected, and this means that they are short-run maximizers. They do not take the long view. This could be disastrous if the long-run impacts of policy are different from the short-run impacts. For instance, to please the electorate, politicians might pursue an expansionary monetary policy resulting in accelerating growth of economic activity, even though the longer-run impact of this policy might increase inflation. Some have even suggested that the term of the Fed chairperson should be increased to further remove that individual from political influences.

Despite the persuasive arguments, to many people the independence of the Fed is inconsistent with democracy. It is argued that the president and Congress are held accountable for the state of economic conditions. If unemployment is rising and inflation is rampant, the president and Congress will be driven from office at election time. Because the president and the Congress are responsible for economic policy, they should have all the tools at their disposal. More generally, opponents of Fed independence argue that monetary policy, like other government policies, should be controlled by people directly responsible to the electorate.

The kinds of reforms that opponents of the Fed's independence would like to see include the following:

1. *A change in the status of Reserve Bank presidents on the FOMC.* Either remove the Reserve Bank presidents from membership on the FOMC, make them nonvoting members, or change the way in which they become Reserve Bank presidents so that they are more representative of the public at large. The concern is that the Reserve Bank presidents represent the interests of the banking community since they are elected by the Reserve Bank directors, two-thirds of whom, in turn, are elected by the member banks.
2. *A broadening of the authority of the General Accounting Office (GAO) to audit the Fed.* At present, GAO audits all aspects of the Federal Reserve with three exceptions: (1) deliberations and decisions regarding monetary policy, (2) transactions directed by the FOMC, and (3) transactions involving foreign exchange operations. Proposals would eliminate these exceptions.
3. *Mandated disclosure of monetary policies and discussions.* Fuller and more immediate disclosure of FOMC discussions and decisions.

In each of these cases, the recommended change would reduce the autonomy of the Fed and make it more accountable. With the Fed often projecting the image that monetary policy is too complicated for the public and the Congress to understand, or that secrecy is essential to successful policy, it

---

[14] Statement by Alan Greenspan, before the Committee on Banking, Finance, and Urban Affairs, U.S. House of Representatives, October 13, 1993.

should not be surprising that Congressional representatives are suspicious. They want to open up the process of formulating monetary policy to examination and debate. They want more timely information about policy decisions.

Today, even though there is not a legislative requirement to do so, the FOMC releases edited minutes of its deliberations immediately following the next FOMC meeting, approximately six weeks later. As previously discussed, in early 1994, Chairperson Greenspan decided to announce several policy changes immediately following the FOMC meetings rather than waiting for the publication of minutes and the policy directive, or for the actual policies to be implemented. This practice was formally adopted in February 1995. Furthermore, in 1993, the Fed agreed to publish "edited" transcripts, not just minutes, of the FOMC meetings with a five-year delay.[15] All of these actions suggest that the Fed is becoming slightly more open, while at the same time maintaining that the present system gives it the proper degree of accountability necessary to carry out monetary policy.

Long-time observers of the political-economic wars believe that the debate over whether the Fed should be independent is more form than substance. On the one hand, it is argued that Congress finds the current system quite convenient. If the economy performs badly, the Congress can engage in Fedbashing— that is, blame the Fed for what went wrong and tell the public that the Fed, insulated by its independence, would not respond to Congress's call to "do the right thing." In 1980, Edward Kane summarized this relationship as follows:

> Whenever monetary policies are popular, incumbents can claim their influence was crucial in their adoption. On the other hand, when monetary policies prove unpopular, they can blame everything on a stubborn Federal Reserve and claim further that things would have been worse if they had not pressed Fed officials at every opportunity.[16]

Kane's synopsis is as true today as it was in 1980. Scapegoats are convenient. If the Fed were directly and completely responsible to Congress, then who would be there to blame when things go wrong?

To sum up, the Fed's independence is in part an illusion. It can only be maintained if the Fed operates within politically acceptable bounds. If it pursued policies at considerable variance from what the president and Congress desired, the Congress could change the law! Since changes have not occurred, we can infer that current arrangements are convenient and attractive. More specifically, political decision makers gain from having the Fed seem independent to the public. This way the Fed can take the heat for unpopular policies and the politicians can share the credit when things go right. At the same time, the Congress and the president are probably confident that if push comes to shove, they can persuade the Fed to pursue policies conforming, at least broadly, to their wishes. This is part of what is popularly referred to as "the political economy of policy making."

In the next chapter, we look at the major financial markets, instruments, and players. It is time to move into the world in which the Fed operates.

---

[15] The editing of the transcripts usually involves deleting a small amount of confidential material that pertains to foreign central banks or entities.

[16] Edward Kane, "Politics and Fed Policymaking: The More Things Change the More They Remain the Same," *Journal of Monetary Economics*, April 1980, pp. 199–211.

Summary of Major Points

1. The Federal Reserve System was established by an Act of Congress in 1913. The original Act was modified and strengthened in 1933 and 1935 following the economic and financial collapse of the Great Depression.

2. The Fed is charged with regulating and supervising the operation of the financial system so as to promote a smooth-running, efficient, competitive financial system and with promoting the overall health and stability of the economy through its ability to influence the availability and cost of money and credit.

3. The Board of Governors, located in Washington, D.C., is the core of the Federal Reserve System. It is composed of seven members appointed by the president, with the approval of the Senate, for 14-year terms. The terms are staggered so that one expires every two years. The president appoints one of the governors as chairperson for a four-year term.

4. The country is divided into 12 districts. Each district is served by a Reserve Bank located in a large city within the district. The framers of the original Federal Reserve Act hoped to decentralize policy-making authority within the Fed through the creation of Reserve Banks.

5. The Federal Open Market Committee (FOMC) is the chief policy-making body within the Fed. It is composed of 12 members: the seven members of the Board of Governors and five of the 12 presidents of the Reserve Banks. The president of the New York Federal Reserve Bank is a permanent voting member, and the other four slots rotate yearly among the remaining 11 Reserve Bank presidents.

6. The Fed's functions can be classified into four main areas: formulation and implementation of monetary policy; supervision and regulation of the financial system; facilitation of the payments mechanism; and acting as fiscal agent for the government.

7. The FOMC directs open market operations, the major tool for implementing monetary policy. These operations involve the buying or selling of government securities—actions that affect the volume of reserves in the banking system as well as interest rates. When the Fed buys securities, bank reserves increase. This, in turn, encourages bankers to expand loans and hence the money supply.

8. The minutes of the FOMC meetings are released to the public immediately after the next FOMC meeting. They contain the policy directive that is the set of instructions regarding the conduct of open market operations that is issued to the New York Fed. The New York Fed, located at the center of the nation's financial markets, executes open market operations on behalf of the FOMC and the entire Federal Reserve System.

9. The discount rate is the rate the Fed charges depository institutions for borrowing reserves from their district Reserve Bank. Since the Fed views borrowing as a privilege rather than a right, institutions are encouraged to borrow only when absolutely necessary and only for short periods of time.

10. In exceptional circumstances the Fed is prepared to serve as a lender of last resort. It will lend for an extended period to an institution experi-

encing severe difficulties. It is motivated by a desire to preserve the public's confidence in the safety and soundness of the financial system.

11. The Fed requires depository institutions to hold reserve assets equal to a proportion of each dollar of deposit liabilities. The Fed's required reserve ratio specifies the proportion.

12. There is an ongoing debate as to whether the Fed should continue to operate as an independent government agency. The Fed and others argue that independence is essential to the pursuit of economic stability. Opponents argue that such independence is inconsistent with our democratic form of government. Others observe that the Congress and the president find the Fed a convenient scapegoat when the economy deteriorates. They further believe that the Fed is really not all that independent and that at times, it does respond to political pressure.

Key Terms

Banking Reform Acts of 1933 and 1935
Board of Governors
Discount Rate
Federal Reserve Act
Federal Reserve System
Fed Open Market Committee (FOMC)
Freedom of Information Act

Lender of Last Resort
Monetary Policy
Open Market Operations
Payments Mechanism
Policy Directive
Required Reserve Ratio
Required Reserves
Reserve Bank

Review Questions

1. Discuss each of the four major functions of the Fed. Which, if any, do you believe requires the most Fed autonomy? Why?

2. Give the major responsibilities of each of the following:
   a. The Board of Governors
   b. The 12 Reserve Banks
   c. The Fed Open Market Committee

3. Why was the Fed created? What effect should the existence of the Fed have on financial crises?

4. Why were 12 Federal Reserve Banks created rather than one central bank?

5. What features of the Fed's structure serve to make it fairly autonomous? Is Congress able to wield any control over the Fed?

6. Why have the responsibilities of the Fed increased since its inception?

7. Discuss the major policy tools that the Fed can use to promote the overall health of the economy. What is the most widely used tool?

8. When and why are changes in the discount rate implemented? Who requests such changes? How often does the Fed make changes in the required reserve ratio? How often does the Fed engage in open market operations?

9. What are the arguments for increasing the autonomy of the Fed? The arguments for increasing the accountability of the Fed?

10. Assume the Fed becomes less independent. How could this affect monetary policy? Assume the Fed becomes more independent. How could this affect monetary policy?

11. Why is the president of the New York Fed a permanent member of the FOMC?

12. Would the Fed be more accountable to Congress or to the president of the United States? Why? Who created the Fed? Who appoints the Fed chairperson?

13. How does each of the following affect the money supply?
    a. The Fed lowers the required reserve ratio.
    b. The Fed lowers the discount rate.
    c. The Fed buys government securities.

Analytical Questions

The Financial System and the Economy

| Back | Forward | Home | Reload | Images | Open | Print | Find | Stop | N |

1. This chapter has described the Federal Reserve System. From the website maintained by the Fed at Minneapolis, (http://woodrow.mpls.frb.fed.US/info/sys/frs.html), answer the following questions:
   a. When and by whom was the Fed created?
   b. What is the Board of Governors of the Fed?
   c. Who are the current members of the Board of Governors?

2. The Federal Open Market Committee (FOMC) directs open market operations that involve the purchase or sale of government securities. The website (http://woodrow.mpls.frb.US/info/policy), maintained by the Federal Reserve Bank of Minneapolis, contains information on the FOMC. Access this site and answer the following questions:
   a. What is the current schedule of FOMC meeting dates?
   b. Who are the current members of the FOMC?

Suggested Readings

For an excellent monetary history and a summary of the events leading up to the legislation establishing the Federal Reserve, see Milton Friedman and Anna Jacobson Schwartz, *A Monetary History of the United States, 1867–1960* (Princeton, N.J.: Princeton University Press, 1963), chap. 4.

The concern about political pressure on the central bank was well founded in the early history of banks in the United States. For a relevant discussion, see Bray Hammond, *Banks and Politics in America from the Revolution to the Civil War* (Princeton, N.J.: Princeton University Press, 1957).

U.S. Monetary Policy and Financial Markets by Ann-Marie Meulendyke (1989) is a readable discussion of Fed procedures and the conduct of monetary policy. It can be obtained free of charge from the Public Information Dept., Federal Reserve Bank of New York, 33 Liberty Street, New York, NY 10045.

"The Independence of Central Banks," by Sun Bae Kim, summarizes a study showing that countries with the most independent central banks have the lowest inflation rates. Furthermore, if the central bank has a reputation for controlling inflation, this can substitute for legal independence. It can be found in the *Weekly Letter of the San Francisco Federal Reserve Bank,* December 13, 1991.

"An Independent Central Bank in a Democratic Country: The Federal Reserve Experience," by William McDonough, offers a historical development of central banking in the United States and a discussion of the need for the Fed to be somewhat independent of the day-to-day control of the government so that it will be less likely to succumb to short-term political pressures. It can be found in the *Federal Reserve Bank of New York Quarterly Review,* 19, Spring 1994, pp. 1–6.

Three articles devoted to the question of central bank autonomy can be found in "The Papers and Proceedings of the 107th Annual Meeting of the American Economic Association in Washington, D.C., January 6–8, 1995" as published in the *American Economic Review,* May 1995. These articles are: "How Independent Should the Central Bank Be?" by Alberto Alesina and Roberta Gaiti; "Central-Bank Independence Revisited" by Stanley Fischer; and "Two Fallacies Concerning Central-Bank Independence" by Bennett T. McCallum.

PART TWO

Financial Markets and Prices

6

Financial Markets, Instruments, and Participants

> *The worst form of inequality*
> *is to try to make unequal things equal.*
> —Aristotle—

Learning Objectives

After reading this chapter, you should know:

◆ The various ways that financial markets can be classified including primary and secondary markets, money and capital markets, and spot and futures markets

◆ The definitions and characteristics of the major financial market instruments

◆ The functions of the key participants—the market makers

◆ How the various sectors of financial markets are connected

Game Talk

To understand the role of money in the financial system, we need to understand the jargon employed by insiders, or market participants, when they describe and discuss the "action" in financial markets. Trade jargon is not unique to these insiders, but is rather pervasive in many aspects of life. Football is a favorite American pastime. The following example points out the need for "players" to understand the lingo in even this traditional activity.

> The time is Saturday afternoon during fall, and the place is the gridiron. When the quarterback reads a blitz (or red-dog) and man-to-man coverage, it is critical to call an automatic at the line of scrimmage and hit the flanker on a fly pattern. Of course, if the blitz does not materialize, the quarterback may find that he has thrown the pass into the teeth of zone coverage where the free safety could easily pick off the ball.

Such is the jargon of football. Much of this lingo is fully understood only by insiders—players, coaches, and football aficionados. Outsiders have difficulty understanding the game because they don't know the jargon, just as outsiders often have difficulty understanding financial market discussions.

In this chapter, we will learn about financial markets (chiefly in the United States) and the language they use so that we too can understand what they are talking about.

Introducing Financial Markets

In general, a market for financial claims (instruments) can be viewed as the process or mechanism that connects the buyers and sellers of claims regardless of where they happen to be physically located. As you will see in this chapter, markets can be classified in many different ways. One of the most popular is to classify financial markets into individual submarkets according to the type of financial claim that is traded: stock market, corporate bond market, Treasury bill market, commercial paper market, and so forth. There is, however, at least one difficulty with classifying markets according to the particular type of financial claim traded; it suggests the individual submarkets are separate, more or less unconnected compartments. A central message of this chapter is that the markets for the individual financial claims are connected and in many respects more alike than different.

Another classification system, which emanates from a recognition of some similarities among the instruments, is to place instruments into one of two compartments—a money market or a capital market. The **money market** includes those markets where securities with original maturities of one year or less are traded. Examples of such securities would be Treasury bills, commercial paper, and negotiable certificates of deposit (CDs). As you might guess, the **capital market** includes those markets where securities with original maturities of more than one year are traded. Examples here include corporate bonds, stocks, mortgages, and Treasury bonds issued by the U.S. Treasury.

Money Market The market for financial assets with an original maturity of less than one year.

Capital Market The market for financial assets with an original maturity of greater than one year.

Not surprisingly, some refer to the money market as the *short-term market* and the capital market as the *long-term market*.

Thus, we can "slice up" financial markets into little pieces, the individual submarkets, and group like items together. In this case, we are grouping instruments by their **term to maturity**—that is, the length of time from when the instrument is initially issued until it matures. Put another way, the various markets may be separate institutionally, but connected analytically through the buying and selling of securities by the participants in the markets.[1]

An alternative way to classify financial markets is into the primary market and the secondary market. The **primary market** is the market in which a security is initially sold for the first time. The security may be called a financial instrument, claim, or IOU; all these terms are interchangeable. For example, if a firm needs to issue new bonds or stocks to finance investment in new equipment, the initial sale of these new securities occurs in the primary market. Thus, the primary market is where the public (individuals or financial institutions) buys newly issued bonds or stocks from the firms issuing them. Once a firm has issued bonds or stocks, further trading, say, a sale of bonds a month later by an initial purchaser, occurs in the **secondary market.** Most of the transactions in financial markets occur in the secondary market as portfolios are continually adjusted. It will be helpful to think of these financial transactions in the secondary market as occurring in the "used-car lots" of our financial system.[2]

The distinction between the primary and secondary markets is somewhat conceptual. In practice, the selling of new securities in primary markets by the firms issuing them and the trading of older securities in secondary markets occurs simultaneously. An analogy may help. The market for autos is made up of the market for new autos and the market for used autos. However, if you go to a GM dealer looking for these parts of the auto market, the only real distinction you will observe is that the used and new cars are located on different sides of the lot.

If this is so, why bother to distinguish analytically between primary and secondary markets? To understand why, we must first learn something about the quality of secondary markets. We assess the quality of a secondary market by the cost and inconvenience associated with trading existing securities. For example, high-quality secondary markets are characterized by trading at relatively low costs and little inconvenience. Such characteristics facilitate the sale and purchase of existing securities, and thereby contribute to an efficient allocation of financial resources and a smoothly functioning savings-investment process.

To illustrate the point, imagine a financial system like those in many less-developed countries where formal secondary markets do not exist. Assume

Term to Maturity The length of time from when a financial security is initially issued until it matures.

Primary Market The market in which a security is initially sold for the first time.

Secondary Market The market in which previously issued financial securities are sold.

---

[1] The nature of the connection leads some to distinguish among financial markets by whether the market facilitates the exchange of funds directly between surplus spending units (SSUs) and deficit spending units (DSUs), or whether funds are channeled through financial intermediaries. In a direct market, funds are exchanged directly; that is, direct finance occurs. In an indirect market, funds flow through financial intermediaries, and indirect finance occurs. As discussed in Chapter 1, indirect finance occurs when financial intermediaries exchange their own liabilities or secondary claims with SSUs for funds and then provide such funds to DSUs. In this latter transaction, financial intermediaries exchange the funds for direct claims on the DSUs.

[2] Note, however, that unlike used cars, securities usually do not fall in value through time.

now that you want to sell a security you purchased several years ago when it was first issued, say, by LHT Inc., an emerging high-tech firm. The absence of a secondary market implies that you would first have to search for someone willing and able to purchase your LHT security and then negotiate a mutually acceptable price with that person. This is obviously quite time consuming and inconvenient, and the experience might discourage you from saving part of your income in this way in the future; that is, you would be less likely to buy LHT bonds in the future. If other people who own securities have similar experiences, this will mean that LHT Inc., and all firms like it, will encounter some difficulty in financing future deficits and the amount of intermediation will be less than what it otherwise would have been. Assuming the deficits were to be used for planned additions to the firms' plant and equipment, the amount of investment falls. Without this investment there will be less future growth of output and employment in the industry and the economy.

The message in this example is that the lack of a smoothly functioning secondary market will inhibit the financing of planned deficits in the primary market and thus have an adverse effect on investment and economic growth over time. In general, the strength and viability of primary markets is a direct function of the quality of secondary markets. Although the secondary market does not generate additional funds for the economy as a whole, its importance stems from the positive effect a well-developed secondary market has on the primary market. Just as selling a used car does not add to the total number of vehicles on the road, the fact that there is a market for used cars improves the market for new cars.

Another way to classify financial markets is according to whether they arrange transactions that occur instantly or transactions that occur in the future where the terms of the transaction are decided today; that is, whether they are spot or futures markets. **Spot markets** are the markets in which the trading of financial instruments takes place instantaneously and the spot price is the price of a security or financial instrument for immediate delivery. We are all familiar with spot markets. For example, if I decide to buy a share of IBM stock, I check with my broker and find out today's price for the stock. Or I may watch the financial news cable channel to check out the price of a bond for immediate delivery, say one issued by LHT Inc.

At other times, I may be interested in buying or selling financial securities for delivery on some date in the future at a price determined today. If this is the case, I enter the **financial futures market** in which transactions are consummated today for the purchase or sale of financial securities at a specified date in the future. Financial futures agreements are traded in organized markets for U.S. government securities of several maturities and for several stock market indexes.[3] These standardized agreements have existed since 1975. In addition, banks and other dealers and brokers often customize financial futures agreements for their customers.

Financial futures markets fulfill two basic functions. First, futures markets may be used to reduce the risk associated with future price changes by "locking in" a future price today. In recent years, financial futures markets have

Spot Market Market in which the trading of financial securities takes place instantaneously.

Financial Futures Markets Organized markets that trade financial futures agreements.

[3] Standardized financial futures also exist for exchanging U.S. dollars and foreign currencies such as the Japanese yen, German mark, British pound, Swiss franc, Australian dollar, Canadian dollar, and European Currency Unit. Chapter 9 looks at these futures contracts and their uses in international trade and finance.

experienced enormous growth. With increased volatility, surplus spending units (SSUs) and deficit spending units (DSUs) have turned to financial futures markets to deal with the greater risk of unanticipated price changes. Second, financial futures markets can also be used to speculate. **Speculation** in financial securities is buying or selling securities in the hopes of profiting from future price changes. The many intricacies and nuances of financial futures markets are covered in detail in Chapter 10.

> **Speculation** The buying or selling of financial securities in the hopes of profiting from future price changes.

Having acquired an awareness of the various ways that financial markets can be classified, we move on to the noteworthy aspects of the major financial securities that are traded in U.S. financial markets.

RECAP

Financial markets can be classified as money or capital markets, as primary or secondary markets, or as spot or futures markets.

Major Financial Market Instruments

Financial markets perform the important role of channeling funds from SSUs to DSUs. Since the action in financial markets involves the trading of financial instruments, in effect, IOUs issued by DSUs, understanding the action requires us to be familiar with what is being traded. We first examine the instruments traded in the money market and then look at those traded in the capital market.

Money Market Instruments

The money market has undergone significant changes in the past 30 years, with new financial instruments being introduced and the amount outstanding of other instruments increasing at a far more rapid pace than the level of economic activity. In Chapter 13, we discuss the reasons for this growth and evolution when we look at the driving forces behind financial innovation. For now, we introduce and briefly describe each of the principal money market instruments. Exhibit 6–1 contains the dollar amount outstanding of each instrument at the end of 1960, 1970, 1980, 1990 and 1995.

U.S. Treasury Bills

U.S. Treasury bills (T-bills) are short-term debt instruments of the U.S. government with typical maturities of 3–12 months. They pay a set amount at maturity and have no explicit interest payments. In reality, they pay interest by initially selling at a discount—that is, at a price lower than the amount paid at maturity. For instance, you might buy a one-year Treasury bill in April 1996 for $9,470 that can be redeemed for $10,000 in April, 1997, thus effectively paying $530 in interest ($10,000 − $9,470 = $530). The yield on such a bill is 3.3 percent or $530/$9,470 [(interest amount)/(purchase price)].

> **U.S. Treasury Bills (T-bills)** Short-term debt instruments of the U.S. government with typical maturities of 3–12 months.

U.S. Treasury bills are the most liquid of all the money market instruments because they have an active secondary market and relatively short terms to

Exhibit 6-1 ◆
The Principal
Money Market
Instruments
Amount
Outstanding, End
of Year Billions of
Dollars

Type of Instrument	1960	1970	1980	1990	1995
Treasury Bills	$37	$76	$200	$482	$743
Negotiable CDs	0	45	260	N.A.*	N.A.
Commercial Paper**	5	35	99	558	678
Bankers' Acceptances	1	4	32	52	23
Repurchase Agreements and Fed Funds	1	22	102	324	546
Eurodollars	1	20	68	N.A.	92

*N.A.—Not available.
**Includes commercial paper issued by financial and nonfinancial firms.

SOURCE: *Federal Reserve Flow of Funds Accounts, Z1*, March 8, 1996. *The Federal Reserve Bulletin*, various issues. *Banking and Monetary Statistics, 1945–1970. Annual Statistical Digest 1971–1975. Economic Report of the President, 1996.*

maturity. They also are the safest of all money market instruments because there is no possibility that the government would fail to pay back the amount owed when the security matures. The federal government is always able to meet its financial commitments because of its ability to increase taxes or to issue currency in fulfillment of its scheduled payments.

Negotiable Certificates of Deposit (CDs)

Negotiable Certificates
of Deposit (CDs) Certif-
icates of deposit with a
minimum maturity of
$100,000 that can be
traded in a secondary
market; first introduced
by Citibank in 1961.

A certificate of deposit (CD) is a debt instrument sold by a depository institution that pays annual interest payments equal to a fixed percent of the original purchase price. In addition, at maturity the original purchase price is also paid back. Most CDs have a maturity of 1–12 months. Prior to 1961, most CDs were not negotiable; that is, they could not be sold to someone else and could not be redeemed from the bank before maturity without paying a significant penalty. In 1961, with the goal of making CDs more liquid and more attractive to investors, Citibank introduced the first **negotiable certificates of deposit (CDs).** Such negotiable CDs could be resold in a secondary market, which Citibank created. Negotiable CDs have a minimum denomination of $100,000 but in practice, the minimum denomination to trade in the secondary market is $2,000,000. Most large commercial banks and many large savings and loans now issue negotiable CDs. In addition, smaller banks are able to borrow in the market by using brokers.[4]

Commercial Paper

Commercial Paper
Short-term debt instru-
ments issued by
corporations.

Commercial paper is a short-term debt instrument issued by corporations such as General Motors, AT&T, and other less well-known domestic and foreign enterprises. Most commercial paper is supported by a backup line of bank credit. Prior to the 1960s, corporations usually borrowed short-term funds from banks. Since then, corporations have come to depend on selling com-

---

[4]To attract investors, brokers offer CDs in $100,000 denominations. Federal deposit insurance coverage for CDs issued by depository institutions is limited to $100,000. CDs of larger amounts can be fully insured by packaging together $100,000 CDs of different depository institutions.

mercial paper to other financial intermediaries and other lenders for their immediate short-term borrowing needs. The growth of the commercial paper market since 1960 has been impressive. The amount of commercial paper outstanding from nonfinancial firms has increased by more than 4,000 percent in the 1960 to 1995 period from $4 billion to more than $160 billion. Initially, only large corporations had access to the commercial paper market. But, in recent years, medium and small firms are also finding ways to enter this market. Some financial intermediaries also get funds to invest and lend by issuing commercial paper.

Bankers' Acceptances

Bankers' acceptances are money market instruments created in the course of financing international trade. Banks were authorized to issue bankers acceptances to finance the international and domestic trade of their customers by the Federal Reserve Act in 1913. Exhibit 6–2 depicts how bankers' acceptances work. A bankers' acceptance is a bank draft (a guarantee of payment similar to a check) issued by a firm and payable on some future date. If, for a fee,

Bankers' Acceptances
Money market instruments created in the course of international trade to guarantee bank drafts due on a future date.

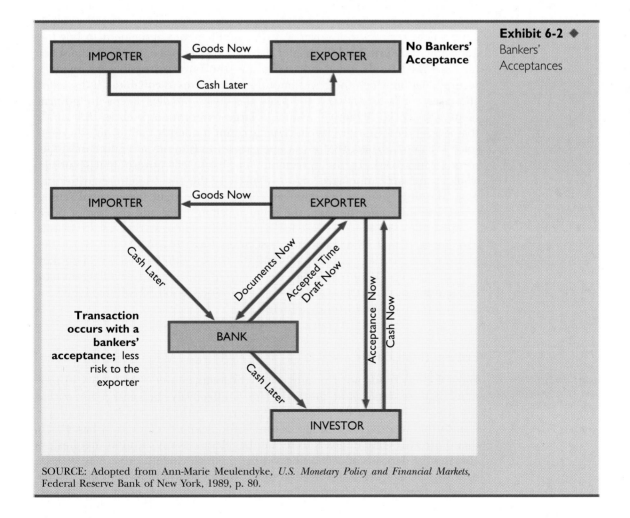

Exhibit 6-2 ◆ Bankers' Acceptances

SOURCE: Adopted from Ann-Marie Meulendyke, *U.S. Monetary Policy and Financial Markets,* Federal Reserve Bank of New York, 1989, p. 80.

the bank on which the draft is drawn, stamps it as "accepted," then the bank is guaranteeing that the draft will be paid even in the event of default by the firm. If the firm fails to deposit the funds into its account to cover the draft by the future due date, the bank's guarantee means that the bank is obligated to pay the draft. The bank's creditworthiness is substituted for that of the firm issuing the acceptance, making the draft more likely to be accepted when purchasing goods abroad. The foreign exporter knows that even if the company purchasing the goods goes bankrupt, the bank draft will still be paid off. The party that accepts the draft (often another bank) can then resell the draft in a secondary market at a discount before the due date or it can hold it in its portfolio as an investment. Bankers' acceptances, which trade in secondary markets, are similar to Treasury bills in that they are short term and sell at a discount. The amount outstanding has increased by nearly 4,000 percent ($2 billion to $75 billion) from 1960 to 1984. However, since 1984, the acceptance market has declined due to the growth of other financing alternatives and the increased trade in currencies other than the dollar. By the end of 1995, the amount of outstanding bankers' acceptances was $22.6 billion.

Repurchase Agreements

Repurchase Agreements
Short-term agreements in which the seller sells a government security to a buyer with the simultaneous agreement to buy it back on a later date at a higher price.

Repurchase agreements are short-term agreements in which the seller sells a government security to a buyer with the simultaneous agreement to buy the government security back on a later date at a higher price. In effect, the seller has borrowed funds for a short term and the buyer ostensibly has made a secured loan in which the government security serves as collateral. If the seller (borrower) fails to pay back the loan, the buyer (lender) keeps the government security. For example, assume a large corporation, such as IBM, finds that it has excess funds in its checking account it doesn't want to sit idle when interest can be earned. IBM uses these excess funds to buy a repurchase agreement from a bank. In the agreement, the bank sells government securities while at the same time agreeing to repurchase the government securities the next morning (or in a few days) at a higher price than the original selling price. The difference between the original selling price and the higher price the securities are bought back for is, in reality, interest. The effect of this agreement is that IBM has made a secured loan to a bank and holds the government securities as collateral until the bank repurchases them when they pay off the loan. Repurchase agreements were created in 1969. The amount outstanding of repurchase agreements is now over $100 billion making them an important source of funds to banks.

Federal (Fed) Funds

Federal (Fed) Funds
Loans of reserves (deposits at the Fed) between depository intermediaries typically overnight.

Federal (fed) funds are typically overnight loans between depository institutions of their deposits at the Fed. This is effectively the market for excess reserves. A depository institution might borrow in the federal funds market if it finds that its reserve assets do not meet the amount required by law. It can then borrow reserve deposits from another depository institution that has excess reserve deposits and chooses to loan them to earn interest. The reserve deposit balances are transferred between the borrowing and lending institutions using the Fed's wire transfer system. In recent years, many large depository institutions have used this market as a permanent source of funds to lend, not just when there is a temporary shortage of required reserve assets. The federal funds rate is closely watched by financial market participants to judge the tightness of credit market conditions in the financial system. When the fed funds rate is high relative to other short-term rates, it indicates that reserves are in short supply. When it is relatively low, the credit needs of depository institutions are also low.

Eurodollars

Eurodollars were originally considered to be deposits denominated in dollars in a foreign bank. The Eurodollar market started in the 1950s when the Soviet bloc governments put dollar-denominated deposits into London Banks. The deposits were made in London because the Soviet governments were afraid that if the deposits were in the United States that they could be frozen in the event of a political dispute. Another example of a Eurodollar would be when an American makes a deposit that is denominated in dollars in a bank in England. U.S. banks can borrow these deposits from foreign banks or their own foreign branches when they need funds. In recent years, Eurodollars have become an important source of funds for domestically chartered banks (over $90 billion in November 1995).[5] Today, the term *Eurodollar* has come to mean any deposit in a foreign (host) country where the deposit is denominated in the currency of the country from which it came rather than that of the host country.[6]

Eurodollars Dollar-denominated deposits held abroad.

Capital Market Instruments

The capital market is extremely important because it raises the funds needed by DSUs to carry out their spending and investment plans. A smoothly functioning capital market influences how fast the economy grows. The principal capital market instruments introduced in this section are listed in Exhibit 6-3, with the amounts outstanding at the end of 1960, 1970, 1980, 1990 and 1995.

Stocks

Stocks are equity claims representing ownership of the net income and assets of a corporation. The income that stockholders receive for their ownership is called *dividends*. Preferred stock pays a fixed dividend and, in the event of bankruptcy, the owners of preferred stock are entitled to be paid first after other creditors of the corporation. Common stock pays a variable dividend, depending on the profits that are leftover after preferred stockholders have been paid and retained earnings set aside. The largest secondary market for outstanding shares of stock is the New York Stock Exchange. Several stock indexes measure the overall movement of common stock prices; the Dow

Stocks Equity claims that represent ownership of the net assets and income of a corporation.

---

[5] *Federal Reserve Bulletin,* February 1996, p. A19.
[6] Eurodollars are to be distinguished from foreign deposits. Foreign deposits are denominated in the currency of the host country—in this case, England. An example of a foreign deposit would be if an American took dollars, converted them to British pounds and deposited them in a bank in England with the deposit denominated in British pounds. In addition to the term *Eurodollar,* we also speak of other *Euro* currency markets, such as the Euroyen and Euromark markets.

Exhibit 6-3 ◆

The Principal Capital Market Instruments Amount Outstanding, End of Year Billions of Dollars

Type of Instrument	1960	1970	1980	1990	1995
Corporate Stock	$451	$906	$1,920	$3,530	$8,345
Mortgages	142	297	965	3,804	4,724
Corporate and Foreign Bonds	75	167	319	1,704	2,760
U.S. Government Securities	178	156	394	1,595	2,532
U.S. Government Agency Securities*	10	51	170	426	837
Municipal Securities					

*Excludes federally sponsored mortgage pools.

SOURCE: Federal Reserve *Flow of Funds Accounts, Z1,* March 8, 1996. The *Federal Reserve Bulletin,* various issues. *Banking* and *Monetary Statistics 1941–1970. Economic Report of the President, 1996.*

Jones Industrial Average, perhaps the best known, is based on the prices of only 30 stocks, while the Standard & Poor's 500 Stock Index is based on the prices of 500 stocks. The value of all outstanding stock was over $8.3 trillion in 1995, exceeding the value of any other type of security in the capital market. The amount of new stock issues in any given year is typically quite small relative to the total value of shares outstanding.

Mortgages

Mortgages Loans made to purchase single or multiple family residential housing, land, or other real structures, with the structure or land serving as collateral for the loan.

Mortgages are loans to purchase single or multiple family residential housing, land, or other real structures, with the structure or land serving as collateral for the loan. In the event the borrower fails to make the scheduled payments, the lender can repossess the property. Mortgages are usually made for up to 30 years and the repayment of the principal is generally spread out over the life of the loan. Some mortgages offer fixed interest rates in which the interest rate charged remains the same over the life of the loan; others offer variable interest rates that are adjusted periodically to reflect changing market conditions. Savings and loan associations and mutual savings banks are the primary lenders in the residential mortgage market, although commercial banks are now also active lenders in this market.

The federal government has played an important role in the mortgage market by sponsoring three government agencies that sell bonds and use the proceeds to purchase mortgages, thus providing funds to the mortgage market. Now would be a good time to look at Exhibit 6-4, which describes the secondary market in mortgages.

Corporate Bonds

Corporate Bonds Long-term debt instruments issued by corporations.

Corporate bonds are long-term bonds issued by corporations usually (although not always) with excellent credit ratings. Maturities range from 2–30 years. The owner receives an interest payment twice a year and the principal at maturity. Because the outstanding amount of bonds for any given corporation is small, bonds are not nearly as liquid as other securities such as U.S.

An ongoing development in the mortgage market is the creation of an active, growing secondary market for mortgages. Because individual mortgages have special characteristics and are typically of small denominations relative to other financial market securities, they were not sufficiently liquid to trade in secondary markets. In 1970 the Government National Mortgage Association (GNMA) began a program in which it guaranteed the timely payment of interest and principal on bundles of at least $1 million of standardized mortgages. This guarantee created a secondary market in mortgages that operates as follows: Private financial institutions gather or pool several federally guaranteed mortgages into a bundle of, say, $1 million. They then sell a $1 million security to a third party (usually a large institutional investor such as a pension fund). Individuals then make their mortgage payments (on the GNMA-guaranteed mortgage) to the private institution. When the mortgage payments for all the mortgages included in the $1 million bundle are received, the institution sends the owner of the security a check for the total of all payments, which constitutes the interest payment on the security.

These securities, which have become known as Ginnie Mae "pass-through securities," have a low default risk because of the GNMA guarantee and provide a steady stream of income to the owner. As a result, they have become highly popular with investors. Other types of mortgage pass-through securities (including Freddie Mac and Fannie Mae) have also developed.[a] This market is now an important source of funds to the mortgage market. In fact, this market has become so important that the bulk of mortgages are now made to lending guidelines that allow them to be packaged and sold as securities, called **asset-backed securities.** When asset-back securities are sold to investors, the lending institution receives additional funds to make new mortgages. The total amount of outstanding debt issued by mortgage pools exceeded $1.7 trillion by mid–1995.

> **Exhibit 6-4 ◆**
> Secondary Markets in Mortgages
>
> Asset-Backed Securities When financial instruments such as mortgages are pooled or bundled together and sold to investors as securities; payments on the securities are backed by the payment streams and worth of the underlying financial instruments.

[a]*Freddie Mac* and *Fannie Mae* are acronyms for the government-sponsored Federal Home Loan Mortgage Corporation and the Federal National Mortgage Association respectively. They actually purchase mortgages and create pools. *Ginnie Mae* does not purchase mortgages directly but guarantees the payment of principal and interest to the lender who creates a pool.

government bonds. However, an active secondary market has been created by dealers who are willing to buy and sell corporate bonds. The principal buyers of corporate bonds are life insurance companies, pension funds, households, commercial banks, and foreign investors.

U.S. Government Securities

U.S. government securities are long-term debt instruments with maturities of 2–30 years issued by the U.S. Treasury to finance the deficits of the federal government. They pay semi-annual dividends and return the principal at maturity. An active secondary market exists, although not as active as the secondary market for T-bills. Despite this, because of the ease with which they are traded, government securities are still the most liquid security traded in the capital market. The principal holders of government securities are the

U.S. Government Securities Long-term debt instruments of the U.S. government with original maturities of 2–30 years.

Federal Reserve, financial intermediaries, securities dealers, households, and foreign investors.

U.S. Government Agency Securities

U.S. Government Agency Securities Long-term bonds issued by various government agencies including those that support commercial, residential, and farm real estate lending, and student loans.

U.S. government agency securities are long-term bonds issued by various government agencies including those that support commercial, residential, and farm real estate lending, and student loans. Some of these securities are guaranteed by the federal government and some are not, even though all of the agencies are federally sponsored. Active secondary markets exist for most agency securities. Those that are guaranteed by the federal government function much like U.S. government bonds and tend to be held by the same parties that hold government securities.

State and Local Government Bonds (Municipals)

State and Local Government Bonds (Municipals) Long-term instruments issued by state and local governments to finance expenditures on schools, roads, etc.

State and local government bonds (municipals) are long-term instruments issued by state and local governments to finance expenditures on schools, roads, college dorms, etc. An important attribute of municipals is that their interest payments are exempt from federal income taxes and from state taxes for investors living in the issuing state. Because of their tax status, state and local governments can issue debt at yields that are usually below those of taxable bonds of similar maturity. They carry some risk that the issuer will not be able to make scheduled interest or principal payments.[7] Payments are generally secured in one of two ways. First, **revenue bonds** are used to finance specific projects and the proceeds of those projects are used to pay off the bondholders. Second, **general obligation bonds** are backed by the full faith and credit of the issuer; taxes can be raised to pay the interest and principal on general obligation bonds. Households in high tax brackets are the largest holders of state and local government bonds.

Revenue Bonds Bonds used to finance specific projects with proceeds of those projects used to pay off bondholders.

General Obligation Bonds Bonds that are paid out of the general revenues and backed by the full faith and credit of the issuer.

Now would be a good time to look at Exhibit 6-5, which covers some of the better-known interest rates for both money and capital market instruments.

In the next section, we discuss market makers. They are among the most important participants in financial markets because they facilitate the flow of funds from SSUs to DSUs, and vice versa.

RECAP

The major money market instruments are U.S. T-bills, negotiable CDs, commercial paper, bankers' acceptances, repurchase agreements, fed funds, and Eurodollars. The major capital market instruments are stocks, mortgages, corporate bonds, U.S. government securities, U.S. government agency securities, and municipals.

---

[7] In mid-1995, investors in Orange County, California, found out firsthand about the risks of municipal bonds after the county declared bankruptcy in December 1994. The bankruptcy resulted from a $1.7 billion loss in the county's investment portfolio due to reckless risk taking in financial markets.

Exhibit 6-5 ◆
Following the
Financial News

The Wall Street Journal publishes daily a listing of interest rates on many different financial instruments in its "Money Rates" column. The interest rates in "Money Rates" that are discussed most frequently in the media are listed here:

Prime Rate: The interest rate that serves as a basis for quoting rates to customers; an indicator of the cost of business borrowing from banks.

Federal Funds Rate: The interest rate charged on overnight loans in the federal funds market; a sensitive indicator of the cost to banks of borrowing funds.

Treasury Bill Rate: The interest rate on Treasury bills; an indicator of general levels of short-term interest rates.

Discount Rate: The rate charged by the Federal Reserve Banks for loaning reserve asset deposits to depository institutions.

Federal Home Loan Mortgage Corp. Rate (Freddie Mac): The interest rate on "Freddie Mac" guaranteed mortgages; an indicator of the cost of financing residential housing purchases.

Federal National Mortgage Association Rate (Fannie Mae): The interest rate on "Fannie Mae" mortgages; an indicator of the cost of financing conventional residential housing purchases.

London Interbank Offered Rate (LIBOR): The interbank rate for dollar-denominated deposits in the London market among international banks; the interest rate that serves as a basis for quoting other international rates.

Although not included in the "money rates," the long-term bond rate (the rate on a 30 year bond) is an important indicator of the level of long-term interest rates. Because of the length of time to maturity, small changes in interest rates cause much larger swings in bond prices. More on this later.

The Role of Market Makers

The participants in financial markets are the buyers, sellers, and market makers. The **market makers** function as coordinators who link up buyers and sellers of financial instruments. The link involves arranging and executing trades between buyers and sellers. They may make markets in only one type of security, say Treasury bills, or they may make markets in several different types of securities, including stocks and corporate and government bonds. Who are these market makers? Where are they located? Why do they exist? What does "making a market" entail? These are some of the questions to which we now turn.

Many have probably heard of large Wall Street firms such as Merrill Lynch, Salomon Brothers, Morgan Stanley, and Goldman Sachs—four leaders of finance. The main offices of these financial firms are in New York City, the financial capital of the United States. These offices are linked by telephone and Telex to other major cities in the United States and the rest of the world where branch offices and regular customers are located. Like most enterprises,

Market Maker A dealer who links up buyers and sellers of financial securities and sometimes takes positions in the securities.

LOOKING OUT

International Financial Markets

In addition to the domestic money and capital markets, it has become much easier for DSUs to tap into international sources of funds and for SSUs to acquire foreign financial claims. The international bond market consists of Eurobonds and foreign bonds. In addition, foreign CDs and Eurodollar CDs are popular money market instruments. We review each briefly.

Eurobonds

Eurobonds are denominated in a currency other than that of the country where they are marketed. For example, dollar-denominated bonds sold outside the United States are called Eurobonds. Like the term *Eurodollar*, the term *Eurobond* has come to mean any bond that is denominated in the currency of the country from which it was issued rather than that of the country where it is sold. The Eurobond market experienced tremendous growth in the 1980s and early 1990s and now makes up over 80 percent of new issues in the international bond market. In addition, the value of dollar-denominated Eurobonds also exceeds the value of new issues in the domestic corporate bond market. No longer do domestic DSUs have to look only to domestic SSUs or domestic financial intermediaries to obtain funds. Likewise, domestic SSUs have opportunities to supply funds denominated in dollars outside the United States. The Eurobond market greatly expands the borrowing sources for domestic borrowers. In addition, Eurobonds have little regulation and some tax advantages over domestic bonds.

Foreign Bonds

Unlike Eurobonds, foreign bonds are underwritten and sold to investors in the currency of the country where the bond is sold, while the issuer of the bond is from a foreign country. An example is a bond issued by a French corporation, denominated in dollars (as opposed to French francs), and marketed in the United States by U.S. investment bankers. Foreign bonds denominated in dollars and marketed in the United States are called *Yankee bonds;* foreign bonds denominated in Japanese Yen and sold in Japan are called *Samurai bonds;* and foreign bonds denominated in British pound sterling and sold in Great Britain are called *Bulldogs.*

Foreign CDs and Eurodollar CDs

In addition to foreign bonds, foreign CDs and Eurodollar CDs (money market instruments) have gained popularity since 1980. Yankee CDs are dollar-denominated CDs issued by branches of foreign banks located in the United States. Yankee CDs are issued by Japanese, Canadian, British, German, and Dutch banks to name a few. Eurodollar CDs are dollar-denominated CDs issued primarily by foreign branches of U.S. banks.

these firms are in business to earn profits. In this industry, profits are earned by providing financial services to the public. These services include giving advice to potential traders, conducting trades for the buyers and sellers of securities in the secondary market, and providing advice and marketing services to issuers of new securities in the primary market.[8]

To better understand the role of market makers it will be helpful to distinguish between brokers and dealers. A **broker** simply arranges trades between buyers and sellers. A **dealer** on the other hand, in addition to arranging trades between buyers and sellers, stands ready to be a principal in a transaction. More specifically, a dealer stands ready to purchase and hold securities sold by investors. The dealer carries an inventory of securities and then sells them to other investors. When we refer to market makers in this text, we will be referring to dealers, the market makers.

As a key player in financial markets, the market maker has an important role in our financial system. Most particularly, a market maker helps to maintain a smooth functioning, orderly financial market. Market makers stand ready to buy and sell and adjust prices—literally making a market. Let us assume that there are 100,000 shares of a stock for sale at a particular price. If buyers take only 80,000 shares at that price, what happens to the remaining 20,000 shares? If the market maker perceives a short-term imbalance, rather than making inconsistent changes in prices, the market maker takes a position (buys them) and holds them over a period of time to keep the price from falling erratically. Or, a market maker may alter prices until all, or most of the shares are sold. Thus, in the short run, market makers facilitate the ongoing shuffling and rearranging of portfolios by standing ready to increase or decrease their inventory position if there is not a buyer for every seller or a seller for every buyer. This serves to enhance market efficiency and contributes to an orderly, smooth-functioning financial system.

Market makers also receive, process, interpret, and disseminate information to potential buyers and sellers. Such information includes the outlook for monetary and fiscal policy; newly published data on inflation, unemployment, and output; fresh assessments of international economic conditions; information on the profits of individual firms; and analyses of trends and market shares in various industries. As all this information is digested by holders of outstanding securities and by potential issuers of new securities, it can bring about a change in current interest rates and the prices of stocks and bonds.

To illustrate, assume the political situation in the Middle East deteriorates, and experts believe a war, which would interfere with the exporting of oil to the rest of the world, is increasingly likely. Analysts employed by the market makers would assess the probable impact on the price of oil, the effect on U.S. oil companies' profits, and so forth. Such information would

Broker A person who arranges trades between buyers and sellers.
Dealer A person who arranges trades between buyers and sellers and who stands ready to be a principal in a transaction; a market maker.

---

[8]The packaging and marketing of new stocks and bonds issued by a corporation are part of what is often called *investment banking*—a function provided by most of the large market makers listed in the text. The term is potentially confusing for it suggests that these market-making firms are banks; in fact they are not full-fledged banks, even though they provide some of the same services banks do. This is a good example of how market jargon can be misleading.

be disseminated to and digested by financial investors and lead some of them to buy (demand) or sell (supply) particular securities.

In general, when something affects the supply or demand for a good, we know the price of that good will be affected. In the financial markets, when something affects the supply of or demand for a security, its price will move to a new equilibrium and the market maker will facilitate the adjustment. As a quick perusal of the newspaper will reveal, security prices change almost every day. Because of the activity of market makers, these changes usually occur in an orderly and efficient manner. Exhibits 6-6 and 6-7 show you how to read the scorecards—that is, the reports of daily activity in the stock and bond markets.

Why Market Makers Make Markets

The willingness of a market maker to make a market for any particular security will be a function of the expected profits and risks associated with buying, selling, and holding that type of security. The profits earned by a market maker flow mainly from the revenue generated by the price it charges for conducting a transaction, the number of transactions engaged in, and any capital gains or losses associated with the market maker's inventory of securities.[9] Generally, a market maker will charge a brokerage fee or commission for each transaction. The fee may be per item, such as 10 cents per share of stock, or perhaps a specified percentage of the total value of the trade, such as 1 percent of the total proceeds from a sale of bonds. Market makers also collect a fee in some markets by buying a particular security at one price—the **bid price**—and selling the security at a slightly higher price—the "offer" or **asked price.** In this case, the revenue received by a market maker is a function of the spread between bid and asked prices and the number of transactions in which the market maker and the public engage. Competition among market makers tends to minimize transactions costs to market participants.

Bid Price The price at which a market maker is willing to buy securities.
Asked Price The price at which a market maker is willing to sell securities.

To sum up, market makers play a key role in facilitating the buying and selling of securities by the public, as outlined in Exhibit 6-8. First, market makers assist in raising funds to finance deficits by marketing a borrower's new securities in the primary market. Secondly, they advise potential buyers and sellers of securities on the course of action likely to minimize costs and maximize returns. Thirdly, they stand ready to buy or sell outstanding securities in the secondary market. To illustrate these various roles, Exhibit 6-9 summarizes the trading of a bond issued by APEI, our old friend from Chapter 4. Note the coordinating and connecting role played by Merrill Lynch and Salomon Bros.

Market Making and Liquidity

The quality and cost of services provided by market makers affect the transactions costs associated with buying or selling various securities. The costs and

---

[9]Market makers assume a large amount of risk when they take positions in long-term bonds. They bear the risk that bond prices will fall and the value of the bonds in their portfolios will decrease. As we will see in Chapter 7, small increases in long-term interest rates can lead to large decreases in long-term bond prices.

Exhibit 6-6 ◆
The Stock Market

CRACKING THE CODE

Here is a typical entry on the stock page of a major newspaper. In this case it is from *The Wall Street Journal* on April 10, 1996. To begin cracking the code, look at the third item, Aetna Lf, which stands for Aetna Life Insurance Co.

The name of the company in the third column is followed by the company symbol and then the annual dividend paid by Aetna Life. In this case it is $2.76. The price of the stock at the close of the day's trading was 71 3/4 or $71.75. The dividend is usually compared with the closing price to get the current yield (or return). The dividend of $2.76 divided by the closing price (71.75) gives a current yield of 3.8 percent on the stock ($2.76/$71.75 = .038).

The next column tells us that the ratio of the price per share to the earnings per share of the company is 33—this is the price-earnings (P-E) ratio. The higher the earnings per share of the company (given the price of the stock), the lower the ratio.

The sales column tells us the number of shares traded (in hundreds) on a given day. On this particular day 1,099,900 shares of Aetna Life were traded. Also, the high price during the course of the day was 74 1/4, the low price was 70 5/8, and the price of Aetna closed at 71 3/4 or $71.75. In the last column, we see that the closing price per share was down 1 7/8 from the close of the previous day.

The final thing to notice is that to the left of the listing of the stock's name are two columns headed "High" and "Low." These are the high and low prices of the stock for the last 52 weeks. Aetna had traded at a low price of 54 ($54.00) and as high as 78 3/4 ($78.75). Those of you who bought in at 54 are allowed to smile.

| 52 Weeks | | | | | | | | | | | |
HIGH	LOW	STOCK	SYM	YLD DIV.	%	PE	100S	HIGH	LOW	CLOSE	NET CHANGE
$78^3/_4$	54	Aetna Lf	AET	2.76	3.8	33	10999	$74^1/_4$	$70^5/_8$	$71^3/_4$	$-1^7/_8$

convenience associated with trading particular securities, in turn, affect the liquidity of these securities. Because transactions costs and liquidity affect portfolio decisions, the market-making function influences the allocation of financial resources in our economy. Some markets, such as the T-bill market, are characterized by high-quality secondary markets. The large volume of outstanding securities encourages many firms to make markets in Treasury securities and the volume of trading and competition among market makers produces a spread between the dealer bid and asked prices of only 0.1 to 0.2

Exhibit 6-7 ◆
The Bond Market

CRACKING THE CODE

Here is a typical example of bond market information as it appears in the newspaper. Again, in this case we have clipped the quotation from *The Wall Street Journal.*

The bond we have chosen to study is one issued by AT&T (American Telephone and Telegraph). AT&T has a number of different types of bonds outstanding. They were issued at different points in time to finance operations such as investment. Accordingly, all these issues are *used* (or *seasoned*) bonds trading in the secondary market. Here we focus on a particular bond maturing in 2022.

First you see the issuing company's name—AT&T. The "8 1/8" next to the name is the coupon yield. It appears on the face of the bond and indicates the amount of interest that AT&T will pay the holder annually; in this case the 8 1/8 percent (8.125 percent) indicates that $81.25 of interest will be paid annually (usually in semi-annual installments) per $1,000 of face (or par) value of bonds held. The $81.25 is 8 1/8 percent of $1,000. Next we see "22"—this means the bond will mature in the year 2022. At that time, AT&T will give the holder of the bond the last interest payment and $1,000 of principal per $1,000 of face (or par) value. As the name suggests, the *face value* appears on the face of the bond.

The Close and Net Change columns refer to the price of the bond. As you will see, the price code in the bond market is different from the price code in the stock market; this is part of a conscious plot to confuse outsiders. To conserve space in the paper, bond prices are stated as percentages of 100, with 100 representing $1,000 face value. Hence, the closing price for the day was 104 1/4 means $1,042.50 (each point is equal to $10). The closing price was up 1/4 from the previous day's closing price, or $2.50 ($2.50 = 1/4 of $10).

The Volume column is simple; 127 of these bonds were traded on April 9, 1996. Not so simple is the Current Yield column. This bond pays $81.25 annually to its holder. At the close on this day, someone could have bought the bond for $1,042.50. As a result, the current yield on the investment—that is, the bond purchased—would be 7.6 percent ($81.25/$1,042.50 = .078 or 7.8 percent). Only if a bond is selling at 100, or at par value, will the coupon yield be equal to the current yield.

BOND			CUR YLD	VOL	PE	CLOSE	NET CHANGE
ATT	$8^{1}/_8$	22	7.8	127	33	$104^{1}/_4$	$+1^{1}/_4$

percent—an amount well below the spread of 0.3125 to 0.5 percent associated with transactions in less actively traded, longer-term government securities.[10]

---

[10] Spreads between dealer bid and asked prices for corporate bonds range up to 2 to 3 percent for securities with relatively low marketability.

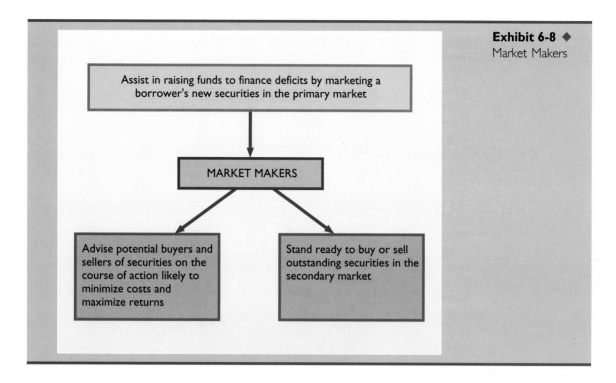

Exhibit 6-8 ◆
Market Makers

Substitutability, Market Making, and Market Integration

An important but less obvious role played by market makers is that they help to integrate the various subsectors of financial markets. Exhibit 6-10 shows the trading room at Salomon Brothers—one of the most important market makers in the world. As you can see, it is a busy place. On the floor of the trading room the specialist in Treasury bills sits near the specialist in corporate bonds, who in turn is no more than 20 feet from the specialist in mortgage-backed securities. Assuming that these people talk to one another, the activity in one market is known to those operating in other markets. With each specialist disseminating information to customers via telephone and continually monitoring computer display terminals, a noticeable change in the Treasury bill market (say a 1/2 percentage point decline in interest rates on Treasury bills), will quickly become known to buyers and sellers in other markets. Such information will in turn influence trading decisions in these other markets and thus affect interest rates on other securities.

This spillover from one submarket to another is important in understanding the ties that bind the various compartments of financial markets together. The key concept underlying these linkages is the notion of substitutability. Whether they be individuals allocating their own savings or bank managers, portfolio managers monitor the expected returns on the array of financial assets available in financial markets. They compare the returns on assets in their portfolios to others available in the market. For example, if a higher, more attractive return becomes available on a Treasury bond as compared to a municipal bond already in the manager's portfolio, the manager may decide to sell the municipal security and buy the Treasury bond. This exchange of a higher-yielding security for a lower yielding one is the essence of substitution. Assuming many portfolio managers undertake similar actions, the net effect

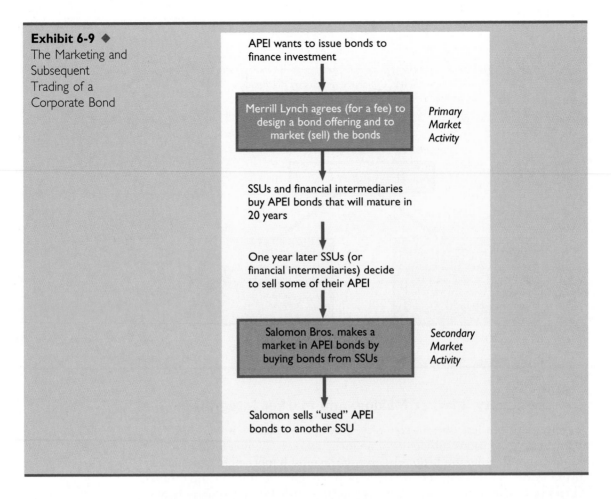

Exhibit 6-9 ◆
The Marketing and Subsequent Trading of a Corporate Bond

is to increase the supply in the municipal securities market and the demand in the Treasury bond market. With our market makers acting in effect as auctioneers, they respond to such changes in supply and demand by changing the prices at which they are willing to buy or sell securities.

So far we have restricted our discussion to domestic financial markets. It is time to point out that for almost every domestic financial market, a corresponding foreign market exists. For example, there are markets for Japanese government securities, Hong Kong stocks, Canadian mortgage-backed securities, and Greek bonds. The same factors that affect the viability of domestic markets affect the substitutability between and among domestic and foreign instruments. Most financial markets are becoming international in scope as improvements in communication technologies have made the world a smaller place. Foreign instruments are good substitutes for domestic instruments in such a world, and vice versa. We hope you can see that the activities of the market maker are critical to "greasing the wheels," which allow for this market integration. More on this in Chapter 9.

Leaving the details aside, the point is that we have come full circle from the beginning of the chapter: there are numerous instruments traded in financial markets and classified in many different ways; the separate markets for the individual instruments are linked by the activities of market makers and the willingness of traders to substitute among the alternative instruments available.

Exhibit 6-10 ◆
The Trading Room
at Salomon
Brothers

Before ending this discussion, note one other aspect of the picture in Exhibit 6-10. There are many computer monitors in this room from which many details on current interest rates and securities prices can be obtained. Among the many bits of data displayed and watched closely by everyone on the trading floor, is information relating to the operations of the Federal Reserve. In fact, if you asked these analysts and traders which type of information they considered most important, they would probably answer, "information on Federal Reserve policy." After studying Chapter 5, we are sure you can see why.

Summary of Major Points

1. The markets for particular types of financial claims are connected, not separate entities. The connectedness of the markets results from the buying and selling (trading) of securities by the participants in the markets—that is, the substitution among available alternative instruments.

2. The money market is where securities with original maturities of one year or less are traded. The capital market is where securities with original maturities of more than one year are traded.

3. Primary markets are where new securities, issued to finance current deficits, are bought and sold. Secondary markets are where outstanding securities (issued earlier) are bought and sold.

4. Secondary markets are important to the operation of an efficient financial system. Well-organized, smoothly functioning, high-quality secondary markets facilitate the trading of outstanding securities at relatively low cost and little inconvenience. This, in turn, facilitates the financing of planned deficits in primary markets.

5. The spot market is the market for the purchase or sale of securities for immediate delivery. In the futures market, contracts are entered into today to purchase or sell securities in the future at a price agreed upon today. Futures markets are used to either hedge or speculate.

6. The principal money market instruments are U.S. Treasury bills, negotiable certificates of deposit, commercial paper, bankers' acceptances, repurchase agreements, federal (fed) funds, and Eurodollars. The major capital market instruments are stocks, mortgages, corporate bonds, U.S. government securities, U.S. government agency securities, and state and local government bonds.

7. Market makers are the specialists who function as coordinators in financial markets and link up buyers and sellers of securities. They serve three important functions: (1) they disseminate information about market conditions to buyers and sellers; (2) they connect the various markets by buying and selling in the market themselves; and (3) they provide financial services that determine the quality of primary and secondary markets. In turn, the quality of the primary and secondary markets affects the ease or difficulty associated with financing deficits, lending surpluses, and, more generally, shifting into and out of various financial instruments.

8. For most domestic financial markets there exists a comparable foreign market, such as a foreign stock market. Market makers have assisted in integrating domestic and foreign financial markets.

Key Terms

Asked Price	Commercial Paper
Asset-Backed Securities	Corporate Bonds
Bankers' Acceptances	Dealer
Bid Price	Eurodollars
Broker	Federal (Fed) Funds
Capital Market	Financial Futures Markets

General Obligation Bonds	Speculation
Market Maker	Spot Market
Money Market	State and Local Government
Mortgages	Bonds (Municipals)
Negotiable Certificates of Deposit (CDs)	Stocks
	Term to Maturity
Primary Market	U.S. Government Securities
Repurchase Agreements	U.S. Government Agency
Revenue Bonds	Securities
Secondary Market	U.S. Treasury Bills (T-bills)

Review Questions

1. Distinguish between primary and secondary markets and between money and capital markets.

2. The secondary market for T-bills is active while the secondary market for federal agency securities is limited. How does this affect the primary market for each security? Why are well-developed secondary markets important for the operation of an efficient financial system?

3. Discuss the major function of market makers in securities markets. What is the difference between a broker and a dealer?

4. If you call a local brokerage firm, you will find that the commission or brokerage fee charged for purchasing $10,000 of Treasury bills is below the charge associated with purchasing $10,000 of, say, municipal bonds issued by the City of Cincinnati. Explain why.

5. Explain why it would be incorrect to view the various sectors of the financial markets as totally separate entities.

6. In Chapter 5, we saw that the Fed can change the amount of reserves available to depository institutions and the required reserve ratio. Why do market makers pay so much attention to what the Federal Reserve is doing?

7. Define commercial paper, negotiable certificates of deposit, repurchase agreements, bankers' acceptances, federal funds, and Eurodollars. In what ways are they similar and in what ways are they different?

8. Define mortgages and asset-backed securities. Which is the more liquid asset?

9. Define and contrast stocks and bonds. What are the advantages of owning preferred stock? What are the advantages of owning common stock?

10. What is the difference between a government security and a government agency security? Which asset would you prefer to own if safety and liquidity were important to you?

11. Would you rather own the stocks or bonds of a particular corporation if you felt that the corporation was going to earn exceptional profits next year?

12. Why are municipals attractive to individuals and corporations with high income or profits?

13. Explain the differences among the fed funds rate, the Eurodollar rate, the discount rate, and the LIBOR Rate. How are they similar?

14. Can the bid price ever be greater than the asked price?

Analytical Questions

15. Rank the following financial instruments in terms of their safety and liquidity:
    a. U.S. Treasury bills
    b. Large negotiable CDs
    c. Mortgages
    d. Government bonds
    e. Government agency securities
    f. Commercial paper
    g. Eurodollars

16. John purchases a one-year Treasury bill in June 1997 for $9,700 that can be redeemed for $10,000. What is the effective interest? What is the yield?

17. A Treasury bond pays 7 1/4 percent coupon yield. What is the coupon payment per $1,000 face value?

18. If a bond pays $80 in interest annually and sells for $1,050, what is its current yield? What would the bond have to sell for to have a current yield of 8 percent?

19. If a share of stock pays a dividend of $3 and closes today at $36, what is the current yield?

20. Compare the current yield on a one-year T-bill that sells for $9,400 and can be redeemed for $10,000 with the yield on a bond with a face value of $10,000 that pays a coupon yield of 8 percent and sells for $9,800.

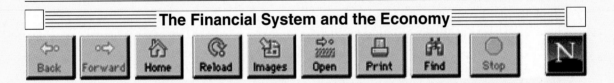

The Financial System and the Economy

1. The Federal Reserve's Statistical Release H-15 reports yields on several financial instruments. Access the website (http://www.stls.frb.org/fred/releases/h15). Can you distinguish between the money market instruments and capital market instruments as reported at this site?

2. From the bank rate monitor website (http://www.bankrate.com/index.html), access the consumer Mortgage Guide and find the local mortgage rates for 15 year fixed, 30 year fixed, and 1 year adjustable (ARM) loans in your hometown.

3. The Wong and Holt Market Report (http://metro/turnpike.net/holt/) describes daily activity in various financial markets. Access the Current Market Report and list some key indices of financial market performances available at this site. What is today's value of the Dow Jones Industrial Average and the Standard and Poor's 500? What were the most actively traded stocks on the New York Stock Exchange?

Suggested Readings

For one of the most comprehensive and readable surveys of money market instruments, see Timothy Q. Cook and Timothy D. Rowe, *Instruments of the*

Money Market, 6th ed., Federal Reserve Bank of Richmond, 1986. Single copies are available for the asking. Write to the Public Service Department, Federal Reserve Bank of Richmond, P.O. Box 27622, Richmond, VA 23262–7622.

Additional free publications that may interest you include *A Pocket Guide to Selected Short-Term Instruments of the Money Market* (1987); *Commercial Paper* (Fedpoints 29); *Basic Information on Treasury Securities* (1988); *Federal Funds* (Fedpoints 15); *Understanding U.S. Government Securities Quotes* (Fedpoints 7); and *Zero Coupons and STRIPS* (Fedpoints 42). Each of these is available by writing the Public Information Department, Federal Reserve Bank of New York, 33 Liberty Street, New York, NY 10045. Fedpoints are available on the internet at (http://www.ny.frb.org/pihome/fedpoint).

For a discussion of recent developments in the commercial paper market, see Mitchell Post, "The Evolution of the U.S. Commercial Paper Market Since 1980," *Federal Reserve Bulletin,* December 1992.

Barbara Kavanagh's article, "Asset-Backed Commercial Paper Programs," *Federal Reserve Bulletin,* February 1992, explains that part of the growth of the commercial paper market since 1983 stems from the evolution of asset-backed commercial paper that is packaged and securitized in a manner similar to the mortgage-backed securities.

7

Interest Rates and Bond Prices: Demystifying the Time Value of Money

> *Change must be measured from a known baseline.*
> —Evan Shute—

Learning Objectives

After reading this chapter, you should know:

◆ Why the interest rate represents the time value of money
◆ What compounding and discounting are
◆ Why interest rates and bond prices are inversely related
◆ The major determinants of interest rates
◆ The relationship between nominal and real interest rates
◆ How interest rates fluctuate over the business cycle

The Present Versus the Future

State University currently charges students $5,000 a year for tuition. Following the appointment of an innovative financial officer, it offers enrolling freshman students a new way to pay four years' tuition—pay $18,000 today rather than $5,000 per year for four years. Would you participate in the plan?

Following her third box office smash, a Hollywood sensation has just signed a multi-picture contract. As compensation, the star has been offered either $6,000,000 today or $7,500,000 in five years. You are her financial advisor; what should she do and why?

You win a million dollar lottery and learn that the million dollars will be paid out in equal installments of $50,000 per year over the next 20 years. Would you be willing to trade this stream of future income for one payment today? How large would that payment have to be?

The purpose of the first half of this chapter is to provide the analytical framework one needs to understand and answer questions such as those just posed, which require one to compare the present with the future. As you will see, the framework developed and questions addressed, while important by themselves, are the key to the second half of the chapter where we will examine the determinants of interest rates and the relationships among interest rates, bond prices, economic activity, and inflation. Even a casual reader of the financial pages of U.S. newspapers has seen headlines such as "Bond Prices Slump as Interest Rates Rise" or "Bond Market Rallies After Weak GDP Report" or "Inflation Fears Result in Lower Bond Prices." Understanding such headlines is the objective of the second part of the chapter.

The Time Value of Money

Interest rates have already popped up in numerous places in the text. In our earlier substantive discussion in Chapter 3, we emphasized that the interest rate is the cost to borrowers of obtaining credit and the reward to lenders for lending surplus funds. Thus, just as rent is the cost to apartment dwellers and the return to the landlord, the interest rate is the rental rate paid by borrowers and received by lenders when money is "rented out."

Money represents purchasing power; if one has money, goods or services can be purchased now. If one does not have money now and wants to make purchases, one can rent purchasing power by borrowing. Likewise, if one has money now and is willing to postpone purchases to the future, one can rent out purchasing power.

Note carefully the role played by the interest rate here. Presumably, the willingness to postpone purchases into the future is a function of the reward—that is, the interest rate. In particular, the higher the interest rate, ceteris paribus, the greater the reward, and hence, the greater the willingness to postpone purchases into the future and lend in the present. Similar reasoning applies on the borrowing side. We can think of someone who wants to purchase goods and services but is short of the necessary funds as having two options: (1) borrow now and purchase now or (2) save now and purchase later. Since the willingness to borrow depends on the cost, among other things, we can conclude that the higher the interest rate, ceteris paribus, the less attractive is option (1) and the more attractive is option (2).

The central point to remember from this discussion is the role the interest rate plays in linking the present with the future. Lending in the present enables spending the sum of what is lent plus the interest earned in the future. Borrowing in the present enables spending in the present, but requires paying back what is borrowed plus interest in the future. Since the interest rate is the return on lending and the cost of borrowing, it plays a pivotal role in spending, saving, borrowing, and lending decisions made in the present and bearing on the future.

The concept we have been discussing is called the **time value of money.** Simply put, the interest rate represents the time value of money because it specifies the terms upon which one can trade off present purchasing power for future purchasing power. In the pages that follow it should become crystal clear that this is one of the most important and fundamental concepts in economics and finance.

Time Value of Money The terms on which one can trade off present purchasing power for future purchasing power; the interest rate.

Compounding and Discounting

Compounding: Future Values

Compounding is a method used to answer a simple question: What is the future value of money lent (or borrowed) today? As illustrated in Exhibit 7-1, the question is forward looking; we stand in the present (today) and ask a question about the future. To see how it works, a few examples will be helpful.

Compounding A method used to determine the future value of a sum lent today.

Suppose Joseph M. Student agrees to lend a friend $1,000 for one year. The friend gives Joe an IOU for $1,000 and agrees to repay the $1,000 plus interest in a year. The amount that is originally lent is called the **principal**—in this case $1,000. If the agreed interest rate is 6 percent, then the friend would pay a total of $1,060 ($1,000 + $60). In this example, the amount of interest is $60 ($1,000 × .06 = $60).

Principal The original amount of funds lent.

This general relationship can be expressed as

(A)   amount repaid = principal + interest

The amount of interest can be expressed as

(B)   interest = principal × interest rate

Substituting Equation (B) into Equation (A) yields

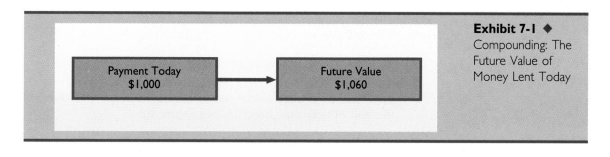

Exhibit 7-1 ◆
Compounding: The Future Value of Money Lent Today

Payment Today
$1,000

Future Value
$1,060

Einstein discovers that time is actually money.

(C)   amount repaid = principal + (principal × interest rate)

Since each term on the righthand side of Equation (C) has a common factor, it can be rearranged and rewritten as

(D)   amount repaid = principal$(1 + i)$

where i is the interest rate. Utilizing Equation (D) and our example, Joe's friend would repay

$$\$1{,}060 = \$1{,}000 \times 1.06$$

For later use, we will rewrite Equation (D) as follows

(7-1) $V_1 = V_0(1 + i)$

where V_1 = the funds to be received by the lender (paid by the borrower) at the end of year one; note this is a future value.

V_0 = the funds lent (and borrowed) now; note this is a present value.

Imagine now that Joe lends to his friend for two years instead of one year and no payments are made to Joe until two years pass. Here is where compounding comes into play. Literally, "compounding" means to combine, add to, or increase. In the financial world, it refers to the increase in the value of funds that results from earning interest on interest. More specifically, interest earned after the first year is added to the original principal; the second year's interest calculation is based on this total. The funds to be received at the end of two years, V_2, consist of the original amount of funds lent out, V_0 plus the interest on the original amount, iV_0 plus the interest on the amount of funds owed at the end of the first year $[i\,(V_0 + iV_0)]$.[1] In our example:

Principal + Interest Earned +	Interest Earned	=
in First Year	in Second Year	
$1,000 + .06($1,000)	+ .06[$1,000 + .06($1,000)] =	
$1,000 + $60	+ $63.60	= $1,123.60

Note that the implication of the last term is that interest is earned on interest; this is compounding. In the second year, Joe earns interest not only on the principal $(.06 \times \$1,000)$ but also on the interest earned in the first year $[.06 \times .06(\$1,000)]$. In effect, the interest earned in the first year is reinvested.

Expressed symbolically:

(7-2) $$V_2 = V_0 + iV_0 + i(V_0 + iV_0)$$

Using some simple algebra, this equation can be reduced to:[2]

(7-3) $$V_2 = V_0(1 + i)^2$$

Equation (7-3) can be generalized for any sum of money lent (invested) for any maturity of n years:

(7-4) $$V_n = V_0(1 + i)^n$$

The future value of a sum of money invested for n years, V_n is equal to the original sum V_0 compounded by the interest rate $(1 + i)^n$. In our last example, $V_0 = \$1,000$, $i = .06$, $n = 2$, and $V_2 = \$1,123.60$.

---

[1] The simple interest rate in this example is 6 percent. If Joe took the interest earned on the loan after one year but left the principal, the total return over two years would be $120, or $60 each year. The average annual rate of return would be 6 percent $[.06 = (\$120/\$1,000)$ divided by 2]. If, as in the example, no interest payment is made after one year—the funds being, in effect, re-lent or reinvested—the total return would be $123.60 and the compound annual rate of return would be 6.18 percent $[.0618 = (\$123.60/\$1,000)$ divided by 2]. The compound rate will always be greater than the simple rate due to the interest earned on interest.

[2] For those who would like to work through all the steps, start with

$$V_2 = V_0 + iV_0 + i(V_0 + iV_0)$$
$$= V_0 + iV_0 + iV_0 + i^2V_0$$
$$= V_0 + 2iV_0 + i^2V_0$$
$$= V_0[1 + 2i + i^2)$$
$$= V_0(1 + i)(1 + i)$$
$$= V_0(1 + i)^2$$

The formula in (7-4) is actually quite easy to use. For example, most calculators have an x^y function and $(1 + i)^n$ is an x^y calculation. Using $(1 + .11)$ for x and 10 for y, you should be able to verify that if Joe lent $1,000 for 10 years, at an interest rate of 11 percent, he would receive $2,839.42 at maturity: $2,839.42 = \$1,000(1.11)^{10}$.

Discounting: Present Values

Compounding is forward looking. It addresses the question: What is the future value of money lent (or borrowed) today? As we shall see, understanding compounding is the key to really understanding what often seems to be a more difficult concept for students to grasp—**discounting.**

In effect, as shown in Exhibit 7-2, discounting is backward looking. It addresses the question: What is the **present value** of money to be received (or paid) in the future?

Perhaps the best way to learn how to answer such questions and to see why such questions and answers are important is to address one of the examples mentioned at the beginning of the chapter. Remember the movie star? She has been signed to a multi-picture deal and the studio offered her either $6,000,000 today or $7,500,000 in five years. Which option should she select?

To calculate the answer we can simply rearrange Equation (7-4). Before, we knew the present value, V_0, the interest rate, i, and the number of years, n, and we wanted to solve for the future value, V_n. Now we want to solve for the present value, V_0, of a sum to be received in the future ($7,500,000), so we can compare it to another present value, the $6,000,000. Accordingly,

(7-5)
$$V_0 = \frac{V_n}{(1 + i)^n}$$

Assuming we know the interest rate—say it's 6 percent—the present value of $7,500,000 to be available in five years is

$$\frac{\$7,500,000}{(1 + .06)^5} = \$5,604,436.30$$

The present value of $6,000,000 received today for signing the multi-picture contract is, obviously, $6,000,000. Given an interest rate of 6 percent, the present value of $7,500,000 to be received in five years is obviously less.[3]

---

[3]We are also assuming that she expects the interest rate to be 6 percent for the next five years.

Discounting A method used to determine the present value of a sum to be received in the future. **Present Value** The value today of funds to be received or lent on a future date.

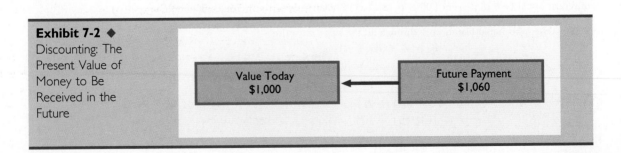

Exhibit 7-2 ◆ Discounting: The Present Value of Money to Be Received in the Future

Value Today $1,000 ← Future Payment $1,060

Accordingly, the movie star should take the $6,000,000 today. To see more clearly why, all you need to do is turn the discounting/present value problem into a compounding/future value problem; if the actress took the $6,000,000 today and invested it at 6 percent, she would have more than $7,500,000 in five years. To be exact, she would have $8,029,353.47 [$6,000,000(1 + .06)^5 = $8,029,353.47]!

To be sure you are completely with us, close the book and ask yourself what the present value of $7,500,000 in five years, given an interest rate of 6 percent really represents. It is the sum you would need to invest today, given a 6 percent interest rate, to have $7,500,000 in five years; that is, to have $7,500,000 in five years given an interest rate of 6 percent, you would have to invest $5,604,436.30 today. To nail everything down, assume the interest rate is 4 percent instead of 6 percent. Would you still advise the movie star to take the $6,000,000 today or does the change in the interest rate point to a different option? Why or why not? The explanation and calculation are in the footnote at the bottom of the page; give the problem a try and then check your answer.[4]

RECAP

Compounding is finding the future value of a present sum. Discounting is finding the present value of a future sum. The future value, V_n, of a sum, V_0, invested today in n years is $V_0(1 + i)^n$. The present value, V_0, of a sum, V_n, to be received in n years is $V_n/(1 + i)^n$.

Interest Rates, Bond Prices, and Present Values

In the previous example, we learned how to compute the present value of a single future payment. How does this help us to understand the relationship between bond prices and interest rates?

While bonds issued by corporations and governments differ in a variety of ways, they generally share the following characteristics: they are issued for a certain number of years (n), have a face or **par value** (F) of $1,000 per bond, and the issuer (borrower) agrees to make equal, periodic interest payments over the term to maturity of the instrument and to repay the face value at maturity. The periodic payments are called **coupon payments** (C) and are equal to the coupon rate on a bond multiplied by the face value of the bond. As we shall see in a moment, the coupon rate, which usually appears on the bond itself, is not the same thing as the interest rate. The distinction between the coupon rate and coupon payment and between the coupon rate and interest rate is often a source of considerable confusion; bear with us and you can avoid the problem.

Par Value The face value printed on a bond; the amount the bond originally sold for.
Coupon Payments The periodic payments made to bondholders, which are equal to the principal times the coupon rate.

---

[4]The present value of $7,500,000 to be received in five years, assuming an interest rate of 4 percent, is $6,164,453.30. This is obviously more than $6,000,000. Put another way, if she took the $6,000,000 today and lent it at 4 percent for five years, she would have only $7,299,917.41 at the end of the period rather than $7,500,000. The $6,164,453.30 is what she would need to lend today at 4 percent for five years to have $7,500,000 at the end of the period. In sum, the actress should take the $7,500,000 in five years rather than the $6,000,000 today.

Given these characteristics, a bond represents a stream of future payments. To find its present value and thus the price it will trade at in financial markets, we need to compute the present value of each coupon payment and the present value of the final repayment of the face value on the maturity date. The appropriate formula is

$$(7\text{-}6) \quad P = \frac{C_1}{(1 + i)^1} + \frac{C_2}{(1 + i)^2} + \cdots + \frac{C_n}{(1 + i)^n} + \frac{F}{(1 + i)^n}$$

where P = the price (present value) of the bond

C = the coupon payment on the bond (C_1 in year one, C_2 in year two, etc.)

F = the face or par value of the bond

i = the interest rate

n = the number of years to maturity (on a five-year bond, $n = 5$)

Notice that this formula is a descendant of Equation (7-5) with $P = V_0$ and $V_n = C$ or F. The only difference is that we use (7-6) to compute the present value of a number of future payments, such as occurs in the case of a bond, while (7-5) is used to compute the present value of a single future payment.

To put some flesh on an otherwise bare-boned formula, let's work through a few examples. Suppose Jane is about to buy a bond that will mature in one year, has a face value of $1,000, carries a coupon payment of $60, and the prevailing interest rate in the market is 6 percent. What is Jane willing to pay for this bond? Utilizing Equation (7-6),

$$P = \frac{\$60}{(1 + .06)} + \frac{\$1,000}{(1 + .06)}$$

$$= \$56.60 + \$943.40$$

$$= \$1,000$$

This tells Jane that the price of the bond or its present value is $1,000.[5] In other words, if the interest rate is 6 percent, the present value of receiving $1,060 in one year is $1,000, and this is what Jane (or anybody else) will pay for the bond. Since the coupon payment is $60, the coupon rate is 6 percent (6 percent = $60/$1,000). You might also note that when the price of a bond is equal to its par value ($1,000), the coupon rate is equal to the interest rate.

Continuing with this example, Jane buys the bond for $1,000 and the next day the prevailing interest rate in the market rises to 8 percent. What effect does this have on the value (price) of Jane's bond? Remember Jane's bond will pay her $1,060 in one year.[6] Imagine yourself with $1,000 to invest. How

---

[5] Are you puzzled by the fact that the price of the bond in the market place equals the present value of the bond? If so, think of what happens in any market when a product is selling for less or more than buyers and sellers think it's really worth. If selling for less, quantity demanded will be greater than quantity supplied and the price will rise in response. If selling for more, quantity demanded will be less than quantity supplied, and the price will fall in response. The *equilibrium* is reached when the prevailing price in the market is such that quantity demanded equals quantity supplied. So too in financial markets.

[6] Technically, the time to maturity is now one year less a day, but to simplify, we ignore the one day.

much would you pay for Jane's bond? Would you pay $1,000? We hope your answer is "no!" You could go out in the market and buy another bond yielding 8 percent for $1,000! Alternatively, you could buy Jane's bond. This would occur if and only if it too was somehow made to yield 8 percent. How could this happen? The maturity of the bond (1 year), the coupon payment ($60 per $1,000 of par value), and the par value ($1,000) are all fixed. They represent the contractual arrangements entered into by the bond issuer (borrower) at the time the bond is initially issued. What's left you ask?—the price of the bond! You and other investors would be willing to pay a price for the bond which, given the receipt of $1,060 at maturity, would represent a yield over the year of 8 percent. Using our Equation (7-5),

$$P = \frac{\$60}{(1 + .08)^1} + \frac{\$1,000}{(1 + .08)^1}$$

$$= \$55.55 + \$925.93$$

$$= \$981.48$$

The figure $981.48 is the present value of $1,060 to be received in one year, given that the interest rate we use to discount the future sum is 8 percent.

Put somewhat more intuitively, if you bought Jane's bond for $981.48, you would receive $60 of interest at maturity plus a capital gain of $18.52; the gain is equal to the par value you get back at maturity ($1,000) minus the price you pay at the time of purchase ($981.48). The $60 + $18.52 = $78.52, gives us an 8 percent yield over the year ($78.52/$981.48 = .08). Thus, in this example, you buy the bond at a price below its par value. This is called a **discount from par** and raises the yield on the bond, called the **yield to maturity,** from 6 percent to 8 percent. In sum, as the market interest rate rises, the price of existing bonds falls. The lower yield to maturity on existing bonds is unattractive to potential purchasers who can purchase newly issued bonds with higher yields to maturity. Therefore, the yield to maturity on previously issued bonds must somehow rise to remain competitive with the new higher level of prevailing interest rates. The yield on existing bonds rises when their prices fall. Hence, bond prices fall until the yield to maturity of the bond becomes equal to the current interest rate.

Discount from Par When a bond sells below its face value because interest rates have increased since the bond was originally issued.
Yield to Maturity The return on a bond held to maturity, which includes both the interest return and any capital gain or loss.

Suppose that instead of rising from 6 percent to 8 percent the day after Jane buys the bonds, the interest rate in the market falls to 4 percent. You should now be able to do the arithmetic with the aid of Equation (7-6); the price (or present value) of Jane's bond will rise to $1,019.23. What does this represent? If any of us bought Jane's bond for $1,019.23, we would be paying a price above the par value. This is called a **premium above par.** At maturity we would get $60 minus a capital loss of $19.23; the loss is equal to what we pay at the time of purchase minus the par value we receive at maturity ($1,019.23 − $1,000 = $19.23). The $60 − $19.23 = $40.77, represents a 4 percent yield over the year ($40.77/$1,019.23 = .04). Thus, as the market interest rate falls, the prices of existing bonds rise. The reason is that the higher yield to maturity on existing bonds is attractive to potential investors and as they buy existing bonds, the bond prices rise, reducing their yield to maturity.

Premium above Par When a bond sells above its face value because interest rates have decreased since the bond was originally issued.

In general then, there is an inverse relationship between the price of outstanding bonds trading in the secondary market and the prevailing level of market interest rates. As a result, one can say that if bond prices are rising, then interest rates are falling, and vice versa. These are different ways of saying the same thing and we need not resort to the formalities of discounting and present value analysis to see the bare essentials of this relationship. For practice, go to the "Bond Markets" section in *The Wall Street Journal,* usually found about ten pages from the back, and read the article. You should now be able to follow the description of the happenings in the market.[7]

Fluctuations in Interest Rates and Managing a Bond Portfolio

In financial circles, one often hears conversation about the interest rate; people will ask, for example, "Do you think interest rates will rise or fall?" In such discussions, reference to interest rates is, in fact, a reference to yields to maturity or *yields* for short.

Why would the manager of a bond portfolio for a large pension fund be concerned with the likely direction of interest rates? Simply put, if rates rise sharply, for example, the value of the manager's portfolio, which contains previously purchased bonds, would fall significantly. This year's bonus for skillful management could go right out the window. Conversely, if rates fall, the prices of previously purchased bonds increase and capital gains are in the offing. Such possibilities are what motivate managers and their advisors to pay so much attention to the factors that determine interest rates. More specifically, a portfolio manager who believes the Fed is about to engage in actions that will raise interest rates is likely to sell a considerable amount of bonds now to avoid the capital losses on bonds held, which will accompany any rise in market yields. Conversely, the expectation of a fall in interest rates would encourage purchases of bonds now in anticipation of the capital gains that will accompany a fall in market rates.[8]

Positioning the pension fund to take advantage of any change in interest rates requires our portfolio manager to understand the major factors determining movements in interest rates. Accordingly, let's take a closer look at the determinants of interest rates. Note it is the expectation of interest rate changes that motivates the portfolio manager into action. After interest rates have changed, it is too late to take advantage of potential capital gains or to avoid potential losses. Of course, it is not too late to try to avoid making the same mistake again and again.

 RECAP

The price of a bond is the discounted value of the future stream of income over the life of the bond. When the interest rate increases, the price of the bond decreases. When the interest rate decreases, the price of the bond increases.

---

[7]You should also be able to verify that the longer the term to maturity is, the greater will be the fluctuation in the price of the bond, and, hence, the larger the premium above par or discount below par.

[8]In Chapter 10, we will see that the managers could also use financial futures markets to reduce the risk of losses from changes in interest rates.

The Determinants of Interest Rates

In previous chapters we have emphasized the role of the financial system in coordinating and channeling the flow of funds from surplus spending units (SSUs) to deficit spending units (DSUs). The interest rate is of paramount importance in this process for the following reasons: (1) since it is the reward for lending and the cost of borrowing, changes in the interest rates influence the amount of borrowing and lending—that is, the behavior of DSUs and SSUs; and (2) conversely, the borrowing and lending behavior of DSUs and SSUs influences the interest rate. In the market for loanable funds, as in other markets, supply and demand will be the key to determining interest rates. This means, of course, that any change in interest rates will be the result of changes in supply and/or demand.

The considerations just discussed were first presented in Chapter 4 and are demonstrated graphically in Exhibit 7-3. The **demand for loanable funds** originates from the household, business, government, and foreign DSUs who borrow because they are spending more than their current income. The downward-sloping demand curve indicates that DSUs are willing to borrow more at lower interest rates, ceteris paribus. Businesses borrow more at lower interest rates because more investment projects become profitable, ceteris

Demand for Loanable Funds The demand for borrowed funds by household, business, government or foreign DSUs.

As in Exhibit 4-8, the interest rate is measured on the vertical axis while the quantity of loanable funds is measured on the horizontal axis. At E_1, the quantity demanded is equal to the quantity supplied and the market is in equilibrium. The supply of and demand for loanable funds determines the interest rate.

Exhibit 7-3 ◆
The Supply of and Demand for Funds

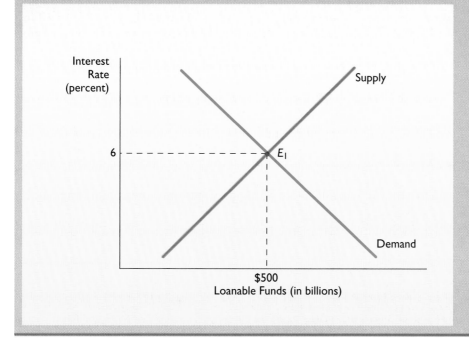

Supply of Loanable Funds
The supply of borrowed funds originating from (1) household, business, government, or foreign SSUs, or (2) the Fed in its provision of reserves in the conduct of monetary policy.

paribus. Projects that are unprofitable if the business had to pay 12 percent to borrow the funds become quite profitable if the funds can be had for only 2 percent. Consumers borrow more at lower interest rates, ceteris paribus, for such things as automobiles and other consumer durables.

The total **supply of loanable funds** originates from two basic sources: (1) the household, business, government, and foreign SSUs who are prepared to lend because they are spending less than their current income, and (2) the Fed in its ongoing attempts to manage the economy's performance, supplies reserves to the financial system that lead to increases in the growth rate of money (and loans). We shall assume that the Fed's supply of funds is fixed at a particular amount for the time being. Adding the funds that SSUs are willing to supply to the Fed's supply of funds produces a supply curve for loanable funds, which is upward sloping.[9] This indicates that SSUs are willing to supply more funds at higher interest rates, ceteris paribus. As Exhibit 7-3 shows, the quantity of funds supplied equals the quantity of funds demanded at point E_1. The equilibrium interest rate in the market for loanable funds is 6 percent and the equilibrium quantity of funds borrowed and lent is $500 billion.

From the point of view of our portfolio manager, it is not sufficient to know the equilibrium or current interest rate. What is really of concern is the potential for future changes in interest rates and the capital gains (increases in bond prices) or capital losses (decreases in bond prices) that will accompany such changes. Since any change in interest rates will be the result of a change in either the supply of funds or the demand for funds, let's take a close look at the major factors that can shift either of the curves.

Changes in the Demand for Loanable Funds

On the demand side, research has shown that movements in gross domestic product (GDP) are a major determinant of shifts in the demand for funds. In particular, when GDP rises, ceteris paribus, for example, both firms and households become more willing and able to borrow. Firms are more willing because the rise in GDP has improved the business outlook, encouraging them to expand planned inventories and engage in more investment spending such as the purchases of plant and equipment. These new activities will have to be financed by borrowing. Households are more willing to borrow because the rise in GDP has increased their incomes and/or improved the employment outlook. These factors encourage them to increase their purchases of goods and services, particularly autos, other durable goods, and houses, which will often require some financing. Both firms and households are more able to borrow because the improved economic outlook and the

---

[9] To illustrate how the behavior of the Fed and SSUs interacts, suppose that during the current period the Fed supplies reserves to the financial system leading to $300 billion of loanable funds being supplied to the market, and that this amount of funds will not increase or decrease as the interest rate changes. As for SSUs, suppose they are willing to lend $100 billion at a 4 percent interest rate, $200 billion at a 6 percent interest rate, and $300 billion at an 8 percent rate. Adding the fixed supply of loanable funds resulting from the Fed's supply of reserves to the interest-sensitive amount that will be supplied by SSUs, we get the total supply of funds of $400 billion at a 4 percent rate, $500 billion at a 6 percent rate, and $600 billion at an 8 percent rate. This is how the supply function shown in Exhibit 7-3 is arrived at. Note that its upward slope reflects the changes in the quantity of funds supplied by SSUs at different interest rates, everything else remaining unchanged.

rise in incomes will make it easier to make the interest and principal payments on any new debt.[10]

The effect of an increase in the demand for funds resulting from a rise in income or GDP is shown in Exhibit 7-4. The demand for funds shifts from DD to $D'D'$. Previously, the quantity of funds supplied was equal to the quantity of funds demanded at point E_1; the equilibrium interest rate prevailing in the market was 6 percent and the quantity of funds borrowed and lent was $500 billion. When the demand curve shifts to the right, ceteris paribus, a disequilibrium develops in the market. More specifically, at the prevailing 6 percent rate, the quantity demanded for funds exceeds the quantity supplied. Given this excess demand, the interest rate rises. As the interest rate rises, this induces SSUs to increase the quantity of loanable funds they are willing to supply (a movement along the supply curve). Such changes in plans help to close the gap between quantity demanded and quantity supplied and a new equilibrium is eventually established at point E_2 where the interest rate is 8 percent and the quantity of funds borrowed and lent is $600 billion. To sum up, we start with an equilibrium, demand increases, ceteris paribus, creating a disequilibrium, the interest rate goes up, and a new equilibrium is established.

---

[10]Traditionally, some students are puzzled by the positive relationship between GDP (income) and the demand for funds discussed in the text. (Remember that a ''positive'' relationship means both move in the same direction—when one rises, the other rises; when one falls, the other falls.) They argue that these variables should be negatively related; for example, a drop in income, given expenditures, will increase a household's deficit, necessitating a rise in the demand for funds (borrowing). The problem with this reasoning is that expenditures are assumed to remain constant. In fact, the drop in income will lead to a reduction in expenditures. More generally, historical experience shows that the willingness and ability to borrow and spend will fall when income falls.

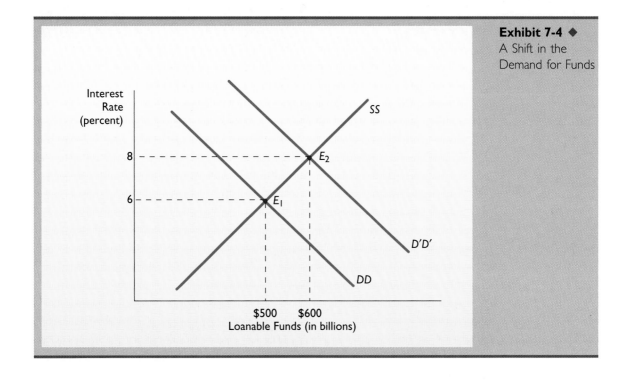

Exhibit 7-4 ◆
A Shift in the Demand for Funds

Changes in the Supply of Funds

On the supply side, as you already know, one of the factors determining the supply of loanable funds is monetary policy. In particular, the Fed's ability to alter the growth rate of money in the economy means it can have a direct effect on the cost and availability of funds. To illustrate, a Fed-engineered increase in the supply of funds, as shown in Exhibit 7-5, shifts the supply curve from SS to $S'S'$, ceteris paribus. This creates a disequilibrium; the quantity supplied of funds exceeds the quantity demanded of funds at the prevailing 6 percent interest rate. The excess quantity supplied puts downward pressure on interest rates. As interest rates fall, DSUs and SSUs revise their borrowing and lending plans. For example, as the cost of borrowing falls, DSUs will be induced to borrow a larger quantity (a movement along a demand curve). Such actions, which serve to narrow the gap between quantity supplied and quantity demanded, will continue until a new equilibrium is established at point E_2. The result is a fall in the interest rate from 6 percent to 4 percent, and an increase in the quantity demanded from $500 to $550. In sum, the money supply growth rate and the interest rate are inversely related, ceteris paribus. Holding other things constant, an increase in the money supply will lower the interest rate, while a decrease in the money supply will raise the interest rate via the effect of changes in the growth rate of the money supply on the supply of loanable funds.[11]

The graphical analysis illustrates the relationship between changes in the supply of loanable funds and interest rates. However, graphs by themselves

---

[11] Later in the text, we shall see that continuous increases in the growth rate of the money supply can lead to inflation, changes in inflationary expectations, and possible increases in interest rates.

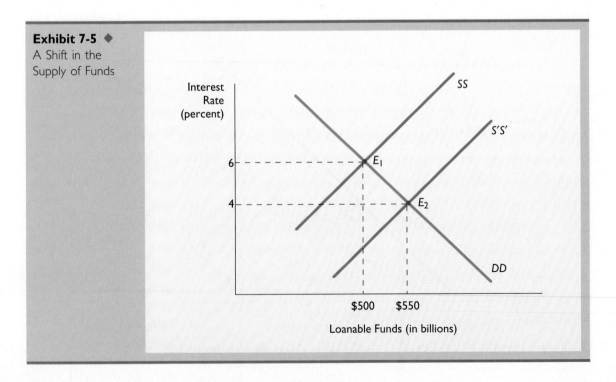

Exhibit 7-5 ◆
A Shift in the
Supply of Funds

explain little and prove nothing. If the illustration is really going to aid your understanding, you need to be able to breathe some life into the picture by knowing how and why the interest rate changes; that is, what is the mechanism or process that produces this result? The answer in this case is really quite simple. Visualize financial intermediaries in the economy, particularly depository institutions, as having more funds to lend as a result of the Fed's actions increasing the money supply.[12] In general, the intermediaries will use these funds to acquire interest-earning assets—securities and loans, in particular. If they demand more securities (bonds), this will raise the price and lower the yield to maturity on outstanding bonds, ceteris paribus. If they want to extend loans, they will have to induce household and firms to borrow more than they are currently borrowing or planning to borrow. How can this be accomplished? If you said "Lower the rates charged on loans" you are correct. Thus, the movement from E_1 to E_2 in Exhibit 7-5 is not a sterile hop to be memorized and reproduced in response to some exam question. It depicts a process and series of transactions including the acquisition of securities, extension of loans, and accompanying changes in interest rates, which are at the heart of the operations of the financial system and its role in the economy.

The discussion of the determinants of interest rates, at least up to this point, can be summarized in a fashion which will prove quite convenient later on.[13]

(7-7)
$$i = f(\overset{+}{Y}, \overset{-}{M})$$

Equation 7-7, which is really a sentence written in shorthand, says the interest rate is a positive function of income or GDP, Y, and a negative function of the money supply, M, ceteris paribus.[14] From the preceding discussion and accompanying graphical analysis you should know that a rise in Y, holding other factors like M constant, will raise the demand for funds, and thus, the interest rate. Likewise, a rise in M, holding other factors like Y constant, will increase the supply of loanable funds and thus decrease the interest rate.

Of course, in the real world, other factors are not constant. Why is this important to keep in mind? Imagine that data released by the Fed indicates that both M and i were increasing. What could explain this seemingly paradoxical result? The reason is that the demand for funds must have increased by more than the increase in supply. This could result from an increase in income, or as you will learn in the next section, from an increase in expected inflation. We suggest graphing this case and others like it to make sure you understand the way in which Y, M, and i interact.

 RECAP

The demand for loanable funds originates from DSUs. The quantity demanded is inversely related to the interest rate. The supply of loanable funds originates from SSUs and from the Fed, which supplies reserves to the

---

[12] We cover the specifics of this relationship in Chapter 16.

[13] The effects of inflationary expectations on interest rates will be added shortly.

[14] This equation is a reduced form equation resulting from simultaneously solving a demand and supply equation for loanable funds.

banking system. The quantity supplied is directly related to the interest rate. If incomes increase, the demand for loanable funds increases and the interest rate rises. If the money supply increases, the supply of loanable funds increases and the interest rate falls: $i = f(Y,M)$.

Inflation and Interest Rates

If you were to lend a friend $100 today and she agreed to pay it back one year from now with 5 percent interest ($100 × .05 = $5), you might consider yourself $5 richer and a shrewd financier. Your $100 will earn $5 of interest income for you. However, if during the year, the inflation rate is 5 percent, the real value—purchasing power—of the funds lent plus interest will be exactly the same as the real value of your funds at the beginning of the year.[15] As a result, the real reward for lending would be zero. In fact, if the inflation rate was greater than 5 percent, your friend would be paying you back an amount of money one year from now which would buy fewer goods and services than the amount you lent would buy today. The real reward would be negative. The shrewd financier in this case would be your friend, not you! You may, of course, still engage in this transaction if this were your absolute best opportunity. If you hold idle cash or money in a low interest earning checking account, you would lose even more in real terms. However, we hope you would be able to find a saving opportunity that paid you a positive real return.

This example suggests lenders are concerned about two things: (1) nominal interest—how many dollars will be received in the future in return for lending now; and (2) inflation—the real purchasing power the funds will be worth upon repayment. For example, a bond bearing even a relatively high interest rate may not be attractive to lenders if, due to price inflation, the money later repaid has less purchasing power than the money originally lent.

The implication of all this is that the market interest rate—something called the **nominal interest rate**—is not an adequate measure of the real return on an interest-bearing financial asset unless there is assurance of price stability. Rather, the appropriate measure is the **real interest rate,** which is the return on the asset corrected for changes in the purchasing power of money. The real interest rate is the nominal interest rate minus the rate of inflation expected to prevail over the life of the asset. For example, if an investor expected inflation of 4 percent, then an asset bearing 7 percent nominal interest will be expected to yield only approximately 3 percent in real terms. If the expected inflation were 7 percent, the asset bearing 7 percent nominal interest would yield nothing in real terms.

Money illusion is said to occur when investors react to nominal changes (caused by price changes) even though no changes in real interest rates or

Nominal Interest Rate The market interest rate, or the real return plus the rate of inflation expected to prevail over the life of the asset.

Real Interest Rate The interest rate corrected for changes in the purchasing power of money; the nominal interest rate minus the expected rate of inflation.

Money Illusion When spending units react to nominal changes caused by changes in prices when real variables such as interest rates have not changed.

---

[15] The calculation is (Funds Received/Price Index) × 100. Assuming the price index was 100 in the previous year, a 5 percent inflation rate produces a price index of 105 at the end of the year (see Exhibit 3-8 in Chapter 3). Thus, the answer is ($105/105) × 100 equals $100. The purchasing power or real value of $105 received one year from now, if the inflation rate over the year is 5 percent, is $100. This implies the real reward for lending is zero.

other variables have occurred. Financial investors who are not victims of money illusion will try to find an investment that pays the highest real return. Wise investors will concern themselves with the nominal market interest rate only insofar as it enters into their calculation of the real interest rate, which is the correct measure of the reward for lending and the cost of borrowing.

The discussion to this point can be summarized with the help of some simple definitions written in the form of identities that are true by definition:

(7-8) $$i = r + p^e$$

Equation (7-8) says that the nominal interest rate is two parts—a real interest rate, r, and an **inflation premium.** The inflation premium is the amount of nominal interest that will compensate a lender for the expected loss of purchasing power accompanying any inflation. Accordingly, the inflation premium is equal to the expected inflation rate, p^e, and therefore, nominal interest rates rise or fall as expected inflation rises or falls, ceteris paribus. Rearranging Equation (7-8) produces

Inflation Premium The amount of nominal interest added to the real interest rate to compensate the lender for the expected loss in purchasing power that will accompany any inflation.

(7-9) $$r = i - p^e$$

One of the first economists to statistically analyze the relationship between inflation and nominal interest rates was Irving Fisher, a prominent economist of the early twentieth century. The available evidence, such as that shown in Exhibit 7-6, does show that nominal interest rates are highly correlated with inflation and inflationary expectations.

The reason for this correlation can be seen by utilizing the equations just presented and graphical analysis developed in the previous section. Suppose the commercial paper rate (remember this from Chapter 6?) is 6 percent and the current and expected rate of inflation is 4 percent. This means that the expected real interest rate is 2 percent. What happens if borrowers and lenders revise their expectation of future inflation upward to 8 percent? If the commercial paper rate remains at 6 percent, they would expect the real interest rate to be minus 2 percent. This is the real cost of borrowing funds. The fall in the expected real cost of borrowing will produce a rise in the nominal demand for funds. The rise in demand should, in turn, put upward pressure on the nominal commercial paper rate.

What about lenders of funds in the commercial paper market? Initially, they would have expected a real return of 2 percent (.06 − .04 = .02). If the lenders also revise their expectations of inflation upward to 8 percent, it seems reasonable to presume that an expected real return of minus 2 percent would make them less willing to lend and thus reduce the nominal supply of funds available in the commercial paper market. The reduction in supply would also put upward pressure on the nominal commercial paper rate.

The combined effect of the increase in demand and reduction in supply, as shown in Exhibit 7-7, is a rise in the interest rate from 6 to 10 percent. With expected inflation rising from 4 to 8 percent, the inflation premium and, therefore, the nominal interest rate rise by 4 percent, from 6 to 10 percent. In this example, the increase in the interest rate is equal to the increase in inflationary expectations. In an imperfect world—the real world—this may not always be the case, but we can be pretty certain that the direction of the change in interest rates will match the direction of the change in inflationary expectations.

Exhibit 7-6 ◆
Inflation and
Interest Rates:
The Data (1960
to 1995)

The inflation rate is measured as the percent change in the Consumer Price Index. The nominal interest rate is represented here by the 6-month commercial paper rate. When the inflation rate rises or falls, nominal interest rates also usually rise or fall.

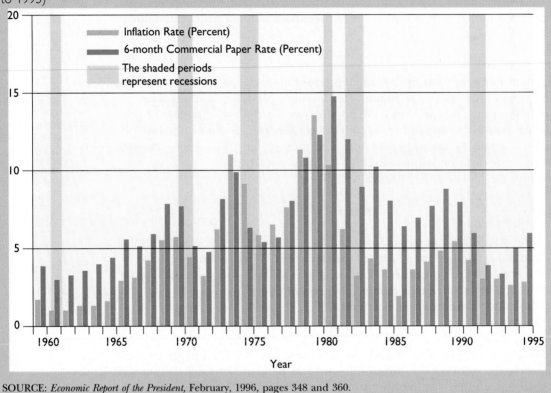

SOURCE: *Economic Report of the President,* February, 1996, pages 348 and 360.

In sum, expectations of inflation affect portfolio choices that help determine the demand and supply of loanable funds. Since interest rates respond to changes in demand and supply, and expectations of inflation affect demand and supply, we can conclude that expectations of inflation affect interest rates. Given this relationship, we can rewrite Equation (7-7) as follows:

$$(7\text{-}10) \qquad\qquad i = f(\overset{+}{Y},\overset{-}{M},\overset{+}{p^e})$$

The nominal interest rate is positively related to the expected inflation rate.

 RECAP

The nominal interest rate is the real interest rate plus the expected inflation rate. Money illusion occurs when investors react to nominal changes when no real changes have occurred. If expected inflation increases, the nominal interest rate will rise. Borrowers are then willing to pay an inflation premium, and lenders demand to be paid an inflation premium. Thus, nominal interest rates are correlated with expected inflation: $i = f(\overset{+}{Y},\overset{-}{M},\overset{+}{p^e})$.

We begin, as in Exhibits 7-3, 7-4, and 7-5, with an initial equilibrium at point E_1 and a prevailing interest rate of 6 percent. If the expected inflation rate, p^e, is 4 percent, this nominal rate, i, implies a real rate, r, of 2 percent ($i = r + p^e$ or 6 percent $= 2$ percent $+ 4$ percent). Assume now that p^e rises to 8 percent, ceteris paribus. At a 6 percent nominal rate, lenders will now expect a lower real rate (-2 percent instead of $+2$ percent). Accordingly, they will be willing to lend less, shifting SS to $S'S'$. As for the borrowers, the rise in p^e means that the expected real cost of borrowing at a 6 percent nominal rate has fallen (from $+2$ percent to -2 percent). In response, they will want to borrow more, shifting DD to $D'D'$. The eventual result of the fall in supply and rise in demand is an increase in the nominal rate equal to the change in inflationary expectations.

Exhibit 7-7 ◆
Inflation and
Interest Rates:
A Graphical
Treatment

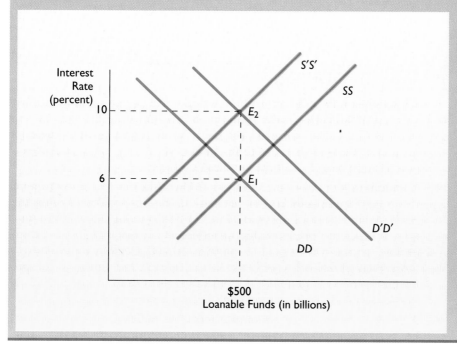

$500
Loanable Funds (in billions)

The Cyclical Movement of Interest Rates

Suppose, like Rip Van Winkle, you slept for a long time and when you woke up you read this chapter and Chapter 1. You would find yourself well rested and—believe it or not—quite able to explain how interest rates move over the business cycle and why they move as they do.

Recall from Chapter 1 that the stages of the business cycle are the recession, trough, expansion, and peak. The recession phase is usually characterized by falling GDP, a drop in the inflation rate (especially in its later stages) and, not surprisingly, given the Fed's desire to stabilize the economy, a rising money supply growth rate. Utilizing Equation (7-10), we hope you would predict such developments generally produce a decline in interest rates during recessions. Conversely, during the expansion phase of the cycle, income is rising, inflation usually re-accelerates (especially in its later stages), and the Fed may be trying to slow money supply growth to prevent an inflationary boom from developing. Again referring to Equation (7-10) you should not be surprised to learn that interest rates usually rise as an economic recovery proceeds. Generally speaking, although not always, interest rates tend to fluctuate pro-cyclically—that is, they move with the business cycle, rising during expansions and falling during recessions.[16]

We have covered much ground. By now you should have a clear understanding of the questions and headlines in the introduction to this chapter. In addition, this chapter contains two appendixes: the first is on the relationship between stock prices and interest rates; the second demonstrates how the price of a special type of bond, called a *consol*, changes as interest rates change.

---

[16]The correlation between the business cycle and interest rates is far from perfect. For example, during the expansion of the early 1990s, interest rates have not behaved in the manner described.

Summary of Major Points

1. The interest rate is the return on lending today (spending in the future) and cost of borrowing today (repaying in the future). It links the present with the future. More directly, the interest rate represents the time value of money and specifies the terms under which one can trade present purchasing power for future purchasing power.

2. Compounding answers the question: What is the future value of money lent today? Specifically, it is the increase in the future value of funds that results from earning interest on interest. Discounting answers the question: What is the present value of money to be received in the future? As long as the interest rate is positive, $1,000 received today is worth more than $1,000 to be received in the future. Discounting is the procedure used to compute the present value of funds to be received in the future. Here again the interest rate links the present with the future.

3. A bond represents a stream of future payments. The price of a bond will be equal to the present value of the discounted future stream of income. When the interest rate changes, the present value of the future payments will also change. More specifically, when interest rates rise, the prices of outstanding bonds will fall. Likewise, when interest rates fall, the prices of outstanding bonds will rise.

4. Ceteris paribus, the quantity demanded of loanable funds is inversely related to the interest rate. Ceteris paribus, the quantity supplied of loanable funds is directly related to the interest rate.

5. Changes in interest rates will be the result of changes in the supply of funds and/or changes in the demand for funds. The supply of loanable funds results from the surpluses of SSUs and the provision of reserves by the Fed to the financial system. The demand for funds originates from the deficits run by DSUs. The demand for loanable funds is positively related to income, Y. In general, anything that increases demand or reduces supply, ceteris paribus, will tend to raise interest rates. Anything that reduces demand or increases supply, ceteris paribus, will tend to lower interest rates. In summary, $i = f(\overset{+}{Y}, \overset{-}{M})$.

6. The nominal interest rate, i, is composed of a real interest rate, r, and an inflation premium, reflecting the expected inflation rate, p^e: $i = r + p^e$. In general, the willingness to lend and the willingness to borrow depends on the real return to lending and the real cost of borrowing where $r = i - p^e$. In summary, $i = f(\overset{+}{Y}, \overset{-}{M}, \overset{+}{p^e})$.

7. Interest rates tend to fluctuate pro-cyclically. As a recession proceeds, income and GDP fall, tending to reduce the demand for funds, and the Fed's efforts to stabilize the economy generally result in a rising growth rate of the money supply. Conversely, as an expansion takes hold, GDP rises, tending to increase the demand for funds. Often inflation re-accelerates and to prevent an inflationary boom from developing, the Fed will slow money supply growth. Reflecting such developments, interest rates will tend to rise.

8. A share of common stock represents a claim on the earnings of a firm. Accordingly, the value of the share depends on a firm's current and prospective earnings. In general, stock prices rise as current and prospective earnings rise. Likewise, stock prices fall as current and prospective earnings fall. (Appendix 7-A)

9. In deciding between stocks and bonds, financial investors will compare the expected rates of return on each type of asset. Assume the interest rate falls relative to the expected return on stocks. Given the substitutability of stocks for bonds, investors will shift their portfolios to stocks given the now higher expected return of stocks. The demand for stocks will rise, tending to increase stock prices. Reinforcing this tendency will be the rise in sales and earnings expected to be associated with the fall in interest rates. (Appendix 7-A)

10. A consol is a perpetual bond with no maturity date. The price of a consol is equal to the dividend divided by the nominal interest rate. (Appendix 7-B)

Key Terms

Compounding	Nominal Interest Rate
Consol	Par Value
Coupon Payments	Premium above Par
Demand for Loanable Funds	Present Value
Discount from Par	Principal
Discounting	Real Interest Rate
Dividends	Supply of Loanable Funds
Inflation Premium	Time Value of Money
Money Illusion	Yield to Maturity

Review Questions

1. Define the concepts of compounding and discounting. Use future values and present values to explain how these concepts are related.

2. Use the concept of present value to explain why a trip to Hawaii next year would mean more to most people than the same trip in the year 2010.

3. Under what conditions will a bond sell at a premium above par? at a discount from par?

4. During the Great Depression of the 1930s, nominal interest rates were close to zero. Explain how real interest rates could be very high even though nominal interest rates were very low. (Hint: Prices fell during parts of the Great Depression.)

5. Assume that after you graduate, you get a job as the chief financial officer of a small company. Explain why being able to forecast the direction of interest rate changes may be critical for your success in that position. Likewise, why are investment bankers concerned about future changes in the interest rate?

6. What factors affect the demand for loanable funds? the supply of loanable funds?

7. In general, discuss the movement of interest rates, the money supply, and prices over the business cycle.

8. A young couple is borrowing $100,000 to buy their first home. An older couple is living off the interest income from the $100,000 in financial assets they own. In what way does the interest rate affect each? If the interest rate increases, could that change the behavior of either one? How and why?

9. Assume that the Fed increases the growth rate of the money supply. How will this action affect stock prices? We suggest graphing this case and others like it to make sure you understand the way in which Y, M, and i interact. (Appendix 7-A)

10. Assume that a company earns a profit but keeps that profit as retained earnings to reinvest rather than paying it out as dividends. Do the stockholders in the company simply lose? (Appendix 7-A)

Analytical Questions

11. What is the present value of the following income streams?
    a. $100 to be received at the end of each of the next three years
    b. $100 to be received at the end of each of the next three years plus an additional payment of $1,000 at the end of the third year

12. What is the price of a bond that pays the income stream in question 11-b?

13. Assume that a bond with five years to maturity, a par value of $1,000, and that pays a $60 dividend annually, costs $1,100 today. What is the coupon rate? What is the current yield?

14. The nominal interest rate is 12 percent and anticipated inflation is 8 percent. What is the real interest rate?

15. Graph the demand and supply for loanable funds. If there is an increase in income, ceteris paribus, show what happens to the interest rate, the demand for loanable funds, and the quantity supplied of loanable funds. If the Fed orchestrates a decrease in the money supply growth rate, cet-

eris paribus, show what happens to the interest rate, the supply of loanable funds and the quantity demanded of loanable funds.

16. As an enrolling freshman, would you have been willing to pay $18,000 for four years tuition rather than $5,000 per year for four years? (Assume you would be able to do so and that you have no fear of flunking out of college before you graduate.)

17. You win a million dollar lottery to be paid out in twenty annual installments of $50,000 over the next twenty years. Assuming an interest rate of 6 percent, how large a payment would you accept today for this future stream of income?

18. Jake is given $10,000 in a CD that matures in ten years. Assuming interest payments are reinvested during the life of the CD, how much will the CD be worth at maturity if the interest rate is 5 percent? if the interest rate is 10 percent?

19. Henry and Sheree just had a baby. How much will they have to invest today for the baby to have $100,000 for college in 18 years if the interest rate is 5 percent? if the interest rate is 10 percent?

20. Use graphical analysis to show that if Y and M both increase, then the interest rate may increase, decrease, or stay the same. In each case, what happens to the equilibrium quantity demanded and supplied?

21. What is the price of a consol with a coupon payment of $200 per year if the interest rate is 10 percent? What is the interest rate on a consol if the coupon payment is $400 and the price of the consol is $8,000? (Appendix 7-B)

22. I purchase a consol with a coupon payment of $100 when the interest rate is 10 percent. When I sell the consol, the interest rate has risen to 20 percent. What is the amount of my capital gain or loss? (Appendix 7-B)

The Financial System and the Economy

⇦	⇨	🏠	🔄	🖼	⇨	🖨	🔍	⬙	N
Back	Forward	Home	Reload	Images	Open	Print	Find	Stop	

1. The realized real interest rate is the nominal interest rate minus actual inflation. Illustrate the relation between actual inflation and nominal interest rates by accessing the following website for nominal interest rates: (http://www.stls.frb.org/fred/data/irates/prime/). Use the prime rate as a measure of nominal interest rates. The actual inflation rate may be obtained from the website at (http://www.stls.frb.org/fred/data/cpi/cpiaucsl).

Suggested Readings

For a very readable article for students who would like more information about real interest rates, see Rosemary and Thomas J. Cunningham, "Recent Views of Viewing the Real Rate of Interest," *Economic Review* of the Federal

Reserve Bank of Atlanta, July/August 1990, pp. 28–37. Current abstracts of the *Economic Review* are available at the following internet site: (http://www.fbratlanta.org/pubaff/pubs).

A classic work dealing with interest rate determination is Irving Fisher, *The Theory of Interest* (New York: Macmillan, 1930).

For an interesting article on the relationship between interest rates and inflation, see Edward Renshaw, "Inflation and the Search for a Neutral Rate of Return on T-Bills," *Challenge,* November/December 1994, pp. 58–61.

A much more technical discussion of stock market prices and inflation can be found in David P. Ely and Kenneth J. Robinson, "The Stock Market and Inflation: A Synthesis of the Theory and Evidence," *Economic Review* of the Federal Reserve Bank of Dallas, March 1989, pp. 17–27.

For an analysis of the relationship between interest rates and bond prices, see Dale Bremmer, "The Relationship Between Interest Rates and Bond Prices," *American Economist,* 36, Spring 1992, pp. 85–86.

The determinants of stock prices are discussed in Robert B. Barsky, "Why Does the Stock Market Fluctuate?" *Quarterly Journal of Economics,* 108, May 1993, pp. 291–311.

APPENDIX 7-A

Stock Prices and Interest Rates

Given the material presented in the body of the chapter on interest rate determination, you are certainly in a better position to see how and why the manager of a portfolio goes about collecting and analyzing economic and financial data in the process of deciding whether to buy or sell bonds. Assuming the manager's portfolio includes stocks as well as bonds, it seems only logical to examine how interest rate developments influence the stock market. The purpose of this appendix is to explain how and why movements in interest rates, either actual or expected, affect stock prices.

The owner of a share of common stock issued by a firm represents ownership of part of that firm. The size of the ownership position depends on the number of shares owned. For example, if there are 1,000 shares outstanding, a stockholder who owns 100 shares, in effect, owns 10 percent of the firm. The value of each share, and therefore, the value of one's holdings in a corporation depends on the prevailing price of the firm's stock. If, for example, the price is $50 per share, and one owns 100 shares, the total value of one's holdings is $5,000. The key question, of course, is What determines the price per share?

As we discussed in Chapter 6, outstanding shares of stocks are often traded on exchanges, of which the New York Stock Exchange is the largest and best known.[a] Stock prices fluctuate daily—some going up, some going down—as financial investors buy and sell the shares of various corporations. To understand the underlying meaning of such fluctuations, it is useful to begin by pointing out that a share of common stock represents a claim on the earnings of a firm. Tangible evidence of this sharing of earnings comes in the form of **dividends,** which are a distribution of profits to stockholders. If earnings prospects are improving, the share price and dividend paid per share are also rising.[b] This will be reflected in a rise in the price of the firm's stock as financial investors are attracted by the improved outlook (profitability) of the firm.

In general, stock prices rise as current and expected future earnings rise, and fall as current and prospective earnings decline. A growing economy means sales, production, and incomes are expanding, while a declining econ-

Dividends Profits distributed to stockholders.

---

[a] Newly issued shares of stock are sold by corporations through investment bankers. Also, stocks that are not traded on organized exchanges are traded in an over-the-counter market in which market makers create a market.

[b] If a company pays out only a small portion of its earnings as dividends, then it has retained earnings it can invest back in the company. Ceteris paribus, this usually leads to larger profits later. If this is so, the company's stock will generally appreciate faster, and the owner will earn a larger capital gain when the stock is sold.

omy means the opposite. Since expected earnings also rise when the economy is expected to grow and tend to fall when the economy is expected to contract, there is often a positive correlation between the growth of real GDP and the Dow Jones Industrial Average (a widely followed index of stock prices).

How Interest Rates Fit into the Picture

Visualize a portfolio consisting of bonds and stocks. How would you go about managing such a portfolio? More specifically, how would you decide whether to purchase stocks or bonds? We hope your answer is that you will compare the expected rates of return on the different types of financial assets, selecting those with the highest expected return.

The expected return on bonds is the prevailing interest rate. What is the expected return on stocks? Generally speaking, the expected return on a share of stock, say over a year, is the expected dividend plus the expected change in the price of the stock, all divided by the share price at the time of purchase. (The expected change in the price is the expected capital gain or loss.) For example, if you pay $50 a share, the expected dividend is $3 per share, and you expect the price to rise $2 over the year, the expected return is 10 percent [($3 + $2)/50 = .10].

To see how interest rates fit into the picture, assume the current interest rate on bonds is 6 percent and the expected return on stocks is also 6 percent with the typical stock costing $50 and the expected dividend equal to $3. We also assume for simplicity that the expected capital gain is zero and that stocks or bonds entail the same amount of risk.[c] If the expected returns on bonds and stocks are equal, the typical portfolio manager is indifferent between stocks and bonds, and will presumably hold some of each.

Suppose now that the Fed decides to pursue a much more expansionary monetary policy and the initial result of this policy is a considerable rise in the growth rate of the money supply and a decline in the interest rate on bonds to 4 percent. The fall in the interest rate will tend to raise stock prices through two channels.

First, the expected return on bonds is now below the expected return on stocks. Given the substitutability of stocks for bonds in investors' portfolios, and the higher expected return on stocks, the demand for stocks will rise, tending to raise stock prices. Within the confines of our simple example, ceteris paribus, we can even say how high stock prices will rise: stock prices will rise until the expected return on stocks is again equal to the expected return on bonds (4 percent). This will occur when the price of our typical share rises to $75.00, because the $3 expected dividend divided by $75.00 equals 4 percent (.04 = $3/$75.00).

Second, the fall in the interest rate will be expected to raise the demand for goods and services, and increase the sales and earnings of firms. With earnings expected to rise, dividends will also be expected to rise. This reinforces the first effect. For example, if the dividend is expected to rise to $4 per share, then financial investors will be willing to bid up the price per share

---

[c]This is a rather bold assumption because in reality, stocks and bonds usually entail different amounts of risk. By making it, however, we do not change the results of the analysis.

even further to $100 because $4 divided by $100 is equal to 4 percent (.04 = $4/$100).[d]

Assuming you and other portfolio managers would like to have owned the stock before all this occurred, you can see now why actual and expected changes in the interest rate get so much attention in the stock market. (Again, to be sure you are "on board," work through an example using numbers and reason where, instead of falling to 4 percent, the Fed pursues a more restrictive policy and the interest rate rises to 8 percent. You can then look at Footnote e to check your results.)[e]

---

[d]A more formal approach to this relationship between stock prices and interest rates makes use of the present value (discounting) analysis developed earlier in this chapter. Within this framework, the share price is viewed as the discounted present value of a firm's expected earnings (or dividends). Accordingly, a fall in the interest rate and/or a rise in the stream of expected earnings increase the expected value of the firm—that is, the share price—in the market.

[e]If the interest rate rises to 8 percent, the price of a typical share will fall to $37.50 because $3/$37.50 = 8 percent. Assuming the higher interest rate reduces demand and hence earnings, the dividend may be expected to fall to $2. If this is the case, the stock price falls further to $25.00 since $2/$25.00 = 8 percent.

APPENDIX 7-B

The Inverse Relationship Between Bond Prices and Interest Rates: The Case of Consols

T he discussion in the text has developed the formal analytical link between changes in interest rates and changes in bond prices. Just in case you are not yet completely comfortable with the analysis, this appendix provides a simpler, helpful example.

Consol A perpetual bond with no maturity date; the issuer is never obliged to repay the principal but makes coupon payments each year forever.

There exists a type of bond called a **consol.** Such securities have no maturity date. The issuer is not obligated to ever repay the principal, and the issuer makes coupon payments each year forever. That is, if I buy a consol today, I am entitled to the coupon payment forever, but never to be repaid the principal. After some mathematical manipulation and simplification of Equation 7-5, which we will mercifully put in footnote a, such characteristics imply the following:[a]

$$i = C/P$$

The yield to maturity, or interest rate, i, on a consol is equal to the coupon payment, C, divided by the price of the bond, P. Suppose a new $1,000 face value consol is issued today and it promises to pay $50 in interest each year. This is the coupon payment each year. Assuming the price of the new consol is $1,000, the $50 divided by the price shows that the consol yields 5 percent ($50/$1,000 = .05).

Now assume that a year later another $1,000 consol is issued by the same company. However, let's suppose the prevailing level of interest rates in the economy has risen so that the new consol will have to pay $60 a year in interest to be competitive. Clearly, the new consol is now a better investment than the one-year-old 5 percent consol.

Suppose now that some unforeseen financial problems lead the owner of the old 5 percent consol to sell it. Who would be willing to purchase the old 5 percent consol, given that they could instead purchase a new 6 percent consol? The answer is nobody, at least not yet. The older consol will have to yield 6 percent to be sold, and it will sell if it can somehow be made to yield 6 percent.

The older consol cannot change the fact that it pays $50 a year in interest. This is a contractual arrangement. However, the old consol can sell for a lower

---

[a]From Equation 7-6, the price of a consol is equal to $P = C/(1 + i) + C/(1 + i)^2 + C/(1 + i)^3 + C/(1 + i)^4 + \ldots = C[1/(1 + i) + 1/(1 + i)^2) + 1/(1 + i)^3 + 1/(1 + i)^4 + \ldots] = C(1/i) = C/i$. Therefore, $i = C/P$.

price. If the price drops to $833.33, then $50 a year interest would represent a yield of 6 percent ($50/$833.33 = .06). In fact, this is exactly what will happen. The owner of the old consol will offer the bond for sale at $1,000—the original price. Because no buyers appear, the market maker handling the transaction will lower the price. Such price cutting will continue until buyers appear; this will occur when the price falls to $833.33 because at this point the yield on the old consols is competitive with the yield on new consols. We suggest closing the book and working through the case where the interest rate on new bonds falls to 4 percent; what will happen to the price of the old consol and why?[b]

---

[b] The old consol represents a future stream of income of $50 per year forever. At an interest rate of 4 percent, the price rises to $1,250 ($50/.04 = $1,250), and the lucky owner makes a capital gain of $250.

8

The Structure of Interest Rates

> *Time gives good advice.*
> —Maltese Proverb—

Learning Objectives

After reading this chapter, you should know:

◆ What a yield curve is

◆ How expectations influence interest rates

◆ What determines expectations

◆ What determines credit ratings and how these ratings affect interest rates

◆ Why interest rates on state and local (municipal) bonds are usually below the rates on other types of bonds

From One Interest Rate to Many

A familiar term we hope you have come to know and understand is the *interest rate*. Before you become too attached, however, the time has come to confess the obvious. Previous chapters have discussed in some detail what determines *the* interest rate as if there is just one interest rate. This simplification allowed us to abstract from many details and focus on the essential factors influencing interest rates, in general. Of course, the real world is more complicated.

As described in Chapter 6, numerous types of financial claims are traded in financial markets—Treasury bills, corporate bonds, municipal bonds, commercial paper, certificates of deposit, Treasury bonds, and so forth. A glance at any newspaper reveals that the interest rates on each type of financial claim differ. Lest you be overwhelmed by such differences, remember that our objective is to bring order to chaos. More specifically, we want (1) to understand the patterns and common threads that link the various interest rates together, which was the major purpose of Chapters 6 and 7, and (2) to identify the factors that explain the differences.

Simply put, interest rates generally move up and down together. However, some rates may move up more than others and occasionally some rates may not move in the same direction as others. As a result of such disparate movements, the spreads between rates can change. For example, the spread between Treasury bill rates and Treasury bond rates, or the spread between the rates on risky corporate bonds and those that are less risky can move in divergent directions. The purpose of this chapter is to study the factors that are primarily responsible for determining the relationship among interest rates. The pattern or spread among interest rates is usually referred to as the **term structure of interest rates.**

Financial analysts have isolated and identified three primary determinants of the relationship among interest rates. These three factors are (1) term to maturity, (2) credit risk, and (3) tax treatment.

Why is it important to know all this you ask? There are many possible responses, but this hypothetical example should suffice. Suppose you have $1 million available to purchase financial claims and you are trying to choose between one-year Treasury notes yielding 7 percent, two-year Treasury notes yielding 8 percent, and two-year municipal notes yielding 5 percent. What would you do? More to the point, what would you need to know before you or any portfolio manager could make a rational decision? This chapter will provide answers to such questions.

Term Structure of Interest Rates The pattern or spread among interest rates determined by the term to maturity, credit risk, and tax treatment.

The Role of Term to Maturity in Interest Rate Differentials

The U.S. Treasury issues different types of securities—bills, notes, and bonds—as it manages the nation's debt and finances the government's budget deficit. The major characteristic distinguishing one type of Treasury security from another is the term to maturity. For example, Treasury bills have short terms to maturity of one year or less, while **Treasury notes** and bonds have long terms to maturity of one year or more. The question we are interested

Treasury Notes Securities issued by the U.S. government with an original maturity of one to ten years.

in is what determines the relationship between interest rates on Treasury securities of different maturities? For example, what is the relationship between the interest rate on a *short-term-to-maturity* Treasury security and the interest rate on a *long-term-to-maturity* Treasury security?

The Yield Curve

A common analytical construct used as a framework for addressing this question is a **yield curve.** Formally, a yield curve is a graphical representation of the relationship between interest rates (yields) on particular securities and their terms to maturity. Put another way, a yield curve is a representation of what is commonly referred to in financial markets as the term structure of interest rates—that is, how interest rates vary with the term to maturity.

When constructing yield curves for the purpose of examining the role of term to maturity in explaining interest rate differentials, analysts traditionally focus on Treasury securities. By focusing on one particular type of security, we can control for factors other than term to maturity such as riskiness and tax treatment, which could also affect the structure of yields. In other words, focusing on Treasury securities permits us to isolate the effects of term to maturity. Although we use U.S. government securities, we could have used other types of assets, such as corporate bonds, junk bonds, and so on, to demonstrate yield curves. Just be sure you understand that each individual asset is usually represented on a single yield curve, even though several yield curves may be drawn on one graph.

To construct yield curves, we begin with Exhibit 8-1. This table shows the interest rates on U.S. Treasury securities of different maturities prevailing on three different dates—January 16, 1981; March 12, 1986; and January 29, 1993. From this information, we can actually construct three different yield curves—one for each of the three dates. Term to maturity is always measured on the horizontal axis, while the return on an asset (yield to maturity) is measured on the vertical.

Utilizing the data in Exhibit 8-1, the yield curves for the three dates are plotted in Exhibit 8-2. Notice that on January 16, 1981, the yield on three-month Treasury bills was 15.19 percent, while the yield on ten-year Treasury bonds was 12.53 percent. Thus, the slope of the yield curve at that time was negative, meaning that yields declined as the term to maturity increased. In contrast, on March 12, 1986, the yield curve had a positive slope, which means

Yield Curve A graphical representation of the relationship between interest rates (yields) on particular securities and their terms to maturity.

Exhibit 8-1 ◆
Interest Rates on Treasury Securities

January 16, 1981		March 12, 1986		January 29, 1993	
Term to Maturity	Interest Rate	Term to Maturity	Interest Rate	Term to Maturity	Interest Rate
3 months	15.19%	3 months	6.8 %	3 months	2.92%
1 year	13.91	1 year	7.01	1 year	3.41
2 years	13.15	2 years	7.18	2 years	4.24
5 years	12.69	5 years	7.49	5 years	6.08
10 years	12.53	10 years	7.66	10 years	6.46

SOURCE: *Federal Reserve Bulletin* (various issues, 1981–1993).

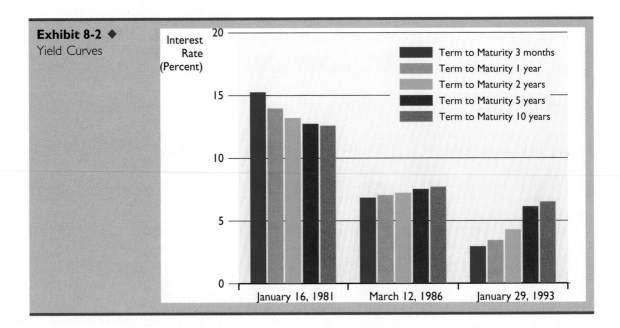

Exhibit 8-2 ◆
Yield Curves

that yields rose with term to maturity. On this day, the yield on three-month Treasury bills was 6.8 percent, while the yield on ten-year Treasury bonds was 7.66 percent. Thus the slope of the yield curve changed over time. Notice also that all the 1986 yields were below all the 1981 yields. This indicates the level of the yield curves as well as the direction of the slope changed. Next look at the yield curve for January 29, 1993. On this day, the yields on three-month Treasury bills and ten-year Treasury bonds were 2.92 and 6.46 percent respectively, resulting in a yield curve that was below and much steeper than the 1986 curve. Even though the slope remained positive, this third yield curve further shows how much variation there can be among yield curves.

The slope (shape) and position (level) of the yield curve are, to repeat, called the term structure of interest rates. We are interested in explaining what determines the term structure— that is, the shape of the yield curve and its level. While much has been written to explain the term structure of interest rates, the conventional wisdom can be boiled down to the expectations theory and some modifications of the theory. To simplify the explanation of the theory and the modifications, we shall assume that there are only two types of Treasury securities: T-bills with a short term to maturity (one year) and Treasury notes with a long term to maturity (two years). We shall develop our analysis in terms of the demand and supply of financial securities of these two maturities.

In Chapter 4, we discussed interest rate determination in terms of the supply and demand for loanable funds. By now you should be able to see that when we supply loanable funds, we demand financial securities and when we demand loanable funds, we supply financial securities. Thus, developing our analysis of the expectations theory in terms of the demand and supply of financial securities is consistent with our previous discussion.

RECAP

The yield curve is a graphical representation of the relationship between the interest rate (yield) and the term to maturity. Yield curves show how interest rates vary with term to maturity.

The Expectations Theory

Simply put, the **expectations theory** postulates that the yield curve is determined by borrowers' and lenders' expectations of future interest rates, and changes in the slope (shape) of the curve result from changes in these expectations. More specifically, the expectations theory postulates that the *long rate* is the geometric average of the current *short rate* and the future short rates expected to prevail over the term to maturity of the longer-term security.

To understand the expectations theory, let us begin by assuming that you have funds to lend for a two-year period and that the current yield, i_1, on a one-year bill—a short-term security—is 5 percent per year, and the current yield, i_2, on a two-year note—a long-term security—is 5.99 percent per year. Now suppose that you and everyone else with funds available to lend expect that the yield on short-term (one-year) securities, i_1^e, will be 7 percent one year from now. Assuming that you have no preference as to holding one-year or two-year securities, that is, you do not have a preference for either short- or long-term securities, which would you acquire now? Drawing on the concept of maximization developed earlier in the text, we predict you will acquire the security with the highest expected rate of return. Think of yourself as having two options: Option A is to buy short-term (one-year) securities today and short-term securities again one year from now; Option B is to buy long-term (two-year) securities now. Which of the options gives the highest expected rate of return?

The answer is derived in two simple steps: (1) calculate the expected return from acquiring the one-year bill now and the one-year bill one year from now; (2) compare it with the 5.99 percent return you would earn by acquiring the two-year note now.

To calculate the expected return of the one-year bill now and the one-year bill one year from now, we find the **geometric average** of the two rates. We use the geometric average instead of the simple arithmetic average to take into account the effects of compounding as discussed in Chapter 7. In other words, use of the geometric average assumes that the interest earned the first year will earn interest during the second year. More precisely, using the geometric average, the long rate, i_2, can be calculated as follows:

(8-1) $$(1 + i_2) = [(1 + i_1)(1 + i_1^e)]^{1/2}$$

Subtracting 1 from both sides of Equation 8-1 yields

(8-2) $$i_2 = [(1 + i_1)(1 + i_1^e)]^{1/2} - 1$$

> **Expectations Theory** A theory holding that the long-term interest rate is the geometric average of the present short-term rate and the short-term rates expected to prevail over the term to maturity of the long-term security.

> **Geometric Average** An average that takes into account the effects of compounding; used to calculate the long-term rate from the short-term rate and the short-term rates expected to prevail over the term to maturity of the long-term security.

Returning to our numerical example, if we perform these calculations, we find that the expected return associated with Option A is 5.99 percent. More specifically, plugging the present one-year rate and expected one-year rate into Equations (8-1) and (8-2) yields:

$$(1 + i_2) = [(1 + .05)(1 + .07)]^{1/2}$$
$$= [(1.05)(1.07)]^{1/2}$$
$$= (1.1235)^{1/2}$$
$$= 1.0599$$

and

$$i_2 = 1.0599 - 1$$
$$= .0599 = 5.99 \text{ percent}$$

This is the geometric average of short rate now, i_1, and the short rate expected to prevail one year from now, i_1^e. The expected return from Option B—acquiring the two-year note—is also 5.99 percent. Since the expected returns from both options are the same, you and other lenders (buyers of securities) will be indifferent between the two options, perhaps resulting in the purchase of both short-term securities and long-term securities. More formally, since the long rate is, in fact, equal to the geometric average of the current short rate and the short rate expected to prevail one year in the future, we have an equilibrium configuration or term structure of interest rates. The associated yield curve is shown in Exhibit 8-3.

Our example does not prove the expectations theory postulated earlier; after all, we chose the numbers in the example. What happens when the numbers change? To get the answer and in the process explain how the theory works, go back to our example and assume the one-year rate and two-year rates initially remain at 5 percent and 5.99 percent, respectively, but that expectations about future rates change such that the one-year rate expected to prevail one year from now rises from 7 to 9 percent. What would you and other potential purchasers of securities do and how would such actions affect the term structure—that is, slope and level of the yield curve in Exhibit 8-3?

You and other financial investors would presumably first recalculate the expected return from Option A (buy short-term securities now and again one year from now) and compare it to the expected return from Option B (buy long-term securities now). We use Equation (8-2) to calculate the geometric average—the expected return—of Option A. Such a calculation reveals that the expected return is 6.98 percent: $.0698 = [(1.05)(1.09)]^{1/2} - 1$. Because this is higher than the 5.99 percent return associated with Option B, you and others will want short-term securities. In fact, those who own long-term securities will want to sell them and buy short-term securities. What will happen as the demand for long-term securities falls in the market? We hope you said the price of these long-term securities will fall and, thus, ceteris paribus, their yields will rise.

How far will this portfolio reshuffling go? Or, to put it somewhat differently, how high will long rates rise? Given our theory, and assuming the short

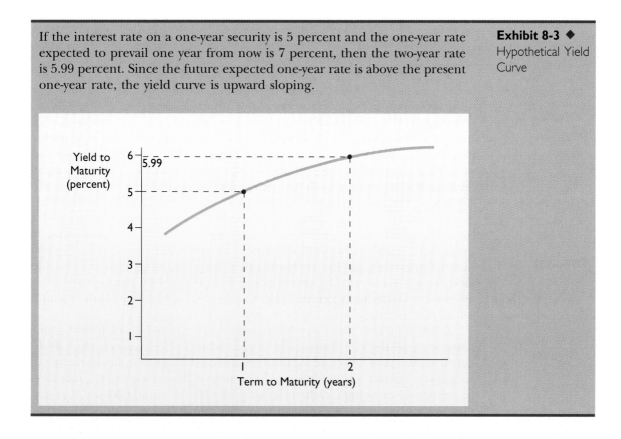

If the interest rate on a one-year security is 5 percent and the one-year rate expected to prevail one year from now is 7 percent, then the two-year rate is 5.99 percent. Since the future expected one-year rate is above the present one-year rate, the yield curve is upward sloping.

Exhibit 8-3 ◆
Hypothetical Yield Curve

rate remains at 5 percent and the expected short rate remains at 9 percent, the long rate will have to rise to 6.98 percent.[1]

Why 6.98 percent? This is the only rate that will equate the expected returns from Options A and B, thus leaving financial investors indifferent between them. If investors are indifferent, there is no tendency to change and an equilibrium configuration or term structure of interest rates is realized. More formally, a 6.98 percent interest rate on the two-year bonds, i_2, will make it equal to the geometric average of the prevailing 5 percent one-year rate, i_1, and the 9 percent one-year rate expected to prevail one year from now, i_1^e. The relationship between long-term interest rates and short-term interest rates depends directly on interest rate expectations; as i_1^e changes, i_2 will change relative to i_1.[2]

In our example, the adjustment in the long (two-year) rate from 5.99 to 6.98 percent as a result of the change in interest rate expectations was developed from the demand side of the market for securities; that is, from the

[1] For simplicity, we are assuming the short-term rate does not change. In reality, because the demand for short-term securities rises, their price would rise. The portfolio reshuffling would result in a fall in the short rate in addition to the rise in the long rate.

[2] Equation (8-2) is easily generalized for a long-term security, with, say, ten years to maturity. In this case, the ten-year rate would be the geometric average of the current short one-year rate and the one-year rates expected to prevail over the next nine years. Thus, $i_{10} = [(1 + i_1)(1 + i_1^e)(1 + i_2^e) \ldots (1 + i_9^e)]^{1/10} - 1$, where i_n^e is the expected one-year rate n years from now.

point of view of the lender. But do not forget, there is also a supply side of the securities market. The expectations of the borrower are also important. Suppose you need funds for two years and the choice is between issuing a security for two years with an interest rate of 5.99 percent or issuing a one-year security at 5 percent and issuing another one-year security one year from now at an expected 9 percent rate. Which option would you choose? Again, drawing on the concept of maximization, we assume you will choose the option that minimizes the cost of borrowing and thus maximizes utility or profits. Accordingly, you would issue a two-year security with an annual interest rate of 5.99 percent rather than sell two consecutive one-year securities having an expected average annual interest rate of 6.98 percent.

When borrowers believe that the average of current and expected future interest rates on short-term securities exceeds the rate on long-term securities, they will increase their current supply of long-term securities, thus tending to raise the long-term interest rate. That is, borrowers will want to issue two-year notes, thus, ceteris paribus, increasing their supply (causing their price to fall) and thereby requiring higher interest rates to be paid on them. The market will be in equilibrium when the quantity of notes supplied equals the quantity of notes demanded.[3]

Taken together, the effects of interest rate expectations of investors and borrowers on the demand for and supply of securities, respectively, will determine the term structure of interest rates. More specifically, if, as in our example, expectations about future interest rates change such that future rates are expected to be higher, the original yield curve in Exhibit 8-3 will turn into the new yield curve in Exhibit 8-4. As the demand for longs falls and the supply of longs rises, the price of longs will fall and the long rate will rise relative to the short rate, resulting in a steepening of the yield curve.

The last few paragraphs have been jam-packed with information. Let's try to summarize and nail down some implications of the key points. First, the hypothetical yield curve accompanying our initial example, shown in Exhibit 8-3, is positively sloped—that is, yields rise with term to maturity. The explanation for the slope of the yield curve is directly related to the interest rate expected to prevail on short-term securities one year in the future—hence the term *expectations theory*. More specifically, the positively sloped yield curve reflects expectations of a rise in the interest rate on short-term securities over the course of the year from the currently prevailing 5 percent to 7 percent.

Second, the new hypothetical yield curve accompanying our second example in which we assumed the expected future rate rose from 7 percent to 9 percent, is, as shown in Exhibit 8-4, even more positively sloped than the original curve. The explanation for the change in the slope is the change in future interest rate expectations. More specifically, the steepening of the slope reflects expectations of an even larger rise in the interest rate on short-term securities over the course of the year—that is, from the currently prevailing 5 percent to 9 percent rather than from 5 to 7 percent as in the previous example.

Third, the change in the slope of the yield curve, which accompanies a change in interest rate expectations, does not come about magically. Rather, it reflects changes in the supply and demand for securities, which are induced by the change in interest rate expectations.

---

[3]For simplicity, we are ignoring the fact that the supply of short-term securities will also be reduced, causing their price to rise and their yield to fall.

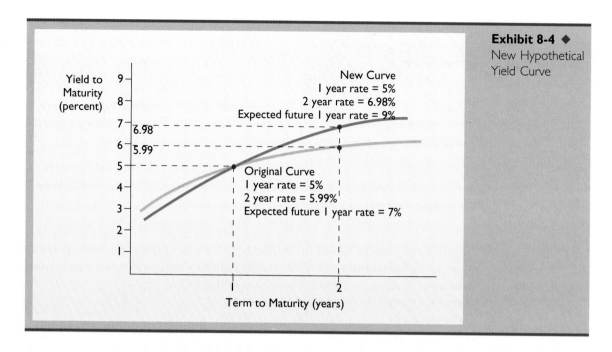

Exhibit 8-4 ◆
New Hypothetical
Yield Curve

Fourth, assuming the expectations theory is basically correct, we can solve for the interest rate expected to prevail in the future by looking at the current structure of rates and doing some simple algebra. We start by squaring both sides of Equation (8-1).

$$(1 + i_2)^2 = \{[(1 + i_1)(1 + i_1^e)]^{1/2}\}^2$$

$$= (1 + i_1)(1 + i_1^e)$$

We then divide through by $(1 + i_1)$ to get

$$(1 + i^2)^2/(1 + i_1) = (1 + i_1^e)$$

Subtracting 1 from both sides of the equation, we arrive at Equation (8-3):

(8-3) $$i_1^e = [(1 + i_2)^2/(1 + i_1)] - 1$$

Returning to our numerical example, if we know that the one-year rate is 5 percent and the two-year rate is 5.99 percent, as in our first example, we can plug the relevant numbers into Equation (8-3) and solve for i_1^e. Specifically,

$$i_1^e = [(1.0599)^2/1.05)] - 1$$

$$= .07 = 7 \text{ percent}$$

Utilizing different numbers, if we observed in the market that the one-year rate was 5 percent and the two-year rate was 4.5 percent, this implies from Equation (8-3) that the expected rate on a one-year security bought one year from now is approximately 4 percent: $i_1^e = [(1 + .045)^2/(1 + .05)] - 1 = .04$. Thus, based on the expectations theory, one can look at the yield curve and infer the market's expectation for the direction and level of future short-term interest rates.

Exhibit 8-5 shows the three most common shapes of the yield curve. Exhibit 8-5a shows a rising or positively sloped yield curve. When a rising yield curve is observed in the market, the implication under the expectations theory is that market participants expect future short-term interest rates, i_s^e, to rise above current short rates, i_s; that is, $i_s^e > i_s$. When a horizontal or flat yield curve is observed in the market, as shown in Exhibit 8-5b, the implication is that interest rates are expected to remain constant, $i_s^e = i_s$. When a declining or negatively sloped yield curve is observed in the market, the implication is that interest rates are expected to decrease in the future, $i_s^e < i_s$.

Believe it or not, you now know enough to say quite a lot about the actual data and yield curves depicted in Exhibits 8-1 and 8-2. With specific reference to the yield curves shown in Exhibit 8-2, the expectations theory tells us the shape of the January 16, 1981, curve indicates that investors expect future short-term rates to decline. Since, according to the expectations theory, the two-year rate is the average of the current one-year rate and the one-year rate expected one year from now, the one-year rate expected to prevail one year from now must be less than the current one-year rate. Utilizing the data in the table in Exhibit 8-1, see if you can figure out the one-year rate that was expected to prevail one year from January 16, 1981.[4]

The shape of the March 12, 1986, yield curve indicates that investors expected future short rates to rise somewhat, and the shape of the January 29, 1993, curve indicates that even a larger increase in short-term rates is expected. See if you can explain how we know this.[5]

RECAP

According to the expectations theory, the long-term rate is the geometric average of the short-term rate and the short-term rates expected to prevail over the term to maturity. Given the one-year rate and the two-year rate, we can solve for the expected one-year rate one year from now.

Now that you have the mechanics of yield curves and expectations nailed down, we are ready for the home stretch. For those who think they have already crossed the finish line, please note that the whole expectations theory is rather empty unless and until we can explain what determines future interest rate expectations and changes in such expectations. Otherwise we have a theory explaining the term structure via expectations that are left unexplained.

---

[4]The answer is 12.395 percent; $i_1 = 13.91$ percent and $i_2 = 13.15$ percent. Plugging these figures into Equation (8-3) yields 12.395 percent: $.12395 = [(1 + .1315)^2/(1 + .1391)] - 1$.

[5]The January 29, 1993, yield curve is steeper than the March 12, 1986, curve. Using the expectations theory to solve for the expected future short-term rate on January 29, 1993, we get 5.08 percent: $[(1 + .0424)^2/(1 + .0341)] - 1 = .0508$. Solving for the expected future short-term rate on March 12, 1986, we get 7.35 percent: $[(1 + .0718)^2/(1 + .0701)] - 1 = .0735$. Hence, according to the expectations theory, in 1993, the short rate was expected to rise from 3.41 percent to 5.08 percent over the course of the year, while in 1986, the short-term rate was expected to rise from 7.01 percent to 7.35 percent.

Exhibit 8-5 ◆
Alternative Yield Curve Shapes

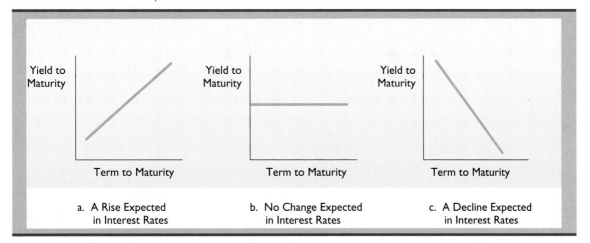

a. A Rise Expected in Interest Rates b. No Change Expected in Interest Rates c. A Decline Expected in Interest Rates

Determining Interest Rate Expectations

Naturally then, the question is what determines interest rate expectations? The answer to this question is much easier than you might think. In the last chapter, we examined the determinants of the interest rate and developed a general expression—Equation (7-10)—that brought together the most important supply and demand influences on the interest rate.[6] This expression is now Equation (8-4):

$$(8\text{-}4) \qquad i = f(\overset{+}{Y}, \overset{-}{M}, \overset{+}{p^e})$$

where Y = national income or gross domestic product, M = the money supply, and p^e = inflationary expectations. The signs over each variable indicate that a rise in income or inflationary expectations would tend to raise the interest rate, and a rise in the money supply would tend to reduce the interest rate.

Now, assuming we want to know what determines the expected short-term interest rate, i_s^e, how can Equation (8-4) be of help? The answer is straightforward; if the current short-term interest rate is determined by Y, M, and p^e, then the expected short-term interest rate must be determined by expectations about Y, M, and p^e. In other words,

$$(8\text{-}5) \qquad i_s^e = f(\overset{+}{Y^e}, \overset{-}{M^e}, \overset{+}{p^e})$$

the expected short-term interest rate, i_s^e, is a positive function of expectations about future income and inflation, and a negative function of expectations about the future money supply.[7]

---

[6] Remember that this equation is a reduced form equation derived from simultaneously solving a demand and supply equation for loanable funds.

[7] An even deeper question is what determines Y^e, M^e, and p^e. This is addressed in a later part of the text.

Tying the Determinants of Expectations to the Changing Shape and Level of Yield Curves

We have learned that a positively sloped yield curve reflects expectations of rising interest rates. Utilizing Equation (8-5), we can be even more specific; a positively sloped yield curve reflects expectations of some combination of future rises in income and inflation and possibly some reduction in the future growth rate of the money supply—developments that would all tend to raise future short-term interest rates. Conversely, a negatively sloped yield curve usually reflects expectations of some combination of future declines in income and inflation, and possibly some accompanying increase in the future growth rate of the money supply—developments that would all tend to lower short-term interest rates in the future.

Everything should now be coming together. To bring the picture into focus, ask yourself at what stage of the business cycle would you expect to observe a positively sloped yield curve. The answer is at that stage when the future appears to hold some growth in income, a rise in prices, and perhaps slower growth of the money supply. This typically occurs at a business cycle trough and during the first half of a recovery. During the previous recession, real income fell, inflation decelerated, and the Fed probably responded with a more stimulative policy, resulting in a rise in the money supply growth rate. All of these developments contributed to a fall in the prevailing short-term interest rate and set in motion the forces of economic recovery. As the economy bottoms out and begins to recover, market participants expect future income and prices to rise as aggregate demand for goods and services increases, and expect the Fed to be less stimulative so as to avoid an inflationary boom.[8] As a result, market participants expect future short-term interest rates to be higher than the prevailing level of short-term rates.

What about a negatively sloped yield curve? At what stage of the business cycle would market participants expect income and inflation to fall in the future, and expect the Fed in the future to take some actions to increase the growth of the money supply? These actions usually occur around business cycle peaks including the late part of a recovery or expansion and the early part of a recession. Typically, income and prices have been rising quickly and the Fed has moved to slow monetary growth—that is, "tighten" policy—to head off further surges in the inflation rate. As Equation (8-4) would lead one to predict, such developments have pushed up the prevailing level of short-term rates and set in motion forces, which in the future are expected to lead to some slowdown in income, deceleration of inflation, and, after a time, a less restrictive monetary policy. Simply put then, future short-term rates are expected to be lower than the prevailing level of short-term rates; hence, we observe a negatively sloped yield curve.

Going back once again to Exhibit 8-2, we hope you are not surprised to learn that January 16, 1981, fell around a business cycle peak (the exact peak was July 1981), that March 12, 1986, fell during an economic expansion, and that January 29, 1993, fell during the lengthy beginning of a weak recovery.[9] The change in the shape of the yield curve among the three dates reflects

[8] In reality, it may be well into the recovery before the Fed puts on the brakes!
[9] Note that negatively sloped yield curves have also been associated with abnormally high levels of interest rates when most market makers expect future interest rates to be lower. This was particularly true in 1981.

changes in interest rate expectations. The change in interest rate expectations, in turn, reflects expected changes in the performance of the economy (income and prices) and expected changes in the stance of monetary policy (specifically, the money supply growth rate). Such changes are typically observed as the economy moves from one stage of the business cycle to another.

RECAP

$$\overset{+\ -\ +}{i = f(Y,M,p^e)}, \text{ then } \overset{+\ -\ +}{i_s^e = f(Y^e,M^e,p^e)}.$$ If Y^e, M^e, or p^e change, then i_s^e changes. Changes in i_s^e cause the yield curve to shift.

Having identified and explained the major factors underlying the different shapes of the yield curves in Exhibit 8-2, we have one task left: to explain the different levels of the yield curves—that is, the reason the level of all the rates prevailing in 1986 was below the level of all the rates prevailing in 1981, and the level of all rates was even lower in 1993. We can address this issue in two parts:

1. Partially, the difference in interest rates is due to the cyclical pattern of interest rates related to real economic activity and the supply and demand for loanable funds. This part of the answer was discussed in Chapter 7, particularly Sections 7.4 through 7.6. Expectations about the returns on financial instruments and the returns to capital, the business outlook, and any other factors that influence the demand and supply for funds will affect the level of the yield curve.

2. The second part of the answer is embedded in Equations (8-4) and (8-5). In March 1986, the inflation rate was about 3 1/2 percent and according to most observers was expected to remain at the same rate or rise only slightly in coming years. By 1993, inflationary pressures were even lower and the economy was experiencing a mild recovery. In January 1981, the inflation rate was about 11 percent and expected to fall into the 7–8 percent area in coming years. Thus, in 1986 with the prevailing and expected inflation rates below the inflation rates prevailing and expected in 1981, the inflation premiums embedded in both short- and long-term interest rates were considerably smaller than the inflation premiums embedded in short- and long-term rates in 1981. By 1993, expectations of future inflation had subsided even more, and combined with slow growth and nonexpansionary monetary policy to produce the lowest interest rates in decades.[10]

Some Necessary Modifications to the Expectations Theory

The expectations theory of the term structure provides a powerful and widely accepted explanation for the relationship between long- and short-

---

[10]The slope of the yield curve decreased significantly during 1993 as long-term rates fell much faster than short-term rates. It was still upward sloping, but flatter. M1 growth increased significantly during 1993, despite lethargic M2 and domestic nonfinancial debt (DNFD) growth. The slow growth of M2 and DNFD is the reason why we characterize monetary policy as nonexpansionary.

term interest rates. However, many researchers, taking note of several historical and institutional features of financial markets, have argued that the expectations theory needs to be modified somewhat to make it a more complete explanation of the term structure. First, it has been observed that over the last 45 years, yield curves have almost always been positively sloped. Taken literally, this would imply that financial market participants have almost always expected short-term interest rates to rise. Given the ups and downs in the economy and the accompanying fluctuations in the supply and demand for funds, this implication is difficult to accept. Second, an assumption underlying the expectations theory is that lenders and borrowers have no preference between long- and short-term securities; they would just as soon lend or borrow for short terms to maturity as for long terms to maturity. The implication that long- and short-term securities are close substitutes for one another has been questioned in light of observations suggesting that (1) many lenders have a preference for liquidity and thus prefer to hold short-term financial claims, which are usually more liquid than long-term financial claims; (2) many borrowers would prefer to issue long-term claims, thereby avoiding the need to issue and reissue short-term claims; and (3) borrowing for short or long terms have different purposes, such as borrowing for inventory versus borrowing for capital expenditures.

The question then is How does the expectations theory need to be modified in view of these observations? There is little doubt that many borrowers and lenders have preferred maturities, or what have come to be called **preferred habitats,** and that this creates a degree of segmentation between the short-term and long-term markets. Nevertheless, abundant evidence exists to support the proposition that the short- and long-term markets are not watertight compartments. More specifically, research suggests that investors, for example, are willing to switch preferred habitats from short-term financial claims to longer-term claims if there is a bonus or a "sweetener" associated with doing so. This sweetener or bonus is referred to as a **liquidity premium;** in essence, it is the extra return required to induce lenders to lend long term rather than short term. In other words, it is the amount of interest that is required to induce lenders to abandon their preferred habitats. The size of the premium is presumed to rise with the term to maturity; the longer the term, the larger the premium must be to induce lenders to give up their preference for liquidity.[11]

How the existence of liquidity premiums modifies the expectations theory of the term structure and yield curves can be illustrated with the help of Exhibit 8-6. Suppose the current short rate and expected short rate are both 5 percent. The expectations approach suggests that the yield curve would be flat (curve A). However, the preceding discussion suggests that the issuers of long-term bonds have to offer an interest premium to get investors to buy bonds having long-term maturities. The size of the premiums is presumed to rise with the term to maturity. Curve B in Exhibit 8-6 depicts the size of such liquidity premiums at each maturity. Curve C represents the yield curve actually observed. The components of the total yield (curve C) are the interest rate expectations (curve A) and the liquidity premiums (curve B).

Preferred Habitats An expectations theory modification hypothesizing that many borrowers and lenders have preferred maturities, which creates a degree of market segmentation between the short-term and long-term markets.

Liquidity Premium The extra return required to induce lenders to lend long term rather than short term.

---

[11] Of course for the lender who goes into the short-term market, there is also the risk that interest rates could fall more than expected or rise less than expected. In this case, the lender would have been better off lending long. This is called the reinvestment risk. In general, it is believed that the liquidity premium outweighs the reinvestment risk.

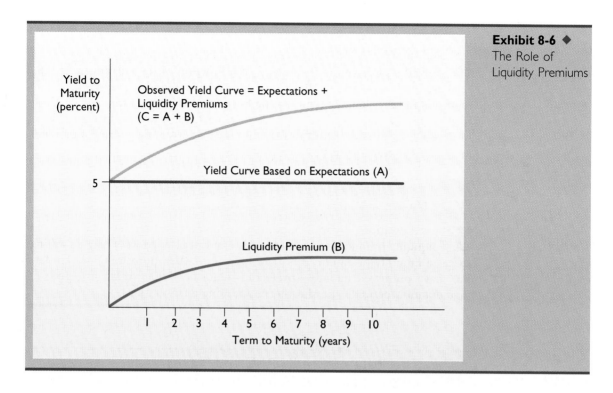

Exhibit 8-6 ◆
The Role of
Liquidity Premiums

By way of contrast, note that the expectations approach would explain the shape of the yield curve depicted by curve C as one that indicates market participants expect rates to rise over time.

The previous discussion looked at the demand side of the market for securities. But let us not lose sight of the behavior of the suppliers of debt securities (borrowers) implied by this approach. Under normal circumstances, the demand for funds (supply of securities) is usually more fickle than the supply of funds. Changes in the demand for funds, which are driven by expectations, probably account for the largest part of the changes in interest rates. The existence of liquidity premiums means that borrowers are willing to pay them. But why would borrowers be willing to pay more to borrow for longer terms than they expect to pay by borrowing and reborrowing for short terms? Simply put, there is some chance that short rates will be higher in the future than the 5 percent expected rate assumed in our example. If higher-than-expected rates were to materialize, then borrowing and refinancing in the future would prove to be more expensive than borrowing for a longer term now. Also, the firm could suffer some difficulty in the future, which might reduce its credit rating and make it difficult to acquire funds later. By borrowing long term, the adverse effects of such problems can be reduced.

In sum, the fact that yield curves have almost always been positively sloped over the past 45 years suggests that liquidity premiums do, in fact, exist. Theoretical considerations on both the supply and demand side of the securities markets and a variety of empirical studies seem to support such a judgment.

Our discussion of the determinants of the relationship between short- and long-term interest rates (the term structure) can be easily summarized with the aid of Equation (8-6).

(8-6)

$$i_1 = f(\overset{+}{i_s}, \overset{+}{i_s^e}, \overset{+}{l})$$

The current long-term interest rate, i_1, is a function of the current short rate, i_s, short rates expected in the future, i_s^e, and the liquidity premium, l. The nature of the relationship between the long rate and each of the determinants is given by the sign over each variable. In particular, we would expect long rates to rise if current short rates rise, if expectations about future short rates are revised upward, or if liquidity premiums rise.

RECAP

The expectations theory is modified by the fact that lenders may demand a liquidity premium to lend long term and that borrowers may be willing to pay a liquidity premium to borrow long term. Also borrowers and lenders may have preferred habitats (preferred maturities) that create a degree of segmentation between the short-term and long-term markets.

The Role of Credit Risk and Taxes in Interest Rate Differentials

The previous section dealt with interest rates on securities that were alike in every respect except one—term to maturity. Now we will extend our discussion and examine the relationship among interest rates on securities with the same term to maturity but that differ with regard to credit risk or taxability.

Credit Risk

Credit Risk The probability of a debtor not paying the principal and/or the interest due on an outstanding debt.

The term **credit risk** refers to the probability of a debtor not paying the principal and/or the interest due on an outstanding debt. In effect, credit risk is a measure of the creditworthiness of the issuer of a security. Treasury securities are considered to have the least credit risk because they are backed by the federal government. The basic idea here is that in the unlikely event the federal government collapses, we can be reasonably sure the rest of the economy has collapsed as well. The reverse is not true since many individual firms can and do fail on a daily basis without the government collapsing. In contrast, corporate and municipal (state and local government) securities are viewed as being risky to some degree and are, therefore, analyzed and rated by firms that specialize in producing credit ratings. The two major credit-rating agencies, **Standard & Poor's** and **Moody's Investors Service,** evaluate a borrower's probability of default and assign the borrower to a particular risk class. With this information, a lender can determine to what degree a borrower will be able to meet debt obligations. Both Standard & Poor's and Moody's distinguish among nine general classes of risk. Exhibit 8-7 reproduces the nine credit ratings with a brief description of each.

Standard & Poor's and Moody's Investors Services The two major credit-rating agencies that evaluate a borrower's probability of default and assign the borrower to a particular risk class.

How are borrowers classified or rated? In the case of business firms, the credit-rating agencies examine the pattern of revenues and costs experienced

Exhibit 8-7 ◆
Credit Ratings

Moody's	General Description	Standard & Poor's
Aaa	Best Quality	AAA
Aa	High Quality	AA
A	Higher Medium Grade	A
Baa	Medium Grade	BBB
Ba	Lower Medium Grade having Speculative Elements	BB
B	Lacks Characteristics of Desirable Investment	B
Caa	Poor Standing	B
Ca	Highly Speculative	B
C	Lowest Grade (in Default)	D

by a firm, its leverage ratio, its past history of debt redemption, and the volatility of the industry, among other things. A firm with a history of strong earnings, low leverage, and prompt debt redemption would get an Aaa rating from Moody and an AAA rating from Standard & Poor. Firms that have experienced net losses, have rising leverage, or have missed some loan payments would get a Baa or lower rating from Moody or a BBB or lower rating from Standard & Poor.

The agencies also assign ratings to securities issued by state and local governments. Factors considered here would include the tax base, the level of outstanding debt, the current and expected budget situation, and the growth in spending.

To see how the credit ratings affect the spread between rates, let us make the reasonable assumption that most potential purchasers of securities would like to be compensated for risk taking. More formally, based on real-world observations, we can say that investors are risk averse and, thus, must be rewarded or compensated with extra interest for accepting more risk. The extra return or interest is called a **risk premium** and its size rises with the riskiness of the borrower. To illustrate, the prevailing rate on securities issued by borrowers rated Aaa is less than the rate on securities issued by borrowers rated Aa, the second highest rating. The spread between the two rates ($i_{Aa} - i_{Aaa}$) is the premium necessary to induce investors to accept the extra risk associated with Aa-rated securities relative to Aaa-rated securities. Similarly, the rates on Baa-rated securities are higher than the rates on A-rated securities, and so on down the credit ratings shown in Exhibit 8-7.[12]

Risk Premium The extra return or interest that a lender is compensated with for accepting more risk.

If we plotted the spread between the interest rates on securities of the same maturity, but possessing different credit risks, we would find that the spread varies over time, as the perceived credit risks among the securities change. For example, if lower-rated bonds are perceived as relatively more risky, say, because of a default in a major market, then, in response, many investors may sell lower-rated issues and purchase higher-rated issues. This movement to higher-rated securities is usually referred to as a "flight to quality." Put another way, if investors perceive that relative risks have changed, they will demand different risk premiums and thus the rate spread among securities will change. Now would be a good time to look at Exhibit 8-8, which

---

[12] For simplicity's sake, we used Moody's ratings in this example. We could have just as easily used Standard & Poor's ratings.

Exhibit 8-8 ◆

The Spread
Between Baa Rated
Municipal Bonds
and Aaa Rated
Municipal Bonds
1960–1996

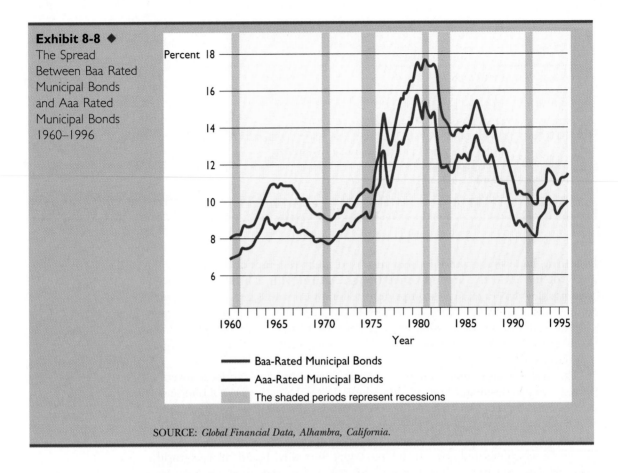

SOURCE: *Global Financial Data, Alhambra, California.*

plots the spreads between the interest rate on Baa- and Aaa-rated municipal bonds and demonstrates how the rate spread between these two securities with different credit risk can vary over time.

Taxability

The last major feature influencing the structure of interest rates is the taxability of securities. As you may know, interest income earned from securities issued by state and local governments is exempt from the federal income tax, while interest earned from corporate securities is taxed at the same rates as other ordinary income.[13]

Marginal Tax Rate The
tax rate that is paid on
the last dollar of income
that the taxpayer earns.

The **marginal tax rate** is the rate paid on the last dollar of income the taxpayer earns. Because we have a progressive tax rate structure, higher rates apply to additional income earned beyond given tax rate brackets. Income under the bracket limits is taxed at lower rates. Interest income from bonds is additional income and is therefore taxed at the highest marginal rate that the taxpayer falls into. For bondholders who do not have much other income,

---

[13] In many states, interest on bonds issued by the investor's home state is also exempt from state income taxes. For example, California residents do not pay state income taxes on interest earned on bonds issued by California, but they do pay income taxes on interest earned on bonds issued by Arizona. Although subject to federal income taxes, interest earned on federal government securities is exempt from state and local income taxes.

interest income is taxed at a lower marginal rate than bondholders whose other income puts them into a higher marginal tax bracket. This means, for example, that if you are in the 33-1/3 percent marginal federal income tax bracket, a 4 percent interest rate on a municipal bond is just as attractive as a 6 percent interest rate on, say, a taxable corporate bond; after taxes, both yield 4 percent.[14]

As we shall see, the tax-exempt status of municipal bonds makes them quite attractive to taxpayers in high marginal tax brackets. Financial intermediaries such as commercial banks and casualty insurance companies, which are subject to the 38 percent marginal corporate income tax rate, have traditionally been heavy purchasers of municipal securities.[15]

To see clearly how the yields on municipals are related to the yields on other types of securities, the following simple equation will be helpful.

$$
\text{(8-6)} \qquad \text{After-tax yield} = i - it
$$

$$
= i(1 - t)
$$

where t is the "marginal" tax rate on interest income. This says that the after-tax yield on a bond is equal to the interest rate earned, i, minus the portion that is taxed away, it; put another way, the after-tax yield is equal to that portion of the interest earned which is not taxed away: $i(1 - t)$.

Just as we care about our after-tax, take-home pay, rather than our before-tax gross pay, financial investors making portfolio decisions care about and, therefore, compare the after-tax returns on securities they might acquire. To see how this matters, suppose the rate on AAA-rated corporate bonds is 6 percent and the marginal tax rate of buyers is 33-1/3 percent, meaning that one-third of the interest income earned will be taxed away. If the only difference between the corporate bond and an AAA-rated municipal bond is that the interest on corporate bonds is taxable while the interest on the municipal bond is not ($t = 0$ percent), we would expect buyers to prefer the municipal securities to the corporate bonds as long as the rate on municipal bonds exceeded 4 percent. If the yield on municipal bonds equaled 4 percent, investors in the 33-1/3 percent marginal tax bracket would be indifferent since the corporate bond yields 4 percent [6 percent − ($.33\frac{1}{3}$ × 6 percent) = 4 percent] after taxes. What if the marginal tax rate of buyers of municipal securities is only 20 percent? What yield on municipal bonds would leave investors in the 20 percent tax bracket indifferent between our 6 percent corporate bond and a municipal bond? We hope that you understand why the answer is 4.8 percent.[16]

In general, we would expect the buying and selling by investors—more formally, the substitution among securities—to result in the yield on municipals being approximately equal to the yield on similarly rated taxable securities, such as corporate bonds, minus that portion of the yield which is taxed away. Close the book for a moment and see if you can explain why. Suppose

[14] For simplicity, we are assuming equivalent safety and maturity.

[15] For commercial banks, there is often subtle pressure to purchase the securities issued by municipalities in the immediate geographical area. With the bank's deposits coming from the local citizens, such purchases are viewed as an investment in the community the bank serves, an investment that demonstrates the goodwill and intentions of the bank.

[16] 4.8 percent = 6 percent − (.20 × 6 percent)

the interest rate on municipals is, for example, above the after-tax yield on corporates for the typical investor; municipals are obviously the more attractive security. The resulting purchase of municipals and sale of corporates will raise the prices and lower the yields on municipals and lower the prices and raise the yields on corporates. In this example, the effect of such substitution toward municipals and away from corporates will be to equalize the interest rate on municipal securities with the after-tax return on similarly rated corporate securities.

We now know that the marginal tax rate that investors pay on interest income is the key to understanding the spread between the interest rates on tax-exempt municipal securities and the interest rates on taxable securities. We can also see that taxpayers, depending on individual incomes, are in different marginal tax brackets, some high and some low. Thus, there is an **average marginal tax rate** somewhere between the high and the low marginal tax brackets. Because of substitution, the interest rate on municipal securities will gravitate to the rate that makes the "average" taxpayer (in the average marginal tax bracket) indifferent between municipals and similarly rated corporate securities.[17]

But why are those in high tax brackets, such as banks and rich individuals, especially attracted to municipals? Simply put, they are subject to a tax rate above the average marginal rate. To see precisely how this matters, assume the average marginal tax rate is 20 percent, and the rate on municipals is 4.8 percent and the rate on corporates is 6 percent. The average investor—that is, the investor in the 20 percent marginal tax bracket—is indifferent between the two securities; both have an after-tax return of 4.8 percent. Not so for the investor in a higher marginal tax bracket. Someone in the 33-1/3 percent marginal tax bracket, for example, would prefer the 4.8 percent return on the municipal security to the 4 percent after-tax return on the corporate security.

Average Marginal Tax Rate The average of the marginal tax rates of all taxpayers.

⬢ RECAP

Other factors that affect the interest rates on different securities with the same maturity are credit risk and taxability of interest income. Taxpayers in marginal tax brackets above the average marginal tax bracket are particularly attracted to tax-exempt securities.

A final example shows how both credit risk and taxability play a part in determining yield to maturity. Under normal circumstances, yields on 20-year general obligation AAA-rated municipal bonds are less than 80 percent of yields on comparable Treasury securities. The yield spread mainly reflects the difference in the credit risk and the tax status accorded the earnings of the two assets. In December 1994, affluent Orange County, California, declared bankruptcy due to bond market losses in its investment pool. The bankruptcy

---

[17]Note that in actuality the yields on municipal securities will be somewhat higher than one would expect after taking account of the average tax rate of all buyers. For the most part, the quality of the secondary market in municipal issues is not as good as the secondary market for Treasuries and many corporate issues. As a result, municipal securities possess somewhat less liquidity than other types of securities and thus the liquidity premium demanded by investors is larger on municipals than on other types of securities.

created widespread uncertainty in the municipal bond market and the perception of greater risk. By year end, the municipal bond market had gone into a tailspin, and according to *Business Week,* "municipal bonds [were] trading at yields unusually close to those on Treasury bonds, so after-tax yields for many long-term muni buyers [were] roughly one-third higher."[18] Although the tax status had not changed, the relative credit risk had, causing the spread between the two categories of securities to narrow. Buyers of municipal bonds demanded a larger risk premium and, as the after-tax yields reflect, they received it.

To sum up, the yields on municipal securities are typically, but not always, well below the yields on other securities with similar credit ratings and similar terms to maturity. The interest rate differentials observed are a reflection of the different tax treatment accorded the interest earned on each type of security and different credit risk.

The appendix to this chapter discusses "cracking the code" in the Treasury securities market. Among other things, it will show you how to read the financial pages of major U.S. newspapers to discover what transpires in the Treasury securities market.

---

[18] *Business Week,* December 26, 1994, p. 140.

Summary of Major Points

1. The yield curve is a graphical representation of the relationship between interest rates (yields) on a particular security and its term to maturity. It is a visual depiction of the term structure of interest rates. A unique yield curve exists for each type of financial asset such as government securities and corporate bonds, among others.

2. The most widely accepted explanation for the shape (slope) and position (level) of the yield curve is the expectations theory.

3. The expectations theory postulates that the long-term rate is the geometric average of the current short-term rate and short-term rates expected to prevail over the term to maturity of the long-term security. The geometric average is the appropriate average to use in explaining the expectations theory because it takes into account the effects of compounding. The interest earned during the first year earns interest during the second year.

4. According to the expectations theory, the slope of the yield curve depends on the interest rates expected to prevail on short-term securities in the future. More specifically, a positively sloped yield curve reflects expectations of a rise in future short-term rates, relative to current short-term rates; a negatively sloped yield curve reflects expectations of a fall in future short-term rates, relative to current short-term rates.

5. Expectations about future short-term rates depend on expectations about future income, the money supply, and inflation. As expectations about these variables change, expected short-term rates will change, resulting in a change in the slope and position of the yield curve.

6. The fact that yield curves have almost always been upward sloping, and that some borrowers and lenders appear to have preferred habitats, has led to the view that the expectations theory is an incomplete explanation of the term structure of interest rates. Accordingly, the expectations theory has been modified to include and take into account term or liquidity premiums—the sweetener or bonus (extra return) needed to induce investors to acquire longer-term financial claims. In general, long-term rates will be determined by current short-term rates, expected short-term rates, and liquidity premiums.

7. Credit risk refers to the probability of a debtor defaulting—that is, not paying the principal or interest due on an outstanding debt. Standard & Poor's and Moody's—the two major credit-rating agencies—evaluate a borrower's probability of default and assign the borrower a risk classification.

8. Since investors are risk averse, they must be offered the "bonus" of extra interest to accept more risk. The extra return or interest is called a risk premium and its size rises with the riskiness of the borrower.

9. Financial investors care about the after-tax return on their investments. Since the interest earned on municipal securities is exempt from the federal income tax, the yields on municipal securities are typically well below the yields on other (taxable) securities with similar credit ratings and similar terms to maturity.

Key Terms

Asked Price
Average Marginal Tax Rate
Bid Price
Credit Risk
Expectations Theory
Geometric Average
Liquidity Premium
Marginal Tax Rate

Moody's Investors Service
Preferred Habitats
Risk Premium
Standard & Poor's Investors
   Service
Term Structure of Interest Rates
Treasury Notes
Yield Curve

Review Questions

1. Discuss the factors that determine the shape and level of a yield curve. How do term to maturity, credit risk, and tax treatment affect the interest rate on a particular asset?

2. Give an explanation of why a yield curve can be negatively sloped. Would interest rates be abnormally high or low? What would be the overall expectation of the direction of future short-term interest rates?

3. According to the expectations theory, how is the long-term interest rate determined? Why is the geometric average used instead of the simpler arithmetic average?

4. Junk bonds are more risky than AAA-rated corporate bonds. Explain where the two yield curves will lie relative to each other. What could cause the spread to widen?

5. What determines expectations? Are expectations about future prices independent of expectations about future money supply growth rates? Why or why not?

6. Could the yield curve for municipals ever lie above the yield curve for government securities? (Hint: Consider all tax rates.) What effect would an increase in marginal tax rates have on the position of the yield curve for municipals?

7. Use the liquidity premium to give an explanation for why yield curves have most often been upward sloping over the past 45 years. Could a yield curve be upward sloping even if short-term rates were expected to remain constant? If interest rates are expected to fall dramatically, under what conditions would the yield curve still be upward sloping?

8. Define preferred habitats. Explain how this modification affects the expectations theory. What could cause market segmentation based on preferred habitats to breakdown?

9. Discuss the following statements: Over a typical cycle, the movement of the yield curve is like the wagging of a dog's tail. The entire tail wags, but short-term rates "wag" more than long-term rates.

10. In late 1995, yield curves became flatter. What does this say about expectations of future interest rates?

11. What would happen to the risk premium if the economy went into a strong expansion? a deep recession?

Analytical Questions

12. If the current short-term rate is 5 percent and the expected short-term rate is 8 percent, what is the long-term interest rate? (Use the expectations theory.)

13. If the current short-term rate is 5 percent and the current long-term rate is 4 percent, what is the expected short-term interest rate? (Use the expectations theory.)

14. Rework questions 12 and 13 assuming there is no compounding. (Hint: Use the simple arithmetic average instead of the geometric average.)

15. Assume that current interest rates on government securities are as follows: one-year rate, 5 percent; two-year rate, 6 percent; three-year rate, 6.5 percent; four-year rate, 7 percent. Graph the yield curve.

16. Given the yield curve in question 15, what is the expected direction of future one-year rates? Under what circumstances would one-year rates be expected to decline?

17. If a taxpayer's marginal tax rate is 33-1/3 percent, what is the after-tax yield on a corporate bond that pays 5 percent interest? If the average marginal tax rate of all taxpayers is 50 percent, will the taxpayer with the 33-1/3 percent marginal tax rate prefer a corporate or municipal security? Assume equivalent safety and maturity.

18. Go to *The Wall Street Journal* and gather data on interest rates for government securities of various maturities for today. Graph the yield curve.

(Hint: Check your answer by looking at the yield curve for Treasury securities that the *Journal* publishes daily in Part C.)

19. What would happen to interest rates, given the following scenarios?

    a. The government increases marginal tax rates.

    b. The tax exemption on municipals is eliminated.

    c. Corporate profits fall severely.

    d. The federal government guaranteed that the interest and principal on corporate bonds will be paid.

    e. A broader secondary market for government agency securities develops.

20. Draw the yield curve assuming future short-term rates are expected to remain constant and the liquidity premium is positive. Now assume that SSUs increase their preference for short-term securities. Show what happens to the yield curve.

21. If the bid price is 110:01 and the asked price is 110:04, what profit does the dealer make when buying and selling a $10,000 security?

The Financial System and the Economy

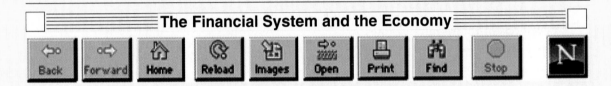

1. Access the *International Financial Encyclopedia* at (http://www.euro.net/innovation/Finance_Base/Fin_encyc.html) and define the following financial terms: security, liquidity, and yield curve.

2. Use the internet site (http://www.stls.frb.org/fred/data/irates.html) to obtain January 1995 and January 1996 data on:

    a. the 3 month CD secondary market rate (a proxy for short-term interest rates)

    b. the 3 year Treasury constant maturity rate (a proxy for medium-term interest rates)

    c. the 30 year FHA mortgage rate (a proxy for long-term interest rates).

    Graph two yield curves: one for January 1995 and one for January 1996. Compare the two curves.

Suggested Readings

For a discussion of the yield curve and the influence of inflation expectations, see C. Alan Garner, "The Yield Curve and Inflation Expectations," *Economic Review of the Federal Reserve Bank of Kansas City,* September/October 1987, pp. 3–15. This article uses the expectations theory (along with several other possible reasons) to seek an explanation for the steepening of the yield curve in the first half of 1987.

Many of the conclusions arrived at in this chapter are discussed in Burton Malkiel, *The Term Structure of Interest Rates,* Princeton, NJ: Princeton University Press, 1966.

For a discussion of yield spreads among different assets, see John Y. Campbell, "Yield Spreads and Interest Rate Movements: A Bird's Eye View," *Review of Economic Studies,* 58, May 1991, pp. 495–514.

Two other articles relevant to the material in this chapter are Mark P. Taylor, "Modeling the Yield Curve," *The Economic Journal,* 102, May 1992, pp. 524–537 and Steven Russell, "Understanding the Term Structure of Interest Rates: The Expectations Theory," *Federal Reserve Bank of St. Louis Review,* 74, July/August 1992, pp. 36–50. Current articles (as far back as 1993) from the *Federal Reserve Bank of St. Louis Review* may be accessed on the internet at (http://www.stls.frb.org/fred/reviewdata.html).

Two articles that deal with bond yields and taxes are Peter Fortune, "The Municipal Bond Market: Politics, Taxes, and Yields," *New England Economic Review,* September/October 1991, pp. 31–36; and Kanhaya L. Gupta, "Interest Rates, Income Taxes and Anticipated Inflation: Some New Evidence," *Journal of Banking and Finance,* 16, September 1992, pp. 973–981.

Two articles that relate growth and inflation to the shape and position of the yield curve are Stephen R. Blough, "Yield Curve Forecasts of Inflation: A Cautionary Tale," *New England Economic Review,* May/June 1994, pp. 3–16; and Campbell R. Harvey, "Term Structure Forecasts Economic Growth," *Financial Analysts Journal,* 49, May/June 1993, pp. 6–8.

APPENDIX 8-A

CRACKING THE CODE

The Treasury Securities Market: In Chapter 6 we cracked the code in the corporate bond and stock markets. Specifically, we decoded the relevant reports in the financial pages of major United States newspapers. In light of this earlier discussion and the subject matter of the current chapter, now is an appropriate time to learn how to read the reports on what transpires in the Treasury securities market.

　　Treasury Notes and Bonds: To understand how to read the accompanying table of developments that occurred on June 21, 1996 (taken from *The Wall Street Journal*), let us take a look at the circled line on the lefthand side. Under Rate (first column) is listed 5-1/8. This is the coupon rate, and it indicates that the holder of this security receives $5.125 per year for each $100 (face or par value), usually paid in semi-annual installments.

TREASURY BONDS, NOTES & BILLS
Friday, June 21, 1996

GOVT. BONDS & NOTES								TREASURY BILLS					
Rate	Maturity Mo/Yr	Bid	Asked	Chg.	Ask Yld.			Maturity	Days to Mat.	Bid	Asked	Chg.	Ask Yld.
5⅝	May 98n	98.09	98:11	+2	6.30			Sep 26 '96	93	5.09	5.07	+0.01	5.21
6	May 98n	99:13	99:15	+2	6.30			Oct 03 '96	100	5.13	5.11	....	5.26
5⅛	Jun 98n	97:25	97:27	+3	6.28								

　　The maturity date (second column) is 1998, June. This simply indicates that the security will mature in June of 1998—exactly two years hence. Thus, it is a two-year security.

　　Following the maturity date is the letter ''n''—this indicates that the security is a note. The only distinction between notes and bonds is that the original maturity (maturity when issued) for notes is ten years or less, while for bonds the maturity is more than ten years.

　　The next two columns give the ''bid'' and ''asked'' prices. The bid price is the price the market maker (dealer) is willing to pay to acquire this security; the asked price is the price the dealer is asking when selling the security. Prices are quoted in thirty-seconds. Thus, 97:25 bid means 97-25/32 or $97.78125 per each $100. Hence for a $1,000 note we need only move the decimal point to find the bid price is $977.8125. The asked price is 97:27 which means 97-27/32 or $97.84375 per $100. For a $1,000 note, the asked price is $978.4375.

　　The column labeled ''Chg'' shows that the bid for this particular government security was up 3 as of the close of business on June 21, 1996, compared with the close on the previous trading day. Changes are also quoted in thirty-seconds, so this means 3/32 per each $100.

The last column gives the yield to maturity on an annual basis for this note. It is 6.28 percent—this is the interest rate, or rate of return on the note. The yield to maturity takes into account the dollar return to the investor resulting from both the coupon payment ($51.25 per year per $1,000 face value), the price appreciation or depreciation between the time when the security is bought and when it matures, and the price paid. In this case, there will be an appreciation at maturity; the security is selling at a discount—that is, the market price of $978.4375 is less than the face value of $1,000.[a]

Whenever the security sells at a discount, the yield to maturity (6.28 percent) is more that the coupon rate (5-1/8 percent). Can you explain why the yield to maturity is less than the coupon rate when the security sells at a premium (market price is more than the face value)? This was discussed in Chapter 7.

Treasury Bills: Quotations for Treasury bills are also shown on the right-hand side of the accompanying table. When issued, all Treasury bills carry maturities of one year or less. However, as we saw in Chapter 6, Treasury bills are issued at a discount from par—that is, at a price less than $100 per $100 of face or par value. The investor pays, say, $99 and at maturity receives $100. The interest received is, in effect, the difference between the face value and the price paid when the bill is purchased—that is, the discount.

Look at the circled bill quotation. The maturity date of the bill is Sep 26 '96. Thus, this bill will mature in ninety-three days. Dealers are bidding 5.09 percent for the issue and asking 5.07 percent. These bid and asked quotations are based on what is called a discount basis or price lower than what is paid at maturity. Comparing the discounts on the bid and asked quotations, the higher discount on the bid side means that a lower price is being offered by the dealers to buy the Treasury bill and the lower discount on the asked side indicates that the dealer is selling the bills at a higher price. The inverse relationship between yields and security prices (bills, notes, and bonds) was discussed in Chapter 7. The last column indicates that the yield to maturity on this bill is equal to 5.21 percent; this is what we mean when we refer to the interest rate on the security.

---

[a] In case you are wondering how the 6.28 percent is determined, note that we know the price of the bond, the coupon payment, the term to maturity, and the face value. With this knowledge, we can plug the relevant figures into the bond price formula in Chapter 7—Equation (7-6)—and solve for i. Thankfully, calculators can be programmed to produce such solutions.

9

How Exchange Rates Are Determined

> *There are three main causes
> that dispose men to madness: love,
> ambition, and the study of foreign
> exchange.*
> —Walter Leaf, 1926—

Learning Objectives

After reading this chapter, you should know:

◆ What exchange rates are

◆ How exchange rates affect prices of imports and exports

◆ How exchange rates are determined by supply and demand in the foreign exchange market

◆ The factors that cause exchange rates to change

◆ What the balance of payments is and why it must balance

The Importance of Exchange Rates

Throughout the early and mid-1980s, typical headlines in *The Wall Street Journal* told of the strong dollar, its detrimental effects on U.S. jobs, and the eventual efforts to bring down the "overvalued" dollar. By the end of 1987, the value of the dollar had decreased to levels experienced in the late 1970s. By the mid-1990s, the dollar had fallen to record lows against many currencies and to less than half its mid-1980's value against the Japanese yen. Headlines such as "Dollar Rises in Foreign Exchange Market as U.S. Interest Rates Surge" have been replaced with "Dollar Sinks to New Low Against Yen."[1] Just what does all this mean to the average person? How do changes in the international value of the dollar affect job opportunities for recent college graduates and other workers? How are domestic interest rates linked with interest rates in the rest of the world and how are domestic prices affected by foreign prices? Perhaps most importantly, how might all these questions and their answers be related?

Not long ago, such questions, and the interactions between the U.S. economy and the rest of the world were largely ignored by most bankers, stock market analysts, economists, accountants, corporate treasurers, policymakers— and textbook writers! The reason was simple but twofold:

1. Trading of goods, services, financial claims (securities), and monies (currencies) between the United States and other countries accounted for only a small portion of total transactions in the United States.
2. Exchange rates between currencies were fixed by the central banks of each country and did not change on a day-to-day basis.

Today the value of the dollar in terms of other currencies changes daily, and questions about its value are often puzzling to the average person. Many diverse opinions exist about whether a strong dollar is good or bad for the economy even though the implications of a strong dollar are not often fully understood. This chapter is included in this section of the text on markets and prices because, as we shall see, exchange rates are merely prices (the price of one currency in terms of another) that are determined in a market (the foreign exchange market). As in all markets, prices (foreign exchange rates) are ultimately determined by the forces of supply and demand.

Defining Exchange Rates

Exchange Rate The number of units of foreign currency that can be acquired with one unit of domestic money.
Foreign Currency (Money) Supplies of foreign exchange.

The **exchange rate** is the number of units of **foreign currency (money)** that can be acquired with one unit of domestic money.[2] In other words, the exchange rate specifies the purchasing power of, say, the dollar in

---

[1] *The Wall Street Journal*, May 27, 1993, p. C15.
[2] Remember our earlier warnings about market jargon? Well, the problem is acute in the international sphere. For example, note that the definition of *foreign currency* in the text refers to foreign coin, paper currency, and checkable deposits, not as is the case in the United States (Chapter 2), where currency includes paper currency and coin only.

terms of how much it can buy of another currency. For example, if the yen/dollar exchange rate is 100 yen, this literally means that $1 will buy 100 yen.[3] If the exchange rate rises to 150 yen, meaning that $1 will now buy 150 yen, then the dollar is said to have **appreciated** relative to the yen. Since it will now buy more yen, the dollar's purchasing power has risen. It has grown stronger. On the other hand, if the yen/dollar exchange rate falls from 100 yen to 50 yen, the dollar is said to have **depreciated** relative to the yen. Since it will now buy fewer yen, the dollar's purchasing power has fallen. It has grown weaker. Supplies of foreign currencies are called **foreign exchange.**

So what does all this have to do with the price a U.S. importer will have to pay for Japanese autos? The following handy formula, linking prices and the exchange rate, provides the ingredients necessary to answer the question:

$$(9\text{-}1) \qquad \frac{\text{U.S. dollar price}}{\text{of foreign goods}} = \frac{\text{foreign price of foreign goods}}{\text{exchange rate}}$$

Appreciated When a currency has increased in value relative to another currency.
Depreciated When a currency has decreased in value relative to another currency.
Foreign Exchange Supplies of foreign currencies.

Exhibit 9-1 utilizes the formula and the hypothetical figures already mentioned to illustrate the key point of this discussion—the U.S. dollar price of a foreign good is inversely related to the exchange rate. More specifically, as the dollar appreciates, ceteris paribus, the price of foreign goods in the United States will fall, even if the foreign price in yen is constant.[4] Conversely, as the dollar depreciates, ceteris paribus, the price of foreign goods in the United States will rise.[5]

Needless to say, the importer and its customers (whether they realize it or not) are affected by changes in the exchange rate. More generally, the exchange rate links the domestic and foreign markets for goods, services, and securities.[6] As a result, changes in the exchange rate will have repercussions in all the domestic and foreign markets, including markets for both inputs and outputs. Thus, if the dollar appreciates, ceteris paribus, then U.S. imports (which are now relatively cheaper than before) increase, and U.S. exports to foreign countries (which are now relatively more expensive) decrease. As the dollar becomes stronger, ceteris paribus, we lose domestic jobs in both the industries in direct competition with the imports and the industries that end up exporting less.

To understand these various linkages and repercussions, we must first examine what determines the exchange rate. Simply put, the exchange rate, like all prices, is determined by supply and demand. The United States and the rest of the world trade goods, services, and securities. This trading gives rise to a supply and demand for the various currencies that are traded in the so-called **foreign exchange market.** More specifically, the supply of dollar-denominated funds comes from the demand by U.S. residents for foreign goods, services, and financial claims during a specific time period; the demand for dollar-denominated funds comes from the demand by foreign residents

Foreign Exchange Market The market for buying and selling the different currencies of the world.

---

[3]Exchange rates can also be expressed from the other direction. For example, if $1 will buy 100 yen, then 100 yen will buy $1 and 1 yen will buy $.01 [$1/(100 \text{ yen}) = \$.01$].
[4]You will recall that, *ceteris paribus* means "other things held constant."
[5]To keep things as simple as possible we are ignoring other factors that might influence the timing and degree to which a change in the exchange rate will actually be passed through into a change in the dollar price.
[6]Does this sound familiar? Recall how the interest rate links the present and the future.

Exhibit 9-1 ◆
How Movements in the Exchange Rate Affect the Dollar Price of Foreign Goods

Suppose a Japanese auto costs 2,000,000 yen in Japan. Ignoring transportation costs, etc., what will it cost in the United States? The answer is that it depends on the exchange rate between the yen and the dollar. The middle row in the following table lists the beginning situation; if the auto costs 2,000,000 yen and $1 buys 100 yen, then as Equation (9-1) indicates, the dollar price will be $20,000 (2,000,000/100).

Yen Price of Japanese Auto (1)	Exchange Rate (2)	Dollar Price of Japanese Auto (1)/(2)
2,000,000 Yen	$1 = 150 Yen	$13,333
2,000,000 Yen	$1 = 100 Yen	$20,000
2,000,000 Yen	$1 = 50 Yen	$40,000

The top row in the table shows that when the dollar appreciates from 100 yen to 150 yen, the dollar price of the Japanese auto falls to $13,333 (2,000,000/150). In contrast, as illustrated in the third row, a depreciation of the dollar results in a rise in the dollar price of the Japanese auto.

for U.S. goods, services, and financial claims over a period of time. For simplicity, in the remainder of this chapter, we will follow common usage and use the term *dollars* to represent *dollar-denominated funds*.[7] Exhibit 9-2 cracks the code for you on how to read the daily reports of exchange rates found in major financial newspapers, such as *The Wall Street Journal*.

 RECAP

The exchange rate is the number of units of foreign currency that can be acquired with one unit of domestic money. The U.S. dollar price of foreign goods is equal to the foreign price of foreign goods divided by the exchange rate.

 Determining Exchange Rates

The purpose of this section is to identify and analyze the most important factors affecting supply and demand in the foreign exchange market and to show how these factors determine exchange rates. Now would be a good time to look at Exhibit 9-3, which gives some of the basics of foreign exchange markets.

---

[7]In Chapter 2, we defined the *dollar* as a unit of account by which exchange values of goods and services could be measured. In this chapter, we are talking about the flow of funds—that is, the supply and demand of dollar-denominated funds—not dollars. So, when we use the term *dollars,* we really mean dollar-denominated funds.

To understand the relationship among supply, demand, and the exchange rates, it will be helpful to abstract from many of the complexities of the real world and to look at how the exchange rate between two currencies is determined. The general framework we develop is directly applicable to the more complex relationships among all national currencies. For example, suppose we know the yen/dollar rate is 100 yen and the mark/dollar rate is 1.5 marks. Then, as demonstrated in Exhibit 9-4, it must follow that the mark/yen rate is .015 marks. This "transitivity" allows us to confine our analysis to two monies. We begin by considering how the exchange rate between the U.S. dollar and the Japanese yen is determined, recognizing that our analysis could easily be extended to relationships among more than two currencies.

Starting with demand, the demand for dollars in international financial markets originates from foreign purchases of U.S. goods, services and securities. Drawing on Exhibit 9-3, we can write:

$$(9\text{-}2) \qquad \begin{array}{c} \text{Demand} \\ \text{for dollars} \end{array} = \overset{+}{F}(\text{foreign demand for U.S. goods,} \\ \text{services, and securities})$$

The plus ($+$) sign over the expression simply means that the foreign demand for U.S. goods, services, and securities and the demand for dollars are positively related; when the former rises, the latter will also rise. When foreign demand for U.S. goods, services, and securities falls, the demand for dollars falls.

Now our task is to consider the question What happens to the quantity demanded of dollars/month when the exchange rate changes?[8] (Note that the quantity demanded is the amount of dollars that will be demanded at a specific exchange rate.) The answer is: ceteris paribus, the quantity demanded is inversely related to the exchange rate as depicted in Equation (9-3).

$$(9\text{-}3) \qquad \text{Quantity demanded of dollars/month} = \overset{-}{F}(\text{Exchange rate})$$

This expression says that when the exchange rate goes up, ceteris paribus, the quantity demanded of dollars/month goes down and vice versa. To see how and why the exchange rate and the quantity demanded of dollars/month are inversely related as shown in this expression, we need to examine how the exchange rate, and changes therein, affect foreign demand for U.S. goods, services, and securities.

Focusing only on goods to simplify matters, the answer will depend on how the exchange rate affects the prices of U.S. goods in foreign markets—that is,

---

[8] In Chapters 3 and 4, we saw that the interest rate can be determined by either a stock model (the supply and demand for money) or a flow model (the supply and demand for loanable funds). Exchange rate determination is an analogous situation in that the exchange rate can be explained using a stock model, dealing with the supply and demand of foreign exchange at a particular moment, or a flow model, dealing with flows of foreign exchange over a particular time period. In this chapter, we have opted for using the flow model, noting that just as with all stock and flow models, each can generally be converted into the other without loss of substance. We hope that you recall that over time flows generate changes in stocks, and by measuring stocks at two points in time, a flow over time can be determined. For simplicity, we arbitrarily picked one month as our time period. The quantity demanded of dollars/month is the amount of dollars that will be demanded at a specific exchange rate.

Exhibit 9-2 ◆
Going Overseas:
Cracking the Code
in the Foreign
Exchange Market

CRACKING THE CODE

Suppose you have an upcoming trip to Germany for which you need marks. You call your local bank, say in Nashville, Tennessee, and place a buy order for 1,000 marks. Most likely your local bank does not itself have a foreign exchange department. As a result, your local bank will probably call its correspondent bank specializing in international transactions and place an order for marks with Citibank's foreign exchange department.[a]

Most foreign currency transactions in the United States are executed by the foreign exchange departments of the largest banks. Performing as market makers, they are linked via modern telecommunications with foreign exchange dealers around the world. Handling transactions from around the globe daily, they stand ready to buy or sell dollars and foreign currencies at the prevailing exchange rate, and, acting as auctioneers, they (and other dealers nationwide and worldwide) are prepared to adjust the exchange rate up as buy orders for dollars rise relative to sell orders, or adjust the exchange rate down as buy orders for dollars fall relative to sell orders. Of course, this is just another way of saying that the exchange rate will change as supply and/or demand changes.

So how much will your 1,000 marks cost? If you could "crack the code" in the relevant table in *The Wall Street Journal*, you could, in fact, figure out the approximate cost. We have reproduced the foreign exchange table that appeared in the *Journal* on March 1, 1996; as noted at the top of the table, it pertains to the exchange rates quoted as of 3 P.M. the preceding day, Thursday, February 29, 1996.

To find the exchange rate between the mark and the dollar on Thursday, look at the column we have labeled (3) and go down to the circled quotations for the mark. The exchange rate was 1.4736, meaning $1 purchased 1.4736 marks. Accordingly, 1,000 marks would have cost $678.61 (1,000 marks/1.4736). Comparing column (4) with column (3), note that the dollar appreciated a bit on Thursday as compared to the previous Wednesday. On Wednesday $1 purchased 1.4653 marks, slightly fewer than the case on Thursday. Accordingly, if you had bought the 1,000 marks on Wednesday, you would have paid slightly more than on Thursday ($682.45 = 1,000 marks/1.4653).

Note that the dollar exchange rate (the number of units of foreign currency one dollar can buy), shown in columns (3) and (4) is simply the reciprocal of the mark exchange rate (the number of dollars that can be purchased with one mark, or equivalently, the number of dollars needed to purchase one mark), shown in columns (1) and (2). That is, on Wednesday, for example, 1.4653 marks to the dollar is the reciprocal of .682454 cents to the mark (.682454 = 1/1.4653).[b] Given this property, a depreciation of the dollar means $1 buys fewer marks, or equivalently, it costs more cents to buy 1 mark. It is crucial for you to see that these are two ways of saying the same thing.

What are the implications of changes in the exchange rate? While Exhibit 9-1 touched on this, and the body of the text will have much to say about the causes and consequences of exchange rate changes, suppose a hotel room in Germany cost 100 marks on February 28, 1995, and the same price one year later on February 29, 1996. If the mark/dollar exchange rate in February 1995 was 2, what does this depreciation of the dollar over this period mean for a U.S. traveler? Simply put, it means that the hotel room cost more in 1996 than in 1995 (100/1.4736 = $67.86, compared to 100/2 = $50.00).[c]

[a]A correspondent bank is nothing more than a large bank, usually located in an important financial center, which provides the smaller bank with various services.

[b].682454 cents rounds to .6825 cents, the figure appearing in *The Wall Street Journal*.

[c]The institutional details should be mentioned. First, the exchange rate quotations in the paper are for large, so-called wholesale transactions of $1 million or more among banks, as noted at the top of the clipping. The "retail" cost of purchasing marks for you or for us would be slightly higher than implied by these quotes.

CURRENCY TRADING

EXCHANGE RATES

Thursday, February 29, 1996

The New York foreign exchange selling rates below apply to trading among banks in amounts of $1 million and more, as quoted at 3 p.m. Eastern time by Dow Jones Telerate Inc. and other sources. Retail transactions provide fewer units of foreign currency per dollar.

Country	(1) U.S. $ equiv. Thu	(2) U.S. $ equiv. Wed	(3) Currency per U.S. $ Thu	(4) Currency per U.S. $ Wed
Argentina (Peso)	1.0004	1.0004	.9996	.9996
Australia (Dollar)	.7646	.7596	1.3079	1.3165
Austria (Schilling)	.09673	.09704	10.338	10.305
Bahrain (Dinar)	2.6532	2.6532	.3769	.3769
Belgium (Franc)	.03309	.03320	30.220	30.120
Brazil (Real)	1.0243	1.0243	.9763	.9763
Britain (Pound)	1.5306	1.5330	.6533	.6523
30-Day Forward	1.5293	1.5318	.6539	.6528
90-Day Forward	1.5276	1.5299	.6546	.6536
180-Day Forward	1.5248	1.5271	.6558	.6548
Canada (Dollar)	.7296	.7263	1.3706	1.3768
30-Day Forward	.7296	.7262	1.3706	1.3771
90-Day Forward	.7291	.7254	1.3716	1.3786
180-Day Forward	.7272	.7213	1.3751	1.3863
Chile (Peso)	.002425	.002426	412.35	412.25
China (Renminbi)	.1207	.1207	8.2880	8.2880
Colombia (Peso)	.0009685	.0009780	1032.50	1022.50
Czech. Rep. (Koruna)	....	....	....	....
Commercial rate	.03683	.03703	27.154	27.006
Denmark (Krone)	.1761	.1768	5.6791	5.6557
Ecuador (Sucre)	....	....	....	....
Floating rate	.0003396	.0003396	2945.00	2945.00
Finland (Markka)	.2205	.2212	4.5356	4.5200
France (Franc)	.1979	.1991	5.0520	5.0220
30-Day Forward	.1981	.1993	5.0474	5.0172
90-Day Forward	.1984	.1996	5.0407	5.0099
180-Day Forward	.1988	.2000	5.0312	5.0003
Germany (Mark)	.6786	.6825	1.4736	1.4653
30-Day Forward	.6799	.6836	1.4709	1.4629
90-Day Forward	.6818	.6858	1.4667	1.4582
180-Day Forward	.6852	.6891	1.4595	1.4511
Greece (Drachma)	.004146	.004158	241.19	240.51
Hong Kong (Dollar)	.1293	.1293	7.7313	7.7313
Hungary (Forint)	.006915	.006956	144.62	143.77
India (Rupee)	.02881	.02845	34.715	35.145
Indonesia (Rupiah)	.0004321	.0004322	2314.25	2313.63
Ireland (Punt)	1.5753	1.5783	.6348	.6336
Israel (Shekel)	.3217	.3220	3.1082	3.1059

Country	(1) U.S. $ equiv. Thu	(2) U.S. $ equiv. Wed	(3) Currency per U.S. $ Thu	(4) Currency per U.S. $ Wed
Italy (Lira)	.0006427	.0006452	1556.00	1550.00
Japan (Yen)	.009498	.009562	105.28	104.58
30-Day Forward	.009537	.009600	104.86	104.17
90-Day Forward	.009650	.009713	103.63	102.96
180-Day Forward	.009875	.009942	101.27	100.59
Jordan (Dinar)	1.4104	1.4104	.7090	.7090
Kuwait (Dinar)	3.3478	3.3523	.2987	.2983
Lebanon (Pound)	.0006297	.0006297	1588.00	1588.00
Malaysia (Ringgit)	.3924	.3926	2.5485	2.5470
Malta (Lira)	2.8011	2.8050	.3570	.3565
Mexico (Peso)	....	....	....	....
Floating rate	.1316	.1325	7.6000	7.5475
Netherland (Guilder)	.6062	.6088	1.6495	1.6425
New Zealand (Dollar)	.6733	.6712	1.4852	1.4899
Norway (Krone)	.1559	.1568	6.4130	6.3761
Pakistan (Rupee)	.02915	.02915	34.300	34.300
Peru (new Sol)	.4237	.4237	2.3600	2.3600
Philippines (Peso)	.03821	.03821	26.170	26.170
Poland (Zloty)	.3898	.3924	2.5655	2.5485
Portugal (Escudo)	.006552	.006573	152.62	152.13
Russia (Ruble) (a)	.0002076	.0002077	4818.00	4815.00
Saudi Arabia (Rival)	.2666	.2666	3.7505	3.7505
Singapore (Dollar)	.7081	.7077	1.4122	1.4130
Slovak Rep. (Koruna)	.03355	.03355	29.810	29.810
South Africa (Rand)	.2590	.2625	3.8605	3.8095
South Korea (Won)	.001277	.001279	783.05	782.00
Spain (Peseta)	.008081	.008095	123.75	123.52
Sweden (Krona)	.1481	.1492	6.7521	6.7007
Switzerland (Franc)	.8322	.8371	1.2016	1.1946
30-Day Forward	.8348	.8397	1.1979	1.1909
90-Day Forward	.8398	.8448	1.1908	1.1837
180-Day Forward	.8469	.8538	1.1808	1.1712
Taiwan (Dollar)	.03637	.03637	27.497	27.495
Thailand (Baht)	.03970	.03972	25.192	25.174
Turkey (Lira)	.00001516	.00001523	65951.50	65678.50
United Arab (Dirham)	.2723	.2723	3.6725	3.6725
Uruguay (New Peso)	....	....	....	....
Financial	.1377	.1377	7.2600	7.2600
Venezuela (Bolivar)	.003509	.003509	285.00	285.00
Brady Rate	.002172	.002212	460.50	452.00
SDR	1.4687	1.4735	.6809	.6787
ECU	1.2585	1.2705	....	....

Special Drawing Rights (SDR) are based on exchange rates for the U.S., German British, French, and Japanese currencies. Source: International Monetary Fund.

European Currency Unit (ECU) is based on a basket of community currencies.

a-fixiang, Moscow Interbank Currency Exchange

SOURCE: *The Wall Street Journal*, March 1, 1996, p. C15.

Exhibit 9-3 ◆ The Foreign Exchange Market

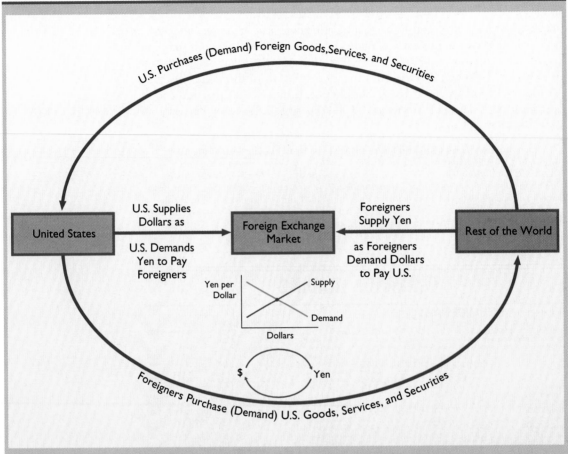

The foreign exchange market facilitates the trading of goods, services, and financial claims (securities) between countries. This global market is woven together by the market makers in foreign currencies—mostly, the foreign exchange departments of the largest commercial banks located in the world's major financial centers, such as New York, London, Frankfurt, and Tokyo. Without the ability to switch funds back and forth among the world's 100-odd currencies, Americans could neither dine in London nor sell hot dogs to Japanese tourists; neither buy imported video cassette recorders nor export computers.

the yen price of U.S. goods in Japan. The following formula provides the key to the entire question:

$$(9\text{-}4) \qquad \frac{\text{Yen (foreign) price}}{\text{of U.S. goods}} = \frac{\text{Dollar price of U.S. goods}}{\times \text{ Exchange rate}}$$

For example, as in Exhibit 9-5, if an IBM computer costs $1,500 in the United States, and the yen/dollar exchange rate is 100 yen—meaning $1 buys 100 yen, or equivalently from a foreign perspective, it takes 100 yen to buy $1—then the computer will cost 150,000 yen in Japan (1,500 × 100 yen = 150,000 yen).

Since \$1 = 100 yen and \$1 = 1.5 marks, then 100 yen = 1.5 marks.
   If 100 yen = 1.5 marks, we can find how much 1 yen is worth by dividing both sides of the equation by 100 to arrive at 1 yen = .015 marks.

$$100/100 \text{ yen} = 1.5/100 \text{ marks}$$

This is the marks/yen exchange rate.
   Likewise, we can find out how much 1 mark is worth by dividing both sides of the equation by 1.5 to arrive at 1 mark = 67 yen.

$$1.5/1.5 \text{ marks} = 100/1.5 \text{ yen}$$

Exhibit 9-4 ◆
Finding the Yen/Mark Exchange Rate

To see how the exchange rate affects the foreign demand for U.S. goods, and thus the quantity demanded of dollars, we need to examine what happens when the dollar appreciates or depreciates. Simply put, an appreciation of the dollar, from say 100 yen to 150 yen, would raise the yen price of the IBM computer from 150,000 yen to 225,000 yen (1,500 × 150 yen). Following standard tenets of consumer demand theory, we can reasonably assume that foreigners, ceteris paribus, will respond to the price rise by reducing the quantity demanded for U.S. computers/month (and U.S. goods, more generally), and thus reducing the quantity demanded of dollars/month.[9] Conversely, a depreciation of the dollar, from say 100 yen to say 50 yen, would lower the yen price of the IBM computer from the 150,000 yen to 75,000 yen (1,500 × 50 yen). Again, it is reasonable to assume that foreigners, ceteris paribus, will respond to the fall in the yen price by raising the quantity demanded for U.S. computers/month, (and U.S. goods, more generally), and thus raising the quantity demanded of dollars/month.[10]

To sum up to this point, the negative sign over the exchange rate in Equation (9-3) reflects the fact that, ceteris paribus, an appreciation of the dollar will raise the yen price of U.S. goods in Japan, and thereby reduce the quantity demanded for U.S. goods and thus the quantity demanded of dollars/month. The reverse is also true.

RECAP

The demand for dollars is directly related to foreign demand for U.S. goods, services, and securities. The quantity demanded of dollars/month is inversely related to the exchange rate, ceteris paribus. The foreign price of U.S. goods is equal to the dollar price of U.S. goods times the exchange rate.

---

[9]Actually, we are also assuming that the demand for computers, and U.S. products in general, is relatively elastic with regard to the exchange rate—that is, as the exchange rate goes up, ceteris paribus, quantity demanded/month goes down by a larger percent than the exchange rate goes up, causing total dollar expenditures to fall. This is a reasonable assumption in the long run, although demand for U.S. products may be relatively inelastic in the short run, causing the quantity demanded of dollars to increase as the exchange rate appreciates.

[10]Again, we are assuming that demand for U.S. computers is elastic with regard to the exchange rate—that is, as the exchange rate goes down, ceteris paribus, the percentage increase in quantity demanded/month is greater than the percentage decrease in the exchange rate and hence total dollar expenditures on U.S. computers by foreigners increase.

Exhibit 9-5 ◆
The Cost of an
IBM Computer in
Japan

If an IBM Computer costs \$1,500 and the yen/dollar exchange rate is 100, then in Japan, assuming transportation costs are zero, the computer will cost

$$\frac{1,500 \times 100 \text{ yen}}{150,000 \text{ yen}} \quad \text{or} \quad 1,500 \times 100 \text{ yen} = 150,000 \text{ yen}$$

If the exchange rate appreciates to 150, then the computer will cost

$$\frac{1,500 \times 150 \text{ yen}}{225,000 \text{ yen}} \quad \text{or} \quad 1,500 \times 150 \text{ yen} = 225,000 \text{ yen}$$

So much for the demand side—what about supply? In international financial markets, the supply of dollars originates from domestic purchases of foreign goods, services, and financial securities, as depicted in Equation (9-5).

$$(9\text{-}5) \quad \frac{\text{Supply}}{\text{of dollars}} = F(\overset{+}{\text{U.S. demand for foreign goods,}} \text{services, and securities})$$

As before, the plus sign over the expression means that U.S. demand for foreign goods, services, and securities, and the supply of dollars in the foreign exchange market are positively related. When the former rises, the latter rises. This results from the fact that when U.S. demand for foreign goods, services, and securities rises, the demand for yen also rises to pay for the foreign goods, services, and securities. But, how do U.S. residents get more yen? The short simple answer is by supplying more dollars! (Remember, dollars are being supplied to purchase yen to purchase foreign goods). You should be able to explain why when U.S. demand for foreign goods (in this case, Japanese goods) drops, the supply of dollars decreases.

The next step is to consider the question How is the quantity supplied of dollars/month affected by changes in the exchange rate? (Note that quantity supplied is the amount of dollars that will be supplied/month at a specific exchange rate.) The answer is: ceteris paribus, the quantity supplied is directly related to the exchange rate as shown in Equation (9-6).

$$(9\text{-}6) \quad \text{Quantity supplied of dollars/month} = F(\overset{+}{\text{Exchange rate}})$$

To see why the exchange rate and the quantity supplied of dollars/month are positively related, ceteris paribus, we need to examine how changes in the exchange rate affect U.S. demand for foreign goods, services, and securities. Focusing again only on goods for simplicity, we can draw on the previous discussion in Exhibit 9-1 and the discussion of Equation (9-1). The dollar price of foreign goods in the United States is equal to the yen price divided by the exchange rate. Thus, as shown in Exhibit 9–1, as the exchange rate rises, the dollar price of foreign goods falls. Accordingly, we would expect U.S. residents to raise the quantity demanded for foreign goods/month, and thus raise the quantity of dollars supplied/month to the foreign exchange market, ceteris paribus.[11] Conversely, a fall in the exchange rate, will raise the dollar price of foreign goods in the United States, lowering the quantity demanded for foreign goods/month and, thus lower the quantity supplied of dollars/month, ceteris paribus.[12]

We have established an inverse relationship between the quantity demanded of dollars/month and the exchange rate, ceteris paribus. In addition, given our assumptions, we have confirmed a direct relationship between the quantity supplied of dollars/month and the exchange rate, ceteris paribus. Now is a good time to look at Exhibit 9-6 where we graph these relationships. With both supply and demand curves in place, Exhibit 9-6 depicts the determination of the equilibrium exchange rate. The foreign exchange market "clears" at the exchange rate where the demand and supply curves intersect. At this exchange rate, the quantity demanded of dollars/month is equal to the quantity supplied of dollars/month and we have market equilibrium (at point A). At any other exchange rate, there is either a surplus or shortage of dollars. Market forces generated by the surplus or shortage will cause changes in the exchange rate, which will continue until equilibrium is reached.

RECAP

The supply of dollars is directly related to U.S. demand for foreign goods, services, and securities. The quantity supplied of dollars/month is directly related to the exchange rate, ceteris paribus.

We have made a good start. But our ultimate objective is to understand the causes and consequences of changes in the exchange rate resulting from changes in supply or demand. We need to examine the factors that can cause the supply and demand curves for dollars in the foreign exchange market to shift.

Changes in Supply and Demand and How They Affect the Exchange Rate

Starting with supply, let's begin our discussion of how and why changes in the supply of dollars in the foreign exchange market affect the exchange rate. The initial question that needs to be addressed is What factors, in addition to the exchange rate, could cause U.S. residents to alter their demand for foreign goods, services, and securities, and thus their supply of

---

[11] We are also making the reasonable assumption that, ceteris paribus, the quantity demanded of foreign goods/month by U.S. residents increases by a larger percentage than the percentage increase in the exchange rate. Thus, as the exchange rate appreciates, the quantity supplied of dollars/month also increases. This assumption, which is reasonable in the long run, may not hold in the short run.

[12] Again, we are assuming that, ceteris paribus, the percent decrease in quantity demanded of foreign goods/month is greater than the percent decrease in the exchange rate, causing the quantity supplied of dollars/month to fall.

Exhibit 9-6 ◆
The Market for
Dollars

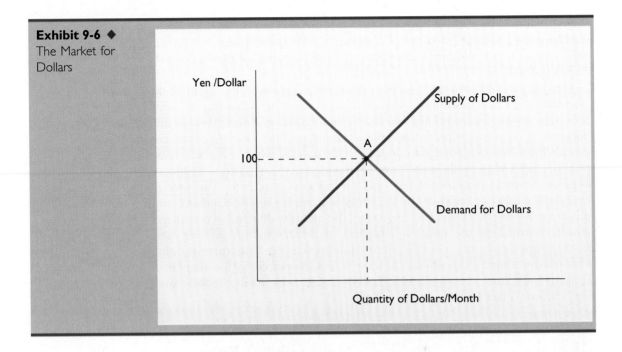

dollars into the foreign exchange market? In other words, what factors could cause the supply curve of dollars to shift? Previous research suggests that the following factors play a major role:

1. Changes in U.S. real income and changes in the supply of dollars are positively related. The reason is that as real income grows in the United States, households and firms have more funds to spend and save. Accordingly, they will demand more U.S. goods, services, and securities and more foreign goods, services, and securities. Thus, as U.S. real income grows, ceteris paribus, the supply of dollars—since Americans now have more income to spend on imports—will increase. Likewise, as U.S. real income falls, ceteris paribus, the supply of dollars will decrease.

2. Changes in the dollar price of U.S. goods relative to the dollar price of foreign goods produces changes in the supply of dollars. Simply put, if the prices of U.S. goods rise relative to the dollar prices of foreign goods, ceteris paribus, U.S. residents will demand more foreign goods and, therefore, supply more dollars into the foreign exchange market because foreign goods are now relatively cheaper than U.S. goods. Holding the exchange rate constant, what could cause such changes in relative prices? If you said a higher inflation rate in the United States than in Japan, you are right! Likewise, using similar reasoning, if the inflation rate in the United States falls relative to Japan, U.S. residents will supply fewer dollars in the foreign exchange market, ceteris paribus.

3. Changes in foreign interest rates relative to U.S. interest rates provide the third factor. As foreign interest rates rise relative to U.S. rates, ceteris paribus, foreign securities become relatively more attractive. Accordingly, U.S. residents will buy more foreign securities and, thus supply more dol-

lars. Likewise, if foreign rates fall relative to U.S. rates, the supply of dollars decreases, ceteris paribus.[13]

For a graphical presentation of the previous analytical discussion pertaining to supply, we refer you to Exhibit 9-7. Study it carefully before moving on to the discussion of the demand for dollars.

Utilizing the same logic and analytical framework already developed, the initial question that needs to be addressed is What factors, in addition to the exchange rate, could cause foreigners to alter their demand for U.S. goods, services, and securities, and thus their demand for dollars in the foreign exchange market? Remember that changes in the demand for dollars cause the demand curve for dollars to shift. We begin by identifying the major factors which can alter demand.

---

[13]To be more precise, U.S. residents will compare interest rates in the United States, i_{US}, with the expected return on foreign securities. The latter consists of the foreign interest rate, i_F, minus the expected appreciation (if any) in the value of the dollar.

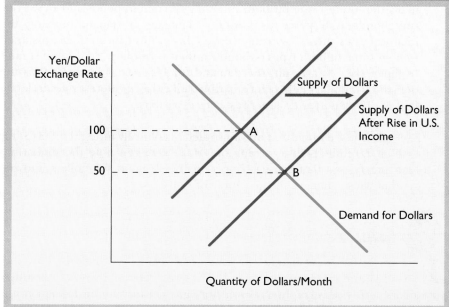

Exhibit 9-7 ◆
Changes in the Exchange Rate: The Role of Changes in Supply

This exhibit begins where Exhibit 9-4 left off, with an initial equilibrium exchange rate of 100 yen. Assume that the equilibrium is now disturbed by a change in one of the factors that affect the supply of dollars, say, a rise in U.S. income, increasing the supply of dollars as shown by the rightward shift of the supply curve. The new equilibrium at point B results in a depreciation of the dollar, as the equilibrium exchange rate falls from 100 yen to 50 yen. Note that a rise in the prices of U.S. goods relative to the dollar prices of foreign goods, or a rise in foreign interest rates relative to U.S. interest rates, would have produced a similar increase in supply and depreciation of the exchange rate.

1. Ceteris paribus, changes in foreign real income and the demand for dollars are positively related. For example, if foreign real incomes rise, ceteris paribus, foreign firms and households will have more funds to spend and save. Accordingly they will demand more of their own goods, services, and securities and also more imported goods, services, and securities. Thus, as foreign real incomes grow, ceteris paribus, the demand for dollars, reflecting the increased supply of yen to execute transactions, will grow.[14] Following similar reasoning, if foreign incomes fall, the demand for dollars also falls, ceteris paribus.

2. Ceteris paribus, changes in the yen price of U.S. goods relative to the yen price of foreign goods and the demand for dollars are negatively related. To see why, assume inflation accelerates in the United States, raising the dollar prices of U.S. goods, while there is no inflation in Japan. The U.S. inflation will raise the yen price of U.S. goods—refer back to Equation (9-4)—relative to the yen price of foreign goods. As a result, foreigners will demand fewer U.S. goods and, thus, fewer dollars, ceteris paribus. If U.S. inflation slows relative to inflation in Japan, foreigners will demand more dollars, ceteris paribus.

3. Changes in foreign interest rates relative to U.S. interest rates and the demand for dollars are also negatively related. For example, suppose initially the interest rate on both foreign government bonds and U.S. Treasury bonds is 6 percent. Portfolio managers in Japan, noticing the identical rates and recognizing the benefits of diversification, are assumed to hold some of both types of bonds in their portfolios. Now, interest rates in Japan rise. As a result, the demand for U.S. securities, and, thus the demand for dollars falls, ceteris paribus. Likewise, if interest rates in Japan fall, the demand for dollars rises, ceteris paribus.

The points just emphasized are illustrated graphically in Exhibit 9-8. Study this exhibit carefully before moving on. Make sure you note the similarities between the factors that cause changes in the demand for dollars and the factors that cause changes in the supply of dollars.

 RECAP

Increases in U.S. real income, in U.S. prices relative to foreign prices, and in foreign interest rates relative to U.S. interest rates all increase the supply of dollars, and vice versa. Increases in foreign real income, in foreign prices relative to U.S. prices, and in U.S. interest rates relative to foreign interest rates all increase the demand for dollars, and vice versa.

We have covered some important material in this section. Now is a good time to stop and see how we can use this analysis.

Imagine a situation in which the U.S. economy is expanding at a relatively slow pace, with real GDP growing at a 1–2 percent annual rate, compared to its potential growth trend of 2-1/2 to 3 percent. Against this background, the

---

[14]We are assuming that U.S. goods are not inferior goods. Recall from your principles class that demand for inferior goods, such as bologna, falls as income increases.

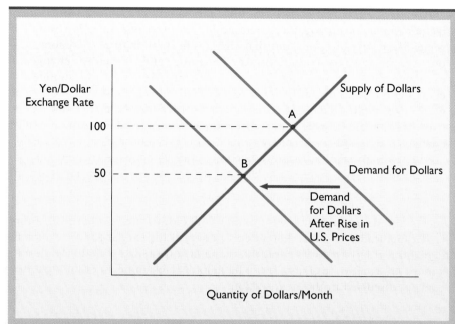

Exhibit 9-8 ◆
Changes in the
Exchange Rate: The
Role of Demand

From the initial equilibrium at point A, assume the equilibrium is disturbed by a change in one of the factors that affect the demand for dollars. In particular, suppose the yen price of U.S. goods rises relative to the yen price of foreign goods, because of inflation in the United States, reducing the demand for U.S. goods by foreigners as shown by the leftward shift of the demand curve. The new equilibrium (point B) results in a depreciation of the dollar from 100 yen to 50 yen. Note that a fall in foreign incomes or a rise in foreign interest rates relative to U.S. rates would have produced a similar leftward shift in the demand curve and depreciation of the dollar.

Federal Reserve decides that a rise in the aggregate demand for goods and services is in order. Accordingly, the Fed decides to pursue a more stimulative monetary policy by increasing bank reserves and the money supply, ceteris paribus. We know from previous discussions that such actions will initially tend to lower interest rates. The question we want to focus on in the present context is How will the fall in U.S. interest rates affect the exchange rate?

Believe it or not, the answer flows directly from the previous discussion in this section. Ceteris paribus, the fall in U.S. interest rates relative to interest rates in Japan will lead to a depreciation of the dollar—that is, a fall in the exchange rate. The reasoning is as follows: the fall in U.S. rates reduces the attractiveness of U.S. securities relative to foreign securities; as a result, foreigners will demand fewer U.S. securities and, thus, demand fewer dollars in the foreign exchange market, while U.S. residents will demand more foreign securities and thus, supply more dollars in the foreign exchange market. In sum, the depreciation of the dollar is a result of the reduction in the demand and rise in the supply of dollars induced by the Fed's actions. Try sketching out this scenario graphically as in Exhibits 9-7 and 9-8. If this policy works, output expands, income grows, and demand for imports rises, all of which potentially further weaken the dollar, especially if such a policy fuels expectations of inflation.

We have examined rather carefully the variety of domestic and foreign factors which, taken together, determine the exchange rate. We would be remiss if we failed to point out that changes in the things we held constant— our ceteris paribus conditions—are ongoing and therefore changes in exchange rates are ongoing. That is, in reality, demands and supplies are changing all the time, and therefore, equilibrium is a constantly moving target. For example, changes in U.S. real incomes lead to changes in other countries' real incomes, which lead to changes in U.S. incomes, which lead to changes in . . . and so on and so on. The interrelationships and interactions are increasingly significant as we become more globally intertwined.

The next logical question is How do developments in international trade and international finance, reflected in the transactions occurring in foreign exchange markets and changes in the exchange rate, affect the U.S. financial system and the output and factor markets? The short, albeit superficial, answer is "Dramatically." (Recall that a depreciation of the exchange rate causes the demand for exports to rise and the demand for imports to fall.) To develop a more informative response, it will be helpful to examine an often mysterious concept discussed in the next section.

Defining the Balance of Payments and Its Influence on the Exchange Rate, the Financial System, and the U.S. Economy

Balance of Payments
The record of transactions between the United States and its trading partners in the rest of the world over a particular period of time.

The supply and demand forces that determine the exchange rate are reflected in the balance of payments. Simply put, the **balance of payments** for the United States is the record of transactions between the United States and its trading partners in the rest of the world over a particular period of time, such as a year. It is a record of the international flow of funds for purchases and sales of goods, services, and securities.

The accounting procedure underlying the balance of payments is based on a standard double-entry bookkeeping scheme, such as that used by business firms or households to record receipts and payments. All this means is that receipts (sources of funds such as income or borrowing) will by definition equal payments (uses of funds). In the balance of payments all transactions that result in payments by foreigners to Americans are recorded as receipts; they are **credit** or plus items. Examples of such transactions would be foreign purchases of U.S. goods called **merchandise exports,** foreign purchases of U.S. securities (in effect, exports of securities), and expenditures by foreign tourists in the United States (in effect, exports of services). All transactions resulting in payments by Americans to foreigners are recorded as payments; they are negative or **debit** items. Examples of such payments include U.S. purchases of foreign goods called **merchandise imports,** U.S. purchases of foreign securities (in effect, imports of securities), and expenditures by U.S. residents traveling abroad.

Credit In the balance of payments, any item that results in a payment to foreigners by Americans.
Merchandise Exports Foreign purchases of U.S. exports.
Debit In the balance of payments, any transaction that results in a payment to foreigners by Americans.
Merchandise Imports U.S. purchases of foreign goods.

Over the years, government statisticians and analysts have found it useful to divide the balance of payments up into several parts by grouping together various types of receipts and payments into particular accounts. These particular accounts are discussed in the following sections and shown in Exhibit 9-9,

Exhibit 9-9 ◆

A Hypothetical and Simplified Balance of Payments for the U.S. Economy in the Year 2001 (in billions of dollars)

Account	Component	Receipts	Payments	Balance
		Uses of $ by Foreigners	Sources of $ by Foreigners	
Current	(2) Merchandise Exports	+$400		(4) Balance of Trade: (2) + (3) = −$200
	(3) Merchandise Imports		−$600	
	(5) Net Exports of Services	+$50		(6) Balance on Goods and Services: (4) + (5) = −$150 = Net Exports
	(7) Net Unilateral Transfers		−$30	(1) Balance on Current Account: (6) + (7) = −$180
Capital	(9) Capital Inflows	+$280		(8) Balance on Capital Account: (9) + (10) = $180
	(10) Capital Outflows		−$100	
		Total Uses	Total Sources	
Balance of Payments		+$730	−$730	(1) + (8) = 0

which provides a simplified and hypothetical balance of payments for the United States. Note that we will ignore for now government transactions in foreign currencies—the so-called "Official Reserve Account" of the balance of payments. This complication will be taken up when we discuss international policy in Chapter 24. This concept is actually less imposing than it may first seem, so let's take a closer look at the various accounts.

The Current Account

The **current account** brings together transactions that involve currently produced goods and services. It is composed of exports and imports of goods and services, and **net transfer payments.** The latter includes U.S. government aid to foreigners, as well as private charitable relief. The difference between merchandise exports and imports, often referred to in news reports as the **trade balance,** is taken by many observers to be an important indicator of a country's ability to compete internationally in the production and sale of goods. When merchandise imports are greater than exports, as they have been in the United States for some years, we have a **trade deficit,** suggesting some deterioration in international competitiveness. It could just as well suggest an improvement in our ability to attract foreign investment. The hypothetical figure in Exhibit 9-9, shows a U.S. trade deficit of (4) $200 billion. In contrast, if exports are greater than imports, as has been the case in Japan for some time, a country has a **trade surplus,** suggesting it is competing successfully in the world economy or that its citizens are heavily investing abroad.

When net exports of services (5), involving tourism, transportation, insurance, and financial services, are added to the trade balance (4), we get the **balance of goods and services** (6); this is nothing more than the "net exports"

Current Account Transactions that involve currently produced goods and services, including the balance of goods and services and net unilateral transfers.

Net Transfer Payments In the current account, the net amount of government aid to foreigners plus private charitable relief.

Trade Balance The difference between merchandise exports and imports.

Trade Deficit When merchandise imports are greater than exports.

Trade Surplus When merchandise exports are greater than imports.

Balance of Goods and Services Net exports of services plus the trade balance.

LOOKING FORWARD

European Currency Unit (ECU) A unit of account made up of a weighted basket of currencies of the countries in the European Monetary System.

A Common Currency for Europe?

In 1991, the Maastricht Treaty of European Union adopted a plan to move in the direction of establishing a single European currency by January 1, 1999.[a] The new currency, to be called the Euro, is to be based on the **European Currency Unit (ECU)**. At the present time, the ECU is an accounting unit made up of a weighted basket of currencies. The weights are determined by the gross domestic product and other real and financial variables of the participating countries. To convert from a system of many currencies to a single currency, fixed exchange rates between participating countries are being phased in, which would then be followed by the adoption of a single currency. In the phase-in period, countries must agree to maintain their exchange rates within a fixed range of the ECU and to allow rates to fluctuate collectively against the U.S. dollar and other currencies.

In order to establish a common currency, countries have to give up much autonomy over their own monetary policy. Countries must surrender their ability to change the money supply and to change exchange rates. In addition, according to the Maastricht Treaty, countries must meet the following criteria to participate:

1. A country's currency must have traded within the fixed range of the ECU for two years without having been devalued.
2. Inflation rates must be no more that 1.5 percent above the average of the three lowest inflation rates of the participating countries.
3. Long term interest rates on government debt have to be within two percentage points of the average of the three lowest long term interest rates among the EU countries.
4. The government's debt has to be less than 60 percent of GDP.
5. Annual budget deficits can be no more than 3 percent of GDP.

As of December, 1995, only Germany and Luxembourg met the above criteria. However, the Netherlands, Austria, Finland, and Ireland can probably meet them by 1997. France is very close also, but must reduce its government budget deficit. Some experts believe that a common currency could still be launched among a few countries with other countries joining at a later date as they meet the monetary and fiscal criteria. Assuming that France is able to meet the criteria, Germany and France, Europe's two largest economies, could be the nucleus of the new currency along with the other four countries that could also meet the criteria. Others suggest that some of the criteria could be relaxed.

Those who support the common currency do so because of the tremendous reductions in the transactions costs of making exchanges with a common currency. Such reductions translate to higher economic growth. According to the European Community, "removing foreign exchange costs could boost annual growth as much as .4 percent."[b]

[a]The following countries participate in the European Union: Austria, Belgium, Denmark, Finland, France, Germany, Great Britain, Greece, Ireland, Italy, Luxembourg, the Netherlands, Portugal, Spain, and Sweden. At this time, not all members of the European Union would participate in a single currency. Noticably absent from the list of countries that would take part are Great Britain and Italy.

[b]See "Now the Hard Part: Imposing a Common Currency," by Peter Gumbel, in *The Wall Street Journal*, July 28, 1995, p. A10.

component of GDP discussed earlier in Chapter 4. If net exports are negative, as they have been in the United States throughout the 1980s and early 1990s, then we are buying more goods and services from foreigners than they are buying from the United States. Relatively speaking, the result is that GDP, and thus production and employment in the United States, are lower than they would have been if net exports had been less negative, ceteris paribus.[15]

Adding the final item, net unilateral transfers (7), such as foreign aid, to the balance of goods and services, or net exports (6), yields the **balance on current account** (1), which in our example is in deficit by $180 billion.

Balance on Current Account The balance of goods and services plus net unilateral transfers.

The Capital Account

The **capital account** summarizes the financial flow of funds and securities between the United States and the rest of the world. The globalization of the U.S. financial system—nothing more than a fancy term to describe the tremendous growth of international lending and borrowing—is reflected in the surge of U.S. investment in international stocks, bonds, and mutual funds, which exceeded $300 billion in the early 1990s, and the increased borrowing abroad by U.S. entities to fund the U.S. current account deficit, which amounted to more than $400 billion during the same period.[16]

Capital Account The financial flow of funds and securities between the United States and the rest of the world.

Purchases of U.S. financial securities by foreigners and, more generally, borrowing from foreign sources by U.S. firms and residents result in **capital inflows** into the United States; these are receipt (credit or plus) items in the capital account, as shown in Exhibit 9-9. Purchases of foreign financial securities by U.S. residents and borrowing by foreigners from U.S. banks and other sources result in **capital outflows** from the United States; these are payment (debit or negative) items in the capital account. In our hypothetical example in Exhibit 9-9, the balance on capital account (8), equal to capital inflows (9) minus capital outflows (10), is in surplus by $180 billion—and the United States is experiencing a **net capital inflow.**

Capital Inflows Purchases of U.S. financial securities by foreigners and borrowing from foreign sources by U.S. firms and residents.
Capital Outflows Purchases of foreign financial securities by U.S. residents and borrowing by foreigners from U.S. banks and other domestic sources.
Net Capital Inflow Capital inflows minus capital outflows.

RECAP

The balance of payments for the United States is the record of transactions between the United States and its trading partners in the rest of the world over a particular time period. The balance of payments consists of the current account and the capital account. The current account brings together transactions involving currently produced goods and services. It includes the balance of goods and services and unilateral transfers. The capital accounts measures the flow of funds and securities between the United States and the rest of the world.

So much for the components of the balance of payments. What does all this have to do with the exchange rate and U.S. markets? Believe it or not,

---

[15] Don't let the terminology confuse you: less negative means a smaller trade deficit of goods and services, meaning either more exports or fewer imports, and hence, ceteris paribus, more U.S. jobs and production in either the domestic exporting industries or those industries competing with imports. If the United States was running a trade surplus of goods and services, the greater the surplus, the greater is the stimulus to U.S. GDP.
[16] "Hot Money," *Business Week,* March 20, 1995, p. 49.

LOOKING BACK

Devaluation Occurs when a country increases the units of currency that equal one ounce of gold under a fixed exchange rate system.

The Gold Standard

During the late 19th and early 20th centuries, the United States along with the other major world economies was on a gold standard that lasted about 30 years. Under the gold standard, the amount of currency in circulation was backed by gold. Each country defined their currency in terms of gold and agreed to buy or sell unlimited quantities of gold at the preestablished price called the *par value.*

A gold standard is a type of fixed exchange rate system. For example, if in the United States, one ounce of gold is equal to $20 and if in England, one ounce of gold is equal to 5 British pounds, then the pounds/dollar exchange rate is .25; that is, $1 equals .25 British pounds. The dollar and the pound will always trade in this fixed ratio as long as both countries redeem their currencies in gold at the par value.

The gold standard comes under strain if countries experienced different growth rates. For instance, if the United States grew faster than its neighbors, it would find that imports were increasing faster than exports. In the foreign exchange market, the quantity supplied of dollars would be greater than the quantity demanded. Foreigners would present the dollars to the U.S. Treasury to be redeemed for gold and the United States would lose its gold supply. As the United States lost gold, its money supply would fall with resulting depressing effects on output, jobs, and so on.

If policymakers wanted to keep the U.S. economy growing faster than the rest of the world, they would be under pressure to devalue their currency. A **devaluation** is an increase in the number of dollars that must be presented to the Treasury to receive an ounce of gold. Fear of devaluation would cause more of the currency to be presented for redemption. Holders of dollars would convert the dollars to gold, and, if devaluation did occur, convert the gold back to more dollars than what they started with! This exacerbated the gold loss and resulted in periodic financial crises as gold redemptions were suspended and the par values among currencies had to be redefined.

the various tools of analysis necessary to answer this question have already been developed. All we need to do is to bring them together.

The Balance of Payments and the Exchange Rate

Take a careful look at the bottom line in Exhibit 9-9. Not surprisingly, it says the balance of payments balances; the hypothetical $180 billion deficit in the current account (1) is exactly offset by a $180 billion surplus in the capital account (8).[17] Another way of saying the same thing is that the sum of all the items in the receipts-from-foreigners column is exactly equal to the sum of all the items in the payments-to-foreigners column.

To see why this equality is not just the result of bookkeeping gimmickry and why it relates directly to the determination of the exchange rate and the

---

[17]Remember, we are ignoring any official government transactions in foreign exchange markets until Chapter 24.

role it plays in our economy, note that all the items in the receipts' column represent foreign demands for U.S. goods, services, and securities—the very items that determine the demand for dollars in the foreign exchange market. Similarly, all the items in the payments' column represent U.S. demands for foreign goods, services, and securities—the very items that determine the supply of dollars in the foreign exchange market. Assuming that the exchange rate is flexible and free to move in response to any change in demand or supply, the exchange rate will move to that rate where the quantity of dollars demanded/month is equal to the quantity of dollars supplied/month. Put in terms of Exhibit 9-9, the equilibrium exchange rate will change until the sum of all the items in the receipts column, which reflects the quantity of dollars demanded/month, is equal to the sum of all the items in the payments column, which reflects the quantity of dollars supplied/month. While the uses of funds are always equal to the sources (for every source there is a use), the intended uses and sources may differ significantly, and these differences in plans and intentions move the exchange rate.

So what's the big deal? Imagine a situation in which U.S. interest rates rise as a result of the combination of a restrictive monetary policy and an expansionary fiscal policy—that is, cuts in taxes and increases in government spending, which expand the budget deficit. The restrictive monetary policy reduces the supply of funds while the expansionary fiscal policy increases the demand for funds. While examining the factors determining exchange rates, we learned that a rise in U.S. interest rates relative to foreign interest rates would tend to increase the foreign demand for U.S. securities, and thus, the demand for dollars, and would tend to reduce the U.S. demand for foreign securities, and thus the supply of dollars. In balance of payments terminology, the relatively higher U.S. interest rates would cause increased capital inflows and reduced capital outflows. The rise in the demand for dollars and the reduction in supply of dollars, in turn, would lead to an appreciation of the dollar.

But wait a minute. If capital inflows rise, and capital outflows fall, the capital account surplus in Exhibit 9-9 would rise. If nothing happens to the current account, the balance of payments would no longer balance. Obviously, something else must change. What happens is this: as the exchange rate appreciates a number of adjustments in foreign demands and U.S. demands will ensue; among the most important will be an increase in the current account deficit, reflecting, in large part, an increase in the trade deficit. To be more specific, the appreciation of the dollar will tend to raise the yen (foreign) price of U.S. goods abroad—refer back to Equation (9-6)—thus reducing U.S. exports. This will tend to lower the dollar price of foreign goods in the United States—refer back to Equation (9-1)—thus increasing U.S. imports and enlarging the trade deficit. From a purely domestic perspective, the rise in U.S. interest rates will attract foreign funds into the U.S. financial system, lead to an appreciation of the dollar, and tend to reduce foreign demand for U.S. output and, thus, U.S. employment relative to what it otherwise would have been.

See if you can write an alternative scenario in which U.S. interest rates fall as a result of expansionary monetary policy and contractionary fiscal policy. For those of you who want to check your answer, see Appendix 9-A where this type of scenario is given.

Again, evidence that such a scenario is not strictly hypothetical is provided in Exhibit 9-10. As a review of this historical experience suggests, international trade and finance do indeed matter for the U.S. economy and financial system.

Exhibit 9-10 ◆
Appreciation and
Depreciation:
Causes and
Consequences of
Dollar Exchange
Rate Movements
Since 1980

The internationalization or globalization of the U.S. economy became apparent to all over the first half of the 1980s. During 1979 and 1980 the international value of the dollar, as measured by an exchange rate index reached a record low.[a] By early 1985 the dollar had appreciated by about 60 percent from its low $[(150 - 95)/95 = 60$ percent$]$.

What caused this appreciation? Most experts agree it was a combination of several factors. First, in late 1979 and early 1980, the Fed embarked on a program of monetary restraint to lower the high inflation rate in the United States. This had the effect of raising interest rates in the United States—in particular, real interest rates—relative to real interest rates in the rest of the world. Second, in 1981, Congress, at President Reagan's urging, enacted a large tax cut. This tended to raise the expected earnings of U.S. firms and, thus, raise the expected return on financial investments, such as stocks, in the United States. At the same time, the tax cut, along with the failure to cut spending, enlarged the budget deficit, which also tended to raise real interest rates in the United States.

The rise in real interest rates in the United States induced by the monetary and fiscal policy actions, in turn, increased foreign demand for U.S. securities, and thus the demand for dollars, while reducing U.S. demand for foreign securities, and thus the supply of dollars in the foreign exchange market. The result was that the rise in U.S. real interest rates relative to real rates in the rest of the world helped produce a substantial appreciation of the dollar, as shown in the following graph. The continued appreciation

[a]An exchange rate index is essentially a trade-weighted average of the exchange rates between the dollar and the currencies of the United States' major trading partners.

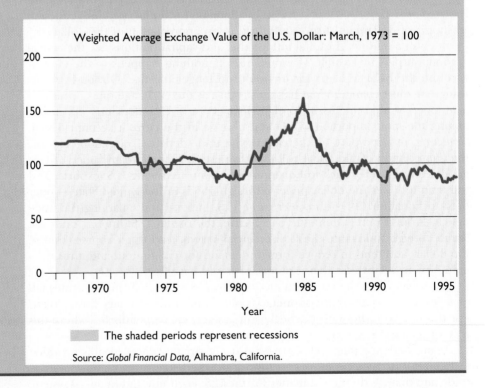

Weighted Average Exchange Value of the U.S. Dollar: March, 1973 = 100

Year

The shaded periods represent recessions

Source: *Global Financial Data*, Alhambra, California.

of the dollar in 1983 and 1984 is thought also to reflect the political and economic stability in the United States and thus the attractiveness of U.S. markets as a "safe haven" for financial investors.

The Value of the Dollar

What were the consequences of the dollar's appreciation? Simply put, the rise in the international value of the dollar had a dramatic effect on the U.S. economy. As one would predict, based on the discussion in this chapter, the appreciation tended to raise the prices of U.S. goods in foreign markets, discouraging exports, and tended to lower the prices of foreign goods in the United States, encouraging imports. The result was a substantial increase in the current account deficit. In other words by 1985, the United States was buying $150 billion more goods and services from abroad than it was selling abroad. Naturally, this deterioration in U.S. international competitiveness reduced employment and output in the United States relative to what it would have been.[b] With import prices lower, the appreciation also tended to dampen the inflation rate in the United States.

But the story does not end there! Beginning in early 1985, leaders of five major industrial nations—called the G-5 nations—agreed to a concerted effort to bring the value of the dollar down.[c] Central banks would supply dollars and demand their own currencies. The pressure to intervene came from the realization that the U.S. economy was in a severely uncompetitive position. The "overvalued" dollar was causing a record trade deficit and the loss of U.S. jobs in domestic exporting industries and industries that suffered from competition from imports. The value of the dollar did consistently fall not only due to central bank intervention in the late 1980s, but also due to falling U.S. interest rates that reduced the demand for U.S. securities. The trade deficit also fell, but not as fast or as far as economists had expected, given the depreciation of the dollar. By the early 1990s, the dollar was about 50 percent lower than in 1985, but a trade deficit, although reduced, still persisted. In the short run, the percentage decrease in the demand for foreign products was less than the percentage decrease in the exchange rate, although this condition was not expected to persist in the long run.

President Clinton came into office promising deficit reduction (contractionary fiscal policy). The Fed pursued a relatively easy monetary policy due to the weak economy and abated inflation fears. These policies produced even lower interest rates and further depreciation of the dollar. During mid-1993, despite these circumstances, the trade deficit again began to widen. No doubt this was due to the mild recovery of the U.S. economy and faltering foreign economies. The demand for imports increased in a recovering domestic economy while the demand for exports decreased in the stumbling foreign economies. With U.S. interest rates at low levels relative to the rest of the world, particularly in united Germany, some economists wondered how far or for how long the dollar would continue to fall.

[b]Actually, employment and output initially decreased but by 1985 both were on the rise. In 1985, the current account deficit was rising, the budget deficit was rising, GDP was rising, and employment was rising!

[c]The G-5 nations include Great Britain, France, Germany, the United States, and Japan.

Summary of Major Points

1. The exchange rate is the number of units of foreign money (currency) that can be acquired with one unit of domestic money. If the exchange rate rises, the dollar is said to have appreciated relative to other currencies. If the exchange rate falls, the dollar has depreciated.

2. The dollar price of foreign goods is equal to the foreign price of foreign goods divided by the exchange rate. The foreign price of U.S. goods is equal to the dollar price of U.S. goods multiplied by the exchange rate. Accordingly, a depreciation will lower the price of U.S. goods in foreign markets and raise the price of foreign goods in the United States. An appreciation will raise the price of U.S. goods in foreign markets and lower the price of foreign goods in the United States.

3. The exchange rate is a price—the price of one national currency in terms of another—and is determined by supply and demand. The demand for dollars in the foreign exchange market reflects the demand by foreign residents for U.S. goods, services, and financial claims. The supply of dollars comes from the demand by U.S. residents for foreign goods, services, and financial claims.

4. The quantity demanded of dollars/month is inversely related to the exchange rate. The demand for dollars is positively related to changes in foreign income and negatively related to changes in the foreign price of U.S. goods relative to the foreign price of foreign goods and to changes in foreign interest rates relative to U.S. interest rates. The quantity supplied of dollars/month is positively related to the exchange rate. The supply of dollars is positively related to changes in U.S. income, to changes in the dollar price of U.S. goods relative to the dollar price of foreign goods, and to changes in foreign interest rates relative to U.S. interest rates.

5. A depreciation of the dollar can result from one or more of the following: a fall in U.S. interest rates relative to foreign interest rates, a rise in U.S. income, a fall in foreign income, and/or more inflation in the United States than abroad. An appreciation of the dollar can result from one or more of the following: a rise in U.S. interest rates relative to foreign interest rates, a fall in U.S. income, a rise in foreign income, and/or less inflation in the United States than abroad.

6. The balance of payments is the record of transactions that keeps track of the flow of funds for purchases of goods, services, and securities between the United States and its trading partners in the rest of the world over a particular period of time. Ignoring official government transactions, it is comprised of the current account and the capital account.

7. If the exchange rate is flexible, and thus free to move in response to any change in the demand for or supply of dollars, the exchange rate will move to that rate where the quantity of dollars demanded/month is equal to the quantity of dollars supplied/month. Using balance of payments terminology, the equilibrium exchange rate will equalize the sum of all receipts from foreigners with all payments to foreigners. The balance of payments always balances.

8. If something, such as a policy-induced rise in U.S. interest rates relative to foreign interest rates, results in capital inflows and, say, a larger capital

account surplus, it will also result in an appreciation of the dollar. In turn, the appreciation of the dollar will tend, among other adjustments, to reduce U.S. exports of goods and services, and tend to raise U.S. imports. These adjustments will tend to produce a larger current account deficit, which will rebalance the balance of payments.

9. Over the first half of the 1980s, monetary and fiscal policies in the United States produced a rise in real interest rates in the United States relative to real interest rates in the rest of the world. In response, the dollar appreciated by an average of 80 percent against the currencies of the other major industrial countries. Among the most noteworthy consequences of this appreciation was a huge increase in the U.S. current account deficit. Over the last half of the 1980s and early 1990s, monetary and fiscal policies in the United States produced falling real interest rates relative to the rest of the world. Subsequently, a fall in U.S. interest rates helped produce a depreciation of the dollar and a reduction in the nation's current account deficit. Although the dollar fell dramatically in the early 1990s, the trade deficit persisted.

Key Terms

Appreciated
Balance on Current Account
Balance of Goods and Services
Balance of Payments
Capital Account
Capital Inflows
Capital Outflows
Credit
Current Account
Debit
Depreciated
Devaluation

European Currency Unit (ECU)
Exchange Rate
Foreign Currency (Money)
Foreign Exchange
Foreign Exchange Market
Merchandise Exports
Merchandise Imports
Net Capital Inflow
Net Transfer Payments
Trade Balance
Trade Deficit
Trade Surplus

Review Questions

1. Define exchange rate, foreign currency, and foreign exchange market.

2. Distinguish between a change in the quantity demanded of foreign exchange and a change in demand for foreign exchange. Do the same for the quantity supplied and supply of foreign exchange.

3. Explain the relationship between the supply of dollars in the foreign exchange market and debit items in the balance of payments. Do the same for the demand for dollars in the foreign exchange market and credit items in the balance of payments.

4. Defend the statement: The balance of payments always balances.

5. Explain the differences between the trade balance, the balance of goods and services, and the balance of payments.

6. How is a surplus in the current account related to a deficit in the capital account? How is a deficit in the current account related to a surplus in the capital account?

7. If interest rates in the United States were lower than in the rest of the world, would the United States be more likely experiencing a net capital inflow or net capital outflow? Ceteris paribus, would the current account be in surplus or deficit?

8. If the demand for U.S. exports falls, what will happen to the exchange rate? What will happen to the trade balance and the balance of goods and services?

9. What would happen to the exchange rate if foreigners decided to sell U.S. securities?

10. What is the difference between the trade balance and the current account balance?

Analytical Questions

11. If a hotel room in downtown Tokyo costs 20,000 yen per night and the yen/dollar exchange rate is 100, what is the dollar price of the hotel room? If the yen/dollar exchange rate increases to 150, what happens to the dollar price of the hotel room?

12. If a hotel room in downtown Los Angeles costs $100 per night, and the yen/dollar exchange rate is 100, what is the yen price of the hotel room? If the yen/dollar exchange rate increases to 150, what happens to the yen price of the hotel room?

13. Assume that the dollar appreciates by 10 percent in terms of the Mexican peso. Explain what happens to the dollar price of tequila from Mexico after the appreciation. Do the same in the case of a depreciation of the dollar.

14. If a bottle of rare French wine sells for 100 francs in Paris and the exchange rate is 2.5 francs, how much will the bottle of wine sell for in New York City? (Ignore transportation costs, etc.)

15. Use graphs to show what happens to the demand for and supply of dollars in the foreign exchange market if
    a. Domestic income rises.
    b. Foreign income rises.
    c. Domestic inflation rises relative to foreign inflation.
    d. Domestic interest rates rise relative to foreign interest rates.

16. Use graphs to demonstrate that when both domestic and foreign incomes are rising, we cannot be sure of the direction of exchange rates.

17. If merchandise exports are $600 and merchandise imports are $500, what is the trade balance?

18. If there is a surplus of $100 in the capital account, there are no unilateral transfers, and there is a $50 deficit in the net exports of services, what is the trade balance?

19. If $1 = 150 yen and 1 yen = 75 British pounds, what is the pound/dollar exchange rate? What is the dollar/pound exchange rate?

20. If the yen/dollar exchange rate is 125, how much will 25,000 yen cost? If the exchange rate appreciates to 150, how much will the 25,000 yen cost?

21. If the yen/dollar exchange rate is 125, how many yen will $15,000 be worth? If the exchange rate depreciates to 100, how many yen will $15,000 be worth?

22. Go to today's *Wall Street Journal* and find the marks/dollar exchange rate. Has the dollar appreciated or depreciated since Exhibit 9-2 was written (March 1, 1996)?

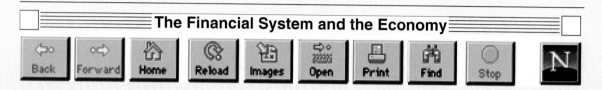

The Financial System and the Economy

1. The Holt page (http://metro.turnpike.net/holt/index.html) provides daily information on major exchange rates. From the internet side (http://metro.turnpike.net/holt/testcurr.htm) examine the pound/dollar exchange rate as well as the mark/dollar exchange rate. Access the historic data chart (http://metro.turnpike.net/holt/loft-gw.zone.org/jason/CUSTOM.html) to determine whether the dollar has appreciated or depreciated since January 1995.

2. Currently monthly trade statistics may be accessed at the following site: (http://www.census.gov/ftp/pub/foreign-trade/www/ustrade.html). What is the current trade balance?

Suggested Readings

Although we ignored (for the time being) government transactions in foreign currencies, the *Federal Reserve Bulletin* reports on "Treasury and Federal Reserve Foreign Exchange Operations" on a quarterly basis. We cite these articles here because they entail an in-depth discussion of the reasons for recent movements in exchange rates.

Are you interested in sampling Big Macs around the world? (We understand that local customs and tastes dictate the spices.) Refer to *The Economist,* which since 1986 has been tracing the dollar price of Big Macs around the world. For the 1994 report, see "Big MacCurrencies," *The Economist,* April 9, 1994, p. 88. Information about the *Economist* can be found on the internet by accessing (http://www.enews.com/magazines/economist).

We also suggest two free publications from the New York Fed. Or you may order or browse *Fedpoints* over the internet by accessing (http://www.ny.frb.org/pihome/fedpoint/). They are *Basics of Foreign Trade and Exchange* (revised in late 1992) and *Balance of Payments* (Fedpoints 40). For those of you who prefer comic books, request *The Story of Foreign Trade and Exchange.* All are available by writing the Federal Reserve Bank of New York, Public Information Department, 33 Liberty Street, New York, NY 10045.

For two articles that look at some other factors affecting international trade and investment, see Harry Harding and Edward J. Lincoln, "Rivals or Partners? Prospects for U.S.–Japan Cooperation in the Asia-Pacific Region," *The Brookings Review,* Summer 1993; and Martin Baily, "Made in the U.S.A.: Productivity and Competitiveness in American Manufacturing," *The Brookings Review,* Winter 1993. You may order this article over the internet by accessing (http://www.brook.edu/PUB/REVIEW/REV_HP.HTM).

For an article that concludes that exchange rate volatility reduces international trade, but only by a small amount, see Vikram Kumar and Joseph A. Whitt, "Exchange Rate Variability and International Trade," *Economic Review of the Federal Reserve Bank of Atlanta,* May 6, 1992, pp. 17–32.

APPENDIX 9-A

Expansionary Monetary Policy and Restrictive Fiscal Policy: A Scenario

The example in the body of the chapter considered the case in which U.S. interest rates rose as a result of restrictive monetary policy and expansionary fiscal policy. In this appendix, we review the opposite scenario.

Imagine a situation in which U.S. interest rates fall as a result of the combination of an expansionary monetary policy (increasing the supply of funds) and a restrictive fiscal policy—that is, increases in taxes and decreases in government spending, which reduce the budget deficit and, therefore, the demand for funds. While examining the factors determining exchange rates in Section 9.2, we learned that a fall in U.S. interest rates relative to foreign interest rates would tend to decrease the foreign demand for U.S. securities and thus, the demand for dollars—that is, decrease capital inflows using balance of payments terminology—and would tend to increase the U.S. demand for foreign securities, and, thus the supply of dollars—that is, increase capital outflows. The fall in demand and increase in supply, in turn, would lead to a depreciation of the dollar.

But wait a minute. If capital inflows fall, and capital outflows rise, the capital account surplus in Exhibit 9-9 would fall. If nothing happens to the current account, the balance of payments would no longer balance. Obviously, something else must change. What happens is this: as the exchange rate depreciates a number of adjustments in foreign demands and U.S. demands will ensue; among the most important will be a decrease in the current account deficit, reflecting, in large part, a decrease in the trade deficit. To be more specific, the appreciation of the dollar will tend to lower the foreign price of U.S. goods abroad—refer back to Equation (9-4) thus increasing U.S. exports. This will tend to raise the dollar price of foreign goods in the United States—refer back to Equation (9-1), thus decreasing U.S. imports and reducing the trade deficit. From a purely domestic perspective, the fall in U.S. interest rates will divert foreign funds from the U.S. financial system, lead to a depreciation of the dollar, and tend to increase foreign demand for U.S. output, and thus U.S. employment relative to what it otherwise would have been.

10

Futures, Options, and Swaps: Modern Ways to Manage Risk

> *Never let the future disturb you. You will meet*
> *it, if you have to, with the same weapons of*
> *reason which today arm you against the present.*
> —Marcus Aurelius—

Learning Objectives

After reading this chapter, you should know:

◆ The difference between a forward transaction and a futures contract

◆ The scope and nature of organized financial futures and options markets

◆ The relationship between spot and futures prices

◆ The difference between put and call options

◆ How swaps can also be used to reduce risks

◆ The reasons for the astounding growth of financial futures, options, and swaps

A Single Solution

It is 5:10 P.M. on Friday, the last day of a month in late 1995. The meeting with the CEO and his staff has run later than usual and a sense of uneasiness pervades the room. Doz-All, a newly emerging conglomerate, is involved in diversified financial and manufacturing areas. The mortgage banking division has committed to make $10 million in loans at 8 percent to be funded in 60 days; $25 million in bonds issued ten years ago for startup money are maturing in three months and the company plans to pay off the existing bondholders by issuing new bonds. The newly formed international division is converting $20 million to Japanese yen to invest in Japanese securities over the next few months. The stock adviser states that although the corporation has a diversified portfolio, there is a general fear that the market may be heading down.

All of these situations expose the corporation to risks—the risks that interest rates (and hence bond prices), stock prices, or foreign exchange rates will move in an unexpected direction causing the corporation to experience a loss. The senior vice president appears tired. She cannot help but perceive that the risks associated with everyday business seem to have escalated in recent years.

The past two decades have brought more volatility to commodity prices, as well as to interest rates, stock prices, and exchange rates. This greater volatility has created greater risks.[1] The chief financial officer is a young business school graduate that the senior management has come to rely on. He assures them that although it will cost money, there are ways to deal with the increased risk. In this case, however, his recommendations are the source of the tension felt in the room. To reduce the risk exposure in the preceding cases, he is recommending that the corporation use the financial futures or options markets. In days long past, futures and options on agriculture products and commodities were considered to be highly risky. Could these new financial futures and options markets that have emerged in the past 20 years actually be used to reduce or manage the risk inherent in everyday business?

In this chapter, we explore financial futures, options, and swaps. We shall see that risk-averse financial intermediaries and corporations increasingly use these markets in their everyday business for just this purpose—that is, to reduce the risks associated with price fluctuations. The adage ''necessity is the mother of invention'' aptly applies because financial futures, options, and swaps have experienced incredible growth in the past two decades in response to increased price volatility.

Forward Transactions and Financial Futures

Forward Transactions
Transactions in which the terms, including price, are completed today for a transaction that will occur in the future.

Forward transactions deal with completing today the terms for a transaction that will occur on a specified date in the future. Financial intermediaries, acting as brokers or agents, often link two parties in a forward

---

[1] For example, small changes in interest rates can lead to large changes in the prices or value of long-term fixed rate assets such as bonds or mortgages.

transaction. For example, suppose a farmer borrows from a bank to cover the operating expenses of growing 10,000 bushels of wheat. To cover the costs incurred today and to make an adequate profit, the farmer must be able to sell the wheat for $50,000 in three months. At the present time, 10,000 bushels are selling for $50,000 but the farmer is worried that the price of wheat could fall between now and harvest time. If the price does fall, the farmer will incur a loss.

At the same time, the owners of a bakery that mills its own flour are planning to produce bread over the course of the next holiday season, and need to know how much wheat will cost in the future—say, in three months. This knowledge can guarantee a profit from selling the bread to the gourmet bakeries they are contracting with today.

For a fee, an intermediary links up the farmer, who is selling wheat, and the bakery owners, who are buying wheat, and they come to terms (including price) today for delivery of wheat in three months. Such a forward transaction will remove the risk of an adverse price change for both parties. In this case, the farmer is protected from a price decrease, and the bakery is protected from a price increase. Note that the farmer needs to sell the wheat on a future date and the bakery needs to buy the wheat on a future date. Both parties have successfully reduced or **hedged** their risks through entering into the forward transaction.

Hedged Reduced risk.

Forward transactions can reduce the risks of future price changes, which reduce profit. But, as with most things in life, appearances may not reveal the whole picture. Even though the risk is reduced for both the farmer and the baker, two problems remain:

1. It may be difficult to find partners; the transaction costs may be high and outweigh the possible gain.
2. One party to the agreement may default, that is, not keep its part of the agreement.

In the previous example, the farmer may not deliver, particularly if the spot price (the price for immediate delivery) three months from now is higher than the forward price. The farmer could sell the wheat in the spot market for a higher price rather than fulfilling the forward transaction. On the other hand, if the spot price is lower, the bakery may renege on the agreement and buy at the lower price in the spot market rather than honoring the forward agreement.[2] Getting compliance in either case may require legal action or be impossible altogether.

But all hope is not lost! To minimize the costs and risks involved with arranging forward transactions, standardized agreements called **futures contracts** have been developed. Because agriculture and commodity markets historically experience large price fluctuations, futures evolved more than a century ago in these markets. In the case of agriculture products, with a relatively stable demand, price fluctuations are related to weather—bad weather causing greatly reduced supply and hence higher prices, and vice versa. Prices of commodities such as oil, copper, and gold fluctuate because of large changes in supply or demand.

Futures Contracts Standardized agreements in agriculture and commodity markets to trade a fixed amount of the asset on specific dates in the future at a price determined today.

---

[2] Recall that the spot market is the market for immediate completion of the transaction and the spot price is the price for immediate delivery.

Financial Futures Markets
Organized markets that trade financial futures, including the Chicago Board of Trade, the Chicago Mercantile Exchange, the London International Financial Futures Exchange, and so on.
Financial Futures Standardized contracts between two parties to trade financial assets at a future date, in which the terms including the price of the transaction are determined today.

During the past 20 years, prices of financial securities, stocks, and foreign currencies have become more unstable. Consequently, **financial futures markets,** which trade financial futures, appeared and are now used by most major financial institutions and other large corporations to manage risk.

Financial futures are contracts between two parties to trade financial assets at a future date, in which the terms (including the price) of the transaction are determined today. Like agriculture and commodity futures, financial futures can be used to reduce the risk associated with future price changes. In the case of financial futures, these contracts reduce the risk associated with price changes of financial instruments.

Financial futures markets trade a wide variety of contracts in underlying assets such as government securities (Treasury bills, notes, and bonds), stock market indexes, Eurodollars, and numerous foreign currencies.[3] They are traded on major exchanges around the world. For example, financial futures are traded on the Chicago Board of Trade, the Financial Instrument Exchange Division of the New York Cotton Exchange, the International Monetary Market of the Chicago Mercantile Exchange, the London International Financial Futures Exchange, the Sydney Futures Exchange, and the Singapore International Monetary Exchange. Futures markets for various currencies and U.S. government securities are available virtually 24 hours a day, somewhere in the world. Look at Exhibit 10-1 at this time for a listing of the most actively traded financial futures, the exchanges that trade them, and the contract size that is traded.

A futures contract trades a fixed amount of the asset for delivery on specific dates in the future. For example, Treasury bond futures trade in contracts of $100,000 face value for delivery in March, June, September, and December, over the course of the next two years. There are eight prices today for delivery of $100,000 of Treasury bonds on the eight future dates. Likewise, Treasury bill futures, which trade in contract amounts of $1,000,000, are also available for delivery on the same eight dates at prices set today. Note that the futures contract can be bought or sold on any given day between now and the future delivery date. The quandary is that the spot price on the delivery date may be different from the futures price agreed upon today.

The seller of a September $1,000,000 T-bill future has the right and obligation to deliver $1,000,000 in T-bills in September for a price set today. The purchaser of the $1,000,000 September T-bill future has the right and obligation to buy $1,000,000 in T-bills in September at a price set today. Hence, both parties know the terms of a transaction that will occur in September, a point in time in the future, and the risk to either party of a price change between now and then is eliminated.[4]

---

[3] As we saw in Chapter 6, Eurodollars are dollar-dominated deposits held abroad.

[4] Note that the buyer rarely takes physical possession of the securities or any futures contract instrument for that matter on the delivery date. Likewise, the seller rarely delivers. If the price changes, the buyer or seller merely settles up financially for any changes in value, usually by executing an opposing transaction. For example, if Suzanne purchases a futures contract, rather than taking delivery on the delivery date, she can sell a futures contract involving the same asset for the same delivery date. The sale effectively cancels out the purchase. Or, if she had sold a futures contract, she can purchase a futures contract with the same delivery date, effectively canceling out the sale. Most futures contracts are settled in this manner—purchases in the futures market are reversed by sales in the futures market; sales in the futures market are reversed by purchases in the futures market. This fact does not alter the analysis, however.

If the price of T-bills rises between now and September, the seller has given up an opportunity to make a profit because she agrees to sell at the lower futures price established today. If the spot price falls in September, the buyer has given up the right to purchase the securities at the lower price in the spot market because he agrees to the higher futures price today. Without the futures contract, however, either party could lose if the price changes in an adverse direction. Without the agreement, the seller would be worse off if the price falls and the buyer would be worse off if the price goes up.

Let's consider a simple numerical example. Assume the futures price is $96,000 for the delivery of $100,000 of Treasury bonds next December and the seller agrees to deliver and the buyer agrees to pay this much. (Make sure that you are clear that December is the delivery date of the securities and not the maturity date of the securities, which may be several years hence.) When December actually arrives, if the spot price is $97,000, the seller still must sell the Treasury bonds for $96,000, even though he could have sold them for $97,000 in the spot market. The buyer still pays $96,000 for the Treasury bonds, even though she would have had to pay $97,000 in the spot market. In this example, the seller is worse off by $1,000 and the buyer is better off by $1,000.[5]

However, if when December arrives, the spot price is $95,000, then the seller gets to sell at $96,000, even though the spot price is only $95,000. The buyer has to pay $96,000 even though she could have paid $95,000 to buy in the spot market. The seller is better off and the buyer is worse off.

The point is that at the time of the agreement, no one knows what the spot price will be on the future date. Both were willing to accept the known outcome as opposed to an uncertain future spot price even though after the fact one could have been better off without the agreement. Now is a good time to read Exhibit 10-2 on how a small credit union can reduce risk by entering the futures market.

So far, we have been discussing futures through which parties to the agreement are hedging, or reducing the risk of a price change in the future. As we saw in Chapter 6, futures markets can also be used for speculation. Consider the case where ABC Government Securities (a firm that specializes in trading government securities) believes that the spot price of T-bills is going to be much higher in September than today's futures price. If ABC holds this belief firmly, it can put its money behind the belief and buy a futures contract. If ABC is correct, it can resell the futures contract at the higher spot price on the delivery date. Contrarily, if the firm believes the price will be lower, it can sell a futures contract to make its profit.[6] Futures prices are reported daily in most major newspapers. Now would be a good time to read Exhibit 10-3 on "Cracking the Code of Futures Prices."

Because financial futures are written only in standardized contract amounts for delivery on a few specific dates, a perfect offsetting transaction between the buyer and seller, as in forward markets, is rarely made. For example, suppose a bank has loans that will be repaid next August and suspects that interest

---

[5] Remember, the securities are not usually physically delivered.

[6] In case you want to check, the answer is: if they guess right, they can go into the spot market in September and purchase the T-bills at the lower price for immediate delivery to the buyer of the future. The difference between the futures price and what they pay in the spot market is their profit—and they're good at counting this.

Exhibit 10-1 ◆
Futures, Exchanges
That Trade
Financial Futures,
Minimum Amounts,
and Open Interest

Consider for a moment the many types of futures markets that exist: grains and oil seeds (including corn, oats, soybeans, wheat, barley, flaxseed, and canola); livestock and meat (including cattle, hogs, and pork bellies); food and fiber (including cocoa, coffee, sugar, cotton, and orange juice); metals and petroleum (including copper, gold, platinum, palladium, silver, crude oil, heating oil, gasoline, natural gas, brent crude, and gas oil); interest rates (including Treasury bonds, five-year Treasury notes, two-year Treasury notes, 30-day federal funds, Treasury bills, one-month LIBOR, Muni Bond index, Eurodollars, Sterling, Long Gilt, Euromark, Euroswiss, German government bonds, and Italian government bonds); currency (including Japanese yen, German deutschemarks, Canadian dollars, British pounds, Swiss francs, Australian dollars, and U.S. dollar indexes); stock indexes (including S&P 500 Index, M&P Midcap400, Nikkei 220 Stock Average, NYSE Composite Index, and Major Market Index).*

Grain and commodities futures have been around for some 100 years. The financial futures including interest rate, currencies, and stock index futures are a relatively recent innovation (during the last 20 years) that have experienced tremendous growth.

The table below shows the major financial futures, the contract size, the futures exchange, and the total open interest as of April 8, 1996.

*Because we believe you may find it interesting, we include in our list both financial and other futures. Since these are information items only, we are not defining all the terms.

Type of Future	Contract Size	Exchange[a] at which Trading Occurs	Open Interest
			April 8th, 1996
Interest Rates			
U.S. Treasury bonds	$100,000	CBOT	371,397
U.S. Treasury bonds	$ 50,000	MCE	N/A
Municipal bond index	$100,000	CBOT	11,099
U.S. ten-year Treasury notes	$100,000	CBOT	287,093

rates are heading down. The bank may have to reinvest the funds at a lower rate. The bank can buy a September T-bill futures contract today to hedge this risk. If interest rates do move down, the funds will be reinvested in August at a lower rate, but the reduction in earnings from the level the bank is presently receiving will be at least (partially) offset by the profit made on the September futures contract. (Recall that T-bills are sold at a discount, and, like other securities, if interest rates go down, the price of the newly issued T-bills goes up.) Even though the standardized contracts do not provide an exact match (either by amount or by date), they do provide an offsetting transaction that reduces risk. Because a perfect match need not be found, the high transactions costs of finding a unique trading partner as in forward agreements are greatly reduced.[7]

---

[7]Because the contracts are standardized with respect to quality (90-day T-bills, 15-year Treasury bonds, etc.), and quantity ($1,000,000 and $100,000 contract sizes), and because volume is large, brokerage fees for buying and selling futures are relatively small.

Type of Future	Contract Size	Exchange[a] at which Trading Occurs	Open Interest
			April 8th, 1996
U.S. five-year Treasury notes	$100,000	CBOT	193,019
U.S. two-year Treasury notes	$200,000	CBOT	16,526
U.S. Treasury notes	$1 million	IMM	13,603
Eurodollar rates	$1 million	IMM	2,404,532
Thirty-day interest rate	$5 million	CBOT	17,911
LIBOR—one month	$3 million	CME	24,418
Currencies			
U.S. dollar index	500 × index value	FINEX	6,498
Japanese yen	12.5 million yen	IMM	78,243
German mark	125,000 D. mark	IMM	55,592
Canadian dollar	$100,000 Canadian	IMM	44,546
British pound	£62,500 British	IMM	49,326
Swiss franc	125,000 S. francs	IMM	30,172
Australian dollar	$100,000 Australian	IMM	13,932
European currency unit	1000,000 ECU	FINEX	N/A
Stock Indexes			
S&P 500	500 × Index	CME	177,435
NYSE Composite Index	500 × Index	NYFE	2,930
Major Market Index	500 × Index	CBOT	169
K.C. Value Line Index	500 × Index	KC	538
K.C. Mini Value Line	100 × Index	KC	3,031
Nikkei 225	5 × Index	CME	28,281
Price Indexes			
Commodity Research Bureau (CRB) Index	500 × Index	NYFE	2,135

[a]Exchanges: CBOT (Chicago Board of Trade); CME (Chicago Mercantile Exchange); FINEX (Financial Instrument Exchange Division of New York Cotton Exchange); IMM (International Monetary Market of the Chicago Mercantile Exchange); KC (Kansas City Board of Trade); MCE (MidAmerica Commodity Exchange); and NYFE (New York Futures Exchange).

SOURCE: Barrons, April 8, 1996.

The futures price is set by bidding and offering in an auctionlike setting on the floor of the exchange. Each financial instrument that is traded usually has its own **pit** (trading area on the floor) where authorized brokers gather to buy and sell for their customers. Bidding and asking prices (to buy or sell) are called out until the brokers become aware of the prices in the market. The most favorable transactions (from the point of view of both the buyers and sellers) are consummated. Once an agreement is struck in the pit, the transaction becomes depersonalized and the agents of the buyer and seller never meet again for that transaction. Rather, the exchange operates a **clearinghouse,** which takes on the responsibility of enforcing the contract. Both the buyer and the seller rely on the clearinghouse to execute the transaction. Specifically, the seller looks to the clearinghouse to deliver and the buyer looks to the clearinghouse to pay the amount due on the delivery date. In this way, the default risk associated with a forward transaction is greatly reduced since the obligation is taken on by the clearinghouse of the exchange.

Pit The trading area on the floor of an exchange where authorized brokers gather to buy and sell for their customers.

Clearinghouse After the agreement is struck, the part of the exchange that takes on the responsibility of enforcing the contract.

Exhibit 10-2 ◆
A Credit Union
Enters the Futures
Market

A small credit union has made some two-year auto loans. To fund these loans, the credit union uses one-year time deposits from its members. That is, it borrows money from its depositors and then re-lends this money to some other members who are purchasing cars. In one year, these time deposits will have to be repaid before the auto loans are repaid. In a year, the credit union plans to induce current time depositors to deposit for another year or to attract additional one-year time deposits to replace those that are withdrawn.

The profit the credit union makes is the difference between what it earns on its two-year loans and what it pays for its one-year deposits. In a year, the credit union will have to issue new one-year time certificates to fund the loans. The cost of the new time certificates will depend on the interest rate at that time. If the interest rate goes up, this will reduce the profit of the loans. The risk that the interest rate will rise causing the credit union to incur a loss is called *interest rate risk.*

To protect itself from an interest rate increase, the credit union can sell a T-bill future today. The T-bill future is a contract that obliges the credit union to deliver T-bills one year from now at a price determined today. The credit union does not own the T-bills but will buy them in the spot market in one year. If the interest rate has gone up, the credit union will be able to buy the T-bills at a lower spot price than what it sold the T-bill future for and hence make a profit. The profit made on the T-bill future offsets the increased costs of paying a higher rate on the new one-year time deposits.

The T-bill future is a way that the credit union has hedged or reduced the risk that the interest rate paid to depositors would increase while the interest rate earned on loans would remain unchanged. Note in this example, if the credit union purchases the future and if interest rates go down, then the T-bills in the spot market will cost more than the futures contract and the credit union will incur a loss on the futures contract. However, the credit union will be able to issue the new one-year time deposits at the lower rate and therefore be no worse off than at the start. Futures markets can protect lenders from losses resulting from unexpected increases in interest rates but they also limit gains if interest rates move in the other direction. In this case, if interest rates move down, the credit union passes up the chance to be better off. Of course, if rates fall, the borrowers will refinance their cars and the credit union will be stuck with the loss on the futures and they will be without the lock on high-rate loans.

Performance Bond A bond required by the exchange of both the buyer and seller of a futures agreement to insure that both parties abide by the agreement.
Margin Requirement The amount that brokers must collect from their customers before they make any futures purchases or sales.

The futures contract is an agreement to make a trade at a later date. The clearinghouse of the organized exchange guarantees that the terms will be met. To facilitate this guarantee, the exchange requires buyers and sellers of futures to put up a **performance bond,** called a **margin requirement,** set by the exchange. Brokers are required to collect margin requirements from their customers before they make any futures purchases or sales. Note that the performance bond or margin is required of both the seller and buyer. A final example of how financial futures can be used to hedge is given in Exhibit 10-4.

In summary, we have seen that the primary reason financial futures markets experienced such spectacular growth in the past 20 years is because the world has become a much more volatile place and financial futures can be used to reduce risks associated with this volatility. Because interest rate swings are larger, the prices of government securities (or the value of any fixed rate asset) oscillates more rapidly and over a broader range. Stock prices now fluctuate over a wider range and, as we saw in Chapter 9, flexible exchange rates have increased the movement of currency prices while foreign trade in goods, services, and securities has escalated sharply. Futures markets may be used to hedge all of these risks. We now turn to how the futures price is determined.

RECAP

Financial futures are standardized contracts between two parties to trade financial assets at a future date in which the terms of the agreement including the price are determined today. Financial futures markets exist for government securities, stock market indexes, Eurodollars, and foreign currencies. The buyer and the seller both have obligations and rights. Financial futures can be used to hedge the risk of future changes in prices or to speculate. Organized exchanges trade the standardized contracts.

Determining the Futures Price

As we have seen, financial futures are traded each day on exchanges around the world. The exchange delivers or accepts for delivery the futures contract at the specified future time and place at a price agreed upon today. The buyer or seller merely accepts the risk of a price change of the contract and agrees to pay off any financial losses or to receive any financial gains.

Looking at Exhibit 10-2, again, we see that there are several different futures prices depending on the expiration date of the futures contract. The question we will attempt to answer in this section is How are those prices determined? We hope that buzzers and alarms are going off in your head and your immediate response is "supply and demand." Of course, you are right! But, in this case, it may prove beneficial to look a little more closely at what determines the supply and demand for financial futures and hence, their prices.

Perhaps the first and most important thing to point out is that the futures price and the spot price are highly correlated—that is, they move up and down together. This is not accidental, but rather due to actions of individuals called **arbitrageurs** who seek a riskless profit.

Consider what happens if a futures contract for Treasury bonds to be delivered in three months is much higher than the present spot price. An arbitrageur could purchase the Treasury bonds in the spot market while selling a futures contract. She could hold the bonds purchased in the spot market for delivery at the later date to fulfill the futures contract. Granted, she would incur some **carrying costs** in holding the Treasury bonds, (or the gold, etc.), but as long as the futures price was greater than the current spot price plus the carrying costs, she would make a riskless profit. (Carrying costs generally consist of the interest costs for the use of the funds to purchase the securities less the interest earned on the securities while the arbitrageur is holding them

Arbitrageurs Traders who make riskless profits by buying in one market and reselling in a another market.

Carrying Costs Interest costs for funds used to purchase the security underlying a futures contract plus any transactions costs.

Exhibit 10-3 ◆
Cracking the Code
on Futures Prices

CRACKING THE CODE

If you open *The Wall Street Journal*, midway through the Money and Investing Section you will find a section titled "Futures Prices," a part of which is reproduced in this exhibit. We can crack the code to futures prices by understanding how to read the futures table. To illustrate, look at the section on Interest Rate Futures. Glance down to the section titled "Treasury Bills (CME)" and to the row starting on the far left with Sept. On March 1, 1996, that row was as follows:

	Open	High	Low	Settle	Chg	Discount Settle	Chg	Open Interest
Sept	95.19	95.23	95.09	95.16	−.01	4.84	+.01	1,394

This means that on March 1, the agreed upon opening price for September delivery of Treasury bills is 95.19 percent of the face value of the contract. Remember T-bills sell at a discount, which is reflected in the price being less than 100 percent of the contract amount. For Treasury bills contracts, the contract amount (face value) is $1,000,000. Likewise, the low price for that day (fourth column) is 95.09. The high for the day (third column) is 95.23 percent, and the settle for the day (fifth column) is 95.16. The change from the previous day (sixth column) is -.01. To verify this, we would have to check yesterday's newspaper to see if the settle price was 95.17 (95.16 − 95.17 = −.01). The seventh column deals with the percent discount on the settle price. Note the settle price is 95.16 percent of the face value of the contract and 100 minus 95.16 equals 4.84, or 4.84 percent discount. Therefore, a T-bill futures contract sells at a 4.84 percent discount. The open interest is the number of contracts outstanding for the month of September.

plus other transactions costs of the exchange.) On the other hand, if the futures price is below the spot price plus carrying costs, then arbitrageurs (who owned some of the securities) would buy futures, driving the futures price up, and sell in the spot market, driving the spot price down. Can you explain how a riskless profit would be made?

When and if such an opportunity for riskless profit opens up, arbitrageurs move in and purchase in the spot market (driving up the price) and sell in the futures market (driving down the price), and vice versa. As the time comes closer to the delivery date of the futures contract, the length of time funds are borrowed to establish the position is reduced. Therefore, the carrying costs are reduced and the futures price approaches the spot price as the delivery date nears. Arbitrage continues until the futures price is bid up (down) to the spot price plus carrying costs—and the phenomenon called **convergence** occurs. Thus, on the last day before the expiration date, the futures price is practically equal to the spot price, because the carrying costs are negligible since only one day is left. Hence, because futures prices are highly correlated with spot prices and because of convergence, futures prices are ultimately

Convergence The phenomenon in which the futures price is bid up or down to the spot price plus carrying costs; the futures price approaches the spot price as the expiration date draws nearer.

To give some meaning to these numbers, let's assume we purchased a T-bill future for September delivery at the settle price. We pay a small brokerage fee (on March 1) for the right and obligation to purchase $1,000,000 face value in Treasury bills (of 90-day maturity) for $951,600 in September. ($951,600 = $1,000,000 × 95.16 percent). If the spot price of $1,000,000 in T-bills in September is greater than $951,600, we win. If it's less, we lose!

FUTURES PRICES

Thursday, February 29, 1996
Open Interest Reflects Previous Trading Day

INTEREST RATE

TREASURY BONDS (CBT)—$100,000; pts. 32nds OF 100%

	Open	High	Low	Settle	Change	Lifetime High	Low	Open Interest
Mar	114-25	115-05	113-29	114-27	+4	122-04	93-13	186,185
June	114-09	114-22	113-14	114-10	+2	121-23	93-06	207,294
Sept	113-26	113-29	112-30	113-24	+2	120-29	102-06	13,447
Dec	112-14	113-10	112-14	113-05	+2	120-15	107-25	2,026
Mr97	112-11	112-20	112-09	112-20	+2	120-00	108-04	999

Est vol 625,000; vol Wd 611.541; op int 410,002, −2,845.

TREASURY BONDS (MCE)—$50,000; pts. 32nds of 100%

	Open	High	Low	Settle	Change	Lifetime High	Low	Open Interest
Mar	114-21	115-02	113-30	114-27	+5	122-04	98-00	3,482
June	114-03	114-17	113-14	114-10	+4	121-09	98-10	1,521

Est vol na; vol Wd 8,190; open int 5,009, −892.

TREASURY NOTES (CBT)—$100,000; pts. 32nds of 100%

	Open	High	Low	Settle	Change	Lifetime High	Low	Open Interest
Mar	111-14	111-27	110-29	111-15	+2	115-14	98-20	146,547
June	110-29	111-03	110-07	110-24	+1	114-26	102-10	126,188
Sept	110-13	110-26	110-11	110-23	+1	114-26	108-04	11,754

Est vol 126,500; vol Wd 144,648; open int 188,282, +3,241.

5 YR TREAS NOTES (CBT)—$100,000; pts. 32nds of 100%

	Open	High	Low	Settle	Change	Lifetime High	Low	Open Interest
Mar	108-23	108-31	108-12	08225	+0.5	11145	10603	91,923
June	108-19	08225	108-03	108-13	+1.0	111-07	10730	88,730
Sept	108-00	108-11	107-31	08055	+1.0	10305	08275	7,629

Est vol 5,000; vol Wd 14,719; open int 27,837, +116.

2 YR TREAS NOTES (CBT)—$200,000, pts. 32nds OF 100%

	Open	High	Low	Settle	Change	Lifetime High	Low	Open Interest
Mar	04115	104-14	04062	104-10	−0.7	105-16	10319	11,253
June	104-13	104-15	04067	104-10	−2.2	105-19	103-27	16,584

30-DAY FEDERAL FUNDS (CBT)—$5 million; pts of 100%

	Open	High	Low	Settle	Change	Lifetime High	Low	Open Interest
Feb	94.795	94.795	94.750	94.770	.035	94.820	94.330	4,526
Mar	94.74	94.76	94.74	94.75	....	94.79	94.46	3,483
Apr	94.83	94.84	94.82	94.83	....	94.98	94.08	3,848
May	94.85	94.87	94.83	94.85	....	95.05	94.49	2,052
June	94.89	94.92	94.85	94.89	....	95.20	94.48	2,656

	Open	High	Low	Settle	Change	Lifetime High	Low	Open Interest
July	94.91	94.95	94.90	94.91	−.01	95.34	94.78	551
Aug	94.89	94.95	94.89	94.91	−.02	95.39	95.01	273
Sept	94.85	94.95	94.85	94.90	−.03	95.43	95.05	154
Dec	94.85	94.88	94.83	94.80	−.08	95.47	95.05	68

Est vol 3,885; vol Wd 4,257; open int 17,764, +251.

MUNI BOND INDEX (CBT)—$1,000; times Bond Buyer MBI

	Open	High	Low	Settle	Chg	High	Low	Open Interest
Mar	117-23	118-02	117-15	118-01	+6	122-09	110-20	12,211
June	115-29	116-07	115-15	116-02	−2	121-00	113-28	1,311

Est vol 6,000; vol Wd 6,384; open int 13,522, +423.
The Index: Close 118-23; Yield 5.99.

TREASURY BILLS (CME)—$1 mil; pts. of 100%

	Open	High	Low	Settle	Chg	Discount Settle	Chg	Open Interest
Mar	95.19	95.20	95.18	95.19	+.01	4.81	−.01	5,138
June	95.20	95.25	95.15	95.22	+.01	4.78	−.01	7,231
Sept	95.19	95.23	95.09	95.16	−.01	4.84	+.01	1,394

Est vol 2,633; vol Wd 2,584; open int 13,790, +726.

LIBOR—1 MO (CME)—$3,000,000; points of 100%

	Open	High	Low	Settle	Chg	Discount Settle	Chg	Open Interest
Mar	94.70	94.70	94.69	94.70	+.01	5.30	−.01	8,220
Apr	94.77	94.79	94.74	94.76	−.01	5.24	+.01	9,126
May	94.79	94.82	94.77	94.79	....	5.21	....	2,819
June	94.81	94.86	94.77	94.83	+.02	5.17	+.02	1,081
July	94.82	94.86	94.81	94.83	....	5.17	....	492
Aug	94.82	94.86	94.79	94.82	+.01	5.18	−.01	368
Sept	....	....	....	94.81	−.01	5.19	−.01	505
Oct	....	....	....	94.81	−.01	5.19	+.01	155

Est vol 4,830; vol Wd 6,593; open int 21,847, 2,198.

SOURCE: The Wall Street Journal, March 1, 1996, p. C14.

determined by the spot prices of the underlying contract assets. Now would be a good time to look at Exhibit 10-5, which discusses stock index futures and the October 1987 crash of the stock market.

RECAP

The futures price is determined by supply and demand. If the futures price is above the spot price plus the carrying costs, an arbitrageur will sell a futures agreement while at the same time purchasing securities in the spot market. The increased supply of futures will push the price down until the difference between the spot and the futures price is equal to the carrying costs. If the futures price is below the spot price plus carrying costs, arbitrageurs (who own some of the underlying assets) would buy futures and sell in the spot market. The futures price would go up and the spot price come down until the difference was the carrying costs. As the delivery date nears, the spot and the futures prices converge.

Exhibit 10-4 ◆

LHT Inc. Enters the
Futures Market

Let's consider an example in which financial futures can be used to hedge. Assume that LHT Inc. issued bonds ten years ago and that those bonds will mature in a year. LHT Inc. will not be in a position to pay off the debt. When the bonds come due, LHT Inc. will issue new bonds (borrow) to raise the funds to pay off the owners of the original bonds.[a] Let's further assume that LHT Inc. fears that interest rates could rise over the next year causing the new bonds to be issued at a higher interest rate. If this scenario materializes, the firm will have to make higher interest payments on the new bonds—something that will cut sharply into profits. But something as important as profits need not be left to the vicissitudes of unknown interest rates one year from now! There are ways that LHT Inc. can protect itself against an undesirable increase in rates by selling a T-bill future today. The T-bill futures agreement will oblige LHT to deliver so many T-bills on a later date, say in one year, at a price set today. If the interest rate does rise over the course of the year, as LHT expects, the spot price of the T-bills will fall. Remember the inverse relationship between the price of securities and the interest rate as discussed in Chapter 7. LHT Inc. can buy the T-bills in the spot market at the lower price for delivery to the purchaser of the futures contract who pays the higher price agreed upon earlier. If the interest rate does rise, the loss due to issuing new bonds at a higher interest rate is offset by the profit made by LHT Inc. on the T-bill futures contract.

But, what happens if LHT Inc. is wrong about the increase in the interest rate over the course of the next year and the interest rate falls or equivalently, the price of T-bills rises? LHT Inc. takes a loss on the T-bill future because it can buy the T-bills in the spot market at the higher price to deliver to the buyer of the futures contract for the lower previously agreed upon price. However, LHT Inc. is not really worse off. The loss in the futures market is offset by the savings on the new bonds the corporation issues at a lower rate since interest rates have fallen.

As we have seen, actual physical delivery of the securities does not usually take place. Rather, any price difference between the spot price and the futures price is merely paid between the buyer and seller of the futures agreement. In this case, if the interest rate does go up, LHT Inc. receives a payment from the seller of the T-bill futures agreement that offsets the loss by having to issue bonds at the higher interest rate. If the interest rate goes down, LHT Inc. makes a payment to the seller of the T-bill futures agreement, but issues the new bonds at the lower interest rate.

LHT Inc. has successfully used the futures market to reduce the risk of losses if interest rates go up while sacrificing the possibility of gains if interest rates go down—a trade that they may be happy to make. Can you explain what happens if interest rates stay the same over the course of the next year? Think about it before checking the answer in the footnote.[b]

---

[a]Borrowing to repay maturing debt is called *rolling over* and is actually quite common.
[b]LHT Inc. buys T-bills in the spot market to deliver to the purchaser of the futures contract at the same price for which they sold the contract. Aside from a small brokerage fee to purchase the futures contract (that can be thought of as an insurance premium), LHT Inc. is no worse off.

Options

In the previous section, we discussed the idea that business firms (financial and nonfinancial) or individuals can use the futures market to reduce the risk of price changes inherent in everyday business. That is, if they need to buy or sell a financial instrument in the future, the futures market can be used to offset any possible loss due to an unanticipated price change between now and the day when they will be making the purchase or sale. However, an unattractive feature of the futures market is that it also eliminates a possible gain from a price change.

For example, consider the case in which John needs to borrow $1 million dollars in a month. He knows what the interest rate is today, but is concerned that it will be higher in a month. He can sell a T-bill future for $1 million dollars that gives him the right and obligation to sell the T-bills in 30 days at a price determined today. If interest rates go up, he borrows at a higher rate, but the price of the T-bill futures contract falls and he makes a profit. This profit offsets the higher borrowing costs (and accomplishes his goal of reducing the risk of losses if the interest rate goes up). If interest rates go down, John gains by borrowing at a lower rate. However, he loses money on the T-bill future (since lower interest rates cause the T-bill futures price to rise and he is locked into selling at the lower price). Therefore, to reduce the risk of losses from the interest rate rising, he forgoes the chance of a gain if the interest rate falls.

Could there be another way of getting risk protection from a loss without giving up the possibility of a gain? If you said, "Surely there must be, since markets are so quick at responding to changing needs and conditions," you are correct (or, as we shall see, almost correct). We now turn our attention to options to demonstrate just how our friend John can use options to reduce the risk of an interest rate increase over the next month without foregoing a gain if rates fall.

Options are similar to futures in that they are used to reduce the risk of future price changes or to speculate. Options give the buyer the right but not the obligation to buy or sell an asset in the future for a price determined today. The agreed-upon price is called the **strike price.** This right continues until an expiration date in the contract. Options exist for many agriculture products, commodities, individual stocks (such as AT&T, IBM, and EDS), and other financial instruments. In addition, options are also available on the major types of futures contracts including stock index futures, currency futures, and interest rate futures. These options are called **options on futures** and give the buyer of the option the right (but not the obligation) to buy or sell a futures contract up to the expiration date of the option. Financial options are available for specific dates in the future, often for the two nearest months, and then for March, June, September, and December for the next nine months. As in the case of futures, the clearinghouse of the exchange enforces the contract, and, for a fee, takes on the default risk. In many ways, the similarities between futures and options stop here.

There are two kinds of options and we briefly outline each, focusing our discussion mainly on financial options. Look at Exhibit 10-6 for a listing of the major U.S. options and the exchanges they are traded on.

Options Standardized contracts that give the buyer the right but not the obligation to buy or sell an asset in the future at a price determined today.

Strike Price The agreed-upon price in an options contract.

Options on Futures Options that give the buyer the right but not the obligation to buy or sell a futures contract up to the expiration date on the option.

Exhibit 10-5 ◆
Stock Index
Futures and the '87
Crash

Stock Index Futures
Contracts that give the
buyer or seller the right
and obligation to pur-
chase or sell a multiple of
the value of a stock index
at some specific date in
the future at a price de-
termined today.

A stock market index such as the Dow Jones Industrial Average is an index that measures price changes of a market basket of stocks included in the index. **Stock index futures** are contracts that give the purchaser (seller) the right and obligation to purchase (sell) a multiple of the value of the index at some specified date in the future at a price determined today. Stock index futures are available for several indexes of stock market activity and the futures contract calls for the delivery of the cash value of a multiple of a particular stock index.

Perhaps the two most prominent stock index futures are the futures contracts for the S&P 500 and the NYSE Composite Indexes. In both cases, the contract size is $500 times the index on the delivery date. The financial futures contracts are available for the quarterly dates (during March, June, September, and December) over the next two years. For example, if John purchases a December contract for the S&P 500, this gives him the right and obligation to receive on the delivery date $500 times the value of the S&P 500 stock index on this date. The price for the future delivery is negotiated today. Let's say John negotiates a price today of $275,000, which he will pay on the delivery date. Consider the two cases for the delivery date on which the S&P Index is (1) 525 or (2) 575. If it is 525, the seller pays $262,500 (500 × $525) but receives $275,000 from John. If it is 575, John pays $275,000 but receives $287,500 (500 × $575). In the first case, the seller makes a profit. In the second case, John makes a profit. If $500 times the value of the index is greater than the futures price, then the buyer of the futures makes a profit. If it is less, the seller makes a profit.

Just as in all futures, the spot and futures prices move up and down together. In the case of stock indexes futures, arbitrage prevents the futures price from deviating a tremendous amount from the spot price. For instance, if the futures price is far above the spot price, an arbitrageur could make a riskless profit by buying a market basket of stocks that made up the index while simultaneously selling a futures contract. As long as the futures price exceeded the spot price plus the cost of carrying the inventory of stocks, the arbitrageur could make a riskless profit. But, by doing so, she would be increasing the demand for stocks in the spot market (pushing up the index) and increasing the supply of futures contracts (pushing down their price). As in other futures markets, arbitrage would keep the spot and futures price in close alignment with one another.

But wouldn't it be difficult to recognize every opportunity for arbitrage and go into the spot market to purchase the market basket of stocks that make up the stock index? After all, in the case of the S&P 500, one would have to purchase (or sell) 500 different stocks. Not even the largest of most

Put Options

Put Options Options
that give the buyer of the
option the right but not
the obligation to sell a
standardized contract of a
financial asset at a strike
price determined today.

Put options give the buyer of the option the right but not the obligation to sell a standardized contract of a financial asset or a futures agreement at a strike price determined today. The seller has the obligation but not the right to buy the contract if the buyer exercises it before the expiration date.[8] There-

---

[8] In this chapter, we are limiting our discussion to *American options*, which can be exercised any time before their expiration date. *European options* can be exercised only on the expiration date of the option.

small investors can do this. However, the advent of sophisticated computer technology has allowed brokerage houses and institutional investors (such as mutual funds and pension plans) to program automatic purchases and sales of stock index "market baskets" into a computer. Sales or purchases can be automatically triggered when the stock index futures price gets out of alignment with the spot price. This **program trading** allows every opportunity for arbitrage to be immediately exploited. As advantageous as this may seem to the brokerage house that uses it, it may entail some controversies, as we shall see shortly.

Program Trading The preprogramming of computers to automatically issue buy and sell orders for stocks as stock prices change.

During the week of October 12–16, 1987, the Dow Jones Industrial Average (another widely quoted index of stock values) fell 250 points. On Monday, October 19, 1987, it fell a whopping 508 points or more than 20 percent. Not only was this the largest point drop in history, but also by far the largest percent drop. To give you some idea of its magnitude, the next largest percent decline occurred October 28, 1929, when the market fell 12.8 percent near the start of the Great Depression. Could program trading have been the culprit in this major downturn?

Consider what would happen if a stock index futures suddenly fell steeply. Program trading would trigger spot market sales of the stocks that made up the index, and purchases of index futures. A major fall in the futures price could bring about large sales (and plummeting prices) in the spot market for stock. **Stop orders** (or orders to automatically sell if the stock price fell to a certain price) would be triggered, which would cause further plummeting of spot prices and could reverse the trend of purchases in the futures market. Indeed it was program trading and stop orders that triggered the October 1987 crash.

Stop Orders Orders to automatically sell if the stock price falls to a certain level.

To prevent such an occurrence, many exchanges have put in restrictions that limit computerized program trading if the index falls more than a certain amount on any day. These limitations were put in place after the 1987 crash. They have been activated many times since.

Other analysts are less concerned about program trading and more concerned about the cause of the fall in futures prices to begin with. If futures prices fall because of the expectation that spot prices will be falling, then the arbitrage causing the present spot price to fall may simply be rational price adjustment in a declining market. By restricting computerized trading, we may only be treating the symptoms of a problem without treating the cause. Maybe the market, like a virus, should be allowed to run its course, or maybe a little preventive medication will stop a mild virus from turning into a severe infection. Opinions about the extent of intervention needed continue to be numerous.

fore, John, who has to borrow $1 million in the next month can hedge the risk of a future interest rate increase, by buying a put option on, say, a T-bill or Treasury bond futures contract. If the interest rate does go up, he exercises the option at a profit to offset the loss incurred by having to borrow at the higher rate. Like futures, financial options are written only in standardized contract amounts for delivery on a few specific dates and a perfect offsetting transaction is rarely found. However, risk is still reduced. Unlike futures, put options allow the risk of an interest rate increase to be hedged without losing the possibility of a gain if the interest rate goes down. If rates do fall, John

Exhibit 10-6 ◆ Major Options, Exchanges, and Open Interest

Types of Options	Exchange[a] at which Trading Occurs	Indexes or Currencies Traded	Open Interest April 8th, 1996
Individual Stock Options	CBOE	Stock options	6,811,574 Calls 4,681,323 Puts
	AMEX	Stock options	4,367,098 Calls 2,247,645 Puts
	PHLX	Stock options	1,765,560 Calls 912,040 Puts
	PSE	Stock options	2,383,748 Calls 1,179,845 Puts
	NYSE	Stock options	880,959 Calls 402,168 Puts
Stock Index Options	CBOE	S&P 500, Leaps & Caps	619,311 Calls 1,193,402 Puts
	CBOE	S&P 100, Leaps & Caps	306,186 Calls 543,560 Puts
	AMEX	MMI, Leaps & Caps	14,398 Calls 45,469 Puts
	AMEX	Institutional & Caps	38,375 Calls 48,781 Puts
	AMEX	Comp Tech	2,091 Calls 2,658 Puts
	AMEX	Oil	3,138 Calls 4,038 Puts
	PHLX	Gold/Silver	12,336 Calls 7,171 Puts
	PHLX	Nat'l OTC	880 Calls 790 Puts
	PHLX	Value Line	1,104 Calls 629 Puts

simply does not exercise the option. He has used put options to reduce the risk of an interest rate increase when he has to borrow in the future. We should note that put options can also be used to reduce the risk of a price decrease by anyone who has to sell a financial asset in the future.

Call Options

Call Options Options that give the buyer of the option the right but not the obligation to buy a standardized contract of a financial asset at a strike price determined today.

Call options give the buyer the right but not the obligation to buy the financial asset at a strike price determined today at any time before the expiration date. Note, the buyer has the right but not the obligation to buy. The buyer exercises the option (buys the asset or futures contract at the strike price) only if it is in his interest—that is, only if the price of the financial asset is greater than the strike price. If the price of the financial asset or futures contract falls, the buyer does not have the obligation to exercise the option and will let it expire. The option allows the buyer to limit his losses from a price increase without limiting his ability to take advantage of a price decrease.

Types of Options	Exchange[a] at which Trading Occurs	Indexes or Currencies Traded	Open Interest April 8th, 1996
	PHLX	Top 100	3,121 Calls 10,658 Puts
	PHLX	Utilities	4,331 Calls 2,656 Puts
Options on Stock Index Futures	CME	S&P 500	178,547 Puts 108,094 Calls
Interest Rate Options on Futures	CBOT	U.S. T-Bonds	343,541 Puts 438,096 Calls
	CBOT	U.S. T-Notes (5)	95,757 Puts 100,105 Calls
Currency Options—Options on Futures	CME	Japanese Yen	38,559 Puts 35,738 Calls
	CME	German Mark	49,712 Puts 38,431 Calls
	CME	Canadian Dollar	5,502 Puts 8,078 Calls
	CME	British Pound	43,542 Puts 34,609 Calls
	CME	Swiss Franc	13,733 Puts 12,022 Calls
	CME	Eurodollar	872,072 Puts 755,316 Calls

[a]Exchanges: AMEX (American Stock Exchange)   NYSE (New York Stock Exchange)
        CBOE (Chicago Board Options Exchange)   PHLX (Philadelphia Exchange)
        CME (Chicago Mercantile Exchange)   PSE (Pacific Stock Exchange)

SOURCE: *Barron's*, April 8th, 1996 (pgs. MW81 to MW87).

RECAP

O ptions give the buyer of the option the right but not the obligation to buy or sell an asset in the future for a price determined today. Put options give the buyer the right but not the obligation to sell a standardized contract, at a price determined today, anytime before the expiration date on the option. A call option gives the buyer the right but not the obligation to buy a financial asset at a price determined today, anytime before the expiration date on the option.

The Option Premium

But, you might ask, why would any firm or individual hedge risk with futures that limit both losses and gains when they could use options which limit only losses? If you said, "Because futures must be cheaper," you may have a future as a great economist! Futures cost very little—basically only a small brokerage fee, which is low because the contracts are standardized, and there is very large volume in the market. Both parties to the agreement have rights and obligations. With options, however, one party has rights with no obligations, and the other party to the agreement has obligations with no rights. From the buyer's position, put or call options give the right but not the obligation to sell or buy the contract at the agreed-upon price if the buyer exercises the option. In addition to paying the exchange a brokerage fee, an **option premium** is paid by the party with the rights but no obligations (the buyer) to the party with the obligations but no rights (the seller).[9] The premium is the reward to the seller of either a put or call option for accepting the risk of a loss with no possibility of a gain.[10]

So far, we have been discussing situations in which options are used to hedge. As you might have guessed, put and call options can also be used to speculate. Needless to say, speculation in this manner can be extremely costly, since option premiums are often quite substantial (several thousands of dollars). If the option is not exercised, the buyer of the call or put option merely loses the option premium. In the case of hedging, this can be thought of as an insurance premium, limiting the amount of losses that will be incurred if a financial instrument must be purchased or sold at a later date. For the speculator, the option premium is the amount that he is willing to bet when he believes that the price will change significantly from the strike price creating potential profit.[11]

In summary, someone who needs to buy a financial security or asset in the future can hedge the risk of an inopportune price increase by paying a premium to purchase a call option—which gives the buyer the right to purchase the asset at a price agreed upon today up to the expiration date of the option. On the other hand, someone who needs to sell a financial security or asset in the future can hedge the risk of a price decrease by paying a premium to purchase a put option—which gives the buyer the right to sell the contract at a price agreed upon today up to the expiration date. The sellers of the call or put options are not hedging, but merely accepting risk for a price—in this case, the option premium. For the buyer of a call or put option, risk is hedged without giving up any potential for gains, as in the case of futures. Like futures, options can also be used to speculate about future price changes. The downside to options, of course, is the option premium, which can be quite substantial, as compared to the usually small brokerage fee for buying or selling the futures contract.[12] Economists are famous for saying "There is no such thing as a free lunch!" If options are used to exploit gains while limiting losses, this is certainly true.

Option Premium The premium paid by the buyer of the option to compensate the seller for accepting the risk of a loss with no possibility of a gain.

[9] Make sure you are clear that the buyer of a put option has the right but not the obligation to sell while the buyer of a call option has the right but not the obligation to buy.

[10] For the hedger to be better off, the loss from the interest rate increase must be larger than the put option premium.

[11] Like hedgers, for the speculator to benefit from the option, the price must increase (in the case of call options) or decrease (in the case of put options) enough to more than cover the option premium.

[12] The option still entails a small brokerage fee for arranging the option in addition to the option premium.

Like futures, option prices are quoted in many daily newspapers. Now would be a good time to read Exhibit 10-7 on cracking the code on option prices.

In this section, we looked at financial options and saw that they also can be used by business firms for managing risk due to price changes. Like futures, options can be used to reduce the risks of price changes in future time periods. We turn our attention now to swaps, which can be used by some businesses (primarily intermediaries) to manage risks over much longer periods of time.

RECAP

The option premium is paid by the party who has rights but no obligations. The seller of the option receives the premium to compensate for accepting the risk of a loss with no possibility of gain.

Swaps

So far, we have seen that financial futures and options can be used to manage the risk of inopportune future changes in prices, interest rates, or exchange rates. These instruments have developed in recent years because of increased price volatility in financial markets. They are similar to futures and options agreements in agriculture and commodity markets, which have existed for more than 100 years.

Swaps are another vehicle that can be used to reduce the risk of future interest rate changes. Originating in 1982, they are a totally new instrument used mainly by entities such as commercial banks, saving and loans, other intermediaries, government agencies, and securities dealers to reduce interest rate risk.[13] Swaps involve two parties who trade interest payment streams to guarantee that the inflows of payments will more closely match outflows. Swaps are growing fast, particularly at large banks. Swaps make markets more efficient and reduce risks, but they are often complex agreements. Because of their complexity, we are limiting our discussion to a simple case.

Consider an example involving two commercial banks. One bank—Bank One—has long-term fixed rate loans such as mortgages, which they fund with floating or variable rate money market accounts. The interest payments on money market accounts fluctuate with market interest rates, but the interest payments earned on the loans do not.

The other bank—Bank Two—has made floating or variable rate loans. The interest payments on these loans go up and down with an index of market interest rates, such as rates on government bonds. The bank funds these loans with long-term fixed rate deposits. The interest payments on these deposits do not change.

Swaps Agreements in which two parties trade interest payment streams to guarantee that the inflows of payments will more closely match outflows.

---

[13] Swaps also exist for foreign exchange where future streams of currencies are traded. For simplicity, we limit our analysis to interest rate swaps.

Exhibit 10-7 ◆
Cracking the Code
on Options

CRACKING THE CODE

Here is a typical example of the way option market information appears in the newspaper. Again, in this case, we have clipped the quotations below from *The Wall Street Journal* on March 1, 1996. In this example, we are considering options on $100,000 of Treasury bond futures with a coupon rate of 8 percent and 15 year maturity. Look at the section on "Futures Options Prices" from the following newspaper clipping. Glance down to the T-Bonds (CBT) section and the row (reproduced below) that starts with the strike price of 112. The 2nd through 4th columns give the settle (final of the day) option premium for call options for April, June, and September, respectively. The 5th through 7th columns give the settle option premium for put options on March 1, 1996 for April, June, and September.

T-Bonds (CBT)
$100,000; points and 64ths of 100%

Strike	Calls-Settle			Puts-Settle		
Price	Apr	Jun	Sep	Apr	Jun	Sep
112	2-44	3-28	4-03	0-24	1-09	2-22

This means that on March 1, for a strike price of 112, or 112 percent of the face value of the contract, (in this example $100,000) the option premium for an April call option is $2,015.63 or (2 44/64 percent × $100,000). For a June put option with a strike price of 112, the option premium is $1,140.63 or 1 9/64 percent times $100,000. If no price is given, such as for a June call option with a strike price of 113, then the contract did not trade on this day.

Both banks make a profit on the spread, the difference between what is earned on their loans and what is paid depositors for the use of their deposits. But there is a problem; the loans and deposits are now configured in such a way that both banks have some interest rate risk. That is, both banks are in a position where a change in interest rates can cause them to experience a loss. If interest rates go down, Bank Two (with variable rate loans and fixed rate deposits) may end up paying more for the use of its deposits than what it is earning on its loans. If interest rates go up, Bank One (with fixed rate loans and variable rate deposits) may end up paying more for the use of its deposits than what it is earning on its loans.

However, all hope is not lost. These two intermediaries can get together and arrange an interest rate swap. Actually, the swap is usually arranged by a bank. They can trade the interest payments, but not the principal payments on their deposits (liabilities). Bank One, the first intermediary, would then be funding fixed-rate assets with fixed-rate liability interest payments, and Bank Two, the second intermediary, would be funding variable-rate assets with variable-rate instruments. Both would be hedging risk by engaging in the swap. The interest payments Bank One receives are fixed, since they have fixed-rate loans. After the swap, the interest payments they make to fund the loans would also be fixed. A rise in interest rates would no longer put them in a losing

To give some meaning to these numbers, let's assume we purchased an April Treasury bond call option with a strike price of 112 for $2,015.63 on March 1. We pay a brokerage fee (on March 1) for the right (but not the obligation) to purchase $100,000 face value in Treasury bond futures (15 year maturity and 8 percent coupon rate) for $112,000 in April. ($112,000 = $100,000 × 112 percent). If the spot price of $100,000 in Treasury bond futures in April is greater than $112,000 we win. If it's less, we do not exercise the option. In this case, we lose the option premium of $2,015.63. However, we can consider the $2,015.63 like an insurance premium, insuring us against having to pay much more for the T-bonds futures in April.

FUTURES OPTIONS PRICES

Thursday, February 29, 1996
INTEREST RATE

T-BONDS (CBT)
$100,000; points and 64ths of 100%

Strike	Calls-Settle			Puts-Settle		
Price	Apr	Jun	Sep	Apr	Jun	Sep
112	2-44	3-28	4-03	0-24	1-09	2-22
113	1-61	....	....	0-41	....	....
114	1-21	2-16	3-00	1-01	1-60	3-16
115	0-55	....	....	1-35	....	....
116	0-32	1-24	2-09	2-12	3-02	4-22
117	0-18	....	....	2-62	....	....

Est. vol. 117,000;
Wed vol. 50,406 calls; 28,033 puts
Op. Int. Wed 372,587 calls; 263,643 puts

111	0-39	0-18	0-48	0-55	1-26	2-05
112	0-17	0-10	0-34	1-33	2-00	2-40
113	0-06	0-05	0-23	2-21	2-44	3-16
114	0-02	0-03	0-16	3-17	3-31	3-61

Est. vol. 211,112 Wd; 19,185 calls; 22,314 puts
Op. int. Wed 208,854 calls; 197,485 puts

5 YR TREAS NOTES (CBT)
$100,000; points and 64ths of 100%

Strike	Calls-Settle			Puts-Settle		
Price	Apr	Jun	Sep	Apr	Jun	Sep
10700	....	....	....	0-08	0-25	....
10750	....	....	....	0-13	0-33	....
10800	0-48	1-06	....	0-22	0-45	1-16
10850	0-30	0-53	....	0-36	0-59	....
10900	0-18	0-39	0-60	0-55	1-12	1-49
10950	0-10	0-28	0-49	1-16	1-33	2-04

Est. vol. 26,000 Wd 5,617 calls; 7,776 puts
Op Int. Wed 75,784 calls; 72,458 puts

T-NOTES (CBT)
$100,000; points and 64ths of 100%

Strike	Calls-Settle			Puts-Settle		
Price	Apr	Jun	Sep	Apr	Jun	Sep
109	1-59	0-48	1-24	0-12	0-40	1-14
110	1-11	0-30	1-01	0-27	0-61	1-39

SOURCE: *The Wall Street Journal*, March 1, 1996, p. C15.

position. For Bank Two, the earnings on their loans would move up and down with market interest rates, but the interest payments they make to fund the loans would also be flexible. A fall in interest rates would no longer put them in a losing position. Now would be a good time to look at Exhibit 10-8.

We have described a simple case of a swap, but as noted previously, these instruments can be and usually are complex. A swap is often arranged for up to fifteen years and has the advantage over futures and options of allowing the participants to hedge for longer periods of time.

The resourcefulness and ingenuity of financial market participants who are risk averse and profit seeking are common occurrences. When risks increase (as they do when markets become more volatile), new ways to "handle" or manage the risk are developed. Thus, we have witnessed the phenomenal growth of futures, options, and swaps. Financial and nonfinancial corporations must now be aware of and take every opportunity to reduce risks. If they fail to do so, they may find that they are not playing on a level field. Even the most skeptical of players—such as Doz-All in the chapter introduction—may become convinced that using the new flashy futures, options, and swaps, rather than being vulnerable to risk, is an avenue that must be exploited by anyone who will be buying or selling financial instruments in the future. If prices settle down (become less volatile), we could expect the growth of these

Exhibit 10-8 ◆	This Year	
A Simple Interest Rate Swap	Bank One Two-year loans earn 9% fixed Deposits cost 5% variable	Bank Two Two-year loans earn 8% variable Deposits cost 6% fixed
	Next Year	
	Rates Go Up—No Swap ☹ Loans earn 9% fixed Deposits cost 9% variable	Loans earn 12% variable ☺ Deposits cost 6% fixed
	Rates Go Down—No Swap ☺ Loans earn 9% fixed Deposits cost 2% variable	Loans earn 5% variable ☹ Deposits cost 6% fixed
	Rates Go Up—They Swap ☺ Loans earn 9% fixed Deposits cost 6% fixed	Loans earn 12% variable ☺ Deposits cost 9% variable
	Rates Go Down—They Swap ☺ Loans earn 9% fixed Deposits cost 6% fixed	Loans earn 5% variable ☺ Deposits cost 2% variable
	The swap allows both banks to be happy all the time!	

markets to slow; however, it is doubtful they would ever disappear. Once such markets are highly developed, they will continue to be used to capitalize on even small opportunities to reduce risk.

RECAP

Swaps entail two parties trading interest payment streams to guarantee that the inflows of payments will more closely match the outflows. Thus, an intermediary with fixed rate assets and variable rate liabilities will trade with another intermediary that has variable rate assets and fixed rate liabilities. By trading interest payment streams, both reduce risk.

We are finishing our section on markets and prices. Our goal was to help you learn something about how prices influence behavior. This chapter contains two appendixes: the first discusses foreign exchange futures markets; the second covers how the mysterious option premium is determined.

Summary of Major Points

1. In forward markets, the terms of a transaction (including the price) that will occur on the future date are arranged today. Forward transactions are used to reduce the risk that future price changes will eliminate profit. Forward agreements can have high transactions costs because they require the exact matching of two parties and because each party has a default risk in that the other party may not fulfill the agreement.

2. Financial futures are standardized contracts between two parties to buy or sell financial securities such as government securities, stock indexes, Eurodollars, and numerous foreign currencies at a future date with the price determined today. They are traded on major exchanges and are used to hedge interest rate risks, exchange rate risks, and the risk that stock prices will change. They can also be used to speculate about future price changes.

3. Because futures contracts are standardized, they have low transactions costs and high volume. Often they do not provide an exact offsetting match with regard to the quality, the quantity, or the due date of the contract. The clearinghouse of the exchange enforces the contract, and, for a fee, takes on the default risk. Both the buyer and seller put up performance bonds. Arbitrageurs insure that the futures price is equal to the spot price plus carrying costs. The futures price converges to the spot price on the delivery date.

4. Options are financial contracts that can also be used to hedge or speculate. They are available for many of the same financial assets as futures. In addition, two kinds of options are offered for either buying or selling futures contracts. A call option gives the buyer of the option the right but not the obligation to purchase the contract by the expiration date at a price determined today. A put option gives the buyer of the option the right but not the obligation to sell the contract by the expiration date at a price determined today. The buyer of a call or put option pays an option premium because she has rights but no obligations. The seller of the call or put option takes on the risk that the option will be exercised for a price, the option premium. Futures limit both gains and losses, while options limit losses without limiting gains.

5. Swaps are a new innovation that involves the trading of interest payment streams (usually by two intermediaries) for a long period of time. They can be used to reduce risks when financial institutions have a mismatch between fixed and floating rate assets and liabilities.

6. During October 1987, the Dow Jones Average fell 508 points. Program trading has been implicated in the fall. The collapse was triggered by declines in the prices of stock index futures. Since that time, reforms have been put in place to limit a collapse from program trading.

7. A foreign exchange futures market trades standardized contracts to buy or sell some amount of foreign exchange on a future date at a price determined today. These futures are widely used to hedge risks involving the delivery of one currency that must be converted to another currency at a later date. (Appendix 10-A)

8. The option premium is dependent on the volatility of the financial instrument in the contract (such as T-bills), the difference between the

strike and the spot price, and the length of time until the expiration date on the option. (Appendix 10-B)

Key Terms

Arbitrageurs
Call Options
Carrying Costs
Clearinghouse
Convergence
Financial Futures
Financial Futures Markets
Forward Transactions
Futures Contracts
Hedged
Margin Requirement

Option Premium
Options
Options on Futures
Performance Bond
Pit
Program Trading
Put Options
Stock Index Futures
Stop Orders
Strike Price
Swaps

Review Questions

1. Define financial futures, forward agreements, options, and swaps. What are the advantages and disadvantages of each?

2. How are spot markets different from futures markets?

3. A government report comes out forecasting both higher inflation and higher interest rates in the future. Yvette needs to borrow money in six months. How can she, as a borrower, protect herself from the risk of an increase in the interest rate before she does borrow? What if she is the lender?

4. Why do both the buyer and seller of futures contracts have to put up performance bonds? When does the seller profit? When does the buyer profit? How is the clearinghouse protected from losses?

5. On the day before the delivery date of a futures contract, explain why the futures price is very close to the spot price.

6. How do arbitrageurs and speculators differ?

7. Explain the process by which arbitrage causes the futures and spot prices to converge.

8. Explain the difference between call and put options. In the case of options, who pays the option premium, the buyer or the seller? Why does the seller of an option take on the risk?

9. What are options on futures?

10. What advantages do swaps have over options or futures? Who are the usual participants in a swap transaction?

11. Explain how an investor could use a stock index future to hedge the risk of a fall in stock prices.

12. Assume an intermediary uses futures only to hedge risk and never to speculate. Is it as vulnerable to losses as an intermediary that uses futures to speculate? Explain.

13. What factors determine the size of the option premium? (Appendix 10-B)

Analytical Questions

14. Mary buys a Treasury bond futures agreement for $94,000. On the delivery date, the spot price is $95,000. Does she win or lose? How much? If Mary bought the futures contract to hedge, can she lose? Explain. (Hint: What if she is willing to give up the opportunity for gain to reduce the risk of loss.)

15. IBM sells a Treasury bond futures agreement for $94,000. On the delivery date, the spot price is $95,000. They sold the futures agreement to speculate. Do they win or lose? Explain.

16. A firm buys a December $100,000 Treasury bond call option with the strike price of 110. If the spot price in December is $108,000 is the option exercised?

17. An investment firm buys a December $100,000 Treasury bond put option with the strike price of 110. If the spot price in December is $108,000 is the option exercised?

18. If the settle price for a T-bill futures contract is 96.75, what is the percent discount?

19. A brokerage house purchases a S&P 500 futures agreement for $300,000. On the delivery date, the S&P 500 index is 575. Does the brokerage house make a profit? What if the S&P 500 is 625?

20. If I buy a T-bill future for $950,000 and interest rates go up between now and the delivery date, what will happen to the price of the T-bill future? Will I make money or lose money? Explain.

21. Assume you inherit a $1,000,000 trust fund from your family when you turn 21 next year. Interest rates are high right now and you fear they may be lower in a year. Explain in detail how you can use futures or options to alleviate your fears.

22. Ruben is importing Colombian coffee to the United States. He will be paid $100,000 in six months, but is really interested in how much of his domestic currency (Colombian pesos) he will receive for the $100,000. Explain in detail how he can reduce the risk that, in six months, the peso will depreciate in value against the dollar and he will receive fewer pesos than he anticipates. (Appendix 10-A)

The Financial System and the Economy

| Back | Forward | Home | Reload | Images | Open | Print | Find | Stop | N |

1. The Chicago Mercantile Exchange (CME) is the world's largest financial exchange where firms buy and sell financial assets. From the internet site (http://www.cme.com/exchange/glossary.html), locate the meaning of futures and options. From the informatioin at this site, explain the difference between a call option and a put option.

Suggested Readings

An article by Charles S. Morris that may be of interest is "Managing Interest Rate Risk with Interest Rate Futures," *Financial Market Volatility and the Economy*, Federal Reserve Bank of Kansas City, 1990.

Two comprehensive and somewhat technical articles are "Money Market Futures" and "Options on Money Market Futures," both found in *Instrument of the Money Market*, 7th ed., edited by Timothy Q. Cook and Robert K. LaRoche, Federal Reserve Board of Richmond, 1993.

For a clear discussion of interest rate swaps, see either Anatoli Kuprianov, "The Role of Interest Rate Swaps in Corporate Finance," *Economic Quarterly of the Federal Reserve Bank of Richmond*, Summer 1994; or J. Gregg Whittaker, "Interest Rate Swaps: Risk and Regulation," *Economic Review of the Federal Reserve Bank of Kansas City*, March 1987.

For those of you who would like to know more about investing in futures and options (not that we recommend it), there are some recent books out on how to get started in investing in futures and options. We suggest Ira Kawaller, *Financial Futures and Options: Managing Risk in the Interest Rate, Currency, and Equity Markets*, Chicago: Probus, 1992; Todd Lofton, *Getting Started in Futures*, 2nd ed. New York: Wiley, 1993; and Michael Thomsett, *Getting Started in Options*, 2nd ed. New York: Wiley, 1993.

For a recent book on swaps, see Mary S. Ludwig, *Understanding Interest Rate Swaps*, New York: McGraw Hill, 1993. It reviews the mechanics and pricing of the swap market, swap jargon, and several potential applications of swaps. For those of you who are really diehards, it also has a standardized swap agreement.

APPENDIX 10-A

The Foreign Exchange Futures Market

In Chapter 9, we discussed how exchange rates were determined in the foreign exchange market. In that chapter, the exchange rates we were referring to were spot rates—that is, the exchange rate of foreign currency for immediate delivery. But large futures markets that trade foreign exchange futures contracts have also developed because they facilitate trade in goods, services, and financial claims. The purpose of this appendix is to look at these foreign exchange futures contracts.

A foreign exchange futures contract is a standardized contract to deliver so much foreign exchange on a date in the future at a price determined today. The agreed-upon price is the futures price. Like spot markets, the growth in foreign exchange futures markets can be attributed to the tremendous growth in trade, the increase in foreign investment, and the increased volatility of exchange rates. Foreign exchange futures markets have been organized since the mid-1970s and allow importers, exporters, and investors in foreign securities to hedge. Like other futures markets, they also provide the opportunity for speculation.

Foreign exchange markets, including both spot and futures, are actually the largest market in the world in terms of the volume of transactions. Spot markets do not have a unique location like the New York Stock Exchange, but rather are located at large banks in the world's financial centers, such as London, New York, Tokyo, and Frankfurt. Large banks in financial centers in other countries are usually linked to the major banks in one of the four financial centers, which in turn are linked by telephone and telex. Standardized futures contracts are traded on the Chicago Mercantile Exchange and require a relatively large minimum purchase. In reality, one worldwide foreign exchange market (either spot or futures) is open somewhere in the world 24 hours each day. Since supplies and demands change from day to day, exchange rates (both spot and futures prices) fluctuate day to day, hour to hour, and even minute by minute![a]

Foreign exchange futures markets, like all futures markets, offer the opportunity to hedge risk or to speculate. Importers and exporters often enter into agreements to deliver goods in the future for a price determined today. Because the price is agreed upon today without knowing the future spot exchange rate, there is a risk that the exchange rate between the two currencies will change between now and the delivery date. There is a possibility that the anticipated profit could be eliminated, or worse yet, a loss could occur.

---

[a] In Chapter 10, we investigate the relationship between the spot and futures exchange rate.

This risk is referred to as exchange rate risk. To hedge, an importer can enter the foreign exchange futures market. An example will help to clarify.

Assume Jean is exporting computers to a firm (Choca Firm) in Switzerland that plans to resell them at a profit.[b] She agrees to deliver 500 computers in September, three months from now, and to be paid $1,000 per computer or $500,000. Choca Firm will have to come up with $500,000 in September to pay for the computers.[c] Checking the exchange rate today, they find that the Swiss franc/dollar rate is 1.5025 Swiss francs. If the exchange rate stays the same (something highly unlikely), Choca Firm would have to pay 751,250 Swiss francs (500,000 × 1.5025) in September for the $500,000. This is great, because Choca Firm is confident that they can resell the computers for 800,000 Swiss francs, making a nice profit. But then, the importer wonders what will happen if the Swiss franc depreciates (or in other words, if the dollar appreciates) between now and September. If the Swiss franc/dollar rate changes to 1.6 Swiss francs (a depreciation of the Swiss franc and appreciation of the dollar), then Choca Firm will have to pay 800,000 Swiss francs (500,000 × 1.6) for the $500,000 and be robbed of any and all profits. Worse yet, if the dollar exchange rate appreciates to 1.75 Swiss francs the importer will have to come up with 875,000 Swiss francs (500,000 × 1.75), incurring a sizable loss! Thanks to organized futures markets, Choca Firm can hedge this risk by buying a standardized foreign exchange futures contract in dollars.

For example, today a futures contract for delivery of dollars in September is selling for 1.508 Swiss francs. If the importer purchases this contract, then he knows that he will pay 1.508 Swiss francs for the delivery of $1 in September, or 754,000 (500,000 × 1.508) Swiss francs for $500,000, regardless of what the spot exchange rate is in September. For Choca Firm or any importer who is interested in importing computers rather than speculating on future spot exchange rates, this offers a simple way to reduce exchange rate risk.

Another use of foreign exchange futures markets is to hedge risk when foreign securities are purchased. For example, foreign purchasers of U.S. government securities know they will be delivered so many dollars in, say, 90 days when the security matures. Can you explain how selling a futures contract hedges the exchange rate risk in this case?[d] No wonder the growth of these markets parallels the growth of trade in goods, services, and financial securities.

---

[b] Choca Firm is a company that has specialized in Swiss chocolates and is trying to diversify into importing computers.

[c] In this example, we are assuming that the importer must exchange domestic currency for the foreign currency—that is, Choca Firm pays for what it imports with the currency of the exporting country. The situation could work in reverse. In that case, the exporter would be paid in the currency of the importing country and have to exchange it for the exporting country's currency. Either way, the risk is the same; the only difference is who bears the risk.

[d] For example, assume a Japanese firm purchases a U.S. government T-bill for $9,900. The T-bill sells at a discount and the Japanese firm knows it will receive $10,000 in three months. The yen/dollar exchange rate on the date of the purchase was 110. That is, the Japanese firm paid 1,089,000 yen (110 yen × $9,900) for the T-bill. If the exchange rate is the same in three months, the T-bill will return 1,100,000 yen for a profit of 11,000 yen. But, it is highly unlikely that the exchange rate will be the same, and if the yen depreciates, the profit could be reduced or a loss could even occur. To hedge this risk, the Japanese firm can sell a futures contract today that agrees to deliver $10,000 three months from now at a yen price agreed upon today. In this way, the firm will know exactly how many yen it will receive for the $10,000.

APPENDIX 10-B

Determining the Option Premium

As in all unregulated markets, the price to buy either a call or put option (the option premium) is determined by the forces of supply and demand.[a] Unlike futures markets where both parties to the transaction can be hedgers, in the case of options, only one party to the transaction can be a hedger. For call and put options, the buyer can be a hedger. Both of these parties could also be speculators, but the point is, the seller of a call or put option can never be hedging. The seller is merely accepting risk for a premium—the option premium.

For any given options contract, the option premium will generally be larger when

1. The price of the contract asset is more volatile.
2. The expiration date of the option is further away.
3. The strike price relative to the spot price for put options is higher and the strike price relative to the spot price for call options is lower.

We will consider the first reason first. If the price of Eurodollars fluctuates more than the price of T-bills (all other factors equal), then the option premium for the Eurodollar option would be greater than the option premium for the T-bill option.[b] Because of the greater volatility, the seller of the Eurodollar call or put option would have a greater probability of losing and therefore the premium would have to be higher to compensate.

Secondly, time is a factor in determining the option premium since the further away the expiration date, the more time there is for the price to fluctuate and hence the more risk that the option will be exercised. Also, the further we look into the future, the more uncertain things become. Hence, the further away the expiration date is, the higher the option premium.

Finally, the strike price also affects the premium. If the strike price for a call option is very low relative to the spot price, it is much more likely that the spot price will go above the strike price, and that the option will be exercised. Hence, the lower the strike price for a call option, the higher the option premium will be. For a put option, the higher the strike price, the more likely it is that the spot price will be below the strike price and that the buyer will exercise the option. Hence, the higher the strike price is for a put option, the higher the option premium will be.

---

[a] Be careful not to confuse the price or option premium *for* the option contract with the strike price *of* the contract.

[b] In this case, both Eurodollars and T-bills are available in $1,000,000 contracts for delivery on the same dates.

PART THREE

Financial Institutions

11

Financial Intermediaries: Some Specifics

Presume not that I am the thing I was.
—William Shakespeare—

Learning Objectives

After reading this chapter, you should know:

◆ The characteristics common to all types of financial intermediaries (FIs)

◆ The services provided by FIs and the types of risks they must manage

◆ The major types of depository institutions and other FIs

◆ The principal assets and liabilities of the various FIs

◆ The characteristics that distinguish one type of FI from another type

Are All Financial Intermediaries More or Less Alike?

It is the thirtieth of the month. Sandi and Dave have both been paid by their employers and it's now time to pay the family's bills and save something for their upcoming vacation. Sitting at the kitchen table they write checks on their account at HLT National Bank to the Prudential Insurance Co. for the premium due on Sandi's life insurance policy, the APEI Credit Union for the car loan payment, and the local savings and loan (S&L) association for the mortgage payment. When these and other bills are paid, a check for the surplus funds to be saved is sent to their money market mutual fund account at Merrill Lynch.

In this hypothetical series of transactions, Sandi and Dave dealt with five different financial intermediaries (FIs)—a commercial bank, an insurance company, a credit union, an S&L, and a money market mutual fund. Why five instead of one? Can't one provide all the relevant services? Put another way, how are these intermediaries similar to one another and how do they differ? These are the questions to be addressed in this chapter. In essence, the plan is to provide an assessment of the functioning and role of those institutions that provide the public with a wide range of financial services and play a central role in coordinating and channeling the flow of funds in the economy.

Aside from our effort to make the material interesting, we recognize that institutional detail can make for dry reading. Don't succumb to the temptation to dismiss such detail as unimportant. You need to know what positions FIs occupy on the playing field and how these positions have evolved in the past 30 years. In fact, as we begin, it should be emphasized that **financial innovation,** which is the creating of new financial instruments, markets, and institutions, has often been the key to growth and survival in the financial services industry.[1] This has been particularly true during the past 30 years. As it is for many other firms and industries in a state of change in our society, institutional details in the financial services industry are continuously evolving. Thus, we can only provide you with a snapshot of the current state of affairs and summarize how and why this snapshot differs from the picture of the financial landscape prevailing in the recent past. This will lay the groundwork for subsequent chapters in which we analyze the forces that have previously produced major changes in the financial system and are likely to remain influential in the future.

Financial Innovation The creation of new financial instruments, markets, and institutions in the financial services industry.

Common Characteristics

To the untrained eye, an insurance company and a commercial bank would appear to be quite different institutions. However, the trained eye should see more. Both are FIs that link up deficit spending units (DSUs) and surplus spending units (SSUs), and in the process provide the public with a wide range of financial services. The linking or channeling function involves the acquisition of financial claims on DSUs by the FIs and the acquisition of

---

[1] We look in depth at financial innovation in Chapter 13.

claims on the FIs by the SSUs. (You might want to take a quick look at Exhibit 1–1 in Chapter 1.) The DSUs sell financial claims against themselves, which the intermediaries purchase. The financial claims may be signed loan papers, equities, or securities. In this context, when we say FIs make loans to DSUs, the FIs are purchasing financial claims, which are the signed loan papers, from the DSUs. The intermediaries get the funds to lend by selling their own financial claims that the SSUs purchase. The financial claims against the FIs include checking, time, and saving deposits, among others. Even though funds flow ultimately from SSUs to DSUs, the intermediaries do more than act as a go-between. The SSUs acquire claims against the FIs, who sell their own liabilities, and the FIs are in debt to the SSUs.[2]

The characteristics common to intermediaries can be identified with the aid of Exhibit 11-1, which conceptualizes the notion that FIs are firms producing services just as nonfinancial firms in the economy produce goods—

---

[2]For the time being, we are ignoring the money creation process by depository institutions, which may also generate funds that are lent to DSUs. This process will be covered in depth in Chapter 16.

FIs are firms. We generally think of, say, manufacturing firms as acquiring inputs including labor, capital, and natural resources, and using these inputs to produce outputs. In the case of FIs, their inputs or sources of funds are found on the liability side of their balance sheets. These funds are used to extend loans and acquire securities. Such financial claims appear on the asset side of their balance sheets and represent the outputs of the FI. Banks, for example, incur deposit liabilities as a source of funds and use the funds to increase their asset holdings of loans and securities. Insurance companies receive premium payments from policyholders and provide benefits (protection) in return. The funds received are used to acquire assets—mainly loans and securities.

Exhibit 11-1 ◆
FIs as Firms

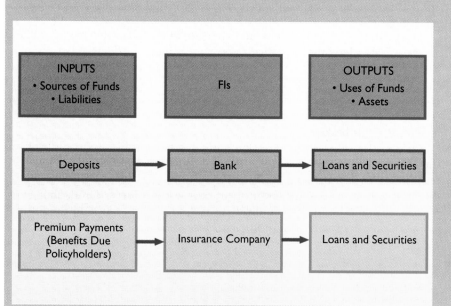

thus we call these firms, collectively, the financial services industry. More specifically, in the process of acquiring and providing funds, FIs provide the public with a wide range of financial services. Two questions are pertinent: (1) Why do FIs do this? and (2) What types of services are we talking about?

The answer to the first question is straightforward and represents a feature common to FIs and nonfinancial corporations. Intermediaries are by and large profit seeking.[3] In this context, this means that FIs provide financial services because engaging in such activity is profitable. By extension, it means that the quantity, quality, and type of financial services offered will expand or contract as the perceived profitability of such activity grows or shrinks.

To illustrate, banks "hire" funds from depositors. The interest they pay on these deposits is a cost of doing business, akin to the wages a manufacturing firm pays its workers. The funds acquired are lent out to farmers, consumers, businesses, and governments. The interest earned on the loans represents revenue to the bank, akin to the sales of a manufacturing firm. Leaving some details aside, the difference between the interest earned and the interest paid is a primary determinant of the bank's profitability. If funds can be hired more cheaply by providing a new type of deposit service, FIs have an incentive to act accordingly. Similarly, if a particular type of lending is turning out to be less profitable than expected, FIs have an incentive to lend less in this area or to attempt in some way to increase the expected revenue associated with such lending.[4] As we shall see, the link between expected profitability and the specific services provided by FIs is a crucial part of the explanation of why FIs change over time.

Let's turn to the second question raised concerning what types of services FIs provide. In general, FIs provide services to the public for the following purposes:

1. To reduce the risks and costs associated with borrowing, lending, and other financial transactions.
2. To fulfill the demand for various financial assets and services, including protection against the financial losses associated with various exigencies.

More specifically, FIs use their expertise to appraise the risk of default associated with lending to particular borrowers and usually do a better job of assessing these risks than individuals could do on their own. FIs pool the surpluses of many SSUs and lend to thousands of DSUs. Diffusing this risk in effect spreads out the individual surpluses of SSUs among numerous borrowers, and further reduces risk. The SSUs are no longer putting all of their eggs in one or a few baskets.

On the flip side, DSUs have much greater borrowing opportunities from the FIs who buy their financial liabilities. The liabilities may be long- or short-term loans, equity, or debt. Without the FIs, these DSUs would be relying on direct finance and have far fewer or no borrowing sources. Think about how difficult it would be for most individuals to find someone to lend them funds to purchase a new car if there were no FIs—or for most firms to borrow to

---

[3] The exceptions, such as credit unions, will be discussed later in the chapter.
[4] As you may know, the default rate on student loans has been on the rise. If you are following the discussion, you should now understand why banks have been increasingly reluctant to make such loans in recent years.

purchase new machinery and equipment. Undoubtedly, DSUs would be charged higher interest rates to compensate for the greater risks when they did borrow. Consequently, the significant overall economic function of financial intermediation is to facilitate borrowing and lending that result in the allocation of resources to capital (plant, equipment, etc.) formation and other spending—the investment and spending processes.

In addition, FIs provide a menu of financial claims and depository services tailored to meet the needs of SSUs, and, more generally, society at large. The menu includes (1) relatively safe and liquid claims, such as checking, time, and savings deposits at banks and other depository institutions, and (2) **contingent claims** on FIs, such as casualty and life insurance benefits, which offer the public some protection from the often catastrophic financial effects of theft, accidents, natural disasters, and death. Thus, the wide array of menu choices fulfills the demand for various financial assets by the SSUs.

Contingent Claims
Claims such as casualty and life insurance benefits that offer the public protection from the often catastrophic financial effects of theft, accidents, natural disasters, and death.

With FIs playing such a vital role in the economy, it should not be surprising that they share another common feature. They are regulated by various levels and agencies of government. Aimed at promoting a smooth-running, efficient financial system and protecting the public from fraud and other abusive practices, government regulators establish and enforce operating regulations. They seek to promote competition in the market for financial services, while preserving the public's confidence in the safety and soundness of the system.

By their nature, regulations represent an attempt to constrain or restrict an activity that might otherwise occur. In the financial system, regulations take on many forms. Entry into the industry may be tightly controlled. For example, one cannot just open a bank. One needs a charter from the federal government or relevant state government to engage in the business of banking. There are also restrictions on the particular types of assets and liabilities specific FIs can acquire. S&Ls, for example, cannot acquire common stock. In the past, regulations limited the interest rates FIs could pay to hire certain types of deposits and charge on certain types of loans. Lastly, regulations have restricted the geographic areas in which some FIs can operate. Until recently, for example, banks could not establish branches across state lines.

Such regulations, examined in detail in Chapters 13 and 15, have had at least three major effects.

1. For quite a while, they tended to reinforce and encourage specialization by FIs in particular financial services. For example, life insurance companies stuck pretty much to providing life insurance and S&Ls stuck to purchasing mortgages. More directly, the regulations tended to limit competition among different types of FIs.

2. Such specialization helps to explain the different types and mix of assets and liabilities found on FIs' balance sheets, the details of which are covered in Section 11.4.

3. Over time, FIs increasingly saw the benefits of diversifying. That is, they saw the profitability of providing the public with a wider range of financial services. Attempts to move in such a direction often involved innovation around some existing regulations, particularly those restrictions that limited the range of services FIs could provide and the competition among FIs, in general.

These more recent developments, which include the emergence of what have been called *financial supermarkets,* are discussed in this and the next chapters.

In addition to the regulatory effects already mentioned, the 1990s brought increasing competition for FIs from nonfinancial institutions and from direct finance through the commercial paper market.[5] For example, many nonfinancial corporations such as General Motors, AT&T, Sears, and General Electric, to name a few, now offer financial services and products such as consumer loans and credit cards. Whereas most firms used to rely on bank loans for the funds they needed to finance inventories and day-to-day expenses, firms of all sizes now have much greater access to borrow through the commercial paper market than in the past.[6]

To sum up to this point, FIs possess many common traits. In general, they are regulated, profit-seeking firms that provide the public with a wide range of financial services. These services help to reduce the risks associated with channeling funds from SSUs to DSUs. The services provided include the appraisal and diversification of risk, the pooling of funds, and the provision of a menu of claims, including contingent claims, tailored to the needs of customers.

To get a clearer picture of how the services that FIs provide reduce the risks associated with borrowing and lending, it is useful to visualize the various FIs as being exposed to and having to deal with several types of risks and uncertainties. FIs face each type of risk in varying degrees depending on the composition of their assets and liabilities. Before turning to the composition of the balance sheets of the specific intermediaries, we first review the types of risks common to all intermediaries and SSUs and DSUs in general.

Types of Risks Faced By All FIs

Credit or Default Risk

If a stranger knocked on your door at 1 A.M. and asked to borrow $1,000, you would probably react quite negatively, regardless of the interest rate the stranger was willing to pay. Your reluctance is, of course, tied to the risk or likelihood that the borrower will default and not repay the loan. You don't know the person's financial history and current situation, and anyone who shows up at this hour making such a request is unusual, thus, raising your suspicions. How would one use a loan of $1,000 at 1 A.M.?

Default Risk The risk that the DSU is unwilling or unable to live up to the terms of the liability it has sold.

But every time an intermediary makes a loan or purchases a security issued by a DSU, it faces the same risk. Credit or **default risk** is the risk that the DSU is unwilling or unable to live up to the terms of the liability it has sold. Perhaps the DSU has unfulfilled expectations and the business it thought would boom turns out to be a bust because of some unanticipated complication or a general slowdown in the economy. Perhaps the borrower is morally unscrupulous

---

[5] In Chapter 6, we saw that commercial paper is short-term IOUs issued by creditworthy corporations to finance short-term borrowing needs.

[6] The commercial paper may be issued through a broker who places it with a large corporation or other lender.

and takes the money and runs. Thus, for whatever reason, when making a loan or buying a financial asset issued by a DSU, the intermediary, whether it be a bank, mutual fund, or insurance company, is exposed to the risk that the DSU will default.

We have already seen that a primary function of the management of an intermediary is to evaluate or assess the credit risk associated with purchasing the financial claims of DSUs such as firms, individuals, and domestic and foreign governments. To do this, FIs employ experts in risk assessment who generally do a better job of assessing default risks than individuals could do on their own. Cynics say it is quite easy to get a loan as long as you can prove you don't really need the funds. In reality, managing credit risk does not mean denying loans to all borrowers who may default or failing to make any investments that could go sour. Maintaining and enhancing profitability in the financial services industry, as in other industries, entails taking some risks. The future is uncertain. Unforeseen events can turn an otherwise profitable endeavor into a losing and perhaps bankrupt situation. Thus a "good" credit risk can become a "bad" investment. A fact of economic life is that despite good intentions, decent planning, and a successful track record, some borrowers will default. Conversely, some who have experienced financial difficulties in the past will "turn the corner" and become quite profitable.

Given this background, the task of financial managers is to lend and invest prudently. In general, this means gathering all relevant information on potential borrowers and using this information to avoid exposing the FI to excessive risk. The information should include balance sheets, income statements, credit checks, how funds are to be used, and so on. Recognize that the terms *prudent* and *excessive* are somewhat nebulous. One cannot find a precise quantitative definition in the dictionary. This means that an FI's management team must establish guidelines that quantify the terms. This is what management is all about. Losses will occur. The trick is to cover the losses with profits on other loans and investments.

Interest Rate Risk

Another type of risk that must be managed is the **interest rate risk,** which we met in Chapter 10. This is the risk that the interest rate will unexpectedly change so that the costs of an FI's liabilities exceed the earnings on its assets. This risk emanates from the relationship between the interest rate (return) earned on assets and the cost of or interest rate paid on liabilities. An FI's profitability is directly related to the spread between these rates. FIs obviously strive for a large positive spread in which the return on assets significantly exceeds the cost of liabilities.

The potential problem is that a positive spread today can turn into a negative spread when the cost of liabilities exceeds the return on assets. For example, whenever intermediaries borrow short through passbook savings deposits or commercial paper and make long-term loans or purchase long-term fixed rate financial assets, such as bonds or mortgages, they are exposed to an interest rate risk. This risk has been a chronic problem for some intermediaries, particularly for the S&L industry during the 1970s and 1980s as deregulation of the financial system occurred and interest rates fluctuated over a fairly wide range. FIs have responded to this changing environment in

Interest Rate Risk The risk that the interest rate will unexpectedly change so that the costs of an FI's liabilities exceed the earnings on its assets.

a variety of ways, which include becoming much more aggressive in utilizing financial futures, options, and swaps. As discussed in Chapter 10, all three instruments are now extensively used to hedge interest rate risk.[7]

In addition, as first discussed in Chapter 7, any intermediary that holds long-term bonds is subject to the risk that the value of these bonds will fall if interest rates rise. The value of other long-term fixed rate assets will also fall when rates rise.

Liquidity Risk

Liquidity Risk The risk that the FI will be required to make a payment when the intermediary has only long-term assets that cannot be converted to liquid funds quickly without a capital loss.

Liquidity risk is the risk that the FI will be required to make a payment when the assets that the intermediary has available to make the payment are long term and cannot be converted to liquid funds quickly without a capital loss. Such a situation could occur when depositors unexpectedly withdraw funds or when an insurance company incurs unexpectedly high claim losses as a result of an earthquake, fire, flood, or hurricane. All intermediaries may experience a sudden unexpected need for funds. However, because reserves of depository institutions are only a fraction of their liabilities and because their liabilities are often payable on demand, they are particularly vulnerable to a deposit run that can cause a financial crisis. In Chapter 5, we saw that for depository institutions, the Fed stands ready to provide liquidity by acting as lender of last resort. Intermediaries can reduce the liquidity risk by holding highly liquid assets that can be quickly converted into the funds needed to meet unexpected withdrawals or contingencies. They can also make other arrangements to mitigate this risk such as backup lines of credit to meet unexpected needs.

Exchange Rate Risk

Exchange Rate Risk The risk that changes in the exchange rate can adversely affect the value of foreign exchange or foreign financial assets.

Lastly, financial markets have become increasingly international in scope. As a consequence, many large intermediaries as well as other large corporations maintain stocks of foreign exchange that are used in international transactions. In addition, some FIs may hold financial assets (investments) that are denominated in foreign currencies, such as foreign stocks or bonds, for example. In either case, the FI is exposed to a risk that the dollar exchange rate between the two currencies will appreciate, causing the dollar value of the foreign currency or foreign financial assets to fall. Thus an FI, like any holder of foreign exchange or foreign financial assets, is subject to an **exchange rate risk**—that is, the risk that changes in the exchange rate will cause the dollar value of foreign currency or foreign financial assets to fall.[8] In this case, the FI incurs a loss that is proportional to the amount of foreign currency or foreign financial assets that it holds and to the change in the exchange rate. As we saw in Chapter 10, foreign exchange futures and options can be used to mitigate this risk.

---

[7] An FI can be exposed to losses if it has fixed rate liabilities and variable rate assets. An example of such interest rate risk would be if its liabilities are fixed rate CDs and its assets are variable rate loans. In this case, if interest rates fall, the return on assets falls while the cost of liabilities does not.

[8] For example, assume an intermediary holds 10,000,000 yen or a financial asset valued at 10,000,000 yen. If the exchange rate is $1 = 100 yen, then the 10,000,000 yen are worth $100,000. If the dollar exchange rate appreciates to $1 = 200 yen, then the 10,000,000 yen are worth only $50,000.

RECAP

FIs are profit-seeking firms that provide the public with financial services to reduce the risks of channeling funds from SSUs to DSUs. All FIs face several risks in varying degrees. Default risk is the risk that the borrower will not pay the financial claim. Interest rate risk is the risk that changes in the interest rate will turn a profitable spread into a loss. Liquidity risk is the risk that funds will not be available when needed. Exchange rate risk is the risk that changes in exchange rates will cause the FI to experience losses in the dollar value of foreign currency or foreign financial assets.

By now you should have a clearer picture of the similarities among FIs. In addition, you should be aware of the risks that all FIs are exposed to in differing degrees. We turn now to the differences among FIs. These disparities among FIs are manifested in the composition of their balance sheets. Such balance sheet examinations will not only highlight these differences but also make clear why FIs are exposed to the sundry risks in varying degrees.

A Guide to FIs and Their Balance Sheets

Thus far in the chapter we have stressed some of the features common to virtually all FIs and the risks that they must manage. In this section, we examine the balance sheets of the major FIs. A **balance sheet** is an accounting statement that presents the monetary value of an economic unit's assets, liabilities, and net worth at a specific point in time such as the last day of a year. In this case, the economic unit is an FI; the assets are financial assets such as loans, securities, and so on, while the liabilities are financial liabilities such as deposits and borrowed funds. The fundamental balance sheet identity is that assets equal liabilities plus net worth. If each dollar of assets is matched by a dollar of liabilities, net worth is zero. If the value of liabilities exceeds the value of assets, call the bankruptcy lawyer!

As we examine the balance sheets of the major FIs, it will be convenient and helpful to group FIs according to the nature of their liabilities or the major financial service they provide. Classifying "like with like" will facilitate the development of a lucid "snapshot" and help bring the relationship between past and current snapshots into clearer focus. We shall see that the nature of the liabilities sold by a particular type of FI bears a close relationship to the nature of the assets acquired. More specifically, the maturity, stability, riskiness, and liquidity of an FI's liabilities affect the maturity, liquidity, and safety of the assets it acquires. In other words, the structure of its assets and liabilities affects the degree to which it manages each of the specific risks discussed in the preceding section.

Balance Sheet An accounting statement that presents the monetary value of an economic unit's assets, liabilities, and net worth on a specific date.

Deposit-Type FIs

Depository institutions include commercial banks, S&Ls, savings banks, and credit unions. The S&Ls, savings banks, and credit unions are called **thrifts.**

Thrifts Depository institutions known as S&Ls, savings banks, and credit unions.

As their classification implies, a large portion of the liabilities issued by these institutions are deposits. Let's take a closer look at the institutions within this category.

Commercial Banks

The word *bank* is derived from the Italian word *banca*, which refers to the table, counter, or place of business of a money changer. While modern banks bear little physical resemblance to ancient money changers, their functions remain quite similar. In modern parlance, **commercial banks** are typically defined as institutions that issue deposit liabilities that are checkable and extend loans to commercial businesses. Of course, banks do many other things too, but these two characteristics help to differentiate banks from other FIs. For example, banks also issue time and savings deposits and offer many other types of loans. They also provide electronic funds transfers, debit cards, international trade-related payments, credit cards, leasing, trust services, financial guarantees, and advisory and accounting services. More on this in Chapter 12. For now, Exhibit 11-2 presents aggregate balance sheet data for all banks in the United States.

A bank's success depends on many factors, but an especially important one is its ability to attract funds by offering deposit liabilities. Deposits fall into three categories: transactions deposits, savings deposits, and time deposits. **Transactions deposits** can be exchanged for currency and are used in transactions to make payments to others through transferring the deposit claim by

Commercial Banks Depository institutions that issue checkable, time, and savings deposit liabilities and, among other things, make loans to commercial businesses.

Transactions Deposits Deposits that can be exchanged for currency and are used to make payments through writing a check or making an electronic transfer.

Exhibit 11-2 ◆ Financial Assets and Liabilities of Commercial Banks (in billions of dollars) Monthly Average— Seasonally Adjusted All Commercial Banks December, 1995		Total*	Percent of Assets*
	Assets	**$4,168**	**100%**
	Loans	2,790	67
	Commercial	711	17
	Real Estate	1,074	26
	Consumer	493	12
	Other	313	8
	Interbank Loans	199	5
	U.S. Government		
	Securities	709	17
	Other Securities	275	7
	Reserves	221	5
	Other	173	4
	Liabilities	**$3,803**	**91.2%**
	Deposits	2,649	64
	Transaction	770	18
	Large Time	421	10
	Other	1,457	35
	Borrowings	674	16
	Other liabilities	480	12
	Net Worth (Capital)	**$ 365**	**8.75%**

*Details may not sum to totals because of rounding.

SOURCE: *Federal Reserve Bulletin,* March 1996, A18.

writing a check or using an electronic transfer. **Savings deposits** can not be withdrawn by writing a check, but are highly liquid. By custom, a bank usually allows withdrawals on demand, although banks could require a waiting period. **Time deposits** have a scheduled maturity and if funds are withdrawn before that date, there is a penalty—usually the forfeiture of some interest that has already been earned. As we first saw in Chapter 2, another kind of account, a money market deposit account, has the characteristics of both transactions and savings deposits.[9] Since deposits are by far the principal source of bank funds, banks will continually strive to increase deposits. In addition, in recent years, banks have developed other nondeposit sources of funds such as fed funds, repurchase agreements, and Eurodollar borrowings. A bank's success depends on local and regional factors, such as the population and economic vitality of the bank's service area, and their ability to attract deposits away from competing FIs or from banks in other geographic regions.[10]

Turning to the asset side of the balance sheet, banks must decide how best to use their funds to meet their objectives. One obvious objective is to maximize profits. Stockholders will see to it that the bank's management will not lose sight of this goal. However, banking can be a risky business, and the management and stockholders will want to minimize the risks faced in the pursuit of profits. In particular, banks will try to diversify their portfolios in a way that will ensure a considerable margin of liquidity and safety for the bank. They seek safety because they are highly leveraged institutions. That is, their assets are overwhelmingly supported by borrowed funds, which are either deposit or nondeposit liabilities. As Exhibit 11-2 shows, liabilities account for 91.2 percent of bank assets in December 1995. The exhibit also shows that banks hold a mix of loans (including business, consumer, real estate, and interbank), government securities, and other assets.

In addition to these interest-earning assets, banks also hold reserve assets in order to help meet their liquidity and safety objectives. Another reason banks hold reserve assets is because the Fed forces them to do so. As we first saw in Chapter 5, the Fed sets reserve ratios requiring banks to possess reserve assets equal to a certain percentage of checkable deposit liabilities.

Bank concerns about liquidity are generated in part by the nature of their sources of funds. For example, checkable deposits, which are obviously payable on demand, can and often do fluctuate widely. Nondeposit liabilities have the potential to fluctuate even more. For example, if the solvency of a bank is questioned or if another depository institution offers more attractive rates, banks can quickly lose some nondeposit funds such as fed funds, repurchase agreements, and Eurodollar borrowings that are usually placed for a relatively short time period.[11] When deposits and nondeposit liabilities fall, even the most solvent banks must have a cushion of liquidity to enable them to meet these withdrawals. Such liquidity needs can be satisfied by the holding of some highly liquid assets, such as Treasury bills and noninterest-bearing cash

Savings Deposits Highly liquid deposits that can usually be withdrawn on demand but not by writing a check.
Time Deposits Deposits that have a scheduled maturity and a penalty for early withdrawal.

---

[9] To refresh your memory, money market deposit accounts are individual accounts authorized by Congress in 1982 that offer limited check writing (say, up to three checks per month) and generally pay higher interest than other checkable deposits.

[10] National factors, such as monetary policy, are also an important determinant of a bank's success.

[11] Small depositors do not have to worry about the solvency of their bank as long as it is a member of the FDIC. Presently, the deposits of all FDIC member banks are insured up to $100,000.

reserves.[12] If profits were all that mattered, a bank would never hold a Treasury bill yielding, say, 4 percent if another, equally safe asset such as a guaranteed student loan yielding, say, 6 percent were available.[13] However, the liquidity of Treasury bills in effect provides an implicit return to banks in addition to its explicit yield.

Guided by its liquidity, safety, and earnings objectives, a bank must make portfolio decisions regarding the optimal mix of loans, securities, and reserves it will hold. Simply put, this means the bank must decide on the best way to use its funds.

The capital base is the value of the bank's assets less the value of its liabilities. In general, the smaller the capital base, the more vulnerable the bank is to adverse developments. Assume that some of a bank's larger loans go sour. That is, borrowers default and fail to pay the principal and interest due. This will reduce the cushion provided by the bank's capital base and push the bank toward insolvency and bankruptcy. For example, if the capital base amounted to 8.4 percent of assets then for every $1,000,000 in assets, banks would be holding only $84,000 in capital. If loans were 65 percent of assets, then capital would be gone if 12.9 percent of loans went sour.[14] We hope you can see why regulators are concerned that banks maintain adequate capital.

That's enough on banks for now. Let's turn briefly to the other depository institutions.

Savings Associations

Savings Associations
S&Ls and savings banks.
Savings and Loan Associations (S&Ls) Depository institutions established for the purpose of pooling the savings of local residents to finance the construction and purchase of homes; have offered checkable deposits since 1980.
Savings Banks Depository institutions located mainly on the East Coast set up to help finance the construction and purchase of homes.

Savings associations include S&Ls and savings banks. **Savings and loan associations (S&Ls),** originally known as building and loan associations, were founded in the United States in the early 1830s. Their express purpose was to pool the savings of local residents to finance the construction and purchase of homes. **Savings banks** predate the S&Ls by about 20 years and are located mostly on the East Coast of the United States. Sixty percent are in New York and Massachusetts. Like S&Ls, savings banks were founded to encourage thrift and to help finance the construction and purchase of homes.[15]

In the mid-1990s, the assets of S&Ls were over three times as great as those of savings banks. However, because the composition of the assets and liabilities are similar and because the institutions share other commonalities, S&Ls and savings banks are lumped together as savings associations. Their combined balance sheet appears in Exhibit 11-3.

---

[12] Banks may also hold liquid assets so that they will be able to accommodate unexpected loan demands from valued customers.

[13] Don't forget that by holding long-term fixed rate financial assets, banks are exposed to an interest rate risk. If the interest rate rises, the value of the asset falls. This risk is minimal for Treasury bills, which will be maturing in the near future.

[14] If loans are 65 percent of all assets and 12.9 percent go bad, then 8.4 percent (= .65 × .129) of the assets would be worthless. This is an equivalent way of saying that banks have lost all of their capital.

[15] The original savings banks were "mutuals," which meant that the depositors were really the owners of the institutions. They were actually benevolent philanthropic institutions set up to encourage the poor and the working class to save to relieve poverty and pauperism. The poor deposited the pennies they could and the funds were managed by wealthy entrepreneurs. Today, roughly two-thirds of the savings banks retain this form of ownership, while one-third have sold stock and converted their ownership to stock savings banks.

	Total*	Percent of Total Assets*
Total Financial Assets	**$1,030**	**100%**
Checkable Deposits and Currency	16	<2
Time and Savings Deposits	1	<1
Fed Funds and Repurchase Agreements	11	1
Corporate Equities	14	1
U.S. Government Securities	185	18
Municipal Securities	2	<1
Corporate and Foreign Bonds	83	8
Mortgages	603	60
Consumer Credit	39	4
Other Loans	13	1
Miscellaneous	63	6
Total Liabilities	**$1,009**	**98%**
Deposits	736	71
Checkable	97	9
Small Time and Savings	559	54
Large Time	81	8
Repurchase Agreements	46	4
Corporate Bonds	3	<1
Loans and Advances	113	11
Miscellaneous	111	11
Net Worth (Capital)	**21****	**2%****

*Details may not sum to totals because of rounding.
**This item is not proposed as a measure of capital for use in capital adequacy analysis.

SOURCE: *Flow of Funds Accounts, Z1, Fourth Quarter 1995*, Board of Governors of the Federal Reserve System, March 8, 1996, p. 96.

Exhibit 11-3 ◆
Financial Assets and Liabilities of Savings Associations (Savings Association Insurance Fund (SAIF) Insured Institutions) (in billions of dollars) December 31, 1995

The major sources of funds for savings associations are time, savings, and checkable deposits. In the aggregate, these deposits account for over 71 percent of total liabilities. Like commercial banks, most deposits are insured for up to $100,000. Savings associations were first allowed to issue interest-earning checkable deposits nationwide called Negotiable Order of Withdrawal (NOW) accounts in 1980. Checkable deposits make up a growing source of funds for savings associations. The major use of funds is to acquire mortgage loans, which comprise about 60 percent of total assets held. U.S. government securities make up another 18 percent of assets.

Although still quite specialized in the mortgage lending area, savings associations diversified somewhat during the 1980s into other forms of lending that had previously been prohibited by regulations. Other changes in regulations allowed the institutions to offer time deposits with rates that went up and down with rates on money market instruments, such as Treasury bills.

Prior to the 1980s, savings associations were not only prohibited from offering checkable deposits, but the rates they could pay on time and savings deposits were not allowed to exceed a ceiling rate or cap set by regulators. In this earlier environment, the major source of funds for savings associations was small savings deposits. Small savers found passbook savings accounts attractive relative to the alternatives then available to them. They were liquid, safe, insured stores of value with fixed interest rates. The new environment, which gave savings associations more flexibility, has resulted in a broadening and diversifying of the types of liabilities that these institutions can offer the public and more competition among banks, S&Ls, and savings banks in the arena of attracting checkable and flexible rate time deposits.

During the 1980s, the S&L industry experienced multiple strains that came to be known as the Savings and Loan Crisis or Debacle. More than 500 institutions became insolvent and were seized by the regulators during the late 1980s at the taxpayers' expense.[16] The **Financial Institutions Reform, Recovery and Enforcement Act (FIRREA) of 1989** attempted to resolve the crisis by creating a new federal regulatory structure, limiting the assets S&Ls could acquire, and requiring the S&Ls to maintain adequate capital. The final cost to the taxpayers for the bailout is still unknown, but the present value of the best estimates exceeds $140 billion. This crisis and other strains on the financial system are the subject of Chapter 14.

Although heavily committed to the mortgage market, savings banks were somewhat more diversified than the S&Ls during the 1980s. They held a substantial quantity of federal, municipal, and corporate securities. This diversification, plus greater reserve ratios, allowed the savings banks to avoid some of the strains that the S&Ls experienced.

The changes in the structure of the assets and liabilities of savings associations over time suggest that areas of specialization among FIs increasingly overlap. Furthermore, legislation now pending before Congress would allow banks and savings associations to merge. Reflecting this trend, the term *bank*, is often used generically by the press and the public to refer to commercial banks, S&Ls, and savings banks.

Credit Unions

Credit unions cater almost exclusively to small (in terms of dollars not physical size) savers and borrowers. They are cooperative, nonprofit, tax-exempt associations operated solely for the benefit of members. By law members must share "a common bond" such as an employer, a church, or a labor union. Not just anybody can "join"—deposit in or borrow from—a particular credit union. Although there are about 20,000 credit unions, most are small in size. Seventy-five percent have total assets of $5 million or less. Like other depository institutions, deposits may be insured for up to $100,000. Exhibit 11-4 lists the major assets and liabilities of credit unions.

Credit unions get most of their funds from members' savings accounts. In addition, like S&Ls, regulatory changes first permitted credit unions to offer checkable deposits in 1980. Interest earning checking accounts at credit unions are called share drafts and as Exhibit 11-4 shows, are now a significant liability for credit unions. As of December 31, 1995, 42 percent of the assets held by credit unions were in the form of consumer loans to members while 22 percent were mortgages. The remaining assets were government and agency securities, deposits at other FIs, fed funds, repurchase agreements, and

Financial Institutions Reform, Recovery, and Enforcement Act (FIRREA) of 1989 An act that attempted to resolve the S&L crisis by creating a new regulatory structure, limiting the assets S&Ls could acquire, and requiring S&Ls to maintain adequate capital.

Credit Unions Depository institutions that are cooperative, nonprofit, tax-exempt associations operated for the benefit of members who share a common bond.

[16]We should also note that the bailout benefited the taxpayer by maintaining the solvency of the financial system.

	Total*	Percent of Total Assets*
Financial Assets	**$311**	**100%**
Checkable Deposits	8	3
Time and Savings Deposits	19	6
Fed Funds and Repurchase Agreements	6	2
U.S. Treasury Securities	18	6
Federal Agency Securities	45	14
Mortgages	68	22
Consumer Credit	132	42
Miscellaneous	15	5
Liabilities	**$285**	**91.6%**
Checkable Deposits	31	10
Small Time and Savings Deposits	225	72
Large Time Deposits	24	7
Miscellaneous	5	2
Net Worth (Capital)	**$ 26****	**8.4%****

*Details may not sum to totals because of rounding.
**This item is not proposed as a measure of capital for use in capital adequacy analysis.

SOURCE: *Flow of Funds Accounts, Z1,* Fourth Quarter 1995, Board of Governors of the Federal Reserve System, March 8, 1996, p. 96.

Exhibit 11-4 ◆
Financial Assets and Liabilities of Credit Unions (in billions of dollars) December 31, 1995

miscellaneous items. Can you explain why credit unions don't generally hold municipal securities?[17]

While these proportions have been remarkably stable over time, the total funds acquired and lent by credit unions have grown rapidly over the years. In 1970, for example, their assets totaled only $18 billion. The comparable 1995 figure totaled $311 billion. Thus, credit union assets increased roughly seventeen-fold while prices roughly quadrupled! Being nonprofit institutions, credit unions have often offered depositors slightly higher rates and loan applicants slightly lower rates than competing FIs. This, along with the convenient locations of many credit unions (close proximity to actual business locations or the company cafeteria, for example) helps to explain their growth.

The deposit-type FIs, or depository institutions, are an important and evolving group of institutions. Let's see how they compare with nondeposit types of FIs.

Contractual-Type FIs

As the name suggests, the liabilities of contractual-type FIs are defined by contract. In general, these contracts call for regular payments into these FIs in exchange for future payments under specified conditions. Thus, as mentioned before, these claims are often referred to as contingent claims. More specifically, life and casualty insurance companies require premium payments

---

[17] Hint: It has something to do with the tax status of credit unions and the fact that municipals pay a lower rate of interest because their interest is exempt from federal taxation.

in exchange for insurance coverage. Public and private pension funds require regular contributions, usually with each paycheck, in exchange for retirement benefits.

Life insurance companies offer the public protection against the financial costs, losses, and reductions in income associated with death, disability, old age, and various other health problems. Based on the principle of risk sharing, the public makes payments, generally called *premiums,* in exchange for this protection, and the companies lend out the funds collected to other households, businesses and governments. The interest and dividend income received on the loans made and the stocks and bonds acquired, along with the premiums, is, in turn, used to pay benefits to policyholders as they come due. Given their relatively steady and predictable influx of premium payments, and the fact that statisticians (actuaries) can predict fairly well life expectancy, retirement, the proportion of policyholders likely to become disabled in a given year, and so forth, life insurance companies have a reasonably predictable stream of benefit payments to policyholders distributed over time. This allows these institutions to use a fairly large portion of their funds to acquire longer term assets or financial investments. Longer term instruments generally provide higher yields than shorter term assets, but are not as liquid. Given the nature of their liabilities, holding a large portion of liquid assets is not as essential as it is for banks, for example.

On December 31, 1995, as Exhibit 11-5 shows, 41 percent of life insurance companies' assets were corporate and foreign bonds, 17 percent were equities, 11 percent were mortgages, 17 percent were government and agency securi-

Life Insurance Companies Intermediaries that offer the public protection against the financial costs associated with events such as death and disability in exchange for premiums.

Exhibit 11-5 ◆
Financial Assets and Liabilities of Life Insurance Companies (in billions of dollars) December 31, 1995

	Total*	Percent of Total Assets*
Financial Assets	**$2,085**	**100%**
Money Market Mutual Funds & Checkable Deposits	32	2
Corporate Equities	353	17
Mutual Funds	14	<1
U.S. Government & Agency Securities	361	17
Municipals	14	<1
Corporate & Foreign Bonds	858	41
Mortgages	219	11
Other	235	11
Liabilities	**$1,966**	**94.3%**
Life Insurance Reserves	535	26
Pension Fund Reserves	1,023	49
Miscellaneous	407	20
Net Worth (Capital)	**$ 119****	**5.7%****

*Details may not sum to totals because of rounding.
**This item is not proposed as a measure of capital for use in capital adequacy analysis.

SOURCE: *Flow of Funds Accounts, Z1,* Fourth Quarter 1995, Board of Governors of the Federal Reserve System, March 8, 1996, p. 98.

ties, and the remainder were miscellaneous items. The liabilities are the policy benefits (reserves) that are due and will be paid to policyholders in the future.

Pension funds are tax-exempt institutions set up to provide participants with income at retirement that will supplement other sources of income, such as Social Security benefits. Some pension plans are run by private corporations while others are associated with governmental units. As in the case of life insurance companies, there is little need for large portions of liquid assets. The number of people likely to retire each year is quite predictable. As a result, private pension funds and those associated with governments place about 73 percent of their funds acquired through contributions by employees and employers in U.S. government securities, corporate and foreign bonds, and corporate equities. As Exhibit 11-6 shows, on December 31, 1995 of the approximate $4 trillion of assets held by these funds, $658 billion were in U.S. government securities, $439 billion were in corporate and foreign bonds, and $1,851 billion were in corporate equities. In fact, pension funds are the largest single class of investors in equities![18] The liabilities are the policy benefits that will be paid out to policyholders in the future.

In contrast to life insurance companies which provide financial protection against some of the adverse developments which can affect individuals, **casualty companies** provide protection in exchange for premiums received against the untoward effects of unexpected occurrences on property, particularly

Pension Funds Tax-exempt intermediaries set up to provide participants with income at retirement in exchange for premiums.

Casualty Companies Intermediaries that provide protection against the effects of unexpected occurrences on property in exchange for premiums.

---

[18] This being the case, it is worth nothing that often heard calls to "tax corporations more" may, if implemented, have the effect of reducing corporate profits and, thus, dividends paid to shareholders, such as pension funds. The result would be a smaller pension for retirees. This is an example of the interdependencies we have been emphasizing.

	Total*	Percent of Total Assets*	
Financial Assets	**$4,013**	**100%**	
Checkable Deposits & Currency	8	<1	
Time & Savings Deposits	52	1	
Security Repurchase Agreements	88	2	
Money Market Mutual Funds	33	<1	
Mutual Funds	269	7	
Corporate Equities	1,851	46	
U.S. Government Securities	658	16	
Municipals	1	<1	
Corporate & Foreign Bonds	439	11	
Mortgages	33	<1	
Commercial Paper	89	2	
Miscellaneous	492	12	
Liabilities	**$4,013**	**100%**	
Pension Funds Reserves	**$4,013**	**100%**	

Exhibit 11-6 ◆ Financial Assets and Liabilities of Public and Private Pension Funds (in billions of dollars) Amounts Outstanding, December 31, 1995

*Details may not sum to totals because of rounding.

SOURCE: *Flow of Funds Accounts, Z1,* Fourth Quarter, 1995, Board of Governors of the Federal Reserve System, March 8, 1996, p. 100.

automobiles and homes. Two factors are relevant in trying to understand the composition of assets held by these FIs: (1) unlike pension funds which are nontaxable, and life insurance companies which are taxed at a very low rate, casualty companies are taxed at the full 35 percent corporate rate; and (2) compared to life companies and pension funds, the stream of benefit payments made by these companies is less predictable. Accidents and natural disasters do not follow the more regular patterns characterizing retirement and death. Hurricane Andrew in 1992 was followed by the Great Mississippi Flood of 1993, the Northridge earthquake in 1994, and Hurricane Opel in 1995. Tax considerations lead these companies to hold 22 percent of their assets, which totaled $743 billion on December 31, 1995, in the form of tax exempt municipal securities, as seen in Exhibit 11-7. The need for liquidity helps to explain the 30 percent of assets held in the form of Treasury securities, checkable deposits, currency, and repurchase agreements.

Investment-Type FIs

Mutual Funds
Investment-type intermediaries that pool the funds of SSUs, purchase the financial claims of DSUs, and return the income received minus a management fee to the SSUs.

The major types of intermediaries in this category are mutual funds, also known as investment companies, and money market mutual funds. Generally speaking, **mutual funds** acquire and pool funds from the public, invest the funds in capital market instruments, and return the income received minus a management fee to the investors. Some funds invest in particular types of securities, such as corporate stocks and bonds, while others have broader asset portfolios that include stocks, bonds, mortgages, gold, and so on. In the early 1990s, mutual funds experienced tremendous growth. Small depositors poured funds into mutual funds seeking higher returns than the low rates depository institutions were offering at the time. Mutual funds began expanding to offer other financial services previously provided by banks. Concern has been expressed regarding the adequacy of regulation, given their tremendous growth in the 1990s. More on this in Chapter 15.

Exhibit 11-7 ◆
Financial Assets and Liabilities of Casualty Companies (in billions of dollars) December 31, 1995

	Total*	Percent of Total Assets*
Financial Assets	**$743**	**100%**
Checkable Deposits, Currency, and Repurchase Agreements	35	5
Corporate Equities	149	20
U.S. Treasury Securities	187	25
Municipals	164	22
Corporate & Foreign Bonds	117	16
Other Assets	92	12
Liabilities	**$496**	**67%**
Net Worth (Capital)	**$247****	**33%****

*Details may not sum to totals because of rounding.
**This item is not proposed as a measure of capital for use in capital adequacy analysis.

SOURCE: *Flow of Funds Accounts, Z1,* Fourth Quarter 1995, Board of Governors of the Federal Reserve System, March 8, 1996, p. 98.

Money market mutual funds, mentioned briefly in Chapter 2, are a good example of a type of fund that limits the range of financial claims it purchases. They acquire funds from individual investors and pool them to purchase money market instruments such as Treasury bills, bank CDs, and commercial paper. They pay the interest earned, minus a management fee, to investors. Exhibit 11-8 gives the major assets and liabilities of mutual funds and money market mutual funds.

Money Market Mutual Funds Mutual funds that invest in money market instruments.

Finance Company-Type FIs

Finance companies such as Household Finance Corporation, Beneficial Finance, Commercial Credit Corporation, and the General Motors Acceptance Corporation lend funds to households to finance the purchase of automobiles, appliances, furniture, etc., and to businesses to finance inventories and the purchase or leasing of equipment. In the past, finance companies often lent to borrowers considered risky by other types of FIs, particularly depository institutions. As Exhibit 11-9 shows, finance companies held assets totaling $824

Finance Companies Intermediaries that lend funds to households to finance consumer purchases and to firms to finance inventories; receive funds to lend by selling commercial paper, issuing long-term bonds, and obtaining bank loans.

	Total*	Percent of Total Assets*
Mutual Funds		
Financial Assets	**$1,865**	**100%**
Repurchase Agreements	47	3
Corporate Equities	1,041	56
U.S. Government and Agency Securities	321	17
Municipals	208	11
Corporate & Foreign Bonds	195	10
Commercial Paper	47	2
Other Assets	7	<1
Liabilities	**$1,865**	**100%**
Mutual Funds Shares	**$1,865**	**100%**
Money Market Mutual Funds		
Financial Assets	**$ 745**	**100%**
Small Time & Savings	$52	7
Repurchase Agreements	88	12
Deposits Abroad	20	3
U.S. Government & Agency Securities	161	22
Municipals	128	17
Commercial Paper	236	32
Corporate and Foreign Bonds	22	3
Other	39	5
Liabilities	**$745**	**100%**
Money Market Fund Shares	**$745**	**100%**

Exhibit 11-8 ◆
Financial Assets and Liabilities of Mutual Funds and Money Market Mutual Funds (in billions of dollars) December 31, 1995

*Details may not sum to totals because of rounding.

SOURCE: *Flow of Funds Accounts, Z1,* Fourth Quarter, 1995, Board of Governors of the Federal Reserve System, March 8, 1996, p. 102.

Exhibit 11-9 ◆
Financial Assets
and Liabilities of
Finance Companies
(in billions of
dollars)
December 31, 1995

	Total*	Percent of Total Assets*
Financial Assets	**$824**	**100%**
Checkable Deposits	$ 13	1
Mortgages	87	11
Consumer Credit	152	18
Other Loans	375	46
Other Assets	197	24
Liabilities	**$737**	**89.4%**
Corporate Bonds	$285	35
Bank Loans	23	3
Commercial Paper	185	22
Miscellaneous	244	30
Net Worth (Capital)	**$ 87****	**10.6%****

*Details may not sum to totals because of rounding.
**This item is not proposed as a measure of capital for use in capital adequacy analysis.

SOURCE: *Flow of Funds Accounts, Z1,* Fourth Quarter 1995, Board of Governors of the Federal Reserve System, March 8, 1996, p. 102.

billion on December 31, 1995. Their major sources of funds come from selling commercial paper and issuing long-term bonds.

Pulling Things Together

FIs can be classified into four groups:

1. Deposit types (banks, S&Ls, savings banks, and credit unions)
2. Contractual types (insurance companies and pension plans)
3. Investment types (mutual funds and money market mutual funds)
4. Finance company types

As Exhibit 11-10 shows, contractual type FIs are now the largest group of FIs in terms of total assets, while banks still are the largest FI. Each group can be distinguished from other groups by the financial services they specialize in and the composition of their balance sheets. Such factors also help to distinguish one member of a group from other members of the same group. More specifically, the composition of each FI's balance sheet mainly depends on: (1) the range of financial services offered to the public; (2) any specialization in particular services offered to the public, perhaps as a result of custom; (3) the tax status of the institution; (4) the nature of the institution's liabilities; and (5) legal constraints or regulations governing the types of assets and liabilities which can be acquired.

Examples of the above factors at work are:

1. Tax-exempt FIs, such as credit unions and pension funds, do not generally hold tax exempt municipal securities, while institutions subject to the full

	1970	1984	December 31, 1995
Deposit-Type			
Commercial Banks	$505	$1,951	$4,168
Savings Associations	252	1,180	1,030
Credit Unions	18	116	311
Contractual-Type			
Life Insurance Cos.	201	697	2,085
Casualty Cos.	50	251	743
Pension Funds	170	1,211	4,013
Investment-Type			
Mutual Funds	47	368	2,610*
Finance Co. Type	64	306	824

Exhibit 11-10 ◆ Total Financial Assets of Principal FIs (Billions of Dollars)

*Includes money market mutual funds.

SOURCE: Figures for 1984 and 1995 are from the *Flow of Funds Accounts, Z1*, Fourth Quarter, 1995, March 8, 1996, and *Federal Reserve Bulletin*, April, 1996, various pages. Figures for 1970 are from the *Annual Statistical Digest*, Federal Reserve Board, 1991, various pages.

   corporate income tax, such as banks and property-casualty insurance companies, do hold such assets.
2. FIs such as life insurance companies with a relatively steady and predictable inflow of funds and fairly predictable stream of liabilities (payment outflows) hold more long-term and less-liquid assets that those FIs, such as banks, which have a greater need for liquidity due to the considerable portion of their liabilities (deposits) being payable on demand.
3. Banks do not hold corporate equities because regulations prohibit it.
4. S&Ls, reflecting custom and regulations, have a perceived competitive advantage, and some tax advantages, specialize in mortgage lending.

   In addition, we can see that the nature of an FI's assets and liabilities determines the degree to which it must manage specific risks. For example, an FI with a high percentage of long-term fixed rate assets must manage interest rate risks to a greater degree than an FI whose assets and liabilities do not have such a maturity configuration. Likewise, an FI with uncertain payment contingencies must manage the liquidity risk to a greater degree than an FI whose payments are more certain and stable.

   A large part of the differences among FIs can be accounted for by customs or long-established practices existing from the time particular types of FIs began operating, along with the structure of regulations. While such specifics and distinguishing characteristics should not be down-played, it is equally important to not lose sight of the "common threads," discussed in Section 11.2, that bind all types of FIs together. Moreover, as has been hinted at throughout the chapter, there are fundamental, ongoing changes in the behavior of FIs.

   At the risk of oversimplification, we can say that banks are increasingly trying to enter the markets for financial services traditionally served by other FIs and other FIs are increasingly trying to enter the markets traditionally served by banks. This process of homogenization and the trend toward financial supermarkets means that Sandi and Dave (and the rest of us) don't really have to deal with five different types of FIs. One may provide the services previously supplied by many. Although not all attempts have been successful, Merrill Lynch is a prime example of a financial supermarket that has been prosperous. It is the nation's largest brokerage firm, the second largest mutual fund company, the largest investment underwriter, and a major insurance broker. In addition, it manages retirement accounts, makes mortgages and other business loans, and manages a successful money market mutual fund. Such supermarket trends have eroded the effectiveness of various regulations and thereby produced fundamental changes in regulations and traditional competitive positions.

Even though banks and other intermediaries have experienced tremendous growth, they are losing ground to other nonfinancial institutions and direct financing venues, which have grown even faster. As previously mentioned, many corporate borrowers, both large and small, now borrow by issuing commercial paper rather than obtaining bank loans; and many nonfinancial corporations such as Sears, AT&T, and General Motors now issue credit cards. In addition, more and more consumers bypass S&Ls to obtain mortgage loans directly from mortgage brokers.

Despite these ongoing developments, the fact remains that banks are still the largest type of FI. They have also been central to the Fed's conduct of monetary policy and the determination of the money supply. They have been at the forefront of innovation and deregulation. The next chapter focuses on banks and the banking industry.

Summary of Major Points

1. In general, FIs are profit-seeking firms that link up DSUs and SSUs, and in the process provide the public with a wide range of financial services. The linking or channeling function involves the acquisition of financial claims on DSUs by the FIs and the acquisition of claims on the FIs by SSUs.

2. The quantity, quality, and type of financial services offered by FIs will vary with the perceived profitability of engaging in various activities.

3. FIs provide services to the public to reduce the risks and costs associated with borrowing and lending and other financial transactions. They also afford the public protection against the financial costs associated with various contingencies and fulfill the demand for various financial claims.

4. Most FIs are heavily regulated. Historically, regulations tended to encourage specialization by certain types of FIs, in particular financial services, thus limiting competition among different types of FIs. More recently, FIs have come to appreciate the benefits of diversifying and providing the public with a wider range of financial services. This has led to various, often successful attempts to innovate around existing regulations and a resulting increase in competition.

5. All FIs are exposed to various risks in varying degrees. Credit or default risk is the risk that the DSU will not live up to the terms of the liability it

has sold. The interest rate risk is the risk that unexpected changes in the interest rate cause the value of fixed rate financial assets to fall or for the FI to experience a negative spread between assets and liabilities. The liquidity risk is the risk that the FI will not have funds available to make required payments and that long term assets cannot be converted to liquid funds quickly without a capital loss. The exchange rate risk is the risk that changes in exchange rates cause the FI to experience losses in the dollar value of foreign currency or foreign financial assets that the FI holds.

6. The differences among FIs manifest themselves in the financial services they specialize in and the composition of their balance sheets. The differing composition of balance sheets depends mainly on the range of financial services offered; any specialization in particular services, perhaps the result of custom; the tax status of the institution; the nature of the FIs' liabilities; and legal constraints or regulations.

7. FIs can be grouped or classified according to the nature of their liabilities or the major activity (financial service) they engage in. The major groups are deposit-type, including banks, S&Ls, savings banks, and credit unions; contractual-type, including insurance companies and pension plans; investment-type, including mutual funds and money market mutual funds; and finance company-type. The contractual-type group is the largest group, and commercial banks are the single largest FI.

8. The major sources of funds for commercial banks are transactions, savings, and time deposits plus nondeposit liabilities. The major uses of funds for banks are loans, government securities, and reserves. The major sources of funds for S&Ls are time, savings, and checkable deposits. The major use of funds is to make mortgage loans. Credit unions are tax-exempt, small in size, and numerous. Their main sources of funds are share drafts and small savings accounts. They primarily make small personal loans and mortgage loans to their members. Savings banks, located mostly on the East Coast, lend heavily in the mortgage market.

9. Contractual-type intermediaries offer contingency claims in return for regular payments. They include life insurance companies, casualty companies, and pension funds. Investment-type intermediaries (mutual funds and money market mutual funds) pool funds from the public, invest the funds, and return the income received, less a management fee, to the investors. Finance company-type intermediaries lend to households to purchase consumer durables and to businesses to finance inventories.

Key Terms

Balance Sheet
Casualty Companies
Commercial Banks
Contingent Claims
Credit Unions
Default Risk
Exchange Rate Risk
Finance Companies

Financial Innovation
Financial Institutions Reform,
    Recovery, and Enforcement Act
    (FIRREA) of 1989
Interest Rate Risk
Life Insurance Companies
Liquidity Risk
Money Market Mutual Funds

Mutual Funds
Pension Funds
Savings Associations
Savings and Loans Associations
   (S&Ls)

Savings Banks
Savings Deposits
Thrifts
Time Deposits
Transactions Deposits

Review Questions

1. List two services that FIs provide to the public. Why do intermediaries provide these services?

2. What is a contingent financial claim? Give two examples.

3. "With financial intermediation, SSUs can earn a higher return on their surplus funds and DSUs can acquire funds at a lower cost." Explain how this seemingly contradictory statement could be true. (Hint: Consider a risk-free return.)

4. How are FIs like other firms? How are FIs similar to each other? How are they different?

5. If an FI has mainly long-term liabilities with few payment uncertainties, in what type of assets is it most likely to invest? Why?

6. What is a depository institution? What are the main types of depository institutions? What distinguishes them from other intermediaries?

7. Why do banks hold reserve assets?

8. Name the major contractual-type FIs. What are their main sources of funds (liabilities) and their main uses of funds (assets)?

9. What are the main sources of funds (liabilities) and uses of funds (assets) for finance company-type FIs?

10. Why does A-1 Student Auto Insurance Co. need to hold more liquid assets than Senior Life Insurance Co.? How do depository institutions manage the liquidity risk?

11. John, a recent college graduate, is buying his first house. From which FIs could he obtain a mortgage loan?

12. How do money market mutual funds differ from mutual funds? How are money market mutual funds similar to depository institutions? As an investor, Sam holds both mutual funds and money market mutual funds. Holding which asset entails greater interest rate risk for him? Why?

13. Would casualty companies hold municipal securities in their portfolio of assets? What about credit unions and life insurance companies? Why or why not?

14. What are the major determinants of an FI's liability structure? Give examples of each.

15. How can diversification reduce credit or default risk? In the event of widespread economic collapse will diversification always reduce this risk?

16. What was the purpose of the Financial Institutions Reform, Recovery, and Enforcement Act (FIRREA) of 1989? Why was the act needed?

17. Which FIs have deposit insurance?

18. What is a mutual savings bank? (Hint: See Footnote 16.)

Analytical Questions

19. If a bank has assets of $100 million and liabilities of $95 million, what is its net worth? If 60 percent of its assets are loans, what percent of its loans could go sour before it would lose all of its capital?

20. Make a chart listing the main sources of funds (liabilities) and main uses of funds (assets) by order of importance for the following depository institutions: commercial banks, S&Ls, mutual savings banks, and credit unions. Describe how sources and uses of funds have changed through the years for the various depository institutions.

21. What type of risk does each situation portray?

    a. After the Northridge earthquake, several major insurance companies did not have available cash assets to meet casualty claims.
    b. ABC Bank, located along the U.S.–Mexican border was holding a large quantity of Mexican pesos when the value of the peso collapsed.
    c. Friendly S&L specializes in fixed-rate mortgages. There is a sharp increase in short-term interest rates.
    d. A family needs funds immediately to meet a medical emergency. All of its assets are tied up in real estate.
    e. I am planning a trip to Europe next summer and have exactly $5,000. At the present exchange rates, I will have a great time. Is there any doubt?
    f. Chad takes a loan for an expensive racing truck and then loses his job.

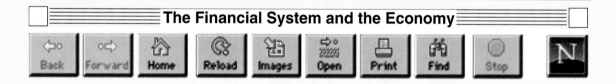

The Financial System and the Economy

1. The FDIC maintains a web page at (http://www.fdic.gov). A useful link at this site provides quarterly banking statistics. Access the latest balance sheet of all FDIC insured depository institutions and answer the following:

    a. What is the total number of commercial banks in the United States?
    b. What is the amount of total assets that are owned by all FDIC insured depository institutions in the United States?
    c. What are the various components on the liability side of commercial banks' balance sheets?

2. Some interesting facts about the FDIC can be found at the website maintained by First Federal Bank (http://www.firstfederal.com/firstfed/fffdic.html). Access this site and answer the following:

    a. Whose deposits does the FDIC insure and what does the federal deposit insurance cover?

b. What is the amount of FDIC insurance coverage? If you have deposits in several different FDIC insured banks will your deposits be added together for insurance purposes?

Suggested Readings

Two rather fun books to read about FIs (and lots of other related subjects) are Tom Wolfe, *The Bonfire of the Vanities*, New York: Farrar, Strauss, & Giroux, Inc., 1987; and Martin Mayer, *The Money Bazaars*, New York: Mentor, 1984.

A recent book about the changes occurring in the financial services industry as we approach the year 2000 is *Financial Services, Perspectives and Challenges*, Samuel L. Hayes, III, ed., Boston: Harvard Business School Press, 1993.

For a practical analysis of the typical assets and funding sources of depository institutions, see J. Austin Murphy, *Research Solutions to the Financial Problems of Depository Institutions*, Westport, CT: Quorum Books, 1992.

12

Commercial Banking: Structure, Regulation, and Performance

> *A holding company is the*
> *people you give your money to while*
> *you're being searched.*
> —Will Rogers—

Learning Objectives

After reading this chapter, you should know:

◆ Who regulates whom in the banking system and why

◆ What a bank holding company is and why virtually all large banks are now organized as holding companies

◆ The competition banks face from other banks and nonbanks

◆ The role of the asset-liability committee in bank management

◆ The profitability of the banking system in recent years

The Biggest Intermediary in Town

The chief operating officer convenes the regular Monday morning meeting of the bank's asset-liability committee. As the heads of the bank's major divisions report, the committee learns that several large corporate customers are in the process of requesting short-term loans and that deposit growth has slowed in recent weeks. In response to this and other information, the committee instructs the manager of the bank's liabilities to borrow more funds in the certificate of deposit (CD) market and directs the senior loan officer to pursue the corporate loan business aggressively by offering attractive terms on the requested loans. Since the slowdown in deposit growth appears to be related to increased competition from other financial intermediaries (FIs) in the area, particularly one large savings and loan (S&L), the committee endorses a major marketing plan designed to inform the public about several new services now available to depositors. Lastly, "the chief" directs the members of the committee to be "on their toes." Bank regulators have arrived to conduct their periodic examination of the bank's books and operations.

This story depicts the start of a fairly normal week. We hope it conveys the flavor of the ongoing action in the dynamic world of banking and helps to introduce the issues to be examined in this chapter. What is an asset-liability committee and how does it function? What risks must banks manage? What competition do banks face in the markets for loans and deposits? What new services might the bank be offering? Who are the regulators and what are the auditors looking for?

As discussed in Chapter 11, banks are the largest type of FI and play an important role in transferring funds from surplus spending units (SSUs) in our economy to deficit spending units (DSUs). They borrow or hire funds from SSUs and pay interest on the borrowed funds. They lend funds to DSUs and earn interest on the loaned funds. Ignoring some of the details for the moment, the excess of the interest earned on the loaned funds over interest paid on the borrowed funds is the profit earned from financial intermediation.

As they "intermediate," commercial banks make a number of decisions. These decisions include (1) the interest rates they will pay to borrow or "hire" funds, (2) the types of deposits they will offer the public, (3) the interest rates they will charge to lend funds, (4) the types of loans they will make; and (5) the type of securities they will acquire. Each of these decisions affects the DSUs' demand for funds (borrowing) from banks and/or the SSUs' supply of funds (lending) to banks.

Ultimately, we need to know much about the macroeconomic and microeconomic aspects of banking. On the macro side, how does bank behavior affect interest rates, the money stock, the volume of credit extended by banks, and economic activity? On the micro side, how do banks make the pricing and quantity decisions just mentioned, how do regulations affect such behavior, and how has bank behavior changed over time? We begin by examining the structure of the commercial banking system, the regulation of banks, and some of the noteworthy aspects of commercial banking. Other issues are covered in succeeding chapters.

As we proceed, we again emphasize that banks are continually changing and attempting to innovate just like many other firms and industries in our society. As a result, many institutional details change somewhat as time passes.

Nevertheless, we can provide a picture of the current state of affairs. We will suggest why banks have evolved into this current position and also be able to see many of the factors that lead to financial innovation.

The Banking Regulatory Structure

As we saw in Chapters 1 and 5, the primary reason the banking system is regulated is to preserve its safety and soundness. From the regulators' perspective, this involves continuous oversight to ensure that banks are operated prudently and according to standing statutes and regulations. The promulgation of regulations is, of course, an activity that complements and defines the supervisory activities. Broadly speaking, regulation involves the formulation and issuance of specific rules to govern the structure and conduct of banks. The purpose of such laws and regulations is to establish a framework for behavior that fosters the maintenance of a safe and sound banking system, and the fair and efficient delivery of banking services to the public.

We have already seen that the Fed is the most important regulator of commercial banks that are members of the Fed. The Fed also sets reserve requirements and provides discount facilities for all depository institutions. In addition to the Fed, two federal bodies share regulatory authority of the banking system with state banking departments. The two federal bodies are the **Comptroller of the Currency** and the **Federal Deposit Insurance Corporation (FDIC).** Prior to the 1980s, the scope of regulation included restrictions on entry, branching, types of assets and liabilities permitted, financial services that could be offered, and interest that could be paid on certain types of deposits and charged on certain types of loans. Today, many of these regulations have been relaxed, although not totally eliminated. Recently, other regulations dealing mainly with bank capital requirements have gained in importance.

To aid in understanding this complex regulatory structure, it is useful to begin with the birth of a bank. Unfortunately, (or should we say fortunately) none of us can just decide to open a bank tomorrow. Commercial banks in the United States are **chartered.** That is, they are given permission to engage in the business of commercial banking by either the federal government or one of the 50 state governments. If a bank's charter is granted by the federal government, the bank is called a **national bank.** The office of the Comptroller of the Currency is the federal government agency charged with chartering national banks. For example, the Wells Fargo Bank of San Francisco is a federally chartered bank. Banks can also be chartered by a state banking authority. This system, in which commercial banks are chartered and regulated by the state or federal government, is usually referred to as the **dual banking system.** Think of it as a dual-chartering system.

Banks that are federally chartered must belong to the Federal Reserve System and must subscribe to federal deposit insurance with the FDIC. The latter provides insurance for individual deposit accounts up to $100,000 per account and charges banks an insurance premium that varies with the reserves that the insurance fund has available. The premium is slightly more for high-risk banks. Thus, national banks are subject to the regulatory and supervisory authority of the Comptroller, the Fed, and the FDIC.

Comptroller of the Currency The federal agency that charters national banks.

Federal Deposit Insurance Corporation (FDIC) The federal agency that insures the deposits of banks and savings associations.

Chartered Given permission to engage in the business of commercial banking; banks must obtain a charter before opening.

National Bank A bank that has received a charter from the Comptroller of the Currency.

Dual Banking System The system whereby banks may have either a national or state charter.

A state-chartered bank will be regulated by its state banking authority. If it chooses to join the Federal Reserve System, the state bank will also have to subscribe to federal deposit insurance since all Fed members must have FDIC insurance. Thus, in this case, the state-chartered bank will be subject to regulation by the Fed and the FDIC. Finally, state banks may also subscribe to FDIC insurance without joining the Fed.[1]

One of the interesting and probably unique features of the system is that those being regulated can choose the regulator. In effect, they can "vote with their feet." By this we mean that banks can apply for either a state or federal charter, or attempt to shift from one to the other.

The decisions banks have made on chartering, branching, membership in the Fed, and deposit insurance are captured in Exhibits 12-1 and 12-2. They are presumably based on expected profitability.

Looking at Exhibit 12-1, the data indicate that as of September 1, 1995, about seventy-two percent of all banks had state charters while about twenty-eight percent had national charters. Despite the fewer national banks, national banks had almost as many total branches as the state banks. Most of the state chartered banks do not belong to the Federal Reserve System. However, larger state banks do tend to be Fed members. Banking offices include the home offices of banks plus branches. Exhibit 12-2 shows that as of December 31, 1994, over 62 percent of all banking offices with FDIC insurance were Fed members, while over thirty-seven percent were not members.

Historically, most banks, especially smaller ones, found it more profitable to be state-chartered nonmembers. State banking departments were often viewed as being more friendly in regulating and supervising institutions and more lenient in allowing nonbanking activities. In addition, the reserve requirements, which specify that reserve assets equal to a portion of deposit liabilities must be held, were often lower for state-chartered/regulated banks than for national banks regulated by the Fed. This meant more potential profits. Since reserve assets were equal to a smaller portion of deposits, loans and other interest-earning investments could be equal to a higher portion. (Reserve requirements for all depository institutions are now the same.) Larger banks, which usually were Fed members, often provided nonmembers

[1] In 1989, the FDIC was also given the responsibility of insuring the deposits of savings associations (S&Ls and savings banks) that wished to join. At that time, the FDIC was divided into two parts. The Bank Insurance Fund insured commercial bank deposits of member banks while the Savings Association Insurance Fund insured deposits of member savings associations.

Exhibit 12-1 ◆ The U.S. Banking System

September 1, 1995	
Chartered Banks Total	10,437
Branches	56,617
Total Banking Offices	67,054
National Banks	2,962
Branches	27,412
State-Chartered Banks	7,467
Branches	29,205

SOURCE: *Banking Industry Statistics*, December 1995–May 1996, p. R19.

Exhibit 12-2 ◆
FDIC Insured
Commercial
Banking Offices

December 31, 1994

Commercial Banking Offices		65,594
Fed Member	40,998	
National Banks	31,633	
State Banks	9,365	
Insured Non-Fed Member	24,596	

SOURCE: *Annual Statistical Digest,* 1995, Board of Governors of the Federal Reserve System, p. 518.

with many of the services the Fed might normally have provided. Fed members also have to buy stock in the Fed equal to 3 percent of their assets. The stock pays dividends that are lower than what banks could earn by making loans.

Although not apparent from the data, as of December 31, 1993, more than 97.5 percent of all banks have elected to be part of the FDIC. Apparently, banks feel it is important to offer depositors the safety and peace of mind federal deposit insurance engenders. For those who think this point is trivial, recall that in the midst of the Great Depression, 1929–1933 to be exact, more than 8,000 banks failed in the United States. As those banks failed, depositors in other banks rushed to withdraw their funds out of a fear that the problems would spread. Such a "run" on even a healthy, solvent bank could cause severe difficulties because the bank's asset portfolio might be illiquid with not enough cash or liquid assets on hand to pay off the many depositors making withdrawals. Limiting cash withdrawals (to say $25 a week) or closing the bank temporarily, as often occurred, reinforced the public's perception that this bank and perhaps all banks were in serious difficulty. As the epidemic spread, such illiquid banks were often forced out of business and the entire financial system was threatened. In what must be judged as one of the most successful pieces of legislation in history, the Congress created the FDIC in 1933. This, by and large, halted the runs on solvent but illiquid banks and thus restored some stability to the banking and financial systems.[2] Deposit insurance was first made a "full faith and credit obligation" of the federal government in 1989. Prior to that year, the FDIC was somewhat on the same footing as other private insurance companies in that the federal government was not required by law to pay off depositors if the FDIC ran out of funds in the face of widespread bank failures.

Clearly, the regulatory structure outlined in the preceding paragraph leads to a considerable overlap of responsibilities, with some institutions subject to regulation and supervision by as many as three regulatory authorities. In an attempt to minimize the degree of overlap, primary regulatory responsibility for each category of banks has been assigned to one regulator with the resulting information shared. Regulatory responsibility has been distributed in the following manner: (1) the FDIC for state-chartered, insured, nonmember banks; (2) the Comptroller for national banks, which also must be FDIC insured and Fed members; (3) the Fed for state-chartered, insured, members of the Fed, and all bank holding companies (more on this later); and (4) the

---

[2] During 1985 some state (as opposed to federally) insured S&Ls in Maryland and Ohio experienced "runs." This, once again, illustrated the attractiveness of federal insurance to depositors.

states for state-chartered, nonmembers of the Fed, non-FDIC insured banks. Exhibit 12-3 gives the number of banks and total assets for each category.

There are some people who believe that the current set of regulations, supervisory authorities, and statutes of the dual-chartering system provides an incentive for local banks with state charters to adapt themselves and structure their services so as to fulfill the needs of the local community, while guidelines for federally chartered banks may relate to national and international concerns. They also argue that the dual system fosters competition and innovation among banks. Opponents of the dual system argue that the overlapping of regulatory agencies breeds considerable confusion and leads to laxity in enforcement; they maintain that this system really gives banks considerable freedom to escape proper supervision and regulation.

As depicted in Exhibit 12-4, bank failures in the mid and late 1980s were at the highest level since the inception of the FDIC in 1933. For example, between 1955 and 1981, bank failures averaged 5.3 per year. For the 1987 to 1990 period, they averaged 189 per year. Even though the early 1990s saw a sharp decline in the number of bank failures and an increase in bank profits, the experience of the 1980s has left many industry observers nervous. In the aftermath, Congress has questioned the various agencies responsible for regulating banks, wanting to know how such failures can occur if regulation and supervision are adequate.[3] Such questions have led to the introduction of several bills in Congress to place all responsibility for regulation and supervision in one federal agency. In Chapter 15, we look at some of the suggestions for streamlining the federal regulatory structure of banking and other financial services.

---

[3] In addition to what appeared to be lax regulation, many banks had problems during years of prosperity because leveraging was high and bad loans had been made to Third World countries.

Exhibit 12-3 ◆
Regulatory
Responsibilities

	Fourth Quarter, 1995	
	Number of Banks	Total Assets (Billions)
The FDIC regulates state chartered insured non-Fed members	6,637	$1,183
The Comptroller of the Currency regulates national banks which are not bank holding companies	2,855	$2,401
The Fed regulates state chartered insured members of the Fed and all bank holding companies	1,042	$ 984
The States regulate state chartered, non-Fed members, non-FDIC insured banks	N.A.*	N.A.

*Not available.

SOURCE: FDIC Division of Research and Statistics, RIS, March 12, 1996.

Exhibit 12-4 ◆ Bank Failures Since the Inception of the FDIC 1934–1994

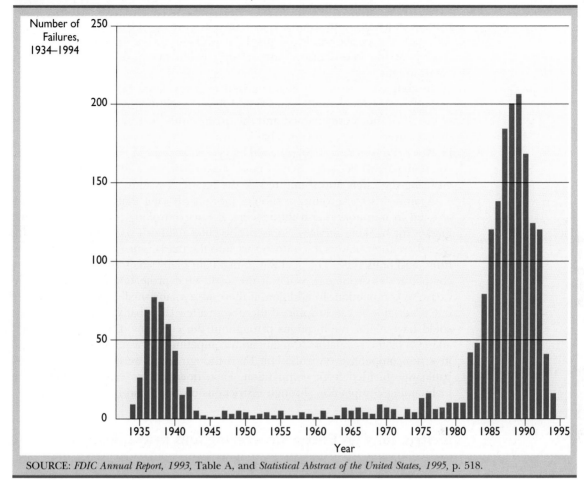

SOURCE: *FDIC Annual Report, 1993,* Table A, and *Statistical Abstract of the United States, 1995,* p. 518.

The Structure of the Commercial Banking System

Having reviewed the institutions making up the regulatory structure, we are now ready to examine the structure of the banking system itself. When economists examine the structure of an industry, they are generally interested in assessing the competitiveness or interfirm rivalry. The basic idea is that the structure of an industry, as reflected in the number and size of firms, has a direct effect on the degree of competition prevailing in an industry. For example, a large number of small firms competing against one another in a market results in a competitive industry. An industry with a few large firms (or where a few large firms dominate) results is a noncompetitive industry.

Going a step further, if an industry is highly competitive, firms are forced to be efficient and to make the best use of resources. The degree of competition and efficiency, in turn, is believed to determine the performance of firms as measured by the prices they charge, the quantity and quality of goods or services they produce, and their profitability.

With regard to the banking system, it was assumed that a large number of small banks would encourage competition and efficiency, which would result in conduct or behavior by firms that was beneficial to the public and society at large. At the same time, the more competitive the market, the greater is the risk of failure of an individual firm from the pressure of intense competition. Although the public would be provided with the largest quantity of financial services at the lowest prices, more banks could fail in a highly competitive environment.

In contrast, a structure characterized by a few large firms, would result in limited competition, inefficiencies, and fewer benefits for the public in terms of the price they were charged and the quality and quantity of financial services they received. At the same time, bank failures in a noncompetitive market would be fewer. Presumably, regulators attempt to balance both considerations by encouraging bank behavior that is beneficial to society while at the same time ensuring the safety and soundness of the financial system.

Against this background, it should not be surprising that regulators were interested in monitoring and influencing, if not controlling, the structure of the market for banking services. Some of the chief methods regulators used in this regard are their powers to control entry into the market, mergers among existing firms, and branching. The goal was to maintain many small firms and a so-called competitive environment, while at the same time protecting small banks from excessive competition. In addition, if there were many small firms, the failure of one would not be catastrophic. If there were a few large banks, the failure of one could have major ramifications throughout the economy. But, as we shall see, attempts by the regulators to maintain a competitive environment often resulted in a noncompetitive environment. Even though there were many banks, each bank was shielded from competition. First, however, we examine attempts at maintaining competition through restrictions on entry and branching.

Restrictions on Entry: Chartering and Branching

As already noted, anyone who wants to engage in the business of banking must apply for a charter. When applying for a charter the applicant must demonstrate a knowledge of the business of banking and have a substantial supply of capital funds.[4]

In practice, the securing of a charter by a new institution is only one of the ways local banks may experience additional competition. Sometimes, existing banks located elsewhere in a state may be able to open a branch office. In the past decade, barriers to branching within states have been significantly reduced. All states now allow some branching and the vast majority of states allow statewide branching. As of January 1991, only nine states substantially limited in-state branching.[5] These states were Arkansas, Colorado, Illinois, Iowa, Minnesota, Montana, Nebraska, New Mexico, and North Dakota.

McFadden Act The 1927 act by Congress that outlawed interstate branching and made national banks conform to the intrastate branching laws of the states in which they are located.

With regard to interstate branching, the **McFadden Act,** passed by Congress in 1927, prohibited federally chartered national banks from branching across state lines. It also required national banks to abide by the branching laws of the state in which they were located. State banks that are Fed members can operate only in the state that grants them a charter. Generally, other state-

---

[4] In addition, the applicant must be free of a criminal record.
[5] Paul S. Calem, ''The Impact of Geographic Deregulation on Small Banks,'' *Business Review of the Federal Reserve Bank of Philadelphia,* November/December 1994, pp. 17–30.

chartered banks cannot open branches across state lines.[6] Although as we shall see, it is soon to be a distant part of history, the McFadden Act is substantially responsible for the structure of the commercial banking system today.

Initially, state and federal restrictions on intrastate and interstate branching were motivated by a desire to prevent undue concentration and reduced competition in banking. For example, it was believed that unrestricted state-wide branching would lead to a few large city banks opening branches across a state. It was feared this would, in turn, drive small community banks out of business and result in a worrisome concentration of economic and perhaps political power in a few large institutions and a reduction in the quality and quantity of financial services available in smaller communities.

The effects of fears concerning the failures that might accompany more competition in local banking markets, and fears concerning ''bigness'' or concentration, have put restrictions on entry and branching, which have led to a large number of small banks located in relatively small communities. Despite the alleged competitiveness, many of these institutions have faced little or no competition in the local market for banking services as larger, and perhaps more efficient banks were prohibited from entering the local market. Thus, entry and branching restrictions have, in the past, served to limit competition, not increase it and were part of the reason why Congress, in 1994, decided to allow interstate branching. The McFadden Act was effectively abrogated in September 1994, when President Clinton signed the **Interstate Banking and Branching Efficiency Act (IBBEA).** IBBEA effectively allows unimpeded nationwide branching beginning June 1, 1997, or sooner.[7]

Another reason the IBBEA was enacted into law was that Congress and the president were merely following the lead of the states. In 1985, the Supreme Court gave states the freedom to form regional banking pacts. Two years later, 45 of the 50 states allowed some form of interstate banking. As we shall see in the next section on bank holding companies, banks had, for all practical purposes, found ways to engage in interstate branching even before the law allowing such branching was passed.

As Exhibit 12-5 shows, in 1993, there were 10,958 FDIC insured banks in the United States. Just over 71 percent of these banks had total assets of less than $100 million, and almost 95 percent had assets of less than $500 million. While $100 million might sound like a lot to us, it is small for a bank. Note also that there is a small number of large banks; 382 banks had total assets of more than $1 billion while 195 banks had assets of $3 billion or more. Although the largest 195 banks account for only 1.8 percent of the total number, collectively they hold about 65 percent of all bank assets. The largest 382 banks—less than 3.5 percent of all banks—hold more than 72 percent of all banking assets. The top ten banks hold more than 26 percent of the total banking assets. As you might guess, most of the industry giants are located in states with liberal branching laws. The nation's second largest bank, the Bank

Interstate Banking and Branching Efficiency Act (IBBEA) Signed into law in September 1994, an act by Congress that effectively allows unimpeded nationwide branching beginning June 1, 1997, or sooner.

---

[6] Seven states have laws permitting entry by state-chartered banks that are not members of the Fed. These seven states are Alaska, Massachusetts, Nevada, New York, North Carolina, Oregon, and Rhode Island. (Paul S. Calem, ''The Impact of Geographic Deregulation on Small Banks,'' *Business Review of the Federal Reserve Bank of Philadelphia*, November/December 1994, pp. 17–30.)

[7] States have the ability to pass a law to override the federal law allowing interstate branching. They must do so before the phase-in date of June 1, 1997. We look more closely at the provisions of IBBEA in Chapter 15.

Exhibit 12-5 ◆
Size Distribution of FDIC Insured Banks: as of December, 1993

	Number of Institutions	%	Total Assets (Billions)	%
Less than $25 Million	2,217	20.2	$ 35.9	.9
$25–$49.99 Million	2,789	25.5	101.5	2.7
$50–$99.99 Million	2,782	25.4	197.7	5.3
$100–$499.99 Million	2,543	23.2	502.6	13.6
$500–$999.99 Million	245	2.2	174.4	4.7
$1–$2.99 Billion	187	1.7	305.6	8.3
$3 Billion or more	195	1.8	2,388.5	64.5

SOURCE: *Statistical Abstract of the United States,* 1995, #791, p. 518.

of America, which merged with Security Pacific in August 1991, for example, is located in California and has more than 1,000 branches.

But the numbers alone conceal additional relevant attributes about banking—namely that virtually all of the large banks are organized as bank holding companies. To this subject we now turn.

RECAP

Federally chartered banks are called national banks and must belong to the Fed and subscribe to FDIC deposit insurance. State-chartered banks can, if they choose, belong to the Fed and/or subscribe to FDIC insurance. Nearly all banks subscribe to FDIC insurance. The McFadden Act outlawed interstate branching by national banks. The McFadden Act required national banks to abide by the branching laws of the state in which they were located. As of June 1, 1997, IBBEA will effectively allow unimpeded nationwide branching.

The Definition of a Bank Holding Company

When we hear the name of the firm Johnson & Johnson, many of us probably think of baby powder, shampoo, and Bandaids. These are major products associated with the J&J brand name. In fact, J&J is a conglomerate, producing numerous other products through its many subsidiaries, including Tylenol, surgical instruments, sausage casings, toys, tranquilizers, and contraceptives. In other words, J&J is a company that owns and operates many firms that produce a wide variety of products.

The situation is similar in the financial system. A **bank holding company** is a corporation that owns several firms, at least one of which is a bank. The remaining firms are engaged in activities that are closely related to banking. If the holding company owns one bank it is called a **one-bank holding company.** If it owns more than one, it is called, not surprisingly, a **multi-bank holding company.**

Many banks organize themselves into holding companies because such an organization is expected to be profitable. More specifically, this corporate form allows banks (1) to circumvent restrictions on branching and thus seek

Bank Holding Company A corporation that owns several firms, at least one of which is a bank.
One-Bank Holding Company A holding company that owns one bank.
Multi-Bank Holding Company A holding company that owns more than one bank.

out sources and uses of funds in other geographic markets and (2) to diversify into other product areas, thus providing the public with a wider array of financial services, while reducing the risk associated with limiting operations to the provision of traditional banking services.

Thus, organizing as a bank holding company allows banks to effectively circumvent prohibitions on intrastate and interstate branching, which have now been virtually eliminated, and to participate in activities that otherwise would be barred. Such activities include data processing, leasing, investment counseling, servicing of out-of-state loans, and so on. For a complete list of activities that bank holding companies can engage in, see Exhibit 12-6. The Fed is charged with regulating their activities. In essence, banks organize as holding companies for more flexibility.

Almost all large banks are owned by holding companies. At the end of 1992, bank holding companies numbered 6,348 and controlled 8,500 commercial banks, which accounted for a remarkable 93 percent of the assets of all commercial banks in the United States. The largest holding company is Chase after its 1995 merger with Chemical Bank. BankAmerica Corp. owns 14 banks, including Bank of America, which together have 2,244 branches. Its nonbank subsidiaries are engaged in providing such services as brokerage services to customers buying or selling stocks and bonds, consumer finance, commercial lending, data processing, leasing, investment advising and management, and insurance. Two years before the 1994 act allowing interstate banking, BankAmerica Corp. operated banks in Alaska, Arizona, California, Hawaii, Idaho, Nevada, New Mexico, Oregon, Texas, Utah, and Washington. It has a presence in virtually every state.[8] As a result, the McFadden Act has lost its effectiveness. Although the list is rapidly changing, the twenty-five largest bank holding companies as of June 30, 1995, are shown in Exhibit 12–7.

In sum, banks, under the holding company corporate umbrella, have been expanding the geographic areas they serve and the array of financial services they offer the public. The expansion by banks into areas traditionally served by other more specialized FIs has been matched, as discussed in the last chapter, by other FIs and other nonfinancial institutions expanding into areas traditionally served mainly by banks such as the checkable deposits offered by S&Ls and the credit cards offered by General Motors.

The breakdown of barriers to intra- and interstate branching and barriers to certain activities has resulted in increased competition in the financial services industry, considerable erosion in the domain and effectiveness of many long-standing financial regulations, and considerable disagreement among the regulatory authorities about how to adapt to the rapidly changing financial landscape. The changes in the structure of U.S. banking and banking laws have been revolutionary and have resulted in a drastic decline in the number of banks in the past few years. In 1995, the trend accelerated and there has been a sizable number of mergers, some by large banks. Some of the notable mergers in the 1990s include BankAmerica Corp. and Security Pacific, Chase Manhattan and Chemical Bank, Wells Fargo and First Interstate, and First Chicago Corp. and NBD Bancorp. With full interstate banking set to begin June 1, 1997, two things are certain: (1) the structure of the banking system looks far different

---

[8] In addition, in 1992, BankAmerica operated in 37 nations. Its Asian operations did $100 million in business.

Exhibit 12-6 ◆ Allowable Activities for Bank Holding Companies

Regulation Y gives activities permitted by regulation.

	Year Added
1. Making or servicing loans	1971
2. Industrial banking	1971
3. Trust company functions	1971
4. Investment or financial advice	1971
5. Leasing personal or real property	1971
6. Community development	1971
7. Data processing	1971
8. Insurance agency and underwriting	1971
9. Operating a savings association	1989
10. Courier services	1973
11. Management consulting to unaffiliated bank and nonbank depository institutions	1974
12. Issuance and sale of money orders, traveler's checks, and savings bonds	1974
13. Real estate and personal property appraising	1980
14. Arranging commercial real estate equity financing	1983
15. Securities brokerage	1982
16. Underwriting and dealing government obligations and money market instruments	1984
17. Arrange and advise foreign exchange transactions	1984
18. Futures commission merchant	1984
19. Investment advice on financial futures and options on futures	1986
20. Consumer financial planning	1986
21. Tax planning and preparation	1986
22. Check guarantee services	1986
23. Operating a collection agency	1986
24. Operating a credit bureau	1986

Holding companies have been allowed to engage in many other activities on an individual basis. A partial list of such activities permitted by order includes:

	Year Added
1. Operating a thrift institution in Rhode Island	1972
2. Buying and selling gold and silver bullion and silver coin	1973
3. Retail check authorization and check guarantee	1979
4. Acquisition and operation of a distressed savings and loan association	1982
5. Acting as a municipal securities brokers' broker	1985
6. Underwriting and dealing in commercial paper, municipal revenue bonds, and mortgage related securities	1987
7. Underwriting and dealing in, to a limited extent, corporate debt and equity securities	1987
8. Acting as agent in the private placement of all types of securities	1989
9. Acting as administrator to mutual funds	1993
10. Providing electronic benefit transfer services, stored value card services, and electronic data interchange services	1993
11. Acting as originator, principal, agent, broker, or advisor with respect to swaps, swap derivative products, and over-the-counter option transactions, based on certain commodities, stock, bond, or commodity indices, or a hybrid of interest rates and such commodities or indices.	1994
12. Trading for the holding company's own account, for purposes other than hedging, in futures, options, and options on futures contracts based on certain commodities or on stock, bond, or commodity indices	1994
13. Engaging in real estate title abstracting	1995

SOURCE: *BHC Supervision Manual*, December 1992, June 1993, and various issues of the *Federal Reserve Bulletin*, 1993 to 1995.

Rank	Bank Holding Companies	Total Assets as of June 30, 1995* (Billions of Dollars)
1.	Citicorp New York, New York	223.9
2.	BankAmerica Corp. San Francisco, California	209.5
3.	NationsBank Corp. Charlotte, North Carolina	172.7
4.	Chemical Banking Corp. New York, New York	167.8
5.	J.P. Morgan & Co. New York, New York	137.8
6.	Chase Manhattan Corp. New York, New York	107.7
7.	First Union Corp. Charlotte, North Carolina	85.1
8.	Bankers Trust New York Corp. New York, New York	82.7
9.	Keycorp Cleveland, Ohio	60.6
10.	First Interstate Bancorp Los Angeles, California	59.0
11.	Norwest Corp. Minneapolis, Minnesota	58.2
12.	First Chicago Corporation Chicago, Illinois	55.1
13.	H.F. Ahmanson and Company Irwindale, California	53.9
14.	PNC Bank Corp. Pittsburgh, Pennsylvania	51.1
15.	Wells Fargo & Co. San Francisco, California	49.8
16.	Bank of New York Co. Inc. New York, New York	43.6
17.	Wachovia Corporation Winston-Salem, North Carolina	41.2
18.	Barnett Banks Jacksonville, Florida	41.1
19.	Bank of Boston Corporation Boston, Massachusetts	41.0
20.	Republic New York Corporation New York, New York	38.9
21.	Fleet Financial Group Providence, Rhode Island	38.8
22.	Mellon Bank Corporation Pittsburgh, Pennsylvania	38.4
23.	National City Corporation Cleveland, Ohio	36.4
24.	First Fidelity Bankcorp. Lawrenceville, New Jersey	35.6
25.	Shawmut National Corporation Hartford, Connecticut	35.4

Exhibit 12-7 ◆
The Giants

Note that only 178 of over 10,000 banks had assets over $3 billion. The top 19 banks had assets over $40 billion!

*Because of the recent wave of bank mergers, this list is undergoing significant change.

SOURCE: *Thomson Bank Directory, North America-1*, December 1995–May 1996, p. R-22.

from how it looked 15 years ago; and (2) profit-seeking banks will continue to adapt to changing regulations and the financial environment in which they operate in ways that will produce further structural changes.

Finally, new legislation has been proposed that would allow banks to enter the securities and insurance industries. These activities have been banned for more than 60 years since the trough of the Great Depression in 1933. If and when such legislation passes, additional changes will occur in the financial services industry.

The Evolution of International Banking

Another area where the environment for banks has changed dramatically is international banking. A striking increase in international borrowing and lending by domestic banks began in the 1970s shortly after the first OPEC oil crisis and with the expansion of world trade.[9] Not only did the amount of international lending increase, but also the number of participating banks. *Petrodollars,* as they came to be known, flowed into the OPEC nations in payment for oil. In turn, the OPEC nations deposited a large part of these funds in U.S. and European banks in exchange for deposit claims. Many U.S. banks began to loan funds denominated in dollars to less-developed countries. In the early 1980s, a crisis developed involving the inability of the less-developed countries to service their loans. This crisis resulted in extensive loan write-offs and loan restructuring for many large banks and subsequent losses that took many years to be absorbed. As a result, the 1990s have brought less emphasis on growth, more caution, and more emphasis on asset quality and rate of return.

In addition, many foreign banks had made significant inroads into U.S. markets by the 1980s. By the end of 1992, 288 foreign banks from 57 countries operated more than 1,000 banking offices in the United States and owned at least 25 percent interest in 117 U.S. commercial banks. All totaled, foreign banks controlled approximately 21 percent of banking assets in the United States. As to be expected, foreign banks in the 1980s got caught up in many of the same types of problem loans as domestic banks and hence, their growth was slowed considerably.

In the 1990s, the banking system has emerged to be truly international in scope. Advances in electronics and telecommunications have allowed domestic and foreign banks to participate in worldwide transactions without leaving home. With this expansion, funds can be easily transmitted virtually anywhere in the world. Deregulation has made it possible for U.S. banks to open offices and enter foreign markets more easily than before, and vice versa.

In this new environment, bankers have discovered that international transactions involving the electronic transfer of funds often result in tremendous competition—and consequently, reduced profit margins. Scores of banks from around the world can bid on loans with the result being that the interest rate, and hence return, is driven to rock bottom levels. What appeared to be new lending opportunities have been somewhat disappointing because of reduced

---

[9] OPEC stands for the Organization of Petroleum Exporting Countries, a cartel dominated by the Middle Eastern oil producing nations.

LOOKING BACK

The Origins of the Dual Banking System

How did we end up with a dual banking system? Actually, it was not the intent of Congress. The National Banking Acts of 1863 and 1864 established the Comptroller of the Currency, which chartered national banks for the first time. The banknotes issued by the national banks circulated at full value and were backed by government bonds.

Prior to this time, all banks were chartered by states. The state banks issued their own banknotes, which were often redeemable at less than face value. The Acts also placed a 10 percent tax on banknotes issued by state banks. The purpose of the restrictive tax was to make state banknotes so undesirable that state banks would be driven out of business. If they were unable to issue notes, then they could not make loans. A financial innovation—the acceptance of demand deposits—saved the state banks from extinction. State banks could stay in business without issuing their own banknotes. The innovation foiled the plans of Congress to drive state banks out of business.

Incidentally, if you have any old state banknotes or national banknotes lying around your house, you may want to check out how much they're worth. At a recent show in St. Louis, a $10 banknote from Platteville National Bank sold for $9,500.[a]

[a]"The Currency Dealer." *Greensheet Newsletter*. Torrance, California: December 1995.

profit margins. As a result, banks once again are looking to more traditional markets for expansion.

The time has come to round out our examination of commercial banking by focusing on the management of individual banks, with particular emphasis on the risks that have to be dealt with. By following this tactic, we will gain a greater appreciation for what banks do and why.

Bank Management: Managing Risk and Profits

After the ribbon is cut and the new bank or branch opens, the bank's managers swing into action. In essence, it is the bank's balance sheet—assets, liabilities, and capital—that is "managed." The decisions involve what kind of loans are to be made, what the prime rate should be, what interest rate to offer on one-year time deposits, and so forth. These decisions reflect an interaction between the bank's liquidity, safety, and earnings objectives, and the economic and financial environment within which banks operate.

To get a clearer picture of this interaction, it is useful to visualize bank management as having to face and deal with several types of risks and uncertainties that include credit or default risk, interest rate risk, liquidity risk, and exchange rate risk. A primary function of a bank loan officer is to evaluate or assess the default risk associated with lending to particular borrowers, such as firms, individuals, and domestic and foreign governments. To do this, a loan officer gathers all the relevant information about potential borrowers including balance sheets, income statements, credit checks, how funds are to be used, and so on.

In addition to developing reports that quantify risks, loan officers must also be aware that they are making decisions about whether to fund a loan under conditions of asymmetric information. **Asymmetric information** means that a potential borrower knows more about the risks and returns of an investment project than the bank loan officer. Thus, the borrower and lender's information is not symmetric or equal. After all, don't all those who apply for a loan obviously try to put their best foot forward and to conceal any blemishes? In addition, those with the most to hide and those willing to take the biggest risks are often the individuals willing to engage in less than forthright behavior and/or who pursue a loan most diligently. If these less desirable loans are then funded, the result is an **adverse selection problem,** which increases the risk of default.

Moreover, after the loan is made, it may be difficult to guarantee that the loan is used only for the stated purpose and not for a more risky venture. This so-called **moral hazard problem** results from the fact that the borrower who gets the funds may afterward have an incentive to engage in a more risky venture.[10] This incentive results from the fact that higher risk ventures pay a higher return.

Asymmetric Information When a potential borrower knows more about the risks and returns of an investment project than the bank loan officer does.

Adverse Selection Problem When the least desirable borrowers pursue a loan most diligently.

Moral Hazard Problem When the borrower has an incentive to use the proceeds of a loan for a more risky venture after the loan is funded.

---

[10] In chapter 14, we shall see that deposit insurance causes a moral hazard problem in a macro sense. The presence of deposit insurance causes financial intermediaries to take more risks than they otherwise would because they know if they lose, their depositors still get their funds back.

"I realize, gentlemen, that thirty million dollars is a lot of money to spend. However, it's not real money and, of course, it's not our money either."

© 1996 Jack Ziegler from The Cartoon Bank,™ Inc.

After all, borrowers are now risking the bank's funds. If borrowers win, they keep the bigger profits, but if they lose, the bank bears the loss. Under these conditions, a bank's management team must be experts at assessing and evaluating risk, recognizing that asymmetric information, adverse selection, and the incentive to engage in more risky ventures are usually facts of life.

Bank managers must also manage interest rate risk. As noted in Chapter 11, a positive spread today can turn into a negative spread later when the cost of liabilities exceeds the return on assets. An example will illustrate the point. Suppose LHT National Bank is about to make a two-year loan to a local restaurant. The loan officer is satisfied that the credit risk is not excessive and an interest rate of 7 percent is agreed upon. The bank, in view of the economic and financial outlook, and its existing balance sheet, plans to, in effect, finance the loan by issuing ("hiring") one-year time deposits paying 4 percent. The 3 percent spread will yield a handsome gross profit over the first year. What about the second year? As a great economic philosopher once said, "It all depends."

At the end of the first year, the time deposit will mature and LHT will have to "rehire" the funds needed to continue financing the outstanding loan to the restaurant. If the funds can be rehired at 4 percent, the spread will not change. However, suppose that the overall level of interest rates has risen dramatically, perhaps due to restrictive policy actions being pursued by the Fed, and the bank must now pay 10 percent on one-year time deposits. A 3 percent positive spread (7 percent minus 4 percent) in the first year of the loan will be exactly offset by a 3 percent negative spread (7 percent minus 10 percent) in the second year. Taking account of various administrative and processing costs, the loan will turn out to be quite unprofitable.

We have already seen that banks can use financial futures, options, and swaps to manage interest rate risk. We have not yet discussed in detail how **adjustable (variable) rate loans** can also be used to hedge interest rate risk. The basic idea is quite simple. The loan contract specifies that the rate charged on a loan—be it a consumer loan, business loan, or mortgage loan—will be adjusted up or down, say once a year, as the cost of funds rises or falls. The aim, of course, is to preserve a profitable spread and to shift the interest rate risk onto the borrower.

Adjustable (Variable) Rate Loans When the interest rate on a loan is adjusted up or down as the cost of funds rises or falls.

Going back to our example, suppose the loan contract with the restaurant called for an adjustable rate of 3 percentage points above the bank's cost of funds, instead of the fixed rate originally assumed. Such an arrangement would produce the same 7 percent rate in the first year (4 percent plus 3 percent), but a 13 percent rate (10 percent plus 3 percent) in the second year. In effect, the bank will have succeeded in shifting the interest rate risk to the borrower.[11] It is worthwhile emphasizing here that the emergence and use of adjustable rate loans has become an important risk management tool. In the early 1990s, interest rates on liabilities fell faster than on assets, resulting in record bank profits. Imagine a positive spread becoming bigger over time.[12]

Like other intermediaries, banks need to manage liquidity risk. As noted in Chapter 11, a fairly large proportion of bank liabilities are payable on de-

---

[11] Note that even though the interest rate risk for the bank has been reduced, default risk increases because the borrower is less certain of future payment obligations.

[12] In a falling interest rate environment, a bank heavily into adjustable loans would be worse off than one that contracted at fixed rates on their assets.

mand. Checkable deposits and savings deposits are two prominent examples. Banks must be prepared to meet unexpected withdrawals by depositors and be prepared to accommodate unexpected loan demands by valued customers. The resulting need for liquidity can be satisfied by holding some highly liquid assets, such as Treasury bills or excess reserves, or by expanding particular types of liabilities as needs develop. One way to expand liabilities is to attract large negotiable CDs, possibly by offering higher rates than the competition. Other ways are to increase the borrowing of reserves from the Fed's discount facility or in the federal funds markets, or to increase borrowing in the repurchase agreements or overnight Eurodollar markets.

Lastly, as banking has become more international in scope, some banks maintain stocks of foreign exchange that are used in international transactions and to service customers when they need to buy or sell foreign currencies. If the exchange rate between two currencies changes, the value of the stocks of foreign exchange will also change. Thus a bank, like any holder of foreign exchange, is subject to an exchange rate risk. As we saw in Chapter 9, banks and other holders of foreign exchange now use exchange rate futures and options to hedge this risk.

Perhaps the business of banking is beginning to sound somewhat more complex and challenging than you originally envisioned. But then again, most senior bank executives don't make six- and even seven-figure incomes just for showing up in grey pinstripe suits.

Managing Risk

Asset-Liability Committee The committee that is responsible for shaping a bank's basic borrowing and lending strategy.

To manage these various risks, most banks utilize an **asset-liability committee.** Simply put, the asset-liability committee is responsible for shaping a bank's basic borrowing and lending strategy. The committee meets several times each month to shape, coordinate, and direct a strategy that will sustain and hopefully enhance profitability without exposing the bank to excessive risk whether it be credit, interest rate, liquidity, or exchange rate risk. The committee is usually composed of senior management including the president, the chairperson, and those in charge of major functions, such as domestic and international lending, liability management, and economic analysis.

Complications aside, the basic issue concerning the asset-liability committee is the rate spread between the return on assets and the cost of liabilities. In the process of reviewing such factors as the bank's current balance sheet, the economic outlook including the stance of monetary policy, loan applications "in the pipeline," and recent deposit growth, the asset-liability committee will make decisions on loan pricing, such as where to set the prime rate and whether to offer loan applicants fixed or variable rate loans. In addition, the asset-liability committee will decide how to raise the funds needed to support the planned expansion of assets. The resulting integrated strategy operates on both sides of a bank's balance sheet and leads to changes in the cost and availability of credit, which have a profound effect on the overall levels of spending, saving, and economic activity. In the 1990s, the emphasis of asset-liability management has shifted from profitability to a combination of profitability and long-term operating viability. The committee reacts to unplanned changes in either assets or liabilities in the least costly, most efficient way without taking on undue risk that would compromise long-term survival.

LOOKING OUT

The Contrast Between Banking Structures Here and Abroad

The structure of the U.S. banking system has no counterpart abroad. Rather, foreign countries have significantly fewer banks, as the following table demonstrates, and generally unlimited branching. As the United States experiences large mergers and unimpeded interstate and intrastate branching in the next few years, our system may soon come to resemble more closely that of other countries.

Country	Number of Banks* (Counted by Bank's Head Office)
France	247
Germany	2,097
Italy	319
Jaspan	182
Russia	495
Spain	112
United Kingdom	217

*Includes foreign and domestic banks.

SOURCE: *Thomas Bank Directory*, December 1995–May 1996.

Given their concern about the safety and soundness of the banking system, it should not be surprising to learn that the regulators will periodically audit banks. Actually, the audit is really more a management appraisal than a financial audit. The examiners pay particular attention to the quality of bank assets and thus how banks are managing risk. The key items examined include the percent of loans that have been defaulted on; the percent of loans that should be classified as "problem" or "nonperforming," indicating a likelihood of default; and the adequacy of the bank's capital base, given the riskiness of the portfolio. The regulators establish various guidelines in these areas and can, in extreme cases, remove a bank's management if fraud is uncovered or if the bank's officers are deemed to be acting imprudently and exposing the bank to excessive risk.

Broadly speaking, the regulators examine and assess the performance of individual banks. To complete our overview of commercial banking, let's take a look at recent industry profitability and what it implies about the performance of banks in the aggregate.

 RECAP

Under the holding company corporate umbrella, banks have succeeded in expanding the geographic areas they serve and the array of financial services they offer the public. Banking has become truly international in scope

LOOKING BACK

The Japanese Banking Crisis

During the late 1980s, the Fed pursued a tight monetary policy while the Bank of Japan followed an expansionary policy. Interest rates in Japan fell to their lowest level in history and the Japanese went on a domestic and international spending spree. In the 1987–1989 period, the Nikkei Index of Japanese stocks, fueled by the spending splurge, went up about 300 percent. Land prices in Japan escalated and the Japanese purchased such desirable U.S. properties as Columbia Pictures, Firestone Tires, Rockefeller Center, and Pebble Beach Golf Resort.

Beginning in 1989, what had been dubbed the "Bubble Economy" burst as the Bank of Japan increased interest rates from 2.5 percent to 6.2 percent. Real estate and stock prices in Japan fell more than 50 percent and the economy moved into recession. The Nikkei Index fell from 40,000 in 1990 to around 19,000 in early 1996. The yen strengthened at the same time Japanese assets in the United States were being sold.[a] When the dollars were converted back to yen, large losses were experienced. By 1996, the Japanese economy was entering an unprecedented sixth year of recession.

What have been the effects on the banking system? As you might guess, a banking crisis that dwarfs the S&L crisis is under way in Japan. Japanese banks hold an estimated $800 billion in problem loans—most of them resulting from bad loans on stocks and real estate.[b] The loans became bad when prices fell and the assets were worth less than what the banks had loaned. As a result, bank lending has declined and the economy is experiencing a credit crunch, which exacerbates the recession. As of December 1995, Japan's finance ministry announced a plan to aid the languishing banks. It may actually turn out similar to the U.S. bailout of the S&L industry. Up to this time, taxpayers have been reluctant to bail out the industry. However, a taxpayer bailout may be inevitable.[c]

[a] Some of the funds to purchase U.S. assets were obtained from loans backed by Japanese real estate. When the value of the real estate fell, some of the U.S. assets had to be sold to repay the loans.

[b] "After the Coverup, the Mop Up," *Business Week*, November 20, 1995, p. 70.

[c] "The Mandarins, the Mob and the American Model," *The Economist*, December 9, 1995, p. 69.

as well. Bank management must deal with the problems of asymmetric information, adverse selection, and moral hazard, as well as default risk, interest rate risk, liquidity risk, and exchange rate risk. Banks use an asset-liability committee to shape a bank's borrowing and lending strategy.

Bank Performance

Banks have faced increasing competition from other FIs and other nonfinancial corporations in a global environment. They have confronted a volatile economic and regulatory environment. In the face of such challenges, bank profitability, which was low in the 1980s, has improved significantly in the 1990s. For example, in 1992, banks earned a record $32.2 billion mostly as a result of falling interest rates on liabilities, which lowered the cost of borrowing.[13] The rate of return on bank equity—a measure of profitability—was 15.48 percent in 1993.[14] Most analysts ascribe the better performance by banks to their more diversified portfolios and to their environment. The problem loans to less-developed countries such as Mexico, Brazil, and Argentina, which caused major loan losses for many large banks in the 1980s, have been somewhat resolved. Banks have shored up capital due to new regulations. As discussed previously, as interest rates declined in the early 1990s, the costs of liabilities fell faster than the earnings on assets. All these factors have led to record profit levels and high bank stock valuations.

Exhibit 12-8 shows the Standard & Poor's Bank Stocks Index since 1980, the relative valuation of bank stock indexes, and the broader Standard & Poor's 500. Basically, bank stocks performed below average in the late 1980s but did very well in the early 1990s. Proceeding on the premise that the market value or price of a firm's stock—be it a bank or a manufacturing firm—is a function of current and expected earnings and the riskiness associated with the firm's operations, the increase in this ratio in the early 1990s suggests that

---

[13] The return on bank assets was also falling during the 1990s, but the cost of liabilities was falling faster, which resulted in increased profits.

[14] Other measures of profitability, such as the return on assets, convey the same picture.

Exhibit 12-8 ◆ Movement in Bank Stock Prices Relative to Stock Prices in General

SOURCE: *Global Financial Data*, Alhambra, California.

financial investors have gradually come to view bank stocks as somewhat more attractive investments than they were in the 1980s. The better performance in the 1990s is partially due to the low interest rate environment, which has contributed to record bank profits. The poor performance in the 1980s reflected troubled loans, which included loans to less-developed countries, and energy and commercial real estate loans. Concerns about the safety of the financial services industry, given the general climate surrounding the savings and loan crisis, were also quite prevalent.

Nonbanks Other intermediaries and nonfinancial companies that have taken an increasing share of intermediation.

The major challenge facing banks in the mid-1990s is competition from other intermediaries and other nonfinancial companies that have taken an increasing share of intermediation. These **nonbanks,** as they have come to be called, face less regulation and often lower costs. The lower costs result from

Exhibit 12-9 ◆

The Declining Share of Commercial Banks in Intermediation

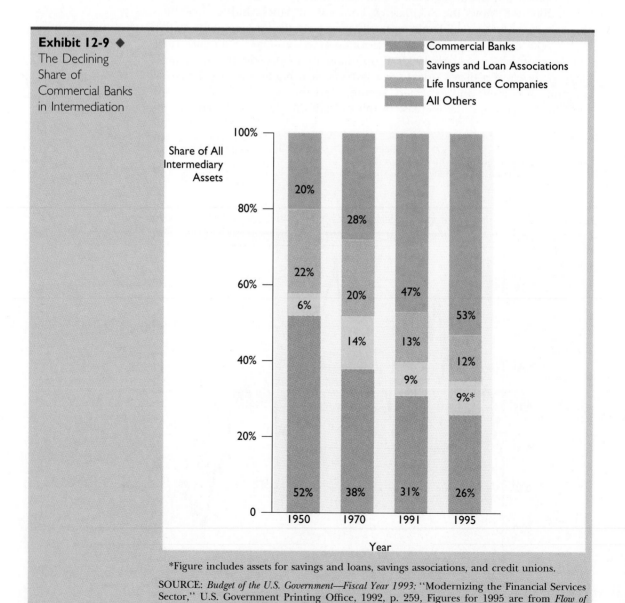

*Figure includes assets for savings and loans, savings associations, and credit unions.

SOURCE: *Budget of the U.S. Government—Fiscal Year 1993:* "Modernizing the Financial Services Sector," U.S. Government Printing Office, 1992, p. 259, Figures for 1995 are from *Flow of Funds Accounts, Z1,* Fourth Quarter 1995, March 8, 1996, p. 72.

the fact that they are not regulated to the extent that banks are with regard to what they can do and where they can locate. They are not faced with reserve requirements. They also don't have to maintain full-service branches. Despite being profitable, Exhibit 12-9 shows that banks are holding a declining share of total intermediation. Banks must increasingly adapt to a changing industry to maintain profits as well as to maintain market share. They must compete effectively with the nonbank organizations. These factors are closely related to the innovation and deregulation discussed in Chapters 13 and 15.

Having examined the structure of the banking system, the changes it is undergoing, and the behavior of individual banks, we can still only guess what the future could bring for banking. As one observer speculated:

> Although financial functions will be the same, they will be looked at differently in the 21st century. Thus we will not refer to "loans," "borrowings," or "securities," but to "claims on wealth" or "financial claims." We will avoid the term "banks" because banks, certainly as we know them, will not exist. . . . A key to the system will be "wealth accounts," in which companies and individuals will hold their assets and liabilities. These accounts will contain today's relatively illiquid assets such as buildings and vehicles as well as what we know today as stocks, bonds, other securities, and new types of financial claims. These accounts would also contain all forms of liabilities. . . . There will be no special need for retail financial branches because everyone will have direct access to his or her financial suppliers through interactive TV and personal digital assistants. True interstate banking will have arrived at last! Or more accurately, true "global banking" will have arrived, as every household will be a "branch."[15]

The aspects of the banking industry and changes therein, which we have highlighted, form the raw material for the discussion of financial innovation and deregulation in Chapters 13 and 14. This chapter contains an appendix that takes a more in-depth look at commercial bank assets.

---

[15] Charles S. Sanford, Jr., "Financial Markets in 2020," *Economic Review of the Federal Reserve Bank of Kansas City*, First Quarter 1994, pp. 19–28.

Summary of Major Points

1. Banking is a heavily regulated industry. Regulatory policy is aimed at promoting competition and efficiency, while preserving the safety and soundness of institutions.

2. Banks in the United States are chartered by either the federal government or one of the 50 state governments. Federally chartered banks are called national banks and must belong to the Fed and subscribe to FDIC deposit insurance. State-chartered banks can, if they choose, belong to the Fed and/or subscribe to FDIC insurance. In fact, nearly all banks subscribe to FDIC insurance. While only about 30 percent have federal charters and belong to the Fed, these banks tend to be the largest.

3. The McFadden Act outlawed interstate branching by national banks. With regard to intrastate branching, the McFadden Act required national banks to abide by the branching laws of the state in which they were located.

4. Restrictions on entry and branching were the result of fears concerning the failures that might accompany more competition in local banking markets and fears of concentration that might result from letting big city banks enter markets served by small community banks. The effect of such restrictions has been to curtail the competition faced by a large number of small banks located in relatively small communities.

5. Under the holding company corporate umbrella, banks have been expanding the geographic areas they serve and the array of financial services they offer the public. The expansion by banks into areas traditionally served by other more specialized FIs has been matched by other FIs and nonfinancial institutions expanding into areas traditionally served mainly by banks. The result has been more competition in the financial services industry and considerable erosion in the domain and effectiveness of many long-standing regulations. As of June 1, 1997, the Interstate Banking and Branching Efficiency Act (IBBEA) of 1994 will effectively allow unimpeded nationwide branching.

6. Banking has become internationalized as U.S. banks have increased their participation in international lending and domestic banks have faced competition from foreign banks. Foreign banks now own 21 percent of U.S. banking assets. Electronic and telecommunication advances have helped to increase the competitiveness of international lending, thereby reducing the profit margin.

6. Bank managers supervise a bank's balance sheet. In the process, they have to face and deal with default risk, interest rate risk, liquidity risk, and exchange rate risk. They must make decisions despite asymmetric information, adverse selection, and moral hazard. Most banks use an asset-liability committee to coordinate and direct a strategy that will hopefully sustain and enhance profitability without exposing banks to excessive risk.

7. Regulators periodically audit (examine) banks. Conducting more of a management appraisal than a financial audit, the examiners pay particular attention to the quality of bank assets and, thus, how banks are managing risk.

8. Banks had some problems in the 1980s because of losses on loans to less-developed countries. In the 1990s, the cost of liabilities has fallen faster than the earnings on bank assets, resulting in record profits. Despite their success, banks are holding a declining share of total intermediation.

9. The major assets of commercial banks are business, real estate, and consumer loans, U.S. government and municipal securities, and reserves. (Appendix 12-A)

Key Terms

Adjustable (Variable) Rate Loans	Asymmetric Information
Adverse Selection Problem	Bank Holding Company
Asset-Liability Committee	Chartered

Comptroller of the Currency

Credit Crunch

Dual Banking System

Federal Deposit Insurance
   Corporation (FDIC)

Interstate Banking and Branching
   Efficiency Act (IBBEA)

McFadden Act

Moral Hazard Problem

Multi-Bank Holding Company

National Bank

Nonbanks

One-Bank Holding Company

Review Questions

1. We have stressed that the goals of efficiency and competition may conflict with the goals of safety and soundness. Give an example of when this could occur.

2. What is meant by a dual banking system?

3. What is a bank holding company? Why have most large banks become bank holding companies?

4. What are the two major provisions of the McFadden Act? What was the motivation behind its passage? What is IBBEA? What was the motivation behind its passage?

5. How did multi-bank holding companies "get around" the McFadden Act before the passage of IBBEA? Defend the statement: IBBEA did nothing more than endorse what was happening in the market place.

6. Critique the following statement: Since there are almost 10,500 commercial banks in the United States, banking is obviously a highly competitive industry.

7. Describe the function of the asset-liability committee. How does it go about its day-to-day business? A bank sustains a large unexpected deposit outflow. Should it adjust assets or liabilities to deal with the situation?

8. What is interest rate risk? Explain several ways banks have found to reduce interest rate risk.

9. What is liquidity risk? Discuss ways in which banks deal with this risk. Does the development of nondeposit liabilities increase or decrease liquidity risk?

10. Identify two factors that contributed to the growth of international banking. What factors contribute to reduced profit margins in this area?

11. What is adverse selection? What is moral hazard? How can a bank manager deal with these risks?

12. Discuss the factors that contribute to the revolutionary changes in the structure of U.S. banking in recent years. Which factors are most important? Could regulators have prevented many of the changes?

13. Will the revolutionary changes in banking increase or decrease the competitiveness of the industry? Why?

14. Dispute the statement: The breakdown of barriers to interstate and intrastate banking means competition in banking is decreasing.

15. What is a credit crunch? What factors contributed to a credit crunch in the early 1990s? Who is most hurt by a credit crunch? Why? (Appendix 12-A)

16. Why do banks hold reserves? Without reserve requirements, would banks hold more or less reserves? (Appendix 12-A)

Analytical Questions

17. In each of the following cases, which regulatory agency supervises the following banks?

   a. Nonmembers of the Fed, and not members of FDIC
   b. Members of the Fed
   c. State-chartered banks that are members of the FDIC
   d. Bank holding companies

18. Explain whether asymmetric information, adverse selection, and moral hazard are involved in the following situations:

   a. I am financing a new car. In applying for a loan, I withhold information about my student loan, and the loan does not show up on my credit report.
   b. Just before quitting my job, I take out all the credit cards I can. I plan to run them up to the limit and declare bankruptcy.
   c. I take out a loan to manufacture a product. My costs end up being higher than expected, and there seems to be little market for my item. I am unable to repay the loan.

19. In 1993, what percent of bank assets did the smallest 94.3 percent of banks control? Approximately what percent of bank assets did the smallest 46 percent of banks control? (Use Exhibit 12-5 to calculate the answers.)

20. Use Exhibit 12-2 to calculate the following:

   a. What percent of state banking offices with FDIC insurance are members of the Fed?
   b. What percent of FDIC insured banking offices are members of the Fed?

21. Assuming a 35 percent tax rate, compare the after-tax return on a Treasury security yielding 5 percent with the return on a tax-free municipal bond yielding 3 percent. (Appendix 12-A)

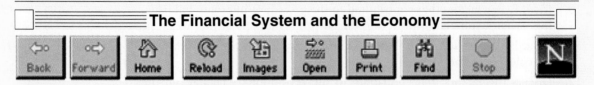

The Financial System and the Economy

1. The U.S. commercial banking system is unique in the sense that it is a dual banking system with side-by-side federal and state chartered commercial banks. Access the gopher site for the FDIC (gopher://gopher.fdic.gov) and obtain data on the current status of commercial banks in the United States.

   a. What percent of commercial banks were operating with a national charter? What percent have a state charter?
   b. From the gopher site (gopher://gopher.fdic.gov:70/00/sob/9509/all/alstru.prn) classify the number of FDIC insured commercial banks by asset size. What do you observe?

2. Browse the quarterly banking profile for the 3rd quarter of 1995 at the internet site (http://www.fdic.gov/research/qbp.fdicqbp.html) and locate information on the total deposits and income of banks with deposit insurance, and the number of bank failures.

Suggested Readings

Several articles on various topics in banking that you may find particularly interesting include:

Amel, Dean F., and Michael J. Jacowski, "Trends in Banking Structure Since the Mid-1970s," *Federal Reserve Bulletin,* March 1989, pp. 120–133.

Bellanger, Serge, "The New Forces in International Banking," *The Bankers Magazine,* July/August 1993, pp. 51–56.

Clair, Robert T., and Paula K. Tucker, "Interstate Banking and the Federal Reserve: A Historical Perspective," *Economic Review of the Federal Reserve Bank of Dallas,* November 1989, pp. 1–20. General information about the publications of the Federal Reserve Bank in Dallas is available on the internet at (http://www.dallasfed.org/publications/pubs.html).

Taylor, Jeremy F., "A New Approach to Asset/Liability Management," *The Bankers Magazine,* March/April 1993, pp. 32–38.

Other interesting banking information may be accessed through the FDIC internet site (http://www.fdic.gov/).

Five books that are very readable and contain a wealth of information include:

Barth, James R. et al., *The Future of American Banking,* Armonk, NY: M.E. Sharpe, 1992.

Koch, Timothy W., *Bank Management,* Hinsdale, IL: Dryden Press, 1988.

Pierce, James L., *The Future of Banking,* New Haven, CT: Yale University Press, 1991.

Rogers, David, *The Future of American Banking—Managing for Change,* New York: McGraw-Hill, Inc., 1992.

Rose, Peter S., *The Interstate Banking Revolution,* Westport, CT: Quorum Books, 1989.

APPENDIX 12-A

A More In-Depth Look at the Major Assets of Commercial Banks

In Chapter 11, we looked briefly at the assets of commercial banks. In this appendix, we take a closer look.

Business Loans

Business loans, commonly referred to as commercial and industrial loans, usually make up a large individual category of earning assets held by banks. Since businesses are not a homogeneous group of borrowers, the interest rate charged on business loans varies from customer to customer. The largest and most creditworthy customers may be charged a rate that is close to the prime rate, which is the benchmark from which rates are quoted.[a] Smaller and less creditworthy customers will be charged some markup over the prime rate. This markup reflects the greater risk of lending to such borrowers as well as the market power banks can exercise over borrowers with lower credit ratings.

Banks have historically played a major role in the financing of business working capital needs, particularly inventories. In the early 1990s, banks, for a variety of reasons we discuss in the next three chapters, withheld funds from businesses. Large businesses had more readily available borrowing opportunities such as issuing commercial paper. However, small businesses were particularly hard hit because of the reduction in bank lending. This so-called **credit crunch,** where the demand for credit outpaces the supply, was particularly harsh on those businesses with few borrowing alternatives. The crunch resulted from new, higher bank capital requirements imposed by the Fed in response to the many bank failures of the late 1980s. Capital is measured relative to assets, and if new sources of capital could not be found, assets would have to be reduced. The higher requirements caused many banks to pull in their lending. More on this in Chapter 14.

Credit Crunch When the demand for credit outpaces the supply of credit.

Real Estate Loans

Real estate loans are usually mortgages that are collateralized or backed by real estate including land as well as structures. Nearly two-thirds of these loans

---

[a] In recent years, banks have been known to offer some of their very best customers rates below their posted prime rate. Obviously, the posted prime rate is less meaningful when this occurs. The prime rate is typically calculated by money center banks through a formula based on the bank's cost of funds and is periodically changed to reflect significant changes in the cost of funds.

are for residential real estate (single-family houses, apartment buildings, condominiums), while the rest are for commercial and agricultural real estate. In recent years, tax law changes have spawned the growth of home equity lines of credit, which grew from close to zero to over 10 percent of real estate mortgages.[b] Home equity lines of credit are simply lines of credit that the borrower can access at any time, usually by writing a check. They are also collateralized by the real estate. Real estate loans are now the most important use of funds by banks. In addition, banks are the second largest provider of funds to the mortgage market.

Consumer Loans

Bank loans to consumers come in many forms. The largest category is installment loans that enable consumers to finance credit card purchases and purchases of automobiles, mobile homes, and other durable goods. The rates on these loans generally exceed the loan rate charged most large, creditworthy businesses. To understand why, consider the relative risk, the market power possessed by banks, and the administrative costs per dollar of loan incurred by banks on each type of loan. Credit card loans are the fastest growing category of consumer loans. In 1991, bank credit card balances amounted to $166.6 billion, up from $25 billion in 1980.

United States Government Securities

U.S. government securities are issued by the federal government to finance budget deficits, which are the excess of government expenditures over receipts. Given that they are highly liquid and free of the risk of default, assuming that the government does not collapse, such securities help banks meet their liquidity and safety objectives.[c] Recall from Chapter 6 that the secondary market is what makes government securities highly liquid. Because of this high liquidity, they are often called secondary reserves. The interest earned on government securities is also exempt from state income taxes.

State and Local Government (Municipal) Securities

State and local government securities are issued by state and local governments to finance budget deficits and are attractive to banks for several reasons. First, unlike other securities, interest payments on municipal securities are exempt from federal income taxes. Since banks are subject to a maximum 35 percent corporate income tax rate, the effective rate of return on, say, a tax-free municipal bond yielding 4 percent is higher than the effective after-tax

---

[b] Prior to 1986, if an automobile was financed, the interest payments could be deducted from gross income for the purposes of arriving at taxable income. Likewise, interest payments on credit cards and other consumer debt could be deducted in the same manner. In 1986, a tax law change phased out interest write-offs except for mortgage interest payments. Home equity lines of credit were devised to allow taxpayers to legally get around the interest write-off exclusion. With a home equity line of credit, a car can be purchased by writing a check against the equity in a home and the interest still is deductible. No wonder home equity lines of credit have experienced such incredible growth.

[c] Again, long-term government securities may be subject to capital losses if the interest rate rises.

return on a Treasury security yielding 6 percent. The after-tax return on the 6 percent Treasury security is 3.9 percent since taxes are 2.1 percent (6 percent × .35 percent = 2.1 percent). The second, more subtle attraction is that banks often find it in their best interests to purchase some securities issued by municipalities in their immediate geographic area. When a considerable portion of a bank's deposits comes from the local economy, the bank is considered to have made an "investment in goodwill." Some may also see the investment in municipals as a necessary political investment.[d]

Reserves

Reserves are perhaps the most familiar of a bank's assets. Banks hold reserves in two forms: the first is called vault cash, which is currency and coin held by banks to accommodate customer needs; the second, held with Federal Reserve Banks, is called deposits with the Fed. The sum of the two is total reserves.

One reason banks hold reserves is to help meet their liquidity and safety objectives. Another reason is because the Fed forces them to do so. The Fed sets reserve requirements, which specify that banks must possess reserve assets equal to a certain percentage of checkable deposit liabilities. These reserve assets are called required reserves. Any reserves that banks choose to hold over and above this figure are referred to as excess reserves. Under normal business conditions, banks manage their reserve position so that excess reserves are close to zero. We can assume that without the Fed requirements, banks would hold fewer reserves.[e]

Note that total reserves can be defined in terms of the form in which they are kept, such as vault cash or deposits at the Fed, or by how they are being used, such as for required reserves or excess reserves. Why all the fuss about reserves? Simply put, as we have seen, by altering the quantity of reserves in the banking system or reserve requirements, the Fed can affect the volume of deposits and the volume of credit extended by banks. Furthermore when loans and investments are affected, interest rates and ultimately economic activity are also affected. We return to the details of these relationships often in later chapters.

---

[d] Banks are also subject to the Community Reinvestment Act, which holds them responsible for investing in their community.

[e] "Under normal conditions" needs to be emphasized. During the mid and latter part of the Great Depression in the 1930s, banks were holding large amounts of excess reserves since they had seen so many banks fail because of insufficient reserves.

13

Financial Innovation and Deregulation

> *Necessity is the mother of invention.*

Learning Objectives

After reading this chapter, you should know:

◆ What financial innovation is and why it has occurred at a rapid pace since the mid-1960s

◆ The major types of financial innovations

◆ How regulations affect the incentive to innovate

◆ The roles of inflation, interest rates, competition, and technological advances in triggering financial innovation

◆ The major provisions of the Depository Institutions Deregulation and Monetary Control Act (DIDMCA) of 1980 and the Garn–St. Germain Act of 1982

The Road from There to Here

Carol, a student at State U. majoring in finance, is about to register for fall semester classes. Interested in working overseas for a large financial institution, she is attracted to a course in the political science department (Pol Sci 505) that examines different political systems and how they influence the conduct of policy. The problem is that it is a graduate course and college rules do not allow undergraduates to register for such courses. Undaunted, Carol meets with the instructor and convinces him that she is fully capable of handling the material. He tells her to register for Pol Sci 296, a listing usually reserved for special independent study courses, and to attend Pol Sci 505. Proceeding in this way, Carol will get to take the course she desires and, in the process, evade the college regulation.

Such adaptive or innovative behavior permeates a college campus. We tell our students that anyone who can't find their way around most university rules isn't trying very hard. Innovation is also widespread in the economy at large. The driving force behind such behavior is reasonably straightforward; university students or other participants in the economy are simply trying to come as close as possible to achieving their objectives. The objective could be a well-rounded education likely to lead to a well-paying, interesting job in the case of a student, or maximum profitability in the case of a firm. This process, referred to as maximization in Chapter 4, is nothing more than the attempt of economic units to do the best they can, given their objectives and the circumstances they face. But what does "doing the best one can" mean in this context? Simply put, if the circumstances pose a barrier to achieving an objective, there is an obvious incentive to find a way to surmount, or otherwise avoid, whatever is standing in the way. As the quotation at the beginning of the chapter suggests, such incentives give birth to the innovation we subsequently observe.

In our discussion of the financial system, we have repeatedly emphasized that change is an enduring characteristic. The system is different from what it was ten years ago, and it will be different ten years hence. Previous chapters have described some of the particularly noteworthy changes. The major forces producing these changes include three influences: (1) innovation in the ways people spend, save, and borrow funds; (2) innovation in the operations and scope of activities engaged in by financial intermediaries (FIs), and (3) changes in financial regulations.

The purpose of this chapter is to develop a more complete understanding of the causes and consequences of the wave of financial innovation and regulatory changes that have altered the U.S. financial system over the past 25 to 30 years. In Chapter 15, we look at the regulatory environment taking shape in the 1990s including some measures that aim at tightening up regulations.

Analytical Foundations and Major Causes of Financial Innovation

A famous economist, Joseph Schumpeter, wrote extensively about the process of economic development. Within this process, he emphasized the key role played by the entrepreneur/innovator. The prototype is a creative, insightful individual or group of individuals willing to take a few risks in the pursuit of higher profits. The innovation may involve the development and adoption of a cheaper method of production or the introduction of an entirely new product. Holding other factors constant, lower production costs will, of course, raise profits. Similarly, if a new product catches on, sales and profits will increase.

Less dramatic but no less important examples of innovative activity include the application of newly developed or existing technology in a new field or product area, and the discovery and adoption of new methods of operating that legally evade rules and regulations. In both cases, profits are increased in the process. As we shall see in a few moments, it was the adoption of new technology and the avoidance of regulations that played key roles in the process of **financial innovation** during the 1960s and 1970s. In addition, two other factors have been important in generating recent financial innovations: (1) FIs face increasing competition from other financial and nonfinancial institutions, causing them to innovate as part of a struggle to survive; and (2) prices, inflation, interest rates, and exchange rates have become more volatile causing the development of innovations that deal with this instability. All told, these factors have caused the period since the mid-1960s to be an era of rapid financial innovation with one innovation leading to another and resulting in a restructuring of the entire financial sector.

Financial Innovation The creation of new financial instruments, markets, and institutions in the financial services industry; new ways for people to spend, save, and borrow funds; changes in the operation and scope of activity by financial intermediaries.

The Beginning Regulatory Structure

Before we can move on to a discussion of the financial innovations that have occurred in the past 30 years, it is first necessary to understand the regulatory structure in place during the mid-1960s and early 1970s at the start of the period. We need a short history lesson to do so.

For the most part, the regulatory structure prevailing at the beginning of the 1970s was inherited from and the product of the 1930s. This structure was put in place as a result of events that occurred at the start of and during the Great Depression. In October 1929, prices on the New York Stock Exchange collapsed. The Dow Jones Industrial Index, a measure of stock market values, stood at 200 in January 1928, rose to 381 in September 1929, and then collapsed. The Dow fell to an eventual low of 41 in July 1932. From 1929 through 1933 more than 8,000 banks failed, industrial production fell more than 50 percent, and the nation's unemployment rate rose from 3 percent to 25 percent. The belief at the time was that these events were intimately connected and that the Great Depression was caused and/or severely aggravated by serious defects in the structure and regulation of the financial system. More specifically, the failure of many financial institutions was alleged to be the result of (1) "excessive and destructive competition" among banks, which had led to the payment of unduly high interest rates on deposits, and (2) the granting of overly risky loans, particularly those extended to stock market speculators. The belief was that seeking out such loans, and the high yields they carried, was necessitated by the high rates being paid on deposits. When the stock market crashed, the value of the speculators' portfolios collapsed, leading them to default on their bank loans. The banks, in turn, found themselves insolvent (bankrupt) or in a weakened position sufficient to generate withdrawals by depositors.

Given this diagnosis, the legislative and regulatory remedies, most of which emerged with the **Glass–Steagall Act of 1933,** are readily understandable.[1] Among the most widespread and ultimately pernicious "cures" was the establishment of maximum ceilings on the interest rates banks could pay on deposits. The ceilings were popularly known as **Regulation Q.** Interest payments on demand deposits, which were the only type of checkable deposit in existence at the time, were prohibited, and interest payments on time and savings deposits were not to exceed the rate ceilings set by the relevant regulatory authority. The Federal Reserve was the regulatory authority for member banks and the Federal Deposit Insurance Corporation (FDIC) for nonmember insured banks. The rationale for such ceilings was seductive and attractive. If the rates on deposits (sources of bank funds) could be held down, this would tend to hold down the rates on loans (uses of funds). The seeking out and granting of high-risk, high-yield loans would be unnecessary.

In addition, to further limit bank failures, the Glass–Steagall Act put deposit insurance into place with the creation of the FDIC. As noted in Chapter 11, the deposits of most banks and other depository institutions are now fully insured up to $100,000. The presence of deposit insurance eliminated bank runs or bank panics in which depositors feared the failure of their bank and "ran" to get their funds out. However, deposit insurance would eventually give banks a greater incentive to make riskier loans and investments, contradicting the presumed intent of Regulation Q. The reasoning goes that if depositors are protected with deposit insurance, banks can take greater risks than if they have to be directly accountable to their depositors. Rather than protecting the safety and soundness of banking, deposit insurance led to a dormant erosion of safety.

Other remedies to the debacle during the Great Depression included (1) tighter control on entry into the banking industry, including chartering and branching laws, so as to limit competition, and (2) the prohibition of so-called "insider loans" to bank officers or directors to minimize conflicts of interest and the possibility of fraud. In addition, investment banking, which is the underwriting and marketing of primary corporate securities, was separated from commercial banking by the Glass–Steagall Act. Banks were no longer allowed to own or underwrite corporate securities. Thus, the assets commercial banks could hold were effectively limited to cash assets, government securities, and loans. The commercial bank was to accept deposits paying up to Regulation Q interest rate ceilings and to make commercial loans predominately. For the purchaser of stocks, limits were put on the proportion of purchases that could be financed by borrowing. These limits were called margin requirements. With this regulatory structure prevailing from the 1930s until the early 1980s, the Fed, the FDIC, and the Comptroller of the Currency exercised broad supervisory and regulatory powers over banks. We now turn to the analytical framework for financial innovation that would generate change in such an environment.

The Analytic Foundations of Financial Innovation

Viewed analytically, the incentive for borrowers or lenders of FIs to engage in innovative activity flows from a comparison of costs and benefits. More spe-

---

[1] Subsequent research has seriously questioned this analysis. For example, it appears that prior to the Great Depression, those banks that paid the very highest rates on deposits were not the ones most likely to later fail.

cifically, an FI, for example, compares the costs and revenues (benefits) associated with some alteration in prevailing portfolio practices. Adopting a new technology or developing a new product, such as a new type of time deposit, can be costly. If the end result is expected to be, say, a reduction in the costs of providing financial services or a rise in the revenue on earning assets—possible benefits of innovation, which exceed the costs of innovation—then there exists a clear profit incentive to innovate and thus alter prevailing practices.

Declining Costs of Innovation

With the preceding discussion as background, understanding the rapid pace of innovation in the financial system will not be difficult. Focusing on the cost side, one factor appears to have been particularly important. Ongoing from the 1970s to the present time, computer and telecommunications technologies are increasingly available and powerful, as well as less costly to adopt. As noted earlier when discussing electronic funds transfer systems, this had the effect of reducing the transactions costs associated with moving and managing funds. Financial claims are particularly receptive to computer advances because they are quite **fungible.** Fungibility is a characteristic referring to the ease with which one item can be transformed into another. How does such a characteristic fit in here? Think back to the story that opened the chapter. Carol and her professor innovated by essentially relabeling a course. This type of change is much easier and less costly than say turning an automobile plant into a computer factory. The situation is similar in the financial world where funds can be moved or transported and, in effect, relabeled relatively easily, making innovation less costly than might be the case in other industries.

Fungible A characteristic referring to the ease with which a financial instrument can be converted to another.

Rising Benefits of Innovation

Turning to the benefits side, the interaction between the prevailing economic environment and the structure of financial regulations initially played the major role. Recall that Regulation Q put interest rate ceilings on bank and savings and loan (S&L) deposits and the activities of banks were fairly tightly controlled. If innovating around these controls could be extremely profitable, then substantial ingenuity would be used to find ways around the restrictions. In the mid-1960s, such an environment developed because of persistent inflation and rising interest rates in a regulatory environment not designed to handle such events. The benefits of avoiding regulations greatly increased in an inflationary environment, and one of the first responses was to develop new products to avoid the binding effects of the regulations. A fatal flaw in the regulatory structure put in place during the Great Depression was in not recognizing the sequence of events that would occur if market interest rates increased and remained above Regulation Q ceilings for a significant period of time. Imagine the following scenarios.

You are a surplus spending unit (SSU) with a savings deposit earning 5 percent, the ceiling rate, at HLT National Bank. Are you satisfied or not? The answer is again, it depends. In particular, it depends on the rate you could earn on the next best option, say on another highly liquid, safe financial claim that would be a substitute for the savings deposit, such as a Treasury bill. Suppose the prevailing rate on Treasury bills in the Treasury securities market is 4 percent. Obviously, you can smile as your rate on the savings deposit is higher.

Alternatively, if the rate on bills was 8 percent, the picture would be quite different. We would expect people to shift funds out of savings deposits and into Treasury bills (T-bills). Such a removal of funds from banks and other intermediaries is called **disintermediation.**[2] The intermediaries are bypassed in the borrowing-lending process. The flaw in Regulation Q then was that there was no way to keep people from withdrawing their funds as they sought out better opportunities. As long as market interest rates are below Regulation Q ceilings, intermediaries subject to Regulation Q can effectively compete against open market instruments such as T-bills, commercial paper, and corporate bonds. However, if rates on the instruments traded in the open market rise above ceiling limits, disintermediation follows as depositors take their funds out of intermediaries and invest them in open market instruments such as T-bills, commercial paper, and so on. The result is that banks are weakened as deposits flow out, subverting the good intention motivating Regulation Q, which was to strengthen the position of banks.

During the 1970s, disintermediation occurred at an alarming rate because market interest rates were substantially above Regulation Q limits. Savers with large balances had always been able to disintermediate and usually did so when market interest rates went above the Regulation Q limit. However, small savers with few alternatives were stuck earning the ceiling rate at depository institutions. Persistently high interest rates in the 1970s caused the development of money market mutual funds, which would change things. Ingenious entrepreneurs who developed these instruments gave small savers an alternative to deposits in banks or other depository institutions also subject to Regulation Q ceiling limits.

As discussed in Chapter 11, money market mutual funds pool funds from small investors, say $5,000 from five individuals, and acquire money market instruments, such as T-bills and commercial paper, that are unavailable to the small saver on her own because of a high minimum denomination. The money market mutual fund passes the higher interest earned, minus a management fee, on to the small investor. For example, suppose you had $5,000 in a savings deposit at a bank and it was yielding the Regulation Q ceiling rate of 5 percent and the rate on commercial paper was 10 percent. You would like to transfer your funds from the depository institution, but if the minimum denomination on commercial paper is $25,000, you don't have enough to acquire the market instrument. After the birth of money market mutual funds, you are able to transfer your funds to a money market mutual fund that pools funds from several small depositors and buys higher denomination instruments while keeping a management fee.

Now put yourself in the position of the bank's president. Profitable lending opportunities exist, but you are losing deposits as disintermediation and the transfer of funds to money market mutual funds proceed.[3] An incentive exists

---

Disintermediation The removal of funds from a financial intermediary.

---

[2] Actually the removal of funds from depository institutions is only half of disintermediation; the other half is the disposing of primary securities by the intermediaries to obtain the funds to pay the depositors. Disintermediation upsets the process by which resources are allocated to capital formation.

[3] Be sure you are clear that disintermediation means the removal of funds from FIs into open market instruments such as government securities, stocks, or bonds. When funds are removed from depository institutions and put into money market mutual funds, disintermediation has not occurred because money market mutual funds are intermediaries.

to find a way to reverse the outflow of funds. A frontal attack is ruled out by Regulation Q. You cannot raise the explicit rate you pay on savings deposits. Putting your head together with the bank's lawyers and accountants you find ways to pay implicit interest. Prominent examples include offering free safe deposit boxes, bonuses such as toasters and dinnerware, and other conveniences to depositors. Let's say these attempts help some, but disintermediation continues, albeit at a slower pace. The breakthrough occurs when your bank and other FIs create new liabilities, many of which represent a relabeling of existing bank liabilities from deposits subject to interest rate ceilings and other regulations to liabilities not subject to such regulations. Thus, the interaction between the prevailing economic environment and the structure of financial regulation, Regulation Q in this case, produced rising benefits of innovation. The level of market interest rates coupled with relatively high inflation produced rising benefits if Regulation Q limits could be avoided. Or, put another way, the changing environment made not complying with such regulations increasingly beneficial in terms of profits, and FIs and their customers were induced to alter prevailing practices. Eventually Regulation Q ceiling limits would be removed, but additional factors would come into play, causing further innovation by banks.

Increasing Competition

As we have seen, since the mid-1970s to the present, banks have been faced with a sharp rise in competition from other financial and nonfinancial institutions. The competition often had lower costs because they were not subject to the same regulations or scrutiny as banks. They did not have to maintain full service branches and could open a financial subsidiary in, say, an existing retail branch.

In any industry with increased competition, profit margins are generally reduced and cost-saving technological advances become more important. This is particularly true for banks when the increased competition comes from firms that already have lower costs. Likewise, because of this increased competition, the benefits of developing a new set of financial and banking products and services are greatly increased. As we saw in Chapter 12, examples of these new products and services include investment and financial advice, leasing, data processing, tax planning, and securities underwriting. Look back to Exhibit 12-6 for a listing of all activities now allowable for bank holding companies. Despite their efforts, banks' share of total intermediation has been declining, and like any business that is losing market share, attempts to stop the "bleeding" become more profitable. Consequently, the greater the competition, the greater is the drive to innovate from both the costs and benefits perspectives.

Greater Volatility

Finally, greater volatility of such things as price indexes, stock values, interest rates, and exchange rates increases the risks and hence the costs associated with intermediation. The increased risks made financial innovation to deal with this volatility much more beneficial. New assets have been and are being developed to mitigate the risks associated with this greater volatility. Chapter 10 was devoted to financial futures and options markets, which are financial innovations that attempt to hedge interest rate and exchange rate risks. Banks now use these instruments to exploit opportunities for profit from even minute price differentials as well as to lessen interest rate and exchange rate risks.

Saving our discussion of the specific types of innovation for the next section, let's sum up the message of this section. Whenever the perceived benefits of innovation exceed the costs, an incentive exists to engage in innovation. The pace of innovation in the United States was rapid over the past 30 years, as the costs of innovation fell and the benefits rose, as depicted in Exhibit 13-1. On the cost side, the malleability of financial claims and the application of emerging computer and telecommunications technology reduced the transactions costs associated with moving and managing funds. On the benefits side, three factors come into play:

1. The rise in inflation and interest rates increased the benefits in terms of greater profits associated with avoiding various regulations. For example, with market rates well in excess of Regulation Q ceiling rates on deposits, SSUs are induced to reduce their holdings of such deposits. The resulting disintermediation and its adverse effect on the profits of banks and other depository institutions prompted these FIs to find ways to pay implicit interest and to create "new" liabilities not subject to such regulation.
2. Additionally, increased competition from other FIs increased the benefits of financial innovation to "meet and beat" this competition. Banks must offer new products and services to compete.
3. Price and interest rate volatility increased the risks of financial intermediation and hence increased the benefits of developing new instruments such as futures and options to deal with these risks.

The regulatory structure played a pivotal role in generating financial innovation, but as we have seen, other forces such as advances in telecommunication technologies, increased competition, and increased volatility of inflation, interest rates, and exchange rates were also significant.

Some Specifics About Financial Innovation

As discussed in earlier chapters, reserve requirements specify the reserve assets banks and other depository institutions must hold as a proportion of their deposit liabilities. Banks would hold some reserves even if there were no formal reserve requirements. Given a desire for liquidity and safety, this would simply reflect prudent management. However, if the reserve requirements set by the regulatory authorities force banks to hold more reserves than they otherwise would, this excess constitutes a tax or drain on bank earnings. That which must be held cannot be lent! What cannot be lent will not earn interest. Accordingly, the higher reserve requirements are relative to what banks would otherwise hold and the higher interest rates are, the larger the foregone profits are.

Prior to 1980, an increasing number of banks decided to give up their membership in the Federal Reserve System and opt for state chartering because the reserve requirements set by the states were, generally speaking, lower. After 1980, Congress changed the law so that the Fed set reserve re-

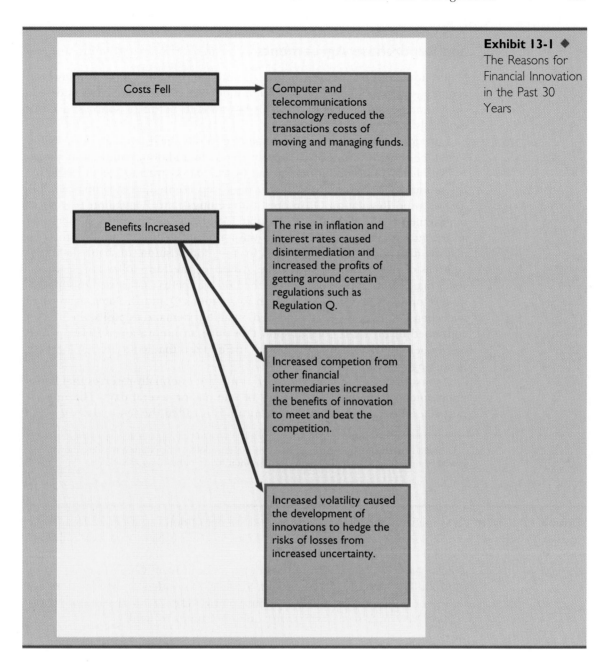

Exhibit 13-1 ◆
The Reasons for Financial Innovation in the Past 30 Years

quirements for all depository intermediaries, thus effectively plugging this hole in the regulatory structure. No longer could banks avoid reserve requirements set by the Fed through exiting the system.

Another way to reduce the burden of the Fed's reserve requirements was to relabel existing liabilities from deposits subject to reserve requirements to so-called **nondeposit liabilities** not subject to reserve requirements. In addition to being exempt from reserve requirements, as we previously saw, such non-deposit sources of funds had another advantage. They were not subject to Regulation Q ceilings. Banks could pay whatever rate prevailed in the market rather than being limited to a maximum rate set by the regulators.

Nondeposit Liabilities Borrowed funds, such as Eurodollar borrowings, fed funds, and repurchase agreements, that are not deposits and not subject to reserve requirements.

Eurodollar Borrowings, Fed Funds, and Repurchase Agreements

Major nondeposit liabilities include Eurodollar borrowings, fed funds, and repurchase agreements. Markets for nondeposit funds were small and relatively unimportant in the early 1970s but grew to be major sources of funds especially for large banks.

Eurodollars are dollar-denominated deposits held abroad. U.S. banks sometimes borrow Eurodollar deposits to obtain additional funds, as depicted in Exhibit 13-2. Eurodollar borrowings by U.S. banks are an excellent example of a nondeposit source of funds that often represented a relabeling of liabilities to avoid Regulation Q (interest rate ceilings) and **Regulation D** (reserve requirements). As explained in Exhibit 13-3, banks and their customers had an incentive to innovate. The result was a significant leak or hole in the regulatory dike and important shifts in the composition of bank liabilities (sources of funds) that spawned the growth of the Eurodollar and Eurocurrency markets.[4] As previously stated, the initial impetus that caused this market to develop was the avoidance of both Regulations Q and D. Later, as we shall see, when Regulation Q was abolished on all but demand deposits, the market continued to thrive. It goes to show that once an innovation is developed, it often does not disappear, even though the impetus that led to its development is no longer present.

As first discussed in Chapter 6, fed funds are essentially reserves that banks trade among themselves for periods of one day or several days. The interest rate determined in the market for fed funds is called the fed funds rate. Like

Regulation D A regulation that prescribed reserve requirements on some deposits.

---

[4]Actually, the Russians were the pioneers of the Eurodollar. For political reasons, they preferred dollar-denominated deposits with London banks rather than U.S. banks.

Exhibit 13-2 ◆

The Anatomy of Eurodollar Borrowing

General Motors converts a $1,000,000 demand deposit at Chase New York to a Eurodollar deposit at Chase London. Chase New York was holding $100,000 in required reserve assets against the $1,000,000 demand deposit. Chase New York borrows the Eurodollar deposit from Chase London. The Eurodollar deposit then becomes a $1,000,000 nondeposit liability, free of reserve requirements. General Motors earns interest on the deposit and Chase New York has $100,000 in additional funds to lend.

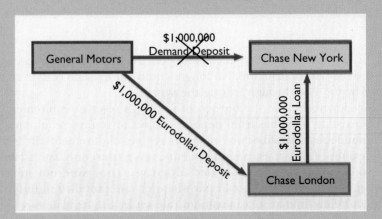

other market interest rates, it is determined by the forces of supply and demand. The demanders are banks that need reserves (funds) to meet their reserve requirements, to meet unexpected withdrawal demands, or to finance loans. The suppliers are banks that have surplus funds and no other immediate use for them.

The fed funds market for overnight borrowing and lending of reserves grew tremendously from the 1960s.[5] It also changed considerably. Rather than borrowing in this market in times of temporary shortfalls in reserves, larger commercial banks came to look to the fed funds market as a permanent source of funds. They borrowed large amounts each and every day and funded assets, including long-term assets, on a continuous basis with this source of funds. Small banks with fewer lending opportunities tended to be net lenders in this market.

Recall from Chapter 6 that an overnight repurchase agreement is an agreement in which a bank takes a government security from its asset portfolio and sells it with the simultaneous agreement to buy it back tomorrow at a price set today. The purchase price tomorrow is higher than the selling price today, with the difference being the interest the lender receives from the bank. In reality, a repurchase agreement is a secured loan with the government security serving as collateral. Like fed funds, repurchase agreements became a significant new source of funds that large banks could access to get new funds to lend. These agreements were often "rolled over" on a daily basis providing a "permanent" source of funds. In early 1994, the amount borrowed each day by large banks in the overnight fed funds and repurchase agreement markets exceeded $130 billion.

Negotiable Certificates of Deposit

Another innovation that does not entail the relabeling of deposit liabilities but is no less important is negotiable certificates of deposit (CDs). The creation of a secondary market for large certificates of deposit in 1961 made them *negotiable* CDs. Thus, a corporation with excess funds, perhaps not having to make payroll until next week, could invest funds in a negotiable CD with the knowledge that if they needed the funds back before the CD matured, the CD could be sold in the secondary market. Although they were subject to the same reserve requirements as other CDs, CDs with maturities of 30 to 89 days were exempted from Regulation Q ceilings in 1970. Reserve requirements on all negotiable CDs were eliminated by the end of 1973. Negotiable CDs are a particularly important source of funds for banks because a bank can advertise and attract additional deposits of negotiable CDs to extend their lending. This was particularly significant when restrictions on branching realistically restricted the growth of checkable deposits to a certain geographic area. A bank could attract CD deposits by advertising high rates.[6]

Now would be a good time to look at Exhibit 13-4, which discusses the changing composition of bank liabilities for large banks. It should be noted that the large money center banks located in major metropolitan areas make

---

[5] The fed funds market was started in the 1920s by some New York banks that borrowed and lent reserves overnight among themselves. The market died out in the 1930s when most banks had excess reserves. It started up again in the 1950s, but was so small that it was virtually insignificant. The market began to grow in the 1960s and by the early 1970s, many large banks began to look to the fed funds market as a permanent source of funds—not just to meet temporary shortfalls in required reserves.

[6] Financially distressed banks have often offered higher rates on CDs to attract deposits.

Exhibit 13-3 ◆
The Development
of the Eurodollar
Market

In the 1970s, market interest rates frequently were above Regulation Q ceilings causing disintermediation. Eventually in 1980, Regulation Q was abolished on all but demand deposits. Corporations were barred by regulation from holding NOW accounts and other interest-earning checkable deposits and, therefore, were left with their funds in short-term, no-interest demand deposits. Can you guess what happened? Corporate treasurers developed cash management techniques that would minimize their holdings of demand deposits. They moved liquid funds to money market instruments, such as commercial paper and T-bills. In response to the cash management techniques, banks fought back in an attempt to maintain their liabilities and to alleviate the disintermediation. They did everything they could to get corporations to convert what would be lost demand deposits into nondeposit liabilities even though banks would have to pay interest on the new liabilities. They did this rather than losing the liabilities altogether, realizing that if they lost liabilities, their ability to make loans would decrease. One of the ways banks used to convert demand deposits to nondeposit liabilities was through the use of the Eurodollar deposit.

After its inception in the 1950s, the Eurodollar market was used to get around both Regulations Q and D. If market interest rates rose above the maximum rate a bank, say Chase, was allowed to offer on time deposits, disintermediation threatened. Rather than sit idly by and see its available funds dwindle and its ability to lend constrained, the portfolio managers at Chase tried to persuade General Motors' financial officer to exchange the deposit at Chase, New York, into a deposit at the Chase branch in London. The deposit would be denominated in dollars and be free of reserve requirements and interest rate ceilings. It would be known as a Eurodollar deposit.* The opportunity to evade some U.S. banking regulations

*Prior to development of the Eurodollar market, a deposit made in a foreign bank was usually denominated in the currency of the host country. For example, an American would take dollars, convert them to British pounds sterling and deposit them in a bank in London. When the funds were withdrawn, the pound sterling had to be exchanged for dollars.

the most extensive use of nondeposit liabilities and other nontraditional sources of funds such as large negotiable CDs.

 RECAP

Financial innovation will occur whenever the benefits are greater than the costs. In recent decades, the rise of inflation and interest rates increased the benefits of innovating around some regulations. Increased competition from other FIs and greater volatility increased the benefits of innovating. A major form of innovation that got around Regulations Q and D was the relabeling of deposit liabilities to nondeposit liabilities. Examples include Eurodollar borrowings, fed funds, and repurchase agreements. The creation of negotiable CDs was another innovation that allowed banks to attract additional funds.

by channeling funds through European banks encouraged the significant growth of the Eurodollar market.

As soon as General Motors deposits the funds in Chase's London branch, Chase's home office in New York borrows the funds from its London branch. This is called a Eurodollar borrowing, a borrowing of dollar-denominated funds from Europe. It is a nondeposit source of funds (liability), which is not subject to reserve requirements. Once Regulation Q was abolished on all but demand deposits, the Eurodollar market became one of the vehicles that banks used to "de facto" pay interest on corporate demand deposits. Corporate demand deposits were simply converted into overnight Eurodollar deposits.

As a net result of this series of transactions, for example, Chase Bank in New York has, in effect, relabeled its demand deposit liability (owed to General Motors) to a Eurodollar borrowing (owed to General Motors) from its London branch. In the process, Chase, New York, reduced the volume of required reserves it had to hold. Assuming the reserve requirement on demand deposits had been 10 percent, this means that Chase, New York, can now lend more even though its total liabilities have not changed. In addition, General Motors earns and Chase pays interest on the deposit.

One last thing—don't get the idea that the funds originally in Chase, New York, were withdrawn by General Motors, packed in a suitcase, flown to London, deposited, borrowed by Chase, New York, and flown back to New York. We have traced out the relevant transactions in slow motion. In fact, the funds would never have left New York and all the transactions could have occurred electronically within minutes using modern telecommunications technology.

The Regulation-Innovation Cycle and Its Influence on Deregulation

In this and previous chapters, where we have discussed the objectives of regulation, the desire for safety and soundness has been emphasized. Given this desire and the despair and disruption accompanying the Great Depression, the financial regulators wrote regulations that limited "price" competition, restricted entry, controlled the various types of products and services banks and other FIs could offer the public, and specified prudent capital positions for intermediaries.[7] The limitations on portfolios were predicated on the alleged benefits of the compartmentalization of FIs into various specialties. Insurance companies were to specialize in insurance and banks in

---

[7]As we have seen elsewhere, these regulations included Regulation Q interest rate ceilings, chartering and branching restrictions, assets and liabilities restrictions, and net worth requirements.

Exhibit 13-4 ◆

The Changing Composition of Liabilities of Large Commercial Banks

Dramatic changes have occurred in the composition of liabilities of large commercial banks since the 1960s. One of the biggest changes is the increasing reliance on nondeposit liabilities such as borrowings in the fed funds market, overnight repurchase agreements, and Eurodollar borrowings. Because these nondeposit liabilities are short term, they can virtually dry up overnight if the lender chooses not to re-lend them each day. Large banks in particular make use of these nondeposit liabilities, which are often merely relabeled deposit liabilities. In addition, transaction deposits, which historically were the most important source of funds, grew less rapidly than other sources of funds.

Another change is the increasing reliance on large negotiable CDs. Large banks can advertise and attract these deposits from a national market and pay a market interest rate on them. Troubled banks sometimes offer a slightly higher or tiered rate to attract CD deposits. Depositors who are willing to accept more risk for the higher return go for the bait. Remember the FDIC insurance limit is $100,000, the minimum amount for a large negotiable CD. In reality, the minimum amount for a CD to be traded in the secondary market is usually $2 million.

The sum of nondeposit liabilities and large negotiable CDs made up less than 1 percent of the liabilities of large commercial banks in 1960. In February 1995, fed funds and repurchase agreements supplied more than 21 percent of the sources of funds for large banks alone.

In general, for all banks, deposits account for a much smaller proportion of liabilities than in earlier decades. In February 1995, total checkable, savings, and time deposits were about 70 percent of bank liabilities. (In 1960, total deposits were 87 percent.) Transaction deposits, which historically were the most important source of funds, have grown less rapidly than other types of deposits. For example, in February 1995, transactions deposits were only about 20 percent of the sources of bank funds whereas in 1960, they were 60 percent.

banking and "never the twain shall meet." Supposedly, competition needed to be limited among the compartments with the results being that financial markets were effectively segmented.

The burdens associated with complying with such regulations and the benefits associated with innovating around them produced numerous forms of adaptive behavior by banks and other FIs. For example, banks developed new types of liabilities to sidestep Regulations Q and D, and used the holding company corporate form to evade certain entry and branching restrictions and to engage in nonbanking activities. With innovations weakening the effectiveness of various regulations, the regulators faced two basic choices: (1) re-regulate by rewriting and revising the regulations, or (2) recognize the difficulty, if not the impossibility, of controlling financial flows and the market for financial services and **deregulate** by dismantling the regulations. Since most regulators believe they are supposed to regulate, the typical response throughout the 1960s and 1970s was to consider and attempt **re-regulation.**

Most economists are quite critical of the regulatory mentality because of their skepticism regarding the possibility of writing "leak-proof" regulations. We assume college students are similarly skeptical about college rules. On an analytical level, when complying with regulations is a burden, an incentive exists to poke holes in a regulation. Recognizing the fungibility of funds helps

Deregulate The dismantling of existing regulations.

Re-Regulation The putting on of new regulations in response to innovations that weakened existing regulations.

us understand why hole-poking is somewhat easier in the financial system than in other parts of the economy. On a practical level, those being regulated will often hire former regulators to help identify both the weak spots in a regulation and how to poke holes most effectively. Since the private sector can pay the best and the brightest much more than they can earn in the government where pay ceilings are in place, it should not be surprising that innovation is often successful. Innovation, loophole mining by those being regulated, was for a time followed by some attempts at re-regulation, loophole plugging by the regulators.

One of the best examples of the dynamic process of adaptation and the regulation-innovation cycle is the nation's experience with Regulation Q (interest rate) ceilings on deposits. As market interest rates rose above the ceilings, depositors were induced to move their funds from the regulated FIs to the open market or to money market mutual funds.

Given profitable lending opportunities in the face of an outflow of funds, and a regulation that limited their ability to pay an explicit competitive return on deposits, depository institutions had an incentive to innovate. As we have seen, this led to the development of new instruments (sources of funds) not subject to Regulation Q, such as Eurodollar borrowings. The initial response of the regulators was to attempt to control the new markets by making Eurodollar borrowings and certain other relabeled liabilities subject to reserve requirements.

Despite these efforts, by the beginning of the 1970s regulators began to realize that controlling the flow of funds into and out of depository institutions was increasingly difficult. More specifically, the regulators recognized that large depositors were able to move their funds into the domestic open market and into the world financial system fairly easily.[8] With U.S. FIs at a competitive disadvantage in international markets where Eurocurrencies could pay market interest rates, a case could be made that maintaining the existing ceilings carried the potential for weakening U.S. FIs, particularly the giants in the banking industry. Accordingly, by 1973, the Regulation Q ceiling on large negotiable CDs with denominations over $100,000 was removed. Banks could now pay a market interest rate when rates went above the Regulation Q ceiling and compete with Eurodollar deposits.

At the same time, we have seen that money market mutual funds provided intense competition for banks. Regulators also toyed with the idea of bringing money market mutual funds under their control. However, there was a growing awareness in and out of government that Regulation Q and the rest of the regulatory structure was being undermined by market forces and in dire need of a substantial overhaul. Many began to recognize that a strong case could be made that existing regulations and the distortions and evasive activity they fostered were weakening the financial system. Eventually, at some point, a political and economic reassessment occurred, and deregulation resulted. Landmark legislation in 1980 and 1982 was the result.[9] The resulting regulation-innovation-deregulation cycle is depicted in Exhibit 13-5.

---

[8] Depositors with large deposits could move their funds out of depository institutions and into open market instruments such as T-bills and commercial paper. In addition, they could enter the equity and bond markets.

[9] In addition to the analytical factors, we should also mention that the general "political wind" had shifted in the late 1970s toward less regulation. We were deregulating airlines, trucking, and even monopolistic cable television operators. This also contributed to the impetus for financial deregulation in the 1980s.

Exhibit 13-5 ◆
The Regulation-
Innovation Cycle

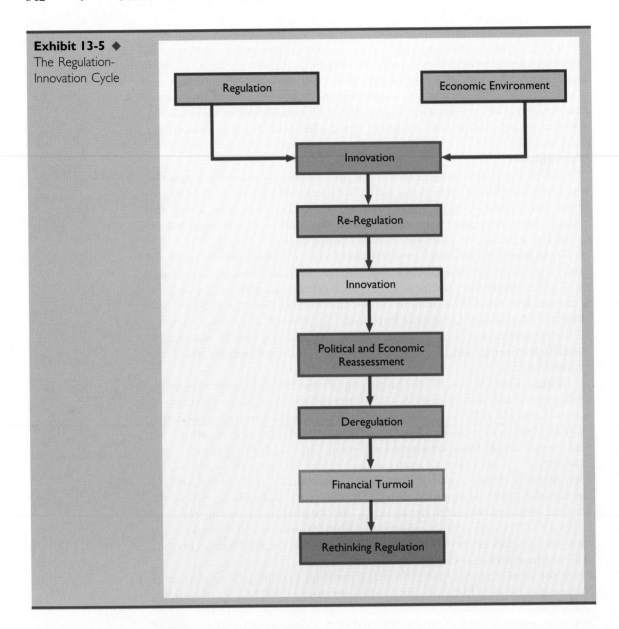

Depository Institutions
Deregulation and Mone-
tary Control Act of 1980
(DIDMCA) The act that
removed many of the
regulations enacted during
the Great Depression,
phased out Regulation Q
and established uniform
and universal reserve re-
quirements, increased the
assets and liabilities depository institutions could
hold, authorized NOW
accounts, and suspended
usury ceilings.

A Wave of Deregulation

The financial regulations and structure that had been designed and erected in reaction to the Great Depression were increasingly ill-suited to the changing economic and technological environment of the 1970s. In belated recognition of this fact the Congress passed the **Depository Institutions Deregulation and Monetary Control Act of 1980 (DIDMCA).** Reflecting the compromises necessary to enact such an all-encompassing piece of legislation, the act contains numerous provisions. However, as the title of the act suggests, the major provisions of interest to us can be classified into two groups:

1. *Deregulation:*
   a. The remaining Regulation Q ceilings were phased out over a six-year period that ended in 1986.

   b. Asset and liability powers for banks and thrifts were expanded.
     — assets: S&Ls and savings banks able to extend loans to businesses and offer more services to customers
     — liabilities: All depository intermediaries permitted to offer households NOW accounts (interest-bearing checkable deposits)
   c. Suspension of state **usury ceilings** (maximum interest rates FIs are allowed to charge borrowers on certain types of loans).

For a discussion of Usury Laws, see Exhibit 13-6.

2. *Monetary Control:*
   a. All depository institutions were subject to reserve requirements (so-called **universal reserve requirements**).
   b. Requirements to be the same on particular types of deposits across institutions (so-called **uniform reserve requirements**) phased in over an eight-year period that ended in 1987.

In general, the deregulation provisions put some explicit price competition back into banking and permitted more competition among depository institutions. In the future, banks and thrifts would be more alike in terms of the products and services offered the public. It was hoped that the net result of more competition would be greater efficiency, an accompanying reduction in the cost, and an improvement in the quantity and quality of financial services.

By mandating universal and uniform reserve requirements, the monetary control provisions of the 1980 act strengthened the effectiveness of the regulatory process and expanded the powers of the Fed. In addition, it essentially eliminated the Fed's membership problem, discussed earlier in the chapter, and accompanying monetary control difficulties. Leaving the Federal Reserve System to become a nonmember bank would henceforth not reduce an institution's required reserves. Therefore, when the Fed changed the amount of funds available for reserves, its control over the money supply and supply of loanable funds would be more direct.

All in all, DIDMCA was a landmark piece of legislation. Many of the long-overdue changes in the financial structure, which had been recommended by numerous federal studies over the previous 20 years, came to pass. However, the timing was no accident. Inflation, high interest rates, technological advances, and the volatile financial environment of the 1970s had unleashed market forces akin to hurricane winds and seas. The result was an increasingly fragile structure in need of a major overhaul.

To understand why only two years later another important piece of legislation, the **Garn–St. Germain Depository Institutions Act of 1982,** was enacted, we need to take note of two facts.[10] First, DIDMCA called for a gradual, six-year phaseout of the Regulation Q ceilings. Regulators have long preferred gradual instead of abrupt changes, believing that such an approach minimizes the disruptions by providing time for those being regulated to adjust to the changing environment. In this case, the rate ceilings on time deposits with the longest maturities, two to four years and over, were scheduled for removal first, with those on shorter maturities and savings deposits to follow several

Usury Ceilings Maximum interest rates that FIs are allowed to charge borrowers on certain types of loans.

Universal Reserve Requirements Reserve requirements established by the Fed to which all depository institutions would be subject.

Uniform Reserve Requirements The same reserve requirements across all depository institutions would apply to particular types of deposits.

Garn–St. Germain Depository Institutions Act of 1982 An additional deregulation act that authorized money market deposit accounts and Super Now accounts.

---

[10] The act was named after Senator Jake Garn and Congressman Ferdinand St. Germain, the chairmen of the Senate and House Banking Committees, respectively. Incidently, Senator Garn also has the distinction of being the only U.S. senator who has gone up in the space shuttle to date.

Exhibit 13-6 ◆
Usury Ceilings

Webster's Dictionary defines usury as "an unconscionable or exorbitant rate or amount of interest." Since at least medieval times governments have worried about lenders charging borrowers usurious rates of interest. Over the years, in response to such concerns, many state legislatures enacted usury ceilings. These regulations set maximum rates of interest lenders (FIs) could charge on certain types of loans granted to consumers, farmers, and businesses. The understandable and laudable intentions leading to the establishment of such ceilings included protecting the public from exploitation and holding down the cost of borrowing to encourage borrowing and spending. Unfortunately, the actual effects of usury ceilings were often the opposite. Borrowing and spending were discouraged. To see how and why such unintended effects prevailed, a simple supply and demand diagram for loanable funds will be helpful.

We assume the supply curve of consumer loans by FIs is upward sloping. As the interest rate rises, ceteris paribus, FIs will lend a larger quantity of funds. We also assume the demand curve for loans by consumers is, ceteris paribus, downward sloping. As the cost of borrowing falls, ceteris paribus, consumers will borrow a larger quantity of funds. In the absence of government intervention in the market such as the enactment of a usury ceiling, equilibrium will be at point A with a prevailing interest rate of 10 percent and the quantity supplied and demanded of $100 billion.

Suppose now that the government enacts an 8 percent usury ceiling because it believes the 10 percent rate is too high, and it wants to lower rates to encourage more borrowing and spending. At the lower rate, ceteris paribus, consumers will naturally demand a larger quantity of loans than previously (point C, $120 billion). At the same time, reflecting their costs of acquiring funds to lend and opportunities to lend elsewhere, ceteris paribus, FIs are willing to supply a smaller quantity of loans than previously (point B, $80 billion). The resulting excess of quantity demanded over quantity supplied will lead FIs to ration the $80 billion they are willing to

years later. Second, market interest rates rose to record levels in 1981 and, in general, remained well above the Regulation Q ceilings on savings deposits and time deposits with shorter maturities. What do you think happened? The size of money market mutual funds at the end of 1979 was about $45 billion. By late 1982 funds deposited with them, and presumably withdrawn from depository institutions, had grown to $250 billion. Although deposits at depository institutions grew in absolute terms between 1979 and 1982, they grew at a much slower rate than the money market mutual funds. Consequently, the market share of banks and thrifts in intermediation declined. Clearly, an incentive to disintermediate or to transfer funds from depository institutions to money market mutual funds still existed and the market would not march to the regulator's slow-paced deregulation beat.

The 1982 Act like its 1980 predecessor had many provisions. Chief among them were those that speeded up the pace of deregulation by allowing depository institutions to offer two types of deposit accounts designed to compete directly with money market mutual funds: (1) money market deposit accounts, which have no rate ceiling and permit six third-party payments transactions per month, and (2) Super NOW accounts, which also have no rate

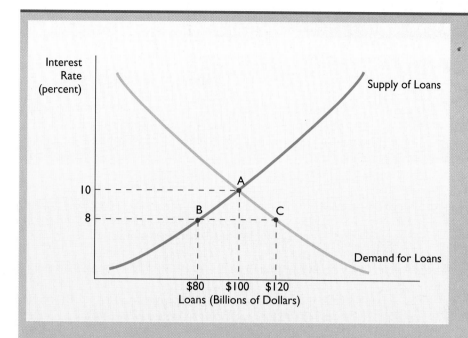

lend by increasing down payment requirements, tightening credit standards, shortening the maturities on loans, and requiring more collateral.

In the end only $80 billion will be borrowed and lent. This is $20 billion less than would have occurred without a usury ceiling. The good intentions that produced the ceilings will have been undermined, producing quite perverse effects. Belated recognition of such unintended and perverse effects led to the Congress suspending such ceilings in the 1980 Act. States were permitted to reenact ceilings in the ensuing three years. Fortunately, most did not.

ceiling, but are fully checkable. The money market deposit accounts proved to be a smashing success, growing to over $520 billion by late 1993. Consumers know a good deal when they see one.

Competition among FIs and between FIs and the open market has increased dramatically. For example, depository institutions offer rates on all deposit liabilities that are closely correlated with market rates. Such dramatic changes in the competitive environment within which banks and other FIs are operating have noticeable effects on the portfolio behavior and operations of depository institutions. Let's take a brief look at some of the directions in which the system is moving.

 ## RECAP

Because market participants had found ways around many regulations, Congress passed two major acts that deregulated financial markets. DIDMCA in 1980 phased out Regulation Q ceilings and expanded the asset and liability powers for banks and thrifts. It also established uniform and universal reserve

LOOKING FORWARD

The Electronic Purse: An Innovation in the Making

During early 1996, many banks began developing a new payments mechanism called the electronic purse or stored-value card. Prepaid cards for a single use have been available for many years. For example, some toll roads accept only a smart card in payment, college dorm cafeterias offer a prepaid smart card, libraries offer prepaid photocopy cards, and in many areas, phone companies sell prepaid calling cards.

The electronic purse would allow a single card the size of a credit card to be used in multiple locations to make many kinds of purchases. When making purchases, the card is passed through the merchant's point-of-sale terminal. Funds are deducted directly from the buyer's card and added to the point-of-sale terminal. Vendors can transfer the balances on their terminals to their bank accounts via a telephone transfer as frequently as they want. When the value on the card is spent, consumers can add additional funds to the card via a telephone transfer, an ATM machine, or a computer transfer. A personal identification number much like an ATM number can be used to validate that the smart card is being used by its owner.

The multiple-use smart card will have one or more computer chips embedded in it capable of storing and transferring information. The main benefit of the smart card to the consumer is convenience. Buying a cup of coffee, a newspaper, or a candy bar from a vending machine would be much easier and faster. For merchants, the electronic card saves time and money in handling cash. Unlike checks, they offer guaranteed payment and will most likely have lower transactions costs than credit cards or debit cards. For the issuer, there may be many benefits. For example, smart cards offer a potential source of fee income and the issuer will earn interest on the unspent balances on smart cards.

Many questions exist with regard to how smart cards will work. For instance, will transactions made on smart cards be traceable? Such record keeping could help the police trace fraudulent use. Or, should use of the smart card be nontraceable like cash? Still other issues are whether the balances on smart cards will be covered by deposit insurance, whether nonbanks can issue such cards, and whether smart cards will effect reserve management and the money supply. By the turn of the new century many of these questions will be resolved.

requirements for all depository institutions. The Garn–St. Germain Act of 1982, among other things, authorized money market deposit accounts and Super NOW accounts.

The Financial Environment Following Deregulation

The 1980s witnessed numerous changes in the financial system. Not all of the changes were driven by technology, inflationary pressure, and/or regulatory avoidance. By the late 1980s, innovation was precipitated by volatile prices in financial markets that encouraged the development of futures, op-

Exhibit 13-7 ◆
Financial Market Changes in the 1990s

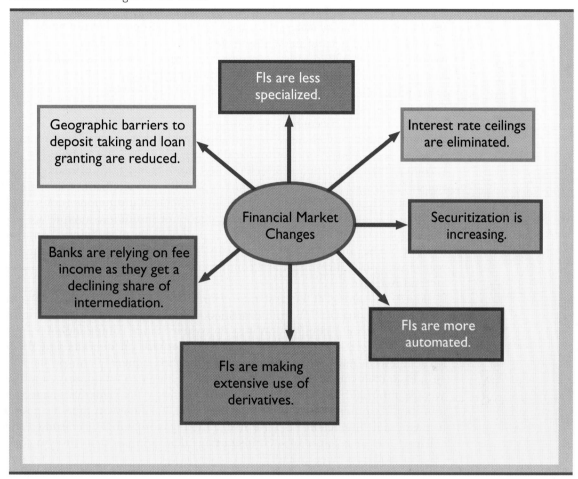

tions, and swaps, and by the banking industry's struggle to survive. Investment bankers developed new financial market instruments such as junk bonds and commercial paper for small and medium businesses that took away short-term and long-term loan business traditionally belonging to commercial banks. Banks responded to this onslaught by getting into nonbank activities such as direct investment in junk bonds and real estate development loans, and by taking equity positions in corporations. Many of these activities were necessarily under the bank holding company umbrella. In the 1990s, innovation within the commercial banking system continues in an attempt to survive unprecedented competition from nonbanks and other nonfinancial institutions.

The 1990s

The major changes are helping to define the characteristics of the financial system in the 1990s. As depicted in Exhibit 13-7, some of these changes were discussed in the last chapter and some in this chapter. They can be grouped under seven main points:

First, geographic barriers to deposit taking, loan granting, and the provision of other financial services are fast eroding. Lenders advertise and solicit credit card accounts and make mortgage loans nationwide. Interstate branching is already permitted within certain regions of the country and some of the largest banks, operating through their holding company affiliates, provide many services nationwide. The move to nationwide banking is also being accompanied by an increasing level of international banking activity.

Second, FIs are becoming increasingly less specialized. More specifically, through mergers and changes in regulations, which have expanded the range of assets and liabilities depository institutions can offer the public, FIs are becoming increasingly more diversified and more competitive in markets previously left to specialized FIs. As we have repeatedly stressed, banks face increasing competition from other financial and nonfinancial institutions (nonbanks) and the characteristics that make each category of institutions unique are becoming blurred. As noted in Chapter 12, proposals are now before Congress to allow banks into the securities industry. This would effectively end the 60-year separation of investment and commercial banking instituted by the Glass–Steagall Act.

Third, the lifting of interest rate ceilings (usury and Regulation Q) has reduced the potential for disintermediation and injected a healthy dose of price (interest rate) competition into the system. Since competing effectively means offering SSUs higher rates and better service on deposits and DSUs lower rates on loans, the competition has, in turn, squeezed the profit margins. Essentially the average spread between the rate earned on assets and the average rate paid on liabilities has fallen for many FIs. This has made the transition to a more competitive environment a bit bumpy at times as poorly managed and inefficient FIs have had difficulty competing successfully. The collapse or near collapse of such institutions demonstrates that "free to compete" also means "free to fail."

The decontrol of the rates paid on deposit liabilities and the resulting correlation between a depository institution's cost of funds and the level of market interest rates has contributed to important changes in the pricing of loans. Increasingly, depository institutions are offering the public so-called adjustable rate loans that we discussed in Chapter 12. An S&L, for example, will agree to grant a potential home buyer a mortgage loan that will carry, say, a 7 percent rate the first year and a rate adjusted up or down in subsequent years as the S&L's cost of funds (rates paid on liabilities) rises or falls. Such an arrangement preserves the S&L's profit margin. If a fixed rate loan had been made and the cost of funds subsequently rose, the S&Ls profit margin on the loan would narrow. It is clear that the use of adjustable rate loans shifts interest rate risk from the FI to the borrower.[11]

Securitization The process whereby relatively illiquid financial assets are packaged together and sold off to individual investors.

Fourth, another financial innovation resulting from the current financial environment is the spread of securitization to many loan markets. **Securitization** is the process whereby relatively illiquid financial assets are packaged together and sold off to individual investors. A market maker agrees to create a secondary market by buying and selling these pass-through securities as they have come to be called. Originating in the early 1980s with the mortgage

---

[11] Adjustable rate loans are often offered with a significant interest rate discount in the early years.

Although it may appear that after 30 years of financial innovations, few unexploited opportunities to significantly reduce costs or increase benefits are left, we can't be too quick to jump to conclusions. A recent innovation in late 1993 deals with the packaging of small business loans into securities (securitization) and the creation of a secondary market. Indeed, a secondary market makes the securitization process much more successful since it increases the liquidity of the new securities. Like all innovations and true to our quote at the beginning of this chapter, "necessity" indeed "gave birth" to this innovation.

In the early 1990s, small businesses were particularly hard hit by a credit crunch due to new capital adequacy requirements imposed on depositories by the Financial Institutions Reform and Recovery Act (FIRREA) of 1989.[a] The lack of loans flowing from FIs to small businesses generated a particularly critical situation because small businesses did not have the same access to the commercial paper market as did medium-sized and large firms. For a long time, securitization of the small business loan market did not seem feasible because small business loans are particularly diverse, and the circumstances surrounding the funding of them are often quite subjective. In other words, small business loans are by nature heterogeneous—a characteristic that did not make them good candidates for securitization. Generally speaking, securitization most easily develops in markets where financial assets are fairly homogenous. For example, to be securitized and sold in a secondary market, mortgages are made to specific criteria regarding income of the borrower and the loan-to-property value ratio. Under these circumstances, pools of mortgages are a fairly homogenous lot. Auto loans, likewise, are made to certain income criteria with the vehicles serving as collateral. In the case of small business loans, which are packaged and sold as securities, the backing includes accounts receivable, inventories, and equipment.

In early 1993, Fremont Financial Corporation of Santa Monica, California, sold $200 million of variable rate certificates backed by a pool of loans to small and medium-sized businesses. Merrill Lynch underwrote the offering, which quickly sold out, with the securities being bought by insurance companies, pension funds, and other large investors.[b]

In general as more small business loans become securitized, the risks involved in lending to small businesses will be spread among many investors, fast-growing companies will be funded, and income will be generated for the innovators. As Fed Chairperson Alan Greenspan puts it, a secondary market for business loans "would be a major contribution to the financial vitality of this country."[c]

[a]We look in depth at the provisions of FIRREA in Chapter 15.
[b]An active secondary market exists for business loans with payments guaranteed by the Small Business Association of the federal government. The novelty about the Fremont offering is that there is no government guarantee.
[c]Kenneth H. Bacon and Eugene Carlson, "Market Is Seen in Small-Business Loans," *The Wall Street Journal*, October 18, 1993.

Exhibit 13-8 ◆
Securitization of Small Business Loans

market, mortgage loans are packaged together and sold off as securities in the secondary market often with government insurance that the principal and interest will be repaid. These **pass-through securities** have been a hit with investors and take relatively illiquid instruments and turn them into quite

Pass-Through Securities Securities that result from the process of securitization.

liquid investments. Securitization has spread because of the greater interest rate risk that lenders experience with the increased interest rate volatility of the 1970s and 1980s. This securitization has spread from the mortgage markets to credit cards, automobile loans, accounts receivable, student loans, and even small business loans. Now would be a good time to read Exhibit 13-8 for a discussion of a recent type of securitization.

Fifth, FIs are becoming increasingly automated as financial firms try to cut costs. The resulting substitution of physical capital (such as automatic teller machines, debit cards, and point-of-sale terminals) for labor is having profound effects on the way transactions are conducted. Other automated payment systems include paying bills by automatic deductions from deposit accounts or paying bills by some form of automatic transfer.

Sixth, because of greater interest rate and exchange rate risks, financial futures and options have developed to allow lenders to hedge these risks. Large banks in particular now make extensive use of these instruments.

Seventh, as banks lose market share in the intermediation business, they are increasingly entering markets that provide services such as data processing, accounting, and loan administration for fees. It is their hope that fee income will help them compete against nonbank FIs from a two-prong perspective. Fee income can reduce the erosion of bank profits resulting from the declining bank market share in financial intermediation. In addition, many of the activities that generate fees, such as data processing, are also offered by nonbanks. By offering such services, banks can more effectively compete in the market for business loans. Banks are becoming more like nonbanks, and vice versa.

Consequently, all this activity has left regulators quite nervous. With many of their regulations discarded, they feel that they have less control over emerging developments and that the financial system is more vulnerable. In response, regulators have required depository institutions, particularly the large and most aggressive banks, to increase their financial capital, seeing this as an important first line of defense against the risks such institutions face. There is a widespread belief that a complete overhaul of the financial regulatory structure is needed. So far, we have just had a tune-up. Not many analysts call for a return to the regulatory regime of past decades, but most believe that the system needs to be rebuilt, perhaps with different kinds of regulation.

Deregulation in the 1980s "let the genie out of the bottle" and taught us that once a financial innovation is introduced, even if the factors that caused its inception disappear, the innovation will not disappear. Two examples come to mind: (1) after the removal of Regulation Q, money market mutual funds did not disappear as many experts predicted; and (2) when interest rates fell and became more stable in the early 1990s, the financial futures and options markets did not disappear, but rather remained to exploit every tiny opportunity to hedge even the smallest risk.

In the next chapter, we shall see that the strains on the financial system in the 1980s have halted the drive toward further deregulation. In fact, attempts have been made starting with the Financial Institutions Reform and Recovery Enforcement Act of 1989 at re-regulation, even though no comprehensive reform plan has been adopted. Chapter 15 completes this section of the text by focusing on regulation in the 1990s.

Summary of Major Points

1. Financial innovation is the adoption of new technologies and products to avoid regulations and to increase profitability. Because financial claims are fungible and because other incentives have been present, the last 30 years have seen a high level of financial innovation. This has occurred because the benefits of innovating exceeded the costs.

2. The incentives to innovate include rising interest rates that led to disintermediation, volatile interest rates that increased interest rate risk, technological advances that affected payments technologies, and increased competition.

3. In the 1970s, much innovation centered around evading regulations. Restrictions included setting reserve requirements (Regulation D) and interest rate ceilings (Regulation Q), limiting entry, separating commercial and investment banking, and specifying margin requirements.

4. The relabeling of deposit liabilities as nondeposit liabilities, which avoided both reserve requirements and interest rate ceilings, represented a major form of financial innovation. Included in this group of innovations are Eurodollar borrowings, fed funds, and repurchase agreements. In addition, the creation of a secondary market for CDs making them "negotiable" was also an important innovation.

5. The initial response to financial innovation by the regulators was to attempt to re-regulate. This response occurred primarily throughout the 1960s and 1970s. During the 1980s, the trend changed and attempts at re-regulation were replaced by deregulation. Loophole mining by those who were successful at getting around regulations was replaced by loophole plugging, later to be replaced by deregulation, which invalidated the need for a loophole.

6. The Depository Institutions Deregulation and Monetary Control Act of 1980 phased out Regulation Q interest rate ceilings, and expanded the asset and liability options for banks and thrifts. All depository institutions were allowed to offer interest-bearing checkable deposits, and S&Ls and savings banks were allowed to make business loans. It also expanded the powers of the Fed by authorizing uniform and universal reserve requirements.

7. The Garn–St. Germain Act of 1982 allowed all depository institutions to offer money market deposit accounts which had no interest rate ceilings, permitted limited check writing, and are fully insured up to $100,000. Also authorized were Super NOW Accounts, which are checking accounts that pay a market interest rate.

8. The financial sector is becoming more competitive because (1) geographic barriers for financial services are disappearing; (2) FIs are becoming less specialized; (3) interest rate ceilings and usury laws have been abolished; (4) securitization is spreading to many markets; (5) financial futures and options are increasingly being used to hedge risk; (6) financial transactions are becoming increasingly automated; and (7) banks are expanding into other areas such as data processing and leasing.

Key Terms

Depository Institutions
   Deregulation and Monetary
   Control Act of 1980 (DIDMCA)
Deregulate
Disintermediation
Financial Innovation
Fungible
Garn–St. Germain Depository
   Institutions Act of 1982
Glass–Steagall Act of 1933

Nondeposit Liabilities
Pass-Through Securities
Regulation D
Regulation Q
Re-Regulation
Securitization
Uniform Reserve Requirements
Universal Reserve Requirements
Usury Ceilings

Review Questions

1. Briefly discuss the incentives that have led to a rapid pace of financial innovation in the last 30 years?

2. What is disintermediation? When is disintermediation likely to occur? What factors can reduce it? If I take my funds out of my credit union and put them in a money market mutual fund, have I disintermediated? Why or why not?

3. Discuss the roles that technology and regulation play in aiding and abetting financial innovation. Will innovation always occur to find loopholes in regulations?

4. What are nondeposit liabilities? Give some examples. What are negotiable CDs? How are nondeposit liabilities different from negotiable CDs?

5. What is Regulation Q? Regulation D? Discuss ways banks have found to get around both regulations.

6. What are the major provisions of the Depository Deregulation and Monetary Control Act of 1980? the Garn–St. Germain Act of 1982? Which act expanded the powers of the Fed? How?

7. What is securitization? How does securitization reduce interest rate risk? Name some types of liabilities that are now securitized.

8. Discuss some characteristics of the financial system of the 1990s that make it different from earlier periods.

9. How have increased competition and price volatility affected financial innovation? What are some specific types of innovation that deal with these factors?

10. Why are usury laws not helpful for all potential borrowers? (Hint: The key word is potential.)

11. Defend the statement: Once an innovation appears, it will remain even after the impetus for its development disappears. Give an example.

12. What are universal and uniform reserve requirements?

13. Are financial claims more fungible today than in the past? Why?

14. Why didn't banks innovate to get around regulations in the 1940s and 1950s?

15. How are money market mutual funds different from money market deposit accounts? If you had $10,000, which would you prefer? Why?

Analytical Questions

16. Graphically show what happens to the quantity supplied and quantity demanded of loanable funds after a usury law is removed. Assume the usury ceiling was below the equilibrium interest rate.

17. Explain the process by which a group of credit card balances could be securitized.

18. Assume a reserve requirement of 10 percent. If Chemical Bank is successful in getting Microsoft to convert a $2,000,000 demand deposit to a Eurodollar deposit, how much can Chemical Bank loan out because of this transaction?

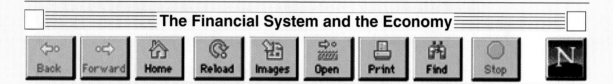

The Financial System and the Economy

1. The internet site (http://www.fdic.gov/library/banklaws.html) describes some important laws that have affected the banking industry in the United States.

   a. What is the Riegle-Heal Interstate Banking and Branching Efficiency Act of 1994?
   b. Which earlier banking act does this act effectively seek to repeal?

Suggested Readings

For an interesting article on the role of banks in a new competitive environment, see "Delivering the Future," *Bank Management,* January/February 1995, pp. 45–48.

In Forrest Capie and Geoffrey E. Wood, *Unregulated Banking: Chaos or Order?* New York: St. Martin's Press, 1991, the authors argue that periods of unregulated banking, although brief, are historically associated with stability and prosperity.

In Frank J. Fabozzi and Franco Modigliani, *Mortgage and Mortgage-Backed Securities Markets,* Boston: Harvard Business School Press Series in Financial Services Management, 1992, the authors present the economic forces that led to the development of secondary mortgage markets.

In M. A. Pawley, *Financial Innovation and Monetary Policy,* New York: Routledge Press, 1993, the author characterizes the development and effects of financial innovation.

Innovative Banking, John Howells and Jim Hine, eds., New York: Routledge Press, 1993, discusses how network technologies have become an important financial innovation for the banking industry.

For an interesting analysis of the topic, see John Wenninger and David Laster, "The Electronic Purse," *Current Issues,* Federal Reserve Bank of New York, April 1995. This article is also available on the internet at (http://www.ny.frb.org/rmaghome/curr_iss/cil-1.html).

14

Strains on the Financial System

> *The advantage of a bad memory*
> *is that one enjoys several times the same*
> *good thing for the first time.*
> —Friedrich Nietzsche—
>
> *Get into a banker for enough money*
> *and you've got yourself a partner.*
> —Billie Sol Estes—

Learning Objectives

After reading this chapter, you should know:

- The ways in which financial intermediaries (FIs) deal with risk and why risk cannot be eliminated

- The reasons why financial intermediation recurrently leads to financial crisis

- The causes of the Savings and Loan (S&L) Crisis

- The causes of the Deposit Insurance Crisis

- Other potential financial stresses in the 1990s including daylight overdrafts, program trading, derivatives, and the Eurocurrency markets

Memory Is the Thing You Forget With[1]

In the 1920s, Charles Ponzi, a Boston financier (or slick con man), convinced people that he was able to make huge sums of money by arbitraging Spanish postage stamps—that is, by buying the stamps in a low-cost market (Spain) and selling them in a high-cost market (Boston). The large difference between the selling price and the buying price would be a capital gain.

Unfortunately for investors, instead of making capital gains, Ponzi was enticing money from new investors to pay off the high anticipated profits of early investors. Inevitably, people lost faith in his capability to pay off their investments and Ponzi's empire foundered and collapsed as he became unable to attract new investors. Later, Ponzi engaged in a land scheme—selling swamp land in Florida—which eventually collapsed also.

In 1909 John Moody issued the first public rating for bonds considered "too risky for investment."[2] He called that rating "below investment grade." These bonds are now called **junk bonds.** During the Great Depression, many bonds originally recommended for investment were downgraded to "below investment grade." After they had been issued, their ratings were lowered because the issuing corporations were not doing as well as expected. At the end of the Great Depression, 42 percent of all outstanding corporate bonds were rated as junk bonds. Even so, new issues of junk were nonexistent, as widespread financial failures—the brute forces of events—caused investors to grow weary of all but the top-rated grades. As a result, by 1977, only 3.7 percent of outstanding corporate debt carried the below investment grade rating.

But the market was ripe for change when, during the 1970s, Michael Milken joined the small unknown brokerage house of Drexel Burnham Lambert. Under Milken's leadership, Drexel Burnham Lambert became a market maker for junk bonds. That is, they began underwriting new issues of junk bonds and created a secondary market, standing ready to buy or sell as needed. The junk bond market grew rapidly throughout the 1980s as financial intermediaries (FIs) and individuals jumped on the bandwagon. By the end of 1989, more than 22 percent of outstanding U.S. corporate bonds were junk bonds. Furthermore, three-quarters of this debt had been issued below investment grade and Drexel Burnham Lambert had grown to rival the largest investment banking firms on Wall Street. But the junk bond market was headed for trouble and two events would lead to its demise:

1. A large issuer of junk bonds defaulted causing panic and large sell-offs among junk bond holders.[3]
2. Congress enacted a law forcing all U.S. thrift institutions—savings and loans (S&Ls), credit unions, and mutual savings banks—to sell off their junk bond holdings by mid-1994.

Faced with these events, the market collapsed and Drexel Burnham Lambert declared bankruptcy. A liquidity crisis ensued and prices plummeted further. Milken, who was indicted on 98 counts of racketeering, and tax and

Junk Bonds Bonds rated below investment grade.

---

[1] Alexander Chase.

[2] When marketing these bonds, brokers refer to them as *high yield bonds*.

[3] The large issuer of junk bonds that defaulted was Campeau Corporation.

securities fraud pleaded guilty to six charges. His sentence included a $600 million dollar fine and ten years in prison. He ended up serving a much shorter time in prison.

How different were the financial institutions and individuals who participated in the junk bond market of the 1980s from those who fell victim to the Ponzi scheme in the 1920s?[4] Perhaps they were not really that different with regards to their desire for a big payoff, their willingness to take a risk, and their refusal to realistically evaluate that risk.[5] Perhaps such behavior is part of human nature and hence endemic to financial institutions controlled by individuals.

In this chapter, we look at some of the reasons why certain strains have recurrently plagued our financial system. We will examine some famous and some not-so-famous stresses that have led to financial crises.

Financial Intermediation, Risk, and Financial Crises

We have seen that FIs have developed numerous ways to manage risk. For example, diversification reduces the risks of insolvency from widespread defaults in one sector or region of the economy. By not putting all of their eggs in one basket, FIs are less likely to run into problems. Another factor that reduces credit risk is the use of experts to evaluate and access the creditworthiness of potential borrowers and potential investments. When all is said and done, there are few substitutes for painstaking credit analysis.

Interest rate risk can be reduced through the use of adjustable rate loans or the judicious use of futures, options, swaps, and securitizations. Coping techniques have become more refined as interest rates have become more erratic. Futures and options are also used to hedge exchange rate risk. In recent decades, foreign exchange rates have become more volatile and finance has become more globalized. Both factors cause this risk to increase significantly. Thus, we have seen the growing use of futures and options to hedge exchange rate risks.

In addition to borrowing funds from the Fed, depository institutions can also rely on their ability to borrow nondeposit liabilities to meet liquidity needs. If liquidity is needed, funds can be purchased in the repurchase agreements, fed funds, or Eurodollar markets. Such ability to borrow reduces the liquidity risk. Depository institutions can also issue new negotiable certificates of deposit. In a liquidity squeeze, all FIs can sell any available liquid assets in secondary markets.

Even though strategies to reduce risks are significantly developed and appear comprehensive, risk is impossible to eliminate because the future is highly uncertain. Risk is simply an inherent part of life. If an FI only makes loans or purchases financial assets with little or no apparent risk, it is passing up opportunities for profit. A relationship between a deficit spending unit

---

[4]There are some differences. The Ponzi scheme was pure fraud. Despite some illegal activities, the crisis in the junk bond market was also aggravated by a liquidity squeeze caused by regulatory changes. Many who rode out the declining market eventually did well. For instance, MCI, the long distance phone company, got started by issuing junk bonds to finance its operations, and the market is active today.

[5]W.C. Fields put it a little stronger when he said, "You can't cheat an honest man!"

(DSU) and an FI that is established today may continue far into the future. The future circumstances the DSU and the FI find themselves in may be far different from what was anticipated. What seems a sure bet today may turn out to be anything but that. Besides, if the entire economy collapses, even the most conservative FI is bound to see the value of its assets fall.

Risk is particularly acute and intensified in financial claims because payments from one party to another are usually dependent on a payment from a third party. For example, to make her house payment to the mortgage broker, Sally is dependent on receiving her paycheck from her employer. To pay the investor, the mortgage broker is dependent on getting the house payment from Sally, and so it goes. Financial claims are layered and dependent on multiple parties fulfilling contracts or making payments that are dependent upon still others fulfilling contracts. If one party defaults, a chain reaction is set off, which can trigger multiple defaults. The more heavily dependent spending units are on payments from others, the greater the risk that a random default will lead to multiple defaults.

Because of its very nature, the financial system will be chronically plagued by various strains, some of which will lead to multiple defaults and a financial crisis. We define a **financial crisis** as a critical upset in a financial market(s) that is characterized by sharp declines in asset prices and the default of many financial and nonfinancial firms.

Financial crises have occurred in the distant past (the Ponzi scheme) as well as the recent past (the junk bond market collapse). They will occur in the future. Like the business cycle, periods of severe strain are recurrent, but not periodic. That is, they recur through time but not on a particular time schedule. Sometimes long periods of time pass with no major strains. At other times, periods of stress occur very close together. Sometimes, financial stresses can be more severe than at other times. Sometimes, strains are isolated in one market and sometimes they spread throughout the entire system. Exhibit 14-1 depicts the anatomy of a financial crisis.

Many interrelationships exist. For example, a general slump in the economy can create a financial crisis. One party defaults because of a downturn in the economy and sets off a chain reaction of defaults. The financial crisis worsens the already existing downturn and can result in a deep recession or depression. At other times, the causation may flow in the opposite direction. In this case, a financial crisis, such as a dramatic fall in stock prices or a random large bankruptcy causing a chain reaction of defaults, leads to a general slump in business activity or a recession.

Because of numerous factors, the probability of a financial crisis may increase. For example, a sharp unexpected rise in interest rates increases the likelihood of multiple defaults. A sharp increase in interest rates raises the monthly payments of homeowners or other borrowers with variable rate loans. Payments may be going up at the same time incomes and property and asset values are falling. (Remember the inverse relationship between interest rates and the value of long-term fixed rate assets.) Moreover, firms that rely on short-term borrowing will see their costs increase and, hence, profits fall. Eventually, declining profits could lead to losses, reduced borrowing, and insolvency.

A fall in stock values can also set off a chain of events that increases the likelihood of a financial crisis. A fall in stock prices makes it more difficult for firms or individuals to borrow. Reduced stock values reduce the net worth

Financial Crisis A critical upset in a financial market characterized by sharp declines in asset prices and the default of many financial and nonfinancial firms.

Exhibit 14-1 ◆
The Anatomy of a Financial Crisis

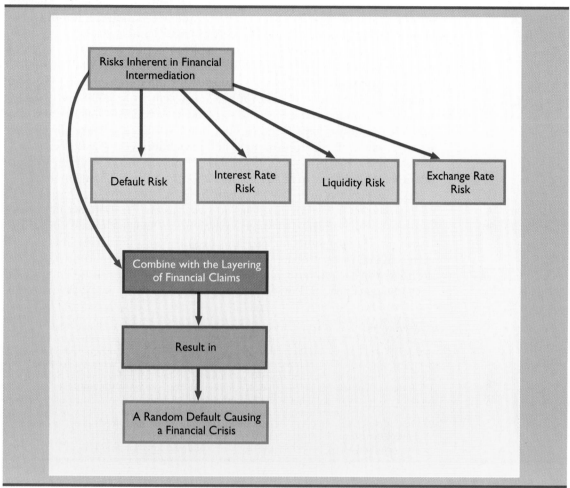

of firms and stockholders. The value of possible collateral falls, the profit outlook dims, and potential borrowers appear less creditworthy. FIs may be hesitant to lend, given the new circumstances and the less certain future.

Moreover, when interest rates are rising and stock values are falling, the most cautious borrowers will drop out of the market, postponing the investment or the large purchase until the future appears more certain. At such times, the adverse selection problem increases; that is, the pool of potential borrowers becomes more heavily weighted with those borrowers who are more willing to take risks, whose financial positions are less secure, and who are less desirable.

Another factor that can intensify the risk of a financial crisis is unanticipated decreases in the overall level of prices. Now would be a good time to look at Exhibit 14-2, which describes a classic situation in which asset and other prices fall leading to a systemwide collapse.

Finally, risks of financial intermediation are exacerbated in a world of sophisticated global electronic funds transfers. Funds can move in and out of markets instantaneously causing widespread losses and gains in various markets. Such fungibility of funds further contributes to financial instability.

Exhibit 14-2 ◆
The Classic Debt
Deflation

Even though deflation sounds seductive to buyers when they think of being able to purchase things for cheaper prices, deflation has many onerous burdens. One of these is debt deflation. A debt deflation is a real increase in debt burdens caused by falling incomes and prices.

For example, assume we are in a "typical" period of general deflation in which both prices and incomes are falling.[a] If I have a $1,000 per month house payment on a house I paid $100,000 for when I was making $30,000, and my income and the value of the house fall to $15,000 and $50,000 respectively, then I am experiencing debt deflation. My income and the value of the house have fallen in half, but I still have to make the higher house payment. In real terms, my house payment has doubled. Because my income and other prices fall, my real debt burden increases, even though my nominal debt payment ($1,000 per month) has not changed.

It is easy to see that debt deflation leads to bankruptcies, foreclosures, and depressed prices for financial and real assets.[b] Individuals in such a situation cannot afford their house payments so they try to sell, just as everyone in a similar situation also tries to sell. With the market glutted and prices falling, there probably are not many buyers, leading to further price declines, and a downward spiral. Lenders move in and foreclose, individuals declare bankruptcy, and prices fall still further. Needless to say, the mood in

[a]Actually periods of deflation have not been "typical" during the middle and late twentieth century. Not since the Great Depression have we experienced widespread debt deflation. In the 1980s and early 1990s, some regions of the country experienced housing debt deflation, which led to foreclosures. For example, in California homeowners who purchased their homes in the late 1980s often found themselves owing more in the early 1990s than what their houses were worth. Despite the fact that interest rates fell to their lowest levels in 20 years, homeowners were unable to refinance.
[b]Businesses can't repay debt on inventories as the value of inventories drops below the amount of debt contracted to purchase them, the value of finished goods drops below the amount of debt contracted to purchase raw materials, etc. As businesses contract, employment and incomes decline and the cycle continues in a downward spiral.

Having considered the reasons why financial crises recurrently plague the economy, and some of the factors that increase the probability of a financial crisis, we now turn our attention to the specifics of two recent financial crises. We begin with the collapse of the S&L industry in the 1980s.

 RECAP

A financial crisis is a critical upset in a financial market and is characterized by sharp declines in asset prices and widespread defaults. Financial crises occur periodically because of the inherent risks in financial intermediation and because financial claims are layered.

 The Savings and Loan Debacle

Throughout most of the 1980s, the savings and loan (S&L) industry in the United States went through a period of severe strain. More than 1,500

the economy takes on an air of pessimism. This is a somewhat exaggerated example, but hopefully you get the picture. If the borrower had an adjustable or variable rate mortgage, the situation may not have been as critical. In a deflation, interest rates and hence the monthly mortgage payments are probably also falling. (In this case, the fall in the monthly payment would reflect the decline in the interest rate but not a decline in the principal, even though the real value of the property has fallen.)

Borrowers with fixed rate loans do not get to lower their monthly payments just because their incomes and other prices have fallen unless they specifically renegotiate their loan contract with the lender. This is sometimes done, although refinancing costs can be high, the property may no longer qualify because the value may have fallen during the deflation, or the borrower may no longer qualify because his income has fallen.[c] What can happen is that the borrower gets squeezed between the constancy of their loan payment (the rock) and falling income (a hard place). The result of this unfortunate turn of events is often foreclosure in which the home is repossessed, and possibly bankruptcy.

If the frequency of foreclosures and bankruptcies accelerates, which it usually does in a deflation, then a debt deflation is under way and losses for bad debts mount at FIs, potentially leading to their collapse. Such a scenario led to the failure of thousands of banks in the 1930s. In response to the collapse, the government put in place safety nets such as the FDIC and FSLIC. Eventually, when prices fall to low levels, the seeds of recovery are planted, as buyers scrape together enough funds to start buying again at the depressed prices. In reality, this occurs when both input and output prices have adjusted to profitable terms of trade.

[c]To relieve the problem of high refinancing costs, many lenders in the 1990s offer no-cost refinance loans where the buyer pays a slightly higher interest rate in lieu of refinancing costs.

institutions failed or went out of existence. Many others downsized and the industry as a whole shrunk considerably. Taxpayers spent billions of dollars to bail out the industry because the financial crisis threatened the health and stability of the entire economy. Today the industry is far different from what it was at the start of the 1980s. The public at large has been disillusioned, questioning the safety and soundness of S&Ls and the financial system as a whole. The honesty and integrity of S&L owners, regulators, and even some members of Congress have been doubted.

Like most crises, the seeds of the S&L debacle were planted long before the first sprouts of trouble appeared. In many ways, the roots of the crisis go back to the way S&Ls do business. Unless interest rates remain fairly stable for long periods of time as they did from the early 1950s until the 1970s, it is risky to fund long-term loans or purchase long-term assets with short-term deposits. If interest rates rise, the cost of the funds borrowed over the short term can increase above what long-term assets are earning. As we saw in Chapter 11, S&Ls were literally established for the express purpose of borrowing short from passbook savers and lending long to finance mortgage loans. That is, they were designed to engage in a dangerous behavior in a setting of volatile or rising interest rates.

From the early 1950s on, the U.S. economy experienced a slow upward drift in interest rates. Regulation Q, which put a ceiling on the interest rate that could be paid on deposits, applied to S&Ls as well as commercial banks. In fact, the ceiling for S&Ls was maintained at one-half percent above the ceiling for commercial banks. The express purpose of this differential was to encourage savers to deposit funds into S&Ls, which then could be used to make mortgage loans, thus encouraging home ownership. With Regulation Q in place, the cost of the funds borrowed mostly from passbook savers was maintained at or below the ceiling limits. Small savers, at least for a time, had few alternatives to passbook savings accounts in depository institutions. Consequently, disintermediation (the removal of funds from FIs) was relatively minor when interest rates on other financial assets such as Treasury bills or commercial paper went above Regulation Q limits. The other financial assets were generally unavailable to small savers because they did not have the required minimum amounts needed to purchase them. For example, $10,000 is the minimum amount needed to purchase a Treasury bill. However by the 1970s, small savers did have money market mutual funds as an alternative to passbook accounts in depository institutions.[6] Still, the situation would ferment for some time before a crisis would occur. By the late 1970s and early 1980s, events began to unfold that would result in total collapse of the industry and, as we shall see, a large taxpayer bailout.

To give some insight to the burgeoning crisis, recall that nominal interest rates are approximately equal to real rates plus the expected inflation rate. In the late 1970s, high nominal rates reflected expectations about inflation and not high real rates. That is, the high nominal rates were the result of large inflation premiums. In fact, in the 1970s, real rates were often abnormally low and sometimes even negative despite the high nominal rates.

In late 1979, the Fed orchestrated a huge spike in already high nominal rates as part of a policy aimed at reducing inflation. Interest rates climbed far above Regulation Q ceilings, which capped nominal rates while ignoring real rates.[7] The spike in nominal rates caused severe disintermediation and/or the transfer of funds from S&Ls to money market mutual funds. Congress responded in 1982 by authorizing the S&Ls to offer money market deposit accounts that competed with money market mutual funds.[8] This legislative change slowed the disintermediation and the transfer of funds from the S&Ls to money market mutual funds, but was probably too little and too late. Also, the S&Ls were left with another problem. S&Ls had mostly long-term fixed rate assets, primarily low-rate mortgages, that were now funded by high-interest variable rate accounts. They were hit with a double whammy: their profits fell as their costs of funds increased faster than their earnings on assets, and the value of their assets fell. Recall that when interest rates rise, the value of long-term bonds falls. Long term, fixed rate mortgages are similar to long-term bonds in that when interest rates rise, the value of long-term fixed rate mortgages goes down.

---

[6]Actually, as we saw in Chapter 13, a person transferring funds from a depository intermediary to a money market mutual fund is not "disintermediating" but is transferring funds from one type of intermediary to another.

[7]Regulators have consistently tried to regulate nominal rates and consistently ignored real rates.

[8]Money market deposit accounts actually had one leg up on money market mutual funds since they were insured by the Federal Savings and Loan Insurance Corporation (FSLIC) whereas money market mutual funds were not.

In 1981, economists estimated that the S&L industry had a negative net worth of $100 billion dollars. This figure was far greater than the assets of the Federal Savings and Loan Insurance Corporation (FSLIC) that insured the deposits of the sickly S&Ls.[9] Estimates of the assets of the FSLIC at the time amounted to only about $6 billion. Rather than confronting the problem head on in the early 1980s, which would have required injecting taxpayer funds into the system at that time, Congress responded with actions that would eventually make the situation much worse. Under the Garn–St. Germain Act, it expanded the lending powers of the S&Ls into product lines that paid a high return but were unfamiliar to S&L managers and entailed a lot of risk. Capital requirements, the cushion against losses, were also lowered so that the S&Ls could aggressively enter new lending arenas. Rather than having capital equivalent to 5 percent of assets, S&Ls were required to hold capital equal to only 3 percent of assets.

With expanded lending powers and lower capital requirements, the industry went for broke and made new high-earning investments in such ventures as junk bonds and commercial real estate. Guess what happened? They ended up losing a lot more and literally went broke. In late 1986, Congress granted the FSLIC $10.8 billion funded by borrowing against future deposit insurance

---

[9] The now defunct FSLIC was the federally sponsored agency that insured the deposits of S&Ls for up to $100,000. It was dissolved in 1989. Since this time, S&Ls can obtain deposit insurance from the Savings Association Insurance Fund (SAIF), which is a part of the Federal Deposit Insurance Corporation (FDIC).

© 1996 Jack Ziegler from The Cartoon Bank,™ Inc.

premiums to be paid by the thrifts themselves. In 1988, the Federal Home Loan Bank, the equivalent of the Fed for S&Ls at the time, liquidated more than 200 insolvent thrifts by selling the institutions to individuals and firms. In the liquidation process, the buyers were compensated for the negative net worth of the institutions with an array of future guarantees and obligations, including tax breaks. None of these compensations required Congressional authorization or appropriation and have been subsequently viewed suspiciously.

Finally in 1989, Congress responded with the Financial Institutions Reform, Recovery and Enforcement Act (FIRREA), which attempted to resolve the problem of widespread failures within the industry and insufficient insurance funds to resolve the crisis. By the end of 1995, the bailout had cost taxpayers over $140 billion.[10] At the time of the bailout, the costs had already been incurred. The bailout shifted the costs from the owners and depositors of the failed thrifts to the public (taxpayers) at large. We look at the specifics of FIRREA and other recent regulatory measures in Chapter 15. Now would be a good time to look at Exhibit 14-3, which gives an account of a rather infamous S&L failure, the Lincoln Savings fiasco.

What can we conclude about the causes of the crisis? It is difficult to apportion blame; and such blame would not be productive anyway. Undoubtedly the inherent problem of lending long and borrowing short when interest rates rise was a major factor. Another factor was the extension of lending powers to the thrifts in the early 1980s. These new powers that allowed for more risk taking also seem to have attracted some dishonest folk to the industry. Finally, regulators were slow to move in and shut down troubled thrifts, which caused eventual losses to be greater than they otherwise would have been. Congress was also slow to act. A lot of hard lessons were learned as taxpayer funds were diverted from potentially building better schools, roads, and infrastructure, among other more positive projects. Now we turn our attention to another crisis within the financial system that was occurring simultaneously.

Crisis Within the Banking System

The most severe financial crisis this country has ever experienced occurred during the Great Depression. During this time period, which predated deposit insurance, more than one-third of the banks in the United States failed. To halt a series of bank runs in early 1933, President Franklin Roosevelt proclaimed a "bank holiday," shutting down all the banks in the nation for one month. During this month, Congress passed the Glass–Steagall Act, which, among other reforms, included deposit insurance and the creation of the Federal Deposit Insurance Corporation (FDIC). For the first time, small depositors did not have to worry about losing deposits if their bank went belly-up. Soon deposit insurance would be available for small depositors in almost all depository institutions.

Ever since the first deposit insurance statutes were enacted, concern has been expressed about the **moral hazard** problem that deposit insurance by its

Moral Hazard The reduction of market discipline experienced by FIs that goes hand-in-hand with deposit insurance.

---

[10] We should point out that the bailout was to the benefit of taxpayers as well as at the expense of taxpayers.

Lincoln Savings was a pristine S&L in the idyllic planned community of Irvine, California. It was purchased for $51 million in 1984 by American Continental of Phoenix, a large real estate development company controlled by Charles Keating. With hindsight, it is surprising that Keating was allowed to buy Lincoln, since he had been accused of fraud by the Security and Exchange Commission only four years earlier. As a state-chartered institution, Lincoln was permitted unlimited direct investment in real estate, a potential gold mine for a real estate developer. Within days of taking the helm, Keating fired moderate loan officers and rushed into high-risk investments including junk bonds, desert land in Arizona, hotels, common stock, currency futures, and real estate developments, including those of American Continental.

The Federal Home Loan Bank was responsible for regulating and insuring Lincoln Savings. Despite the fact that under the state charter Lincoln was free to make unlimited direct investments in real estate, the Federal Home Loan Bank balked and announced a regulation that limited direct investment in real estate to 10 percent of total assets for S&Ls insured with the FSLIC. In 1986, regulators from the Federal Home Loan Bank in San Francisco realized that Lincoln exceeded this limit for federally insured thrifts by some $600 million. By 1987, they realized that Lincoln Savings was in serious trouble, and the regulators wanted to move in and seize the institution.

Keating responded by seeking the help of influential politicians. He made large political contributions, in particular giving $1.3 million to five U.S. Senators who became known as the Keating Five.* They intervened with the Federal Home Loan Bank on behalf of Lincoln and met with Edwin Gray, chairperson of the Federal Home Loan Bank, and top regulators from the San Francisco office. They alleged that the regulators were being too hard on Lincoln and asked for regulatory leniency.

In September 1987, M. Danny Wall had replaced Edwin Gray as chairperson of the Federal Home Loan Bank. He later continued on at the Office of Thrift Supervision, which replaced the Federal Home Loan Bank. Chairperson Wall transferred the regulation of Lincoln out of the San Francisco office to the Washington office, a most unconventional move. A regulator never walked into Lincoln for the next ten months. In early 1987, Lincoln had assets of $3.9 billion. By early 1989 when Lincoln failed, assets had grown to $5.5 billion. Obviously, a lot of lending had been done. The Lincoln failure ended up costing taxpayers about $2.5 billion. M. Danny Wall was forced to resign because of his involvement in the scandal, and both Charles Keating and his son were sentenced to prison for numerous convictions of negligence and fraudulent acts.

Of the many fraudulent practices that Lincoln engaged in, perhaps the most pernicious was misrepresentation in the sale of subordinated debt. Subordinated debt is unsecured debt that in the event of default will not be repaid until other creditors are repaid. Buyers of this debt, who later swore to investigators they had been guaranteed that the debt was insured just like other deposits in an S&L, lost about $200 million. Many of these unsuspecting investors were senior citizens who lost their life savings.

*The senators include Dennis DeConcini and John McCain of Arizona, Alan Cranston of California, John Glenn of Ohio, and Donald Riegle of Michigan. Check the reelection results after the scandal, and you may be surprised at what you find.

Exhibit 14-3 ◆
The Lincoln Savings Scandal

very nature causes.[11] In Chapter 12, we discussed moral hazard in terms of one borrower; that is, after getting the loan, a borrower may use the funds for a different, higher-risk project. In this chapter, the moral hazard problem refers to the reduction in market discipline experienced by FIs that goes hand-in-hand with deposit insurance. For example, deposit insurance encourages banks (and other FIs) to make riskier loans because depositors do not keep tabs on how banks manage their funds as much as they would if their deposits were not insured. The insured banks will take more risks because greater risks offer the possibility of higher returns and after all, banks are highly lever-aged—they are risking depositors' funds, as well as their own, and they get to keep all the winnings. Furthermore, loan officers do not have to lose sleep at night worrying about losing those funds when the funds (deposits) are in-sured. Well-managed banks are penalized because they have to help pay the losses incurred by poorly managed banks.

Even in light of all these concerns, until the 1980s, deposit insurance was widely viewed as an incredible success.[12] Despite the reduction in market dis-cipline that resulted from it, the 1933 Banking Act, which established the FDIC, was probably one of the most successful pieces of legislation this century. The incredible success of the FDIC is often attributed simply to knowledge of its existence. That is, the absence of any significant general run on FDIC insured banks is attributed to the assumption that a run was a waste of time. For 50 years, losses of the FDIC were negligible, its reserves grew, and annually about two-thirds of all the insurance premiums paid in were refunded back to the banks. As a result of its success, Congress raised the insurance limit several times from the original $2,500 in 1934 to $100,000 per account at present.

But all was not well behind closed doors. As we have seen, bank capital is the cushion that banks (depositors) have against calamity if loans start to go bad. The capital-to-assets ratio measures the size of this cushion relative to bank assets. The higher the ratio, the greater the relative losses that could be sustained before the bank would become insolvent. For banks, this ratio was gradually falling throughout the years from 15 percent in 1930 to 7 percent by 1970 and later, to much lower levels. In addition, the level of risk was even greater than the numbers implied because new kinds of bank behavior, **off-balance-sheet activities,** were much greater in 1970 than in 1930.

Off-balance-sheet activities include **standby lines of credit,** overdraft pro-tection, unused credit card balances, and other commitments for which the bank is liable but which do not show up on the balance sheet. They do not affect the capital-to-assets ratio. For example, a standby letter of credit guar-antees that the bank will lend an issuer of commercial paper the funds to pay off creditors on the due date if the issuer cannot. If a bank for a fee gives a standby letter of credit to an issuer of commercial paper and the issuer de-faults, the bank experiences a loss just as if it had made a bad loan. The only difference is that this exposure never shows up on the balance sheet whereas the loan-loss exposure does.[13]

Off-Balance-Sheet Activities Activities such as standby lines of credit, overdraft protection, un-used credit card balances, and other commitments for which the bank is lia-ble but which do not show up on the balance sheet.

Standby Lines of Credit Commitments for which a bank is liable but which do not show up on the balance sheet.

---

[11] The moral hazard problem pertains to any depository institution that offers deposit insurance, including S&Ls. We focus here on commercial banks.

[12] The inception of deposit insurance in the early 1930s resulted in federal examination of state nonmember banks. This in turn caused a sharp decrease in some of the activities that contributed to the bank failures of the 1930s.

[13] In the next chapter, we shall see that banks must now consider off-balance-sheet activities in calculating capital requirements.

In addition to declining capital-to-asset ratios, many other factors contributed to a potential deposit insurance crisis including some of the same factors that caused the S&L debacle. During the 1970s, banks extended their lending to less-developed countries and to highly leveraged business ventures. They made more mortgages, which because of the length of the loan commitments, also increased interest rate risk. Remember the inverse relationship between the interest and the value of long-term fixed rate assets such as mortgages.[14] At the same time, the volatility of the economy was increasing. These factors increased the fluctuations of the value of a bank's assets and, hence, increased risk. The fall in energy prices (particularly oil) caused many loans to go sour. Many large loans including some to less-developed countries could have been repaid only if the price of oil stayed high. In addition, over-building of commercial real estate in the mid-1980s caused a sharp drop in prices, many foreclosures, and large loan losses for banks in the late 1980s. The overbuilding, low occupancy, and foreclosure problems of the commercial real estate market were still prevalent in certain regions of the country well into the mid-1990s.

As we saw in Chapter 12, beginning in the early 1980s, bank failures escalated. Despite suspension of the premium rebates and sharp increases in the premium, the reserves of the FDIC, which peaked in 1987 at $18 billion, were depleted by the end of 1991. A financial crisis occurred, which was not really as severe as that of the S&L industry, but which was a crisis no less. Perhaps the Fed, the lender of last resort, was simply unwilling to let the insurer of last resort, the FDIC, fail. Finally, we must note that FIs were in a market with a high level of competition for funds, which resulted in higher costs. To make the same spread, FIs had to go after higher-risk projects.

Like the S&L regulators, bank regulators were also hesitant to resolve insolvencies quickly, particularly of large banks. Regulators were also timid about imposing losses on uninsured depositors (those with account balances greater than $100,000) and other creditors. With the failure of Continental Illinois National Bank of Chicago in 1984, the doctrine of **"too big to fail"** became the official position of FDIC regulators. Now would be a good time to look at Exhibit 14-4 for a discussion of the Continental Illinois failure.

"Too big to fail" means that the regulators will not allow a "big" bank to fail, but rather use the **purchase and assumption method** to resolve insolvencies. With the purchase and assumption method, another healthy institution is found to take over the assets and liabilities of the failed bank. The insurer, the FDIC in this case, pays the takeover institution the difference between the assets and the liabilities of the failed institution. The takeover bank benefits by ending up with a much larger portfolio. Neither the depositors with uninsured account balances greater than $100,000 nor the creditors lose. When the "too big to fail" doctrine is implemented, all deposits are "de facto" insured. With the **payoff method,** rather than finding a buyer for the troubled institution, the FDIC merely pays off insured depositors up to the $100,000 limit and closes down the bank. When insurers resolve the insolvency with the

"Too Big to Fail" The position adopted by FDIC regulators in 1984 whereby the failure of a large bank would be resolved using the purchase and assumption method rather than the payoff method.

Purchase and Assumption Method The method of resolving a bank insolvency by finding a buyer for the institution.

Payoff Method The method of resolving a bank insolvency by paying off the depositors and closing the institution.

---

[14]We have seen that mortgages are now packaged together and sold off in the secondary market. This securitization reduces the interest rate risk. However, if an FI is holding long-term fixed rate mortgages—before they are sold off—and the interest rate goes up, the value of those mortgages falls.

Exhibit 14-4 ◆

The Collapse of the Continental Illinois Bank: Regulatory Causes, Responses, and Consequences

At the time of its collapse in the spring of 1984, Continental was the eighth largest bank in the nation. The factors contributing to its demise are easily summarized: (1) Continental is located in Chicago, and Illinois was a unit banking state at the time. No branching was permitted. Without an extensive network of branches, deposits by households and local firms, often viewed as comprising the stable core sources of bank funds, were relatively small. (2) Given the small source of deposits and a desire to expand loans (earning assets), Continental borrowed large volumes of funds on a short-term basis in domestic and international money markets in the form of large negotiable certificates of deposit, Eurodollar borrowings, and overnight borrowings in the federal funds market. At the time of its collapse, Continental was funding (financing) its assets with about $9 billion of very short-term borrowings. For it to continue to maintain its asset portfolio, it had to be able to regularly reborrow these funds. (3) Remember that the FDIC only insures deposits up to $100,000. Thus if you are a surplus spending unit (SSU) with a surplus exceeding this figure, you will move your funds out of an FI if you believe the institution is experiencing some difficulty and is in danger of failing. This means the types of funds Continental was relying upon, in contrast to core deposits, were volatile sources of funds.

In essence, Continental Bank was an inverted pyramid. A relatively small core of stable deposits, the bottom point of the pyramid, was supporting a much larger volume of loans, the top of the pyramid. The institution's balance was maintained by the additional support provided by short-term volatile sources of funds. The eventual loss of this additional support and resultant toppling of the institution began with the failure of the Penn Square Bank in July 1982.

Located in a shopping center in Oklahoma, Penn Square Bank was a younger bank that attempted to capitalize on the oil and gas boom of the late 1970s and early 1980s. The rising price of oil and decontrol of natural gas prices had provided a clear incentive for firms and individuals to explore and drill for these fuels. Such activity needed to be financed and Penn Square Bank became a leading financier of the resultant energy boom. Since its own deposit base was relatively small, and the loan applications it had were huge, Penn Square Bank, in effect, became a broker of loans. Such a bank is often called a merchant bank. It would arrange (originate) a loan and then sell the loan to a larger bank, such as Continental, who also wanted to get in on the energy boom and the seemingly profitable lending opportunities it offered. In the process, Penn Square Bank would collect fees from Continental and other large banks for arranging and servicing the loans.

To put it mildly, Penn Square Bank was not a well-managed institution. First, with so many loans in the energy field, its asset portfolio was not

payoff method, creditors, stockholders, and depositors with uninsured balances greater than $100,000 all lose.[15]

---

[15] In Chapter 15, we shall see that a law passed in 1991 requires banks to use the least costly method to handle insolvencies.

diversified. Second, its analysis of the riskiness associated with lending to individual borrowers was shoddy or nonexistent. Not surprisingly then, when oil and gas prices fell in the 1981–82 recession, Penn Square Bank found itself in serious difficulty. The falloff in energy demand accompanying the recession and resultant decline in energy prices meant that many of those suppliers of energy who had borrowed from the bank defaulted on their loans. This left Penn Square insolvent. The value of its liabilities exceeded the value of assets, and the FDIC moved in and closed the bank.

So how does Continental fit in to all this? About $1 billion of the loans Continental had acquired from Penn Square were defaulted on. This huge loss began to weaken confidence in the institution by those providing it with high volumes of funds on a regular basis. With its "balance" increasingly precarious, it wasn't going to take much to topple this banking giant.

In the spring of 1984, rumors about Continental and its troubles swirled. A run began, but it was not an old-fashioned run with individual depositors lined up outside the bank. Rather, it was a modern run in which large providers of funds simply moved their funds electronically to other institutions. Over the course of a week, Continental lost about $9 billion of funds. Regulators were ready with their safety net. The Fed, fulfilling its role as a lender of last resort, lent Continental about $4 billion. The FDIC pledged an additional $2 billion of its funds. Recognizing the threat to the entire industry, other large banks pledged another $3 billion. Despite this extraordinary support, the run continued. Finally, amid fears that a nationwide and worldwide banking crisis would accompany the actual failure of Continental, the FDIC announced that it would extend its insurance coverage to all deposits, not just those up to $100,000. The run ended. Suddenly, Continental went from the most risky bank in America to the safest. Utilizing its powers, the FDIC then took over (nationalized) the institution, replaced its senior management, and set a course it hoped would return the bank to health someday—which did happen.

This episode provides considerable insight into the dynamics of regulation and banking. Part of Continental's troubles were the result of regulations. A desire to grow coupled with branching restrictions led the bank to rely on volatile sources of funds. Once trouble developed, the federal response probably averted a serious financial crisis. This illustrated the primacy of the safety/soundness objective and the system's safety net, including FDIC insurance and the Fed's discount facility (lender of last resort). Lastly, the handling of the Continental bank collapse probably represents a watershed in regulatory policy. The consequence is that large institutions were not "free to fail" between the mid-1980s and the mid-1990s. As we shall see in Chapter 15, a provision of the Financial Institutions Reform, Recovery, and Enforcement Act (FIRREA) of 1989 would change this policy.

As we saw in Chapter 12, the strains of the banking system have been somewhat resolved in the 1990s without the major legislation necessary to resolve the S&L debacle. Banks have earned record profits. Their cost of funds fell faster than their earnings on assets. Indeed, in the mid-1990s, the FDIC is in the process of downsizing because of the improvement in the health of the banking sector. In particular, 15 of 22 liquidation offices nationwide will be closed by 1995, with about one-half of the employees laid off—not good for those affected employees, but good for the industry and economy as a whole.

Despite the turnaround, industry experts believe that only Bandaid solutions have been applied to the problems so far and that many unresolved issues remain to be addressed. They do not believe that the present reforms sufficiently deal with the moral hazard problem inherent in deposit insurance. Many proposals have been made to reform the system of the future to enhance market discipline. In the next chapter, we look at some of the reforms that will undoubtedly become part of an overhauled regulatory system in the future.

More Recent Strains on the Financial System

In addition to the standard risks that financial institutions have experienced in the past, financial institutions in the 1990s face new strains. Some of these new situations result from the changing composition of balance sheets and some result from activities that never show up on financial statements. New modes of behavior create the potential for new strains. We begin by looking at the **daylight overdraft** problem.

Daylight Overdrafts

Daylight Overdraft An overdraft that results from the Fed crediting a payment in the morning regardless of whether the funds are in the account of the payor.

Fedwire The communication network that links large bank computers with the Fed and over which payments can be made.

Fedwire is the communications network that links the computers of most large banks with the Fed. Payments between banks are executed over Fedwire by transferring deposit claims against the Fed. For example, suppose Bank of America wants to make a $10 million payment to Citibank. The Fedwire operator at Bank of America types a message into the computer instructing the transfer to be made from Bank of America's account to Citibank. In usually less than two minutes and for an average cost of $10, Citibank receives the message that a deposit has been made into their account. Bank of America is sent a message that the transfer has been made. The daylight overdraft problem results from the fact that Citibank is credited with the payment now and the payment is made regardless of whether the funds are presently in Bank of America's account. If the funds are in the account, they are immediately withdrawn. If not, the payment is still made and an automatic loan—called an overdraft—is made to Bank of America by the Fed. The overdraft is expected to be repaid by the end of the day and no interest is charged for the use of the funds during the day.

Banks increasingly rely on nondeposit liabilities, whether they be funds borrowed in the overnight repurchase agreements market, the fed funds market, or the Eurodollar market. Funds borrowed the day before are generally paid off by transfers in the morning using Fedwire. For example, in the preceding case, Bank of America could be repaying an overnight fed funds loan from Citibank. Large banks make extensive use of daylight overdrafts when they rollover their overnight borrowings from various sources with the Fed extending an overdraft. Later in the day, the borrowing bank pays off the overdraft by reborrowing in one of the same markets it borrowed from the day before.

Can you guess the source of a potential problem? If a bank that owes daylight overdrafts fails during the day, the Fed is left with a bad debt. Hence the Fed is exposed to a credit risk. Indeed, the failure of Continental Illinois (Exhibit 14-4) left the Fed to convert a $3.5 billion overdraft into a discount loan. The Fed had little choice in this matter, since the funds had already been paid out.

The Fed has been concerned about daylight overdrafts since the late 1970s and has developed measures to reduce them beginning with caps on the maximum amount of overdrafts allowed. In April 1994, the Fed instituted fees on daylight overdrafts which were to be comparable to the costs of avoiding an overdraft. The immediate effect of the fee was that overdrafts dropped about 40 percent from a daily average of $125 billion in the preceeding six months to a daily average of about $70 billion in the six months after the fee was initiated.[16] At the present time, the Fed is studying the possibility of increasing fees to further reduce the amount of daylight overdrafts.

Program Trading

Program trading is the preprogramming of computers to automatically issue buy and sell orders for stocks as stock prices change on organized exchanges such as the New York Stock Exchange. Computers located at large brokerage houses such as Merrill Lynch or Prudential Bache track stock prices and automatically issue buy and sell orders when the price of a stock rises or falls to a certain level. In the case of a price decrease, the seller benefits by limiting his losses and the buyer benefits by guaranteeing the price at which she will purchase the stock. In the case of a price increase, the seller sells his stock at a certain preprogrammed price and thus makes a certain profit.

> **Program Trading** The preprogramming of computers to automatically issue buy and sell orders for stocks as stock prices change.

On October 19, 1987, the Dow Jones Industrial Average, an indicator of the value of stocks traded on the New York Stock Exchange, fell 508 points or 22.8 percent in one day. Traditional economic theory tells us that in response to such a fall, spending would also fall causing a recession. After all, spending units must feel less wealthy after this decline in stock values and will tend to spend less, or so theory would have us believe. The large downward movement in prices on this day was partially the result of program trading. When stocks fell to a certain price, sell orders were generated by a computer causing further price decreases and further computer-generated sell orders. Now would be a good time to look back at Exhibit 10-4, which deals with the causes of the 1987 Crash.

Fortunately, this incident represents a good example of Fed intervention where a downturn was prevented in the wake of a potential financial crisis. Fed Chairperson Alan Greenspan took decisive action to provide liquidity to the markets by increasing bank reserves. Furthermore, the public and market participants were assured that the Fed stood ready to provide whatever liquidity was needed, if indeed any additional amounts were needed. **Margin requirements** are the amount of funds that must be put down to purchase securities. Liquidity may be needed because margin requirements are such that securities may be purchased with only 50 percent down and the rest

> **Margin Requirements** The amount of funds that must be put down to purchase securities; the remainder can be financed.

---

[16]"Daylight Overdraft Fees and the Federal Reserve's Payment System Risk Policy," *Federal Reserve Bulletin*, December 1995, pp. 1065–1077.

LOOKING OUT

Japan Has an Ally at the Fed

We know that the Fed is committed to maintaining the safety and the soundness of the U.S. banking system. But, as the world becomes more globalized, the Fed must increasingly consider the safety and soundness of foreign financial systems. The reason is that a crisis abroad could spill over to the U.S. economy. A case in point is the Fed's response to the Japanese banking crisis. (See Looking Out, in Chapter 12.) On October 16, 1995, the Chairperson of the House Banking Committee disclosed that the Fed had privately assured Japanese officials that the United States stood ready to provide emergency liquidity to Japan to avert a financial crisis.*

But why would the Fed extend this carte blanche offer? Primarily, it fears that, in the event of a severe crisis, Japanese investors will sell off U.S. financial assets. Such a selloff could drive up U.S. interest rates, depress real estate values, send the dollar further down, and be the harbinger of a U.S. recession.

Some analysts say the grounds for such fears are real because of the large holdings of Japanese investments in the United States. For example, Japanese investments in U.S. Treasuries total more than $200 billion, and Japanese banks account for more than 17 percent of all corporate lending and 20 percent of all syndicated business. A pullout or selloff would leave domestic lenders hard pressed to pick up the slack, and interest rates would undoubtedly head north. Given these numbers, we can better understand the rationale for the Fed's assurances.

*See "Why Japan's Banks Have a Friend in Washington," *Business Week*, October 30, 1995, pp. 38–39.

---

financed. Without the ability to obtain liquidity, a downturn could trigger massive defaults and a deeper crisis. More than likely, a potential financial crisis was prevented by the Fed announcing "Have no fear, the Fed is here!"

In response to the October crash, certain reforms have been instituted to prevent what happened in late 1987 but to still allow market participants to take advantage of hedge and arbitrage opportunities. For example, **circuit breakers** were introduced which temporarily slow or halt program trading if prices fall by some specified amount. Market makers then have a chance to take positions and evaluate new information to provide support for the market. Bargains could be snatched up and the free fall in prices stopped. Circuit breakers to slow trading were triggered 29 times in 1995 while program trading was halted once when the market fell 100 points. Program trading accounted for 11.3 percent of overall volume on the New York Stock Exchange and averaged 39.7 million shares traded daily in 1995.[17] Despite the introduction of circuit breakers, program trading is still sometimes responsible for large daily price movements of stocks. However, concern that program trading poses a risk for a financial crisis has become somewhat mitigated.

Circuit Breakers Measures that slow or halt program trading if prices fall by some specified amount.

---

[17] William Power, "Program Trading Volume Reached a Record In Year, But Was Lower in Percentage Terms," *The Wall Street Journal*, January 2, 1996, R36.

Derivatives

Derivatives are financial contracts whose values are derived from the values of other underlying assets, such as foreign exchange, bonds, equities, commodities, or an index. Their values fluctuate with the values of the underlying assets. Examples of derivatives include financial futures, options, and combinations thereof as described in Chapter 10. They are used by banks and others, including virtually every large corporation in the United States to hedge, speculate, or arbitrage price differences.

In recent years, large banks have greatly increased their involvement with derivatives, which at the same time, have become even more complex. Powerful computers are often needed to assess the risks involved if one factor, say, an interest rate or exchange rate, changes by a small amount, perhaps only one-hundredth of one percent. Indeed it is difficult, if not impossible, to understand all the risks that are involved with extremely complex derivatives and all possible scenarios. Despite this, derivatives will undoubtedly get even more complex in the future.

Because of these facts, some analysts worry that derivatives may be too risky for banks. They believe that bank participation in these markets should be limited or that the market should somehow be regulated. Others go so far as to suggest that Congress should ban the use of derivatives by banks altogether. The concern is that not enough is known about how derivatives work and about the risks that are involved. If rates move by a small amount in an unanticipated direction, large losses can occur if derivatives are used for specu-

Derivatives Financial contracts whose values are derived from the values of other underlying assets; examples include financial futures and options.

© 1996 Jack Ziegler from The Cartoon Bank,™ Inc.

Exhibit 14-5 ◆
The Collapse of a
California County
and a British Bank

What do Barings Bank of London and Orange County, California, have in common? Not much to the casual observer, but events in late 1994 and early 1995 will put the two close together in the history books forever. Within the span of a few months, both sustained massive losses in the derivative market, and both institutions were brought to their knees.

We begin in the affluent County of Orange, located just south of Los Angeles. Robert Citron, a Democrat, had served as County Treasurer for more than 24 years in this traditionally Republican County. As such, he managed the county's investment pool. Starting in the late 1980s, the pool began to grow rapidly from less than $1 billion to more than $8 billion as many other municipalities outside the county and other public entities opted to join. The reason for the growth was due to the pool's high return and the impressive earnings record that Citron had amassed. He was considered brilliant for consistently earning an above-average return and others sought to share his good fortunes.

But all was not well, as wise investors should have suspected. After all, what is the probability of earning significantly above-average returns for several years in a row if one is not taking more risks? Unfortunately, as Citron and the county found out all too late, the probability is not high. When all was said and done, Citron claimed to have an "incomplete" understanding of the risks inherent in the financial instruments—or as some would say, exotic derivatives—that he was dealing in. Having leveraged the $8 billion portfolio to $20 billion, he bet that interest rates would continue to fall in 1994. When the Fed began to raise rates in February, Citron failed to reverse his position. Citron owned securities whose value fell as rates rose. As rates continued upward, Citron faced reelection in June and denied to his constituency that the investment pool was in trouble. After his victory, he still tried to hold on and by the time Wall Street refused to extend any more credit, the County was unable to come up with the funds needed to pay bondholders and the County was forced into bankruptcy. The portfolio was liquidated—that is, the securities whose value had fallen were sold—taking a $1.7 billion loss. Thus, the largest municipal bankruptcy in history had occurred in one of the country's wealthiest counties.[a]

Another unlikely candidate for bankruptcy was Barings, a prestigious British investment banking house that had been around for 233 years. Like Orange County, Barings had one individual who was to bring the institution down. Nick Leeson was only 28 years old and by most accounts seemed on the fast track to success if not already there. He headed the futures trading

[a] If the County could have held on, when rates turned back down in mid-1995, the losses would have been much less.

lation.[18] Now would be a good time to look at Exhibit 14-5, which gives a recent example of how derivatives brought down an otherwise healthy British investment bank and a wealthy Southern California County.

---

[18] As described in Chapter 10, derivatives can also be used to offset or counter risks inherent in the regular activities of FIs. Prohibiting the use of derivatives by banks would also prohibit the use of them for this valuable function.

department in Singapore for Barings. In 1994, his bonus topped $1,000,000. Not bad for a kid who had grown up on the other side of the tracks. Who could guess that by late February 1995, he would be on the run and that Barings would be in bankruptcy. Here's how it happened.

Apparently Leeson bought enough futures in a three-week period beginning in late January to have a $27 billion exposure. The transactions appeared normal because Barings had been taking large hedge positions for years in Nikkei Stock index futures—positions that were used to arbitrage even minute price differences between stocks traded in Singapore and Osaka. Around January 26, Leeson switched from a hedged position to a speculative position. No one knows for sure what his thinking was, but it is suspected that he thought that the Kobe earthquake would stimulate the economy and push up the Nikkei. But, as events unfolded, his strategy proved wrong, and he sold put and call options to raise cash for margin calls. In this situation, he was betting the Nikkei would settle into a narrow range. By February 20, his losses had accumulated to $700 million and Barings put up more cash to cover his deficit. Barings believed that the margin call was for a corporate customer whose funds would be deposited in a few days. When Leeson couldn't produce the funds, he fled, leaving behind a note that said, "I'm sorry." By this time, the loss amounted to $900 million and was more than all of Barings' capital. The Bank of England put Barings into bankruptcy. Less than a month had elapsed since the start of the fiasco. Leeson was eventually apprehended, extradited to Singapore, and received a 3-1/2 year prison sentence.

Examples such as Orange County and Barings are not unique.[b] As *Business Week* put it, "In the easy-money boom, too many securities executives lost the ability or will to scrutinize high-energy traders or guard against unethical salespeople. Too many bankers and [chief financial officers] CFOs neglected to ask whether they understood the complexity—or the downside—of the highly leveraged derivatives they were using to hedge financial risks."[c] In such a world, the value of derivative contracts can fluctuate wildly from even small changes in stock, bond, or currency prices. What should be done to protect investors and institutions? For now that remains an unanswered question. But one thing is certain, both Barings' executives and the Board of Supervisors of Orange County regret not keeping a closer eye on the situation.

[b]In April 1994, Procter and Gamble sustained a $102 million after-tax loss in an interest rate swap. Also in April of that same year, Kidder Peabody found that one of its traders had parlayed a $210 million dollar loss. After the loss, Kidder Peabody was sold to Paine Webber.
[c]"The Lesson from Barings' Straits," *Business Week*, March 13, 1995, pp. 30–32.

Could derivatives set off chain reactions in world financial markets that lead to financial instability? Do market participants, including banks, have enough knowledge about them to be heavily involved? Will regulators be able to properly regulate these markets? Risks from derivatives currently do not show up on balance sheets. Will regulators be able to insure that such risks somehow be disclosed? These are questions to be answered in the near future.

The Eurocurrency Market

Eurocurrency Market
Eurodollar deposits and
Eurobonds that are de-
nominated in the cur-
rency of a country other
than the host country
where the deposit or
bond is placed.

Another source of concern in the 1990s is the Eurocurrency market. The **Eurocurrency market** includes Eurodollar deposits and Eurobonds. Eurodollars are deposits that are denominated in the currency of a country other than the host country where the deposit is placed. One example of a Eurodollar deposit is a short-term deposit denominated in dollars and placed in a bank in England.[19] Another example is a deposit originating in Japan and denominated in Japanese yen that is placed in a bank in Australia. Even though "dollars" or "Europe" are in no way involved in the latter example, the term *Eurodollar* has come to be a generic term to refer to any deposit in a foreign (host) country that is denominated in the currency of the country of the owner of the deposit.

The Eurodollar market began in the 1950s in London but has spread around the world with the Caribbean being a particularly large haven for deposits. The Eurodollar market blossomed primarily to escape domestic regulation. Domestic banks could "suggest" Eurodollar deposits in a foreign subsidiary to their customers and then borrow funds from the foreign subsidiary. The depositors earned a higher rate of return than what they could get on domestic deposits, and the banks had a source of funds that was not subject to domestic regulation (primarily Regulation Q and reserve requirements). Indeed, Eurodollar deposits have become an important source of funds for banks in the past 30 years.

The Eurobond market is the market for bonds denominated in one currency but sold in a different country. The Eurobond market also grew to escape regulation and taxation, and to tap into international sources of funds. New bond issues in the Eurobond market now exceed domestic bond issues.

Concern has been expressed about the possibility of a liquidity crisis in the Eurocurrency market. The ramifications of such a crisis are difficult to speculate about since the Fed is at most indirectly involved with Eurodollar deposits in subsidiaries of U.S. institutions only and Eurobonds.[20] This responsibility results only from the potentiality that a liquidity crisis in the Eurocurrency market could spread to domestic financial markets and that the Fed is responsible for maintaining the safety and soundness of the U.S. financial system.

Could a liquidity crisis or default in a foreign subsidiary of a U.S. institution threaten the domestic economy? How much do we really know about the size and activities of these markets? Presumably not as much as we or the Fed would like to know. These questions will probably be answered one way or another in the not too distant future.

 RECAP

Daylight overdrafts are Fedwire payments that are credited to the payee's account even if the payor does not have the funds. An interest-free loan from the Fed is given to be resolved by the end of the day. If the payor goes

---

[19] The term of the deposit is often overnight.
[20] In reality, foreign subsidiaries of U.S. intermediaries are fully responsible for their liabilities, whatever denominations are involved.

bankrupt in the middle of the day, the Fed may be left with a large debt. Program trading, which is the use of computers to issue buy and sell orders for stocks, may increase stock market volatility and financial instability. Derivatives are financial contracts whose values are derived from the values of underlying assets, such as foreign exchange, bonds, equities, or commodities. Large banks are heavily involved in derivatives and may not know enough about the risks. Concern is also expressed about the liquidity of Eurocurrency markets and the possibility of a crisis spilling over into the domestic economy.

In this chapter, we have come full circle from past stresses on the financial system and their resolution to potential strains of the future. In Chapter 15, we look at the specific areas of regulations and reforms as we move towards the year 2000.

Summary of Major Points

1. FIs have developed numerous ways to reduce and deal with risks. FIs use diversification and expert credit analysis to manage credit risk. They use adjustable rate loans, futures, options, swaps, and securitizations to manage interest rate risk. Liquidity risk is managed by the ability to borrow funds, and exchange rate risk is managed with futures and options. Despite this, because of the uncertainty of the future and the interdependence of financial claims, financial crises will periodically occur. A financial crisis is a severe upset in a financial market that is characterized by sharp declines in asset prices and the failure of many financial and nonfinancial firms.

2. During the 1980s, S&Ls experienced a severe financial crisis that resulted in the failure of 1,500 thrifts. The projected industry losses in 1981 were far greater than the assets of the FSLIC. Rather than closing the defunct thrifts down, the regulators extended their lending powers and reduced their capital requirements hoping that they could recover some of the funds that were lost. Instead the losses grew resulting in a much larger taxpayer bailout.

3. Moral hazard refers to the reduction in market discipline that deposit insurance encourages. Banks are given an incentive to invest in riskier loans, which they did gradually over time. This gradual increase in risks resulted in many bank failures in the 1980s. Losses resulted from loans to less-developed countries, energy loans, and commercial real estate loans. Regulators were slow to shut down insolvent banks and the doctrine of "too big to fail" was the official position of the FDIC from the failure of Continental Illinois in 1984 until the early 1990s.

4. Many actions have been taken to deal with the issues surrounding deposit insurance. Despite the fact that the banking industry is earning record profits in the early 1990s, many calls for deposit insurance reform still abound today.

5. Daylight overdrafts are a potential source of financial system stress. Fedwire payments are credited to the payee's account even if the payor does

not have the funds in its account. An interest-free overdraft loan is automatically given to be resolved by the close of business that day. If the payor goes bankrupt in the middle of the day, the Fed may be left with a large debt. Daylight overdrafts have fallen significantly since the Fed instituted fees for the use of overdrafts in April 1994.

6. Program trading is the use of computers to issue buy and sell orders for stocks. Program trading has the potential to increase stock market volatility and hence increase overall instability. Circuit breakers slow or halt program trading if prices fall by a certain amount. Derivatives are financial contracts whose values are derived from the values of other underlying assets, such as foreign exchange, bonds, equities, or commodities. Large banks are heavily involved in derivatives and concern has been expressed as to whether enough is known about the risks involved with this exposure. Concern is also expressed regarding the liquidity of Eurocurrency deposits in foreign subsidiaries of U.S. financial institutions.

Key Terms

Circuit Breakers	Moral Hazard
Daylight Overdraft	Off-Balance-Sheet Activities
Derivatives	Payoff Method
Eurocurrency Market	Program Trading
Fedwire	Purchase and Assumption Method
Financial Crisis	Standby Lines of Credit
Junk Bonds	"Too Big to Fail"
Margin Requirements	

Review Questions

1. Discuss ways in which each of the following risks can be reduced: default risk, interest rate risk, liquidity risk, and exchange rate risk.

2. Why does financial intermediation inherently involve risk? Are FIs better at evaluating risks than you are? Why or why not?

3. What is a financial crisis? Why would an economic downturn often lead to financial crisis? Explain why the reverse is also true.

4. Can sharp increases in interest rates increase the risk of a financial crisis? Explain.

5. Were interest rate ceilings for S&Ls higher or lower than for commercial banks? Why?

6. Is a financial crisis more likely to be triggered by inflation or deflation? Explain.

7. What does "too big to fail" mean? What are the costs of such a policy? Under what circumstances would your funds be safer in a small local bank that only loaned in the local area versus a large bank with a diverse portfolio of loans including foreign loans?

8. Discuss the factors that contributed to the S&L debacle during the 1980s.

9. What is moral hazard? Why does deposit insurance inherently involve moral hazard?

10. Define daylight overdrafts, program trading, and derivatives, and describe the risks that each entails. Who regulates Eurocurrency deposits?

11. What factors led to the collapse of Lincoln Savings? What factors led to the collapse of Continental Illinois?

12. S&Ls had limited experience making commercial loans, while commercial banks are extremely experienced; explain how this could exacerbate the adverse selection problem for the S&Ls.

13. Can derivatives cause massive losses if they are used only to hedge?

Analytical Questions

14. Margin requirements are 50 percent. How much do you have to put down to buy 100 shares of stock that sell for $50 a share?

15. If all prices and my income fall by 25 percent, by what percent does the real value of my debt increase?

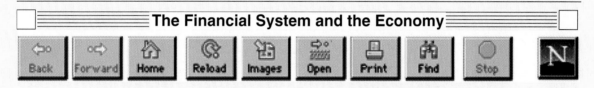

The Financial System and the Economy

1. An interesting chronology of the savings and loan debacle is obtainable from the internet site (http://www.fdic.gov/library/slchron.html). Access the site and answer the following:

   a. What was the Garn St. Germain Act? What was it designed to accomplish in the savings and loan industry? Did this act have its requisite effect on the savings and loan industry?

   b. What is the Financial Institutions Reform, Recovery, and Enforcement Act (FIRREA)? When was it enacted and what are its major provisions? (FIRREA will also be discussed in Chapter 15.)

Suggested Readings

Thomas Parzinger has authored two fairly comprehensive articles: "Key Proposals for Deposit Insurance Reform (Parts 1 and 2)," *The Bankers Magazine*, March/April 1993, and May/June 1993.

Two recent books on the S&L crisis are J.R. Barth, *The Great Savings and Loan Debacle*, Washington, D.C., American Enterprise Institute, 1990; and *The S&L Debate: Public Policy Lessons for Bank and Thrift Regulation*, New York: Oxford University Press, 1991.

For interesting reading on financial instability, try Hyman Minsky, *Stabilizing the Unstable Economy*, New Haven: Yale University Press, 1986.

Martin Wolfson, *Financial Crises: Understanding the Postwar U.S. Experience,* 2nd ed., Armonk, NY: M. E. Sharpe, 1994, gives a comprehensive history of financial crises up through the mid-1980s.

For a discussion of bank involvement in derivatives, see "Derivative Product Activity of Commercial Banks," a joint study conducted by the Board of Governors of the Federal Reserve System, the FDIC, and the Office of the Comptroller of the Currency, 1993.

Financial Conditions and Macroeconomic Performance, Essays in Honor of Hyman P. Minsky, Steven Fazzari and Dimitri B. Papadimitriou, eds., Armonk, NY: M. E. Sharpe, 1992, offers a unique view of financial instability.

E. P. Davis, *In Debt, Financial Fragility, and Systemic Risk,* looks at the increased vulnerability of the financial system since 1970. New York: Oxford University Press, 1993.

15

Regulations in the 1990s

> *The dogmas of the quiet past are inadequate to the stormy present. As our case is new, so we must think anew and act anew. We must disenthrall ourselves, and then we shall save our country.*
> —Abraham Lincoln—
>
> *The people's right to change what does not work is one of the greatest principles of our system of government.*
> —Richard Nixon—

Learning Objectives

After reading this chapter, you should know:

◆ Why regulation is needed in the financial services industry

◆ Who regulates whom in the major financial markets and institutions

◆ Some of the major pieces of legislation important to the financial services industry in the 1990s

◆ Regulatory challenges facing Congress and the regulators

The Role of Regulation

The ability of certain industries within a market economy to regulate themselves has been the subject of controversy for a long time. Some analysts believe that virtually no regulation is needed and that the market can handle practically every situation far better than a government regulatory agency. For example, they believe that airlines can regulate themselves better than a government regulatory agency can.[1] If an airline is unsafe, or so the argument goes, it would experience more accidents than other airlines. Consequently, passengers who became aware of this accident record would avoid flying on it. Thus, the unsafe airline would be driven out of business. Likewise, the market can better regulate the financial services industry than any regulatory agency such as the Fed or the Office of Thrift Supervision (OTS) can. For example, the bank that took too many risks would be driven out of business when cautious depositors became aware of the risks and withdrew their deposits or when the bank sustained losses and was unable to pay back depositors.

At the other extreme are those who believe that society needs a lot of regulation because the quest for profits is strong, and without regulation, consumer welfare will frequently be jeopardized. For example, an airline may skimp on costly maintenance and keep planes in the sky since the planes on the ground do not generate profit. Or, a financial intermediary (FI) might be tempted to take a large risk because the payoff may be big. After all, the bulk of the funds the intermediary is risking belongs to the depositors.[2] However, even if the unsafe airline is driven out of business in a market economy, it doesn't bring back the loved one who was killed in a plane crash because the airline was not taking reasonable safety precautions. Likewise, it is bittersweet if the depository that lost one's life savings is driven out of business. Although it may provide a certain degree of satisfaction, it would not reduce the pecuniary losses.

Despite these examples that suggest the need for some regulation, by the late 1970s, sentiment in the United States had shifted to the belief that the economy had become a victim of overregulation. This change led to a deregulation movement that continues in varying degrees today. Industries such as the airlines, trucking, and financial services have been deregulated.

Since deregulation, some industries have experienced severe stresses and bankruptcies. For example, the financial services sector experienced the collapse of the savings and loan (S&L) industry, the largest wave of bank failures, and the most serious strains since the Great Depression. Some have blamed deregulation at least to some extent for this situation. Still, others believe that the failures were the result of regulations that had protected inefficient operations.

In Chapters 13 and 14, we examined financial innovation, deregulation, and stresses on the financial system. In this chapter, we look at recent regulatory legislation and the regulatory structure of the financial services industry in the mid-1990s. Part of this regulatory structure was implemented in response to the financial crises of the 1980s and to new financial markets and

---

[1] For the airline industry, the regulatory agency is the Federal Aviation Administration (FAA).

[2] In a world with deposit insurance, the problem is even greater since the depositors will be paid off even if the venture fails.

products. A portion resulted from a hodgepodge of legislation inherited from the past. We also look at various regulatory reforms that have been suggested but as of yet, not implemented.

The How and Why of Financial Services Regulation

"Free to compete" means "free to fail." Once one recognizes that the failure of a significant number of banks undermines the public's confidence in the system, the potential conflict between the competition and efficiency objective and the safety and soundness objective emerges. The regulatory authorities attempt to balance these objectives, or at least so they tell us, by issuing regulations governing bank activities.

Most, if not all, bank activities were regulated by various government regulators from the Great Depression in the 1930s until the 1980s. During the 1980s, banks and most other intermediaries were substantially deregulated. A series of financial crises followed that culminated in widespread insolvencies within the savings and loan (S&L) industry and many bank failures.[3] The crises triggered attempts at re-regulation that are still going on to some extent.

Throughout this text, we have repeatedly emphasized the role of regulation in ensuring the safety and soundness of the financial system. Regulations were deemed necessary because of the nature of the financial system and the trade-off between high returns for surplus spending units versus safety and soundness. The FI could earn a higher return if it took more risks. Indeed, some intermediaries offer higher returns for the acceptance of more risks. Depository institutions, however, within limits, offer a guaranteed, albeit lower return.

When deciding how much risk to take on, the FI should evaluate the risks of the activity. Generally speaking, if the expected benefits outweigh the expected costs then it will, on average, be profitable to undertake. However, in the process of assessing the expected costs associated with various levels of risk, the intermediary considers only the costs to the stockholders, creditors, and depositors, which would result from an investment or portfolio of investments going sour.[4] Because they are so highly leveraged, some FIs may fail to adequately consider how much risk they should take. In general, the costs to the community at large that could result from the failure of the institution are ignored. As discussed in Chapters 12 and 14, the collapse of an FI would not only imperil those directly involved, but could also impede the smooth functioning of the entire economy. The failure could lead to a bank run and a simultaneous financial collapse. Here is where the crux of the problem lies: If left to decide the level of risk on their own, banks or other intermediaries would generally be willing to accept too much risk, since they fail to consider the additional costs of failure that the community at large would bear. If banks and other intermediaries were left unregulated, the drive or quest for profits might jeopardize the goals of safety and soundness for the system as a whole.

---

[3] Remember our early warning in Chapter 3 that correlation does not imply causality. Deregulation did not necessarily cause the subsequent insolvencies.

[4] Actually, as we have seen, in a world with deposit insurance, the intermediary may only consider the costs to the stockholders and creditors, since a large portion of the deposits are insured. In reality, bank managers may only consider the risk of losing their own jobs if investments go sour.

Prior to the 1980s, regulations encouraged specialization that resulted in the segmentation of the industry. For many decades, the financial services industry remained highly segmented. However, slowly over time, barriers between intermediaries began to break down as financial institutions found inroads into each others' areas of specialty. The segmentation of the financial services industry gave way as banks increasingly engaged in traditionally non-banking activities, and nonbanks increasingly engaged in traditionally banking activities.

Historically, the regulatory structure was segmented much as the financial services industry. As the industry segmentation broke down, however, the regulatory segmentation did not concurrently break down.[5] Who said government bureaucrats were flexible anyway? Though the historical segmentation of regulatory responsibilities persists into the mid-1990s, it is also in the gradual process of change. Today, we find ourselves in this place of ongoing change.

Regulation can be by either financial market (product) or by financial institutional group. For example, stocks, bonds, and futures are financial products that are regulated, while banks, S&Ls, and insurance companies are financial institutions that are regulated. In addition, sometimes more than one regulatory agency regulates a particular financial product or institution, while at the same time, one regulatory agency may regulate more than one financial product or institution. Given this background, now would be a good time to look at Exhibit 15-1, which surveys the many regulatory agencies in place in the various segments of the financial services industry in the mid-1990s.

We are now in a better position to pull together material from the last several chapters. To summarize, the regulatory structure of the financial services is in a process of ongoing change because of the potpourri of many regulations and regulators, the performance of the industry in recent decades, the ongoing evolution of the industry resulting in new products and markets, technological changes in the delivery of financial services, and the many concerns about the adequacy of regulation. We turn our attention to major pieces of legislation that reflect the most recent changes in regulation of the financial services industry of the 1990s.

 ## Recent Major Legislation

Even though this chapter deals with regulation in the 1990s, we begin our discussion with two acts that were signed into law in the late 1980s.

The Basel Accord

Until 1980, banks were pretty much free to establish their own capital requirements as the Fed and other regulators pursued different avenues of control such as reserve requirements, asset restrictions, chartering, and Regulation Q.

---

[5] Perhaps the only exception to this is the creation of SAIF under the auspices of the Federal Deposit Insurance Corporation (FDIC) in 1989.

Since the deregulation of these traditional avenues of regulation in the early 1980s, regulators have attempted to impose stricter capital guidelines and to use capital requirements as a primary vehicle of regulation. In November 1988, the United States entered into agreement with twelve other countries to set international uniform capital standards for banks. The agreement is known as the **Basel Accord.**

The Basel Accord specified the amount of bank capital that banks must hold relative to assets. Despite the increasing emphasis in this area, the new requirements were stricter than the requirements banks were adhering to at the time. In other words, banks were holding less capital relative to assets than what the new regulations required. This had the effect of causing many U.S. banks to alter their behavior—to somehow shore up bank capital relative to assets—in the early 1990s to meet the stricter standards. Exhibit 15-2 explains the new standards and gives an example of how they are implemented.

Financial Institutions Reform, Recovery, and Enforcement Act of 1989

The **Financial Institutions Reform, Recovery, and Enforcement Act (FIRREA)** was signed into law in August 1989. FIRREA was passed in response to the S&L crisis of the 1980s and was an attempt at re-regulation following the deregulation and subsequent crises of the 1980s (see Chapter 11). The provisions of FIRREA include the following:

1. An initial $50 billion was injected into the newly created Savings Association Insurance Fund (SAIF). SAIF was established to provide deposit insurance for the deposits of S&Ls; in this capacity, SAIF replaced the Federal Savings and Loan Insurance Corporation (FSLIC). Additionally, SAIF was created to provide funding for government takeover of failed S&Ls. The original $50 billion was raised by selling bonds known as *bailout bonds,* and the money was used to compensate institutions that took over a failed S&L by making up the difference between assets and liabilities. This procedure for taking over a failed institution is similar to the purchase and assumption method discussed in Chapter 14 to resolve a failed bank. Administration of SAIF was made the responsibility of the Federal Deposit Insurance Corporation (FDIC). Because of the crisis of the 1980s, the Federal Savings and Loan Insurance Corporation was dissolved. It had virtually gone bankrupt and was unable to cover the losses of insured deposits.

2. Two new government agencies were created. The **Office of Thrift Supervision (OTS)** was created to oversee the S&L industry replacing the **Federal Home Loan Bank Board.** The **Resolution Trust Corporation (RTC)** was created to dispose of the properties of the failed S&Ls. The FDIC was put in charge of the RTC, and the board of the FDIC was expanded from three to five members with the addition of the director of the OTS and an additional appointment by the president of the United States.

3. For the first time, deposit insurance was made a full faith and credit obligation of the federal government, rather than the FDIC. Up until 1989, neither Congress nor the taxpayers were legally required to bailout an insolvent deposit insurance company, whether it be the FDIC or the FSLIC. In reality, the government was de facto required to bail out a failed

Basel Accord An agreement in 1988 between 12 countries, which set international capital standard for banks.

Financial Institutions Reform, Recovery, and Enforcement Act (FIRREA) Legislation passed in 1989 in response to the S&L crisis; injected $50 billion into the newly created SAIF, set up the OTS and the RTC, made deposit insurance a full faith and credit obligation of the federal government, and imposed new regulations on assets and new capital requirements.

Office of Thrift Supervision (OTS) Created by FIRREA to oversee the S&L industry replacing the Federal Home Loan Bank Board.

Federal Loan Home Bank Board The regulatory body of the S&L industry up until 1989.

Resolution Trust Corporation (RTC) Created by FIRREA to dispose of the properties of the failed S&Ls.

Exhibit 15-1 ◆
Regulators in the
Financial Services
Industry

Banks: We have already discussed the dual banking system in which federal and state-chartered banks exist side by side. Federal banks are regulated by the Office of the Comptroller of the Currency, the FDIC, and the Fed. State banks are regulated by the state banking commissioner and possibly the Fed and/or FDIC depending on whether they choose to be members of the Fed and/or subscribe to deposit insurance. With regard to reserve requirements, all banks are regulated by the Fed.

Savings and Loan Associations: S&Ls are regulated by the Office of Thrift Supervision (OTS) of the Treasury and, with regard to reserve requirements, the Fed. Those that subscribe to deposit insurance are also regulated by the FDIC.

Credit Unions: Federally chartered credit unions are regulated by the **National Credit Union Administration** while those with state charters are regulated by state banking commissioners. The **National Credit Union Share Insurance Fund** insures deposits in credit unions up to $100,000. Because they are nonprofit, tax-exempt institutions, credit unions have generally engaged in less risk taking than their for-profit competitors, and consequently they have experienced much milder strains. They have larger reserves and fewer losses. Unlike other depository institutions, credit unions do not pay an insurance premium, but rather put up capital equal to 1 percent of their insured deposits with the insurance fund. If this reserve is ever depleted because of losses, credit unions are required to replenish it out of capital.

National Credit Union Administration The regulating agency of federally chartered credit unions.
National Credit Union Share Insurance Fund The insurance company that insures deposits in credit unions up to $100,000.

Finance Companies: Finance companies must obtain permission to open an office for business from the state in which they want to operate. Once that permission is obtained, there are virtually no restrictions on branching. The **Federal Trade Commission (FTC)** regulates finance companies with regard to consumer protection. However, there are no restrictions on the assets they hold or how they raise their funds, other than those generally applying to the issuance of securities.

Federal Trade Commission (FTC) The commission that regulates finance companies with regard to consumer protection.
Commodity Futures Trading Commission The commission that regulates financial futures.
National Futures Association An association set up by the financial futures industry for self-regulation.

Financial Futures: Financial futures are regulated by the **Commodity Futures Trading Commission** and the **National Futures Association.** The latter is set up by the industry for self-regulation.

Financial Options: Financial options are regulated by the **Securities and Exchange Commission (SEC).** Options on futures are regulated by the Commodity Futures Trading Commission. The **Options Clearing Corporation** is set up by the industry for self-regulation.

Securities and Exchange Commission (SEC) Established in 1933; regulates stocks and bonds, financial options, and security firms.
Options Clearing Corporation An association set up by the financial options industry for self-regulation.
Investment Company Act of 1940 Extended the regulatory responsibilities of the SEC to mutual funds.

Mutual Funds: The SEC was given regulatory control over mutual funds by the **Investment Company Act of 1940.** Regulations include requirements to publicly disclose financial information and restrictions on how business can be solicited. Mutual funds have experienced tremendous growth in the 1980s and early 1990s. Partially as a result of this growth, concerns have been raised that additional regulation may be needed. This seems to be the result of two facts: (1) Sales offices for mutual funds are now allowed to be located

deposit insurer, as it did with the FSLIC, but only because such a failure could cause a systemwide collapse. Despite what most Americans thought, there was no legal responsibility for the bailout. The new deposit insurance funds, SAIF and the Bank Insurance Fund (BIF), both under the FDIC, were required to maintain reserves of at least 1.25 percent of in-

inside commercial banks, even though the funds are not sold directly by the bank. Apparently, a significant portion of customers erroneously believe that mutual funds purchased within a bank are insured by the bank. (2) Mutual funds have grown to be a significant portion of total intermediation while the regulatory structure has not grown at the same pace.

Insurance Companies: Insurance companies are regulated by the insurance commissioner of the state in which they do business.

Pension Funds: Pension funds are regulated by the Department of Labor. The **Pension Benefit Guaranty Corporation** provides insurance if the pension plan will not be able to pay the benefits defined in the pension agreement. The pension rights of more than 40 million Americans are protected by it. In other words, if pension benefits cannot be paid because the pension plan has made with what turned out to be bad investments with the premiums or because the pension plan was not funded properly to begin with, then the Pension Benefit Guaranty Corporation insures that the benefits will be paid according to the contract and makes up any payment deficiencies up to a limit. Like other insurance companies, this responsibility to pay benefits if the plan comes up short also gives them regulatory responsibilities.

Pension Benefit Guaranty Corporation Provides insurance if the pension plan will not be able to pay the benefits defined in the pension agreement.

Stocks and Bonds: The SEC, established in 1933, is a government regulatory agency that oversees securities markets including brokers and dealers. The SEC requires extensive reporting by companies of their financial condition prior to the company's issuance of bonds and while the bonds are outstanding. Likewise, issuers of new securities must register with the SEC and disclose all important financial information. If the equities are to be publicly traded, ongoing disclosure is required, and **insider trading,** which is trading by those who have access to information before it is made public, is forbidden. The Fed sets margin requirements for the purchase of stocks and bonds.

Insider Trading Trading by those who have access to information before it is made public.

Securities Firms: Security firms are regulated by the SEC, the New York Stock Exchange (NYSE), and other exchanges. In addition, security firms are self-regulated by the **National Association of Securities Dealers.** The **Securities Investor Protection Corporation** insures retail customers of securities brokerage firms for up to $500,000 of their portfolios in the event the brokerage firm becomes insolvent.

National Association of Securities Dealers The self-regulating agency of security firms.
Securities Investor Protection Corporation Insures retail customers of securities brokerage firms for up to $500,000 in the event the brokerage firm becomes insolvent.

U.S. Government Securities: U.S. government securities and securities of agencies of the U.S. government are regulated by the Fed and the SEC.

Noticeably absent from this list is a regulator of the money markets including the market for commercial paper, bankers acceptances, negotiable CDs, the mortgage-backed securities market, and the Eurocurrency markets. Since the regulatory structure will continue to change as the financial services industry evolves, innovative regulation for new and existing markets and products may be just around the corner.

sured deposits. Premiums paid are a percent of total domestic deposits including deposits over $100,000. Effective January 1, 1993, premiums ranged from $.23 to $.31 for each $100 of domestic deposits, depending on the risk profile of the insured institution. Higher-risk institutions are charged rates on the higher end of the range.

Exhibit 15-2 ◆
Bank Capital
Standards Under
the Basel Accord

Subordinated Debt
Long-term debt of banks
that is paid off after depositors and other credi-
tors if the institution goes
under.

Under the new standards mandated in the Basel Accord, requirements exist for core capital and for total capital. Core capital is by definition the historical value of outstanding stock plus retained earnings. Total capital is core capital plus supplemental capital (loan-loss reserves plus subordinated debt). **Subordinated debt** is long-term debt that is paid off after depositors and other creditors if the institution goes under. The amount of capital that must be held is based on the larger of two measures: one measure is based on risk-adjusted assets and one on total assets.

The risk-adjusted-assets method assigns different weights to different types of assets according to their risks. For instance, ordinary loans are counted at 100 percent of their value, while mortgages are counted at 50 percent. Mortgages count for less than their full value since the property is held as collateral and repossessed in the event of default. Deposits between banks (interbank deposits) count at 20 percent while T-bills and cash count at 0 percent. In addition to assigning different weights to various assets, off-balance-sheet activities that result in an obligation or potential obligation for the bank are also counted in risk-adjusted capital and at their full value. An example would be a standby letter of credit. If a bank gives a standby letter of credit for $1,000, that letter of credit is counted at its full value ($1,000) in calculating risk-adjusted assets, even though it is not an asset. The reason for this is obvious. If the standby letter of credit is exercised, the bank stands to lose $1,000 just as if it had made a bad loan. For safety purposes, banks must maintain greater capital if they have off-balance-sheet activities that expose the bank to greater risk. The risks of some activities such as futures, options, and swaps may be difficult to evaluate.

Once risk-adjusted assets have been determined, they are subject to two capital constraints: (1) a bank must have core capital equal to at least 4 percent of risk-adjusted assets; and (2) a bank must have total capital equal to at least 8 percent of risk-adjusted assets. At the present time, risk-adjusted assets take into account only credit risk. They do not consider interest rate, liquidity, or exchange rate risks. Additional requirements to consider these risks may be implemented in the future.

In addition to the constraints based on risk-adjusted assets, a leverage requirement is also stated in terms of total assets. In this case, all assets are weighted at 100 percent and there is no accounting for off-balance-sheet activities. (The weight assigned to off-balance-sheet activities is 0.) According to the Basel Accord requirements, a bank must have core capital equal to at least 3 percent of total assets. The use of international capital require-

As of mid-1995, BIF had reserves equal to 1.25 percent of insured deposits, but SAIF was seriously underfunded with reserves of only .38 percent of insured deposits. There is concern that additional taxpayer funds may have to be diverted to the industry. Because BIF has adequate reserves, it is expected that premiums for BIF insured institutions will fall to $.04 per $100 of domestic deposits by the close of 1995. As of late 1995, there are proposals to allow S&Ls to merge with banks. Some S&Ls are expected to request to obtain bank charters. Part of the reason is that the

ments has many desirable effects. All banks from the various countries that abide by them are put, more or less, on an equal footing. The following table provides an example of how such standards are implemented.

CORE CAPITAL	$775,000	
Stock Issued	$500,000	
Retained Earnings	$275,000	
TOTAL CAPITAL	$1,535,000	
Core Capital plus	$775,000	
Loan-Loss Reserves	$260,000	
Subordinated Debt	$500,000	
RISK-ADJUSTED ASSETS		
Loans	$14,000,000 @ 100 percent	$14,000,000
Mortgages	$3,500,000 @ 50 percent	1,750,000
Interbank Deposits	$2,000,000 @ 20 percent	400,000
Government Securities	$3,000,000 @ 0 percent	0
Reserves	$1,800,000 @ 0 percent	0
Standby Letters and		$3,000,000
Other Lines of Credit	$3,000,000 @ 100 percent	
TOTAL RISK-ADJUSTED ASSETS		$19,150,000
TOTAL ASSETS		
Loans	$14,000,000 @ 100 percent	$14,000,000
Mortgages	$3,500,000 @ 100 percent	$3,500,000
Interbank Deposits	$2,000,000 @ 100 percent	$2,000,000
Government Securities	$3,000,000 @ 100 percent	$3,000,000
Reserves	$1,800,000 @ 100 percent	$1,800,000
Standby Letters and	$3,000,000 @ 0 percent	0
Other Lines of Credit		
TOTAL ASSETS		$24,300,000

Core capital must equal at least 4 percent of risk-adjusted assets:
4 percent of $19,150,000 equals $766,000
Total capital must equal at least 8 percent of risk-adjusted assets:
8 percent of $19,150,000 equals $1,532,000
Core capital must equal at least 3 percent of total assets:
3 percent of $24,300,000 equals $729,000

higher proposed premiums for S&Ls are expected to cause a severe disadvantage for these institutions.

4. New regulations restricted the investments of S&Ls by limiting commercial mortgage lending and by phasing out junk bond investments by 1994. Investments in junk bonds had been first authorized in 1982 by the Garn–St. Germain Act. In addition, S&Ls were required to hold at least 70 percent of their assets as mortgages or mortgage-backed securities. Commercial real estate loans were restricted to 400 percent of total capital.

"The big one's the federal government which bailed us out."

© 1996 Harley Schwadron from The Cartoon Bank,™ Inc.

5. Capital requirements were imposed on the S&Ls. The requirements were similar to those placed on banks in accordance with the international regulations of the Basel Accord. Risk-based capital standards were phased in, just as they had been for banks in participating countries. (See the previous section on The Basel Accord.) Core capital for S&Ls was to be 3 percent by 1995, and total capital was to be at least 8 percent of risk-adjusted assets by 1992. These new capital requirements more than doubled the amount of capital that had to be held under the previous standards.

Federal Deposit Insurance Corporation Improvement Act of 1991

Although it may seem that deposit insurance should solve the problem of excessive risk taking by protecting the small depositor in the event of insolvency, deposit insurance increases the problem of excessive risk taking. The fact that depositors are insured reduces market discipline in that depositors do not have to be concerned about the level of risk their bank engages in because if it fails, the insurance company will pay off. This risk, known as the moral hazard problem, was discussed in Chapter 14. A financial institution is encouraged to take on more risks because the greater the risk, the greater the possibility of higher returns, and the depositors are protected in the event of a default. It's like going to Las Vegas to gamble with your neighbor's funds with the caveat that if you win you get to keep the winnings and if you lose, your neighbor still gets paid back, but not by you.

In response to a growing concern about this problem, Congress passed the **Federal Deposit Insurance Corporation Improvement Act (FDICIA)** in 1991. FDICIA attempted to secure the safety and soundness of the banking and thrift industries (S&Ls, savings banks, and credit unions) through regulatory changes and enacted several reforms. These reforms include:

1. Insurance premiums were scaled to the risk exposure of the banks or thrifts. Banks or thrifts that engaged in high levels of risk or had low capital ratios would be charged higher deposit insurance premiums. The result is that higher-risk institutions contribute more to deposit insurance funds than do lower-risk institutions.
2. As of December 31, 1994, FDICIA limited insurance coverage in regular accounts to a maximum of $100,000. On retirement accounts, the limit was $100,000 per depository institution.
3. The FDIC was also required to use the least costly method to resolve any insolvency. This could prevent the FDIC from de facto insuring deposits over $100,000 by using the purchase and assumption method to dispose of insolvent banks that are "too big to fail." The practice, begun in 1984 with the failure of Continental Illinois, was formally ended.
4. Under FDICIA, the FDIC established a system that divided weak banks into different categories such as "undercapitalized," "significantly undercapitalized," and "critically undercapitalized." Banks in each category would be subject to appropriate treatment. The greater the degree of undercapitalization, the more severe would be the restrictions on a bank's operations.
5. FDICIA also set limits on the capability of foreign banks in the United States to use certain categories of deposits. Foreign banks desiring to keep insured deposit accounts could do so only through insured U.S. subsidiary banks.

Thus, as a result of the Basel Accord, FIRREA, and FDICIA, banks and other depository institutions are now subject to both risk-based capital standards and risk-based insurance premiums. We turn now to the Community Reinvestment Act, which was actually passed in 1977 and was not really well known outside the banking industry until recent years.

Community Reinvestment Act

The original purpose of the **Community Reinvestment Act** was to increase the availability of credit to economically disadvantaged areas and to correct alleged discriminatory lending practices. Minority borrowers and neighborhoods had long been the victim of **redlining.** Redlining refers to the practice of drawing a redline (or any colored line) around a certain area on a map and restricting the number or dollar amount of loans made in that area regardless of the creditworthiness of the borrower with respect to income or collateral.

The Community Reinvestment Act did not get much attention because no avenue of enforcement was implemented by the regulators. However, activist groups believed that many banks were not making significant efforts to comply

Federal Deposit Insurance Corporation Improvement Act (FDICIA) Legislation passed by Congress in 1991 to enact regulatory changes to insure the safety and soundness of the banking and thrift industries.

Community Reinvestment Act Legislation passed by Congress in 1977 to increase the availability of credit to economically disadvantaged areas and to correct alleged discriminatory lending practices.
Redlining The practice of restricting the number of or dollar amounts of loans in an area regardless of the creditworthiness of the borrower.

with the law, and in recent years, many mainstream community groups have joined their calls for more stringent enforcement.

At the same time, during the late 1980s, an avenue became available through which the Community Reinvestment Act could be implemented. The wave of bank mergers and acquisitions, that began in the late 1980s, provided this route. In judging whether a bank merger or acquisition should be approved, the Fed presently assesses how well the bank is meeting the lending criteria of the act, and compliance statements are judged critically.[6] Because of this, the law is getting more "teeth" as regulators enforce it more stringently. Banks are finding it in their best interest to take notice. Bank performance in this area often is difficult to judge, since banks are required to practice nondiscriminatory lending while at the same time focusing on safety and soundness.

To clarify some of the confusion of what compliance would entail, a policy statement was issued on March 21, 1989, by the four regulatory agencies—the Fed, the Comptroller of the Currency, the FDIC, and the now defunct Federal Home Loan Bank Board. Some of the guidelines call for

1. Continuing efforts by banks to discover community needs through outreach to local government, business, and community organizations
2. Ongoing efforts to develop, market, and advertise products and services that the community needs, such as low-cost checking accounts
3. Participation in government-insured lending programs
4. Training employees to be responsive to guidelines of the Community Reinvestment Act
5. Directly marketing credit services to target groups such as small business owners and real estate agents in low and moderate income neighborhoods.

The policy statement lists specific activities the bank should engage in to insure compliance. Although banks often thought of the law as a burden, a couple of facts have caused them to reassess this opinion. The nation is experiencing a growing diversity and will continue to do so. To the extent that the Community Reinvestment Act forces financial institutions to recognize and respond to the changing demographics before they would have otherwise done so, the law will be providing an important service to the industry and community. Many bankers are now of the opinion that new markets, products, and services will be developed and that these new activities will turn out to be quite profitable.

We turn now to recent landmark legislation on interstate banking.

Interstate Banking and Branching Efficiency Act of 1994

Interstate Banking and Branching Efficiency Act (IBBEA) A 1994 act which will eliminate most restrictions on interstate bank mergers by June 1, 1997.

The **Interstate Banking and Branching Efficiency Act (IBBEA)** of 1994, described in Chapter 12, eliminates most restrictions on interstate bank mergers and makes interstate branching possible for the first time since the passage of the McFadden Act in 1927. The law permits all bank holding companies to acquire banks anywhere in the nation as long as certain conditions are met.

---

[6]In the next section, we shall see that the Interstate Branching and Banking Efficiency Act of 1994 also emphasized compliance with the Community Reinvestment Act.

In addition, given the same conditions, banks in one state may merge with banks in another state, thus effectively branching. The conditions under which these activities may occur include requirements for the safety and soundness of the institutions involved, and commitments to community reinvestment under the Community Reinvestment Act. Under no circumstances will banks be permitted to use a branch to generate deposits without considering community reinvestment needs. Prior to the law, some states had limited or put additional conditions on the acquisition of banks by out-of-state bank holding companies.

In addition, effective June 1, 1997, bank holding companies will be permitted to convert their multiple banks in various states into branches of a single interstate bank. This is expected to reduce the costs of maintaining a separate board of directors for each bank and of other duplicative overhead costs. Whether significant savings will be realized remains to be seen. States have an opportunity to opt out of the branching-by-merging part of the law if they do so before it takes effect on June 1, 1997. It is expected that most or all will not.

To summarize, many regulatory changes had already occurred by the mid-1990s. Among others, these changes include (1) scaling insurance premiums to the risk exposure of banks, (2) limiting foreign deposit coverage, (3) intervening early when a bank begins experiencing problems so that intervention would usually occur before bank capital is fully depleted, (4) ending the practice of "too big to fail," (5) increasing capital requirements, and (6) expanding interstate banking. We now focus on other concerns that still exist and possible areas of future reform that could alleviate these concerns.

RECAP

The Basel Accord of 1988 established international capital standards for financial institutions. FIRREA of 1989 bailed out the S&L industry and imposed new capital standards and restrictions on assets. FDICIA of 1991 imposed risk-based insurance premiums and eliminated the "too big to fail" practice. The Community Reinvestment Act of 1977 was designed to eliminate discriminatory lending practices. IBBEA of 1994 would allow unimpeded nationwide branching as of June 1, 1997.

Other Concerns and Possible Reforms

Regulation within the financial services industry is a somewhat unsettled issue at this time. The 1990s will bring additional legislation that will result in new regulations and a new regulatory framework. Even though some regulations have been tightened up, regulators and Congress are still attempting to deal with the regulatory lapses of the 1980s and the perceived need to consolidate regulation. Regulations have been tightened up through both FIRREA and FDICIA.

From a conceptual microeconomic point of view, the movement toward higher capital standards and rigorous enforcement has been generally praised as a much needed remedy to the moral hazard dangers of deposit insurance. At the same time, the microeconomic aspects of the tighter regulations can

Exhibit 15-3 ◆

Remedies for a
Credit Crunch

In Chapters 2 and 3 we saw that credit extension (lending) is important in determining the overall level of spending, output, and jobs. During the early 1990s, much media attention was given to an alleged credit crunch in which the quantity demanded of credit for small business loans was greater than the quantity supplied at the prevailing interest rate. This crunch is often blamed for the recession during the second half of 1990 and the unspectacular recovery that persisted until the mid-1990s. Controversy continues over the extent of the credit crunch. Some analysts contend that a credit crunch did not exist and that banks and thrifts were hesitant to lend to small businesses because of dimmed prospects and/or to make real estate loans in the face of falling property values. Others contend that a credit crunch did exist but that it can be attributed to many factors. The factors include cautious lenders and tightened lending practices, increased government regulation, the fallout of the commercial real estate market, and the anemic economic performance of the economy in the early 1990s. Regardless of the causes or cures, the credit crunch seemed to have eased considerably by the mid-1990s as the recovery picked up steam. In 1994, the Fed orchestrated a series of interest rate increases in an attempt to maintain the growth rate of the economy at a level that would not result in upsurges in inflation.[a]

Shortly after taking office, President Clinton and his administration announced a series of bank regulatory initiatives to ease the credit crunch of the early 1990s. The thought was that there was overregulation at the federal level in response to the various financial crises during the 1980s in-

[a]In the period of the crunch, interest rates were falling. Under normal circumstances, during a credit crunch, one would expect interest rates to be rising. The shortage of credit would be attributed to an interest rate that was below the market equilibrium rate. In the early 1990s, market segmentation, combined with nonprice rationing, caused the shortage in the market for small business loans, despite surpluses in other financial markets that led to falling rates.

have undesirable effects of their own. Lenders have been accused of becoming exceedingly nervous and cautious about making loans. Lenders contend that Congress and the regulators have gone overboard in their efforts to improve bank safety and that the FDICIA, combined with rigorous bank examiners, have stifled lending.[7] Now would be a good time to look at Exhibit 15-3, which details an example of how tighter regulations may impinge on credit availability.

The point is that the microeconomic aspects of lenders restricting lending and overall improving their balance sheets, coupled with increasing capital standards, although good for the individual institutions, may for a time have depressing effects on the macroeconomy as a whole. We have come full circle. Lack of effective regulation can jeopardize the entire economy while at the same time too much regulation can depress the macroeconomy.

---

[7]Some analysts even go so far as to suggest some of the tighter regulations are punitive in nature with the goal of "punishing" the financial services industry for excesses in the 1980s.

cluding the S&L debacle and deposit insurance crisis. This overregulation caused the credit crunch.

The Clinton plan was directed initially at lending to small businesses but eventually extended beyond. The goal was to increase lending without weakening regulation aimed at ensuring safety and soundness in banking. A study by the Fed had shown that paperwork for small business loans doubled over the previous decade as examiners required banks to document every aspect of their lending. The Fed and the administration believed that a way had to be found to restore lending to small businesses and, hence, to increase their financial vitality. The administration sought regulatory relief and additional credit extension to achieve increased output and employment. Congress was probably more committed to preventing bank failures. Hence, the administration was concerned about macroeconomic goals while the S&L crisis of the 1980s left Congress more concerned about microeconomic goals.

The Clinton plan required no new legislation, thus bypassing Congressional approval. The primary changes initiated by the plan were reductions in "administrative red tape." Well-capitalized banks would be exempt from current rules requiring extensive documentation for every small business loan. Instead of reviewing every loan, bank examiners would judge performance of the overall portfolio. This approach to regulation allowed strong banks to make "baskets" of loans that were exempt from full documentation requirements. Loans included in the basket could be made solely on the character of the borrower. This led one large bank senior executive to quip, "Unfortunately, when we've loaned on character, we've wound up lending to characters."[b] Another provision eased the requirement to obtain appraisals of real estate as collateral for small business loans. All in all, the plan sought kinder and gentler regulation.

[b]"Crunch Plan Earns Points—So Far, Mostly For Symbolism," *The ABA Banking Journal,* June 1993.

In response to the existing regulatory potpourri and confusion, as well as the new risks and challenges that face the financial services industry in the future, there have been suggestions to consolidate and streamline regulatory agencies. Most analysts believe that a complete regulatory overhaul is inevitable. Look again at Exhibit 15-1. Current regulatory responsibility over the banking system (including banks and S&Ls) is distributed among four supervisory agencies: the FDIC, the Office of the Comptroller of the Currency, the OTS, and the Fed. Many analysts believe that the present system causes duplication of regulatory functions and bureaucratic delays. They believe that multiple decentralized supervisory agencies result in costly systems that potentially decrease the effectiveness and efficiency of bank supervision.

To resolve this situation, the Clinton administration has proposed the consolidation of the four regulatory units into a single independent federal agency, the **Federal Banking Commission.** At the present time, the vast majority of banking organizations are examined by at least two regulators. Under

Federal Banking Commission A proposed agency that would consolidate the regulatory responsibilities of the Fed, the FDIC, the OTS, and the Office of the Comptroller of the Currency into one agency.

Exhibit 15-4 ◆
Other Areas of
Possible Reform

Capping or Limiting Deposit Insurance

A major area for reform includes capping or limiting deposit insurance. Deposit insurance up to $100,000 per account is available for virtually all depository institutions. In reality, deposit insurance is available for larger amounts through the use of brokered accounts. A brokered account involves the use of a broker to break up large sums of money into small amounts not over $100,000 for deposit in a number of banks. A depositor with $1,000,000 could insure the entire amount by opening an account with a broker who would then make deposits in ten different banks each with $100,000 in coverage. Corporations and individuals could obtain coverage for even much larger amounts. Many experts believe that the $100,000 limit per account is too high—particularly for brokered accounts, which in reality result in giving much more than $100,000 coverage to individuals and institutions. Moreover, distressed banks can attract large deposits of brokered funds by advertising high rates. After all, if the deposits are insured, why worry about the health of the institution in which they are placed?

Various solutions have been put forth to deal with this situation. They include:

1. Reducing the insurance limit (it was increased from $40,000 to $100,000 in 1980)
2. Limiting systemwide coverage of deposits by an individual to $100,000, regardless of how many accounts the individual has
3. Scaling deposit insurance; for example, 100 percent coverage for the first $10,000 of deposits, 75 percent coverage for the next $20,000, and 50 percent coverage for all deposits exceeding $30,000
4. Covering only a uniform percentage of all accounts regardless of amount; for example, 75 percent of all accounts would be covered.

Mark-to-Market Accounting

A second area of reform deals with accounting methods for valuing assets. Present accounting methods use historical costs and book value in-

the original Clinton proposal, every bank organization would be supervised and examined by the Federal Banking Commission, which would also issue all regulations.

The new agency would be governed by a five-member board composed of one member from the Treasury Department, one from the Federal Reserve, and three independent members appointed by the president with Senate confirmation. The OTS and the Office of the Comptroller of the Currency would be eliminated. The FDIC would remain as an independent insurer and the Fed would independently determine monetary policy. Neither the FDIC nor the Fed would have any regulatory functions.

Proponents of the proposal emphasize the need for uniform, rapid, and final decisions on important regulatory issues within the banking system. They believe these qualities are now lacking and unlikely to occur without regulatory consolidation. The proposed organization with only one regulator would

stead of current economic values to appraise assets. This method does not necessarily deal with writing down bad loans (which currently is done), but rather valuing assets at their present market value rather than their historical costs. Repeatedly throughout this text, we have emphasized that when interest rates increase, the value of long-term bonds and other long-term fixed rate assets (such as mortgages) decreases. **Mark-to-market accounting** would require that these assets and other hard-to-value assets be properly accounted for.

Mark-to-Market Accounting A procedure that requires long-term assets and other hard-to-value assets to be properly accounted for on balance sheets.

Tiered Deposit Insurance

Another suggestion for reform is the use of **tiered deposit insurance.** Under a tiered deposit scheme, institutions and depositors would get to choose the amount of insurance that they want. By accepting less insurance, a bank would be subject to less regulation and perhaps greater returns as the "tax" of regulation would be reduced. A bank foregoing all insurance would not be subject to any regulation with the exception of consumer disclosure. The benefit is that depositors and banks would get to choose their level of regulation or lack thereof.

Tiered Deposit Insurance Insurance in which depositors and institutions get to choose the amount of insurance that they want.

Narrow Banking

Still another suggestion is an ancient one: it is to institute **narrow banking,** which would eliminate fractional reserve banking for transaction deposits by requiring 100 percent reserve backing for transaction deposits. Advocates believe this would provide a much safer payment system than the present one. Fees would be charged to administer such a payments system.* Fractional reserve banking and thus money creation would still be allowed for savings balances.

Which of these reforms, if any, will be adopted remains to be seen.

Narrow Banking A system that would eliminate fractional reserve banking by requiring 100 percent reserve backing for transactions deposits.

*At the present time, a large portion of the costs of the payments system are passed on to bank customers either in lower rates to depositors or higher rates to borrowers.

also allow banking regulation to be used to achieve social goals such as fair lending to minorities.

Needless to say, the primary opposition to this consolidation comes from the Fed, which stands to lose the most power from the proposal. The Fed argues that the plan would complicate the execution of monetary policy, weaken the ability of the central bank to respond to financial crises, and increase the chances of unnecessarily rigid regulation. State bank regulators contend that the dual banking system would be compromised and perhaps even eliminated.

To counteract the proposal, the Fed offered its own plan calling for far less sweeping reforms of banking regulation. At this time, the Treasury Department (the administration) and the Fed have come to a tentative compromise. Under this compromise, the Fed would continue to oversee bank holding companies and the state-chartered banks that are members of the

LOOKING BACK

A Time Line of Banking Legislation

The twentieth century has seen major banking legislation that has shaped the industry and its evolution.

◆ *The Federal Reserve Act of 1913* created the Federal Reserve System.
◆ *The McFadden Act of 1927* outlawed interstate banking.
◆ *Glass–Steagall Act of 1933* created the FDIC, separated commercial and investment banking, established Regulation Q interest rate ceilings, and set the interest rate ceiling on demand deposits at 0 percent.
◆ *Depository Institutions Deregulation and Monetary Control Act (DIDMCA) of 1980* authorized NOW accounts nationwide, which ended the monopoly of commercial banks on checkable deposits; phased out Regulation Q; established uniform and universal reserve requirements; eliminated usury laws; and increased deposit insurance from $40,000 to $100,000 per account.
◆ *Garn–St. Germain Act of 1982* expanded the asset and liability powers of banks and thrifts, and created money market deposit accounts and Super NOW Accounts.
◆ *Financial Institutions Recovery, Reform, and Enforcement Act (FIRREA) of 1989* authorized a taxpayer bailout of the S&L industry, created the OTS and the RTC, and imposed new restrictions on S&Ls.
◆ *Federal Deposit Insurance Corporation Improvement Act (FDICIA) of 1991.* Abolished the "too big to fail" policy, limited brokered deposits, established capital requirements and risk-based insurance premiums; and restricted activities of foreign banks.
◆ *Interstate Banking and Branching Efficiency Act (IBBEA) of 1994* allowed virtually unimpeded interstate branching by June 1, 1997.

Fed. The supervision of the S&Ls and the remaining banks would be combined under the newly created banking commission. State-chartered banks would be able to choose either the Fed or the banking commission as their regulator. Within the next year or so, the compromise plan, or some version of it, will probably be passed by Congress.

In addition to streamlining and consolidating the regulatory structure, other suggestions have been offered for regulatory and deposit insurance reform. Now would be a good time to look at Exhibit 15-4, which contains some of these specific suggestions.

At the present time, the impetus for major reform is reduced due to the record profits that the banking system earned in the early and mid-1990s. Congress rarely imposes substantial changes without a crisis occurring first. However, there is still the impetus to consolidate and streamline the regulatory structure. Such consolidation is perceived by many to be long overdue. One thing we can be sure of is that the financial services industry, and the regulation thereof, will be different in the 21st century from what it is today.

Summary of Major Points

1. Because the failure of a depository institution has systemwide repercussions, legislation has been passed that resulted in regulation with the goal of averting such a failure. A segmented financial services industry resulted in a segmented regulatory structure.

2. Regulation is by institution group or financial market (product). All depository institutions are regulated by the Fed with regard to reserve requirements. Banks and thrifts that opt for federal deposit insurance also are regulated by the FDIC. Many other regulatory agencies regulate specific institutions. In addition, agencies such as the SEC regulate stocks and bonds. Other agencies regulate other financial products such as futures and options. Some product groups establish self-regulatory bodies. At the present time, there is no regulatory agency in charge of regulating the money market. The regulatory structure is in an ongoing evolutionary process.

3. The Basel Accord, an agreement among 12 countries, sets international uniform capital requirements for financial institutions as a primary vehicle of regulation. Requirements set for core capital and total capital are based upon risk-adjusted assets and total assets. Core capital is the historical value of outstanding stock plus retained earnings. Risk-adjusted assets are calculated by assigning different weights to different types of assets depending upon risk.

4. The Financial Institutions Reform, Recovery, and Enforcement Act (FIRREA) of 1989 attempted to resolve the S&L deposit insurance crisis. It created the OTS and assimilated the defunct FSLIC into the FDIC. New regulations restricted the investments that S&Ls could make, and capital standards similar to those imposed on banks by the Basel Accord were adopted. Deposit insurance was made a full faith and credit obligation of the U.S. government, and bonds, which would eventually be paid off by taxpayers, were sold to obtain the funds necessary to bail out the defunct S&Ls.

5. The Federal Deposit Insurance Corporation Insurance Act (FDICIA) of 1991 required higher deposit insurance premiums for banks or thrifts that undertook high levels of risk. The "too big to fail" doctrine that had been in effect since the failure of Continental Illinois was ended. Weak banks were categorized as either "undercapitalized," "significantly undercapitalized," or "critically undercapitalized" and subject to appropriate treatment.

6. The Community Reinvestment Act of 1977 gained prominence in the late 1980s as the Fed used compliance with this act as a criteria for approving or disapproving bank mergers. It requires banks to lend in economically disadvantaged areas and to end the practice of redlining.

7. The Interstate Banking and Branching Efficiency Act (IBBEA) of 1994 will allow interstate branching by mergers on June 1, 1997. Under the new law, bank holding companies can also convert separate banks into branches.

8. Stricter regulations, despite being good for the health, safety, and soundness of the banking system, may have microeconomic effects on bank lending that can result in a credit crunch in the short run. Other suggestions for reform include (1) reducing deposit insurance coverage, (2) using mark-to-market accounting methods to appraise bank assets, and (3) establishing tiered deposit insurance coverage and/or narrow banking. Many

other suggestions have been offered to streamline and consolidate the regulatory agencies.

Key Terms

Basel Accord
Commodity Futures Trading Commission
Community Reinvestment Act
Federal Banking Commission
Federal Deposit Insurance Corporation Improvement Act (FDICIA)
Federal Home Loan Bank Board
Federal Trade Commission (FTC)
Financial Institutions Reform and Recovery Enforcement Act (FIRREA)
Insider Trading
Interstate Banking and Branching Efficiency Act (IBBEA)
Investment Company Act of 1940
Mark-to-Market Accounting
Narrow Banking
National Association of Securities Dealers

National Credit Union Administration
National Credit Union Share Insurance Fund
National Futures Association
Office of Thrift Supervision (OTS)
Options Clearing Corporation
Pension Benefit Guaranty Corporation
Redlining
Resolution Trust Corporation (RTC)
Securities and Exchange Commission (SEC)
Securities Investor Protection Corporation
Subordinated Debt
Tiered Deposit Insurance

Review Questions

1. How is the failure of an FI different from the failure of a video rental store? What do these differences imply about the need for regulation?

2. Discuss the major provisions of FIRREA and FDICIA.

3. What is *redlining*? How is the Community Reinvestment Act supposed to affect redlining? Discuss some of the difficulties with assessing compliance with the law. Could I be violating the law if my bank fails to lend to businesses located in the deteriorating downtown area?

4. Explain at least three suggestions for deposit insurance reform to deal with the moral hazard problem. What is narrow banking? What is tiered deposit insurance?

5. What is the Basel Accord? Why is it desirable to have uniform international capital standards for banks?

6. When would a bank not want to use mark-to-market accounting?

7. Some contend that the passage of IBBEA will not change much. What is the basis of their argument? On what date will banks be allowed to branch across state lines by merging with a bank in a different state?

8. Would a wealthy individual with bank accounts greater than $100,000 prefer the FDIC to use the purchase and assumption or the payoff method to liquidate bank failures? Why?

9. What is a credit crunch? Would large or small borrowers be affected most by a credit crunch? (Hint: Large borrowers can easily issue commercial paper while small borrowers may be more dependent on bank loans.)

10. What is core capital? How do risk-adjusted assets differ from total assets?

11. Who regulates money markets? Who regulates capital markets?

12. What are the arguments for a single banking regulatory agency? What are the arguments against it?

13. Explain the difference between risk-based capital standards and risk-based deposit insurance premium.

14. What are the regulatory responsibilities of the Securities and Exchange Commission? What is insider trading? Who sets margin requirements?

15. What are three self-regulating agencies and which industries do they regulate? Speculate as to why an industry would self-regulate?

16. Explain the function of each of the following:
    a. The National Credit Union Share Insurance Fund
    b. The Pension Benefit Guaranty Corporation
    c. The Securities Investor Protection Corporation
    d. The FDIC

Analytical Questions

17. Assume a bank has core capital of $1,000,000 and total capital of $2,000,000. Assume that total risk-adjusted assets are $25,000,000 and total assets are $30,000,000. According to the Basel Accord, does the bank have adequate capital?

18. If deposit insurance were scaled so that there was 100 percent coverage for the first $10,000 of deposits, 75 percent coverage for the next $20,000, and 50 percent coverage for all deposits exceeding $30,000, how much coverage would an individual with a $200,000 deposit have? Would the individual be better or worse off than with the present system?

19. Assume a bank has the following:

Stock Issued	$15,000,000
Retained Earnings	2,750,000
Loan-Loss Reserves	2,600,000
Subordinated Debt	5,000,000

What is its core capital? What is its total capital?

The Financial System and the Economy

| Back | Forward | Home | Reload | Images | Open | Print | Find | Stop | N |

1. From the latest Quarterly Banking Profile, (http://www.fdic.gov/research/qbp/qbpcom53.html), access the latest balance sheet for FDIC insured commercial banks and report the numbers for the total assets for all FDIC insured commercial banks in the latest quarter. Compare this number to the assets figure for the same quarter of the previous year.

2. Access the mission statements of the following regulatory agencies:
   a. OTS: (http://www.wings.usps.gov/federal/OTS/html/index.html)
   b. Office of the Comptroller of the Currency (http://www.occ.treas.gov/).
   c. FDIC: (http://www.fdic.gov/mission.html).

Do you believe that the present system involves multiplicity and duplication of regulatory functions? Report the latest data on the equity capital (net worth) of all commercial banks.

Suggested Readings

An interesting article on the future is Charles S. Sanford, Jr., "Financial Markets in 2020," *Economic Review of the Federal Reserve Bank of Kansas City,* First Quarter 1994, pp. 19–28.

Helen A. Garten offers a look at *Why Bank Regulation Failed: Designing a Bank Regulatory Strategy for the 1990s,* Westport, CT: Quorum Books, 1991.

For an international perspective, see David Gowland, *The Regulation of Financial Markets in the 1990s: Issues and Problems in an Age of Innovation,* Brookfield, VT: Edward Elgar Publishing, 1990.

Reforming Financial Institutions and Markets in the United States, George Kaufman, ed., Hingham, Mass.: Kluwer Academic Publishers, 1994 is a collection of essays on the state of the financial system and rationales for reform.

In Anthony Saunders and Ingo Walter, *Universal Banking in the United States* New York: Oxford University Press, 1994, the authors discuss the realities of expanded activities for U.S. banks.

A recent book on the European Community is Jordi Canals, *Competitive Strategies in European Banking,* New York: Oxford University Press, 1993.

For an engaging analysis of the present state of the financial system, along with a blueprint for change, see *Transforming the U.S. Financial System,* Gary Dymski, Gerald Epstein, and Robert Pollin, eds. Armonk, NY: M.E. Sharpe, 1993.

A book that looks at banking and securities regulation in both the United States and the European Community is *International Financial Market Regulation,* Benn Steil, ed., New York: Wiley, 1994.

PART FOUR

Monetary Theory

16

The Role of the Fed and Depository Institutions in the Money Supply Process

> *How do you make a million? You start with $900,000.*
> —Stephen Lewis, to Morton Shulman—
>
> *Make money and the whole world will call you a gentleman.*
> —Mark Twain—

Learning Objectives

After reading this chapter, you should know:

◆ How the Fed can affect the supply of reserves in the banking system

◆ How changes in the supply of reserves or reserve requirements affect the ability of depository institutions to expand loans and deposits

◆ Why changes in loans and deposits are usually a multiple of any change in reserves

◆ What the monetary base is

◆ Why changes in the money supply are a multiple of changes in the monetary base

◆ What affects the Fed's ability to control the money supply and credit

Where Money Comes From

Suppose that during one month, say April, the Fed conducts a large open market operation; it sells government securities through its trading desk at the New York Fed. About a month later, in conjunction with its regular weekly release of pertinent financial data (usually on a Thursday afternoon), the Fed reports that the money stock fell over the month of May. The purpose of this chapter is to help you understand the relationship between these two events—the open market sale and the subsequent fall in the money stock.

Much of the groundwork for this chapter has already been laid. In Chapters 2 and 3, we examined the definition, measurement, and role of money in the economy; in Chapter 5 we introduced the Federal Reserve and the tools it uses in conducting the nation's monetary policy; and in Part III (Chapters 10–15) we examined various aspects of the behavior of financial intermediaries, with particular focus on depository institutions.

As we have seen, depository institutions include banks, savings and loan associations, credit unions, and mutual savings banks. They issue checkable deposits and hold reserve assets equal to a fraction of deposit liabilities. Taken together, depository institutions make up the banking system.

This chapter focuses on the ways in which the operations of the Fed affect the banking system and how depository institutions, in turn, influence the supply of money and credit in the economy.

The Fed and Bank Reserves

Open Market Operations

Open Market Operations
The buying and selling of government securities by the Fed.

Open market operations are the buying and selling of government securities by the Fed. When the Fed engages in open market operations, a link is created between the Fed's actions and the nation's money supply. Open market operations affect the supply of reserves available to depository institutions. The volume of reserves has a direct effect on the banking system's ability to expand loans and thereby expand checkable deposits and the supply of money. In addition to their effect on the money supply, open market operations have an impact on the liquidity of the financial system and, more broadly, affect the supply of credit in the economy. Look at Exhibit 16-1 to make sure you are clear about these steps. We begin with the connection between open market operations and reserves.

The New York Federal Reserve Bank buys or sells U.S. government securities on behalf of the Fed and under the guidance and direction of the Fed Open Market Committee (FOMC). Such day-to-day transactions are the most important monetary policy tool. In general, open market operations initially influence the financial system in two ways. First, they affect the quantity of reserves in the banking system.[1] Second, they affect the level of interest rates,

---

[1] Shortly, we shall see that open market operations usually also affect currency in the hands of the public.

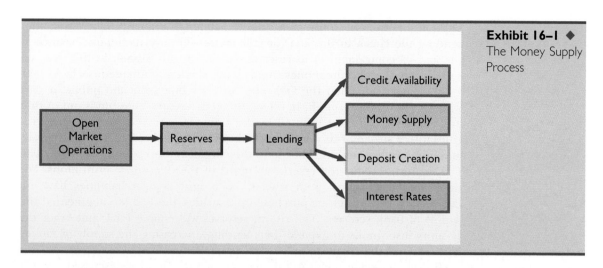

Exhibit 16–1 ◆
The Money Supply
Process

particularly short-term interest rates, such as the federal funds rate and Treasury bill rates. We say "affect" because, as we shall see, changes in other factors can have an impact on both reserves and interest rates. For now, we are going to focus on the effect of open market operations on reserves. There are two rules to remember:

1. When the Fed buys securities, reserves of depository institutions rise.
2. When the Fed sells securities, reserves of depository institutions fall.[2]

Since there is no reason for you to accept these propositions as true without proof, and since so much depends on understanding these rules, we will trace out the mechanics of the relationship between open market operations and reserves of depository institutions.

Suppose the Fed wants to add $1,000 to the supply of reserves in the banking system. The trading desk at the New York Fed, which is run by the manager of the Fed's portfolio of securities, will buy $1,000 of, say, Treasury bills (or Treasury bonds) from a group of dealers (market makers) with whom it does business regularly. The Fed will pay for these securities by issuing checks to the sellers whom we shall treat as part of the public at large. The sellers will, in turn, deposit their checks in, say, HLT National Bank. These checks are then cleared through the Fed's check processing network. See Exhibit 5-5 to refresh your memory about how this process occurs. In this case, HLT will send the checks to the Federal Reserve Bank in its district. The Fed in turn will credit HLT's deposit balance at the Fed. This deposit balance at the Fed is a component of HLT's reserves. (Remember reserves can be held in two forms—vault cash or deposits at the Fed.)

After the open market purchase, the Fed has $1,000 more securities and the dealers, who are the public, have $1,000 less securities. In return for selling the securities to the Fed, the public gets checks worth $1,000 from the Fed, which, for the present time, we assume are deposited in HLT National. The

---

[2]We should point out that when the Fed buys or sells "anything else" such as gold or foreign exchange, that reserves also change. The buying and selling of securities is the primary tool used to change reserves.

deposits are an asset to the public and a liability to the bank. The bank, after sending the check to the Fed for collection, will have its deposit balance at the Fed—a component of its reserves—credited with $1,000. In this case, reserves, deposits, and the money supply have all risen simultaneously by $1,000.

To generalize, when the Fed buys Treasury bills from the public, it pays with checks drawn on itself. In effect, the Fed "creates" the funds out of thin air! Utilizing the power granted by the Congress, the Fed pays for the securities with a stroke of its pen. The public exchanges these checks for deposits at depository institutions. They send the checks to the Fed for collection. The Fed, in turn, credits the reserve accounts of the depository institutions. For depository institutions, both reserve assets and deposit liabilities have increased. Thus, through its purchase of securities, the Fed has augmented the supply of bank reserves. The rise in reserves will enable HLT and other depository institutions to expand their lending, increasing the supply of money and credit in the economy.

To get a better feel for the set of transactions just discussed, simple "T-accounts" can be of considerable help. Here these simplified balance sheets will be utilized to focus on changes in assets and corresponding changes in liabilities.[3] Exhibit 16-2 shows T-accounts for the Fed, the public, and HLT National. It traces the transactions and changes that occur as a result of the Fed's open market purchase. The Fed has experienced an equal change in assets and liabilities. Study this exhibit carefully then close the book and see if you can work through an open market sale of securities by the Fed and the fall in reserves that results.[4]

[3] Recall from Chapter 4 that the basic balance sheet identity is total assets must equal total liabilities plus net worth. Expressed in terms of changes, this identity implies that the change in assets must equal the change in liabilities plus the change in net worth. In the examples employed in this chapter it is assumed that the entity's net worth does not change. Thus in each case a change in assets must be matched by a corresponding change in liabilities. By dealing only with changes, we can ignore other details and concentrate instead on the essential transactions.

[4] If you do it correctly, the entries should be identical to those in Exhibit 16-2, *except* all should carry opposite signs (+ to −, and − to +).

Exhibit 16-2 ◆

Affect of Open Market Operations on Reserves

Fed		Public		HLT National Bank	
Assets	Liabilities	Assets	Liabilities	Assets	Liabilities
(1) + $1,000 securities purchased from the public	(3) + $1,000 deposit due HLT	(1) − $1,000 securities sold to the Fed (2) + $1,000 deposits in the form of checks received from Fed and deposited in HLT		(3) + $1,000 reserves in the form of deposits at the Fed	(2) + $1,000 deposits by the public

Discount Loans

As discussed in Chapter 5, the Fed controls the amount of required reserve assets that depository institutions must hold. Because of this, they also operate a lending facility called the discount window through which depository institutions caught short of reserves can borrow from the Fed. Depository institutions are charged the discount rate to borrow reserves from the discount window.

Like open market operations, changes in discount loans also affect the volume of reserves in the banking system. When the Fed makes a discount loan to a depository institution, reserve assets increase by the full amount of the loan. When a discount loan is extended, the effect on reserves is the same as an open market purchase. Likewise, when a discount loan is paid off and borrowing from the Fed is reduced, the effect on reserves is the same as an open market sale. Exhibit 16-3 illustrates the balance sheet effects of a discount loan to HLT Bank.

Although the Fed has complete control over the volume of open market operations, it cannot totally control the amount of borrowing from the discount window. Borrowing at the discount window must be initiated by depository institutions. The Fed can raise or lower the discount rate to discourage or encourage borrowing, and the Fed can even refuse to make a discount loan. However, the fundamental issue is that decisions by banks to borrow or not to borrow from the discount window affect the volume of discount loans and hence the volume of reserves. Exhibit 16-4 illustrates how open market operations and discount loans influence reserves.

Other Factors That Change Reserves

Before moving on, we need to elaborate on two points. First, open market operations and discount loans are not the only factors that can affect reserves. Other factors can and do affect reserves. Second, the Fed can and does respond to changes in reserves caused by these other factors with **offsetting open market operations.** That is, if an unexpected increase in reserves is caused by a change in another factor that affects reserves, then the Fed can use an open market sale to decrease reserves. Likewise, if an unexpected decrease in reserves occurs, then the Fed can use an open market purchase to increase reserves.

Offsetting Open Market Operations Open market purchases or sales to offset changes in the monetary base from other factors.

To clarify, let us consider an example of how one of the many factors affects the volume of reserves in the banking system and what the Fed can do about the effects. Suppose I live in Los Angeles and send a check from my West Coast bank to my daughter Susie who goes to college in Omaha. Susie receives the check and deposits it in her checking account in Nebraska. Her bank credits her checking account and sends the check to the Federal Reserve Bank in Kansas City for collection. The Kansas City Fed sends the check to the San Francisco Fed, which will return the check to my bank. When the check is returned, my account will be debited. The whole process will take a

Fed		HLT National Bank		
Assets	Liabilities	Assets	Liabilities	
+$1,000 discount loans	+$1,000 deposits due HLT	+$1,000 reserves	+$1,000 discount loans	**Exhibit 16-3 ◆** Affect of Discount Loans on the Monetary Base

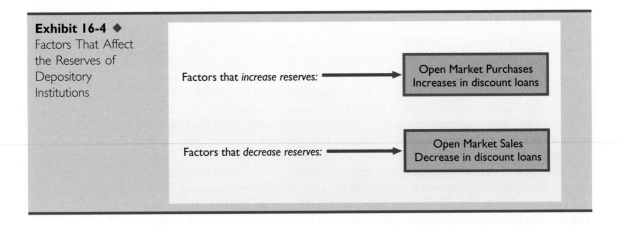

Exhibit 16-4 ◆
Factors That Affect
the Reserves of
Depository
Institutions

Factors that *increase reserves:* ⟶ Open Market Purchases / Increases in discount loans

Factors that *decrease reserves:* ⟶ Open Market Sales / Decrease in discount loans

few days. Because of the time it takes to transfer the check physically, the Kansas City Fed will typically credit the reserve account of the Omaha bank before the San Francisco Fed debits the reserve account of the Los Angeles bank. The net result of this series of transactions is that deposits and reserves in the banking system are higher than what they otherwise would be, during the period (usually a day) when the reserves and deposits appear on the balance sheet of both banks. This is called **Federal Reserve float.**

Federal Reserve Float
The excess in reserves that results from a check being credited to one bank (or other depository institution) before it is debited from another.

Now suppose the Fed, given its current policy stance, does not want reserves and deposits to increase. What can it do? The answer is that it can sell securities to offset the impact on the banking system of the rise in Federal Reserve float. Likewise, if some other factor causes reserves to unexpectedly decrease, the Fed could use an open market purchase to offset the impact on the banking system.

In general, these so-called offsetting open market sales and purchases are designed to counter movements in the reserves of depository institutions caused by other factors so as to maintain existing reserve conditions in the banking system. Since the Fed does not change its policy stance each day, but other factors that affect reserves are always changing, the Fed conducts large amounts of day-to-day offsetting open market purchases and sales. The appendix of this chapter looks in some detail at the other factors that influence reserves.

In sum, even though a variety of factors including discount loans can affect the volume of reserves in the banking system, the Fed's powerful tool, open market operations, enables it to offset the impact of these other factors and thus greatly influence the reserves of depository institutions.

The "rules" we have laid out should now be much clearer. Understand that in examining the first link in Exhibit 16-1 we have traced out the transactions in slow motion. In practice, most of the transactions are conducted electronically and occur quickly. However, regardless of timing, an essential point is that through its open market operations the Fed can inject or remove reserves from the banking system.

Loan and Deposit Expansion by the Banking System

Now that we have seen how the Fed can increase or decrease reserves, we can examine the second linkage in Exhibit 16-1. More specifically, we want to see how changes in reserves affect the volume of deposits and loans in the banking system. To simplify, we will employ a balance sheet (and T-account) for a bank in our hypothetical banking system.[5]

Prototype Balance Sheet
for a Bank

Assets	Liabilities
Reserves Loans	Checkable Deposits

On the assets side, there are reserves and loans. For simplicity, other assets are ignored. On the liabilities side, we shall assume that there are only checkable deposits, the major component of the nation's money supply. Thus, we are ignoring other deposit and nondeposit liabilities and net worth. In addition, we focus only on changes in assets and liabilities resulting from various transactions.

Now would be a good time to look at Exhibit 16-5, which begins where Exhibit 16-2 left off. HLT begins with the $1,000 of new **total reserves** and $1,000 of new deposit liabilities, which resulted from the open market purchase described in the previous section. Where do we go from here? HLT is not in business to hold idle funds as reserves; it uses funds deposited with it to acquire assets that earn interest income. If the Fed insists that HLT hold **required reserves** assets equal to 10 percent of its checkable deposit liabilities, the remaining 90 percent of reserves are **excess reserves.** In this example, required reserves are $100 (10 percent × $1,000) and excess reserves (total reserves minus required reserves) are $900 ($1,000 − $100).

Given their desire for profits, we assume that HLT and other depository institutions in our system will not wish to hold any excess reserves and will, therefore, use such funds to acquire assets. In our simple model, loans are the only assets that are acquired. Assuming new loan customers are readily

Total Reserves Required reserves plus excess reserves.

Required Reserves The amount of reserve assets that the Fed requires a depository institution to hold. **Excess Reserves** Reserves over and above those required by the Fed.

---

[5] Note that we could have chosen to use the balance sheet of any depository institution; we chose to use banks in our example because they make up the largest class of depository institutions.

Exhibit 16-5 ◆
Loan and Deposit Expansion at HLT National Bank

Assets		Liabilities	
Total Reserves	$1,000	Checkable Deposits	$1,000

The total reserve assets and checkable deposits of HLT each increase by $1,000. Assuming the bank was loaned up to begin with, this represents an increase of $100 in required reserves and $900 in excess reserves. The bank can safely loan out its excess reserves. When a loan is made, the proceeds are disbursed by creating a checkable deposit. The bank's assets increase by the amount of the loan.

HLT National Bank

Assets		Liabilities	
Required Reserves	$ 100	Checkable Deposits	$1,000
Excess Reserves	$ 900		
Loan	$ 900	New Checkable Deposits	$ 900
Total	$1,900	Total	$1,900

available, we are ready to consider the first stage of what will be a multi-stage process of loan and deposit expansion.

It just so happens that our old friend J.P. Young from Chapter 4 needs $900 to purchase a new stereo. Given the excess reserves it has on hand, HLT agrees to lend J.P. $900. J.P. signs a loan contract, which HLT puts in its vault, and HLT credits $900 to J.P.'s deposit balance. The loan contract is an asset while the deposit balance is a liability. Exhibit 16-5 also shows the T-account entries for HLT and J.P. after this transaction. Combining this stage with the initial situation, HLT's balance sheet shows a $1,900 rise in assets—$1,000 in reserves plus $900 in loans. On the liability side there is also a $1,900 rise in liabilities—the original $1,000 deposit plus the new $900 deposit in J.P.'s account. Since deposits increase when the $900 loan is made, $900 of money has been "created."

Remember, however, J.P. did not borrow the money to keep in his account. J.P. uses the $900 to pay I.M. Loud, Inc., for the stereo equipment purchased by writing a check. We will assume I.M. Loud, Inc., does its banking at Second National Bank. Accordingly, I.M. Loud deposits the check received from J.P. in its deposit account at Second National. Second National credits I.M.'s account and when the check is cleared, the Fed will debit (decrease) HLT's deposit account at the Fed by $900 and credit (add to) Second National's deposit account at the Fed by the same amount. HLT will, in turn, debit J.P.'s account for $900 for the check written to I.M. This series of transactions is shown in Exhibit 16-6.

So what is the net effect of those transactions on the supply of money and credit in the economy? When J.P. writes a check for $900 against his account at HLT, this reduces HLT's deposit liabilities and reserve assets by $900. (The $900 in reserve assets is credited to I.M. Loud's bank, Second National.) If we sum up the charges on HLT's balance sheet (bottom row), we see that the initial $1,000 deposit inflow is balanced by a $100 rise in reserves and a $900 rise in loans. HLT is now fully **loaned up;** this just means that it has no excess reserves left to serve as a basis for lending. The $100 of reserves it holds are all required reserves. HLT responded to the initial deposit inflow by expanding its loans and deposits by 90 percent of the inflow. Thus, HLT, and indeed any individual depository institution, can make additional loans and thereby "create" deposits equal to its excess reserves.

The process has not ended, however. Take a close look at Second National's balance sheet. It is clearly not loaned up. It has $810 of excess reserves. As was the case with HLT, Second National will react to the deposit inflow ($900) by lending out an amount equal to that portion of the funds received left over after the Fed's reserve requirement has been met. In this case, given our assumption of a 10 percent reserve requirement, it will have to keep $90 as required reserves and will have $810 of excess reserves. The excess reserves

Loaned Up When a bank has no excess reserves left to serve as a basis for lending.

Exhibit 16-6 ◆

Transactions between HLT National and Second National Banks

HLT National Bank				Second National Bank			
Assets		Liabilities		Assets		Liabilities	
Total Reserves	$ 100	Checkable Deposits	$1,000	Total Reserves	$900	Checkable Deposits	$900
Loan	$ 900						
Total	$1,000		$1,000		$900		$900

will serve as the basis of lending to, say, Jane Collins who happens to need exactly $810 to pay her fees at State University. Again, let us assume that Jane gives a check to the university, which then deposits it in the Third National Bank, as depicted in Exhibit 16-7. As was the case before, the clearing of the check will result in the Fed crediting Third National's account at the Fed by the same amount. Second National will, in turn, debit Jane's account by the same $810, leaving it fully loaned up with the original gain of $900 in deposits on the liability side of its balance sheet and a rise of $90 in required reserves and $810 in loans on the asset side of its balance sheet. (Again, $810 in total reserve assets have been credited to Third National, State University's Bank, since Jane's check is written to State.) If you are with us, you should now be able to describe what will happen in the next stage.

We have shown that each individual bank was able to increase its earning assets by the amount of the excess reserves that resulted from a deposit inflow. But why can't an individual bank (or other depository institution for that matter) expand deposits by more than its excess reserves (90 percent of the inflow)? In general, it cannot assume that new deposits created in conjunction with loans will be spent and redeposited in its coffers. Rather, it should expect to lose reserves equal to the loans extended and deposits created. If it lent out, say $1,000 (100 percent of the inflow) and subsequently lost $1,000 of reserves, it would find itself with the original $1,000 inflow of deposits on the liability side. If you think this is okay, you've forgotten one important factor— the Fed's reserve requirements. All depository institutions must have $100 of required reserves for each $1,000 of checkable deposits. To avoid the problem, lending and deposit creation by an individual institution would normally be limited to its excess reserves.

However, as the loans of one depository institution increased, the use of proceeds of the loan by the borrower led to a deposit inflow at another. A deposit inflow increases total deposit liabilities and reserve assets. The depository institution will adjust to the inflow of reserves and deposits by expanding

Exhibit 16-7 ◆ Transactions of Second National and Third National Banks

Second National Bank			
Assets		Liabilities	
Total Reserves	$ 900	Checkable Deposits	$ 900
Loans	$ 810	Checkable Deposits	$ 810
Total	$1,710		$1,710

The proceeds of the loan from Second National are spent and deposited in the university's account at Third National. Second National loses $810 in reserve assets and the $810 deposit of the loan proceeds is extinguished. The resulting balance sheets of Second National and Third National are as follows:

Second National Bank				Third National Bank			
Assets		Liabilities		Assets		Liabilities	
Total Reserves	$ 90	Checkable Deposits	$900	Total Reserves	$810	Checkable Deposits	$810
Loans	$810						
Total	$900		$900		$810		$810

its loans and "creating" additional deposits. Subsequently, the individual in-stitution will lose reserve assets and the additional deposit liabilities as the borrower uses the proceeds of the loan to pay for a purchase. However, one institution's loss is another's gain. Note that as this occurs, the total volume of reserves in the banking system does not change. What does happen at each stage is that deposits rise and the composition of total reserves in the banking system changes—required reserves rise and excess reserves fall.

The size of these changes can be stated precisely. As deposits flow through the banking system, the change in deposits at each depository institution can be represented as the change in required reserves plus the change in excess reserves. The change in required reserves is equal to 10 percent of the deposit inflow while the change in excess reserve assets is equal to 90 percent of the deposit inflow. Hence, the change in loans and deposits "created" by each depository institution is equal to 90 percent of the inflow to that institution. In our example, the $1,000 increase in deposits at HLT is followed by a $900 increase in deposits at Second National, which is followed by a $810 increase in deposits at Third National. Taken together, that is, adding up the changes in each balance sheet, the increase in total deposits in the banking system at each stage as loans are extended is 90 percent of the new deposits "created" at the previous stage. This means that, ultimately, the new deposits created at subsequent stages approach zero and the process ends.[6]

Perhaps the most important aspect of the process to fix in your mind is that the total expansion of loans and deposits ($1,000 + $900 + $810 + ...) is much greater than the initial injection of reserves into the banking system. In fact, the expansion of loans and deposits turns out to be a multiple of the initial injection of reserves. Some simple algebra presented in the next section will help confirm this point.

 RECAP

Open market purchases increase the supply of reserves while open market sales decrease the supply of reserves. When the Fed makes a discount loan, reserves increase. When a discount loan is paid off, reserves decrease. Depository institutions loan out excess reserves and in the process create money. Any one institution can safely lend only its excess reserves. However, when the proceeds of a loan are spent, deposits and reserves flow into another depository institution that responds by expanding loans and creating addi-tional deposits. Loans, deposits, and the money supply expand by a multiple of an injection of reserves.

 ### The Simple Multiplier Model of the Money Supply Process

In our simple example, the process of creating money and credit from increases in reserves will end when all reserves in the banking system become

---

[6]To illustrate .9 × $1,000 = $900; .9 × $900 = $810; .9 × $729 = $656.10; .9 × $656.10 = $590.49; and so on.

"Miss Purvis, would you please check the window of the money room for me?"

© 1996 Robert Mankoff from The Cartoon Bank,™ Inc.

required reserves. This is when the banking system is fully loaned up. This situation is reached gradually as individual depository institutions "create" deposit liabilities and at the same time increase assets (loans in this case) in response to deposit inflows. When there are no excess reserves left in the banking system, new loans cannot be made and new deposit creation ceases. The net result of the actions taken by individual depository institutions for the banking system and the economy as a whole can be illustrated with the aid of a simple model.

Required reserve assets, RR, are by definition equal to the **required reserve ratio,** r_D, multiplied by the amount of deposit liabilities, D.

Required Reserve Ratio (r_D) The fraction of deposits that depository institutions are required to hold as required reserve assets.

$$(16\text{-}1) \qquad RR = r_D \times D$$

Excess reserves, ER, are by definition equal to total reserves, TR, minus required reserves.

$$(16\text{-}2) \qquad ER = TR - RR$$

If total reserves equal required reserves, there are no excess reserves to serve as the basis of lending. As already discussed, this is the case when the banking system is fully loaned up. Therefore, when ER equals zero,

$$(16\text{-}3) \qquad TR = RR$$
$$= r_D \times D$$

Rearranging terms yields

(16-4) $$D = TR/r_D$$

or $$D = 1/r_D \times TR$$

Simple Money Multiplier
The reciprocal of the re-
quired reserve ratio, $1/r_D$.

Total deposits are equal to the quantity of reserves multiplied by the reciprocal of the required reserve ratio. We shall refer to $1/r_D$ as the **simple money multiplier.**

For any change in reserves, TR, the change in deposits, D, is equal to the change in loans, L. Assuming excess reserves equal zero, we can rewrite Equation (16-4) as

(16-5) $$\Delta L = \Delta D$$
$$= 1/r_D \times \Delta TR$$

Since we assumed that r_D was fixed at 10 percent (.1) in our example, the simple money multiplier is $1/.1$, which is equal to 10. Therefore, the increase in deposits resulting from the $1,000 increase in reserves will be $10,000, assuming depository institutions hold no excess reserves. Although in our example, reserves increased by $1,000, make sure you understand that the simple money multiplier works in both directions. If reserves decrease by $1,000, assuming depository institutions hold no excess reserves, there would be a corresponding decrease in deposits of $10,000.

Sometimes students come away from the preceding analysis with the feeling that they do not really understand how an injection of reserves into the banking system by the Fed leads to multiple increases in the money supply and credit. For those of you who fall into this category, we can illustrate this phenomenon without resorting to equations. Here is another way to understand this process.

Fractional Reserve Bank-
ing System A banking
system in which individual
banks hold reserve assets
equal to a fraction of deposit liabilities.

The simple multiplier process is a reflection of what is called the **fractional reserve banking system.** A depository institution must hold reserve assets equal to some fraction of deposit liabilities. The fraction it must hold is determined by the reserve requirements set by the Fed. If the reserve requirement is 100 percent, any increase in deposits would result in an identical dollar-for-dollar increase in required reserves. In this case the simple money multiplier would equal one. If the reserve requirement is less than one, however, a given dollar increase in deposits will result in the need to hold required reserves equal to only some fraction of the increase in deposits. The remaining fraction of reserve assets is excess reserves and can serve as the basis of lending, which becomes new deposits as described before. In this latter case, the total change in deposits is greater than the amount of required reserves and, therefore, the multiplier is greater than one. In general, the change in deposits and credit, which accompanies a given change in reserves, will be inversely related to reserve requirements. That is, for a given change in reserves, the smaller the required reserve ratio is, the larger will be the change in deposits and credit. Exhibit 16-8 shows various combinations of required reserve ratios and the resulting simple money multiplier.

The whole process can be viewed as an inverted pyramid ($\triangledown$). The original injection by the Fed leads to increased reserve assets and deposit liabilities, and provides individual depository institutions with excess reserves. They ad-

Exhibit 16-8 ◆
The Required
Reserve Ratio and
the Simple Money
Multiplier

r_D	Simple Money Multiplier
.05	$1/.05 = 20$
.10	$1/.10 = 10$
.20	$1/.20 = 5$
.25	$1/.25 = 4$
.50	$1/.50 = 2$

As the required reserve ratio increases, the simple multiplier decreases. Intuitively, if the Fed increases the required reserve ratio, depository institutions have to hold more reserve assets and have fewer excess reserves to lend.

just to this abundance of reserves by expanding loans and deposits. The deposits, when spent by loan recipients, flow to other depository institutions (higher up on the pyramid), who, in turn, expand loans and deposits. The process continues because profit-maximizing institutions are, in general, not interested in holding noninterest-earning excess reserves. As a result, the original injection of reserves, the foundation of the inverted pyramid, can support a multiple expansion in loans and deposits, as in Exhibit 16-9. The whole process is not unlike one's family tree. A husband and wife have children, who in turn have children, and so forth.

Exhibit 16-10 shows in tabular form the expansion of loans, deposits and reserves for the banking system based on the example we have been discussing in this chapter when the injection of reserves is $1,000, the required reserve ratio is .1, and the multiplier is 10. Note that excess reserves decline at each stage and required reserves increase at each stage. In the final stage excess reserves have fallen to zero and required reserves are equal to the initial reserves supplied. Exhibit 16-11 presents the same process and example in graphical form. At each stage deposits expand by 90 percent of the deposit expansion at the previous stage. This process occurs because at each stage when the proceeds of a loan are spent and redeposited in another depository institution, required reserve assets equal to 10 percent of the new deposits must be held and 90 percent can serve as the basis of lending.[7] Again, the cumulative process continues until there are no excess reserves left to serve as the basis of lending—a point attained in our example when the total expansion of deposits has reached $10,000.

RECAP

$ER = TR - RR$. If depository institutions are loaned up, then $TR = RR = r_D \times D$. The simple money multiplier is $1/r_D$ since $\Delta L = D = 1/r_D \times TR$. An expansion of loans and deposits equal to a multiple of the increase in reserves results from fractional reserve banking. If depository institutions lose reserves, loans and deposits fall by a multiple of the loss.

---

[7] In reality, the same expansion occurs whether the proceeds of a loan are spent and redeposited in another depository institution or the same institution that made the loan.

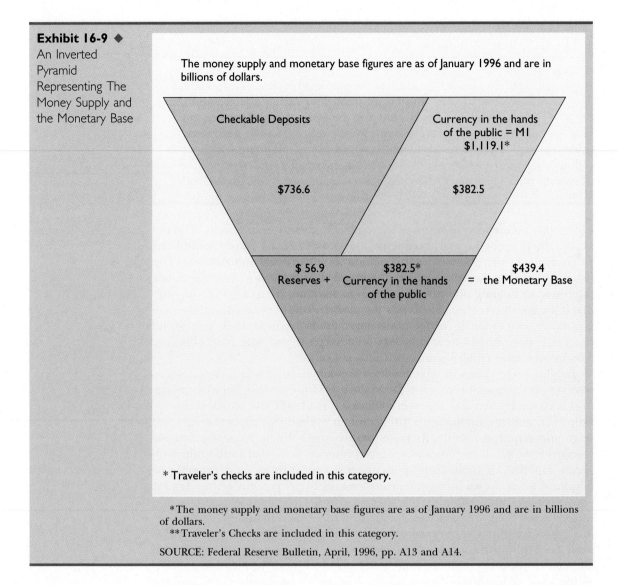

Exhibit 16-9 ◆
An Inverted Pyramid Representing The Money Supply and the Monetary Base

The money supply and monetary base figures are as of January 1996 and are in billions of dollars.

Checkable Deposits

Currency in the hands of the public = M1
$1,119.1*

$736.6

$382.5

$ 56.9
Reserves +

$382.5*
Currency in the hands of the public

$439.4
= the Monetary Base

* Traveler's checks are included in this category.

*The money supply and monetary base figures are as of January 1996 and are in billions of dollars.
**Traveler's Checks are included in this category.
SOURCE: Federal Reserve Bulletin, April, 1996, pp. A13 and A14.

Policy Implications

Even though we have ignored many real-world details, several policy implications flow from the preceding analysis. First, a given dollar change in reserves will lead to a larger (multiple) change in the money supply and credit extension. Since the Fed can ultimately control the supply of reserves in the banking system with its open market operations, the Fed has considerable influence on the lending activity of depository institutions and, therefore, the availability of funds in the financial system. Second, if the multiplier were really as simple as $1/r_D$, the Fed could actually control the money supply precisely. Simple arithmetic is all that would be required. If the Fed can control total reserves, TR, and it sets reserve requirements, r_D, it can make deposits, D, in Equation (16-3), or more generally, the money supply, do anything it wants to, assuming depository institutions wish to maintain zero excess reserves.

Exhibit 16-10 ◆

The Multiple Expansion of Deposits and Loans in the Banking System With an Initial Increase in Reserves of $1,000 and a Multiplier of 10

	Total Deposits	Required Reserves	Excess Reserves	Total Reserves	Loans	Total Assets RR + ER + Loans TR + Loans
Initial Reserves Provided	$1,000	$100	$900	$1,000	—	$1,000
Expansion						
Stage 1	$1,900	$190	$810	$1,000	$900	$1,900
Stage 2	2,710	271	729	1,000	1,710	2,710
Stage 3	3,440	344	656	1,000	2,439	3,439
Stage 4	4,100	410	590	1,000	3,095	4,100
Stage 5	4,690	469	531	1,000	3,690	4,690
Stage 6	5,220	522	478	1,000	4,221	5,200
Stage 7	5,700	570	430	1,000	4,680	5,700
Stage 8	6,130	613	387	1,000	5,130	6,130
Stage 9	6,510	651	349	1,000	5,517	6,510
Stage 10	6,860	686	314	1,000	5,859	6,860
⋮	⋮	⋮	⋮	⋮	⋮	⋮
Stage 20	8,900	890	110	1,000	7,902	8,900
Final	$10,000	$1,000	$0	$1,000	$9,000	$10,000

Through a multistage, multiple expansion process, deposits grow to a total of ten times the new reserves supplied to the banking system by the Fed through the open market purchase. When the reserves are provided initially, this results in HLT National Bank and the banking system as a whole having an additional $1,000 of reserves, of which $100 are required reserves and $900 are excess reserves. In Stage 1, HLT makes a $900 loan and in the process expands deposits by a like amount. As a result, deposits in the banking system have now risen by $1,900—the initial $1,000 plus the $900. The deposits (proceeds of the loan) are spent and flow to another bank (Second National). The $900 inflow of deposits and reserves will raise Second National's excess reserves by $810 and its required reserves by $90. For the banking system as a whole, the change in total reserves remains $1,000, but required reserves are now $190—the $100 held by HLT plus the $90 held by Second National—and excess reserves are $810 (remember that HLT lost its $900 of excess reserves when it made a loan). In Stage 2, Second National makes a loan for $810, raising the total expansion of loans in the system to $1,710 ($900 + $810) and the total expansion of deposits to $2,710 ($1,000 + $900 + $810). The process continues at each stage until excess reserves equal zero, and required reserves equal the amount of initial reserves supplied.

SOURCE: Adopted from *Modern Money Mechanics*, Federal Reserve Bank of Chicago.

The next section explains that the multiplier is actually more complicated than $1/r_D$ and is not under the Fed's complete control. However, such complications should not obscure two features of monetary control: (1) the Fed's enormous influence on the value of borrowing and lending in the economy, and (2) the cumulative process linking Fed actions to deposit creation and hence, the money supply. Simply put, whenever the Fed reports a large monthly decrease in the money supply, such as the one described at the beginning of the chapter, you can be reasonably sure this is to a large extent the result of prior Fed actions, particularly open market sales.

Exhibit 16-11 ◆

The Multiplier Effect of an Increase in Reserves

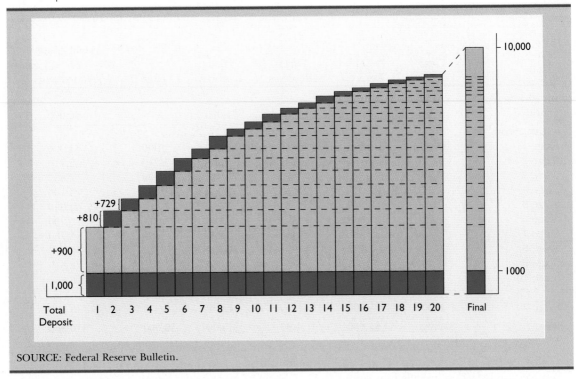

SOURCE: Federal Reserve Bulletin.

Some Complicating Realities in the Multiplier Model

Let us take a look at the simplifying assumptions we made in developing the preceding model of how money and credit are created and their implications.

First, we assumed that depository institutions never hold any excess reserves. When deposits flow in and reserve assets increase, depository institutions continue to lend by creating new deposit liabilities until excess reserves equal zero. In fact, depository institutions do hold excess reserves, and the excess reserves they hold fluctuate over time. The excess reserves are a leakage from the flow of increases in deposits and credit extension. The effect of this leakage is similar to the effect of an increase in reserve requirements. The amount of loans and deposits created at each stage will be reduced by the volume of excess reserves held. The net effect will be to lower the simple money multiplier.

Second, we have ignored currency. If the stereo dealer (I.M. Loud) in the example in the previous section exchanges J.P.'s $900 check for a $675 deposit at Second National and $225 of currency from the vault at Second National, then the net change in the reserves of Second National is less than J.P.'s check. Second National has an increase in its reserve account at the Fed of $900, a reduction in vault cash of \$225, and a net change in reserves of \$675.[8] In other words, the stereo dealer exchanges the \$900 check for a deposit equal to three-fourths of the amount of the check and currency equal to one-fourth of the amount. This will reduce the flow of reserves and deposits from Second National to subsequent depository institutions by 25 percent and hence reduce the overall expansion of the money supply.[9]

Modifying the Multiplier Model

As a result of these implications, the actual multiplier is clearly not as simple as the one presented in Equation (16-4). We can develop a somewhat more realistic multiplier model by taking into account the factors already mentioned. Let us see what happens when we recognize that depository institutions hold excess reserves. Now total reserves, TR, are equal to required reserves RR, against checkable deposits, $r_D D$, plus excess reserves, ER.

(16-6)
$$TR = RR + ER$$

or
$$TR = r_D D + ER$$

Next, assume that depository institutions hold excess reserve assets equal to a constant proportion of checkable deposit liabilities, D. For example, say they hold a few cents of excess reserve assets per dollar of deposits. Given this assumption, we can define ER as equal to eD, where e is the ratio of excess reserves held to checkable deposits, ER/D. More directly, e is the ratio of excess reserves depository institutions choose to maintain relative to the size of their deposit liabilities. Substituting this expression into Equation (16-6) yields

(16-7)
$$TR = r_D D + eD$$
$$= (r_D + e)D$$

Solving this equation for D yields

(16-8)
$$D = 1/(r_D + e) TR$$

---

[8] Second National exchanges the \$900 check for an increase of \$900 in its reserve account at the Fed. However, the vault cash of Second National has gone down by \$225. If Second National replenishes its vault cash by drawing on its account at the Fed, its reserve account has a net change of \$675.

[9] Other factors also complicate the simple multiplier. For example, until December 1990, depository institutions were required to hold required reserves against some time and saving deposits. If State University decided to hold, say, one-fifth of the tuition payments it received from Jane and others in the form of large negotiable CDs rather than checkable deposits, then required reserves, checkable deposits, and M1 would initially fall. Reserve requirements on large negotiable CDs were less than on checkable deposits. The narrowly defined money aggregates fell as checkable deposits were exchanged for CDs, which are not included in M1. Total reserves in the system did not change while required reserves decreased. In late 1990 and early 1991, reserve requirements on virtually all time and savings deposits were eliminated. However, to the extent that checkable deposits are exchanged for time and savings deposits as checkable deposits grow, the multiplier can still be affected.

LOOKING BACK

The Money Multiplier During the Great Depression

You might be interested to learn that between 1929 and 1933 bank holdings of excess reserves rose from $25 million to over $2 billion and that the currency-to-deposit ratio increased from approximately 17 percent to 33 percent.

Why do you think these changes occurred? Borrowers were defaulting on loans as the Depression deepened, and depositors became wary as thousands of banks failed. Solvent banks found few attractive loan opportunities and tried to regain the public's confidence by staying liquid—that is, holding excess reserve assets. The public on the other hand had lost confidence in the banking system and responded by withdrawing funds and thus increasing their holdings of currency.

In this chapter we have seen that the multiplier is equal to $(1 + c)/(r_D + e + c)$ and that the multiplier times the monetary base is equal to the money supply. Without knowing any of the facts, the multiplier tells us that if r_D and total reserves remained roughly unchanged, checkable deposits, and therefore the money supply, would decline as e rises. Although it is not as clear from the formula, if c rises, the multiplier would also decline, as the public withdraws deposits and reserves from the banking system.

Since these processes were not really understood in the 1930s, the money supply fell by about one-third between 1929 and 1933 due to the rise in both e and c and the resulting fall in the money multiplier. The drop in the money supply was hardly the type of anti-Depression policy one would have hoped for.

It is possible that the Fed could have moderated or reversed the decline in the money supply by sufficiently lowering r_D or raising total reserves. The Fed could have provided banks with additional reserves through open market purchases or by lending reserves to depositories and serving as a lender of last resort. Thus they could have offset the drop in the multiplier by increasing the monetary base. A sufficient volume of such actions would have forestalled the decline in the money supply. The fact that the Fed did not respond in this fashion is one of the reasons the Fed is often blamed for aggravating the Depression. In fact, it actually raised reserve requirements, believing this would help to restore the public's confidence in the banking system.

Of course, today our understanding of what determines the money supply and its importance in the economy is much greater than it was during the Great Depression. Thus, it is likely such a rise in e and c today would produce a much more aggressive Fed reaction.

*Until 1980, banks were the only financial intermediary that issued checkable deposits.

And in terms of changes in reserves and deposits, we have

$$(16\text{-}9) \qquad \Delta D = 1/(r_D + e)\Delta TR$$

Equation (16-9) defines the new relationship between deposits and reserves. Two things are important to note about this relationship. First, the multiplier in Equation (16-9), $1/(r_D + e)$, is smaller than the simple multiplier, $1/r_D$, in Equation (16-5). For example if r_D is .10 and e is .02, the multiplier is 8.33, $[1/(.10 + .02) = 8.33]$, rather than 10 $(1/.10 = 10)$. Second, the multiplier is not under the complete control of the Fed. Depository institutions can control the excess reserve ratio, e, which suggests that control by the Fed is not a matter of simple arithmetic.

In recent years (1994 and 1995), the holdings of excess reserves by depository institutions have generally fluctuated between $.75 billion to $1.5 billion. (During this time, total reserves fluctuated between $60 and $65 billion.) The changes in excess reserves contribute to fluctuations in the multiplier and make it difficult to predict precisely. This difficulty is especially relevant in the short run (week to week and month to month). Over a longer period, say three to six months, the fluctuations largely average out. That is, a large increase during one week is offset by a large decrease during another week. Hence, controlling the money supply is less difficult for the Fed over longer periods than over shorter periods.

Having shown that depository institutions can affect the multiplier through e, let us examine how the public can affect the money supply through its currency holding behavior. Recall that the total money supply (M) is equal to checkable deposits, D, plus currency in the hands of the public, C. Let us assume that the public also desires to maintain its currency holdings as a constant proportion of its checkable deposits. Currency held by the public, C is equal to cD where c is the desired ratio of currency to checkable deposits, C/D. Thus we can write

$$M = D + C$$

(16-10)
$$= D + cD$$

$$= (1 + c)D$$

Taking account of the fact that the public desires to maintain its currency holdings equal to cD, we can see that open market purchases of securities by the Fed may result in a combination of both reserves and currency in the hands of the public increasing. As the public sells securities, their checkable deposits increase and they exchange some of those deposits for currency to maintain the desired currency-to-deposit ratio, c.

We define the **monetary base,** MB, as the sum of reserves and currency in the hands of the public, $TR + C$.[10] While initially open market purchases show up as increases in reserves, which lead to new lending and deposit creation, the reserves become severely depleted as the newly created deposits are exchanged for currency to maintain the desired currency-to-deposit ratio. Thus, when the Fed engages in open market operations, both reserves and currency in the hands of the public can change. In reality, open market operations change the monetary base. The multiplier is affected by the fact that some of the newly created deposits are exchanged for currency. Making the appropriate substitution for reserves from Equation (16-8) and substituting cD for C, as noted previously, we arrive at Equation (16-11):

Monetary Base Reserves plus currency in the hands of the public, denoted as MB.

---

[10] The monetary base can also be defined as reserve deposits at the Fed, DF, plus currency outside the Fed, C^*. This is so because currency outside the Fed is either in the vaults of depository institutions where it is part of reserves or in the hands of the public. Thus, reserves include deposits at the Fed plus vault cash, VC, and vault cash plus currency in the hands of the public is currency outside the Fed. The following equation summarizes this relationship and illustrates the difference between C and C^*: $TR + C = DF + VC + C = DF + C^*$, and $VC + C = C^*$.

$$MB = TR + C$$

(16-11)
$$= (r_D + e)D + cD$$

$$= (r_D + e + c)D$$

Rearranging terms, we get

(16-12)
$$D = [1/(r_D + e + c)]MB$$

Equation (16-12) shows the relationship between the monetary base and deposits. By combining Equations (16-10) and (16-12), we can derive the relationship between the monetary base and the money supply, M:

$$M = D + C$$

$$= [1/(r_D + e + c)]MB + C$$

(16-13)
$$= [1/(r_D + e + c)]MB + cD$$

$$= [1/(r_D + e + c)]MB + c\,[1/(r_D + e + c)]MB$$

$$= [1/(r_D + e + c)]MB\,(1 + c)$$

$$= [(1 + c)/(r_D + e + c)]MB$$

In terms of changes in the monetary base and the money supply, we have

(16-14)
$$[(1 + c)/(r_D + e + c)]\Delta MB = \Delta M$$

Equation (16-14) defines the change in the money supply in terms of the monetary base and the expanded multiplier, which we will now refer to as simply the **money multiplier.** Taking account of another complication (the currency drain) has reduced the multiplier; if c is equal to .3, the multiplier is $(1 + .3)/(.1 + .02 + .3) = 3.1$, rather than the 8.33 in Equation (16-9). Because we are using M1 as our measure of the money supply, our money multiplier is actually the M1 multiplier. In Appendix 16B, we develop the M2 multiplier. Exhibit 16-12 illustrates the factors that cause the money multiplier to change.

To summarize, in this more complete model, the money multiplier is the multiple of the change in the monetary base by which the money supply will change. For example, in the preceding illustration, if the Fed uses open market purchases to increase the monetary base by $1,000, the money supply will increase by $3,100. The new money multiplier takes account of excess reserves and the currency drain. In the simple money multiplier case, the simple multiplier is the multiple by which a change in reserves leads to a change in deposits and loans, without consideration of other factors.

Money Multiplier The multiple of the change in the monetary base by which the money supply will change.

 RECAP

The monetary base is reserves, TR, plus currency in the hands of the public, C. The money supply will be equal to the monetary base, MB, times the money multiplier. The actual money multiplier is more complicated than the

LOOKING BACK

The Evolution of the Money Multiplier[a]

Perhaps it took you careful thought and study to assimilate the material on the money multiplier presented in this chapter. If so, you should not feel alone. Economists grappled with ideas about how an increase in reserves led to a multiple increase in deposits and money for a long time before a clear and complete explanation emerged.

During the 18th century, writers such as John Law (1671–1729) and Alexander Hamilton (1755–1804) noticed that bank deposits were a multiple of the underlying cash base and inferred from this that banks create deposits. They did not see that the multiple resulted from the successive lending and redeposit of excess reserves. This idea was first put forth in 1826 by James Pennington (1777–1862), who recognized that a given increase in the reserve base causes deposits to multiply as the reserve increase shifts from bank to bank. It was left to Robert Torrens (1780–1864) to trace Pennington's notion of deposit expansion to its logical conclusion in 1837 (resulting in what we referred to as the simple money multiplier in this chapter). Thomas Joplin (1790–1847) clarified how expansion proceeds as one bank loses excess reserves to another that then also expands. Alfred Marshall (1842–1924) provided the algebraic model for the simple multiplier that takes into account excess reserves—Equation (16-9) in this chapter. Finally, in 1921, Chester Phillips (1882–1976) "stated the theory with a power, precision, and completeness unmatched by his predecessors."[b]

Two steps remained to complete the analysis. First, the notion of a currency drain as deposits expand was developed by several economists between the 1930s and the 1950s. Finally, the work of James Meade, Milton Friedman, Anna Schwartz, and Phillip Cagan in the 1950s and early 1960s incorporated a currency drain into the money multiplier and fully explained the relationship between changes in the monetary base and changes in money. Thus, not until the early 1960s was the money multiplier fully expounded.

Don't you think you mastered the material rather quickly?

[a]Much of the material presented in this Looking Back feature is based on Thomas M. Humphrey, "The Theory of Multiple Expansion of Deposits: What It Is and Whence It Came," *Economic Review of the Federal Reserve Bank of Richmond*, March/April 1987, pp. 3–11.

[b]Thomas M. Humphrey, "The Theory of Multiple Expansion of Deposits: What It Is and Whence It Came," *Economic Review of the Federal Reserve Bank of Richmond*, March/April 1987, pp. 3–11.

simple money multiplier because depository institutions may hold excess reserves, ER, equal to some fraction of deposits and the public may withdraw cash as deposits expand to maintain a desired currency-to-deposits, C/D, ratio. Taking both effects into account the money multiplier is $(1 + c)/(r_D + e + c)$. $\Delta M = \Delta MB[(1 + c)/(r_D + e + c)]$.

The Fed's Control over the Money Supply

We could go on adding complications, but we hope you get the point. When the Fed engages in open market operations, reserves and the monetary base change.

Exhibit 16-12 ◆
Factors That Affect
the Money
Multiplier

An Increase in . . .	Caused by . . .	Results in . . .
c (the desired ratio of currency to checkable deposits)	The decision by the public to increase their holdings of currency relative to deposits	
e (the ratio of excess reserves held to checkable deposits)	The decision by depository institutions to hold more excess reserves	A decrease in the money multiplier and a decrease in the money supply
r_D (the required reserve ratio)	The decision by the Fed to increase the required reserve ratio	

A Decrease in . . .	Caused by . . .	Results in . . .
c	The decision by the public to decrease their holdings of currency relative to deposits	
e	The decision by depository institutions to hold fewer excess reserves	An increase in the money multiplier and an increase in the money supply
r_D	The decision by the Fed to decrease the required reserve ratio	

Compare Equations (16-5) and (16-14). In Equation (16-14) the multiplier is smaller and the Fed's control of the money supply is not so straightforward. The public, rather than the Fed, controls c and depository institutions determine e.

Since c and e vary over time, the multiplier linking the monetary base and the money supply is not perfectly stable or predictable, especially in the short run. And what does that mean? It means that even if the Fed can control the monetary base, it may find controlling the money supply somewhat more difficult, especially in the short run. Over a longer period, fluctuations in the c and e ratios and, thus, the multiplier tend to offset one another. That is, a large increase is offset by a large decrease in some other period. Consequently, the Fed's ability to predict the money multiplier and, thus, control the money supply improves considerably over a longer time period.

The multiplier model presented in this chapter yields many insights into the money supply process, the interaction among depository institutions, and the effect of Fed actions. You should recognize, however, that it is really a "sausage grinder" model—the Fed increases the monetary base, you crank the handle, and loans, deposits, and currency held by the public come out at the other end. This leaves out some of the points developed in earlier chapters. Nevertheless, when the Fed engages in open market operations or when discount loans change, the effects ripple through the entire financial system including loans, deposits, credit availability, currency held by the public, and the monetary aggregates.

Remember that depository institutions are firms, and like other firms they are interested in maximizing profits. Such an objective will lead firms to consider the costs and revenues associated with alternative courses of action, such as lending versus not lending or borrowing reserves versus not borrowing reserves. The multiplier model simplifies away such notions. In particular, the cost of deposits and the return on loans—in other words, interest rates—were ignored. It is simply assumed that depository institutions always have customers ready, willing, and able to borrow.

The model also neglects to consider the creative ways that banks and other depository institutions develop to get around reserve requirements if the banking system is demanding more reserves than what the Fed is willingly supplying to them. For example, the Eurodollar market is a prime example of a way that a bank could change a deposit liability with a corresponding reserve requirement into a nondeposit liability free of a reserve requirement. Credit extension could continue, even without the Fed feeding additional reserves.

Also remember the role of the discount window in affecting the supply of reserves and the monetary base. Acting as the lender of last resort through its discount facility, the Fed could supply depository institutions with all the reserves they demand. In reality, the Fed can discourage discount window borrowing by raising the discount rate and making it uncomfortable for depository institutions to borrow from the discount window. Borrowing, after all, is a privilege, not a right, and should be exercised only to cover temporary shortfalls of reserves, never to extend new loans.

In the next chapter, we look at the demand for money and credit. We also put demand and supply together to see how the public, the Fed, and the banking system jointly interact to determine a money market equilibrium. This chapter contains two appendixes. The first is on other factors that affect the monetary base. The second develops the relationship between changes in the monetary base and changes in M2 (the M2 multiplier).

Summary of Major Points

1. The Fed's open market operations affect the quantity of reserves in the banking system: when the Fed buys securities, reserves of depository institutions rise; when the Fed sells securities, reserves of depository institutions fall. Reserve assets in the form of vault cash or deposits at the Fed must be held equal to a certain percent of deposit liabilities. The amounts that must be held are required reserves; any amounts held greater than that are excess reserves. When the Fed makes a discount loan, reserves increase by the full amount of the loan. When a discount loan is paid off, reserves fall by the full amount of the loan.

2. For a depository institution, a deposit inflow increases total deposit liabilities and total reserve assets. Part of the reserves will be required and part will be excess. A depository institution can adjust to the inflow of reserves by expanding its loans and "creating" additional deposits equal to the amount of excess reserves that result from the deposit inflow.

3. As the proceeds of a loan are spent, the lending institution will lose reserves. However, another depository institution will gain reserves. The re-

serves lost by the lending institution will flow to another as the funds are spent. The new depository institution gains deposit liabilities and reserve assets. This depository institution, too, can expand loans and "create" additional deposits in the amount of the excess reserves that flow to it.

4. Following an initial injection of reserves, the total volume of reserves in the banking system does not change. However, the composition of reserves changes; as deposits expand at each stage, required reserves rise and excess reserves fall.

5. The total expansion of loans and deposits is a multiple of the initial injection of reserves into the banking system. In the simplest model ignoring excess reserves and currency, the multiplier is equal to $1/r_D$, that is, the reciprocal of the reserve requirement ratio. The simple multiplier is the multiple of the change in reserves by which deposits and loans change. Thus, the lower reserve requirements are, the larger is the multiplier. The higher reserve requirements are, the smaller is the multiplier.

6. The monetary base is reserves plus currency in the hands of the public. In a more elaborate model, excess reserves and currency drains are taken into account; the money multiplier is the multiple of the change in the monetary base by which the money supply will change. It is smaller than the simple multiplier and is influenced by the behavior of the Fed, deposit institutions, and the public. This means the money multiplier is not totally under the Fed's direct control and is not perfectly stable or predictable, especially in the short run.

7. Even if the Fed can control the monetary base, it may have difficulty controlling the money supply in the short run. Over a longer period (3–6 months), as the fluctuations in the multiplier tend to offset one another, the Fed's ability to predict the multiplier and thus control the money supply improves considerably.

Key Terms

Excess Reserves
Federal Reserve Float
Fractional Reserve Banking System
Loaned Up
Monetary Base
Money Multiplier
Offsetting Open Market
 Operations

Open Market Operations
Simple Money Multiplier
Repurchase Agreement
Required Reserves
Required Reserves Ratio (r_D)
Reverse Repurchase Agreement
Total Reserves

Review Questions

1. Briefly explain why the Fed does not have precise control over the money supply.

2. If the public chooses to hold no currency, does the Fed control the money supply? If depository institutions choose to always "loan up," does the Fed have precise control? If both of these situations occur, does the Fed have control?

3. In what form can a depository institution hold its required and excess reserves? What are the possible uses of currency outside the Fed?

4. If a depository institution has excess reserves, how much can it safely loan?

5. What are offsetting open market operations? When would the Fed use an offsetting open market purchase? an offsetting open market sale?

6. Explain how open market purchases and sales influence interest rates. To increase the money supply should the Fed use an open market purchase or sale?

7. Assume your parents live and do their banking on the East Coast while you attend school on the West Coast. Suppose you deposit the monthly check you receive from your parents into your checking account on the West Coast. How is the money supply affected? What is Federal Reserve float?

8. Comment on John D. Rockefeller's statement, "I believe that the power to make money is a gift from God." Do depository institutions really create money? Explain.

9. If the Fed lowers the discount rate, ceteris paribus, what will happen to the monetary base? Does the Fed have absolute control over the volume of discount loans?

10. If e increases given c and r_D, how can the Fed offset this change in e?

11. If discount loans increase, what happens to the monetary base?

12. What are the major assets and liabilities of the Fed? (Appendix 16A)

Analytical Questions

13. Assume the Fed sets the required reserve ratio equal to 10 percent. If the banking system has $20 million in required reserve assets, what is the amount of checkable deposits outstanding?

14. If $r_D = .25$, what is the simple money multiplier? If reserves increase by $100, how much do loans and deposits increase?

15. If $c = .35$, $r_D = .10$, and $e = .10$, what is the money multiplier? If a depository institution's excess reserves increase by $400, how much can it safely loan? Ceteris paribus, how much money will the banking system create?

16. If $c = .25$, $r_D = .10$, $e = .05$, and the Fed sells $100 in securities to the public, what happens to reserves, the monetary base, and the money supply after the change has worked its way through the entire banking system? Use T-accounts to explain your answer.

17. Using the same ratios as in question 16 and again using T-accounts, what happens to reserves, the monetary base, and the money supply if the Fed buys $100 in securities from the public?

18. In each of the following fictitious examples, tell whether the money multiplier will increase, decrease, or stay the same.

    a. Depositors become concerned about the safety of depository institutions, and there is no deposit insurance.
    b. Depository institutions do not see any creditworthy borrowers.
    c. The required reserve ratio is lowered by the Fed.

    d.   Larger amounts of currency are demanded by the public to use in the "underground economy."[11]

    e.   Depository institutions believe that overall default risk has decreased.

19.   Assume a depository institution has excess reserves of $100 and the required reserve ratio is 10 percent. What is the amount of checkable deposits at the depository institution resulting from new loans based on the excess reserves? Why is this amount different from the maximum amount of $1,000 in checkable deposits that can be generated by the banking system as a whole?

20.   Suppose you find $100 in the attic of an old house you have just purchased. You deposit the $100 in your checking account at Bank of America. Use a T-account to show what happens to the bank's assets and liabilities. What is the maximum amount Bank of America can loan from this deposit given a required reserve ratio of 10 percent?

21.   Suppose you withdraw $1,000 in cash from your Bank of America checking account for a weekend trip to Las Vegas. Use a T-account to show the impact on the bank's assets and liabilities. Given a required reserve rate of 10 percent, what is the impact on bank lending?

22.   Recall from Chapter 15 that narrow banking requires 100 percent reserve backing for checkable deposits. What is the money multiplier in this case?

23.   If M2 is $4 trillion and the monetary base is $500 billion, what is the M2 multiplier? (Appendix 16-B)

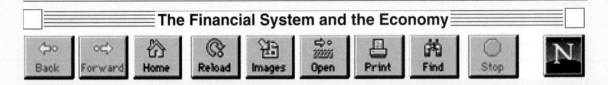

The Financial System and the Economy

1.   Access Fedpoint 32 from the New York Fed's internet site (http://www.ny.frb.org/pihome/fedpoint/fed32.html) and answer the following:

    a.   What are open market operations?

    b.   Who makes the decisions to conduct open market operations and who executes these operations?

2.   Access Fedpoint 18 (http://www.ny.frb.org/pihome/fedpoint/fed18.html) that pertains to the discount window of the Fed. What is this window? From this internet site, access the link to the discount rate (Fedpoint 30) and list some of its features.

3.   Access Fedpoint 15 (http://www.ny.frb.org/pihome/fedpoint/fed15.html) that describes federal funds. What role does the federal funds market play in the execution of monetary policy?

---

[11] The underground economy consists of activities including cash transactions to avoid taxes and illegal activities that are not reported in the National Income and Product Accounts and hence do not show up in gross domestic product (GDP) and other measures of economic activity.

Suggested Readings

For a description of the money creation process using T-accounts and a discussion of the factors affecting reserves, see *Modern Money Mechanics*, revised, published by the Federal Reserve Bank of Chicago, 1992.

For a look at how money is created and how it works in our economy with emphasis on the Fed and commercial banks, see *Money: Master or Servant?*, revised, published by the Federal Reserve Bank of New York, 1992. This is also available on the internet at (http://www.ny.frb.org/pihome/fedpoint/fed01.html).

Another valuable source for the material in this chapter is Tom Humphrey, "The Theory of Multiple Expansion of Deposits: What It Is and Whence It Came," *Economic Review* of the Federal Reserve Bank of Richmond, March/April 1987, pp. 3–11.

APPENDIX 16-A

Other Factors That Affect the Monetary Base

So far we have seen that the Fed, through open market operations, can change reserves and the monetary base. Although initially altering reserves, ultimately open market operations tend to change both reserves and currency held by the public. Although the Fed undoubtedly has enormous influence over reserve assets, other factors also affect them. The purpose of this appendix is to identify the various other factors that can affect reserves (and the monetary base) and to show how, despite these other factors, the Fed still exerts a great deal of influence over reserves, the monetary base, interest rates, and lending. The Fed monitors the net effect of movements in the other factors and uses open market operations to offset any net increase or decrease in the monetary base resulting from movements the Fed deems undesirable. Because the monetary base is the ultimate source of liquidity for the entire financial system, we frame our analysis in terms of it, rather than reserves, recognizing that reserves are merely the monetary base less currency in the hands of the public. Since the whole story flows from an examination and subsequently a rearrangement of the consolidated balance sheet for the entire Federal Reserve System—shown in Exhibit 16-13—let us begin by describing the major items shown there.

Gold and Special Drawing Rights (SDRs) Certificate Account

The gold and special drawing rights (SDRs) account reflects the Fed's holdings of international reserves. Changes in this account involve fairly complex transactions among the Fed, Treasury, International Monetary Fund, and foreign governments. Nevertheless, you need to simply recognize that acquisitions of gold, SDR, or foreign currency will raise this asset account for the Fed and raise international reserves in the United States. Conversely, sales of gold, SDRs, and foreign currency will lower this asset account for the Fed and lower international reserves.

Loans

As discussed in the body of Chapter 16, discount loans are made by the various Federal Reserve Banks to depository institutions via the discount facility. Any changes in discount loans also change the volume of reserves and the monetary base.

Account	Jan. 3, 1996
ASSETS	
1. Gold certificate account	11,050
2. Special drawing rights certificate account	10,168
3. Coin	412
Loans	
4. To depository institutions	299
5. Other	0
6. Acceptances held under repurchase agreements	0
Federal agency obligations	
7. Bought outright	2,634
8. Held under repurchase agreements	1,592
9. Total U.S. Treasury securities	390,494
10. Bought outright[1]	378,749
11. Bills	183,667
12. Notes	151,013
13. Bonds	44,069
14. Held under repurchase agreements	11,745
15. Total loans and securities	395,019
16. Items in process of collection	15,725
17. Bank premises	1,125
Other assets	
18. Denominated in foreign currencies[2]	21,102
19. All other[3]	10,756
20. Total assets	465,357
LIABILITIES	
21. Federal Reserve notes	401,236
22. Total deposits	43,525
23. Depository institutions	38,316
24. U.S. Treasury—General account	4,787
25. Foreign—Official accounts	165
26. Other	257
27. Deferred credit items	8,137
28. Other liabilities and accrued dividends[4]	4,328
29. Total liabilities	457,225
CAPITAL ACCOUNTS	
30. Capital paid in	3,976
31. Surplus	3,964
32. Other capital accounts	192
33. Total liabilities and capital accounts	465,357

[1] Includes securities loaned—fully guaranteed by U.S. Treasury securities pledged with Federal Reserve Banks—and excludes securities sold and scheduled to be bought back under matched sale-purchase transactions.
[2] Valued monthly at market exchange rates.
[3] Includes special investment account at the Federal Reserve Bank of Chicago in Treasury bills maturing within ninety days.
[4] Includes exchange-translation account reflecting the monthly revaluation at market exchange rates of foreign exchange commitments.

SOURCE: *Federal Reserve Bulletin*, April, 1996, p. A11.

Exhibit 16-13 ◆ Consolidated Balance Sheet of the Federal Reserve

Securities

Government securities are acquired or sold by the Fed through its open market operations. The Fed can buy or sell securities in either of two ways. First, it can buy or sell securities outright. An outright trade, other things being equal, represents a permanent addition or subtraction of reserves from the banking system. Second, the Fed can buy or sell through what are called **repurchase agreements** or reverse repurchase agreements. As discussed in Chapter 6, a repurchase agreement is an arrangement whereby the buyer, in this case the New York Fed, agrees to buy securities from the securities dealers with whom it regularly does business, and the dealers agree to repurchase the securities on a specific day in the near future.[a] Most repurchase agreements are for one day, but from time to time they run for more than one day. By using the repurchase agreement, the Fed can increase reserves temporarily, other things being equal, for a specific period of time.

Also as discussed in Chapter 6, nonbank dealers are highly leveraged firms that generally borrow funds to finance their holdings or inventories of government securities. A repurchase agreement, from the dealer's point of view, is a method by which the Fed finances the dealer's inventory of securities. Securities sold to the Fed under repurchase agreements will be available to the dealer to sell when the repurchase agreement matures.

The New York Fed can also execute the opposite of a repurchase agreement, called a **reverse repurchase agreement.** In this case, the Fed agrees to a temporary sale of securities to dealers, which is matched by an agreement to repurchase the securities on a specific day in the near future. Again, most reverse repurchase agreements are for one day. Such transactions temporarily reduce reserves in the banking system. You will see in a few moments how repurchase agreements can come in handy.

Float

As discussed in the chapter, float is an asset item arising from the accounting conventions underlying the Fed's check-clearing procedures. To review, suppose you live in New York and you send a check for $100 drawn on your account at a New York City bank or other depository institutions to your mother who lives in Chicago. She receives the check and deposits it in her bank account. Her bank credits her checkable deposit balance and sends the check to the Federal Reserve Bank of Chicago for collection. At this point, the check becomes a cash item in the process of collection for her bank. The Chicago Fed will send the check to the New York Fed, which will return the check to your bank. At that point, your deposit account will be debited. For the two commercial banks (yours and hers), the Fed will complete the transfer of funds arising from the check by increasing the deposit account of the Chicago bank at the Chicago Fed and lowering the deposit account of the New York bank at the New York Fed. Remember, deposit accounts at the Fed are part of reserves and the monetary base. When all these transactions are com-

Repurchase Agreement An arrangement whereby the New York Fed agrees to buy securities from the securities dealers with whom it regularly does business and the dealers agree to repurchase the securities on a specific day in the near future.

Reverse Repurchase Agreement An arrangement whereby the New York Fed agrees to sell securities to the securities dealers with whom it regularly does business and the Fed agrees to repurchase the securities on a specific day in the near future.

---

[a]The Fed's open market operations are executed with government security dealers (see Chapter 5), which the New York Fed has certified as fit to make markets in such securities and to conduct business with the Fed. There are about 30 such dealers; about half of them are departments of large commercial banks and the rest are nonbank dealers, such as Salomon Brothers and Merrill Lynch.

pleted, the total amount of deposits, reserves in the banking system, and the monetary base will, other things being equal, be as they were before. The difference will be in the location of the deposits and reserves (commercial bank deposits at Federal Reserve Banks). Chicago will have gained and New York will have lost deposits and reserves. Because of the time it takes to transfer the check physically, the Fed will typically credit the Chicago commercial bank's account at the Chicago Fed before it debits the account of the New York Bank at the New York Fed. This means that for a short time (usually a day), the deposit and reserves in question appear on the balance sheets of both banks. As a result, the Fed is, in effect, providing credit to the banking system through this procedure.[b] As electronic technology is applied to the check-clearing process, we would expect the volume of float to fall.[c]

Now that we have sorted out the major asset accounts, let us briefly examine the major liability and net worth entries.

Federal Reserve Notes

Federal Reserve notes are the paper money in circulation. These notes constitute about 90 percent of the currency in circulation in our economy. The other 10 percent of total currency in circulation consists mainly of coins minted by the Treasury. Federal Reserve notes may be either currency in the hands of the public or vault cash. If held as vault cash, they are part of reserves.

Bank Deposits

As we have already learned, banks may hold reserves in the form of vault cash or in the form of deposits at the Fed. Such deposits, which account for the majority of bank reserves, are assets for the institutions and liabilities for the Fed. These deposit balances are held at the banks' district Reserve Bank, and they rise or fall as the Fed credits or debits banks' balances.

Deposits of the U.S. Treasury

Deposits of the U.S. Treasury are the Treasury's money account. The Treasury pays its bills by writing checks on its deposit balance at the Fed. When this happens, Treasury deposits decline. If tax receipts rise (as they do around major tax dates, such as April 15) or the Treasury issues and receives payment for securities to finance a deficit, the Treasury's deposits at the Fed will rise. The level of Treasury deposits rises and falls with the ebb and flow of government receipts and expenditures.

---

[b]All this is analogous to the way in which individuals use "float." Many of us write checks and send them off to pay bills and so forth, even though at that specific moment we do not have enough funds in our account to cover the check. Knowing that it takes time for the check to "clear," we plan to add funds to our accounts in time to cover the check.

[c]On the Fed's balance sheet, float is actually the difference between cash items in the process of collection (an asset) and deferred-availability cash items (a liability). The asset item always exceeds the liability item because the Fed credits the deposit (reserve) account of the bank sending a check for collection to the Fed before it debits the deposit (reserve) account of the bank on which the check is drawn.

The Monetary Base Equation

With all the relevant items defined, we can develop a monetary base equation, which states the monetary base according to the factors that increase or decrease it. As previously stated, we frame the analysis in terms of the monetary base because the monetary base is the foundation of liquidity for the economy. By subtracting currency held by the public from each side of the equation, we could express the equation in terms of reserves instead of the monetary base. The first thing to notice about Exhibit 16-13 is that the largest asset item is the securities account and the largest liability accounts are Fed notes and deposits (reserves) of depository institutions. The second thing to notice is that, although the values of all items on the balance sheet change somewhat over time, the largest and therefore the most significant changes occur in the largest items.

To bring together all the key items that affect the monetary base and thus derive the monetary base equation, we can rearrange the Fed's balance sheet. We know that total assets, TA, equal total liabilities and capital, TL.

$$(16A\text{-}1) \qquad\qquad TA = TL$$

On the liability side of the Fed's balance sheet, we have currency issued by the Fed, C^*, Treasury Deposits, TD, depository institution deposits at the Fed, DF, and all other liabilities and capital, OL.

$$(16A\text{-}2) \qquad\qquad TL = C^* + TD + DF + OL$$

Note that in this case, C^* includes both currency in the hands of the public plus vault cash. Because total reserves, TR, include vault cash, VC, plus deposits at the Fed, DF, while C is currency in the hands of the public, if we add DF to C^*, we get the monetary base, $TR + C$. Therefore, substituting $TR + C$ into Equation (16A-2) for $DF + C^*$, we get

$$(16A\text{-}3) \qquad\qquad TL = TR + C + TD + OL$$

Rearranging terms, we can express the monetary base, reserves, TR, plus currency in the hands of the public, in terms of the other items.

$$(16A\text{-}4) \qquad\qquad \begin{aligned} MB &= TR + C \\ &= TL - TD - OL \end{aligned}$$

Using Equation (16A-1), we can rewrite Equation (16A-4) substituting TA for TL:

$$(16A\text{-}5) \qquad\qquad \begin{aligned} MB &= R + C \\ &= TA - TD - OL \end{aligned}$$

Total assets are equal to the gold and SDR account, reflecting international reserve holdings, IR, plus loans, L, plus government securities held, GS, plus float, F, plus other assets, OA.

$$(16A\text{-}6) \qquad\qquad TA = IR + L + GS + F + OA$$

The final step is to substitute Equation (16A-6) into Equation (16A-5), which gives us the monetary base equation:

(16A-7) $$MB = TR + C$$
$$= IR + L + GS + F + OA - TD - OL$$

Increases in any of the items with a plus sign before them will raise the monetary base (and most likely reserves), while increases in any of the items with a minus sign before them will lower the monetary base. Note that all the items with a plus sign are from the asset side of the Fed's balance sheet, while the items with minus signs are from the liability side of the Fed's balance sheet.[d]

---

[d] The plus items are sometimes called *factors supplying reserves* or *sources of reserves,* while the minus items are called *factors absorbing reserves* or *uses of reserves.* A table in the *Federal Reserve Bulletin* reports the data in this fashion.

APPENDIX 16-B

The M2 Multiplier

In the body of the chapter, we developed the money multiplier to calculate a change in the monetary base. In reality, since we were considering money to be currency, C, plus deposits, D, we were developing the multiplier for M1.* The M1 multiplier tells us how much M1 will increase when there is an increase in the monetary base; M1 will increase by the multiplier times the change in the monetary base.

In carrying out monetary policy, the Fed may be more interested in the behavior of M2 or another aggregate than in the behavior of M1. In this appendix we develop the M2 multiplier, which tells us how much M2 will increase when the Fed increases the monetary base. In other words, the M2 will increase by the M2 multiplier times the change in the monetary base. As we saw in Chapter 2, M2 is:

$$
\left.
\begin{array}{l}
\text{Currency in the Hands of the Public } (C) \\
\text{Checkable Deposits } (D) \\
\text{Small Savings and Time Deposits } (D^*) \\
\text{Overnight Repurchase Agreements} \\
\text{Overnight Eurodollars} \\
\text{Money Market Deposit Accounts} \\
\text{Individual Money Market Mutual Funds}
\end{array}
\right\} = MI
$$

To simplify, we will consolidate the last four items together as money market instruments, MI. Equation (16B-1) illustrates this relationship.

(16B-1) $$ M2 = C + D + D^* + MI $$

We also assume that spending units have desired D^*/D and MI/D ratios, just as they had a desired C/D ratio. The M2 multiplier is the ratio of M2 to the monetary base, MB. With the use of Equations (16-2), (16-11), and (16B-1), we can derive the M2 multiplier:

(16B-2) $$ M2/MB = (C + D + D^* + MI)/(RR + ER + C) $$

To express this multiplier in notation that is similar to the M1 multiplier developed in the chapter, we multiply Equation (16B-2) by $(1/D)/(1/D)$, which is equal to 1. The result is derived in Equation (16B-3).

---

*For simplicity, we are following our convention of ignoring traveler's checks.

$$M2/MB = (C/D + D/D + D^*/D + MI/D)/(RR/D + ER/D + C/D)$$
$$\text{(16B-3)} \quad = (c + 1 + D^*/D + MI/D)/(r_D + e + c)$$

Rearranging the terms yields Equation (16B-4).

$$\text{(16B–4)} \quad M2/MB = (1 + c + D^*/D + MI/D)/(r_D + e + c)$$

Multiplying both sides of Equation (16B-4) by the monetary base and expressing the result in terms of changes yields:

$$\text{(16B-5)} \quad \Delta M2 = [(1 + c + D^*/D + MI/D)/(r_D + e + c)] \, \Delta MB$$

Equation (16B-5) defines the relationship between changes in the monetary base and changes in M2. Thus, the M2 multiplier is equal to $(1 + c + D^*/D + MI/D)/(r_D + e + c)$. It is similar to the M1 multiplier except that the numerator is larger by the magnitude $D^*/D + MI/D$. Therefore, the M2 multiplier is larger than the M1 multiplier, which was also apparent because M2 is larger than M1. As can be seen from Equation (16B-5), the M2 multiplier is positively related to both the D^*/D and MI/D ratios. Like the M1 multiplier, the M2 multiplier is inversely related to the required reserve ratio, r_D, the currency-deposit ratio, c, and the excess reserve ratio, e.

17

The Demand for Real Money Balances and Market Equilibrium

Money is like muck—not good unless it be spread.
—Francis Bacon—

Learning Objectives

After reading this chapter, you should know:

◆ Why the demand for money is really a demand for real money balances

◆ What transactions and precautionary demand for real balances are

◆ How the demand for real balances is related to the level of real income and the interest rate

◆ Other determinants of the demand for real money balances

◆ How changes in the demand and/or supply of real balances affect the market equilibrium and the interest rate

◆ The theories of monetarism and Keynes' speculative demand for money

Where Is All the Money?

During 1995, M1 averaged $1,123 billion. Of this, roughly $372.5 billion was currency and the remainder, checkable deposits. This money was used to support a gross domestic product (GDP) of $7,247.7 billion, resulting in a velocity of 6.45. Given that there were about 97 million households in this country at that time, the average holding of M1 was $11,577 per household while the average holding of currency was $3,840 per household.

If you are from an "average" household, you probably find these figures relatively high. The authors and the people we know who are mostly professors, students, government bureaucrats, and other professionals just don't seem to hold that much in money balances. Although our evidence is hardly scientific, we have been asking our students, colleagues, and friends for many years and get answers that leave us in a quandary. So, you may wonder, where is all this money?

Possibly a little investigation can shed some light on the situation. Corporations, as we know, are forbidden by law to hold interest-earning checkable deposits. We can speculate that a large portion of outstanding demand deposits, which totaled $389.1 billion in 1995, are held by corporations. We also know that other checkable deposits, which totaled $352.5 billion in 1995, must be held by households. Thus, the average household balance held in interest-earning checking accounts amounted to $3,634. This certainly seems like a more realistic figure.

Although we have given a "somewhat reasonable" explanation of where outstanding checkable deposits are, we still have not resolved the question of where the large outstanding holdings of currency are located. Most businesses (particularly the corner grocer, dry cleaner, etc.) need some currency. Additionally, estimates are that more than 50 percent, and perhaps as much as 60 percent of U.S. currency in circulation, is held outside the United States, while some currency, particularly coin, is held by collectors.[1] Moreover, many speculate that large amounts of currency are needed to support the underground economy that deals in illegal activities such as drug trafficking. In addition, otherwise legal activities are conducted with currency in order to evade taxes, which is illegal. However, the mystery remains as to why the amount of currency outstanding per household has been growing consistently since 1960.

In this chapter, we discuss the determinants of how much money households and firms want to hold at a given moment in time. Additionally, we analyze equilibrium in the market for money balances. Although the enigma presented in the preceding paragraphs may be difficult to resolve conclusively, we do explain a lot about the demand for money and equilibrium in the money market.

The Demand for Real Money Balances

Wealth may be held in either real assets, such as houses, gems, and rare oil paintings, or in financial assets, such as stocks, bonds, mutual funds,

---

[1] "New Currency Aims to Counter Counterfeiters," *Los Angeles Times,* July 14, 1994.

and money. From this perspective, money is viewed as just one of many real or financial assets in which households may hold their wealth. When relative rates of return on the various assets change, households adjust their portfolios toward those real or financial assets that offer a relatively higher return.[2] Therefore, as the returns on some assets rise, ceteris paribus, households will hold relatively more in those assets (either real or financial) that yield a higher return and less in the assets whose relative yield has decreased. Money, however, is exceptional among financial assets because it alone functions as a means of payment (medium of exchange), as well as a store of value. Therefore, we single money out for special attention.[3]

The demand for money is actually a demand for **real money balances** or the quantity of money expressed in real terms. Real money balances, or real balances for short, are adjusted for changes in purchasing power. We can define a real money balance as the nominal money supply, M, divided by the overall price level, P, as in Equation (17-1).

Real Money Balances The quantity of money expressed in real terms; the nominal money supply, M, divided by overall price level, P, or M/P.

(17-1) $$\text{Real Money Balances} = M/P$$

P is a price index that measures changes in the overall price level. Examples of price indexes include the consumer price index (CPI) or the producer price index (PPI) introduced in Chapter 3.

To see why the demand for money is really a demand for real balances, consider the following example. What would happen if all prices including input prices and output prices quadrupled tomorrow? In nominal terms, everything would cost four times as much, but households and firms would be making four times as much money. Households and firms would demand to hold four times as much nominal money to make the same real transactions as before. The demand for nominal money balances would quadruple. Referring back to Equation 17-1, the numerator and the denominator both increase by a factor of four, leaving the demand for real balances unchanged ($M'/P' = 4M/4P = M/P$).

Note that we are ignoring the effect of price changes on financial assets and liabilities. When the overall price level rises, deficit spending units (DSUs) pay back their debts with "cheap" dollars while the surplus spending units (SSUs) receive back less in real terms than what they lent. Since for every financial liability there is a corresponding financial asset, the benefit to the DSU that owes the financial liability offsets the loss of the SSU that owns the financial asset.

Since the demand for money is a demand for real money balances, nominal money demand is proportional to the overall level of prices. If the price level increases by 10 percent, the nominal demand for money increases by 10 percent and the demand for real balances remains unchanged. Likewise, if the price level decreases by 10 percent, nominal demand decreases by 10 percent and the demand for real balances remains unchanged.[4] Sometimes

---

[2] The yield or return on real estate includes the value of the stream of services the assets provide plus any capital gain.

[3] The value of money itself is measured in terms of the unit of account, which is an abstract measure of the exchange value. Another unique feature of money is that it has a fixed price in terms of the unit of account. For example, the value of a NOW account (money) is measured in dollars, which is the unit of account.

[4] In this example, we are considering a one-time increase in the price level as opposed to inflation, which is a sustained increase in the price level. As we shall see, changes in inflation affect the demand for money.

we use the expression *the demand for money* for short to mean the demand for real money balances or just real balances. But don't be confused; the demand for money is always a demand for real balances because of the proportionality between nominal money demand and the overall price level. Having established this relationship, we turn our attention to the factors that motivate households and firms to hold real money balances.[5]

Household Demand for Real Money Balances

Households have basically two motives behind their demand to hold real money balances. First, households need money to consummate transactions. Someone who purchases real assets, nondurable goods and services, or financial assets must supply in exchange a means of payment that is generally acceptable to the seller. Money is the means of payment. Since financial transactions occur frequently (probably several times a day) and income is typically received less frequently (say weekly or monthly), households hold an inventory of real balances to get from one income-receiving period to the next. We call this first motive for holding real money balances the **transactions motive.**

Transactions Motive A motive for holding money based on the need to make payments.

Exhibit 17-1 illustrates the transactions motive for holding real money balances by showing a typical relationship between income receipts, financial

---

[5] Chapter 19 contains a brief discussion of the demand for Treasury deposit balances used for transactions by the government.

Exhibit 17-1 ◆
Real Money
Holdings by a
Typical Household

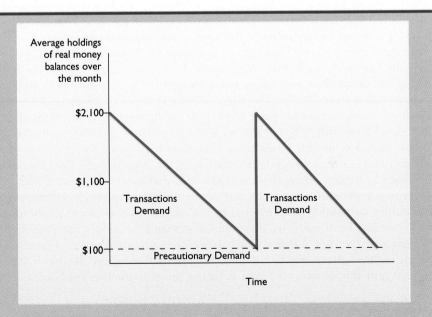

Assume that the typical household receives an income of $2,000 once each month and engages in transactions that consist of expenditures on goods and services, more or less on a continual basis. Over time, the household is also assumed to maintain a small amount of real money balances as a precaution against unforeseen contingencies. The demand for real money balances is the average amount of money balances held over the month.

transactions, and holdings of real money balances. The peaks in the holdings of real balances each month represent paydays, and the gradual decline in the holdings of real balances between paydays reflects spending on goods and services and other transactions. Note the exhibit shows that the "typical" household will have some real money balances left over at the end of each month. This reflects the second motive for holding real money balances, the **precautionary motive.** Households will try to hold some real money balances—the most liquid asset there is—as a precaution against unforeseen developments.

The transactions and precautionary motives for holding an inventory of real money balances are analogous to the factors that give rise to the holding of an inventory of food by households. In general, it is costly and inconvenient to run to the store every time we want to eat. Accordingly, the typical household buys groceries once a week and then uses them several times a day throughout the week. As in Exhibit 17-1, the inventory of food runs down and is replenished at the next shopping trip. Since we don't like an empty refrigerator, especially when guests drop in unexpectedly, most of us try to keep some food on hand as a precaution.[6]

In addition to fulfilling the transactions and precautionary motives, we can think of real money balances as yielding a stream of services to households and, in the case of interest-earning checkable deposits, some interest income. These are the **benefits of holding real money balances.** The stream of services that real balances yield are defined by the time and distress saved by having money on hand for immediate use. The value or benefits of such services can be seen by examining what would happen if a household did not hold an inventory of real money balances, instead holding all its financial assets in the form of bonds. This would mean that when the household wanted to purchase goods or to make a payment, it would have to first sell bonds and acquire money. More specifically, the household would have to call a brokerage firm, pay a brokerage fee, and wait for the money to actually arrive.[7] The benefits of holding real money balances are both monetary (saving the brokerage fee and the interest earned on checkable deposits) and nonmonetary (the time and inconvenience of waiting for the money if one wants it and it is not there).

The **cost of holding real money balances** is the additional foregone interest that holding nonmonetary financial assets, such as stocks or bonds, would have yielded. When money does pay interest, as in the case of interest-earning checkable balances, the interest rate yield on real money balances is generally less than what could be earned on other less liquid financial assets. These

Precautionary Motive A motive for holding money based on a precaution against unforeseen developments.

Benefits of Holding Real Money Balances The stream of services that real balances yield defined as the time and distress saved by having money on hand for immediate use.

Costs of Holding Real Money Balances The additional foregone interest that holding nonmonetary financial assets would have yielded.

---

[6] As for the role of risk, note that we generally choose not to store food with a tendency to spoil quickly because when we need it, the food might not be usable. The poorer and more susceptible our refrigeration system is to breakdowns, the greater this risk. Likewise, the greater the probability of inflation, the greater is the risk that money held for transactions and precaution will lose value. The more prone the economy is to bouts of inflation, the greater this risk and the fewer money balances we will hold. In such a case, people might store value in the form of real assets to hedge the risk of inflation.

[7] The household could also hold savings or time deposits at banks or other financial intermediaries. In the case of savings accounts, the household would have to make a trip to the bank to remove the funds, or transfer the funds over the phone or from a home computer. The household would incur record keeping, time, and other transactions costs. In the case of time deposits, the same costs would be incurred and, in addition, the depositor could experience a penalty for removing the deposit before its maturity date.

other assets must pay a higher return, ceteris paribus, to compensate for the loss in liquidity and greater risk.[8]

But how much money should a household *hold* given both the benefits and costs to holding real money balances? From an economist's point of view, the household should increase its holdings of real money balances as long as the benefits of doing so outweigh the costs. With regard to the transactions demand for real balances by households, when we apply the benefits-greater-than-costs rule, two conclusions follow:

1. Ceteris paribus, the interest rate on nonmonetary assets and the quantity demanded of real money balances are inversely related; that is, as the interest rate increases, quantity demanded decreases, and vice versa. The result follows from the fact that if the interest rate on nonmonetary assets increases, the opportunity cost of holding real money balances increases, and households will demand to hold less.
2. Ceteris paribus, the brokerage fee (the cost of transferring from nonmonetary to monetary assets) and the quantity demanded of real money balances are directly related. This result follows from the fact that if the brokerage fee increases, the household will make fewer calls to the broker and hence hold a larger quantity of real money balances.

We leave the mechanics of demonstrating this particular result to the appendix. Although the analysis is quite cumbersome, our abstract rules translate into behavior in the real world fairly easily. We now turn to the demand for real money balances by business firms.

A Firm's Demand for Real Money Balances

Production, investment spending, and sales generate a variety of financial transactions. Over the past 25 years, universities have graduated large numbers of capable graduates trained in the intricacies of money and finance. In addition, the use of new technologies—computers, spreadsheet software, telecommunications—have become routine necessities for firms. Cash management, in particular, and balance sheet management, more generally, have become highly sophisticated. Given the growth of foreign activity by U.S. firms, international financial transactions have expanded in size and importance. Nevertheless, the basic factors determining business holdings of real money balances can still be viewed in fairly straightforward terms.

Firms, like households, want (demand) real balances to consummate transactions. Examples of such transactions are the regular, expected payments for factor services and tax payments. The payments to the factors include such things as wages, salaries, and rent. In addition, firms need money for transactions that cannot be perfectly anticipated. The timing of some transactions may be uncertain. A firm may not know when a certain delivery will be made or when it will have to pay for that delivery. Transactions balances are used

---

[8] Indeed, prior to the Depository Institutions Deregulation and Monetary Control Act of 1980 (DIDMCA), checkable balances paid no interest. Since that time, interest is allowed on nonbusiness checking accounts, but it is less than the market rate of interest on other less liquid assets.

to make payments for normal day-to-day operations, even though the exact time of these payments may be difficult to predict.

Some transactions may be totally unexpected such as a bill for repairing an equipment breakdown or expenses related to an unforeseen strike. Expenses, whether anticipated or not, must be paid. As a result, firms will need some money and/or liquid assets such as Treasury bills as a precaution against these contingencies. Like households, firms have both transactions and precautionary motives for demanding real money balances.

Firms experience two flows of real money balances: expenditures that generate outflows of funds and receipts that generate inflows of funds. The basic problem is that these flows are not synchronized. Thus, when expenditures exceed receipts, firms must either have money on hand or have immediate access to it to meet their financial obligations. Of course, if receipts exceed expenditures, the firm's financial manager must decide how much of the surplus to hold as real money balances and how much should be used to acquire interest-bearing financial assets, such as Treasury bills and certificates of deposit (CDs).

The points just made are fairly obvious. But what determines the amount of real money balances firms should hold? In essence, the basic framework is similar to that employed by households in deciding the size of real money balances to hold. That is, firms analyze the benefits and costs of holding real money balances.

For firms, the benefits of holding real money balances are the stream of services that money balances provide. Being able to make payments when they are due is a definite plus and a necessity for a firm to retain its business reputation and integrity.[9] Indeed, long-run survival often depends on making payments in a timely fashion. The opportunity cost of holding real money balances is the foregone interest related to retaining money in lieu of less liquid, higher earning assets. Real money balances held by firms (currency and demand deposits) do not, as of this writing, earn explicit interest. In any case, the relative interest rate differential between money and nonmonetary assets is the opportunity cost.

In deciding the optimum amount of money balances to hold, the cash manager will want to minimize money holdings, subject to the constraint of having enough money on hand or access to it when it is needed. A cash manager will also attempt to maximize the return earned on the other financial assets held in place of money. In reality, the firm, like households, will hold additional real money balances only if the benefits of doing so are greater than the costs, as depicted in Exhibit 17-2. We turn now to a discussion of interest rates, income, and real money balances.

RECAP

The demand for money is a demand for real money balances (M/P). Real money balances are adjusted for changes in purchasing power. Households demand real money balances to fulfill the transactions and precautionary

---

[9] Some firms may also be able to take a discount if they pay within a certain time period. The discount often amounts to 1–2 percent of the invoice. This translates into an annual return of 12–24 percent on the funds used to make the payment.

Exhibit 17-2 ◆
How Households
and Firms Decide
What Amount of
Real Balances to
Hold

The benefits of holding real money balances are:

◆ To fulfill a stream of services related to having money available when needed, including not having to pay a brokerage fee to get money and not having to wait to get money
◆ To be able to make payments when due

The costs of holding real money balances are:

◆ The foregone interest that the nonmonetary balances of households and firms would have earned

Decision Rule:

◆ Hold real money balances as long as the benefits are greater than the costs

motives. The benefit of holding money balances is the stream of services that having money on hand provides. The cost is the foregone interest that holding nonmonetary financial assets would have yielded. Firms demand real balances to make transactions because inflows and outflows are not perfectly synchronized. The firm will minimize its holdings of money subject to the constraint of having money balances available when needed. Both households and firms will demand money balances as long as the benefits are greater than the costs.

The Interest Rate, Real Income, and Real Money Balances

The opportunity cost of holding currency or checkable deposits is the foregone interest that one gives up when money balances are held. Currency and demand deposits earn no interest while other checkable deposits earn less than differentiated liquid financial assets. As the interest rate increases, ceteris paribus, the opportunity cost also increases.[10] Likewise, if rates fall, ceteris paribus, the opportunity cost falls.

At higher interest rates, spending units substitute into other less liquid assets that yield a higher return.[11] In other words, at higher interest rates,

---

[10] In this discussion, following our analysis in Chapter 8, we are referring to "the interest rate" as representative of the overall level of interest rates, assuming that rates move up and down together depending on risk, liquidity, maturity, and tax treatment.

[11] Even if interest rates on checkable deposits increase by the same percentage amount as on other market instruments, the opportunity cost of holding funds in checkable deposits increases. For example, assume the Treasury bill rate is 5 percent and the rate on checkable deposits, 2 percent. If rates rise by 10 percent, the Treasury bill rate rises to 5.5 percent and the rate on checkable deposits to 2.2 percent. After the increase, the opportunity cost of holding checkable deposits, assuming that T-bills are the next best alternative, is 3.3 percent (5.5 percent less 2.2 percent). Before the increase, the opportunity cost is 3 percent (5 percent less 2 percent).

households and firms will conserve on the quantity of real money balances they hold because there is a greater reward for doing so. J.P. (our friend from Chapter 4) is not concerned about the idle $2,000 sitting in his checking account earning 2 percent if the rate on money market deposit accounts is 3 percent. However, if the rate on money market deposit accounts goes up to 10 percent while the rate on checkable deposits only increases to 3 percent, then he will try to get by with holding a smaller average balance in his checking account.

In light of the preceding discussion, we can see the inverse relationship between the quantity demanded of real money balances and the interest rate, ceteris paribus. This relationship is summarized in Equation (17-2). The negative sign over the interest rate specifies the inverse or negative relationship between the interest rate and the quantity demanded.

(17-2)   Quantity Demanded of Real Money Balances = f(Interest Rate)

In this analysis, we are following the convention of defining the quantity demanded as the amount of real balances that will be demanded as a function of a *specific* interest rate. If the interest rate increases, ceteris paribus, the quantity demanded of real money balances decreases, and vice versa. If any other factor affecting demand changes, the demand for real balances changes.[12] The demand for real balances is the quantity demanded at *every* interest rate.

Now would be a good time to look at Exhibits 17-3 and 17-4. Exhibit 17-3 is a demand curve showing an inverse relationship between "the interest rate" and the quantity demanded of real money balances. Real money balances are

---

[12] In this section, we shall see that income is one of these "other factors" that will cause demand to change. In the next section, we look at additional factors.

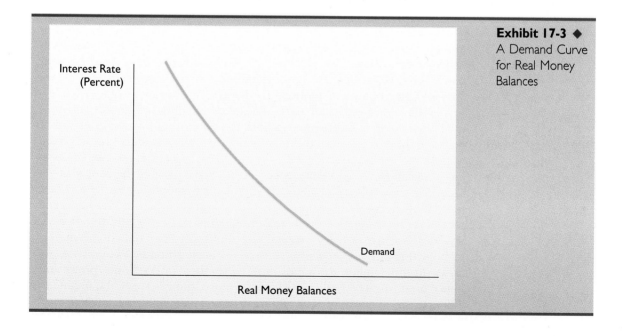

Exhibit 17-3 ◆
A Demand Curve for Real Money Balances

Exhibit 17-4 ◆
Keynes' Speculative Demand for Money

Liquidity Preference A theory of the demand for money developed by John Maynard Keynes that results in an inverse relationship between the quantity of money demanded and the interest rate.

Speculative Demand for Money The theory that individuals will demand to hold money when interest rates are low (bond prices high) to avoid capital losses when interest rates rise and to hold bonds when interest rates are high (bond prices low) to capture capital gains when interest rates fall.

So far, we have considered the quantity demanded of money to be inversely related to the interest rate, ceteris paribus, because of the fact that money earns a lower rate of interest than nonmonetary financial assets. As the interest rate increases, the opportunity cost of holding money increases, and vice versa. Money is one of many financial assets that an individual may hold. As interest rates change, so do the relative rewards of holding various financial and real assets. Individuals adjust their portfolios to reflect these changes.

But, we would be remiss here if we did not introduce you to another theory that also results in an inverse relationship between the quantity demanded of money and the interest rate, ceteris paribus. This theory is known as **liquidity preference.** It involves the **speculative demand for money** and is attributable to John Maynard Keynes, perhaps the most influential economist of the twentieth century.

To simplify, Keynes assumed that individuals can hold their wealth in either bonds or money. Bonds earn the market rate of interest while money earns no interest or less than the market rate of interest. Moreover, the price of bonds fluctuates when interest rates change. As we saw in Chapter 7, when interest rates rise, bond prices fall and vice versa. Hence, when interest rates fall, individuals holding bonds experience capital gains and, when rates rise, individuals holding bonds experience capital losses. Consequently, from this analysis, Keynes concluded that if individuals expect interest rates to rise in the future, they are hesitant to buy bonds today because if their expectations are fulfilled, that is, if interest rates do rise, these individuals will experience capital losses. Hence they prefer to hold money instead of bonds if they expect interest rates to rise. Likewise, if individuals expect interest rates to fall, individuals prefer to buy bonds today to experience a capital gain if interest rates do indeed fall.

The caveat of the theory is that if interest rates are high, more and more individuals will come to believe that rates will be going down in the future and will therefore prefer to buy bonds today in hopes of a capital gain when interest rates do fall. Consequently, because individuals hold either bonds or money, when interest rates are high, the quantity demanded of money will be low. If interest rates are low, more and more individuals will believe rates will be rising in the future and will prefer to avoid holding bonds today out of fear of future capital losses. Hence when interest rates are low, ceteris paribus, the quantity demanded of money will be high.

Keynes added one final twist. When interest rates are abnormally low, virtually everyone could come to hold the belief that interest rates would be going up in the future. If this were the case, all individuals would prefer to hold money balances instead of bonds. This has a theoretically interesting implication for monetary policy. If the Fed increases the supply of reserves to the banking system and the money supply in turn increases, individuals normally take the increase in money and would choose to use part of it to buy bonds, thus increasing the demand for bonds. In this case, however, because of fear of capital losses, individuals would choose merely to hold the increase in money instead of buying bonds. Without the increase in the demand for bonds pushing up their prices, bonds prices and hence interest rates would not change. Hence, the Fed would be unable to increase the quantity of real output demanded by lowering interest rates and increasing interest sensitive spending. When the Fed increased the money supply, individuals would merely hold the increase as "idle" money balances. The economy would be flooded with liquidity and hence would be in what is known as a **liquidity trap.**

Although economists can describe a liquidity trap, it is not known if the economy has ever actually been in one. (Keynes couldn't find one.) However, this possibility was one reason Keynes preferred an active fiscal policy, changing government spending or taxes, to a policy that worked solely through changing interest rates. If the economy were in a recession and liquidity trap, monetary policy would be unable to lower interest rates and stimulate interest-sensitive demand. To see why, take a look at the following graph.

Liquidity Trap When interest rates are very low (bond prices are very high), the demand for money becomes perfectly horizontal and the economy is in a liquidity trap; the Fed is unable to lower interest rates by increasing the supply of money.

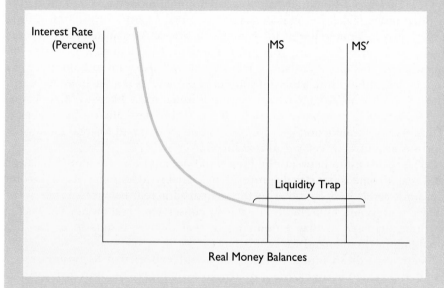

Note that "the interest rate," which measures the overall level of rates, is measured on the vertical axis. In a liquidity trap, the demand for real money balances curve becomes horizontal.

Later economists questioned the validity of Keynes' speculative demand for money altogether. They point out that the theory implies that when interest rates are low, individuals prefer to hold money as opposed to bonds, waiting to buy until interest rates are up and bond prices down. The problem is that the theory just did not seem realistic for the average person. How many "average people" do you know who hold money, say in their checking account, in lieu of bonds when interest rates are low because they fear a capital loss?* Apparently, many economists did not feel they knew any. The point became somewhat moot, because other economists showed that, ceteris paribus, there would still be an inverse relationship between the quantity demanded of money and the interest rate, if money is viewed as one of many financial assets in which wealth can be held.

*Keynes was also writing in the Great Depression, when a liquidity trap seemed particularly unlikely. If the Fed was successful in increasing the money supply, how plausible is it that people would just hold this money and not spend it in the middle of a depression?

measured on the horizontal axis while the interest rate is measured on the vertical axis. If the interest rate changes, ceteris paribus, we move along the demand curve, as the quantity demanded of real money balances changes. Note that the demand curve is drawn holding other factors, including the price level, constant. Exhibit 17-4 discusses an alternative theory of why the quantity of real money balances demanded and the interest rate are inversely related. This historically significant theory is Keynes' theory of liquidity preference.

So far, we have considered the demand for real money balances for a given income. Now we want to look at what will happen to demand if income changes. We begin with households. We first saw in Chapter 3 that the amount of nominal money that a household demands at a point in time is directly related to its income. We can now extend that analysis to real money balances by recalling that real money balances are nominal money balances divided by a price index. Likewise, **real income** is nominal income divided by a price index. It is income adjusted for changes in prices. As real income increases, households on average are going to make more transactions and, hence, demand more real money balances. Households will also want to hold more real money balances to fulfill the precautionary motive. As real income decreases, the reverse is true. A high-income person is much more likely to carry around a few $100 bills in a purse or wallet for a "rainy day" than a poor person. Thus, like the transactions motive, precautionary demand for real money balances is also directly related to real income.

The relationship between the household demand for real money balances and real income is not strictly proportional. That is, a doubling of real income does not result in a doubling in the demand for real balances. From an intuitive standpoint, households are able to conserve on real money balances as income increases so that a doubling of real income results in a less than doubling in the demand for real balances.[13]

With regards to business firms, we would expect that as businesses expanded production and sales, transactions would increase, thus giving rise to increased demand for real money balances. Taking our analysis a step further, as real output expands and contracts, real income, in the aggregate, moves in the same direction. That is, if production and sales increase, real income also increases while if production and sales decrease, real income decreases. Hence, the demand for real balances by firms is directly related to real income, as in the case of household demand.

This direct relationship between real aggregate income and the demand for real money balances by business firms appears to be borne out by the data. However, the data also strongly suggest business money holdings have generally risen less than might have been expected as output and sales rose. Can you guess why? The most important reason is that during the 1970s and 1980s interest rates generally trended up. Higher interest rates increased the opportunity costs of holding money balances and encouraged firms, like households, to economize on their cash positions. Among the innovations firms developed, with the aid of their banks, were better management of inflows and outflows resulting in better synchronization of the flows and more certainty about the timing of cash payments. As a result, a portion of the funds

Real Income Nominal income divided by a price index.

---

[13] Note that for prices, a doubling of prices led to a doubling in the demand for nominal money and no change in the demand for real money balances.

that normally would have been held as money balances were used to expand operations, acquire other financial assets, pay off existing debts, and so forth. When interest rates fell in the 1990s, the innovations that firms had developed in response to the high interest environment of the 1970s and 1980s did not disappear. Rather, firms continued to use these techniques to exploit even minute price differentials.

The desired accumulation of real money balances for both households and business firms is summarized in Equation (17-3). The plus sign over real income signifies the direct or positive relationship between real income and demand.

(17-3)   Demand for Real Money Balances = $f(\overset{+}{\text{Real Income}})$

Now would be a good time to look at Exhibit 17-5, which is a graph of various demand curves for real money balances. Real money balances are measured on the horizontal axis while the interest rate is plotted on the vertical axis. For every level of real income, there is a different demand curve showing an inverse relationship between the quantity of real money balances demanded and the interest rate, ceteris paribus. If real income increases, the demand curve for real money balances shifts to the right and there is an increase in demand. If real income decreases, the demand curve shifts to the left and there is a decrease in demand.

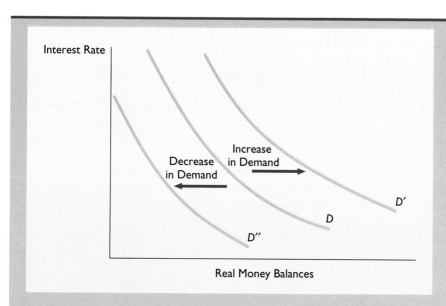

Exhibit 17-5 ◆
The Demand for Real Money Balances

Each demand curve is drawn for a different level of real income. For simplicity, we are referring only to real income as a determinant of the position of the demand curve, recognizing that the level of production and sales is also a determinant. (Because production and sales are highly correlated with real income, this analysis is not significantly affected.) Since there is a direct relationship between the demand for real money balances and real income, if real income changes, the demand curve shifts. If the interest rate changes, ceteris paribus, there is a change in the quantity demanded of real money balances and a movement along a single curve.

RECAP

The demand for real money balances by households and firms is directly related to real income. That is, increases in real income increase demand while decreases in real income decrease demand. Likewise, ceteris paribus, quantity demanded is inversely related to the interest rate. The interest rate is the opportunity cost associated with holding real money balances. Increases in the interest rate, ceteris paribus, decrease quantity demanded, while decreases in the interest rate, ceteris paribus, increase quantity demanded.

Additional Factors Affecting the Demand for Real Money Balances

Although real income is the major factor that determines the demand for real money balances, other factors can also affect demand. In turn, changes in these other factors cause the demand curve for real money balances to shift. They include:

1. Wealth
2. Payment technologies such as the introduction of ATM machines, debit cards, and credit cards
3. Expected inflation
4. The risk and liquidity of other financial assets.

Like real income, changes in wealth are directly related to changes in the demand for real money balances. As wealth increases, ceteris paribus, the demand for real balances also increases, and vice versa. At the same time, the widespread availability of ATM machines, allowing funds to be easily transferred between checking and savings balances, reduces the demand for real money balances. J.P. will hold fewer real balances if he can transfer funds from his savings to checking account 24 hours a day at an ATM machine. Likewise, the widespread availability of credit cards may reduce the need to hold money balances by firms and households and, thereby reduce both the precautionary and transactions motives for holding real money balances from what they otherwise would be.

Inflation reduces the value and purchasing power of money. Assuming a household starts out with a given amount of nominal money balances, if inflation occurs, the value of real money balances falls. The larger the money balances that are held initially, the greater is the risk of incurring losses if inflation should occur. Expectations of higher inflation, therefore, reduce the demand for real money balances, ceteris paribus. Increased uncertainty about future inflation rates would also reduce the demand for real money balances.

As discussed in Chapter 13, increases in the liquidity of other financial assets reduce the demand for real money balances. Thus, as financial innovations, which increase the liquidity of other assets and create new highly

LOOKING FORWARD

Will Checks Go the Way of the Dinosaur?

Throughout this text, we have seen that it has become easier for consumers to make payments electronically, thus bypassing the use of checks or currency. For example, in Chapter 2, we described how point-of-sale terminals allow consumers to make purchases using debit cards and how consumers can pay some bills using phone transfers. In Chapter 13, we understood that a general-use prepaid card called an *electronic purse* is just around the corner and may replace currency in many uses. The electronic purse will most likely also reduce the use of checks.

In addition to these innovations, many banks now issue check cards. A check card allows the user to pay for a purchase by making a withdrawal from their checking account without writing a check. Check cards look like ATM cards but have a credit card symbol (such as VISA) in a corner. Instead of writing a check to make a purchase, a check card can be presented anywhere the VISA credit card is accepted. But it is not a credit card because there is no borrowing. A personal identification number is needed for use.

The advantages of a check card are many. It is convenient because it is similar to paying with a credit card. It is flexible in that it may be used in places that accept credit cards but won't take checks. It saves the time of writing a check and usually doesn't require additional identification as checks do. It allows the owner to get cash from a huge network of ATM machines around the world. Some check cards also offer other carrots such as travel insurance when tickets are purchased with the card, warranty services on goods purchased with the card, and so on. A monthly statement of every transaction makes record keeping easy. The costs vary from bank to bank but most banks offer deals that for the majority of people would be cheaper than using debit machines or paper checks.

What are the disadvantages? Identifying the disadvantages seems rather difficult at this time, which suggests that checks may indeed be going the way of the dinosaur.

liquid substitutes for money, occur, the demand for real money balances decreases from what it otherwise would be.[14]

If the risk of holding other assets increases, the demand for real money balances increases, ceteris paribus. For example, if the stock and bond markets become more volatile, the demand for real money balances increases. Likewise, if the risk of holding money increases, then the demand for other financial assets increases. Can you explain what happens if the risk of holding other financial assets decreases?

Exhibit 17-6 summarizes the factors that affect the demand for money. Having completed our discussion of the demand for real money balances, we are ready to put demand and supply together. After all, it takes both to make a market.

---

[14] These innovations include home equity lines of credit on homes, which make even real assets more liquid.

Exhibit 17-6 ◆

Factors That Affect
the Demand for
Real Money
Balances

An increase in . . .	Will cause the demand for money to . . .
Income	Increase
Wealth	Increase
Payment Technologies	Decrease
Expected Inflation	Decrease
Risk of Other Financial Assets	Increase
Liquidity of Other Financial Assets	Decrease

A decrease in . . .	Will cause the demand for money to . . .
Income	Decrease
Wealth	Decrease
Payment Technologies	Increase
Expected Inflation	Increase
Risk of Other Financial Assets	Decrease
Liquidity of Other Financial Assets	Increase

RECAP

Other factors that affect the demand for real balances include wealth, payment technologies, expected inflation, and/or the risk and liquidity of other financial assets. If wealth increases or if the risk of other financial assets increases, the demand for real money balances increases. If payment technologies improve, if inflation is expected to increase, or if the liquidity of other financial assets increase the demand for money decreases.

Equilibrium in the Market for Real Money Balances

In Chapter 16, we saw that the Fed, through the use of open market operations, exerts a great deal of influence over the supply of nominal money balances and interest rates. This implies that they also exert a great deal of influence over the supply of real money balances, since real money balances are nominal balances divided by a price index. We can depict the supply of real money balances curve as a vertical line on the demand-supply plane.

So far in this chapter, we have seen that, ceteris paribus, the quantity demanded of real money balances is inversely related to the interest rate. By putting the supply and demand curves together, we can describe how the interest rate is determined as depicted in Exhibit 17-7. Real money balances are measured on the horizontal axis while the interest rate is on the vertical axis. Equilibrium occurs where the two curves intersect at the interest rate of 6 percent. At this rate, the quantity of real money balances demanded is equal to the quantity of real money balances supplied. If the interest rate is above 6 percent, quantity demanded is less than quantity supplied and there is a surplus of real balances. Because of this surplus, the price of real money balances (the interest rate) will fall. If the interest rate is below 6 percent, quan-

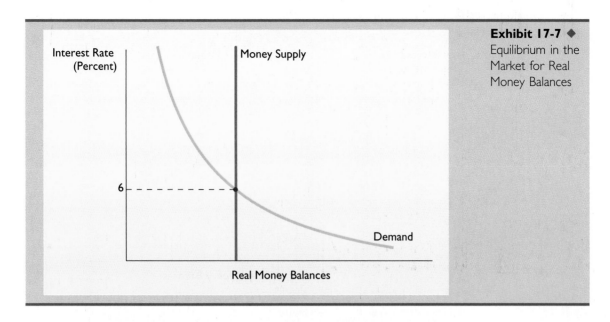

Exhibit 17-7 ◆
Equilibrium in the
Market for Real
Money Balances

tity demanded is greater than quantity supplied and there is a shortage of real money balances. Because of this shortage, the interest rate will rise. Thus, interest rate is that rate at which the quantity demanded is equal to the quantity supplied and the market for real money balances is in equilibrium.

A couple of life's few absolutes are that the future is uncertain and that change is an inherent part of life. Consequently, either demand or supply will be constantly changing in the dynamic world in which we live. Let's observe how interest rates will change in response to changes in the demand or supply of real money balances. We begin with changes in supply.

Open market operations lead to changes in reserves that change the nominal money supply. If prices remain constant when the nominal money supply changes, then the supply of real money balances will also change. But is it reasonable to assume that the price level will remain the same when the nominal supply of money increases? Recall from our peek at the data in Chapter 3 that changes in the money supply are correlated with changes in the price level. However, changes in the rate of inflation today are most highly correlated with changes in the money supply one-to-two years ago. The immediate response to an increase in the growth rate of the nominal money supply is a less than proportional increase in the price level. Therefore, if the nominal money supply increases at a faster rate, then, because price changes usually lag, the supply of real balances also increases, as depicted in Exhibit 17-8. When the Fed increases the supply of reserves, ceteris paribus, the vertical supply curve of real money balances shifts to the right. When the Fed decreases the supply of reserves, ceteris paribus, the vertical supply curve shifts to the left. We should also note that as discussed in Chapter 16, other factors including changes in discount loans can and do change the supply of bank reserves, the monetary base, and the supply of real money balances.[15] If any of these factors change, ceteris paribus, the vertical supply curve of real money balances shifts.

---

[15] Recall from Chapter 16 that the Fed can use offsetting open market operations to offset the impact of these factors.

Exhibit 17-8 ◆
A Change in the
Supply of Real
Balances

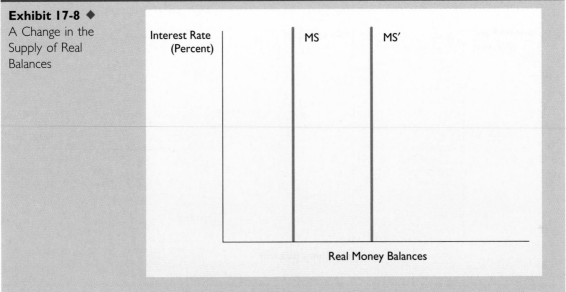

Assuming a given price level, when the money supply changes relative to a given price level, the supply of real money balances also changes. If supply increases, the supply curve shifts right; if supply decreases, the curve shifts left. On the other hand, if the price level increases, the supply of real balances decreases, shifting the vertical supply curve to the left. If the price level decreases, the supply of real balances increases, shifting the vertical supply curve to the right.

Assume that economic activity seems sluggish, that growth has been disappointing, and that the Fed has become convinced of the need to do something to speed up the economy. It decides to use open market purchases to increase bank reserves. The supply of real balances increases and, in turn, the supply curve shifts to the right. Assuming the demand for real money balances does not initially change, the interest rate falls and the market for real money balances moves to the intersection of the demand and new supply curves, (point B) as depicted in Exhibit 17-9.

But, a change in reserves or the monetary base is not the only factor that can change the supply of real money balances. Another factor is the price level. If the price level changes for a given nominal money supply, the supply of real money balances also changes.[16] Such a situation could be caused by a supply shock, such as a drought or a new labor contract. Prices rise without necessarily a corresponding increase in the nominal money supply. In this case, the supply of real balances falls. For example, assume that overall prices increase 2 percent while nominal money remains at $1 trillion. In this case, the real money supply (M/P) would fall since the denominator increased 2 percent while the numerator remained unchanged. On the other hand, if the

---

[16]This discussion applies to a one-time change in the price level and not to inflation which is a sustained increase in the price level. As noted previously, if there is a change in expected inflation, the demand for real money balances also changes.

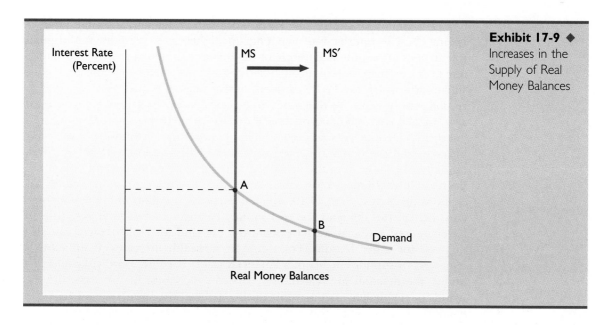

Exhibit 17-9 ◆
Increases in the
Supply of Real
Money Balances

overall price level falls, the supply of real balances increases. In any case, when the supply of real money balances changes, ceteris paribus, a corresponding change in the interest rate follows.

Return again to our reference to a sluggish economy. We have seen that if real income increases, the demand for real money balances increases, and if real income decreases, the demand for real balances decreases. If the Fed engages in expansionary policy to relieve a sluggish economy and if this Fed policy leads to lower interest rates, then real income would hopefully also increase. At the lower interest rate, interest-sensitive spending rises, and real incomes and jobs expand, achieving the desired results. As real income goes up, however, so does the demand for real money balances, and hence the demand curve shifts to the right, as shown in Exhibit 17-10. The market moves

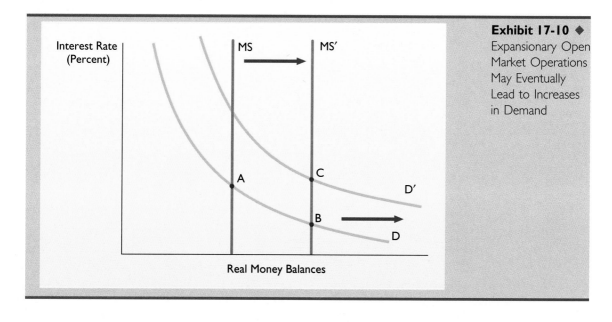

Exhibit 17-10 ◆
Expansionary Open
Market Operations
May Eventually
Lead to Increases
in Demand

to a new equilibrium at the intersection of the new demand and supply curves (point C). The interest rate may end up higher or lower than the original rate depending on the magnitude of the increase in demand for real balances due to the increase in real income. See if you can work through the analogous situation in which the Fed uses open market sales to reduce bank reserves in response to an economy that seems to be overheating. In this case, the interest rate initially rises, choking off interest sensitive spending, and resulting in a fall in real income. As real income falls, so does the demand for real money balances and the demand curve shifts to the left. The interest rate may end up higher or lower than the original rate depending on the magnitude of the decrease in the demand for real balances due to the decrease in income.

Look again at Exhibit 17-10, which depicts the situation where real income and, hence, the demand for real money balances increases in response to lower interest rates. As we have seen, the demand for real balances can also increase for other reasons. For example, if wealth increases, if inflation is expected to subside, or if other financial assets become more risky and less liquid, the demand for real money balances increases. In this case, the demand for real balances curve shifts to the right. If the supply of real balances curve does not change, the interest rate rises. Such a situation is depicted in Exhibit 17-11. Likewise, if income decreases, or other factors (say payment technologies) improve, the demand curve shifts to the left and, ceteris paribus, the interest rate falls.

In any case, the market for real money balances always gravitates to that interest rate at which quantity demanded is equal to quantity supplied. When we observe interest rates constantly changing in our economy, they are responding to changes in supply and/or demand. That is, they are moving up or down in response to increases or decreases (shifts) in supply and/or demand. Now would be a good time for you to read Exhibit 17-12, which looks at the theory of monetarism, which is historically important in the development of monetary theory. Monetarism relates the nominal supply of money and changes therein with the level of economic activity.

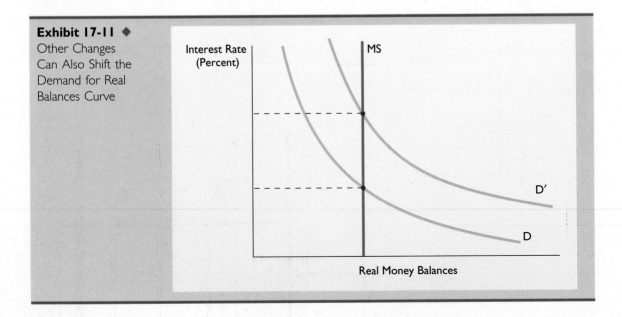

Exhibit 17-11 ◆
Other Changes Can Also Shift the Demand for Real Balances Curve

Monetarism is a school of thought in economics that, not surprisingly, emphasizes the importance of changes in the nominal money supply as a cause of fluctuations in prices, employment, and output. Leading monetarists are Milton Friedman (who received the Nobel Prize in economics in 1976), Karl Brunner, and Allan Meltzer. Monetarist analysis of the role of money usually begins with the **equation of exchange,** which can be written as

$$M \times V = \text{GDP} = P \times Y$$

This equation is really an identity—that is, it is true by definition; it says that the nation's nominal GDP (the overall price level, P, multiplied by the real level of output, Y) is equal to the money supply, M, multiplied by **velocity, V**—the number of times the money supply must "turn over" during a year to "mediate" all the purchases of goods and services comprising GDP.* In effect, V is the average number of times the typical dollar component of the money supply is spent on final output through the economy in a year. An analogy may help: If there are nine players on a baseball team and the team scores 18 runs in one game, then each player, on average, scored twice—that is, circled the bases twice. In this illustration, the total runs scored, 18, are akin to GDP, the nine players are analogous to the money supply, and the average "velocity" for each player is two.

As the equation of exchange suggests, velocity is the crucial link between the money supply and economic activity. To illustrate, if the money stock is $1 trillion and velocity is 6, then GDP will be $6 trillion ($1 trillion × 6 = $6 trillion); if velocity is 5.5, then GDP will be $5.5 trillion. If we assume that the Federal Reserve can control M—that is, can make the quantity of money equal to $1 trillion or whatever figure it believes is best for the economy's health—and we assume that the Fed would like to conduct monetary policy so that GDP turns out to be as close as possible to a "full employment" figure, say $6 trillion, then the key to pulling this off will be the predictability of V. Will it be 5.5, 6.0, or some other figure? If the Fed has a GDP target of $6 trillion, and believes velocity will be 6.0, it will aim for a money supply of $1 trillion. If, however, velocity turns out to be only 5.5, then GDP will be $5.5 trillion—far short of the Fed's objective.

The **quantity theory of money** is the intellectual heart of monetarism. The equation of exchange, which, as it stands, is just a definitional identity, is transformed into a theory linking money and economic activity by first hypothesizing that V is reasonably predictable and then gathering evidence supporting this assertion. Why is this important? Let's take the simplest case. Suppose V is stable (fixed). If policymakers could always count on V to be 6, then they could be sure that a money supply of $1 trillion would produce GDP of $6 trillion. More generally, they would know that, for example, a $100 increase in the money supply would produce a $600 rise in GDP; that is, changes in the money supply would lead to proportional changes in GDP—this is in essence the quantity theory of money.

In many respects, the role of money within both monetarism and the quantity theory of money is not very different from that illustrated within

Exhibit 17-12 ◆
Monetarism

Monetarism The school of thought that emphasizes the importance of changes in the nominal money supply as a cause of fluctuations in prices, employment, and output.
Equation of Exchange $M \times V = P \times Y = \text{GDP}$

Velocity The number of times the money supply turns over during a year to mediate all the purchases of goods and services comprising GDP.

Quantity Theory of Money The theory that velocity is stable or fixed and that changes in the money supply lead to proportional changes in GDP.

*Consistent with general economic usage, when the term GDP is used, it is understood to refer to nominal GDP and is equal to the total dollar value of all final goods and services produced by the economy during a year.

Exhibit 17-12 ◆
Monetarism
(continued)

Exhibit 3-1. Monetarists tend to prefer the simpler and more direct quantity theory approach because of their belief that the detailed linkages between money and economic activity are either relatively unimportant or, given the complexities and interdependencies characterizing the economy, too hard to figure out. Thus, it is argued, focusing on *M* and *V* is appropriate and sufficient for analyzing the general role of money in the economy.

As we have noted previously, major structural changes in financial markets have not only skewed the relationship between narrowly defined monetary aggregates and the level of economic activity, but have also made it difficult for a central bank to use monetary targeting in the execution of monetary policy, as the theory of monetarism suggests. Because credit now emanates from so many nondepository-institution sources such as mutual funds and finance companies, the degree of credit restraint in operation at any particular time is difficult to measure by a standard money supply such as M1, M2, or M3, or broader credit aggregate such as domestic nonfinancial debt (DNFD).

 RECAP

Open market operations or a one-time change in the overall price level for a given nominal money supply causes the supply of real balances to change. The market for real balances always gravitates to the interest rate at which quantity demanded is equal to quantity supplied.

A Final Note

In this chapter, we extended our discussion introduced in Chapter 3 by developing a theory of interest rate determination based on the supply and demand for real money balances. Real money balances are measured at a point in time and refer to actual stocks. The interest rate adjusts to equate the quantity supplied (stock) of real money balances with the quantity demanded.

In Chapter 4, we developed the loanable funds theory in which the interest rate is determined by the supply and demand for loanable funds. The supply and demand for loanable funds are measured through time and refer to actual flows. The interest rate adjusts to equate the quantity demanded of loanable funds with the quantity supplied. As in Chapter 4, we can reconcile the two theories by recognizing that when there is a change in a stock measured at different times, a flow has occurred. Correspondingly, changes in the flow of loanable funds entail changes in the stock of real money balances as measured at two different points in time. Make sure you are clear about the difference between stocks and flows and that interest rates equate both the supply and demand for loanable funds and real money balances.

In the last two chapters, we have analyzed the supply and demand of real money balances. This chapter has one appendix about the transactions demand for money by households. In the next chapter, we look at financial aspects of household and firm behavior in the hopes of understanding how spending and financial decisions affect economic activity.

Summary of Major Points

1. The demand for money is really a demand for real money balances. Real money balances are the nominal supply of money divided by the price level. Changes in the overall price level lead to proportional changes in the demand for money and no change in the demand for real balances. Households demand real money balances to consummate transactions (transactions motive) and to fulfill the precautionary motive.

2. There are benefits and costs with regards to holding real money balances. The benefits are the interest payments that are earned on checkable deposits plus the stream of services that money balances provide. The costs are the foregone interest payments that holding nonmonetary financial assets would have yielded. Households and firms should adjust their holdings of real balances to the point where the marginal benefits of doing so are equal to the marginal costs.

3. Household demand for real balances is directly related to real income. Ceteris paribus, the quantity demanded of real balances is inversely related to the interest rate. A firm's demand for real money balances is directly related to production and sales, and the need to make transactions. Both are highly correlated with real income. Other factors affect the demand for real money balances. These factors include changes in wealth, payment technologies, expected inflation, the availability of near money substitutes, and the risk and liquidity of other financial assets.

4. The interest rate is determined by the demand and supply for real money balances. If either demand or supply changes, the interest rate changes. The supply of real balances changes when the Fed uses open market operations to change the supply of reserves to depository institutions. Changes in the overall price level for a given nominal money supply also cause the supply of real balances to change. In response to a sluggish economy, if the Fed is successful in speeding up the economy through increasing the supply of real balances, the demand for real balances will also increase as real income increases.

5. Keynes' liquidity preference theory asserts that there is a speculative demand for money in which the quantity demanded of money is inversely related to the interest rate. The inverse relationship results from the fact that when interest rates are low, people will demand to hold money instead of bonds because they fear a capital loss when interest rates rise. Likewise when interest rates are high and bond prices low, they will hold bonds instead of money to take advantage of a capital gain when interest rates fall. When interest rates are abnormally low, the economy may be in a liquidity trap where the money demand curve becomes horizontal. In this case, increases in the supply of money do not cause the interest rate to fall and monetary policy is less effective in affecting economic activity.

6. Monetarism is a theory that stresses the relationship between changes in nominal money and changes in GDP. It stresses that the primary determinant of changes in GDP is changes in the supply of money because velocity is highly stable. More modern monetarists stress that although velocity may not be stable, it is sufficiently predictable.

7. The benefits of holding additional real money balances decline as additional calls are made to the broker each month. The cost of each call to the broker, however, is a constant amount per call. Calls to the broker should be made as long as the benefits of doing so are greater than the costs. The optimum number of calls determines the average daily holding of real balances and hence, the transactions demand for real money balances by households. (Appendix 17-A)

Key Terms

Average Daily Holding of Funds

Benefits of Holding Real Money
  Balances

Costs of Holding Real Money
  Balances

Equation of Exchange

Liquidity Preference

Liquidity Trap

Monetarism

Precautionary Motive

Quantity Theory of Money

Real Income

Real Money Balances

Speculative Demand for Money

Transactions Motive

Velocity

Review Questions

1. What is a real money balance? If the nominal money supply increases by 20 percent while prices increase 20 percent, what happens to the demand for real money balances? What happens to the supply of real money balances?

2. If real income increases 20 percent, what happens to the demand for real money balances? Is the change in demand proportional to the change in real income?

3. What is the difference between a one-time increase in prices and inflation? How does a one-time increase in prices affect the demand for real money balances? How does expected inflation affect the demand for real balances? How does a one-time increase in prices affect the real money supply?

4. Why do firms want to hold real money balances? Why do households? What factors determine the quantity of real balances that each wants to hold?

5. What happens to the demand for real balances if interest rates on time deposits rise relative to interest rates on checkable deposits?

6. Correct the statement: "When the interest rate increases, the demand for real money balances decreases."

7. In Chapter 3, our initial peek at the data showed that changes in money were more highly correlated with changes in nominal GDP than with changes in either real GDP or inflation. Does this support or refute monetarism? Explain.

8. Using the liquidity preference theory, explain why the quantity demanded of money is inversely related to the interest rate. What is a liquidity trap?

9. When is the market for real money balances in equilibrium? If the Fed engages in open market sales, what happens to the supply of real balances?

10. Explain the transactions and precautionary motives for demanding real money balances.

11. What are the benefits of holding real money balances? What are the costs? What is the optimum amount of real money balances that households and firms will demand?

Analytical Questions

12. Graph the supply and demand curves for real money balances. Explain what happens to the interest rate if:

   a. Credit cards become more widely used and accepted to make transactions.
   b. The economy is growing faster than what the Fed thinks is desirable, and therefore the Fed sells bonds to the public.
   c. Many new near money substitutes are created.
   d. The overall price level falls while the nominal money supply remains constant.
   e. ATM machines become more accessible and more widely used.
   f. The secondary markets for negotiable CDs and junk bonds collapse.
   g. Inflation is expected to pick up in the coming year.

13. The graph in Exhibit 17-1 shows the relationship between real money holdings and a typical household, assuming real money balances are gradually depleted over the course of the month. Jacques gets paid on the first of each month, but parties extensively over the next week and is broke for the remainder of the month. Graph Jacques' real money holdings over the course of a month.

14. Graphically show what happens to the interest rate if the Fed takes action that leads to a decrease in the supply of real money balances while the economy is in a liquidity trap.

15. What is the equation of exchange? If nominal GDP is $6.5 trillion and the money supply is $1 trillion, what is velocity? If the Fed increases the nominal money supply, what happens to nominal GDP? (Hint: First assume that velocity is constant and then relax this assumption.) Can we be sure of the direction of change in prices and real GDP?

16. Graphically show what happens to the real money supply if the price level rises while the nominal money supply remains constant. What happens to the real money supply if both the nominal money supply and the price level rise by the same percent?

17. If J.P. earns $4,000 per month, the interest rate is 4 percent, and the cost of a call to the broker is $.75, what should his transactions demand for real balances per month be? (Appendix 17-A)

18. Referring to question 17, if J.P.'s income goes up to $6,000 per month, what happens to his demand for real money balances? (Appendix 17-A)

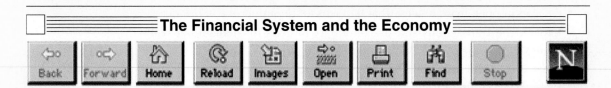

1. Tabulate the relationship between interest rates and money (M1) growth for the years from 1962 to 1976. For data on interest rates use the 3-month Treasury bill rate from the world wide web site (http://www.stls.frb.org/fred/data/irates/tb3m). For data on the rate of growth of M1 use the world wide web site (http://www.stls.frb.org/fred/data/monetary/m1sl). Verify that an increase in the rate of growth of the money supply during the mid 1960s and 1970s did not lead to a decline in interest rates. Is this possible? Why? (Hint: see Exhibit 17-10 in the text for a possible explanation.)

Suggested Readings

For a more in-depth look at the demand for money and the supply of money, see K. Bain, *Monetary Economics,* Brookfield, VT: Edward Elgar Publishing, 1994.

William J. Frazer, Jr., *The Legacy of Keynes and Friedman,* Westport, CT: Praeger Publishers, 1994, looks at the monetary theories of each.

Thomas Mayer, *Monetarism and Macroeconomic Policy,* Brookfield, VT: Edward Elgar Publishing, 1990, is easy-to-read coverage of the topic.

For a history of the uses and abuses of money and debt, see G. Leigh Skene, *Cycles of Inflation and Deflation,* Westport, CT: Praeger Publishers, 1992.

For a technical and empirical approach to the demand for money see Neil Thompson, *Portfolio Theory and the Demand for Money,* New York: St. Martin's Press, 1994.

For some engaging reading on monetarism, see Milton Friedman's classic article titled "The Quantity Theory of Money: A Restatement," in *Studies in the Quantity Theory of Money,* Chicago: University of Chicago Press, 1956.

For an early discussion about the determination of velocity, see Irving Fisher, *The Purchasing Power of Money: Its Determination and Relation to Credit, Interest, and Crises,* New York: MacMillan, 1911.

Monetarism is explained at the Economic Policy Institute's world wide web page at (http://epn.org/idea/economy.html).

APPENDIX 17-A

The Transactions Demand for Money by Households

We have seen that a household should demand real balances for transactions as long as the benefits of doing so are greater than the costs. A problem arises in that both the benefits and costs increase as more real balances are held. The purpose of this appendix is to shed light on how this abstract rule can be translated into behavior in the real world. We use a numerical example to illustrate this procedure. Again, we are assuming that the household can hold money balances or bonds and that it must call its broker, pay a fee, and wait to liquidate the bonds when it is in need of funds.

Let's consider a simple example in which the household earns a fixed income, say $2,000 per month, and can make a varied number of calls to its broker each month, ranging from 0 to say 2, as described in Exhibit 17-13. For simplicity, we will also assume that the price level is one.

If the household makes no calls, it puts $2,000 in its checking account and spends the funds evenly over the course of the month. On average, the household is holding half of its monthly income ($1,000) as nominal money balances. During the first 15 days of the month, the household is holding more than half of its income ($1,000) and during the last 15 days, it is holding less. Since the price level is one, the household's **average daily holding of funds** ($1,000/1 = $1,000) is its demand for real money balances during the month.

If the household makes one call to the broker during the month, initially, half of its income ($1,000) is used to buy bonds and the other half is spent evenly over the first 15 days of the month. On the sixteenth day, the household calls the broker to sell the bonds and the household receives back the half of its income ($1,000) originally invested in bonds. It then spends these funds ($1,000) over the last 15 days of the month. On average, the household holds one-fourth of its income ($500) as checkable funds. Since the price level is one, this is its demand for real money balances ($500/1 = $500).

If the household makes two calls per month, it initially puts two-thirds of its income in bonds ($1,333) and spends the other one-third ($667) during the first third of the month. One-third of the way through the month, the household calls the broker to sell ($667) in bonds for funds to spend during the middle third of the month. The household calls the broker a second time two-thirds of the way through the month for the remainder of the funds ($667). Since it is removing one-third of its income each time it calls the broker and spending that amount equally over one-third of the month, (approximately ten days) its average holdings of real money balances is half of each withdrawal which is one-sixth of its income ($333.33). Since the price level is one, the demand for real money balances is $333.33/1 = $333.33.

Average Daily Holding of Funds A household's demand for real money balances during the month; the amount of each withdrawal divided by two.

Exhibit 17-13 ◆
The Number of
Broker Calls Per
Month and the
Average Holdings
of Real Balances
(Transactions
Demand for Real
Balances)

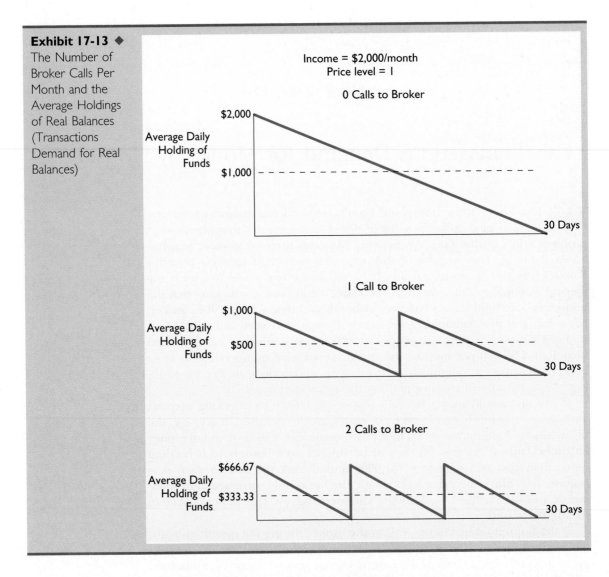

Following the same methodology, if three calls per month are made, the demand for real money balances is $250/1 = $250. Having completed this rather mechanical exercise, let's now consider the benefits and the costs of making additional calls to the broker. We can make a few simplifying assumptions that will not change the conclusions:

1. We assume that the cost of a call to the broker (the brokerage fee and time and inconvenience) is a constant amount per call regardless of how many calls an individual makes.*

2. We assume that the benefit of an additional call to the broker is the additional interest that is earned on the larger amount of funds held in bonds during the month because of the call.

---

*For example, if the cost per call is $1 and 3 calls are made, total cost is $3. If 4 calls are made, total cost is $4.

Armed with these two assumptions, we are now in a position to describe how many calls the household should make to the broker each month. Once we know this, we can determine the average daily balance and hence the real money balances that the household will demand each month for transactions. How so, you may ask? The number of calls determines how many time periods the month is divided into. If two calls are made, the month is divided into three time periods. If three calls are made, the month is divided into four time periods, and so on. The monthly income divided by the number of time periods gives the amount of funds at the start of each time period. Since the funds are spent evenly over the period, one half of this amount is the average holding of funds. If we divide the average holdings of funds by the price level, we get the quantity of real money balances that the household will demand for transactions.

In the preceding example if the household makes one call to the broker, the demand for real money balances decreases by $500 from $1,000 to $500. The benefit of that first call is the interest earned on the $500 that is kept in bonds over the course of the month. If the household makes a second call, the demand for real money balances falls from $500 to $333.33 and the benefit of that second call is the interest that is earned on the additional $166.67 ($500 − $333.33) that is held in bonds over the course of the month. If the household makes a third call to the broker, the demand for real money balances falls from $333.33 to $250 and the benefit of the third call is the additional interest earned on $83.33 ($333.33 − $250). We could keep going but hopefully you see the point. *As additional calls to the broker are made, the benefit of each additional call, although positive, is decreasing.* Total benefits are increasing but at a decreasing rate.

We now have all the pieces in place to make a decision. Recalling that we assumed that the cost of calls to the broker is a constant amount per call regardless of how many calls are made, we can say that calls should be made as long as the marginal benefits (the interest earned on the additional funds kept in bonds) are greater than the cost of the additional call. Because marginal benefits decrease as additional calls to the broker are made and costs per call are constant, the household will be exploiting all opportunities to be better off if it makes all calls where the marginal benefits are greater than the marginal costs. Now would be a good time to look at Exhibit 17-14. Assuming the interest rate on bonds is 6 percent above the rate on money balances, and a brokerage cost of $1 per call, one call should be made to the broker where the benefit is $2.50. If a second call is made, the benefit is $.83 while the cost is $1. In this case, the quantity demanded of real money balances for transactions would be $500. In addition, the household will demand to hold a small amount of real money balances, say $100, to fulfill the precautionary motive. If this is the case, then, the total quantity demanded of real money balances is $600 ($500 + $100).

In this simple example, two factors can change the optimum number of calls to the broker per month—a change in either the cost per call or the interest rate. First, consider changes in the cost of brokerage calls.

Returning to Exhibit 17-14, if the cost of brokerage calls falls to $.50 per call, then it is advantageous to make the second call, which has $.83 in benefits. Again, the third call is not made. On the other hand, if the cost per call increases to $3, zero calls are made because the benefit of the first call is only $2.50. In this case, the household puts all of its income into its checking

Exhibit 17-14 ◆
Benefits and Costs
of Additional Calls
to the Broker

Benefits: The benefit of a call to the broker is the interest that is earned on the additional funds held in bonds because of the call. To illustrate, we will assume the interest rate is 6 per year or approximately 1/2 percent per month.

Call	(A) Transactions Demand for Money If Call Not Made	(B) Transactions Demand for Money If Call Made	(A) − (B)	Benefit: Interest on Additional Bonds Held
0	$1,000	—	—	
1	1,000	$500	$500	$2.50 ($500 × .005)
2	500	333	167	.83 ($167 × .005)
3	333	250	83	.43 ($83 × .005)
4	250	200	50	.25 ($50 × .005)

Costs: Assume costs per call are constant at $1.00 per call. Eventually the costs of an additional call will be greater than the benefits and the call should not be made. In this example, only one call to the broker should be made because the second call costs $1.00 and the benefits are only $.83.

account and spends it evenly over the course of the month. Consequently, if the cost per call to the broker increases, households will make fewer calls. The average holdings of real money balances and, hence, demand will be greater. You should be able to analyze what will happen to the demand for real money balances if the cost per call to the broker decreases. Now would be a good time to look at Exhibit 17-15, which illustrates what happens to the

Exhibit 17-15 ◆
Benefits and Costs
of Calls to Broker
If the Interest Rate
Increases to 1
Percent Per Month

Call	(A) Transactions Demand for Money If Call Not Made	(B) Transactions Demand for Money If Call Made	(A) − (B)	Benefit: Interest Earned on Additional Bonds Held
0	$1,000	—	—	
1	1,000	$500	$500	$5.00 ($500 × .01)
2	500	333	167	1.67 ($167 × .01)
3	333	250	83	.83 ($83 × .01)
4	250	200	50	.50 ($50 × .01)

Costs: Assume costs per call are constant at $1.00 per call. In this case, the household should make two calls to the broker per month because the benefits of the second call ($1.67) outweigh the costs ($1.00). Hence, the quantity demanded of money for transactions is $333.

quantity demanded of real money balances if interest rates per month increase from 1/2 percent to 1 percent. In this case, the benefits of each additional call double. If the cost per call is $1, the household makes two calls per month and the quantity demanded of real money balances is $333. Hence, as the interest rate increases, the quantity demanded of real money balances for transactions decreases from $500 to $333.

18

Financial Aspects of Household and Firm Behavior

> *The farmer's way of saving money: to be owed by someone he trusted.*
> —Hugh MacLennan—

Learning Objectives

After reading this chapter, you should know:

- ◆ What motivates household consumption and saving
- ◆ How economic and financial conditions influence household spending, saving, borrowing, and lending
- ◆ What determines the volume of investment spending in the economy
- ◆ How firms finance current production and investment
- ◆ The sources and uses of funds for the household and business sectors

To Spend or Not to Spend

Reflecting the weak economy, sales of new cars have been disappointing and inventories of unsold cars are piling up on dealer lots. Given this situation, General Motors, among others, decides to take some bold action. The prevailing interest rate on consumer loans for new automobiles is 7 percent. Beginning next Monday and lasting for the next 30 days, buyers of new General Motors cars will be able to finance their purchases by borrowing funds from General Motors' finance company subsidiary at an interest rate of only 3.5 percent, and the price of all cars purchased will be reduced by $1,000.[1] Jan and Dave, who had been planning to buy a new car next year, believe this deal is too good to pass up and decide to buy now. Since they must come up with $2,000 as a down payment on the $20,000 auto they want to buy (borrowing the other $18,000 from General Motors), Jan and Dave will withdraw the necessary funds from their savings deposit at HLT National Bank.

After discussion, study, and months of agonizing, it's time to act. The Board of Directors of All Purpose Enterprise, Inc. (APEI), one of the ten largest companies in the nation, decides to undertake three separate actions: (1) sell a subsidiary whose profitability has consistently trailed other parts of the firm, (2) construct a new plant in Arkansas, and (3) extend an offer to purchase a medium-sized firm specializing in telecommunications. With the economic outlook expected to improve in the months ahead and interest rates relatively low, APEI, in effect, decides to restructure itself. The firm-specific forces driving these actions are the increased competition from both domestic and foreign firms and the resulting need to boost profitability by enhancing productivity, efficiency, and the firm's position in the marketplace. APEI expects to raise its earnings in an improving economic climate by redeploying its assets. Since these actions will, on balance, require APEI to raise $2 billion of new funds, the company hires Salomon Brothers of New York, a preeminent investment banker, to manage the tender offer for the telecommunications firm, the finding of a buyer for the subsidiary, and the issuance of the new bonds and stock necessary to finance the actions undertaken.

Although superficially different, the scenarios above have some similarities that may escape the notice of even a discriminating eye. Both scenarios are motivated by the economic environment that each of the parties perceives and both result in the restructuring of balance sheets in response to the discernible changes in that environment. That is, in response to perceptions and realities, our couple (Jan and Dave) and the business firm (APEI) both alter their holdings of assets and liabilities. The resulting changes enable the household and firm, given their constraints, to achieve their goals—either maximum satisfaction for the household or maximum profit for the firm.

In this chapter, we examine the spending, saving, borrowing, and lending behavior of households and firms. We see that although individual behavior is motivated by individual perceptions, the aggregate behavior of each group has a profound effect on the health of the economy and the functioning of the financial system. We look at the causes and consequences of changes in each sector and how they relate to changes in the economy. We use balance

---

[1] General Motors' finance subsidiary is General Motors Acceptance Corporation.

sheets to help flesh out the role that the financial system plays in facilitating these changes.

Household Behavior from a Financial Perspective

When General Motors lowers the price of its automobiles and improves the financing terms, Jan and Dave revise their plans in the direction of more consumption spending on goods and services and fewer funds available to lend. The changes in spending, saving, borrowing, and lending behavior in turn alter Jan and Dave's portfolio of assets and liabilities. That is, flows of spending, saving, borrowing, and lending result in changes in real assets, and financial assets and liabilities. In this case, real assets and financial liabilities (the auto and the loan, respectively) increase while financial assets (the savings deposit) decrease.

The collection of real assets (houses, autos, etc.) and financial assets (money, stocks, bonds, savings accounts, etc.) and liabilities (mortgages, consumer loans, etc.) is called a **portfolio.** One's portfolio can be displayed on a balance sheet, introduced in Chapter 11, which measures the monetary value of a household's assets, liabilities, and **net worth** on a specific date. A portfolio is a stock concept, since it measures the value of assets and liabilities held at a particular point in time. Aggregating over all households gives a balance sheet for the household sector, which reflects assets, liabilities, and net worth. See Exhibit 18-1 for the balance sheet of the household sector as of December 31, 1996. Flows of spending, saving, borrowing, and lending occur between given points in time that cause balance sheet changes. The balance sheet transformations summarize the millions of spending, saving, borrowing,

Portfolio The collection of real and financial assets and liabilities.
Net Worth The difference between assets and liabilities at a point in time.

Assets	Liabilities
Real Estate	Real Estate Mortgages
Other Real Assets	Installment Debt
Money	Other Personal Debt
Other Financial Assets	Net Worth
Total Assets	Total Liabilities plus Net Worth

Exhibit 18-1 ◆
The Balance Sheet of the Household Sector December 31, 1996

Like all balance sheets, the balance sheet for the entire household sector is arranged according to the fundamental identity that assets equal liabilities plus net worth. This means the dollar value of the left column is identical to the dollar value of the right column. Other financial assets include time and savings deposits, stocks, bonds, mutual funds, money market mutual funds, and so forth. Not surprisingly, real estate holdings comprise the largest portion of household assets, and mortgages on such real estate, the largest component of liabilities. Net worth measures the degree to which the value of assets exceeds the value of liabilities, which is exactly analogous to the capital entry on FIs' balance sheets, which is viewed as a measure of the financial health or wealth of households.

and lending decisions that households make in light of their objectives and constraints.

We first introduced the concepts of aggregate demand and aggregate supply in Chapter 4 where we saw that fluctuations in aggregate demand and aggregate supply lead to changes in the overall price level and the level of real economic activity as measured by real GDP. Consumption expenditures by households are by far the largest component of aggregate demand. In addition, when households spend money on investments such as houses, they also increase aggregate demand.[2] Since household spending makes up more than 70 percent of aggregate demand, by its sheer size, household spending is extremely important in the macroeconomy. Our focus is on how and why the household flows of spending, which are measured over an interval of time, change. Now would be a good time to look at Exhibit 18-2, which shows how

---

[2] Recall that income not spent on consumption is saving. A portion of household saving may be directly invested in real assets such as housing and the remainder is surplus funds available to be lent in financial markets.

Exhibit 18-2 ◆
Household Portfolio Changes over Time
J.P. Young
(Figures are in thousands of dollars.)

(1) January 1, 1996		(2) Actions During Year		(3) December 31, 1996	
Real Assets	$100	Purchase computer, stereo, and TV	$5	Real Assets	$105
Money	$3	Increase in money holdings	$.3	Money	$3.3
Other Financial Assets	$30	Acquisition of stocks and bonds	$2.7	Other Financial Assets	$32.7
Total Assets	$133	Change in total assets	$8	Total Assets	$141
Total Liabilities	$53	Change in total liabilities	$2	Total Liabilities	$55
Net Worth	$80	Change in net worth	$6	Net Worth	$86

The figures above trace out the changes in a hypothetical portfolio for our typical consumer J.P. Young. The left hand side of the table, column (1) shows the value of J.P.'s assets, liabilities and net worth as of January 1, 1996. The middle of the table, column 2), summarizes J.P.'s spending, saving, borrowing, and lending during the year. Spending on so-called nondurables such as food and clothing and services such as haircuts are not shown since they are in effect "consumed" or used up as purchased. Note that part of J.P.'s purchases of assets have been financed by borrowing $2,000. Liabilities increase from $53,000 to $55,000.

J.P.'s portfolio at the end of the year, shown in column 3, is the sum of the beginning of the year portfolio (column 1) and J.P.'s spending, saving, borrowing, and lending actions during the year (column 2). For example, real asset holdings at year end were $105,000 reflecting holdings totaling $100,000 at the beginning of the year and purchases of durables (computer, stereo, and TV) totaling $5,000 during the year. For simplicity, we have assumed that none of the real assets held at the beginning of the year wore out (depreciated) during the year and that there were no changes in the value of any of his financial assets (stocks and bonds).

flows throughout the year change a typical balance sheet.[3] In this case, the flows are those of J.P. Young whom we first met in Chapter 4.

Research into consumer attitudes and behavior suggests that household portfolio decisions are guided by certain objectives, such as happiness, good health, and a high standard of living. Leaving happiness and good health for the psychologists and physicians, economists traditionally focus on living standards, arguing that as households strive for a better quantity and quality of life, they will develop desired portfolios. Operationally, they will then spend, save, lend, borrow, or work so as to move their actual portfolios toward their desired portfolios. The point is that household behavior is not haphazard, but rather purposeful. The result is a process characterized by consideration of alternatives, calculation of costs and benefits, and careful planning. Let's take a closer look at the process with regards to financial decisions, and what lies behind it.

Asset Accumulation: Spending and Saving

Households acquire **real assets** when they engage in consumption spending on durable goods or investment spending on newly constructed houses.[4] If they have surplus funds left over to lend in financial markets, they acquire financial assets. In general, they desire real assets for the flow of services such assets provide. For example, a house (an investment good) provides shelter services over time. An auto provides transportation services, while a television provides entertainment services. Both are consumption goods. In addition, certain real assets such as houses and antiques may also be desired because of expected capital gains. The benefit or return associated with the acquisition of real assets is comprised of the value of the flow of services together with any capital gain or loss. Such returns are analogous to and, as we shall see, comparable with the returns on financial assets.[5]

Real Assets For households, durable goods and houses.

Financial assets, from the household perspective, serve as a store of value or purchasing power that can, for example, be used in the future to acquire real assets, pay for children's education, and so forth. Financial assets, other than money, generally provide income to the holder in the form of interest and dividends, and sometimes, capital gains. This income supplements wages and salaries during the working years, and supplements pensions during retirement. In fact, retirement constitutes a strong motive for households to be surplus spending units (SSUs) and thus accumulate financial assets during the working years. By doing so, households will be better able to maintain living standards in the retirement years.

Financial Assets Financial instruments such as stocks, bonds, and money, which serve as a store of value or purchasing power.

Of course, retirement and future spending plans are not the only things that motivate the accumulation of financial assets. Equally important is the fact that we live in an uncertain world. Anyone can get laid off from a job, the frostfree refrigerator can break down, a medical emergency can occur, and so on. To cushion itself from the adverse effects of such happenings, a

---

[3] Balance sheet changes are also caused by capital gains or losses on assets through time. Capital gains accrue when assets increase in value, while capital losses occur when assets fall in value.

[4] As we saw in Chapter 1, investment in houses is expenditure for new residential construction, which renders a service over a period of time.

[5] Note that because nondurables and services are used up in the period in which they are purchased, households do not accumulate them.

household will typically want to acquire some financial assets, especially liquid and safe assets, such as savings deposits, Treasury bills, and money market mutual fund shares. These near monies can be converted into money quickly at little cost and involve little risk.[6] Changes in the size and composition of financial assets over time also reflect capital gains or losses on assets owned, and household decisions to spend, save, borrow, or lend. The important role that risk and the aversion to risk play in choosing among financial assets is discussed in Exhibit 18-3.

Money is also one of many financial assets households may possess. As we saw in the last two chapters, money is unique among financial assets in serving as a means of payment. Because of its unique position, we devoted all of Chapter 17 to the demand for real money balances. For now, we are merely reminding you that money is one of an array of financial assets a household

---

[6]The need for households to hold liquid assets for "a rainy day" has diminished somewhat in recent years as financial intermediaries (FIs) have made so-called lines of credit increasingly available to consumers. In essence, a line of credit is a promise by, say, a bank, to lend you funds as you need them, up to the amount you have been approved for. Thus if you have a $10,000 line of credit (including home equity lines of credit), all or part of these funds are available to you if and when you need them. The availability of such prearranged loans reduces the need to hold liquid savings for contingencies. In effect, the household gets liquidity from the liability rather than the asset side of the balance sheet. Households up to their credit limit have no liquidity remaining from this source.

Exhibit 18-3 ◆

Choosing Among Financial Assets: The Role of Risk Aversion

A financial investor can acquire many different types of financial claims. The claims differ by type of issuer, maturity, liquidity, and riskiness. Most financial experts agree that the average investor is risk averse. In practice, this tendency means that individuals will avoid assets and portfolios with higher risk vis-à-vis assets and portfolios with lower risk unless the expected return on the high-risk assets exceeds the return on the low-risk assets by a sufficient amount. Simply put, risk-averse investors must be rewarded with higher returns for bearing additional risk.

So what does this have to do with choosing among financial assets? Suppose a household is in the process of deciding which of two financial assets (A or B) to acquire. Assume the expected rate of return on both assets over the next five years is 10 percent. However, suppose the probability of earning 10 percent on asset A is 100 percent, while asset B has three possible outcomes including 10 percent, 20 percent, and 0 percent. For asset B, the probability of earning 10 percent is 50 percent, the probability of earning 20 percent is 25 percent, and the probability of earning 0 percent is 25 percent. The expected return is calculated by summing the product of each possible outcome and its associated probability over all possible outcomes. For asset A, since there is only one possible return, the expected value is 10 percent (10 percent × 1.0 = 10 percent). Using the same formula, we see that the expected rate of return for asset B is also 10 percent, (10 percent × .5) + (0 percent × .25) + (20 percent × .25) = 5 + 0 + 5 = 10 percent. In this context, risk is defined as the possible fluctuation of the return on an asset around its expected value. Thus, in this example, the greater variance of the return on asset B makes it more risky; accordingly the risk-averse investor will prefer asset A.

may hold and that the demand for real money balances is directly related to income while, ceteris paribus, the quantity demanded of real money balances is inversely related to the interest rate.

Liability Accumulation: Borrowing

Periodically, throughout their lifetimes, households like Jan and Dave's consider spending (consuming) more than their current income or portfolio of financial assets can finance at that time. This is where borrowing and the accumulation of debt, or **financial liabilities,** comes in. By examining the motives for borrowing and what limits the ability and willingness of households to borrow, the important interdependencies inherent in household portfolio decisions will be highlighted.

Financial Liabilities Debt incurred through borrowing.

A decision to borrow today is really two decisions: a decision to borrow today and a decision to repay what is borrowed plus interest in the future. The borrower is willing to trade off or borrow against future purchasing power for current purchasing power. Why would a household want to do this? Visualize a student couple whose current income is low, but whose future income is expected to be higher. They desire to consume more now. Borrowing and spending now will raise consumption relative to current income and lower consumption in the future relative to income as the debts accumulated now are paid off. In the process, borrowing facilitates the smoothing out of house-

Do not jump from this example and discussion to the conclusion that risk-averse investors will never acquire risky assets. Financial investors learned long ago that risks can be minimized while still earning a handsome overall return in a well-diversified portfolio. To see how and why, and to tie in some of the previous discussion on household spending, imagine three portfolios. Portfolio A consists only of asset A, say, government bonds yielding 10 percent. Portfolio B consists entirely of asset B, say shares in companies producing consumer durable goods and lumber. Reflecting the tendency of consumer spending on durables and housing to fluctuate fairly widely over the business cycle, the prices of these shares, and thus the return on portfolio B, also fluctuate cyclically in a fairly wide range (0 to 20 percent), while, like portfolio A, averaging a 10 percent return. In contrast, portfolio C consists of shares in a wide variety of companies. In particular, and in addition to shares in companies producing consumer durables and lumber, the portfolio contains shares in food, health, and chemical firms—industries hardly affected by cyclical fluctuations in income and interest rates because consumer spending on the products produced by such firms is less affected by such fluctuations. Why is this important? The relatively good earnings performance of the food, health, and chemical firms during recessions offsets the relatively poor performance of the consumer durables and lumber firms by enough to raise the overall return on the portfolio over the business cycle to 11 percent and reduces the variance of the return on the portfolio (that is, the riskiness of the portfolio) significantly relative to portfolio B. In such a situation, risk-averse financial investors will, of course, be attracted to portfolio C and thus be willing to hold some risky assets as part of a diversified portfolio.

hold spending and consumption over time. Of course, households may also borrow to acquire knowledge and skills (education), which will lead to a higher future income. Likewise, they may borrow to acquire real or financial assets that are expected to rise in value over time.

Sounds great—but one question still needs to be answered. Since borrowing facilitates the acquisition of real and financial assets, and we generally prefer more rather than less, why not borrow continually and without limit? The answer, of course, is that households will not be able to borrow an unlimited volume of funds at the prevailing interest rate. The impediment to continuous borrowing, a **borrowing constraint,** comes from both the lenders such as banks, for example, and the households themselves.

It is generally believed that as the ratio of debt or debt payments to income rises, the ability of a household to "service" or pay off additional debt is reduced. More specifically, the probability of default or delinquent payments on a loan rises. This, of course, makes financial intermediaries (FIs) reluctant to grant new loans to heavily indebted borrowers. FIs require potential borrowers to fill out forms and undergo credit checks so that information on the balance sheet position of the household and the household's current and future income are available and can be used to gauge the riskiness of a potential loan. A household with little debt, a comfortable net worth position, and a steadily growing income is obviously a more attractive borrower from a lender's perspective than a household with considerable debt, small net worth, and a highly volatile income stream.[7]

The considerations that influence a lender's willingness to lend also influence a household's willingness to borrow. After all, households understand that if they become overextended and default on a loan, their future ability to borrow and spend will be severely impaired. Even if we disregard any legal repercussions, such a credit history will clearly make future potential lenders more reluctant to lend.

To summarize, households accumulate assets and liabilities in the process of attempting to maximize their well-being. The decisions they make and actions they take are the product of their objectives and the economic and financial environment within which they operate. Assuming that the objectives still remain relatively constant, it is changes in the economic and financial environment that will lead to more or less spending and/or saving and thus more or less accumulation of real and financial assets and liabilities. The process is depicted in Exhibit 18-4.

How Economic and Financial Conditions Influence Household Accumulation of Assets and Liabilities

Household spending must be financed, whether via income, existing holdings of money, or borrowing. In addition, other financial or real assets can be a source of funds for spending, but they must be liquidated. Accordingly, fluctuations in household income and net worth (wealth) are usually directly associated with household willingness and ability to spend and borrow. It is

Borrowing Constraint The impediment to continuous borrowing that may come from the lender's unwillingness to keep lending or the borrower's unwillingness to keep borrowing.

---

[7]As mentioned previously in the text, cynics have suggested that the typical banker is someone who will lend you money as long as you can prove you don't really need it.

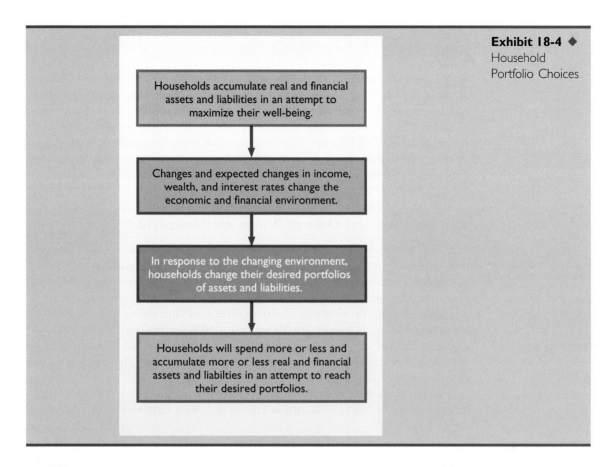

Exhibit 18-4 ◆
Household
Portfolio Choices

important to note that although these variables tend to move together, the relationship between the aggregate variables is quite complex with causation running in both directions. For example, while increases in household incomes surely encourage more consumption, it is also true that increases in aggregate consumption spending raise aggregate income.

Perhaps the most obvious financial determinant of spending and saving or borrowing and lending is the interest rate. A point emphasized throughout the text has been that the interest rate connects the present with the future. More specifically, it specifies the terms under which present purchasing power can be traded off for future purchasing power. To review, for the borrower who gets funds now and pays principal plus interest in the future, the interest rate is the cost of borrowing and spending. For the lender who gives up funds now (forgoes some spending) and is paid principal plus interest in the future, the interest rate is a reward for saving and lending. Thus, if interest rates rise as the result of the behavior of firms, government, or the foreign sector, then the cost of borrowing as well as the reward (return) for lending increase. Intuitively, we should expect households to respond by reducing their borrowing and spending on durables and housing, and to increase their saving and, thus, lending. In summary, changes (and expected changes) in income, wealth, and interest rates are the key forces driving household portfolio adjustments. We now turn to the sources and uses of funds for the household sector to shed some light on these adjustments.

RECAP

Households accumulate assets and liabilities in an attempt to maximize their well-being. Assets may be real or financial. Households compare relative returns on real and financial assets. Money is one financial asset that is demanded for the stream of services that it yields. Households also incur financial liabilities. Changes and expected changes in income, wealth, and interest rates cause households to alter the composition of their assets and liabilities through portfolio changes.

The Sources and Uses of Funds for Households

Flow of Funds A social accounting system that divides the economy into a number of sectors and constructs a sources and uses of funds statement for each sector.

Sources and Uses of Funds Statement A statement for each sector of the economy, such as the household, firm, government, or foreign sectors, that lists the sources and uses of funds.

The **flow of funds** is a social accounting system, which divides the economy into a number of sectors and then constructs a **sources and uses of funds statement** for each sector. The four main sectors are the household, business, government, and foreign sectors. For any sector, spending may be more or less than income or receipts, which implies that borrowing can be more or less than lending. However, for all sectors combined, borrowing (the issuance of financial liabilities) must equal lending (the acquisition of financial assets). This is so because each financial liability in turn implies the existence of a complementary financial asset.

For the household sector, the sources of funds are income and borrowing. These sources of funds, as shown in Equation (18-1), have several possible uses.

	Sources of Funds	Uses of Funds
(18-1)	Disposable Income + Borrowing =	Consumption spending on nondurables and services
		+
		Consumption spending on durables and investment spending on houses (changes in real assets held)
		+
		Changes in financial assets held

Households can use funds (1) to purchase nondurables and services, (2) to purchase durable goods or new houses, and thus add to their holdings of real assets, or (3) to add to their holdings of financial assets including money. To simplify our analysis, borrowing—the change in financial liabilities—can be moved to the "uses" side of Equation (18-1) and subtracted from the change in financial assets (money, stocks, bonds, and time deposits). The resulting net change in other financial assets held—in effect, net household lending— is normally a positive number reflecting the fact that the household sector as a whole is a surplus or lending sector. Within the household sector, some individual households will be net borrowers (deficit spending units, DSUs), while others will be net lenders (surplus spending units, SSUs). Furthermore, the economic and financial environment will affect the degree of borrowing and may induce some households to switch from borrowing to lending, or vice versa. The fact remains, however, that for many decades, all households taken together have had surplus funds—that is, increased their holdings of net financial assets—by an amount equal to about 5 percent of yearly disposable income. The increase in net financial assets is **net financial investment.** We should also note that an additional source of funds could be a selling off of real assets. Since households generally have increased their holding of real assets, we consider changes in these two items to be uses of funds.

Net Financial Investment The increase in net financial assets.

Subtracting borrowing from both sides of Equation (18-1) yields:

	Sources of Funds	**Uses of Funds**
(18-2)	Disposable Income =	Consumption spending on nondurables and services
		+
		Consumption spending on durables and investment spending on houses (changes in real assets held)
		+
		Net changes in financial assets held

As Equation (18-2) implies, households must decide how to allocate income among various possible uses. This allocation decision, as already stated, is guided by a household's desired portfolio. Anything that alters desired portfolios—more formally, the demand for assets—such as changes in interest rates, will, in turn, influence how much income is allocated to each of the possible uses of funds. Given this framework, we can logically proceed by bringing together the key determinants of household demand for real and financial assets.[8]

Household Demand Equations for Real and Financial Assets

The following equations constitute the demand functions for assets by households. (In this case, we separate money from other financial assets.)

$$\text{(18-3)} \qquad \text{Demand for Real Assets} = f(\overset{+}{Y}, \overset{+}{W}, \overset{+}{r}, \overset{-}{i})$$

$$\text{(18-4)} \qquad \text{Demand for Real Money Balances} = f(\overset{+}{Y}, \overset{+}{W}, \overset{-}{i})$$

$$\text{(18-5)} \qquad \text{Net Demand for Nonmonetary Financial Assets} = f(\overset{+}{Y}, \overset{+}{W}, \overset{-}{r}, \overset{+}{i})$$

---

[8]We ignore consumption spending on nondurables and services. Since such goods and services are "consumed" or used up as purchased, they do not directly affect portfolios. In addition, such spending, although large, is a relatively stable proportion of income.

where Y = Household disposable income

W = Household wealth or net worth

r = The yield or return on real assets; the sum of the value of the flow of services from real assets plus any capital gain, all divided by the price of the real asset

i = The market interest rate (return) on financial assets

These equations are less imposing than they look, so let's examine the role of each variable. Income is the most familiar and most straightforward determinant of asset demands. A rise in income—the major source of household funds—will permit or encourage an increase in real and financial asset holdings. Hence, the income variable in Equations (18-3), (18-4), and (18-5) has a positive sign over it, indicating the existence of a positive relationship. A rise in income will lead to more spending on real assets and the accumulation of financial assets including money; the latter is needed for the additional transactions the rise in income induces.

The story is similar in the case of wealth. If, for example, households experience capital gains on assets they hold, the resulting rise in wealth tends to increase household demand for assets. Thus, here again, the wealth variable has a positive sign over it in Equations (18-3), (18-4), and (18-5). As we noted in Chapter 17, wealth also directly influences the demand for money.

The role of the interest rate is a bit more involved. As shown in Equation (18-5), the interest rate is positively related to the net demand for nonmonetary financial assets (financial asset demand minus borrowing). The reasoning is as follows: assume the interest rate—the reward for lending—rises because of the action of firms, government, or the foreign sector. Many households will want to lend more, thus increasing the demand for financial assets; at the same time, other households, for whom the rising interest rate represents an increase in the cost of borrowing, will want to borrow and spend less. The result is that the net demand for financial assets, such as bonds and time deposits, rises as interest rates rise, ceteris paribus. To be a bit more specific, ceteris paribus, the rise in the interest rate encourages households to rearrange their portfolios by holding more net financial assets. However, this rearranging or process of substitution means households will choose to hold less in real assets. Thus, as is shown in Equation (18-3), the interest rate is inversely related to the demand for real assets.

In Chapter 17, we saw that, ceteris paribus, the quantity demanded of real money balances was inversely related to the interest rate. In this chapter, we are no longer holding all other factors constant to isolate the relationship between the interest rate and the quantity demanded of real money balances. In Equation (18-4), there is a negative sign over the interest rate variable indicating an inverse relationship between changes in the interest rate and the demand for real balances. If changes in other factors cause the interest rate to increase, then the demand for real money balances is lower than what it would be if rates had not increased.[9] Likewise, if changes in other factors

---

[9] In Chapter 17, we discussed other factors in addition to income and wealth that affect the demand for real money balances. In this chapter, we are considering the key determinants only.

cause the interest rate to decrease, the demand for real money balances is greater than what it otherwise would be.

To summarize, if we assume real assets, money, and other financial assets are substitutes for one another in household portfolios, a rise in the interest rate will, ceteris paribus, lead households to substitute. They will hold more bonds, say, fewer real money balances, and a smaller quantity of real assets. The equations aside, the intuition behind this result flows from the purposeful, calculating behavior of households as they try to do the best they can in achieving their objectives. In effect, households compare the return (interest rate) on financial assets with the returns available on other assets (money and real assets specifically). If the return on nonmonetary financial assets such as bonds rises relative to the return on other assets (real assets and money), then the typical household trying to maximize its current and future well-being will have an incentive to acquire more bonds and fewer goods now.

Conversely, if interest rates fall and/or the return on, say, real assets, to be discussed in a moment, rises, then households will be induced to hold more real assets and fewer financial assets. The return on real assets is equal to the value of the flow of services from real assets plus any capital gain, all divided by the price of the real assets. Note carefully the positive relationship between the return on real assets and the demand for such assets in Equation (18-3) contrasted with the negative relationship between the return on real assets and the net demand for financial assets in Equation (18-5). These relationships are depicted in Exhibit 18-5. This type of household reaction is illustrated by Jan and Dave's story at the beginning of the chapter. The cut in the interest rate on car loans by General Motors made borrowing more attractive; the fall in market interest rates made lending—that is, acquiring financial assets—less attractive, and the $1,000 price reduction on General

Exhibit 18-5 ◆
Household Demand for Real and Financial Assets

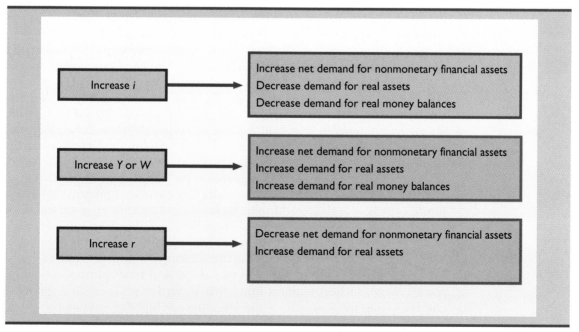

Motors cars, in effect, raised the return on this type of real asset. Comparing the return on financial assets, the cost of borrowing, and the return on real assets, Jan and Dave responded as the simple model embodied in Equations (18-3) to (18-5) predicts. They increased consumption and their holdings of real assets by borrowing and withdrawing funds from their account at HLT National.

The basic forces driving household behavior have now been laid out and linked. A typical reaction by students at this point is "Ok, I understand what happens, for example, if either income or interest rates change. But, what happens when they both change at the same time as is likely to be the case in the real world?"

Suppose, for example, we are interested in what happens to the demand for real assets, and thus consumption spending on durables, when income and interest rates both rise. We know that the rise in income will raise spending and the rise in interest rates will depress spending. At a minimum we know that spending will rise less than it would have if interest rates had remained unchanged. Beyond that, we need to consult the results of empirical research on the relationships embedded in Equations (18-3) to (18-5). Generally speaking, this research suggests that proportional changes in income and wealth have much larger effects on household decisions to consume and save than do equally proportional changes in interest rates. For example, if income and wealth fell by one-half and interest rates fell by one-half, we can say confidently that the depressing effects of the declines in income and wealth on overall consumer spending, including nondurables and services, would be much larger than any boost to spending provided by the fall in interest rates. This does not mean that changes in interest rates are unimportant. For some types of spending, such as the purchase of new homes, the impact of a change in interest rates can be large indeed. For other types, such as spending on durables, changes in interest rates are also important. One must be careful, however, not to overemphasize the role of interest rates and thus conclude, for example, that the Fed, through its ability to affect the supply of funds and interest rates, really controls everything that goes on in the economy including household spending and saving.

The last point that needs to be made concerns the impact of household decisions on the financial system. Until now we have been examining how the financial system affects households. In 1993, the financial surplus (the net financial investment) of the household sector amounted to $190.4 billion dollars, making households by far the largest surplus sector. Given the large role played by households, it should not be surprising to learn that changes in monetary or fiscal policy, or expectations about the future, cause households to alter their spending and thus saving plans, which can have a dramatic effect on the cost and quantity of funds available to the deficit sectors and, therefore, their behavior. If, for example, households become more optimistic about the future or believe inflation will soon accelerate and decide to spend more on consumption or investment goods such as houses and to lend less now, such actions will reduce the size of the household surplus available to prospective borrowers. Ceteris paribus, the resultant fall in the supply of funds will raise the overall level of interest rates and thus the cost of funds to prospective borrowers. Some, such as business firms, will, in turn, reevaluate their spending and borrowing plans in light of the less attractive financial conditions. It is to the behavior of business firms from a financial perspective that we now turn.

RECAP

The flow of funds is an accounting system that constructs a sources and uses statement for major sectors in the economy including the household, business, government, and foreign sectors. The source of funds for households is disposable income. The uses of funds are spending on durables, nondurables and services, investment spending on new houses, and net changes in financial assets. The household demand equations for real and financial assets are:

$$\text{Demand for Real Assets} = f(\overset{+}{Y}, \overset{+}{W}, \overset{+}{r}, \overset{-}{i})$$

$$\text{Demand for Real Money Balances} = f(\overset{+}{Y}, \overset{+}{W}, \overset{-}{i})$$

$$\text{Net Demand for Nonmonetary Financial Assets} = f(\overset{+}{Y}, \overset{+}{W}, \overset{-}{r}, \overset{+}{i})$$

Financial Aspects of the Behavior of Nonfinancial Firms

Having devoted all of Part III to financial institutions, in this section we are restricting our analysis to nonfinancial firms. As in Chapter 4, we assume that firms are in operation to earn profits and that everything they do is guided by the desire to maximize the stream of profits over time.[10] For example, firms maximize profits by expanding production as long as the extra revenue from selling an additional unit of output is expected to be greater than the extra cost of producing the additional unit. In other words, as long as the extra or **marginal revenue** is greater than the extra or **marginal cost,** total revenue minus total cost (profit) rises. Conversely, a firm should reduce production if the marginal revenue from producing and selling an additional unit of output is expected to be less than the marginal cost. Taken together, the rules governing the expansion or reduction of production imply that firms will choose the level of production at which the marginal revenue generated by the last unit of output produced is expected to be just equal to the marginal cost associated with producing that unit.

As costs change, perhaps because wage rates change, or as revenues change, perhaps because output prices change, the output level that yields maximum profits will also change. Firms adjust production accordingly. Such adjustments have repercussions elsewhere because decisions to expand or contract output may be associated with increases or decreases in employment and wages. After all, more or less output will require more or less input. For example, constructing and bringing on-line the new plant in Arkansas will lead APEI to use more inputs as well as to produce more output. Against this background, it should not be surprising that household income depends

Marginal Revenue The additional revenue from selling an additional unit of output.
Marginal Cost The additional cost of selling an additional unit of output.

---

[10] As economists, we use the term *maximize profit* realizing that there may be some practical problems including how to adjust for risk and the time value of money and how to measure profit. In reality, firms may pursue some other goal such as maximizing shareholder's wealth or the firm's value. To do so, firms maximize return, given an acceptable level of risk.

directly on the behavior of firms and the economic environment within which they operate.

To this point, we have focused on how the profit-seeking motive of firms drives production decisions. Happily, the basic logic and analytical framework are applicable to the full range of business decisions, including inventory levels, pricing, investment spending, and borrowing. As was the case with households, the multitude of decisions made by businesses are reflected in firms' balance sheets—that is, in their assets and liabilities. Accordingly, by examining the factors that influence the accumulation of assets and liabilities by firms, the causes and consequences of business actions should come into clearer focus.

Business firms hold real assets such as plant and equipment and inventories. They also hold financial assets, including demand deposits and currency, as well as other highly liquid short-term financial assets such as money market mutual funds, negotiable certificates of deposit (CDs), foreign deposits, and trade credit. In addition, they hold time deposits, mutual funds, and other miscellaneous longer-term assets. Because business receipts and expenditures are not synchronized, firms use cash management techniques through which funds are moved in and out of highly liquid short-term financial assets to minimize the costs of holding real money balances. We looked at the determinants of the demand for real money balances by firms in Chapter 17. Taken together, these real and financial assets are what a firm owns.

Since World War II, the nonfinancial business sector has been a fairly consistent deficit sector and the "average" business firm has been a DSU. Unlike households, firms in the aggregate were net borrowers. Starting in 1991, however, the nonfinancial business sector showed positive net financial investment, meaning that it was a surplus sector—supplying funds rather than demanding them in the aggregate. This anomaly, reflected in the market for loanable funds, was a factor that contributed to interest rates being lower than what they otherwise would be during the early 1990s. Since the second quarter of 1994, the business sector has turned back to being a deficit sector.

Liabilities such as bonds outstanding, long-term mortgage loans owed, short-term debt including business loans from banks and other FIs, and commercial paper outstanding represent what the firm owes. The funds acquired through such borrowing are used to finance current operations and the acquisition of new capital. The difference between the value of assets and liabilities is a business's net worth or owners' equity. As with households, changes in balance sheets at different points in time are caused by flows. Aggregating over all business firms gives a balance sheet for the business sector that reflects assets, liabilities, and net worth. See Exhibit 18-6 for the balance sheet of the business sector as of December 31, 1996.

With this primer as background, it is natural to ask why firms wish to accumulate real assets. The simple answer is that real assets are utilized to produce goods and services and, therefore, earnings. Let's take a closer look at the key factors that underlie the accumulation of real assets.

The Accumulation of Real Assets by Firms: Capital and Inventories

A firm's most important real assets are its capital stock and inventories. We already know that capital is a key factor in the production process and that

Assets	Liabilities
Real Assets	Equity
Capital Goods	Common Stock
Inventories	
Financial Assets	Debt
Currency, Checkable	Long-term
Deposits	
Money Market Mutual	Short-term
Funds	
Certificates of Deposit (CDs)	
Mutual Funds	
Trade Credit	
Other Financial Assets	Other Financial Liabilities
Total Assets	Total Liabilities plus Net Worth

Exhibit 18-6 ◆ The Balance Sheet of the Business Sector (December 31, 1996)

expanding production, once existing factors are fully utilized, will require additional quantities of capital and/or other factors of production. If a firm is only using half of its existing capital, it would seem unlikely that investment spending would be high on the corporate priority list.

As depicted in Exhibit 18-7, business spending on new equipment, the construction of a new plant, and/or an increase in inventories is called **investment spending.** A firm's decision to invest, just like a firm's decision to expand production, depends crucially on expected profits. If firms find that they can increase their profits by expanding production, then output and sales rise. As production expands, capacity utilization increases and at some point, firms find they must undertake investment spending to expand further. If new equipment or a more modern plant can be expected to raise profits over time, firms invest. Depreciation is the amount of investment that would be required to replace the capital stock worn out in the current production process. As a firm's existing capital stock depreciates, the firm must decide whether to replace it. If a firm's investment spending on capital is only as large as depreciation, the capital stock does not increase. **Net investment** increases the capital stock or inventories. Since the factors affecting decisions regarding replacement are essentially the same as those affecting net investment, there is no real need for a separate analysis of investment spending that replenishes worn-out capital. Therefore, we shall focus on net investment, which is gross (total) investment minus depreciation.

From an economywide perspective, firms' decisions to invest play two key roles in the economy. First, investment spending is an important component of aggregate demand. Again, fluctuations in aggregate demand lead to changes in the overall price level and level of real economic activity. Even though investment spending is a much smaller component of aggregate demand than consumption, it is much more volatile than consumption spending. Hence, changes in investment spending are usually associated with fluctuations in business activity. Therefore, policymakers monitor investment spending closely because decisions to invest or not to invest have important effects on real gross domestic product, unemployment, and prices. Second, increases in the capital stock raise the nation's productive capacity and enhance our standard of living and competitive position in the world economy.

Investment Spending For businesses, spending on new equipment and capital or net additions to inventories.

Net Investment Gross investment minus depreciation.

Exhibit 18-7 ◆
Business
Investment

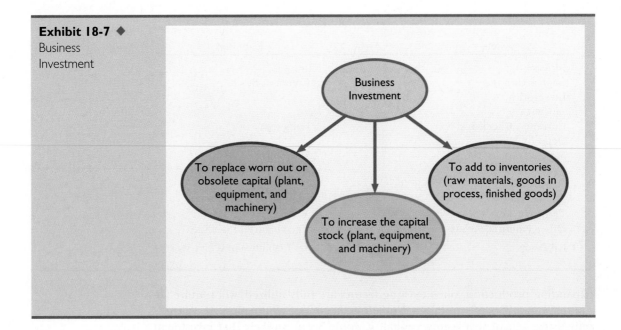

Let's assume that a firm, which is presently using all of its existing capital, finds that it can increase profits by expanding production, but must invest in new capital to do so. It begins by assessing the costs and revenues associated with various investment projects. Specifically, firms will compare the rate of return on particular projects with the cost of financing them. To make this comparison, both the rates of return and the costs of financing projects are typically expressed in annual percentage rates.

The cost side, specifically the cost of financial capital, can be kept fairly simple at this point. Suppose a firm were considering a project that would cost $1,000,000 to purchase. The firm could borrow the funds to finance the project, or it could use funds accumulated from past profits (retained earnings). If the firm borrowed the $1,000,000, the cost of funds would be the prevailing interest rate. If the firm used funds from past profits, the cost of using such funds should be measured by the return the firm could earn if it lent out the funds instead. Since the firm could lend out the funds at the prevailing interest rate, the interest rate is the cost of using the funds even though the firm is spending and not lending them. This is an application of the notion of **opportunity cost.** The opportunity cost of holding or spending money is the return one could have earned by using it in the next best alternative or opportunity. Whether the firm borrows or uses accumulated profits, the cost of funds is the prevailing interest rate. A final point should be noted: the interest rate that matters for investment decisions is the real interest rate, which is approximately the nominal interest rate minus the expected inflation rate. This is so because the real interest rate has been adjusted for expected inflation and represents the true opportunity cost of using funds.[11]

Opportunity Cost The return one could have earned by using funds in the next best alternative; for investment spending, the real interest rate.

---

[11] Another reason why the real interest rate is the relevant rate for investment decisions is because debts are denominated in dollars. A firm would be able to pay a higher nominal interest rate if inflation is expected because the real value of its debt would also be expected to fall. For example, if 5 percent inflation is expected, the firm would be willing to pay a 5 percent higher rate because the value of its outstanding debt would be falling by 5 percent in real terms.

As already discussed, whether firms are willing to invest depends on a comparison of the cost of funds with the returns expected on the purchase of new capital goods. In general, the business outlook and the government's tax policy are important aspects of how firms assess the expected return on any particular investment project. The expected return is the present value of the future stream of returns likely to be associated with a particular project. The value of that stream is determined by the expected profits a project generates. Profits are a function of the productivity of the capital good, the price of the firm's output, the costs associated with operating and maintaining the capital good, and federal, state, and local taxes. If the business outlook is good, firms will expect demand for output to continue to grow, prices to rise, and therefore, revenues to increase. On the other hand, if firms expect a long-lasting recession to begin shortly, the situation and outlook will not be conducive to investment: lower expected future sales will mean lower future profits. Similarly, if the government is expected to raise corporate taxes, this too will lower the future value of profits.

In sum, the accumulation of capital by individual firms, and therefore firms in the aggregate, depends on the degree of capacity utilization, the business outlook, the government's tax policy, and the cost of financial capital (borrowing). Given firms' estimates of the returns on potential investment projects, the amount of investment spending on capital that will actually occur depends crucially on the prevailing financial environment including the level of interest rates and the stance of monetary policy.

As previously noted, firms may also make investments in inventories. Firms hold inventories of raw materials and finished goods to facilitate smooth and efficient production and to satisfy consumer demand. If over a particular time period, such as a year, inventories increase, then investment in inventories is positive. If inventories decrease over the course of the year, then this decrease reduces the net amount of investment spending.

Like sales, planned inventories fluctuate over the business cycle. In particular, inventory investment picks up as the economy expands in anticipation of higher sales. It may also slow down as the economy contracts in anticipation of slower sales.[12] Firms must also finance their inventory stocks. Accordingly, firms take account of the cost of financing and holding inventories. A large portion of that cost is the interest rate. In general, the higher the interest rate, the smaller is the upward adjustment in the stock of desired inventories in response to a surge in sales. The lower the interest rate, the larger is the upward adjustment in response to a surge. In sum and ignoring the details, we can conclude that current and expected sales are the primary determinant of the stock of planned inventories held by firms. Of course, the cost of financing inventories, the interest rate, also contributes to the decision.

 RECAP

Firms maximize profits by producing as long as marginal revenue is greater than marginal cost. In the process, they acquire real assets such as capital

---

[12] If a recession is caused by a drop in aggregate demand, then firms would experience unwanted inventory accumulation at the beginning of a recession. Sophisticated inventory control techniques, made possible by the development of powerful computer systems, have moderated cyclical fluctuations in inventories during the last 10–15 years.

and additions to inventory. They also acquire financial assets (including money) and financial liabilities. Investment spending by the business sector is spending on capital or additions to inventories. The accumulation of capital depends on capacity utilization, the business outlook, the government tax policy, and the cost of borrowing.

The Accumulation of Liabilities by Firms

Firms, in the process of investing and operating on a day-to-day basis, experience periods when expenditures exceed receipts. As a result, several portfolio decisions, summarized in Exhibit 18-8, must be made regarding the financing of excess spending. First, should the spending be financed internally or externally? **Internal financing** is simply the spending of money balances on hand, or the liquidation of financial or real assets owned by firms to finance the excess. Internal financing is the largest source of funds for business firms. As for **external financing,** there are two types: expanding equity or debt. Thus, assuming external financing is decided upon, say because the financing needs exceed the internal funds available, the second decision is whether to issue new debt and/or equity.

External financing via equity involves issuing shares of common stock, expanding the ownership in the firm. If the firm chooses external financing through borrowing, the third decision is whether to issue long-term or short-term debt. For example, the firm must choose between loans or market instruments, such as commercial paper and corporate bonds. In general, each decision is motivated primarily by profit maximization and the existing structure of financial liabilities. A firm will choose the option that minimizes the cost of funds.

Internal Financing The spending of money balances on hand or the liquidation of financial or real assets to finance spending that exceeds current receipts.
External Financing Financing spending that exceeds current receipts by expanding either debt or equity.

Exhibit 18-8 ◆
Business Finance

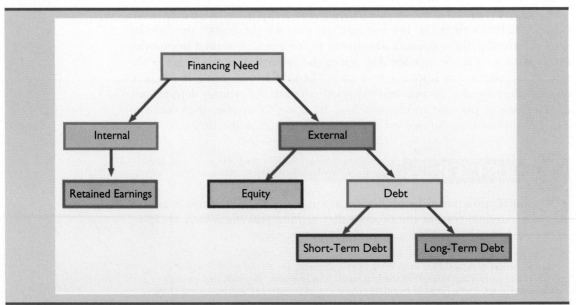

For each firm, the overall cost of funds will be determined by the prevailing financial environment, the stance of monetary policy, and so forth. The relative cost of alternative sources of financial capital and, therefore, the particular financing decision reached will be influenced by several considerations: (1) the particular type of expenditures being financed, (2) the current financial environment and expectations about the future environment, (3) a firm's financial structure, and (4) the tax laws. The accumulation of financial liabilities can be related algebraically to the earnings of firms and the accumulation of assets. A firm's balance sheet can be summarized as follows:

$$(18\text{-}6) \qquad \text{Assets } (A) = \text{Liabilities } (L) + \text{Net Worth } (NW)$$

Converting stocks to flows gives:

$$(18\text{-}7) \qquad \Delta \text{Assets } (A) = \Delta \text{Liabilities } (L) + \Delta \text{Net Worth } (NW)$$

Ignoring capital gains on assets owned, the change in net worth equals net earnings after taxes minus dividends paid to stockholders. In other words, the change in net worth is equal to retained earnings. Substituting this result into (18-7) and rewriting yields:

$$(18\text{-}8) \qquad \Delta \text{Liabilities} = \Delta \text{Assets} - \text{Retained Earnings}$$

Sometimes called the **corporate financing gap,** the increase in a firm's liabilities must be equal to the increase in assets held minus retained earnings.

Traditionally, borrowing to finance inventories has taken the form of either short-term bank loans or the issuance of commercial paper. The usual maturity of the bank loans or commercial paper is one to six months, which coincides with the fact that inventories are typically not held for long periods of time. Fluctuations in inventory investment over the business cycle explain much of the variation in short-term debt accumulated by firms. However, the correlation is not perfect. For example, if prevailing long-term rates are perceived by many firms to be temporarily high relative to short-term rates, some firms will issue short-term debt to finance the initial phases of their investment spending on new capital. These firms expect long-term interest rates will soon drop, enabling them to then issue long-term debt to pay off the maturing short-term debt and finance subsequent phases of their investment spending. Thus, we see how current and expected financial environments play a role in the financing decisions of firms.

From the mid-1970s until 1991, a substantial portion of externally financed investment spending, which by definition is the acquisition of capital (new plant and equipment), was financed by issuing long-term debt. Why long-term debt instead of equity? The answer is that U.S. tax laws tend to bias the financing decisions of business firms toward debt and away from equity. Interest paid on debt is a tax deductible cost and thus is subtracted from gross revenues before the corporate income tax is computed. However, dividends paid equity holders are not tax deductible. Dividends must be paid out of after-tax earnings.[13] Thus debt financing will initially be cheaper, on average, than

Corporate Financing Gap
The increase in a firm's liabilities, which is equal to the increase in assets held minus retained earnings.

---

[13] Thus, there exists the so-called double taxation of dividends. They are taxed as part of business income and taxed again as part of household income.

equity financing, which may also have higher flotation costs. Equity financing also dilutes the ownership of current shareholders.

There is a downside to debt financing. Increasing debt is believed to expose a firm to more risk and therefore to weaken a firm's financial structure. The exposure to more risk can ultimately raise the overall cost of capital as the suppliers of funds require higher returns to compensate them for the additional risk.

The relationship between debt finance, risk, and the cost of capital is rooted in a common measure of the financial structure. This measure is known as the **leverage ratio,** which is the ratio of debt to equity on a firm's balance sheet. Other things equal, the higher the leverage ratio, the greater is the risk to bondholders and stockholders. The reason is because a substantial decline in earnings for a highly leveraged firm could force it into bankruptcy if it were to default on its debt obligations. This could leave its stockholders with nothing. A firm with a low leverage ratio could weather a decline in earnings by cutting dividends. These are not contractual obligations, but rather residual claims. This is not so for the leveraged firm. It must pay its debt costs or fold. Hence, ceteris paribus, the risk-averse investor will typically demand a higher yield on funds they lend to highly leveraged corporations. Firms that have considerable debt relative to equity will find the cost of debt financing (as well as equity financing) to be relatively high. This may in turn lead them to issue equity to both raise funds and strengthen their balance sheets.

Another reason new debt was issued in the 1980s was to acquire in whole or in part the equities of other firms. This activity is often referred to as mergers and acquisitions and has sometimes been financed by the issuance of junk bonds that carry yields above prevailing yields on higher-rated conventional corporate bonds. In this case, debt increases but no new investment occurs. Whatever the benefits of this activity, the resulting expansion of debt relative to equities will increase the leverage ratio of the corporate sector as a whole. This in turn generates concerns about increased risk—that is, an increased vulnerability of individual firms and the economy as a whole to adverse developments.

Starting in 1991 and lasting until early 1994, firms altered the trend of debt financing and issued record levels of new stocks. Because of lower interest rates on CDs, savers poured funds into mutual funds that soaked up the new stock issues. With stocks trading at high values, large amounts of funds could be raised by issuing relatively fewer shares. By mid-1994, the trend seemed to have reversed itself.

In sum, we have examined in some detail how the accumulation of financial liabilities by firms is influenced by the desired accumulation of assets in particular, and their profit-seeking activities more generally. Firms choose the financing option that minimizes the cost of funds.

Having considered how several factors individually affect the accumulation of assets and liabilities by business firms, we are now in a position to consider what happens when expected profits, capacity utilization, and interest rates are all increasing simultaneously. These events are just what would be expected to occur in the expansion phase of the business cycle. We know that the rise in expected profits and capacity utilization will tend to increase the demand for real assets and hence, the demand for financial liabilities, while the rise in interest rates will tend to depress spending and increase the quan-

Leverage Ratio The ratio of debt to equity on a firm's balance sheet.

tity demanded of financial assets. At a minimum, investment and net financial liabilities will go up less than what they would have if interest rates had remained unchanged. Generally speaking, however, research suggests that investment spending is much more sensitive to expected profits than to interest rates. This reality is responsible for the fact that investment spending and the issuance of financial liabilities is often highest when interest rates also peak.

To shed some light on how firms can make adjustments to achieve their goal of profit maximization, we pull together the sources and uses of funds for the business sector. Decisions to spend, save, borrow, and lend to achieve the desired balance sheet configuration are reflected in the sources and uses of funds statements.

 RECAP

Firms may use internal or external financing. Internal financing is the spending of money balances on hand. External financing is expanding debt or equity financing. The change in assets plus the change in liabilities equals the change in net worth. Firms adjust assets and liabilities in response to changes in expected profits, the business outlook, or interest rates.

The Sources and Uses of Funds for the Business Sector

The sources of funds for firms are revenues and borrowing. These sources of funds, as shown in Equation (18-9) have several possible uses.

Sources of Funds	**Uses of Funds**
(18-9) Net Revenues[14]	= Net Spending on real assets such as plant and equipment
+	
Borrowing	+
	Net Spending on real assets such as inventories[15]
	+
	Changes in financial assets held

Firms can use funds to purchase real assets such as plant and equipment or to change their inventories. They can also add to their holdings of money and other financial assets. To simplify our analysis, the "change in financial assets held" can be moved to the lefthand-side of Equation (18-9) and subtracted from borrowing. The result is net borrowing—in effect, net business borrowing of nonfinancial firms—which is normally a positive number reflecting the fact that the business sector as a whole is most often a deficit or

---

[14] Net revenue is gross revenue minus operating expenses such as wages, raw materials, and other operating expenses.
[15] Net spending on real assets whether capital or inventory is gross spending on new real assets minus liquidation of previously owned real assets. Since this is usually a positive number, at least in the aggregate, we keep it on the right side of the equation as a use of funds.

borrowing sector. As we noted previously, this is not always the case. For example, in the 1991–1993 period, the business sector actually experienced surpluses and the net acquisition of financial assets (net financial investment). Despite the fact that the business sector was a surplus sector during that particular period, as of the first quarter in 1994, financial assets of the nonfinancial business sector were just under $3.2 trillion while financial liabilities were just over $5.4 trillion.

Within the business sector, some individual firms will be net lenders who purchase financial assets, while others will be net borrowers. The economic and financial environment will affect the degree of borrowing by the net borrowers and may induce some firms to switch from borrowing to lending and acquiring financial assets, or vice versa. The fact remains, however, that in most post-World War II years, all firms taken together have borrowed—that is, increased their financial liabilities more than their financial assets.

As with households, an additional source of funds could be a drawing down (dis-hoarding) of money holdings or a selling off of real assets. Since businesses have generally increased their holdings of both, we consider changes in these items to be uses of funds.

Subtracting the "changes in other financial assets held" from both sides of Equation (18-9) yields:

Sources of Funds	**Uses of Funds**
(18-10) Net Revenues	= Net spending on real assets such as plant and equipment
+	+
Net Borrowing	Net spending on real assets such as inventories

As Equation (18-10) implies, a firm must decide how to allocate income among its various possible uses. This allocation decision, as in the case of households, is guided by a firm's desired portfolio. Anything that alters desired portfolios—more formally, the demand for assets and liabilities—such as changes in expected profits, the business outlook, or interest rates, will, in turn, influence how much borrowing is done and how borrowing and income are allocated to each of the possible uses of funds. The causal relationship running from desired portfolios to borrowing and investment reflects the fact that it is by borrowing and investing that firms make balance sheet adjustments. We cannot underestimate the importance of the prevailing financial environment and the stance of monetary policy in affecting desired portfolios and business decisions.

RECAP

The sources of funds for firms are net revenues plus net borrowing. The uses of funds are net spending on real assets such as capital and inventories.

In the next chapter, the analysis is extended to the government and foreign sectors. For now, in reviewing this chapter's major themes, keep in mind the pivotal roles of the household and business sector in the overall economy.

Summary of Major Points

1. Households accumulate assets and liabilities in the process of attempting to maximize their well-being. Spending and saving decisions are based on their objectives and the economic and financial environment within which they operate. Assuming that the objectives remain relatively constant, it is changes in the economic and financial environment that lead to more or less spending and saving and thus more or less accumulation of assets and liabilities. Changes in income, wealth, and interest rates are the key forces driving household portfolio adjustments. Consumption spending by households is the largest component of aggregate demand.

2. Investment spending by individual firms, and therefore firms in the aggregate, depends on the degree of capacity utilization, the business outlook, the government's tax policy, and the cost of financial capital (borrowing). Given firms' estimates of the returns on potential investment projects, the amount of investment spending that will actually occur depends on the financial environment including the level of interest rates and the stance of monetary policy. Like consumption spending, investment spending is also a component of aggregate demand. Investment spending is more volatile than consumption spending.

3. Firms also hold inventories of raw materials and finished goods to facilitate smooth and efficient production and to satisfy consumer demand. Like sales, inventories fluctuate over the business cycle. Firms must also finance their inventory stocks. Accordingly, firms take account of the interest rate, which is the cost of financing and holding inventories. In general, the higher the interest rate, the smaller will be the upward adjustment in the stock of desired inventories in response to a surge in sales, and vice versa.

4. Firms experience periods when expenditures exceed receipts. They must decide if the spending should be financed internally or externally. Assuming external financing is decided upon, the second decision is whether to issue new debt or equity. There are tax advantages to debt financing but at the same time, financial leverage and its accompanying risks increase. Short-term borrowing is often used to finance inventories. Long-term borrowing is usually used to finance investment. If interest rates are expected to fall, short-term borrowing may sometimes be used for investment.

5. The sources and uses of funds statement shows that households are net lenders while businesses are usually, but not always, net borrowers. Thus, the household sector's accumulation of financial assets is greater than their issuance of financial liabilities while the business sector's issuance of financial liabilities is usually greater than their accumulation of financial assets. Although the amount of financial assets acquired by a sector is usually not equal to the amount of financial liabilities issued for that

sector, if we aggregate over all sectors, the financial assets for the entire economy are equal to the financial liabilities. Each financial liability in turn implies the existence of a comparable financial asset.

Key Terms

Borrowing Constraint
Corporate Financing Gap
External Financing
Financial Assets
Financial Liabilities
Flow of Funds
Internal Financing
Investment Spending
Leverage Ratio
Marginal Cost

Marginal Revenue
Net Financial Investment
Net Investment
Net Worth
Opportunity Cost
Portfolio
Real Assets
Sources and Uses of Funds
    Statement

Review Questions

1. What is a balance sheet? Are assets equal to liabilities for an individual household? for the household sector as a whole? for the economy as a whole? Explain.

2. What are the commonalities regarding decision making between households and business firms? How does each react to external changes? How do internal decisions affect the economy?

3. Both changes in income and changes in the interest rate affect spending. Which has a greater effect? Explain.

4. Explain the circumstances under which the business sector can be a net accumulator of financial liabilities. In such a situation, must the household sector be a net accumulator of financial assets?

5. Explain the role of each of the following variables in affecting household and/or business spending or saving:
   a. Income
   b. Wealth
   c. The interest rate
   d. Capacity utilization
   e. Expectations
   f. Monetary policy
   g. Tax policy

6. Define the following terms: depreciation, net investment, and the corporate financing gap.

7. Is money a financial asset?

8. What are some of the factors that determine whether a firm chooses internal or external financing? How is the leverage ratio related to the borrowing constraint?

9. Give the stock balance sheet identity. Do the same for flows. What factors cause real assets to change?

10. Why do firms produce output up to the point at which marginal revenue is equal to marginal cost?

11. Do most college students face a borrowing constraint? Explain.

12. My income is going up, but interest rates are also higher. Will I buy a new car?

13. Why don't purchases of nondurable goods show up on balance sheets?

14. What is net revenue for a firm?

15. Will risk averse investors ever acquire risky assets? Explain the role of diversification.

16. Would a firm ever use short-term debt to finance long-term capital expenditures? (Hint: Consider all possibilities for expected long-term rates.)

Analytical Questions

17. Assume at the end of the year that Rosemarie and Jack have the following assets:

House	$150,000	Jewelry	$ 2,000
Stocks and bonds	10,000	Savings deposits	1,000
Money	1,500	Car	10,000
Furniture	3,500		

What is the total of their real assets? What is the total of their financial assets? What are total assets?

18. Assume at the end of the year that Rosemarie and Jack have the following liabilities:

Mortgage loan	$120,000
Credit card debt	4,000
Car loan	6,000

What are their total liabilities? Assuming assets from question 17 and liabilities from question 18, what is their net worth?

19. Assume a hamburger stand sells 10,000 hamburgers at $2 each. Assume also that they paid $.75 for the hamburger, buns, and condiments. What is net revenue?

20. What is the expected return from owning an asset with a 50 percent probability of earning 100 percent and a 50 percent probability of becoming worthless?

21. What is the expected return from owning an asset with a 50 percent probability of earning 100 percent and a 50 percent probability of earning 0 percent?

The Financial System and the Economy

1. From the international financial encyclopedia at the world wide web site (http://www.euro.net/innovation/Finance_Base/Fin_encyc.html), check out the meanings of the following terms:

    a) balance sheet and balance sheet accounts

    b) liquidity risk

    c) portfolio

2. Browse the 1994 annual report for IBM at the world wide web site (http://www.ibm.com/ibm/ibmar94/finance.html)

    a) What are the total assets of IBM equal to? What are total liabilities?

    b) How much is the net worth (stockholders equity) of IBM?

    c) What percent of IBM's total assets is in cash and cash equivalents?

Suggested Readings

For a look at the issue of consumption, see Ben Fine and Ellen Leopold, *The World of Consumption,* New York: Routledge Publishing, 1993.

For a related topic, look at *Personal Saving, Consumption, and Tax Policy,* Marvin H. Kosters, ed., Waldorf, MD: AEI Press, 1992.

A recent approach to understanding the relationship between monetary policy and investment, is found in Laura S. Novak, *Monetary Policy and Investment Opportunities,* Westport, CT: Quorum Books, 1992.

Capital Choices, Michael E. Porter, ed., Boston: Harvard Business School Press, 1994, looks at aspects of the U.S. system of investment decision making including the economic environment, cost of capital, financial markets, executive compensation, and capital budgeting practices.

A classic article on the flow of funds between sectors is Lawrence Ritter, "The Structure of the Flow-of-Funds Accounts," *Journal of Finance,* 17, no. 2, May 1963.

For a discussion of household and business behavior, see Chulho Jung and Barry J. Seldon, "The Macroeconomic Relationship Between Advertising and Consumption," *Southern Economic Journal,* 61, January 1995, pp. 577–587.

19

Financial Effects of the Government and Foreign Sectors

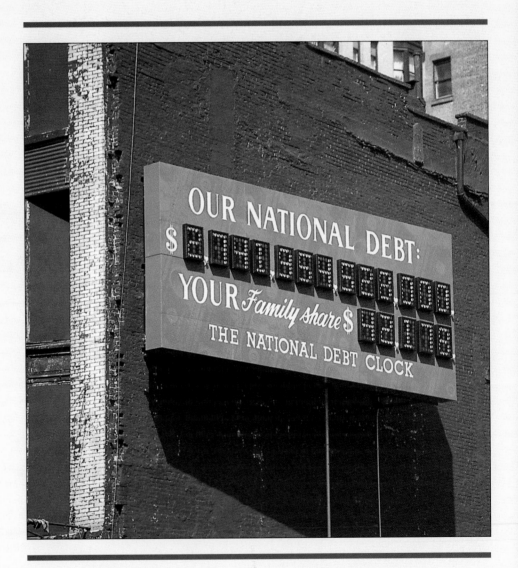

> *The supply of government exceeds the demand.*
> —Lewis H. Lapham—
>
> *Today's interest rates are higher and our [foreign] trade position worse because of our budget situation. There are strong reasons to believe the trend of interest rates should be lower. But we have this big force coming from the U.S. government.*
> —Paul Volcker, January 13, 1984—
>
> *[Deficit reduction] has been the principal factor in the dramatic decline in long-term interest rates.*
> —Bill Clinton—

Learning Objectives

After reading this chapter, you should know:

♦ How the government's spending, taxing, and borrowing broadly affect the financial system and interest rates

♦ How net exports affect aggregate demand and, hence, output and prices

♦ How the spending, saving, borrowing, and lending of the foreign sector affect the financial system and the interest rate

♦ How the federal government deficit may be linked to the trade deficit

Optimism and Dismay

Many newly elected presidents come to Washington, D.C., believing they can make good government financing decisions. Indeed, the last few presidents asserted that they could significantly reduce the government budget deficit and come close to balancing the federal budget. They quickly learned how difficult such tasks can be. Unlike monetary policy, where the Fed is the only body that formulates and directly puts policy actions into effect, no single government body formulates and implements fiscal policy. Actions affecting taxes, transfers, and government expenditures on goods and services, which determine the federal budget balance, are jointly the result of compromises reached between the executive and legislative branches of government. These compromises often result from pressures of organized special interest groups who have access to both the president and Congress. Moreover, voters may suffer from near-sightedness and pressure their elected representatives not to cut spending or to raise taxes. The resulting federal budget balance, the difference between federal receipts and expenditures, in turn affects financial developments in the United States and abroad, including interest rates and exchange rates. Since 1980, the federal budget has been in a uniquely high deficit position. Although the deficit has fallen in the mid-1990s, the recent fiscal experience has had a profound effect on financial developments.

In the mid-1990s, the value of the dollar in terms of the Japanese yen repeatedly fell to record lows causing Judy Shelton to comment, "How many times can you note that the dollar 'reached a post-World War II record low' before it loses its power to shock?"[1] For more than 15 years, the United States has run a continual deficit in the current account, dominated by a continuing deficit in the balance of trade. Despite a depreciated dollar, the trade deficit has persisted. Currently, in an environment in which U.S. interest rates have risen since the early 1990s, it seems that the Japanese are not aggressively purchasing U.S. financial assets. Hence the dollar remains far below its mid and late 1980s value in terms of the yen. Apparently, supply has increased more than demand. Other causes have also been bantered about in the press by those who were alarmed by such events and those who gave them nothing more than a fleeting thought. What forces caused the dollar to depreciate so drastically and what were the implications? How is the value of the dollar related to the government's fiscal or monetary policy?

In this chapter, we discuss the financial repercussions of government spending and taxation policies. In addition, we look at how the spending, saving, borrowing, and lending decisions made by foreigners affect the domestic economy. We see how the government and foreign sectors affect the entire economy, and vice versa. We also consider how the behavior of each affects the other.

Financial Aspects of Government Behavior

The most important macroeconomic objective of government action is the stabilization and growth of the economy. This function involves design-

---

[1] "How to Save the Dollar," *The Wall Street Journal,* July 15, 1994.

ing and implementing taxing and spending policies, usually referred to as **fiscal policy** (introduced in Chapter 1), or to designing and implementing monetary policy by the Fed. In theory, these policies are designed to affect **aggregate demand** and **aggregate supply** (discussed in Chapter 4) in a way that will improve or maintain the overall health of the economy, as measured by the rate of inflation, the unemployment rate, the pace of economic growth, and the competitive position of the United States in the world economy. In this section of the chapter, we focus on fiscal decisions and their effect on the economy and the financial system. Monetary policy is the subject of Part V (Chapters 21–24).

As we have implied, government spending on goods and services is a component of aggregate demand, just as consumption and investment expenditures are components. Note that it is changes in government spending on goods and services, not government outlays, that affect aggregate demand. Government outlays include government purchases of goods and services plus transfers, such as social security and unemployment benefits, and interest on the public debt, sometimes referred to as the national debt. Transfers merely shift purchasing power from one group to another. Unlike changes in government purchases of goods and services, they do not represent changes in the demand for output.

If government spending increases, ceteris paribus, aggregate demand increases and the public benefits from the increased spending whether it be for higher education, national defense, better roads, or the space station. If the economy is at less than full employment, then the increase in government spending may also lead to increases in income and employment as well as more consumption and investment spending. If the economy is at full employment and presently using all of its productive resources, then an increase in real government spending on goods and services will, of necessity, reduce real private spending or result in real borrowing from abroad.[2] The latter scenario may or may not lead to increased benefits for society as a whole.

Unfortunately, all increases in government spending must be financed either by tax increases or by the issuance of government securities, both of which can have a detrimental effect on the private sector. Ceteris paribus, increases in tax rates reduce disposable income. Since spending units have less income, consumption and investment spending decrease. Consumers and business firms are worse off, and aggregate demand is depressed from what it would be otherwise. If government securities are issued, we shall see that regardless of who purchases these securities, the economy can be adversely affected. Interest rates may end up higher and interest-sensitive spending on such things as investment in capital, inventories, and new houses may be negatively impacted. Likewise, the increased government spending may lead to higher inflation which, if unanticipated, has detrimental effects on creditors and may debilitate the whole economy. Note that the real government expenditures on goods and services—rather than taxes—transfer goods from private to public use. Taxes in the aggregate merely influence whether the government allocates the goods with inflationary consequences.

Fiscal Policy Government spending and taxing decisions to speed up or slow down the level of economic activity.

Aggregate Demand The total quantity of final goods and services that will be demanded at various prices, including consumption, investment, and government purchases of goods and services.

Aggregate Supply The total quantity of final goods and services that will be supplied at various prices.

---

[2] As in previous chapters, the use of the term *real* before a variable means that the variable has been adjusted for changes in the price level. In this case, the real amount of government spending (adjusted for price changes) has increased.

Because the positive and negative impacts of increased government spending on the private sector are difficult to measure, judging whether the benefits outweigh the costs is a difficult task. In either case, before government spending is increased, the trick is to be sure that the benefits of that spending are indeed greater than the costs.

The process of making decisions with regard to government taxing and spending is complicated and frequently based on political rather than economic considerations. Taken together, individual policies aimed at many laudable objectives can add up to more government spending, and thus a larger budget deficit than either the president or Congress believes is economically sensible. Politicians are often reluctant to raise taxes and to cut spending on specific programs since both actions are likely to cost them votes. A moment's reflection on the implications of such behavior for the federal budget will make the picture conveyed by the data on federal government outlays and receipts readily understandable. When examining data on government outlays and receipts, analysts have found it useful to view these figures in relation to the general economy as a whole. Such a perspective provides a relative gauge of the growth of the government sector. Now would be a good time to look at Exhibits 19-1 and 19-2, which show federal outlays and receipts as a proportion of GDP from 1960 until 1995.

Borrowing directly connects government actions to the financial system. Building on earlier discussions in the previous chapter, the government sector is similar to the household and business sectors in that if outlays exceed receipts, the resulting deficit must be financed by borrowing. Equation (19-1) ties government deficits to the government securities the Treasury must issue to finance the excess of outlays over receipts.

$$\text{Government Outlays} - \text{Government Receipts} = \text{New Borrowing}$$

$$(19\text{-}1) \quad = \text{Net New Debt Issued by the Treasury (bills, notes, and bonds)}$$

$$= \text{Net Government Demand for Loanable Funds}$$

Rolled Over Borrowing to pay off maturing debt.
Refunding The refinancing of past government debt that is maturing.
Public Debt The sum of all past government deficits less past surpluses.

In addition to borrowing to finance the current deficit, if some previously issued past debt is maturing and the government is not in a position to pay it off, that debt must be **rolled over.** That is, new borrowing called **refunding** must occur to refinance that part of the debt that is coming due. This part of new borrowing does not add to the **public debt,** which is the total of all past deficits less past surpluses.[3] Reflecting the paucity of surpluses after World War II and the large recent deficits, federal government debt outstanding totaled about $5 trillion dollars in 1996. Given approximately 97 million households, this translates to more than $51,500 per household. Only the new borrowing to finance a current deficit adds to the public debt.

The U.S. Treasury is the department responsible for managing the debt of the government. Since outlays have risen faster than receipts, the budget has moved from a small surplus in 1969 to large deficits in the 1980s and still relatively large deficits in the 1990s. Exhibits 19-3 and 19-4 show the federal budget balance since 1960.

---

[3] Sometimes the public debt is referred to as the national debt, but we follow the convention used by the Treasury, Fed, and the Department of Commerce.

Exhibit 19-1 ◆
Federal Outlays
and Receipts as a
Share of GDP
1960 to 1995

Year	Receipts (1)	Outlays (2)	Difference (1) − (2)
1960	18.3%	18.3%	0 %
1961	18.3	18.9	− .6
1962	18.0	19.2	−1.2
1963	18.2	19.0	−1.0
1964	18.0	19.0	−1.0
1965	17.4	17.6	− .2
1966	17.8	18.3	− .5
1967	18.8	19.8	−1
1968	18.1	21.0	−2.9
1969	20.2	19.8	.4
1970	19.6	19.9	− .3
1971	17.8	20.0	−2.2
1972	18.1	20.1	−2
1973	18.1	19.3	−1.2
1974	18.8	19.2	− .4
1975	18.5	22.0	−3.5
1976	17.7	22.1	−4.4
1977	18.5	21.3	−2.8
1978	18.5	21.3	−2.8
1979	19.1	20.7	−1.6
1980	19.6	22.3	−2.7
1981	20.2	22.9	−2.7
1982	19.8	23.9	−4.1
1983	18.1	24.4	−6.3
1984	18.0	23.1	−5.1
1985	18.5	23.9	−5.4
1986	18.2	23.5	−5.3
1987	19.2	22.5	−3.3
1988	18.9	22.1	−3.2
1989	19.2	22.1	−2.9
1990	18.8	22.9	−4.1
1991	18.6	23.3	−4.7
1992	18.4	23.3	−4.9
1993	18.4	22.5	−4.1
1994	19.0	22.0	−3.0
1995*	19.3	21.6	−2.3

*Value for 1995 is estimated.

SOURCE: *Economic Report of the President*, February 1996, p. 368.

In financing the current deficit and refunding maturing debt, the Treasury must consider the timing of the sale of new issues and what maturity distribution of securities should be issued. In other words, how many notes, bills, and bonds should be issued and when should they be issued?

The Treasury is by far the largest single borrower in the financial markets and, as we have seen, it dominates the market for securities because of the large outstanding volume of securities as well as their large initial offerings. To minimize the disruptions that its financing operations can cause in the market, the Treasury has **regularized** a large part of its financing activity. By

Regularized The advanced announcements of Treasury intentions to borrow at standard intervals.

Exhibit 19-2 ◆
Federal Outlays
and Receipts as a
Share of GDP
(1960 to 1995)

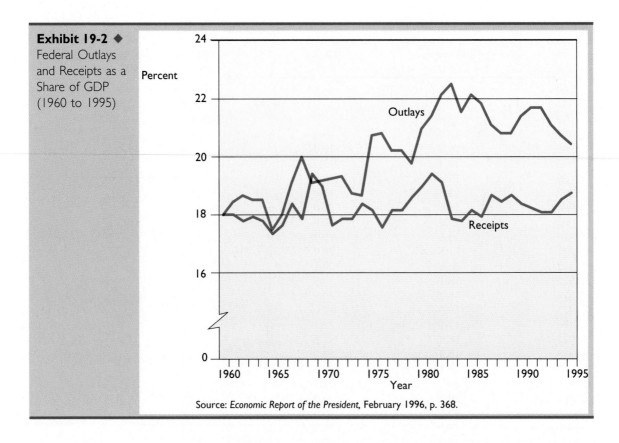

Source: *Economic Report of the President,* February 1996, p. 368.

this we mean that the Treasury announces its borrowing intentions well in advance and tends to borrow at regular intervals. For example, every Monday the Treasury sells new debt consisting of Treasury bills carrying three- and six-month maturities. These weekly sales of bills are used by the Treasury to re-finance bills—issued three or six months previously—that are maturing and to help finance part of the current budget deficit. The latter is done by selling, say, $14 billion of bills on Monday. Of this, $500 million is net new debt and will be used to cover the current budget deficit. The rest will be used to pay off the $13.5 billion of maturing bills. In effect, the government "rolls over" its old debt by paying with newly borrowed funds.

The debt is sold to the public through an auction process. The typical bidders are domestic and foreign financial intermediaries, market makers, and individuals. *The Wall Street Journal* regularly reports the announcements and results of Treasury financing operations. We turn now to the effects of these financing operations.

Financial Effects of Government Borrowing

Simply put, government borrowing, and thus the budget deficit that generates it, can have a considerable impact on the availability and cost of funds to other borrowers. The effect on the spending plans of other borrowers will, in turn, affect the overall pace of economic activity and inflation.

A rise in government borrowing, as spelled out in Equation (19-1), rep-resents an increase in the government's demand for funds. Recall that a rise

LOOKING OUT

How the United States Stacks Up Against the European Union

As discussed in Chapter 9, the European Union is attempting to launch a common currency called the *Euro* by the year 1999. To launch the currency, the member nations have established certain criteria that must be met before a country can participate. Among other criteria, the government deficit as a percent of GDP cannot exceed 3 percent. At the present time, the U.S. government deficit as a percent of GDP for 1996 is estimated to be 2%. The following table shows how the United States stacks up against the 15 nations in the European Union.*

Country	Deficit as a Percent of GDP (Estimated for 1996)
Austria	3.8
Belgium	4.1
Denmark	2.0
EMU Criteria	3.0
Finland	1.5
France	4.6
Germany	2.8
Greece	10.0
Ireland	2.3
Italy	7.5
Luxembourg	2.0
Netherlands	3.0
Portugal	4.8
Spain	5.0
Sweden	6.4
United Kingdom	2.9
United States	2.0**

**Investor's Business Daily*, November 22, 1995, p. B1.
**Figure for the United States is from the *Economic Report of the President*, February 1996, p. 21.

in the demand for funds will, ceteris paribus, raise the interest rate.[4] Again, as in Chapter 8, we assume *the* interest rate refers to the overall level of interest rates. In this case, the interest rate on government securities initially rises because of the increase in government borrowing. In turn, interest rates on other securities such as corporate bonds, municipal bonds, and perhaps even mortgages are also pulled up. As the yield on government securities rises, financial investors seeking higher returns will be attracted to these securities. Some will rearrange their portfolios by selling, say, corporate bonds and buy-

---

[4]Recall from Equation (8–2) that $i = f(\overset{-}{M}, \overset{+}{Y}, \overset{+}{p^e})$ where i equals the interest rate, Y equals income, and p^e equals expected inflation. You can also think of the rise in government spending or cut in taxes, which necessitates more government borrowing, as raising Y and thus the demand for funds.

Exhibit 19-3 ◆
The Difference Between Federal Outlays and Federal Receipts 1960 to 1995 (billions of dollars)

Year	Receipts	Outlays	Surplus or Deficit (−)
1960	$ 92.5	$ 92.2	$ .3
1961	94.4	97.7	-3.3
1962	99.7	106.8	− 7.1
1963	106.6	111.3	− 4.8
1964	112.6	118.5	− 5.9
1965	116.8	118.2	− 1.4
1966	130.8	134.5	− 3.7
1967	148.8	157.5	− 8.6
1968	153.0	178.1	− 25.2
1969	186.9	183.6	3.2
1970	192.8	195.6	− 2.8
1971	187.1	210.2	− 23.0
1972	207.3	230.7	− 23.4
1973	230.8	245.7	− 14.9
1974	263.2	269.4	− 6.1
1975	279.1	332.3	− 53.2
1976	298.1	371.8	− 73.7
1977	355.6	409.2	− 53.7
1978	399.6	458.7	− 59.2
1979	463.3	503.5	− 40.2
1980	517.1	590.9	− 73.8
1981	599.3	678.2	− 79.0
1982	617.8	745.8	− 128.0
1983	600.6	808.4	− 207.8
1984	666.5	851.8	− 185.4
1985	734.1	946.4	− 212.3
1986	769.1	990.3	− 221.2
1987	854.1	1,003.9	− 149.8
1988	909.0	1,064.1	− 155.2
1989	990.7	1,143.2	− 152.5
1990	1,031.3	1,252.7	− 221.4
1991	1,054.3	1,323.8	− 269.5
1992	1,090.5	1,380.9	− 290.4
1993	1,153.5	1,408.7	− 255.1
1994	1,257.7	1,460.9	− 203.2
1995*	1,350.6	1,514.4	− 163.8

*Value for 1995 is estimated.

SOURCE: *Economic Report of the President*, February 1996, p. 367.

ing government bonds. This selling of corporate bonds will tend to raise the rate on corporate bonds (lower the price), and the purchase of government bonds will tend to lower the rate on government bonds (raise the price). It is this process of substitution that binds together all the interest rates in financial markets and generally causes all interest rates to move up and down together. Thus we can refer to the overall level of interest rates or *the* interest rate as moving up and down.

Why are we interested in this financial effect of government borrowing? Simply put, the rise in interest rates generated by the government's deficit

financing will, ceteris paribus, tend to reduce the funds flowing to private borrowers such as firms and households, as well as municipal and state governments. This phenomenon is known as **crowding out,** which means that the rise in rates could induce some who had planned to borrow and spend to cancel, postpone, or reduce their spending and borrowing plans. More specifically, the rise in interest rates will tend to lower investment spending by some firms relative to what it otherwise would have been because firms may find that the higher cost of financial capital now exceeds the expected return on some previously planned investment projects. Similarly, the rise in rates on mortgage and consumer loans will lower spending by some households, particularly on consumer durables and housing, relative to what it otherwise would have been.[5] Utilizing a now familiar tool, Exhibit 19-5 illustrates the effect of federal government borrowing on the interest rate. Loanable funds are measured on the horizontal axis while *the* interest rate is measured on the vertical axis.

The initial equilibrium is point A. The equilibrium interest rate is 6 percent and the quantity of funds supplied and demanded is $500 billion. Now assume, ceteris paribus, the government raises spending or cuts taxes such that the deficit and, therefore, government borrowing increases by $50 billion. The increase in the government's demand for funds will shift the total demand for funds by all deficit spending units (DSUs) in the economy to the right. If

Crowding Out The reduction in private borrowing and spending due to higher interest rates that result from government deficit financing.

---

[5] The phrase, "relative to what it otherwise would have been," is included to emphasize the fact that consumption and investment may increase even in the face of rising interest rates. However, the rise in rates will result in the increase in spending being smaller than what it otherwise would have been.

Exhibit 19-4 ◆
The Differnce Between Federal Outlays and Receipts Since 1960

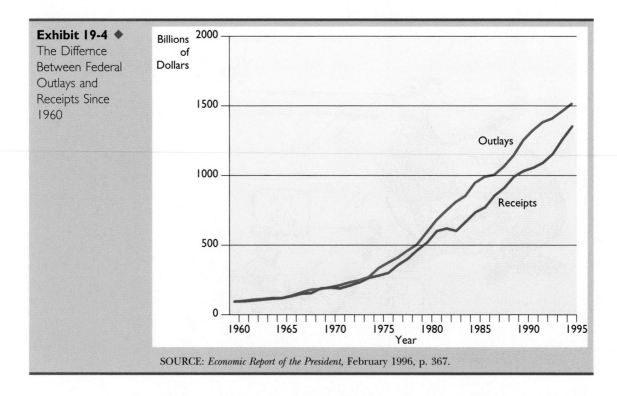

SOURCE: *Economic Report of the President,* February 1996, p. 367.

the interest rate remained at 6 percent, the total quantity demanded of funds would rise by $50 billion to $550 billion. Of course the interest rate will not remain at 6 percent because the quantity of funds now demanded ($550) exceeds the quantity of funds supplied ($500). In response to this disequilibrium, the interest rate rises to 8 percent and the quantity of funds supplied and demanded rises to $530 billion to reach a new equilibrium. The government is borrowing $50 billion more while total borrowing increases by only $30 billion from 500 billion to $530 billion. Hence, the rise in the interest rate reduces the total amount of funds borrowed by households and firms by $20 billion relative to what they would have borrowed in the absence of a rise in rates. This reduction in borrowing and the associated reduction in consumption and investment spending that results from the rise in rates induced by increased government borrowing is crowding out.

But don't let Exhibit 19-5 lull you into the complacent belief that interest rates and deficits always move up and down together. Here, as elsewhere, our ceteris paribus assumption is critical. In the real world where thousands of factors are changing at once, the relationship between interest rates and deficits can be obscured by a variety of factors. For example, on the demand side, decreases in the demand for funds by households and firms may offset the increase in the demand for funds by government. Indeed, this is exactly what we expect could happen in a recession. A cyclical drop in production and employment during a recession can lead, ceteris paribus, to an increase in the federal budget deficit. Tax receipts fall as household and business income falls, while government outlays rise mostly from increases in transfer payments such as unemployment compensation. The same cyclical drop in production that enlarges the deficit produces a reduction in household spending, particularly on housing and durable goods, and in business investment spending.

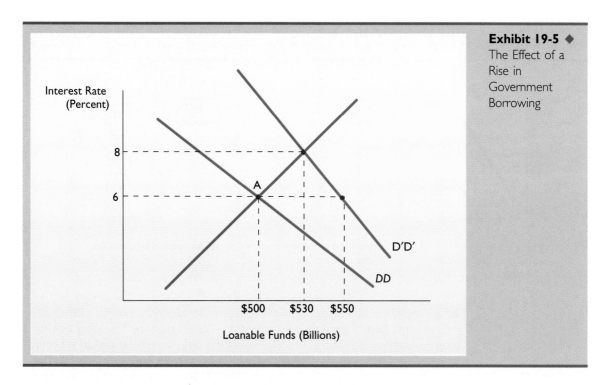

Exhibit 19-5 ◆
The Effect of a
Rise in
Government
Borrowing

Interest Rate
(Percent)

8

6

A

$500 $530 $550

D'D'

DD

Loanable Funds (Billions)

Since less spending typically means less borrowing, the increase in the government's demand for funds will offset a fall in demand by others and interest rates can fall despite the rise in the budget deficit.

On the supply side, a rise in the total demand for funds, reflecting, say, a rise in the budget deficit, may not result in a rise in interest rates if, at the same time, there is an increase in the supply of funds. That would be a shift to the right of the supply curve in Exhibit 19-5. How could this occur? The supply of funds reflects the willingness of surplus spending units (SSUs), both domestic and foreign, to supply funds and the Fed's provision of reserve assets to the economy.[6] Accordingly, if a rise in the government's deficit and thus, borrowing, is accompanied by an increase in the amount of funds supplied by the Fed, interest rates may not rise at all. Interest rates could even fall if the rise in the supply of funds generated by the increase in reserves is relatively larger than the rise in demand. Similarly, if foreign SSUs judge U.S. financial claims as more attractive than foreign claims, there could be a rise in the foreign supply of funds. Large inflows of foreign funds into the United States during the 1980s played an important role in financing the historically high U.S. government budget deficits. This inflow of funds from abroad limited the rise in U.S. interest rates and the crowding out of consumption and investment spending which could have otherwise occurred. Now would be a good time to look at Exhibits 19-6 and 19-7. Exhibit 19-6 demonstrates that given an increase in the supply of loanable funds along with the increase in the government deficit, the interest rate may increase, decrease, or stay the

---

[6]A rise in the government deficit will increase, correspondingly, the surplus of other sectors combined since the aggregate deficit of all sectors is zero. This will possibly lower the demand for funds by other sectors.

Exhibit 19-6 ◆

Increases in the Supply of Funds May Accompany Increases in the Government Deficit

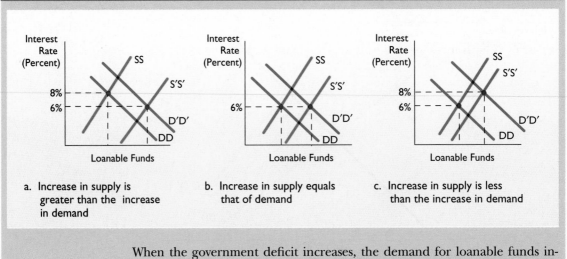

a. Increase in supply is greater than the increase in demand

b. Increase in supply equals that of demand

c. Increase in supply is less than the increase in demand

> When the government deficit increases, the demand for loanable funds increases, and, ceteris paribus, the interest rate rises crowding out some private interest-sensitive spending. But this crowding out may not necessarily occur if the Fed increases the supply of loanable funds by providing reserves to the banking system. SS shifts to the right to S'S'. The interest rate may increase, decrease, or stay the same depending on the magnitude of the shift.

same depending on the magnitude of the shifts. Exhibit 19-7 shows who the federal debt is owed to.

Expectations and the Timing of Interest Rate Changes

Recall that a rise in interest rates lowers the price of bonds. Now suppose that analysts suspect that the budget deficit three months down the road is going to be larger than previously believed and that interest rates may rise. All those individuals and institutions holding bonds may want to sell bonds to avoid pending capital losses, perhaps planning to buy them back later after rates rise and bond prices stop falling. The market effect on those selling bonds is that rates will rise in the market. The rates rise today well before the Treasury actually borrows the larger-than-previously expected volume of funds.

The key point illustrated is the pivotal role played by expectations of future events in determining current conditions in the financial system. In particular, changes in expectations will lead to changes in interest rates, especially longer-term rates, well before the event to which the expectations pertain actually occurs. For example, after the Deficit Reduction Act was passed in 1993, interest rates on long-term bonds fell dramatically. Some analysts attributed this fall in interest rates to the fact that perceptions changed about the size of future deficits. Rates went down long before any real impact on the deficit as a result of the legislation's effect on expectations.

In reality, the correspondence, or lack thereof, between expectations of future Treasury borrowing and what the Treasury actually borrows can lead to at least three different interest rate responses as the Treasury issues new debt: in

Case 1, the Treasury's borrowing is entirely expected and thus, prevailing interest rates are not affected by the financing (rates have risen previously as expectations of the Treasury's borrowing were folded into expectations and portfolio decisions); in Case 2, the Treasury borrows more than is expected and this unexpected increase in the demand for funds raises the prevailing level of interest rates; and in Case 3, the Treasury borrows less than is expected and this unexpected decrease in the demand for funds lowers the prevailing level of interest rates.

While the considerable attention accorded pending government actions by the press and financial market participants suggests Case 1 is typical, all three cases have been in evidence during recent years. Even though the third scenario could be particularly baffling to the naive observer, only when Case 2 occurs do we actually observe the tendency for rates to rise contemporaneously as the Treasury borrows more funds. At a minimum, the supply, demand, and timing considerations discussed here should serve to reemphasize the fact that interest rates are jointly determined by the behavior of deficit spending units (DSUs), surplus spending units (SSUs), and the Fed. Expectations about such behavior and the economy more generally play a key role in the financial system. For now, let's turn to the sources and uses of funds for the government sector.

The Sources and Uses of Funds in the Government Sector

The sources of funds for government are primarily tax receipts and borrowing. These sources of funds, as shown in Equation (19-2), have several possible uses.

	Sources of Funds	**Uses of Funds**
(19-2)	Tax Receipts + Borrowing =	Government spending on goods and services
		+
		Government spending on transfer payments
		+
		Interest payments on the public debt
		+
		Changes in financial assets held[7]

Governments can use funds to purchase goods and services, to make transfer payments such as social security payments and welfare, to pay interest on the public debt, and to acquire financial assets. The government holds some financial assets as Treasury deposit account balances to engage in the normal

---

[7] Part of the changes in financial assets held may be changes in Treasury deposit accounts at the Fed. As we saw in previous chapters, the Fed is the fiscal agent for the government and as such maintains Treasury deposit accounts from which the Treasury makes disbursements (payments). The balances in these accounts, although there for the purpose of making transactions, were not included in any monetary aggregate and, thus as we have defined them, are not money.

Exhibit 19-7 ◆
Who the Federal
Debt Is Owed To
2nd Quarter 1995

	Dollar Value (billions)	Percent
Total National Debt	$4,951.4	100.0%
U.S. Government Agencies	1,316.6	26.6
Federal Reserve Banks	389.0	7.9
Domestic Investors	2,460.9	49.7
Foreign Investors	783.7	15.8

SOURCE: *Federal Reserve Bulletin*, February, 1996, A30.

transactions involved in running the government. Other financial assets are also held by the government.

To simplify our analysis, the "change in financial assets held" can be moved to the left-hand-side of Equation (19-2) and subtracted from the change in borrowing. The resulting net change in other financial liabilities owed—in effect, net government borrowing—has been a positive number in most of the years since the end of World War II and continuously since 1980, reflecting the fact that the government sector as a whole is a deficit or borrowing sector.[8] Within the government sector, including federal, state, and local jurisdictions, some states and local government bodies have run surpluses, thus offsetting the large government deficits of the federal government. However, in the 1990s, these state and local surpluses have decreased as state and local governments have run into some of the same funding problems that have plagued the federal government for a longer period of time. The fact remains, however, that over the past 20 or so years, all government units taken together have borrowed—that is, increased their net financial liabilities by relatively large amounts.

Since net borrowing is equal to "borrowing" minus "changes in financial assets held," Equation (19-2) simplifies to Equation (19-3):

Sources of Funds   **Uses of Funds**

(19-3)   Tax Receipts + Net Borrowing = Government spending on goods and services

+

Government spending on transfer payments

+

Interest payments on the public debt

Net new borrowing by the government is usually termed the *government deficit*. When the government borrows, the Treasury issues new government

---

[8] In fact, the last time the federal government ran a surplus was 1969, while the last time the government sector as a whole (including state and local governments) ran a surplus was 1979. In the last 26 years, the federal government has run a deficit, thus increasing its financial liabilities.

bills, notes, and bonds, all of which are financial liabilities. If the public buys the bills, notes, and bonds, they are financial assets to the purchaser and liabilities to the federal government. If the Fed buys the government securities, the Fed has in effect **monetized** the government deficit. That is, the Treasury's deposit account with the Fed is credited and the Treasury disburses the funds, just as if the government had printed money. In this case, the government securities are assets to the Fed and liabilities of the federal government. In either case, the supply and/or demand of loanable funds can change, which will have repercussions throughout financial markets and indirectly affect the behavior of participants in other sectors through the effect on interest rates. It is important to note that the Fed, and not the Treasury, decides which part of the deficit gets monetized and which part is borrowed from the public.

Monetized When the Fed purchases newly issued Treasury securities, which credits the Treasury's deposit account.

The discussion in this section has focused on the short-run financial effects of government borrowing. Over time, reflecting the government's chronic budget deficits, the nation's total indebtedness has increased dramatically. Exhibit 19-8 includes a discussion of the long-run effects of government borrowing. For now, we move on to look at the impact of the foreign sector on the economy.

RECAP

Government spending on goods and services is a component of aggregate demand. Government spending must be financed either by taxes or borrowing. Increases in taxes reduce consumption and investment expenditures. Since 1960, government outlays have grown faster than taxes. Government outlays minus receipts equal the government demand for loanable funds. Increases in government spending may increase interest rates and crowd out private spending. The sources of funds for the government are taxes and net borrowing. The uses of funds for the government are spending on goods and services, spending on transfer payments, and interest payments on the public debt.

The Foreign Sector and Its Effect on the Financial System

In Chapter 9, we saw that the exchange rate is the number of units of one currency that can be acquired with one unit of another. Like other prices, the exchange rate is determined by the forces of supply and demand. We found the demand for dollar-denominated funds to be directly related to changes in foreign income, and to be inversely related to changes in the foreign price of U.S. goods relative to the foreign price of foreign goods and to changes in foreign interest rates relative to U.S. interest rates. In turn, the supply of dollar denominated funds is directly related to changes in U.S. income, to changes in the dollar price of U.S. goods relative to the dollar price of foreign goods, and to changes in foreign interest rates relative to U.S.

Exhibit 19-8 ◆

The Long-Term Effects of Government Deficit Spending

When outlays exceed tax receipts, the government runs a deficit, borrowing occurs, and the public debt increases by the amount of the shortfall. Our public debt—that is, the total amount of U.S. government debt outstanding—is about $5 trillion. When the debt becomes a topic of discussion, one question inevitably comes up: "Is this enormous public debt a burden that will have to be paid off by future, still unborn generations of Americans?" Let us examine the issue more closely.

If we owe that much money, to whom do we owe it? For every creditor (holder of a financial asset) there must be a debtor (owner of a financial liability). To answer the question, let us suppose that all holders of government bonds are Americans. In this case the debt is, in effect, owed to ourselves! More specifically, Americans owe those Americans owning government securities. The net debt burden on the society is nil. There are, of course, distributional effects within society. Those who own bonds will be receiving the interest income. The bondholders are better off and the taxpayers without bonds are worse off. On balance, however, there would be no current net debt burden on society. Of course there is the real burden of the frictional costs and resources necessary to administer it. Further, there are potential disruptive effects on production if the debt burden grows exponentially—that is, when borrowing has to be increased to pay the interest and the new borrowing raises the debt, which raises the interest, which raises the borrowing, which raises the debt which. . . . This could result in financial crises.

In assessing the burden of the debt, one must keep in mind the fact that the debt comes into existence and rises when the government's spending exceeds it receipts. What does the government purchase? In general, it purchases resources (factors of production) that enable it to produce goods and services such as highways. Thus, in exchange for the debt, we get benefits in the form of goods and services provided by the government. Obviously, the debt looks less burdensome when we recognize and take account of these benefits. A portion of the current debt resulted from deficits incurred during World War II. If you think this debt is a burden on society, consider what would have happened if the government had not spent and incurred these deficits. Of course, if the government borrows and spends money frivolously or its spending crowds out private spending lowering real capital formation and generating considerable inflation, then the notion that its debt in some way burdens society is more credible.

The debt can be burdensome in another way. In the preceding discussion, we assumed that the outstanding debt is owed to Americans. This, of course, is not true. A significant share of the debt is owed to foreigners—about 16 percent or $783.7 billion in mid-1995. The debt owed to foreigners is a financial claim they have on future U.S. wealth. If and when foreigners exercise these claims by using the purchasing power accumulated, our domestically owned national wealth will be reduced and future generations will bear that burden. This is one aspect of the growing importance of international considerations in the United States.

interest rates.[9] Hence, changes in the exchange rate can come about from either changes in the foreign or domestic economy.

Let's consider how changes in the exchange rate will feed back into the domestic economy regardless of their source. Think about the relationship between the exchange rate and the balance of trade in goods. Ceteris paribus, as the dollar appreciates, exports become more expensive for foreigners while imports become cheaper for domestic residents. Being rational, foreigners reduce their purchases of the now more costly exports while spending units in the domestic economy substitute into the now cheaper foreign goods. The result is that as the dollar appreciates, exports decrease while imports increase. Given that net exports are by definition equal to exports minus imports, as the dollar appreciates, net exports fall and as the dollar depreciates, net exports rise. Consequently, ceteris paribus, the relationship between net exports and the exchange rate is inverse.[10]

We first discussed aggregate demand in Chapter 4, where for simplicity, the government and foreign sectors were ignored. Aggregate demand within our simplified economy reflected the behavior of households and firms planning to engage in consumption and investment spending. In the last section, we noted that government spending on goods and services and taxes also affect aggregate demand. Now we are in a position to see that net exports are also a component of aggregate demand along with consumption, investment, and government spending.

Let's consider what happens to aggregate demand when the exchange rate changes. For example, if the dollar depreciates, then, ceteris paribus, net exports increase. Foreigners are purchasing more goods from the U.S. while domestic residents are purchasing fewer imports from abroad.[11] In the United States, a depreciation in the dollar could mean more jobs and production, and higher income than if the exchange rate remained unchanged. On the other hand, if the dollar appreciates, U.S. residents will, ceteris paribus, purchase relatively more goods from abroad; demand for domestic goods and services is lower than what it would be otherwise. This change could translate to fewer jobs, less production, and lower income in the United States. In other words, increases in the exchange rate, ceteris paribus, could lead to decreases in U.S. production, employment, and income, while decreases in the exchange rate could lead to increases in U.S. production, employment, and income. So changes in the exchange rate are, ceteris paribus, inversely related to U.S. production and employment. Exchange rate changes feed back to the domestic economy via their effect on net exports, which are directly related to changes in aggregate demand.

---

[9] Remember that there is an inverse relationship between the quantity demanded of dollar-denominated funds, ceteris paribus, and the exchange rate. Likewise, there is a direct relationship between the quantity supplied of dollar-denominated funds, ceteris paribus, and the exchange rate.

[10] If the value of goods a country is exporting is greater than the value of goods it is importing, then the country is running a trade surplus. Likewise, if the value of goods it is importing is greater than the value of goods it is exporting, then the country is running a trade deficit.

[11] If the United States is initially running a trade surplus when the dollar depreciates, then the trade surplus grows. Conversely, if the current account was initially in a deficit position, then the deficit declines or turns into a surplus.

Now we can begin to see clearly the linkages among economies. In addition to domestic factors such as monetary or fiscal policy or changes in the behavior of households and firms, any factor that affects net exports also affects aggregate demand and hence domestic GDP and the domestic price level. For example, if foreign income (or the foreign price level relative to the U.S. price level or foreign interest rates relative to U.S. rates) changes, aggregate demand changes, causing domestic GDP and the price level to change. These changes then feed back to the foreign economy, which will in turn affect the domestic economy, and on it goes.

The foreign sector clearly adds additional complications that policymakers face in managing the domestic economy. Any policy action that affects the domestic economy will also affect the international economy, and the effects on the international economy will then feed back into the domestic economy. Likewise developments in the international economy will affect the domestic economy. If a domestic economy is somewhat isolated from the rest of the world, then indeed this effect may be rather small. However, as international trade and finance become more significant, as they have to the United States in the past 25 years, this effect also becomes more significant. Exhibit 19-9 shows exports and imports relative to gross domestic product. Striving (and sometimes failing) to manage such effects so as to preserve the health and stability of the economy must necessarily involve international considerations. More on this in a later policy chapter. For now we turn to the effects of foreign demand for U.S. securities on domestic financial markets.

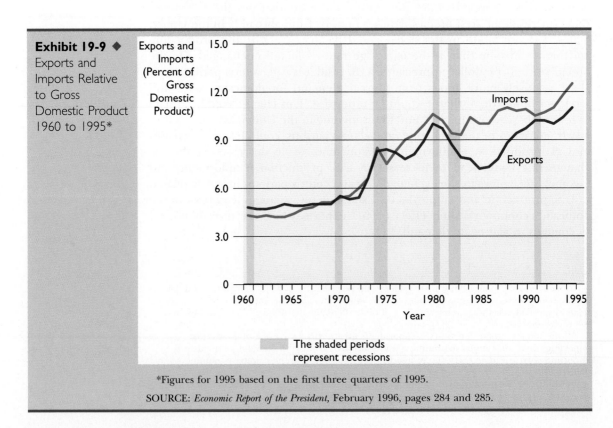

Exhibit 19-9 ◆ Exports and Imports Relative to Gross Domestic Product 1960 to 1995*

Exports and Imports (Percent of Gross Domestic Product)

The shaded periods represent recessions

*Figures for 1995 based on the first three quarters of 1995.

SOURCE: *Economic Report of the President*, February 1996, pages 284 and 285.

The Effects of International Events on the Interest Rate

Changes in the exchange rate affect net exports as measured in the first account of the balance of payments. The first three accounts of the balance of payments constitute the current account, which measures international transactions in currently produced goods and services.[12] In recent decades, the current account has been dominated by a deficit in net exports. Since the balance of payments always balances, if a deficit in net exports causes the current account to be in deficit, then the balance in the capital account, which measures international capital flows, must be in surplus.[13]

When purchases of U.S. financial claims by foreigners and borrowing, more generally, from foreign sources by U.S. firms and residents exceed purchases of foreign financial claims (securities) by U.S. residents and borrowing by foreigners from U.S. banks and other sources, the U.S. is experiencing **net capital inflow.** The result is that, ceteris paribus, the supply of loanable funds is greater and the domestic interest rate is lower than what they would be without the capital inflow. If net exports are positive (resulting in a surplus in the current account), then there is a net capital outflow and the supply of loanable funds is less than what it would be otherwise. Thus, net capital flows affect domestic interest rates through their impact on the supply of loanable funds. Exhibit 19-10 shows capital flows relative to gross domestic product.

In previous chapters, we considered the supply of loanable funds as consisting of the surplus funds generated by SSUs and increases in credit extension through financial intermediaries. Credit extension is often triggered by increases in reserve assets initiated by the Fed. We now are in a position to see that when foreigners purchase U.S. financial assets, they too are increasing the supply of loanable funds. Ceteris paribus, the inflow of funds from abroad leads to decreases in the interest rate. Likewise, decreases in foreign purchases of domestic financial assets lead to decreases in the supply of loanable funds and increases in the interest rate.

But you may ask, why would foreigners want to increase or decrease their purchases of domestic financial assets? An obvious reason would be that U.S. interest rates changed relative to the rest of the world, making U.S. securities more or less attractive relative to foreign securities.[14] For example, if U.S. rates increased, ceteris paribus, funds would flow in from abroad to get the higher return. Note the enigma of the situation: the capital inflow causes interest rates to be lower than what they would be otherwise, but it occurs because interest rates are relatively high to start with. In addition, high U.S. interest rates relative to the rest of the world would increase the demand for dollar-denominated deposits and hence cause the dollar to appreciate relative to other currencies—and, as we have seen, changes in the exchange rate feed into net exports. It seems we have come full circle. Changes in the exchange rate affect net exports, which change aggregate demand. Changes in domestic interest rates affect capital flows, which also affect the exchange rate and, hence, net exports and aggregate demand.

Net Capital Inflow The purchases of U.S. financial claims by foreigners exceed purchases of foreign financial claims by U.S. entities.

---

[12] These three accounts include merchandise exports and imports, trade in services, and unilateral transfers.

[13] We ignore any official reserve transfers in this discussion.

[14] Another reason could be that demand for U.S. securities is high because the U.S. is perceived to be a safe haven for investment due to its political and economic stability.

Exhibit 19-10 ◆
Capital Flows
Relative to Gross
Domestic Product
1960 to 1995

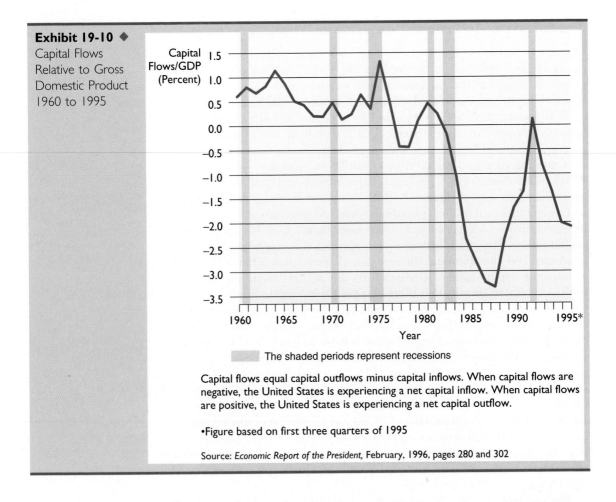

The shaded periods represent recessions

Capital flows equal capital outflows minus capital inflows. When capital flows are negative, the United States is experiencing a net capital inflow. When capital flows are positive, the United States is experiencing a net capital outflow.

•Figure based on first three quarters of 1995

Source: *Economic Report of the President,* February, 1996, pages 280 and 302

A related question is Why would domestic interest rates be high relative to the rest of the world? Perhaps the supply and demand for loanable funds provides the answer. If the interest rate equates the quantity demanded of loanable funds with the quantity supplied, then any factor that affects either demand or supply would also affect the interest rate. On the demand side, changes in the spending plans of households, firms, or government would all affect the demand for loanable funds. On the supply side, changes in the surplus funds available from SSUs, credit extension by financial intermediaries, and capital flows from abroad would all change the supply of loanable funds. In addition, changes in domestic inflationary expectations relative to foreign inflationary expectations would also change the level of domestic rates relative to foreign rates.

Since 1983, the United States has experienced relatively large net capital inflows. Reports suggested that the nation quickly went from being the world's largest creditor nation to a debtor nation.[15] Many suspected that these capital

---

[15]There are major questions with regard to whether the United States is really a debtor nation. These questions result from how assets are valued. It seems that both foreign and domestic assets are valued by their acquisition costs. Many foreign assets held by Americans were acquired many years ago while a higher proportion of American assets held by foreigners were acquired in recent years. The thought is that the foreign assets acquired years ago and still valued at their acquisition price may be undervalued.

LOOKING OUT

The Stock Boom and the Globalization of Finance

Eurobonds are bonds denominated in currencies other than that of the country in which they are sold. As we saw in Chapter 6, the Eurobond market has experienced incredible growth since the 1980s. U.S. firms will borrow wherever the cost of funds is lowest. Such "offshore" financing is an obvious example of the globalization of finance.

Another example of financial globalization deals with equities and the recent surge of the stock market. On November 21, 1995, the Dow Jones Average (an index of stock prices) closed above the 5,000 mark for the first time in history. This represents a five-fold increase since 1982 and one of the greatest boom periods for stocks in history. By March, 1996, the index had climbed to above 5,600.

In the past, many analysts would suspect that such a strong bull market would be followed by a collapse, a correction, or stagnation. For example, the boom period of the 1920s ended with the stock market crash of 1929 and the start of the Great Depression. In addition, many other rallies have been followed by corrections or downturns.

This recent swell of stock prices may be different from previous surges or so suggests G. Pascal Zachary in an article in the *Orange County Register.** Zachary believes the stock market will continue to rise because "many economists and corporate chieftains see a new era of steady growth and productivity gains related to global integration and technological advances—a climate especially suited to large, well-capitalized U.S. corporations."

Such globalization benefits domestic companies because of the inflow of capital, which helps to finance U.S. investment. With the United States having experienced large gains in productivity in the 1990s, stock prices may continue to climb as funds flow in from all corners of the globe seeking the highest return.

*G. Pascal Zachary, "Global Answer to Stock Surge," *Orange County Register*, November 24, 1995.

inflows were the result of U.S. interest rates being higher than the rest of the world due to the high demand for loanable funds. A major source of the lofty demand for loanable funds was the large federal government deficit. In what came to be known as the **twin deficits,** the record high trade deficit was related by many economists to the record high government deficit. The mainstream scenario went as follows: the high government deficit (together with a low savings rate) led to large increases in the demand for loanable funds. Increases in demand pushed U.S. interest rates above those in the rest of the world. This in turn made U.S. financial assets highly desirable and increased the demand for dollar-denominated funds in international financial markets. The exchange rate of the dollar rose, which led to a deficit in the balance of trade. (Recall that a strong dollar means import prices fall, increasing demand, while export prices rise, decreasing demand.) Thus, the suspicion was that the high government deficit led to an appreciation of the dollar, which resulted in the trade deficit. Although this scenario was widely accepted as a possibility, it was not all that evident in the data because of the many other causal factors for both deficits. Now would be a good time to look at Exhibit 19-11, which shows

Twin Deficits During the 1980s, the high trade deficit and the high government deficit.

the federal government balance along with the trade balance. Although far from perfectly correlated, the data suggest that at times (particularly in the 1980s) large trade deficits are correlated with large government deficits. At other times, the correlation has not been as great.

In early 1993, Congress passed the Deficit Reduction Act, which was to reduce the federal deficit by $500 billion over the next five years. Long-term interest rates fell dramatically as inflation expectations seemed to subside.[16] By mid-1994, however, interest rates started to rise again as the relatively strong performance of the U.S. economy generated new fears of inflation.[17] By mid-1995, fears of inflation had subsided as the level of economic activity slowed and interest rates again turned downward. The value of the dollar, which had peaked in 1985, also fell, reaching record lows against the Japanese yen in mid-1994. Despite the depreciated dollar, the trade deficit, after falling to below $30 billion per year in 1991 and 1992, began to increase again, fueled by the relatively good performance of the U.S. economy. With expectations that the Fed would have to raise interest rates again to halt the dollar's slide, foreigners' willingness to purchase U.S. financial assets diminished. Many analysts believed that the long-run solution to the persistent trade deficit was for Japan to open its economy to U.S. exports. Time will tell how the situation will resolve itself as rates and flows continue to adjust to a changing economic environment.

---

[16]Apparently expectations of inflation, fueled by the large government deficits, had kept long-term rates above what they would have been. Market participants were suspicious that chronic record deficits would lead to a monetizing of those deficits by the Fed. Monetizing the deficit would in turn lead to higher inflation and hence an inflation premium on long-term rates.

[17]The economy showed few signs that inflation was rekindling, but the episode demonstrates how the Fed must not only be concerned about actual inflation but also the expectation of it.

Exhibit 19-11 ◆ The Federal Government Balance and the Trade Balance

SOURCE: *Economic Report of the President,* February 1996, pp. 392 and 367.

To summarize, net exports affect the U.S. economy through their effect on aggregate demand. Output and prices are directly affected by changes in net exports. With regards to the financial side of the economy, ceteris paribus, net foreign demand for U.S. securities directly affects the supply of loanable funds and interest rates. If there is a net capital inflow, ceteris paribus, then the exchange rate could be higher and net exports lower than what they would be otherwise. Because of the large inflow of funds from abroad in recent years, we have focused on the net foreign demand for U.S. securities. Keep in mind that changes in the net domestic demand for foreign securities also affect the supply of loanable funds. Try working through the effects of an increase in foreign interest rates relative to U.S. rates. Can you explain what happens to the domestic supply of loanable funds and the interest rate? For now, we turn to the sources and uses of funds for the foreign sector.

The Sources and Uses of Funds for the Foreign Sector

Equation (19-4) gives the sources and uses of funds for the foreign sector.

	Sources of Foreign Exchange	Uses of Foreign Exchange
(19-4)	Foreign purchases of U.S. goods and services	U.S. purchases of foreign goods and services
	+	+
	Net transfers from foreigners	Net transfers to foreigners
	+	+
	Net foreign purchases of U.S. financial assets	Net U.S. purchases of foreign financial assets

In the balance of payments terminology, the equilibrium exchange rate will equalize the sum of all receipts from foreigners—which reflects foreigners' demand for U.S. goods, services, securities, and thus, dollar-denominated funds—with the sum of all payments to foreigners, which reflects U.S. residents' demand for foreign goods, services, and securities and thus, the supply of dollar-denominated funds in the foreign exchange market. Suffice it to say, exchange rates adjust so that the identity of the sources and uses of funds reflects the desires of the market participants. For example, if the current account is in a deficit position and at the same time foreigners reduce their demand for U.S. securities, then the deficit in the current account will be reflected in the depreciation in the value of the dollar.

 RECAP

Net foreign demand for U.S. securities directly affects the supply of loanable funds and interest rates. If there is a net capital inflow, ceteris paribus, then the exchange rate could be higher and net exports lower than what they otherwise would be. Changes in the net domestic demand for foreign securities also affect the supply of loanable funds. The sources of foreign exchange are foreign purchases of U.S. goods and services plus net transfers from foreigners plus net foreign purchases of U.S. financial assets. The uses of foreign exchange are U.S. purchases of foreign goods and services plus net transfers to foreigners plus net U.S. purchases of foreign financial assets.

In the last two chapters, we have considered the financial aspects of the behavior of the household, business, government, and foreign sectors. In the next chapter, we will pull together material from these and earlier chapters to take a closer look at aggregate demand and supply.

Summary of Major Points

1. Fiscal policy results from compromises reached between the president and Congress. They are sometimes reluctant to raise taxes or cut spending. Government outlays have risen faster than tax receipts since 1960, and the budget has moved from a small surplus in 1960 to large deficits in the 1980s and 1990s. Borrowing directly connects government actions to the financial system. If outlays exceed receipts the resulting deficit must be financed by borrowing, which the U.S. Treasury carries out. Other maturing government debt must also be refunded.

2. Increases in the government deficit, ceteris paribus, push interest rates up by increasing the demand for loanable funds. Other factors operating on both the demand and supply side of the market for loanable funds may affect whether interest rates will indeed rise when the government deficit rises. Expectations about the government deficit affect the interest rate, particularly for long-term bonds, before the deficit changes. If the government deficit causes interest rates to rise, some private spending may be crowded out.

3. Net exports add to domestic demand. If net exports are positive, output and the price level could be higher than what they would be otherwise. If net exports are negative, output and the price level could be lower than what they would be otherwise. Net exports are inversely related to the exchange rate, ceteris paribus. If the exchange rate increases, ceteris paribus, net exports decrease, and vice versa. Therefore, if the exchange rate increases, income could decrease. Likewise, if the exchange rate decreases, income could increase.

4. Foreign demand for U.S. financial assets has a significant effect on the domestic supply of loanable funds. To the extent that foreigners demand U.S. securities, the supply of loanable funds is increased and interest rates are lower than what they would be otherwise.

5. Throughout the 1980s, record trade deficits were offset by capital inflows. Because of their hypothesized relationship, the trade deficit and the government deficit became known as the twin deficits. Although the dollar has relatively depreciated from its high levels in the 1980s, a trade deficit still persists. When implementing stabilization policy, the international effects on net exports and net capital flows must be taken into account.

Key Terms

Aggregate Demand
Aggregate Supply
Crowding Out
Fiscal Policy
Monetized
Net Capital Inflow

Public Debt
Refunding
Regularized
Rolled Over
Twin Deficits

Review Questions

1. How should the government decide whether to change government purchases of goods and services? How does this procedure compare with the political process that is used?

2. How will reductions in the government deficit affect aggregate demand? Do changes in transfer payments affect aggregate demand?

3. How can government expenditures be financed?

4. Assume a constant supply of loanable funds. When government deficit spending leads to increases in the demand for loanable funds, do interest rates always rise? Explain. (Hint: Consider the role of expectations.)

5. If the economy is at full employment and the government increases its purchases of goods and services, does this always lead to crowding out? Is this good or bad for the economy?

6. Distinguish between the public debt and the deficit.

7. When the Treasury issues government securities, who buys the securities? Explain the different impacts of government deficit spending depending on who buys the securities.

8. Will increased government spending always involve crowding out? (Hint: Be sure to consider the two cases when the economy is at full employment and when the increased spending involves transfer payments rather than the purchase of goods and services.)

9. Refute the statement: Because the Treasury increases its borrowing today, interest rates will always go up.

10. Briefly discuss the long-term effects of government borrowing and the public debt.

11. What are the twin deficits and what is the alleged relationship between them? Does it always exist?

12. What is the relationship between net exports and aggregate demand? between net exports and capital flows? If net exports increase, ceteris paribus, what happens to real GDP? If the domestic price level increases, ceteris paribus, what happens to net exports?

13. If the government's deficit increases, what does this imply about the combined surpluses of the other sectors?

14. Is the government always a deficit sector? If the government balance was in surplus, would the debt still have to be rolled over?

15. Why has the government regularized its borrowing?

16. What would happen to U.S. interest rates if, ceteris paribus, foreigners decided to sell some of the U.S. financial assets that they own?

Analytical Questions

17. Graphically depict the situation in question 4. Consider two cases: (1) expectations are unaffected by increases in government deficit spending; (2) increases in government deficit spending cause people to expect higher taxes in the future.

18. Graphically show how interest rates change if the Fed increases the supply of funds at the same time the government deficit is increasing. Graph three possibilities.

19. Graphically show what would happen to interest rates if the Fed decreases the supply of funds at the same time the government deficit is increasing. Are there three possibilities as in question 18?

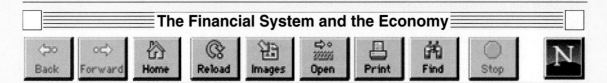

The Financial System and the Economy

1. Fedpoint 40 available on the world wide web at (http://www.ny.frb.org/pihome/fedpoint/fed40.html) contains information about the Balance of Payments accounting framework. Access this web site and answer the following:

   a. What are the sub-accounts under the current account?
   b. What are the sub-accounts under the capital account?

2. Access the Bureau of Census world wide web site at (http://www.census.gov/ftp/pub/statab/www/freq.html). Obtain the summary statistics for the federal deficit from 1960 to 1990. Obtain data for the U.S. merchandise trade balance for the same period.

   a. Do you see any correlation between the federal deficit and the trade deficit?
   b. What are your observations about the correlation over the 1980s?
   c. What is meant by the term "twin deficits"?

Suggested Readings

Many articles about the government and trade deficits are found in the popular press. A recent survey includes the following:

Keith Bradsher, "Greenspan Says Weak Dollar Is Caused by Federal Deficits," *The New York Times,* May 17, 1995, p. D2.

The *New York Times* has a world wide web home page at (http://www.nytimes.com/pope/).

Willem H. Buiter, "Who's Afraid of the Public Debt?" *The American Economic Review,* 82, May 1992, pp. 290–294.

"Can Anyone Fix This Country?" *Business Week,* May 8, 1995, p. 56+.

Business Week has a world wide web home page at (http://www.enews.com/magazines/bw/).

"The Cutting Edge of the Next Congress," *Economist,* 333, December 3, 1994, p. 40.

"The Deficit: Better Than Expected," *Congressional Quarterly Weekly Report,* 52, June 25, 1994, p. 1684.

G. A. Mackenie, "The Hidden Government Deficit," *Finance and Development,* 31, December 1994, pp. 32–35.

Peter Truell, "Dollar Surges on New Plan to Cut Deficit," *The New York Times,* May 12, 1995, p. D1+.

Another interesting article, "Dollars, Deficits, and Trade," is available on the world wide web. It can be accessed at (http://www.cato.org/main/dollars.html).

In addition, many books also contain relevant discussions.

The relationship between the federal deficit and the trade deficit is explored in Robert A. Blecker, *Beyond the Twin Deficits: A Trade Strategy for the 1990s,* Armonk, New York: M.E. Sharpe, 1992.

Albert Gailor Hart and Perry G. Mehrling, *Debt, Crisis, and Recovery: The 1930s and the 1990s,* Armonk, New York: M.E. Sharpe, 1994.

Balancing Act: Debt, Deficits, and Taxes, John H. Makin, Norman J. Ornstein, and David Zlowe, eds., Waldorf, MD: AEI Press, 1990, looks at fiscal policy in the 1980s and the challenges of the 1990s.

For a recent analysis of the business cycle and its influence on the trade balance, see David Rich *The Economics of International Trade,* Westport, CT: Quorum Books, 1992.

For a look at the relationship between government budget deficits and inflation in developing countries of the Western Hemisphere, see Wassin N. Shahin, *Money Supply and Deficit Financing in Economic Development,* Westport, CT: Quorum Books, 1992.

20

Aggregate Demand and Aggregate Supply

> *One man's wage rise is another man's price increase.*
> —Harold Wilson—

Learning Objectives

After reading this chapter, you should know:

◆ The determinants of aggregate demand and aggregate supply

◆ Why the aggregate demand curve is downward sloping and what causes it to shift

◆ Why the short-run aggregate supply curve is upward sloping and the long-run aggregate supply curve is vertical

◆ What causes the short-run and long-run aggregate supply curves to shift

◆ How short-run and long-run aggregate supply are related

◆ How the sources and uses of funds can be used to integrate financial flows between sectors

◆ Why the economy is in equilibrium when net financial investment is zero and when intended aggregate demand is equal to aggregate supply

"GDP up 8 Percent": Is This Indicative of an Economy in Good Health?

Over the four-year period 1979–1982, nominal GDP increased, on average, by about 8 percent per year. Over the two-year period 1991–1993, nominal GDP grew, on average, by about 5.5 percent per year. To the casual observer, these data might suggest that although performing well in both periods, the economy performed better in the early period. Nothing could be further from the truth!

The composition of the growth in nominal GDP was dramatically different across the two periods. Over the 1979–1982 period, prices rose about 8 percent per year, on average, while real GDP growth was essentially nil. In contrast, over the 1991–1993 period, prices rose about 3 percent per year, while real GDP rose about 2.5 percent per year. With inflation lower and real growth higher, the economy obviously performed considerably better over the 1991–1993 period. Armed with these facts, it is natural to ask what accounted for this improvement. Was it good luck, deft policy adjustments by the Fed, or clever fiscal decisions by Congress and the President?

To get at the answers to these and related questions, we shall build on material developed in the two previous chapters that focused on the behavior of households, firms, government, and the foreign sector. We will see that an increase, for example, in demand, regardless of the source, will initially tend to lead firms to raise some combination of production, employment, and prices (depending on the shape of aggregate supply). In this chapter, we will show how changes in aggregate demand and/or supply combine to produce changes in the overall price level and real GDP—the two factors that make up nominal GDP. Within the context of this overall discussion, particular focus and emphasis will be placed on understanding why the short-run effects of changes in aggregate demand or supply on output, employment, and prices differ markedly from the long-run effects. As we shall see, this point is absolutely crucial in explaining fluctuations in the economy's performance and the role of policymakers in aggravating or moderating such fluctuations.

Aggregate Demand

As the term itself implies, *aggregate demand* is the quantity of real goods and services that will be demanded at various price levels over a specific time period such as a year. We can arrive at aggregate demand by summing the total demands of each sector in the economy at a myriad of price levels. These demands, which have been discussed in some detail in the previous two chapters, flow from the various spending, saving, borrowing, and lending decisions made by the household, firm, government, and foreign sectors. Equation (20.1) illustrates the various components of aggregate demand.

(20.1)   Aggregate Demand = Consumption + Investment + Government + Net Exports

Consumption demand originates with the household sector and includes intended purchases of durable goods, nondurable goods, and services. Consumer spending, which has a relatively stable growth rate (or stable with respect to income), is directly related to income and inversely related to the interest rate, ceteris paribus.

Gross investment demand emanates from the business or household sectors and includes intended expenditures for replacement and new capital, increases in inventories, and additions to the stock of houses. Like consumption, it is directly related to income and inversely related to the interest rate, ceteris paribus. Unlike consumption, investment demand is relatively volatile, and swings in investment spending have been associated with turns in the business cycle.

Government demand includes intended purchases of goods and services whether they be at the federal, state, or local level. Examples include intended purchases of roads, national defense, and education. Transfers, such as social security payments and unemployment benefits, are excluded from aggregate demand because transfers merely shift purchasing power from one group to another without adding to or subtracting from the level of aggregate demand. Ceteris paribus, increases in government purchases increase aggregate demand while decreases in such purchases reduce it. As we have seen, government purchases of goods and services are determined by a complex decision-making process involving Congress and the president. Government purchases, including state and local, make up more than 20 percent of real GDP.

Net exports are the difference between exports and imports. Changes in net exports can be negative or positive. If the intended changes are positive, they add to aggregate demand and, if negative, they reduce aggregate demand from what it otherwise would be. Ceteris paribus, net exports are inversely related to the exchange rate and to capital inflows.

The Aggregate Demand Curve

So much for the definitions; we now turn to how the quantity demanded of real GDP (aggregate demand) is related to changes in the overall price level. Look at Exhibit 20-1, which plots the relationship between the price level and aggregate demand using hypothetical figures. Real GDP is measured on the horizontal axis while a price index, such as the **GDP deflator,** is measured on the vertical axis. The GDP deflator measures the overall changes in prices of everything in GDP. Like other demand curves, the fact that the aggregate demand curve is downward sloping means that, ceteris paribus, there is an inverse relationship between the aggregate quantity of real goods and services demanded and the overall price level. Thus, points on the **aggregate demand curve** show combinations of a price index and the quantity of real GDP that will be demanded assuming all other factors except the price level are held constant. These other factors include the nominal money supply, expectations about future economic conditions, interest rates, taxes, and government purchases, among others.

Demand curves for individual products, such as hamburgers, baseballs, and dry cleaning, are downward sloping because of the substitution effect. As the price of hamburgers changes, ceteris paribus, hamburgers become either relatively cheaper or relatively more expensive than other goods and services.

GDP Deflator A price index that measures the overall changes in prices of everything in GDP.

Aggregate Demand Curve A curve showing an inverse relationship between the overall price level and the quantity of real output that will be demanded at various price levels, ceteris paribus.

Exhibit 20-1 ◆
The Aggregate
Demand Curve

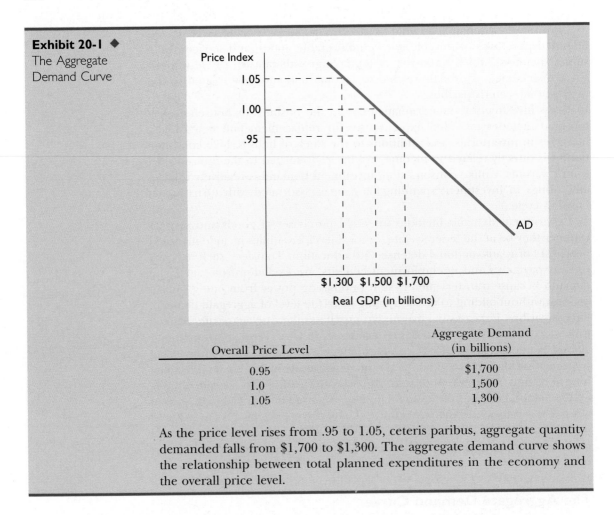

Overall Price Level	Aggregate Demand (in billions)
0.95	$1,700
1.0	1,500
1.05	1,300

As the price level rises from .95 to 1.05, ceteris paribus, aggregate quantity demanded falls from $1,700 to $1,300. The aggregate demand curve shows the relationship between total planned expenditures in the economy and the overall price level.

J.P. (who we first met in Chapter 4) and his friends substitute toward goods that are relatively cheaper and away from goods that are relatively more expensive. The result of such rational behavior is an inverse relationship between price and quantity demanded, ceteris paribus. For example, when the price of hamburgers goes up while the price of hot dogs remains unchanged, prudent shoppers substitute out of hamburgers and into hot dogs, which are now relatively cheaper.[1] The reverse happens when hamburger prices decrease. Hamburgers are now relatively cheaper than hot dogs and consumers find themselves enjoying more of the comparably cheaper burgers. Thus, when the price of hamburgers goes up, quantity demanded goes down, ceteris paribus, and when the price goes down, quantity demanded goes up.

But the substitution effect cannot be a reason why the aggregate demand curve is downward sloping. With regards to aggregate demand, a price index and not a relative price is measured on the vertical axis. When an individual price changes while other prices stay the same, relative prices change. When

---

[1] Note that the nominal price of hot dogs has not initially changed even though their relative price has changed.

the price index moves up or down, overall prices change while relative prices remain unchanged. There is no substitution effect. Despite this, economists believe that the aggregate demand curve is indeed downward sloping and that there is an inverse relationship between the quantity of real GDP demanded and the overall price level, ceteris paribus. As summarized in Exhibit 20-2, three of the main reasons, among others, usually given for the inverse relationship are:

First, when the overall price level changes for a given nominal money supply, the supply of real money balances changes. (Remember the nominal money supply was one of the factors we held constant when we drew our aggregate demand curve downward sloping.) For example, if the price level increases while the nominal money supply remains constant, the supply of real money balances decreases. When the supply decreases, ceteris paribus, spending units experience a loss in wealth since real balances are a component of wealth. At the higher price level, a smaller quantity of real GDP will be demanded because spending units are poorer. Likewise, if the price level decreases, the supply of real balances increases. Ceteris paribus, when the supply of real balances increases, spending units experience a gain in wealth and demand a larger quantity of real output. This effect, which leads to the inverse relationship between the price level and real GDP, ceteris paribus, is called the **wealth effect** or **real balances effect.** Consequently, with the money supply unchanged and prices down, people can and do demand (buy) more, ceteris paribus. The reverse is also true.

> **Wealth Effect or Real Balances Effect** The change in the supply of real balances, which causes an increase or decrease in wealth, when the price level changes for a given supply of nominal money balances.

Second, when the overall price level changes, ceteris paribus, domestic goods and services become relatively cheaper or relatively more expensive than foreign goods, which can lead to changes in net exports. For example, if the U.S. price level rises relative to the foreign price level, then U.S. goods are relatively more expensive than foreign goods. Purchasers substitute out of the relatively more expensive domestic goods and into the relatively cheaper foreign goods. Likewise, if the U.S. price level falls relative to the foreign price level, then U.S. goods are relatively cheaper than foreign goods. Purchasers substitute out of the relatively more expensive foreign goods and into the relatively cheaper U.S. goods and services. As the price level rises, ceteris paribus, net exports fall while as the price level falls, net exports rise. As the price level rises, quantity demanded of real GDP falls because of the decline in net exports and as the price level falls, quantity demanded increases. This effect which, ceteris paribus, leads to the inverse relationship between the price level and the quantity of real GDP demanded is called the **substitution-of-foreign-goods effect.**

> **Substitution-of-Foreign-Goods Effect** When changes in the domestic price level cause consumers to substitute into relatively cheaper foreign goods or out of relatively more expensive foreign goods.

Third, when we draw an aggregate demand curve, we consider what happens to the quantity demanded of real GDP as we vary the overall price level. Other factors, including nominal income, remain constant. By the equation of exchange, which we first discussed in Chapter 17, nominal income is equal

1. The real balances or wealth effect 2. The substitution-of-foreign-goods effect 3. The constant nominal income effect	**Exhibit 20-2** ◆ Why the Aggregate Demand Curve Slopes Downward

to the overall price level multiplied by real GDP.[2] Hence, when the price level rises, the quantity demanded of real GDP must fall in accordance with the constant nominal income constraint. Simply put, less is demanded at higher prices because the funds run out sooner. We call this effect the **constant nominal income effect.**

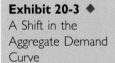

Constant Nominal Income Effect When changes in the price level necessarily cause the quantity demanded to change in the opposite direction to maintain the constant nominal income.

Having established reasons why the aggregate demand curve is downward sloping—that is, why there is an inverse relationship between the price level and the quantity of real GDP demanded—we now turn to the factors that cause aggregate demand to change and the aggregate demand curve to shift.

When aggregate demand changes, the entire set of relationships between the various price levels and the quantities demanded at those prices change. Simply put, if aggregate demand changes, the entire aggregate demand curve shifts. For example, if aggregate demand increases, the aggregate demand curve shifts to the right while if aggregate demand falls, the aggregate demand curve shifts to the left. The mechanics of such shifts are shown in Exhibit 20-3. To complete our discussion of aggregate demand, we need to address briefly one last but crucial question.

---

[2] In Chapter 17, we introduced the equation of exchange, which can be written as $M \times V = GDP = P \times Y$. This equation says that the nation's nominal gross domestic product (GDP) (the overall price level, P, multiplied by the real level of output, Y) is equal to the money supply, M, multiplied by velocity, V.

Exhibit 20-3 ◆

A Shift in the Aggregate Demand Curve

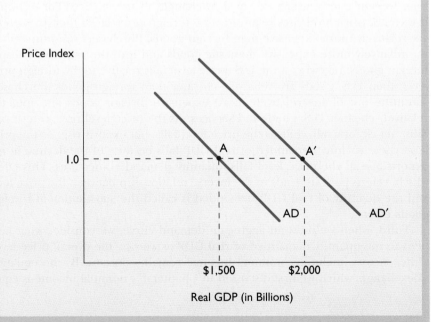

The first aggregate demand curve (AD) is identical to the one in Exhibit 20-1. If aggregate demand increases, the aggregate demand curve shifts to AD'. More specifically, the quantity demanded for goods and services at price level 1.0 rises from $1,500 billion to $2,000 billion, that is from point A to point A'. The other points can be derived similarly.

What Causes Aggregate Demand to Change?

Changes in aggregate demand are the key to understanding one side of the economy.[3] Therefore, wrapping up our examination of aggregate demand requires us to identify the primary causes of changes in aggregate demand. Like any demand curve, the shape and position of the aggregate demand curve were initially determined by the factors we held constant, and it will change when and only when any of these factors change.

From Equation (20-1), we can see that aggregate demand changes when any of the four components change. If a component of aggregate demand increases while the others at least remain the same, aggregate demand is given a boost. Analogously, if a component falls, aggregate demand also falls, and this may have undesirable ramifications for the economy as a whole.

Changes in taxes, government spending, the money supply, interest rates, expected inflation, the economic outlook, and exchange rates can each individually trigger changes in aggregate demand. We have touched on how many of these catalysts activate fluctuations in the components of aggregate demand already. For example, increases in government spending, ceteris paribus, increase aggregate demand. Ceteris paribus, increases in income tax rates decrease consumption expenditures while increases in corporate tax rates reduce the expected profitability of investment. Both would decrease aggregate demand. Changes in the money supply lead to changes in interest rates and liquidity within the entire financial system which impact consumption and investment spending. Changes in expected inflation change the demand for real money balances, ceteris paribus, and lead to changes in interest rates and stock prices. Moreover, changes in any of the factors usually affect the economic outlook, which then impacts on spending decisions.

To round out our picture of what causes changes in aggregate demand at this time, we can safely link changes in any of the factors to changes in government spending and taxing decisions and to changes in the money supply and interest rates as initiated by the Fed. That is, monetary and fiscal policy can and do cause aggregate demand to fluctuate. The linkages between fluctuations in demand in the United States and the various stabilization policies of the federal government and the Fed will be taken up in greater detail in several of the policy chapters in Part V. However, it is important to note that sustained changes in aggregate demand have usually been the result of monetary and fiscal policy actions in the United States and, on occasion, monetary and fiscal policy actions abroad.

To summarize, the schematic diagram in Exhibit 20-4 brings together the essential parts of the story. Changes in U.S. monetary policy—and changes in fiscal policy—have a powerful impact on spending and hence the components of aggregate demand through the effects on the financial system (interest rates and stock prices), international competitiveness (exchange rate), income, and expectations of future economic and financial developments.

One-half of our demand and supply framework is in place. To understand what happens to the price level and real output when aggregate demand shifts and how the price level and real GDP are ultimately determined, we need to develop the other half—a theory of aggregate supply.

---

[3] Shortly we shall see that aggregate supply is the other side.

Exhibit 20-4 ◆
A Schematic
Overview of the
Movements in
Aggregate Demand

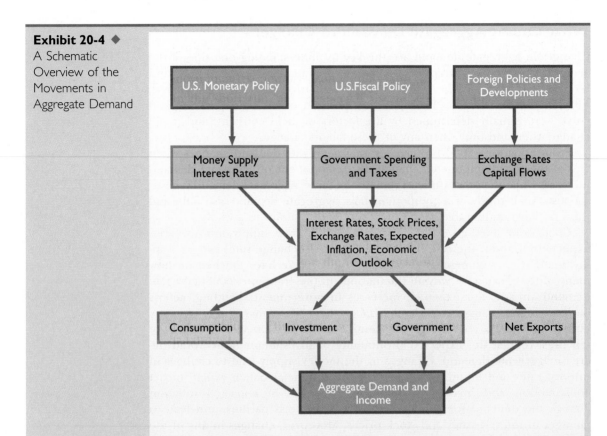

Policy actions in the United States and abroad are typically the source of major movements in aggregate demand. A policy action, such as a rise in the money supply engineered by the Fed, may lower interest rates in the United States. The resulting fall in the cost of financial capital will encourage consumption and investment spending, particularly the acquisition of real assets including durable goods, houses, and plant and equipment. The increased spending will tend to increase production, sales, and profits which will in turn tend to boost stock prices.

On the international side, the fall in U.S. interest rates relative to foreign interest rates will tend to lower (or depreciate) the international value of the dollar. With import prices denominated in dollars rising and export prices denominated in foreign currencies falling, imports will tend to fall and exports will tend to rise, boosting U.S. net exports. Thus, by affecting interest rates, exchange rates, stock prices, and, perhaps expectations about future values of these magnitudes, policy alters aggregate demand in the United States.

 RECAP

Aggregate demand is the quantity of real goods and services that will be demanded at various price levels over a specific time period. There is an inverse relationship between the overall price level and the quantity of real output that will be demanded. The aggregate demand curve is downward sloping because of the real balance effect, the substitution-of-foreign-goods effect, and the constant nominal income effect. The components of aggregate demand are consumption, investment, government purchases of goods and services, and net exports. Aggregate demand changes when any of the four components change. Catalysts that change aggregate demand include changes in taxes, government spending, the money supply, expected inflation, the economic outlook, and exchange rates.

Aggregate Supply

At the level of the individual firm, the concept of supply is fairly straightforward. It is the level of production of goods and services planned by a firm at various prices per unit of output over a specified time period such as a year. For example, at a price level of $10 per unit of output, a firm might plan to produce 1,000 units of output. At a price level of $11, ceteris paribus, the firm might plan to supply 1,010 units of output. Put another way, supply tells us the price level a firm must receive in order to induce it to produce various levels of output during a specified time period.

So far so good. But what lies behind a firm's supply plans? Simply put, it is the price of output relative to the expected costs of production. If a firm is willing over time to produce 1,000 units of output per year at a price of $10 per unit, we can be sure this price covers the expected costs of production per unit.

What would lead our firm to alter its production? Again, the answer follows fairly directly. If the price of output continues to fall relative to the expected price of inputs (which we will hold constant for now), the firm will ultimately reduce production because revenues are falling relative to costs.[4] Conversely, if the price of output rises relative to the fixed prices of inputs, the firm will increase production because revenues per unit of output will be rising relative to costs per unit. Make sure that you are clear about the fact that the price of the firm's output is changing while input prices remain constant.

The central analytical point of our discussion thus far is the key role played by relative prices. More specifically, the price of the output relative to the expected price of inputs drives a firm's production decisions; anything that alters this relative price will alter a firm's quantity produced. In the preceding example, output prices rise, ceteris paribus, and thus we get our direct relationship between output price and quantity supplied.

From the Individual Firm to the Aggregate

These "micro-foundations" of supply by individual firms provide the basics of aggregate supply. Taking all firms together, the **aggregate supply curve** for the economy as a whole depicts the level of output firms and others will produce at alternative price levels over a specified time period such as a year.

Aggregate Supply Curve The curve graphically depicting the relationship between the overall price level and the quantity of real GDP that will be supplied at various price levels.

---

[4] When we invoke the ceteris paribus assumption, we hold all other factors including input prices constant and only allow output prices to vary.

The price level at the aggregate level is not the price of a particular unit of output but rather the average of all output prices as captured by a price index. The quantity is not of a particular good but rather real output for the entire economy. As with aggregate demand, such a price index is the GDP deflator, and our measure of real output is real GDP.

To see and understand how firms in general and, therefore, aggregate supply react to a change in the price level, let's work through an example. Suppose aggregate demand for goods and services increases unexpectedly. What will happen? The answer—which can initially be confusing and a bit frustrating—is that some combination of prices, output, and employment will rise in the short run. But, given the same factors of production, state of technology, and full employment, only prices will rise in the long run.

It should be noted that over time, the "givens" (the factors of production and technology) do not remain constant and, thus, the long-run response changes. In Chapter 21, we take up the dynamic nature of this analysis. In this chapter, we restrict our analysis to a more static situation in which the givens remain constant.

What accounts for the different short- and long-run responses of the economy? The brief answer is the behavior of firms as reflected in aggregate supply. A little more detailed answer is the dynamics of firms' behavior and the resulting adjustments in aggregate supply over time. Soon we shall visualize what lies behind major fluctuations in the economy. Hopefully, we will gain insight into the difficulties policymakers face in achieving the nation's goals.

Short-Run Aggregate Supply

Long-Run Equilibrium When all prices (including wages) have fully adjusted to previous shifts in aggregate supply or demand and the flow of spending, saving, borrowing and lending continues until something else changes.

Real Wage The nominal wage divided by the overall price level.

The analysis begins with the economy in **long-run equilibrium.** This means that all prices (including wages) and quantities in the economy have fully adjusted to previous shifts in aggregate supply or demand, and the configuration of interest rates, exchange rates, expectations, and relative prices is producing a flow of spending and saving, borrowing, and lending that will continue unless and until something changes. Included in the relative prices that have adjusted is the **real wage,** which is the nominal wage deflated by the price level. An important characteristic of this analytical convention called long-run equilibrium is that expected values are equal to actual values. Sales are coming in as expected and thus there are no unexpected changes in inventories. Actual inflation is equal to expected inflation, resulting in no unexpected changes in real interest rates or real wages. Resources, including labor, are fully employed. There is no tendency for the real wage to fall since there are no involuntarily unemployed workers who would be willing to accept jobs for slightly lower nominal wages thus bidding the real wage down.

Seldom, if ever, is the economy precisely in such a state. But that's less of a problem than you might think. The concept and characteristics of equilibrium will enable us to isolate and trace the effects of major shocks to the economy.

With the economy in long-run equilibrium, the Fed moves unexpectedly to raise aggregate demand by increasing the reserves of depository institutions through substantial open market purchases. The resulting rise in the money supply and initial fall in interest rates stimulates nominal spending and sales. The question we are focusing on is What happens to aggregate supply? Or, more specifically, How do firms respond to the increase in aggregate demand?

As in our introductory discussion in Chapter 4, the rise in firms' sales produces an unexpected decline in inventories and unexpected upward pressure on output prices. Holding the prices of inputs fixed for now, firms in the aggregate, just like the individual firm already discussed, respond to the decline in inventories and rise in output prices relative to input prices by expanding output. Since more output requires more inputs, employment of labor and other factors of production will also expand. But, given that we started at a position of full employment, it becomes impossible for firms in the aggregate to hire more workers without increases in the nominal wage. So, rather than remaining fixed, as we initially assumed, the nominal wage begins to rise, albeit at a slower rate than output prices. Employment temporarily goes above sustainable full employment.[5] Workers temporarily perceive the increase in nominal wages, even though it is less than the increase in prices, to be an increase in real wages and agree to supply more labor.[6] To sum up, the initial or short-run effect of a rise in demand will be an increase in the price level and an accompanying increase in output and employment. In other words, the quantity of goods and services supplied increases when the price level rises. The explanation is that output prices are assumed to rise relative to input prices providing the requisite incentive to raise production. Be certain that you are clear that a price index is measured on the vertical axis. When output prices rise, the overall price level rises. However, in this situation, we are assuming that, since input prices do not rise as quickly as output prices, relative prices are also changing.

What happens to the quantity of goods and services supplied in the short run if aggregate demand falls unexpectedly? The short answer is that there will be downward pressure on both the price level and quantity of goods and services supplied. The reasoning parallels the preceding discussion: the unexpected fall in demand will produce an unexpected rise in firms' inventories and downward pressure on output prices.[7] Firms respond to the rise in inventories and fall in output prices relative to input prices by reducing output. Reflecting the production cuts, employment of labor and other factors of production will fall. Thus, the initial or short-run effect of a fall in demand will be downward pressure on the price level and a reduction in output and employment. Here again, we see that the aggregate quantity of goods and services supplied would fall if the price level falls, reflecting a decline in output prices relative to input prices.

The basic and essential features of short-run aggregate supply are nailed down graphically in Exhibit 20-5, which depicts the **short-run aggregate supply curve,** which shows the direct relationship, ceteris paribus, between the overall price level and the quantity of real GDP supplied. The short-run aggregate supply curve is positively sloped; the aggregate demand curve shifts along a given positively sloped short-run aggregate supply curve. By tracing the short-run response of firms and thus the economy to shifts in aggregate demand,

Short-Run Aggregate Supply Curve A curve showing the direct relationship between the overall price level and the level of real output that will be supplied in response to changes in demand before full adjustment of relative prices has taken place.

---

[5] Sustainable full employment is the level that can be maintained without upward or downward pressure on wages and prices.

[6] If a large percentage of workers work under a contractual collective bargaining agreement, since nominal wages do not rise over the course of the agreement, an unexpected rise in the price level will result in increases in nominal wages, which lag increases in the price level.

[7] In the post-World War II period, prices have been much less flexible downward than upward. That is, prices are much more likely to rise in response to increases in demand than they are to fall in response to decreases in demand.

Exhibit 20-5 ◆
Short-Run
Aggregate Supply

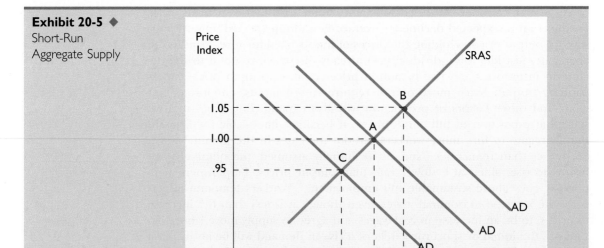

Overall Price Level	Aggregate Supply (in billions)
0.95	$1,300
1.0	1,500
1.05	1,700

In the short-run, shifts in aggregate demand will generally lead to movements in the same direction in output, employment, and prices. Assume the economy is in equilibrium at point A and aggregate demand increases (AD to AD′). With sales increasing, inventories falling, and output prices under upward pressure, firms respond by expanding output and employment. Input prices are assumed to be fixed or increasing relatively slower than output prices in the short run. Thus, output prices rise relative to input prices. The result for the economy as a whole is depicted by the movement from point A to point B. Output rises to $1,700 and the price level increases to 1.05. Starting over again from point A, the result of a decline in aggregate demand (AD to AD′′) is that the economy moves from point A to point C; output and the price level fall.

we, in effect, trace out the short-run aggregate supply curve. Again, hypothetical figures are used. Study it carefully before moving on.

 **RECAP**

Aggregate supply is the amount of output that firms will supply at various prices for the economy as a whole. In the short run, there is a direct relationship between the overall price level and the level of output supplied.

In response to an increase in aggregate demand, firms will supply more output in response to higher output prices. In the short run, input prices are fixed and firms respond to higher output prices by offering more for sale. If aggregate demand falls, there will be downward pressure on the price level and the quantity of real goods supplied. Since output prices fall relative to input prices, firms will produce less.

Long-Run Aggregate Supply

As already discussed, it is completely possible for the economy to move from one level of real output supplied (and demanded) to another in the short run. More generally, it is perfectly feasible for the economy to move from a position of long-run equilibrium (remember this is where we started our discussion of short-run aggregate supply) to a short-run equilibrium wherein the level of real output has changed.

The task before us is to explain (1) why at any particular time, there is just one level of real output—called the **natural level of real output**—at which long-run equilibrium with a stable price level is possible, (2) why a short-run equilibrium, wherein the level of real output differs from the long-run, natural level of real output, is a temporary, nonsustainable situation, and (3) how the economy moves back to long-run equilibrium. Put more simply, we want to understand what the natural level of output is and how and why the economy tends to move back toward this long-run norm whenever the level of output deviates from this norm.

Natural Level of Real Output The level of real output that is consistent with long-run equilibrium given the economy's quantity and productivity of the factors of production.

As summarized in Exhibit 20-6, an economy's natural level of real output is determined by the quantity and productivity of its factors of production. These factors include the economy's capital stock, natural resources, and labor force. In addition, the natural level is influenced by the technological know-how that production techniques embody and the institutional arrangements governing the operation of the labor market and other input markets. The natural level should not be thought of as an absolute limit on what the economy can produce. Rather it is the level to which the economy would move, given its factors of production and current technology.[8] As discussed previously, the actual level of real output can increase in the short run if, for example, firms respond to a rise in demand by operating overtime using standby plant capacity and if more people than usual are employed. More people than usual may accept jobs because they mistake an increase in nominal wages for an increase in the real wage. That is, they fail to recognize for

---

[8]As the factors of production and technology change over time, the natural level of real output will also change.

The Economy's Capital Stock	**Exhibit 20-6** ◆
Natural Resources	Determinants of
The Labor Force	the Natural Level
Technological Know-How	of Real Output
Institutional Arrangements Concerning the Labor Market and Other Input Markets	

a time that output prices are actually going up faster than the nominal wage. Similarly, the actual level of real output can fall for a time, as in a recession when workers are laid off and some portion of plant capacity lies idle.

As we shall see, however, short-run equilibrium in which the actual level of output differs from the natural level of real output is not a long-run equilibrium and thus is not sustainable over time. When an economy is in long-run equilibrium the prices of goods and services sold by firms will bear a consistent relationship with the prices of the inputs employed by firms. In particular, the prices of goods and services must be high enough to allow firms to cover their costs of production and earn a normal profit. Similarly, the prices of inputs—wages and salaries, in particular—must be high enough relative to "the cost of living" to make work worthwhile. The nominal cost of living can be measured by the prices of consumer goods, such as the consumer price index.

A helpful way to summarize the discussion to this point is to say that the economy is in long-run equilibrium when relative prices are correct—more specifically, when output prices are consistent and sustainable relative to input prices. As pointed out at the beginning of the subsection on short-run aggregate real supply, the implication of saying "relative prices are correct" is that all input and output prices in the economy have fully adjusted to previous shifts in aggregate supply or demand. The resulting configuration of interest rates, exchange rates, relative prices, and expectations is producing a flow of spending, saving, borrowing, lending, production, and employment which will continue unless and until something changes. A key characteristic of such a situation, which is crucial to everything that follows, is that actual values are equal to expected values. There are no surprises or unexpected developments. Actual sales are coming in as expected, and thus there are no unexpected changes in inventories or production, because if output prices are expected to rise, input prices will rise proportionately to maintain the real incomes of the suppliers of the factors of production. With input prices rising in proportion to output prices, there will be no change in relative prices and thus no incentive for firms to produce more or for workers to work more. The end result, depicted by the movement from point A to point B, will be a doubling of the price level from 1.0 to 2.0 with the economy continuing to operate at its natural level of real output. Actual prices will again be equal to expected prices and thus there will be no unexpected changes in real wages or real interest rates, and the economy will continue to operate at its natural level of real output, as shown in Exhibit 20-7.

In contrast, if actual values differ from expected values, adjustments in production, employment, spending, and so on, will occur. For example, if the actual price level turns out to be higher than expected, workers who bargained for and accepted a particular nominal wage rate based on an expected price level of 1.0 will, in time, come to realize that their real wages are lower than they anticipated. For example, if the price level turns out to be 1.05 rather than 1.0, workers will find their real wage and real purchasing power are lower. Among other things, this will lead them to seek higher nominal wages in an effort to restore their real wages and purchasing power. Any resulting wage increase will raise production costs which in turn will affect employment, production, and output prices. By definition then, when actual values differ from expected values, such a situation cannot be a long-run equilibrium.

To sum up, we first discussed short-run aggregate supply in which input prices are initially assumed fixed or slower to change than output prices. In

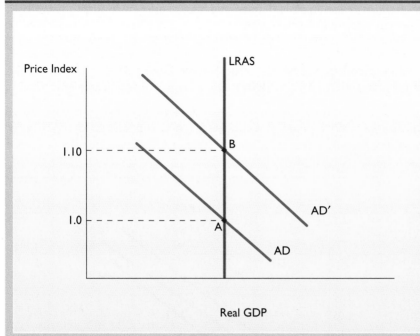

Exhibit 20-7 ◆
Long-Run Aggregate
Real Supply

Suppose the economy is in long-run equilibrium at point A with the actual price level of 1.0 equal to the expected price level and with the economy operating at its natural level of real output. Now assume firms and suppliers of factors of production expect aggregate demand to increase and this in fact occurs (with AD shifting to AD′). The economy responds to the anticipated rising demand by moving up a given vertical long-run aggregate supply curve to point B.

this situation, changes in output prices result in changes in relative prices and thus changes in production and employment. Secondly, we examined long-run aggregate supply in which input prices are not fixed and all input and output prices (and price expectations) have completely adjusted to various developments. The **long-run aggregate supply curve** is vertical at the natural level of real output.[9] Along the long-run aggregate supply curve, there is no change in relative prices and the economy is operating at its natural level of real output, given technology and a given quantity of the factors of production. With these two building blocks in place, the final crucial step in our discussion of aggregate supply should be obvious: How is short-run aggregate supply related to long-run aggregate supply?

Long-Run Aggregate Supply Curve The vertical curve through the natural rate of output to which the economy will return in the long run regardless of the price level.

 RECAP

In the long run when input prices are flexible and full adjustment has occurred, the economy will gravitate to the natural level of real output. The

---

[9] Note that the vertical long-run aggregate supply curve will shift if the quantity and productivity of the factors of production change. More on this in Chapter 21.

natural level of real output is determined by the quantity and productivity of the economy's factors of production.

The Relationship Between the Short Run and the Long Run: Shifts in Short-Run Aggregate Supply

The task before us is, in effect, to integrate Exhibits 20-7 and 20-8. More specifically, we need to show two things: (1) how the short-run response of the economy to, say, a rise in aggregate demand compares to the long-run

Exhibit 20-8 ◆

Shifts in Short-Run Aggregate Supply

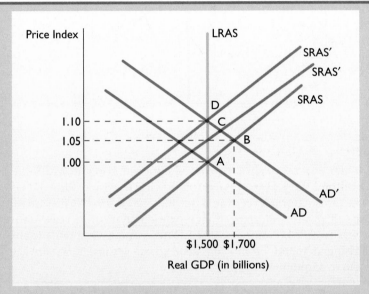

Initially, the economy is in long-run equilibrium at point A. The actual price level (1.0) is equal to the expected price level underlying the short-run aggregate supply curve, and the economy is operating at its natural level of real output ($1,500). Subsequently, aggregate demand increases unexpectedly shifting the aggregate demand curve from AD to AD'. In the short run, the economy will move to point B with output rising to $1,700 and the price level increasing to 1.05. Point B is not a long-run equilibrium, however, because the actual price level (1.05) is above the expected price level (1.0). As input suppliers respond to the unanticipated increase in prices (to 1.05), input prices increase, price expectations are revised upward to 1.05, and the short-run aggregate supply curve shifts from SRAS to SRAS'. As SRAS shifts, firms revise their initial reaction to the rise in demand. The new equilibrium at point C is also not a long-run equilibrium because here again the actual price level has risen above the expected price level (1.05). This inequality induces another series of adjustments by input suppliers and firms, resulting in further shifts of the short-run aggregate supply curve to the left. With no further shifts in aggregate demand, the economy will settle at a new long-run equilibrium at point D. In effect, the economy moves along the path A-B-C-D as successive shifts in short-run aggregate supply alter the initial, short-run effects of a rise in aggregate demand on the economy.

response of the economy; and (2) how the different short- and long-run responses depend on changes in price expectations and associated shifts in short-run aggregate supply. Believe it or not, we have already developed the requisite analytical tools.

To begin, assume the economy is in short- and long-run equilibrium at point A, as depicted in Exhibit 20-8. The actual price level is equal to 1.0 and the economy is operating at its natural level of real output—$1,500 billion in our hypothetical example. Since this is a long-run equilibrium, the actual price level is equal to the expected price level. All prices—input as well as output prices—have completely adjusted to previous developments. Therefore, the aggregate demand curve intersects the long-run aggregate supply curve and the short-run aggregate supply curve at point A. Note carefully that it is assumed that input prices, especially wage rates, reflect the price level expectations prevailing at the time. Thus, the short-run aggregate supply curve reflects price level expectations of 1.0 at point A, and since the actual price level is also equal to 1.0, we have a short- and long-run equilibrium. By definition, short-run aggregate supply always intersects the short-run aggregate supply curve at the expected price level governing the setting of input prices.

So far so good. But what happens to output, employment, and the price level if there is an unexpected rise in the money supply and aggregate demand increases unexpectedly from AD to AD'? In the short-run, the economy will move to point B. Intuitively, the rise in demand results in an unanticipated fall in inventories and a rise in the level of output prices relative to the level of input prices, which are assumed fixed in the short run or to rise more slowly than output prices. Firms respond to the rise in output prices and fall in inventories by expanding production and employment. They quickly find that nominal wages rather than remaining fixed as initially assumed, start to rise, albeit at a slower rate than prices. The result in our hypothetical example is a rise in the price level to 1.05 and a rise in real output to $1,700 billion.

At point B the economy is in a short-run equilibrium. But this is not a long-run equilibrium and, therefore, is not sustainable. The reason is that the actual price level (1.05) is above the expected price level (1.0). Accordingly, input suppliers, such as workers, have suffered a decline in real income relative to what they expected even though nominal wages may have risen. They will attempt to negotiate even higher wages and salaries as will other input suppliers. The decline in their real income is the result of the unexpected price level increase, which exceeds the increase in nominal wages. With employment up and thus unemployment down, labor markets and the markets for other inputs, more generally, have tightened up such that the bargaining position of workers and other input suppliers has improved. We assume for now that firms and input suppliers base their revised expectations about future prices on the newly prevailing level of output prices—that is, 1.05. As a result of such adjustments, firms will experience a rise in current and expected input prices, leading to a shift in the short-run aggregate supply curve to SRAS'. (Note SRAS' intersects the short-run aggregate supply curve at price level 1.05.) Again, the adjustment stops when the increase in wages catches up with the increase in the price level.

To fully understand why the short-run aggregate supply curve shifts as it does, it is useful to recall that the supply curve tells us what price level is required to induce firms to produce any particular level of output, given the level of expected input prices. Accordingly, if input prices are expected to rise, then firms will require a higher output price to produce the same level of output. That is, the short-run aggregate supply curve will shift to the left.

In other words, firms revise their initial reaction to the original rise in demand. With input prices now expected to rise, they do not find it profitable to expand their output by as much as they did initially. The reduction in the quantity of real output supplied and accompanying increase in the price level produce a new equilibrium at a point such as point C in Exhibit 20-8. Here again, the actual price level (that is, the average of output prices) has risen above the expected price level (1.05) This, in turn, means there will be additional adjustments in price expectations, input prices, and firm's production decisions. Without tracing out all the intermediate steps, we can say the short-run aggregate supply curve will continue to shift to the left until the economy reaches point D, which intersects SRAS" and the long-run aggregate supply curve. Assuming no further shifts in demand, this is a point of long-run equilibrium; the expected price level is equal to the actual price level (1.10), relative prices are correct in the sense that the level of output prices is consistent with the prevailing and expected level of input prices (input prices have caught up), and the economy is operating at its natural level of real output, given the quantity and productivity of its factors of production. The short-run aggregate supply curve shifts left until this occurs.

So what is the end result of the rise in aggregate demand? In the short run, output, employment, and the price level rose. In the long run, output and employment were unaffected, returning to their natural levels, given the quantity and productivity of the factors of production. Prices, however, rose from 1.0 to 1.1.

What explains the differing short- and long-run effects? In the short run, price expectations, and thus expected input prices, are assumed fixed or to change more slowly than output prices. As a result, the economy moves up along short-run aggregate supply (point A to B in Exhibit 20-8) as demand increases. Over time, as actual prices rise, expectations and thus firms' production decisions and the workers' decisions to supply labor adjust, resulting in successive shifts in short-run aggregate real supply. Reflecting these adjustments and assuming there are no further shifts in demand, the economy moves back to the natural rate of unemployment (point B to D in Exhibit 20-8).

Demand-Pull Inflation
Sustained increases in the overall price level due to high levels of demand.

What has just been described and analyzed is a case of **demand-pull inflation.** Demand increases and "pulls" up prices. Note that from a policymaker's perspective the short-run outcome (point B) is fairly attractive. Output rises, unemployment drops, and the increase in prices is not dramatic. In the long run (point D), the situation is much less pleasant. The result of boosting demand with, say, monetary or fiscal policy is that prices have risen while employment and output have returned to the natural levels prevailing initially (at point A). If policymakers are nearsighted, they would tend to focus on (and value) the short-run effects on the economy of boosting demand, ignoring or downplaying the longer-run inflationary effects. More on this point will follow in the next chapter when we examine the effects of other economic scenarios and the Fed's response (monetary policy) from an aggregate demand and supply framework.

RECAP

From a position of long-run equilibrium, if there is an increase in aggregate demand, the economy will initially respond by moving to a short-run equilibrium at a higher price and output level above the natural rate of real output. Since this level of output is not sustainable, input prices will start to rise, shifting the short-run aggregate supply curve leftward. Over time, as input prices catch up with the higher output prices, the economy will move back to the natural rate of output at a higher price level.

The aggregate demand and supply framework developed in this chapter so far is powerful. It brings together the major determinants of the price level and real GDP, the major causes of economic fluctuations, and their short- and long-run consequences. However, the analysis has basically occurred in the absence of a financial system. To remedy this and to pull together our discussions in Chapters 18 and 19, we return to the sources and uses of funds for the various sectors. In the next section, we look at a theory of macroeconomic equilibrium, which draws on the role of finance and the flows of funds among sectors. Rather than contradicting the aggregate demand and aggregate supply model, the flow of funds model will extend and complement the analysis so far.

Equilibrium and Financial Flows Among Sectors

We have already met the sources and uses of funds statements for the household, business, government, and foreign sectors. By adding a fifth sector, the financial sector, along with the others, we can see how intermediation facilitates the flows of funds from the surplus to the deficit sectors and impacts on intended aggregate demand and aggregate supply. In addition, we can develop a model of macroeconomic equilibrium in which the interest rate and income are simultaneously determined via the interaction of the flows of funds among sectors.

In reality, the net financial deficits (financial liabilities) of the deficit sectors get intermediated to become the net financial investments (financial assets) of the surplus sectors. Following the flow of funds terminology, going into debt is the **net incurring of financial liabilities,** while the purchasing of financial assets is the **net acquisition of financial assets.** If the net acquisition of financial assets is greater than the net incurring of financial liabilities for a sector, then this sector has made a positive **net financial investment** and is a surplus sector. If the net acquisition of financial assets is less than the net incurring of financial liabilities for a sector, then this sector has a positive **net financial deficit** and is a deficit sector.

Because every financial liability is a corresponding financial asset for someone else, it is always true that in the aggregate the net acquisition of financial assets will equal the net incurring of financial liabilities, and consequently both the net financial investment and the net financial deficit will always equal

Net Incurring of Financial Liabilities The incurring of debt.
Net Acquisition of Financial Assets The purchasing of financial assets.
Net Financial Investment When the net acquisition of financial assets is greater than the net incurring of financial liabilities within a given sector.
Net Financial Deficit When the net incurring of financial liabilities is greater than the net acquisition of financial assets within a given sector.

zero. It is impossible for someone to have a financial liability that is not also a financial asset to someone else. However, as we have seen, in each individual sector, it would be highly unlikely if the net acquisition of financial assets was to equal the net incurring of financial liabilities.

The household sector has consistently been a surplus sector and still is. Since 1982, the foreign sector has also been a surplus sector. The government sector has been a deficit sector in almost all of the years since 1960 and the deficit escalated during the 1980s. The business sector was consistently a deficit sector with the exception of a few years in the early 1990s. We expect that in future years it will invariably be a deficit sector.

Given this framework, let's consider when the economy would be in equilibrium. Equilibrium, as we know, is a stable state with no tendency to change. As depicted in Exhibit 20-9, such a situation would be characterized by the equality between the desired aggregate intentions to acquire financial assets and the desired aggregate intentions to incur financial liabilities. If the economy is not in equilibrium, then these intentions are not equal, and vice versa. For example, if the sum total of all intentions to spend (aggregate demand) is less than income (aggregate supply), then the desire to acquire financial assets is greater than the desire to incur financial liabilities. In the aggregate, spending units desire to have a positive net financial investment. In such a situation, because the desired aggregate demand is less than aggregate supply and the demand for financial assets is greater than the supply, both income and the interest rate will fall. As rates fall, more spending units will be enticed to incur financial liabilities and fewer will be offered. Also, as the interest rate falls, interest-sensitive spending is stimulated and the fall in the level of income is arrested.

Likewise, if aggregate demand is greater than aggregate supply, spending units in the aggregate are attempting to spend more than their incomes, and the intentions to incur financial liabilities are greater than the intentions to

Exhibit 20-9 ◆
The Mechanics of Macroeconomic Equilibrium

From a framework of aggregate demand and aggregate supply, the macro-economy is in equilibrium at the price level where the quantity demanded of real GDP is equal to the quantity supplied.

From the flow-of-funds framework, the macroeconomy is in equilibrium when the desired aggregate intentions to acquire financial assets are equal to the desired aggregate intentions to incur financial liabilities—when net financial investment and net financial deficits both equal zero.

If aggregate demand is greater than aggregate supply, then the intentions to incur financial liabilities are greater than the intentions to acquire financial assets.

If aggregate demand is less than aggregate supply, then the intentions to acquire financial assets are greater than the intentions to incur financial liabilities.

If either of these two cases exists, there is a tendency for interest rates and spending and income to change until the intentions to acquire financial assets are just equal to the intentions to incur financial liabilities and the quantity of real GDP demanded is equal to the quantity of real GDP supplied.

acquire financial assets. The desired net incurring of financial liabilities is greater than the desired net acquisition of financial assets. In such a situation, both the interest rate and income will rise. Consequently, if either of the two states exists, there is a tendency for interest rates and hence spending and income to change until the desired net acquisition of financial assets is just equal to the desired net incurring of financial liabilities and desired aggregate demand is equal to aggregate supply. In such a world, interest rates reflect both the willingness to incur financial liabilities and the desire to acquire financial assets. Thus, in equilibrium, the planned acquisitions of financial assets by the surplus sectors are just equal to the planned incurring of financial liabilities by the deficit sectors, for only then have interest rates and spending flows adjusted so that there will be no tendency to change. The macroeconomy is in equilibrium when the planned net financial investment for the economy as a whole, including the foreign sector of the United States, is equal to zero (and intended aggregate demand is equal to aggregate supply).

Recall that the uses of funds by one sector become the sources of funds for another. Each sector usually has two major sources of funds. For example, for households, the sources are income and going into debt; for business firms, the sources are net revenues and net borrowings; and for the government, the sources are taxes or net borrowing. Likewise, each sector has two major uses. For example, for households, the uses are spending on consumption and investment assets or acquiring financial assets; for the foreign sector, the uses are to purchase foreign goods or services or to invest in foreign securities. Although the flow of funds accounts divide the economy into nine sectors, we simplify to the five sectors mentioned above. The numbers we use are hypothetical but somewhat representative of the financial flows between sectors in the mid 1990s. As can be seen, the surpluses of the household and foreign sectors exactly offset the deficits of the business and government sectors.

<table>
<tr><td>Sources of Funds</td><td>Uses of Funds</td></tr>
<tr><td colspan="2" align="center">(Billions of Dollars)</td></tr>
</table>

Household

Disposable income $5,306

Consumption spending on nondurables, durables, and services $4,777

+

Investment spending on real assets $265

+

Net change in other financial assets held $264

Surplus = $264

Business Firms

Net revenues $638

+

Net borrowing $115

Net spending on real assets (plant and equipment) $715

+

Net spending on real assets (inventories) $38

Deficit = $115

Government

Tax receipts $2,266	Government spending on goods and services $1,135
+	+
Net borrowings $247	Government spending on transfer payments $1,053
	+
	Interest payments on the national debt $325

Deficit = $247

Foreign Sector

Foreign purchases of U.S. goods and services $805	U.S. purchases of foreign goods and services $903
+	+
Net foreign purchases of U.S. financial assets $427	Net U.S. purchases of foreign financial assets $329
	Surplus = $98

Financial Intermediaries

| Net acquiring of financial assets $1,225 | Net incurring of financial liabilities $1,225 |

The use of this format allows us to analyze flows of funds among sectors, how those flows are intermediated, and how the Fed can monitor and influence them. During expansions, both income and interest rates normally rise along with the relative intentions to incur financial liabilities. Likewise in recessions, the reverse happens. Nevertheless, no sector of the economy can incur increasing financial liabilities without the acceptance of increasing financial assets on the part of the other sectors.

 RECAP

Because every financial liability is a corresponding financial asset for someone else, it is always true that in the aggregate the net acquisition of financial assets will equal the net incurring of financial liabilities, and consequently both the net financial investment and the net financial deficit will always equal zero. The economy is in equilibrium when the desired aggregate intentions to acquire financial assets equal the desired aggregate intentions to incur financial liabilities. If desired aggregate demand is not equal to aggregate supply, then the demand for financial assets is not equal to the supply, and both income and the interest rate will change. The process of adjustment continues until the desired intentions to acquire financial assets are just equal to the desired intentions to incur financial liabilities, and desired aggregate demand is equal to aggregate supply.

In this chapter, we have completed a rather static analysis of aggregate demand and aggregate supply. We have augmented this with a model of macroeconomy equilibrium based on the flow of funds among sectors. In Part V, we turn to the role of monetary policy. Chapter 21 begins with some dynamic applications of aggregate demand and aggregate supply, which makes the following summary of major points particularly important.

Summary of Major Points

1. Aggregate demand is the sum of the quantities of goods and services demanded by each sector of the economy at various price levels. The aggregate demand curve shows the quantity of real GDP that people, business, and government plan to purchase at alternate price levels. Ceteris paribus, quantity demanded is inversely related to the overall price level. Reasons for this inverse relationship include the real balances or wealth effect, the substitution-of-foreign-goods effect, and the constant nominal income effect.

2. The major causes of changes in aggregate demand (shifts of the aggregate demand curve) are changes in U.S. monetary and fiscal policies as reflected in changes in taxes and government expenditures, or changes in interest rates and the money supply. Such policy changes have a powerful impact on spending plans through their effects on the financial system (stock and bond prices), our international competitiveness (exchange rates), and expectations of future economic and financial developments.

3. Firms' production decisions are guided by the price of their output relative to expected costs of production. A rise in output prices relative to input prices will lead firms to expand production, while a fall in output prices relative to input prices will lead firms to reduce production.

4. The short-run aggregate supply curve is positively sloped, ceteris paribus. It depicts the level of output firms will produce at alternate output price levels, assuming input prices are constant or that changes in input prices lag changes in output prices. The assumption of constant or lagging input prices is what defines the short run and distinguishes the short run from the long run. Starting from a position of long-run equilibrium, an unexpected rise in demand will lead to a rise in output prices relative to input prices, an unexpected fall in inventories, and an accompanying increase in output and employment. In long-run equilibrium, expected values of sales, inventories, and prices are equal to actual values.

5. The long-run aggregate supply curve is vertical at an economy's natural level of real output. An economy's natural level of real output is determined by the quantity and productivity of its factors of production. What makes such a level of output "natural" is that it is sustainable in the sense that once output prices and input prices have fully adjusted to previous shifts in supply or demand, there is no tendency for the economy to move away from this equilibrium level of output and employment.

6. If something causes actual values to differ from expected values, an economy's long-run equilibrium is disturbed and adjustments in production, employment, spending, and so forth, will occur. More specifically, after a disturbance (such as an increase in aggregate demand), some initial ad-

justments occur, producing a short-run equilibrium. As time passes, further adjustments occur, particularly in price expectations, input prices, and in the short-run aggregate supply curve, that cause the economy to move toward a new long-run equilibrium.

7. In the short run, an unexpected rise in aggregate demand will, ceteris paribus, lead to a rise in output and employment and some rise in output prices. Subsequently, there will be an increased demand for inputs that results in higher input prices. The short-run aggregate supply curve shifts to the left and firms post higher prices and produce less. In the long run, when output prices and input prices have fully adjusted to the initiating increase in demand, the economy will return to its natural level of real output. This is a case of demand-pull inflation. In the long run, a rise in demand pulls up prices but does not affect output and employment.

8. The net financial deficits (financial liabilities) of the deficit sectors get intermediated to become the net financial investments (financial assets) of the surplus sectors. If the net acquisition of financial assets is greater than the net incurring of financial liabilities for a sector, then this sector has made a positive net financial investment and is a surplus sector. If the net acquisition of financial assets is less than the net incurring of financial liabilities for a sector, then this sector has a positive net financial deficit and is a deficit sector. Because every financial liability is a corresponding financial asset for someone else, it is always true that in the aggregate the net acquisition of financial assets will equal the net incurring of financial liabilities, and consequently both the net financial investment and the net financial deficit will always equal zero.

9. The economy is in equilibrium when the desired aggregate intentions to acquire financial assets equal the desired aggregate intentions to incur financial liabilities. If the economy is not in equilibrium, then these intentions are not equal. For example, if desired aggregate demand is greater than aggregate supply, then the demand for financial assets is less than the supply, and both income and the interest rate will rise. If desired aggregate demand is less than aggregate supply, then the demand for financial assets is greater than the supply, and both income and the interest rate will fall. The process of adjustment continues until the desired intentions to acquire financial assets are just equal to the desired intentions to incur financial liabilities, and desired aggregate demand is equal to aggregate supply.

Key Terms

Aggregate Demand Curve
Aggregate Supply Curve
Constant Nominal Income Effect
Demand-Pull Inflation
GDP Deflator
Long-Run Aggregate Supply Curve
Long-Run Equilibrium
Natural Level of Real Output
Net Acquisition of Financial Assets
Net Financial Deficit

Net Financial Investment
Net Incurring of Financial
    Liabilities
Real Balances Effect
Real Wage
Short-Run Aggregate Supply Curve
Substitution-of-Foreign-Goods
    Effect
Wealth Effect

Review Questions

1. Explain the difference between aggregate demand and the quantity demanded of real output. Ceteris paribus, how is quantity demanded related to the overall price level?

2. Explain the wealth effect, the substitution-of-foreign-goods effect, and the constant nominal income effect.

3. What are the major sources of changes in aggregate demand? What are the short-run effects? the long-run effects?

4. What does investment spending consist of? How is investment spending related to the interest rate? Which is more volatile, consumption or investment? Which makes up a larger component of GDP?

5. Explain why only government purchases of goods and services and not transfers are a component of aggregate demand.

6. What are net exports? How are they related to the exchange rate?

7. If prices and wages always change and are expected to always change by exactly the same percentage, how is the short-run aggregate supply curve shaped? Make an argument that in this case, there is no such thing as a short-run aggregate supply curve. What is the real wage?

8. What is the GDP deflator?

9. Using the flow of funds framework, explain when the economy is in equilibrium? Why?

10. If the household, firm, and government sectors were all deficit sectors, what would this imply about the foreign sector?

11. Can the natural level of real output ever change? If so, when? How is the natural level of real output related to the long-run aggregate supply curve?

12. How do price expectations affect the position of the short-run aggregate supply curve?

13. If desired aggregate demand is greater than aggregate supply, what does this imply about the demand for financial assets relative to the supply?

14. In the situation described in question 13, what will happen to income and interest rate?

15. If the aggregate intentions to incur financial liabilities exceed the aggregate intentions to acquire financial assets, what does this imply about desired aggregate demand relative to aggregate supply?

16. In the situation described in question 15, what will happen to income and interest rates?

Analytical Questions

17. Graphically illustrate the difference between a change in aggregate demand and a change in the quantity demanded of real GDP. Illustrate an increase in aggregate demand and an increase in the quantity demanded of real GDP.

18. Use aggregate supply and aggregate demand curves to explain what will happen to prices, output, and employment if, ceteris paribus,

   a. Government cuts spending.
   b. The Fed makes open market purchases.
   c. Corporate tax rates are increased.
   d. Interest rates abroad increase.

19. Why is the demand curve for wheat downward sloping? Why is the aggregate demand curve downward sloping? Explain why the reasons are different.

20. Draw a short-run aggregate supply curve. Why is the curve upward sloping? What causes the short-run aggregate supply curve to shift?

21. Use graphs to explain demand-pull inflation.

22. Assume that the economy is originally in long-run equilibrium and that there is a drop in demand. Use graphs to explain how and why the economy initially moves to a short-run equilibrium with unemployment. How does the economy return to long-run equilibrium?

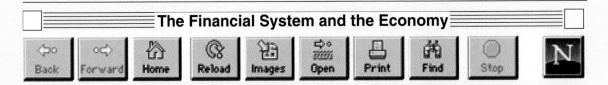

The Financial System and the Economy

1. Access the world wide web site of the Federal Reserve Bank in Minneapolis at (http://woodrow.mpls.frb.fed.us/economy/beige/beigeb.html) which sums up the "state of the economy." Check out your Federal Reserve District by clicking on the map of the United States provided at the site. Keeping Chapter 20 in perspective, comment on the following with regard to your Federal Reserve District:

   a. overall economic growth
   b. manufacturing activity growth in your Federal Reserve District
   c. inflationary pressures
   d. retail spending
   e. banking.

Suggested Readings

E. P. Davis, *Debt, Financial Fragility, and Systemic Risk*, New York: Oxford University Press, 1993, looks at the financing behavior of households and businesses, which has generated high levels of debt since the 1970s, and its relationship to instability.

Many principles of economics texts contain developments of aggregate demand and aggregate supply. We recommend Richard Lipsey, Paul N. Courant, Douglas D. Purvis, Peter O. Steiner, *Economics*, 10th ed., New York: Harper Collins, 1993.

Some recent articles on inflation that touch on many of the topics in this chapter are:

Dawn Blalock, "Jump in Price Doesn't Worry Many Analysts," *The Wall Street Journal,* May 15, 1995, p. A2+.

James Cooper, "Why Inflation Isn't Sprouting in Mr. Greenspan's Neighborhood," *Business Week,* May 8, 1995, pp. 29–30.

Franklin J. Chu, "The Golden Rule: Gold, Inflation, and Monetary Policy," *The Bankers Magazine,* March/April 1995, pp. 16–19.

Robert D. Hershey, Jr., "Producer Prices Hold the Line, Calming Jitters About Inflation," *The New York Times,* April 12, 1995, p. D1+.

Other articles may be assessed on the world wide web by visiting the following web sites:

Business Week (http://www.enews.com/magazines/bw/)
The New York Times (http://www.nytimes.com/pope/)
The Economist (http://www.economist.com)
The Wall Street Journal (http://www.wsj.com)

In addition, a listing of business journals with web sites may be accessed at:

(http://www.businessjournals.com/rolodex/online.html).

PART FIVE

Monetary Policy

21

The Challenges of Monetary Policy

> *Listen, there is no courage or any extra courage*
> *that I know of to find out the right thing to do.*
> *Now, it is not only necessary to do the right*
> *thing, but to do it in the right way and the only*
> *problem you have is what is the right thing to do*
> *and what is the right way to do it. That is the*
> *problem. But this economy of ours is not so simple*
> *that it obeys to the opinion of bias or the*
> *pronouncements or any particular individual. . . .*
> —Dwight D. Eisenhower—

Learning Objectives

After reading this chapter, you should know:

◆ The goals of monetary policy, including economic growth, stable prices, full employment, and satisfactory external balance

◆ How numerical goals are formulated and why they can differ in the short run and long run

◆ The monetary policy goals in terms of aggregate demand and aggregate supply

◆ Monetary policy options in response to fluctuations in aggregate demand and aggregate supply

Can the Business Cycle be Mitigated?

The Great Depression of the 1930s was by far the most severe downturn of the U.S. economy during the 20th century. For more than a decade, output and employment remained considerably below the natural rate. Measured unemployment averaged more than 20 percent, while prices fell by over one-quarter. During this painful period, macroeconomics experienced profound changes. Led by John Maynard Keynes, a school of thought was born that emphasized the need for government intervention to stabilize the level of economic activity. The problem according to Keynes was that it would be an accident if the level of aggregate demand was just sufficient to achieve full employment and stable prices. The more likely situation would be that aggregate demand would be either too great or too little. Moreover, relative price adjustments would occur only slowly so that the economy could experience long bouts of either unemployment (too little demand) or inflation (too much demand).

The buildup for World War II in the early 1940s seemed to validate Keynesian theory. Almost overnight, the economy went to full employment and measures were needed to "control" inflation. Based on such events, much of the academic community accepted Keynesian theory in the post-war period. During the 1960s, Keynesian policy prescriptions were put into practice by the government with some apparent degree of success.[1] Although voices of dissent were always there, they became louder during and after the 1970s when the economy was plagued concurrently with a condition of both high unemployment and high inflation that came to be known as **stagflation.** Economists struggled to understand the causes and remedies for such a dilemma, which Keynes believed could not happen.

Stagflation A condition of concurrent high unemployment and inflation.

Since the Great Depression, the U.S. economy has experienced ten recessions. During these periods, output declined, unemployment increased, and the growth rate of prices generally fell. The economy also has experienced periodic bouts of rapid inflation. Some analysts believe that the government has been successful in reducing the length and magnitude of cyclical downturns and in lengthening cyclical expansions. Although a repetition of the Great Depression has been avoided, there is less consensus now than before about the extent to which government intervention can or should be used to mitigate the business cycle. Despite these observations, researchers are in general agreement that the vast majority of these economic contractions and expansions resulted from fluctuations in aggregate demand. Nonetheless, shocks to aggregate supply (shifts of the aggregate supply curve) have been occasionally responsible for both recessions and inflations. In these cases, analysis simply focusing on aggregate demand may not be appropriate.

Since the early 1970s, the economy has experienced dramatic growth of international trade and finance and a breakdown of barriers to capital flows. At the same time, a flexible exchange rate system has replaced the fixed exchange rate system that was put into place in 1945. Both factors contributed to the increased volatility and relevance of exchange rates. The Fed has chosen

---

[1] Keynes viewed fluctuations as originating with aggregate demand, and, as we have seen, both fiscal and monetary policies under normal circumstances affect demand. Although we consider both policies to be Keynesian, Keynes' preference was for fiscal policy.

on occasion to intervene in the foreign exchange market to smooth the adjustment of changes in the value of the dollar. Such intervention may interfere or conflict with the pursuit of other monetary policy goals. As we shall see, the Fed must be aware of the effects of its policies on the external balance of trade and capital flows.

In this chapter, we look first at the macroeconomic goals and challenges of monetary policy. We then use an aggregate demand and supply framework to examine the specifics of what needs to be done to achieve these goals if the economy experiences either a recession or excessive inflation. As implied in the preceding discussion, what "should" be done in response to fluctuations in aggregate demand or aggregate supply is often unclear and controversial.

The Goals of Monetary Policy

Macroeconomic policy consists of (1) monetary policy, through which the Fed uses its policy instruments to affect the cost and availability of funds in the economy, and (2) fiscal policy, through which Congress and the President propose and enact alterations in government spending or taxes.[2] As illustrated by Exhibit 20-3, the changes in fiscal and monetary policies that lead to changes in aggregate demand interact in turn with aggregate supply to produce changes in prices, real output, and employment.

In conducting monetary policy, the Fed works through the financial system. Recall that the primary tools of the Fed to influence the financial system include control of the monetary base, the required reserve ratio, and the discount rate. Monetary policy in turn influences the borrowing, lending, spending, and saving behavior of the household, firm, government, and foreign sectors. As depicted in Exhibit 21-1, the specific goals of monetary policy are to design and implement policies that will achieve sustainable economic growth, full employment, stable prices, and satisfactory external balance.[3] Now let's take a closer look at the various rationales underlying each of the specific goals guiding policymakers' actions.

Economic Growth

The size of the "economic pie" divided up among a nation's citizens is determined by the quantity of goods and services produced. That is, the size is determined by real output, or specifically, real GDP. Simply put, if the size of a nation's economic pie and thus its potential standard of living are to rise over time, the productive capacity of the economy must expand. To use the terminology of Chapter 20, the natural level of real output (long-run aggregate supply) must increase.

Most economists agree that the growth of aggregate supply over time is determined primarily by the growth of capital, the labor force, and productivity. Thus, growth of the key inputs in the production process and techno-

---

[2] Fiscal policy is the subject of the first half of Chapter 19.
[3] In recent years, many members of the Fed Open Market Committee and other analysts have stressed that maintaining stable prices is the primary goal of the Fed. Others have continued to emphasize that employment levels in the economy must not be ignored.

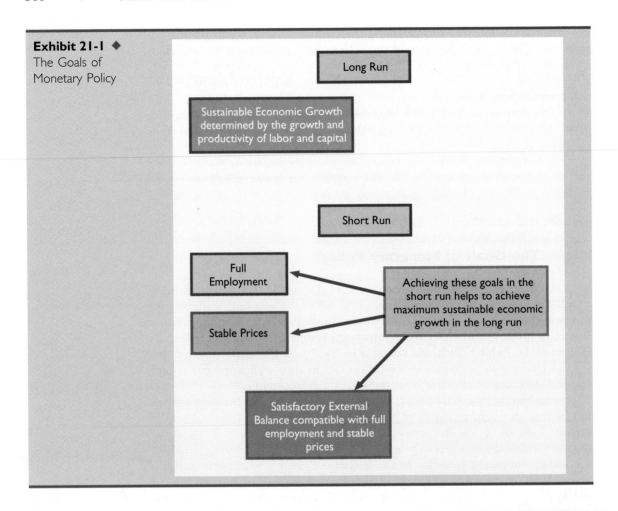

Exhibit 21-1 ◆
The Goals of
Monetary Policy

logical improvements are the key to long-run growth of output. So far so good, but what determines the growth of capital, labor, and productivity?

The growth of the capital stock depends directly on the amount of investment spending undertaken by firms. By definition, the change in the capital stock is equal to net investment spending. The productivity of capital is thought to depend on the amount of resources devoted to research and development and on the resulting technological advances that lead to new and more productive plants and machines. Labor force growth flows from the growth of the population and from increases in the proportion of the population that participates in the labor force. The productivity of labor is thought to depend on the educational attainment and health of workers, the quantity and quality of the capital stock with which they work, and, perhaps, the competitive environment faced by firms and their employees.

In general, a thriving nation's productive capacity grows over time. Research shows that macroeconomic policy, through its effects on the determinants of economic growth, influences the pace of growth in a number of ways. While ignoring many of the detailed relationships and linkages, it is worth noting here that the government's tax policy will affect both the willingness of firms to invest and engage in research and development and the willingness of households to work and save. Similarly, the level of interest rates resulting from the interaction of monetary and fiscal policies pursued will have a decisive influence on spending and saving decisions. Over time, such decisions affect an economy's growth potential and therefore affect aggregate supply.

Beyond these fairly obvious influences, we should also include the overall economic environment within which firms and households are making decisions. More specifically, a stable environment is likely to be more conducive to farsighted planning and decision making that enhance an economy's long-run growth potential. Such a situation is characterized by consistently high rates of capacity utilization and employment, and thus real output growing at a steady, sustainable pace. Exhibit 21-2 depicts such a situation.

On the other hand, an unstable environment characterized by a series of inflationary booms and deflationary recessions is likely to inhibit long-run growth. In such a situation, aggregate demand almost always grows faster or slower than aggregate supply, thereby generating either inflationary pressures or an economic slowdown. Hence, the shorter-run stabilization objectives in the following discussion are not really separate and distinct but rather

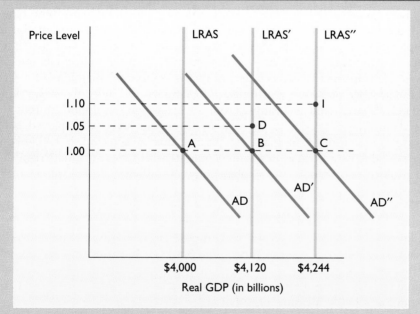

Exhibit 21-2 ◆
Steady
Noninflationary
Growth

On the vertical axis is a price index, and on the horizontal axis is the level of real GDP. Assume that each year a nation's natural level of real output, as measured by the long-run aggregate supply (LRAS), grows by 3 percent. Thus, in year 1, LRAS is $4,000 billion; in year 2, LRAS is $4,000 billion × 1.03 = $4,120 billion; and in year 3, LRAS is $4,120 × 1.03 = $4,244. If aggregate demand also grows by 3 percent per year, then the economy will follow the path A-B-C with 3 percent real GDP growth, a stable price level (1.0) and zero inflation. Alternatively, aggregate demand could grow faster than 3 percent, say, for example, 8 percent per year. Then, the economy would follow path A-D-I with prices rising 5 percent per year. Thus, in general, the growth in aggregate demand relative to aggregate supply determines the price-output performance of the economy.

support and complement a nation's pursuit of economic growth over the long run. Short-run fluctuations around the long-term trend influence the trend itself.

RECAP

The goals of monetary policy are sustainable economic growth, full employment, stable prices, and satisfactory external balance. Sustainable economic growth is determined by the growth and productivity of the labor force and capital stock. Policies that achieve full employment and a noninflationary environment help to achieve maximum sustainable growth.

Stabilization of Unemployment, Inflation, and the External Balance

Recent and expected movements in unemployment and inflation dominate discussions about the health of the economy. Rarely do the evening news and political speeches fail to note what's happening on these fronts. One reason why the nation is concerned about unemployment, as measured by the unemployment rate, is fairly obvious. As a society, we understand that if the nation is to reach its full economic potential, then all individuals must be given the opportunity to become productive, employed members of society. In the absence of such opportunity, poor families and individuals experience financial distress and hardships. From an economic standpoint, output that could have been produced last year by those who were unemployed is lost forever and can never be made up. Against this background, it is readily understandable why our nation's leaders operate with a clear mandate regarding unemployment. Exhibit 21-3 explains how the official unemployment rate is measured.

What is less clear is why inflation generates so much concern. Simply stated, inflation is the rate of increase in the general price level. The Consumer Price Index (CPI), which is discussed in Exhibit 3-10, is the most frequently cited measure of the price level in the United States. It measures the average level of prices of a typical market basket of goods and services that consumers purchase. The month-to-month percentage change in this index gives us a somewhat reliable measure of inflation.[4]

Measurement aside, why is inflation a problem policymakers worry about? After all, if the prices of all goods and services double, but so do wages and salaries, isn't everyone, and thus the nation as a whole unaffected? The short answer is no. To see why, it is useful to distinguish between expected inflation and unexpected inflation.

Suppose it's 1998 and households expect inflation to be about 4 percent in 1999. How will this affect household behavior? First and foremost, the work-

---

[4]Although being widely used and as we have implied "fairly reliable," the CPI has recently been criticized for overstating inflation by the chairperson of the Fed who recommended that it be refigured to eliminate its upward bias. See "Greenspan Says Flaws in Data Hurt Fed Policy-Making Ability," *Investor's Business Daily*, August 11, 1994. Economists believe the upward bias is between .2 and 1.5 percent per year.

Statistics on the labor force, employment, and unemployment in the United States are gathered and published by the Bureau of Labor Statistics. Each month more than 65,000 households nationwide are surveyed. Based on the responses to a series of questions, individuals are classified as

1. Unemployed (16 years or older, out of work, and actively looking for work)
2. Employed
3. Labor Force Participant (Employed plus Unemployed)
4. Not in the Labor Force (out-of-work and not actively looking for work; includes individuals who are under 16, retirees, disabled persons, and so called "discouraged" workers who have lost their jobs and stopped looking for a job).

Exhibit 21-3 ◆
Measuring Unemployment

These data are then used to compute the unemployment rate, which is the percent of the labor force unemployed.

Unemployment Rate = Number of Persons Unemployed/Labor Force

To illustrate, in 1995 there were 7.404 million people unemployed, and the labor force totaled 132.3 million. As a result, the unemployment rate was 5.6 percent.

To fully appreciate the dynamics of the labor market and the relationship between the growth of the economy and unemployment, it is helpful to view the state of unemployment as a pool. Flowing into the pool are the new entrants to the labor force who have not yet found work and those who have recently lost or quit their jobs. Flowing out of the pool are those who have found jobs. If the inflow exceeds the outflow, the number in the pool rises. Conversely, if the outflow exceeds the inflow, the number in the pool falls. To understand the dynamics of unemployment, we must examine the causes and amounts of inflows relative to outflows. For example, over the 1982–1990 period, the U.S. civilian labor force, reflecting the ongoing growth of the population, expanded by about 14.6 million people. Fortunately, the economy grew rather steadily over this period, with real GDP expanding at an annual rate of 2.7 percent. About 18.4 million new jobs were created. As a result, the number of people in the unemployment pool decreased and the unemployment rate fell from 9.5 percent to 5.4 percent. In contrast, during the 1991 recession, the labor force continued to grow but job creation slowed dramatically as firms reacted to the fall in demand for their output and rising inventories by slashing production and laying off workers. The result was a large increase in the pool of unemployed people and the unemployment rate rose sharply to 7.4 percent. Clearly, economic growth and unemployment are tightly connected.

ers in the households will try to secure wage increases of at least 4 percent so that the purchasing power of their incomes will not decline. Ideally, of course, they would hope for a wage increase of more than 4 percent so that their real incomes would rise. Second, if they are net lenders, they will be looking for financial assets with nominal interest rates or nominal returns high enough to produce an adequate expected real return. For example, as discussed in Chapter 7, a nominal return of 7 percent, given that the expected inflation is 4 percent, is expected to produce a real return or real interest rate of about 3 percent. If inflation turns out to be close to 4 percent, as was expected, all is well. But what happens if prices actually rise by 8 percent?

First, the real wage of workers will fall because nominal wages will rise by a smaller percent than prices. The resulting change in output prices relative to input prices will, ceteris paribus, lead to an increase in firms' profits and encourage them to alter production and employment. As we saw in Chapter 20, the short-run aggregate supply curve slopes upward. That is, until expectations adjust to the higher, unanticipated price level, firms will offer more for sale than the natural level of real output. Second, the real return on financial assets acquired will be below what was anticipated and perhaps even negative. In this case, the beneficiaries will be borrowers who find that the actual real cost of borrowing is well below what they expected. Beyond these types of redistribution, citizens living on fixed incomes, such as many retirees, find their purchasing power shrinking.

These simple examples illustrate a central reason why inflation, particularly unexpected inflation, is viewed as worrisome. Inflation redistributes income in arbitrary and unpredictable ways from workers to firms, from lenders to borrowers, and from those on fixed incomes to those with variable incomes that increase with inflation.

In addition, many firms and households will find that several features of the U.S. tax system result in proportionately more taxes being paid to the government in an inflationary environment. To illustrate, if a household earns 4 percent interest on its surplus funds, if the actual and expected inflation rate is zero, and if the household is in the 25 percent tax rate bracket, then the after-tax real return is .03 or 3 percent, as in Equation (21-1).

$$(21\text{-}1) \quad \begin{array}{ccccc} \text{Nominal} & - & \text{Expected} & - & \text{Taxes} & = & \text{Real} \\ \text{Interest} & & \text{Inflation} & & & & \text{After-Tax} \\ \text{Rate} & & \text{Rate} & & & & \text{Return} \end{array}$$

$$.04 \quad - \quad 0 \quad - \quad .25 \times .04 =$$

$$.03 = 3 \text{ percent}$$

Now suppose that, ceteris paribus, expected and actual inflation rises to 2 percent and the nominal interest rate rises from 4 to 6 percent to compensate lenders for the loss in purchasing power. The real after-tax return will again be the nominal rate (0.06) minus the expected inflation rate (.02) and taxes (.25 × .06). In this case, the real after-tax return equals .025 or 2.5 percent of the nominal interest rate, as in Equation (21-2).

$$(21\text{-}2) \quad \begin{array}{ccccc} \text{Nominal} & - & \text{Expected} & - & \text{Taxes} & = & \text{Real} \\ \text{Interest} & & \text{Inflation} & & & & \text{After-Tax} \\ \text{Rate} & & \text{Rate} & & & & \text{Return} \end{array}$$

$$.06 \quad - \quad 0.2 \quad - \quad .25 \times .06 =$$

$$.025 = 2.5 \text{ percent}$$

Since nominal returns rather than real returns are taxed, inflation results in government taxes taking a larger portion of interest income than in a non-inflationary environment.[5]

As for firms, standard accounting procedures base depreciation allowances on the historical cost of equipment and structures rather than on the replacement cost. In an inflationary environment, firms' depreciation allowances, which are deducted from revenues before taxable income is computed, are too small to replace the capital wearing out as production occurs. More to the point, they result in taxes being proportionately higher than in a noninflationary environment. Again, as in the prior examples, inflation redistributes income and can distort economic decision making.

Returning to the uncertainty theme already discussed with regard to economic growth, we note that research has also shown a tendency for the variability of inflation to rise and a tendency for the relationship among relative prices to become more volatile and difficult to predict as the inflation rate rises. The result is that pricing, production, saving, and investment decisions have to be made in a more uncertain environment. Firms and households are likely to be much more cautious about making long-term commitments to spend, save, produce, or invest, focusing instead on near-term opportunities. Such a perspective does not enhance long-run stability and growth and can aggravate short-run instabilities and cyclical fluctuations.

Lastly, inflation can have an adverse effect on the nation's international competitiveness and thus its role in the world economy and in world affairs. For example, if the prices of U.S. goods rise relative to prices of similar and thus competing goods in the rest of the world, U.S. producers will, ceteris paribus, find the demand for their products falling with attendant effects on domestic production and employment, as discussed in Chapter 19. While the resulting depreciation of the dollar will help to offset and reverse the negative effects on the trade balance over time, there is no assurance this will occur quickly. In the meantime, a nation's firms will lose a portion of their share of world markets.

As the U.S. economy becomes more globalized, monetary policymakers must be aware of the international effects of policy. For example, if the Fed embarks on a program of monetary restraint to slow the growth rate of the U.S. economy, real interest rates could rise relative to foreign rates. A substantial appreciation of the dollar and augmented capital inflows can result. The dollar's appreciation may have a dramatic effect on the economy through its effect on net exports. Net exports fall as the foreign prices of U.S. goods increase and the domestic prices of foreign goods decrease. The result would be reduced employment and output in the United States relative to what they would have been otherwise.

If monetary policymakers establish policy goals for inflation and growth that are widely divergent from other countries, substantial fluctuations in exchange rates can result. In addition to the price effects on net exports and the interest rate effects on capital flows, fluctuations in exchange rates greatly increase the exchange rate risks of international trade and finance. These

---

[5] Inflation also reduces the real value of nominal money balances held. In this way, it acts as a tax on such holdings.

fluctuations may result in the need for central bank intervention to stabilize exchange rates. Such intervention can dampen or conflict with the pursuit of other policy goals.

To summarize, monetary policy can cause dramatic changes in exchange rates and the balances on the current and capital accounts—that is, the external balance—which then feed back to the domestic economy. Exchange rate volatility can necessitate central bank intervention. The bottom line is that in designing and implementing monetary policy, monetary policymakers must seek to achieve an acceptable external balance compatible with the domestic goals of full employment and stable prices. In Chapter 24, we take a more in-depth look at the international effects of monetary policy. We shall see that this increasingly globalized environment will necessitate increased coordination among countries as they establish policy goals.

But monetary policymakers do not simply make policy decisions in a vacuum aiming at abstract, long-run theoretical goals. They are not oblivious to the domestic and international environment. Rather, they have specific numerical objectives in mind for unemployment and inflation when they make policy adjustments that are consistent with the economic environment. It is to these objectives that we now turn.[6]

RECAP

Full employment is necessary for a nation to reach its economic potential. A stable price level is desirable because unexpected inflation redistributes income in arbitrary and unpredictable ways and causes distortions in the U.S. tax system. Monetary policy can cause changes in exchange rates and the external balance that feed back to the domestic economy. Monetary policymakers must secure an external balance that is consistent with the domestic goals of full employment and stable prices.

Employment Act of 1946 The first act that directed policymakers to pursue policies to achieve full employment and noninflationary growth.
Humphrey–Hawkins Full Employment and Balanced Growth Act of 1978 An act that required policymakers to pursue policies to achieve full employment and noninflationary growth.
Natural Rate of Unemployment The rate of unemployment consistent with stable prices; believed to be about 5.5 percent.

The Source of Numerical Objectives for Unemployment and Inflation

General guidelines for policymakers are contained in the **Employment Act of 1946** and the **Humphrey–Hawkins Full Employment and Balanced Growth Act of 1978.** Both direct policymakers to pursue policies consistent with achieving full employment and noninflationary growth. Briefly, this legislation, in effect, leaves it to policymakers, their staffs, and the economics profession at large to determine, for example, what unemployment rate is consistent with full employment and nonaccelerating inflation.

As we look forward to the 21st century, most estimates of sustainable employment go along with an unemployment rate of about 5.5 percent. Also called the **natural rate of unemployment,** this rate is believed to be the un-

---

[6]In compliance with the 1978 Humphrey–Hawkins Act, the Fed reports the long-term goals for unemployment and inflation to the Congress twice each year in February and July.

employment rate that is consistent with stable prices in the late 1980s.[7] Economists believe that a measured unemployment rate much below this level will trigger inflation as shortages appear in some markets driving up prices. The natural rate can change over time for various reasons including the changing gender and age composition of the labor force, and the changing safety net of benefits available to the unemployed.[8]

On the inflation front, the problem is a bit more complicated. In 1971, President Nixon imposed a 90-day freeze on wages and prices because the inflation rate had "surged" to 3.5 percent.[9] Even today's moderate inflation rate of 2 to 3 percent was worrisome then to policymakers. In contrast, the inflation rate fell dramatically during President Reagan's term from the double-digit levels prevailing at the beginning of the 1980s to below 3 percent by 1986. President Reagan claimed "victory" over inflation as the inflation rate settled down to the 3 to 4 percent range. In 1994, the Fed raised interest rates several times out of fear that inflation might again increase despite the fact that it still hovered in the 3 to 4 percent range. Rapid economic growth kindled renewed fears that inflation would again reappear.

Over time policymakers desire price stability and often stress that this should be the primary objective of monetary policy. Some analysts believe that price stability means zero inflation while others associate inflation rates in the 1 to 2 percent range with price stability. However, the inflation goal over the near term, such as the next year or two, is dependent upon recent experience and a balancing of the desire to reduce inflation further with the desire to minimize the accompanying and possibly adverse near-term effects on unemployment and output growth. Consequently, goals, such as for inflation, are not selected in a vacuum. The recent historical experience, judgments about what is feasible, and the political environment all play a role. Times change and so do economic goals.

In the long run, after all adjustments are completed, the goals of stable prices and full employment are believed to be perfectly compatible. Thus, balancing among some goals does not arise. However, we all live, and policymakers act, in the short run. History, as well as theory, tells us that policymakers' attempts to lower inflation can reduce output growth and raise unemployment for a time, while attempts to raise output growth and employment can aggravate inflation. In this context, concern about the short-run versus long-run effects of policy actions and the price versus output effects of policy actions in the short run do arise.

Finally, the potential long-run growth rate for real GDP is estimated to be around 2.5 to 3 percent per year over time. This estimation results from our historical experience. Growth beyond 3 percent per year does not seem to be sustainable over a long period of time. Sustainable growth in the 2.5 to 3 percent range is compatible with the other numerical goals for full employment and stable prices. If the economy grows at this sustainable rate, the vertical long-run aggregate supply curve shifts to the right by 2.5 to 3 percent per year.

---

[7] In the late 1980s and early 1990s, the natural rate of unemployment was believed to be in the 5.5 to 6.0 percent range. Low unemployment in the mid-1990s with moderate inflation convinced many economists that the natural rate had fallen to the 5.2 to 5.5 percent range.

[8] The natural rate of unemployment is the unemployment rate that corresponds with the natural level of output discussed in Chapter 20.

[9] During the 1950s and 1960s, inflation had averaged 1 to 2 percent.

In sum, the prevailing economic and political environment and the nation's historical experience all play a role in setting the priorities that guide policy actions. Since the policymakers and the environment can change over time, so can the weight given to each priority. We turn now to the aggregate demand and supply framework to look at policy alternatives.

RECAP

General guidelines for numerical objectives are found in the Employment Act of 1946 and the Humphrey–Hawkins Full Employment and Balanced Growth Act of 1978. Full employment is believed to be about 5.5 percent. The goal for inflation depends upon recent experience and the political and historical environment. Sustainable growth is thought to be in the 2.5 to 3 percent range.

Changes in Aggregate Demand and Policy

From an aggregate demand and aggregate supply framework, the obvious goals of monetary policy are to achieve successive long-run equilibriums with sustainable noninflationary growth. Such a situation occurs when the aggregate demand and long-run aggregate supply curves are both shifting

CLAY BENNETT
Courtesy St. Petersburg Times

to the right by the same relative magnitude. Look again at Exhibit 21-2 in which steady noninflationary growth is achieved because aggregate demand and long-run aggregate supply are both growing by 3 percent per year. Unfortunately, due to the extremely dynamic nature of the world, the economy may often fall short of achieving those goals. Consequently, a role for policymakers is to react to changes or to initiate changes that guide or sometimes push the economy in the right direction.

In Chapter 20, we discussed demand-pull inflation, when an excessive level of aggregate demand pulls up the overall price level. Ceteris paribus, starting from a long-run equilibrium position, an unexpected shift to the right in the aggregate demand curve—an increase in demand—initially leads to increases in both output and the price level. The economy moves to a new short-run equilibrium along an upward-sloping short-run aggregate supply curve. The output level is not sustainable and price level adjustments bring the economy back to long-run equilibrium at full employment and a higher price level.

Look at Exhibit 21-4, which illustrates the adjustment of the economy in response to an increase in aggregate demand. Initially, the economy is in long-run equilibrium at point A. The actual price level (1.0) is equal to the expected price level underlying the short-run aggregate supply curve and the economy is operating at its natural level of real output ($1,500). Subsequently, aggregate demand increases unexpectedly shifting the aggregate demand curve from AD to AD′. In the short run, the economy will move to point B with output rising to $1,700 and the price level increasing to 1.05. Point B is not a long-run equilibrium, however, because the actual price level (1.05) is above the expected price level (1.0). As input suppliers respond to the unanticipated increase in prices, the expected price level increases to 1.05 and input prices increase. The short-run aggregate supply curve eventually shifts from SRAS to SRAS′. With input prices and thus production costs rising, firms will require a higher output price than was initially the case to induce them

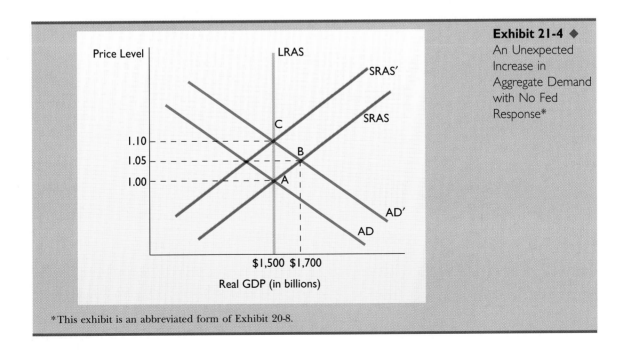

Exhibit 21-4 ◆
An Unexpected Increase in Aggregate Demand with No Fed Response*

*This exhibit is an abbreviated form of Exhibit 20-8.

to produce a particular level of output. When the adjustment is completed, the economy will settle at a new long-run equilibrium at point C. (See if you can explain why this is the case.) In effect, the economy moves along the path A-B-C as shifts in short-run aggregate supply alter the initial short-run effects on the economy of a rise in aggregate demand. In the end, the rise in aggregate demand results in a rise in the price level (1.0 to 1.1) and no change in real GDP.

Normally, we would hope that the Fed would not unexpectedly increase the growth rate of the money supply when the economy was in a long-run equilibrium with stable prices and full employment. However, as we have pointed out, myopic policymakers may have an incentive to do so because of short-run, unsustainable gains in employment despite concurrent and subsequent increases in the price level. In an election year, some politicians may find it is desirable to push the unemployment rate below its natural level. If no other action is taken, price increases would eventually move the economy to a new long-run equilibrium with a higher price level as in Exhibit 21-4.

Unexpected increases in aggregate demand can also come from other sources such as swells in household, business, or government spending, or surges in export demand. Regardless of the source, Congress can use fiscal policy and/or the Fed can use monetary policy to reduce the level of demand. For example, tighter monetary policy would reduce the growth rate of the monetary aggregates and at least temporarily increase short-term interest rates from what they would be otherwise. Or, the appropriate fiscal policy would be to slow government spending or increase tax rates. In either case, the level of spending and thus aggregate demand would be reduced. In such a case, the economy would return to long-run equilibrium at a lower price level, and perhaps more quickly, than if the government did nothing. Now would be a good time to look at Exhibit 21-5, which illustrates the path the economy would take to return to long-run equilibrium if the government intervenes.

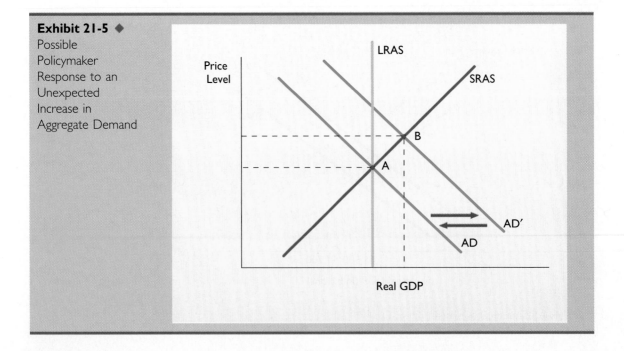

Exhibit 21-5 ◆
Possible Policymaker Response to an Unexpected Increase in Aggregate Demand

LOOKING BACK

How History Affects U.S. and German Policy Goals

A nation's priorities depend in an important way on its history. In the United States, for example, the trauma surrounding the Great Depression contributed to a political environment in which policymakers tended to emphasize the economic growth and unemployment objectives for many decades after World War II. In contrast, the former West Germany experienced economic and political dislocations, including Hitler's rise to power because of the German hyperinflation following World War I. This past ordeal led the former West Germany to emphasize the price stability objective. These tendencies in turn govern policymaking in the sense that they condition the direction in which policymakers are generally prepared to err. Accordingly, and not surprisingly, the tendency for policymakers to err on the expansionary side in the United States and the tendency for German policymakers to err on the restrictive side, have resulted in the U.S. inflation rate generally being above the German inflation rate over the past 35 years.

In addition to a nation's long-run historical experience, there is no question that recent history also influences the priorities assigned various policy objectives. For example, the significant acceleration in inflation in the United States during the late 1970s clearly influenced priorities and actions. More specifically, the appointment of Paul Volcker as chairperson of the Board of Governors of the Fed in 1979 and the two recessions the nation endured in 1980 and 1982 can all be linked to some degree to a consensus that inflation had to be brought down even at the cost of a temporary rise in unemployment and a retardation of economic growth. Reminiscent of the difficulty in curbing inflation if inflationary expectations take hold, the Fed took actions that increased interest rates five times during 1994 despite little concrete evidence that inflation was or would be much above 3 percent in the foreseeable future.

A united Germany, on the other hand, did not lose sight of the preeminence of the price stability goal in the 1990s. The German inflation rate remained below 4 percent despite the 1990 unification of East and West Germany. By 1995, German inflation was below 2 percent.*

*In mid-1990, residents of the former East Germany turned in their ostmarks, the currency of East Germany, for deutsche marks, the currency of West Germany.

In response to an unanticipated increase in aggregate demand, the economy moves from long-run equilibrium at point A to point B, ceteris paribus. Output is above the sustainable full employment level and the price level has risen. If policymakers respond by using fiscal or monetary policy to reduce the level of demand, this will move the economy back to long-run equilibrium at a price level (point A) which is lower than what it otherwise would be if the government failed to act.

Note the irony of this situation when the increase in aggregate demand is due to an unexpected increase in the money supply. After having generated the increase in aggregate demand, the Fed engages in contractionary policy to bring the economy back to long-run equilibrium at the original point. We turn now to the equally sinister demand-induced recession.

RECAP

Starting from full employment, an increase in aggregate demand initially leads to increases in both output and prices as the economy expands along the short-run aggregate supply curve. The higher level of output is not sustainable in the long run. Such unexpected increases in demand cause demand-pull inflation and can come from increases in spending in any sector. If policymakers do nothing, the economy returns to full employment at a higher price level. If policymakers engage in contractionary policies, the economy returns to full employment at the original price level.

Demand-Induced Recession

Whatever the source, the initial effect of an unexpected fall in aggregate demand is an unanticipated rise in inventories, ceteris paribus. In response, business firms cut production, employment, and prices. In the aggregate, output prices tend to fall relative to input prices, including wages, which do not immediately fall or which fall slower than output prices in response to the reduction in demand. Exhibit 21-6 illustrates the case of a demand-induced recession.

Initially, the economy is in long-run equilibrium at point A which is the intersection of the aggregate demand and long-run aggregate supply curves. The short-run aggregate supply curve is in the initial position of SRAS. The economy moves along the short-run aggregate supply curve (from point A to point B in Exhibit 21-6) into a recession.[10]

Once in a recession, there are two possible paths the economy can take from this short-run equilibrium back to a long-run equilibrium. First, with the actual price level (0.95) below the expected price level, firms and workers presumably will adjust their price expectations downward. This, along with the fact that the employment of labor and other factors of production has declined, will lead to decreases in nominal wages and other input prices. The short-run aggregate supply curve will shift to the right, reflecting the fall in production costs, and the economy will return to a long-run equilibrium at the natural rate of output (point C). The end result of a fall in aggregate demand (10 percent in Exhibit 21-6) will be a proportional fall in the price level (1.0 to .9) and no effects on real output or employment.

An important question to ask about this first possible path is How long will it take? The answer is that it depends on how quickly input and output prices adjust downward. This adjustment is a process, which, in turn, depends on how individuals (firm managers as well as workers) formulate and thus adjust their price expectations. Suffice to say that the adjustment of prices and price expectations in the United States during recessions has usually been a sluggish process. Accordingly, policymakers have found it economically and politically difficult to wait for the economy to take the B-C path back to long-run equilibrium. Exhibit 21-7 discusses how individuals form price expectations.

---

[10]Technically speaking, a recession is usually defined as a fall in real GDP lasting at least two consecutive calendar quarters. In actuality, the government maintains a Business Cycle Dating Committee to decide when the economy officially enters and leaves a recession.

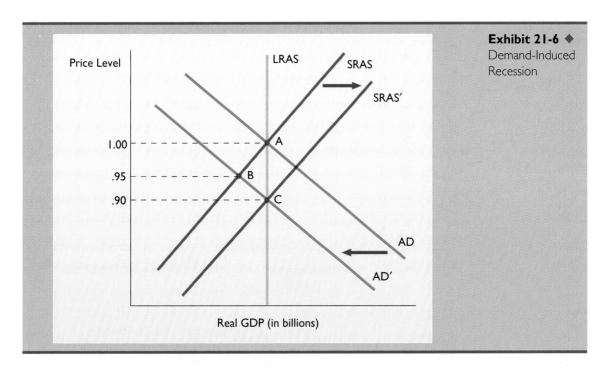

Exhibit 21-6 ◆
Demand-Induced
Recession

Such considerations suggest a second possible route out of the recession. Aggregate demand can be boosted, for example, through expansionary monetary and fiscal policies such that aggregate demand rebounds (from AD′ back to AD in Exhibit 21-6). The economy returns to the natural level of real output and the initial price level (point A). Again, the appropriate monetary policy would be to increase the growth rate of the monetary and credit aggregates and to lower interest rates from what they would be otherwise. Likewise, the appropriate fiscal policy would be to increase the growth of government spending and/or reduce tax rates.

 RECAP

Starting from full employment, an unexpected drop in aggregate demand causes a demand-induced recession. Output and prices fall as the economy moves down a short-run aggregate supply curve. If policymakers do nothing, the short-run aggregate supply curve will eventually shift to the right as firms and workers adjust their price expectations downwards. The economy returns to full employment at a lower price level. Policymakers can also choose to boost demand through fiscal or monetary policy. The economy returns to full employment at the original price level.

Which route does the economy usually take out of a recession? Modern history shows that the second route, a policy-induced rebound in aggregate demand, has predominated. The reasons are two-fold:

1. Recessions generate political pressures "to do something" and policymakers generally respond to such pressures eventually.

Exhibit 21-7 ◆
Formation of Price
Expectations

The expected price level is a major determinant of the interaction between aggregate supply and aggregate demand. Therefore, it is also a major determinant of the relationship between prices and real output. One important factor is how fast the public adjusts its price expectations to actual price developments. The slower and less complete this adjustment is, the slower the response of wages and other input prices, and the more likely we are to observe output and employment changing in the short run as aggregate demand and aggregate supply change.

The weight of current research on the formation of price expectations suggests that the public does not adjust its expectations instantaneously. However, the evidence also suggests that as the public has come to develop and understand the process of inflation, the lag in adjusting expectations has shortened considerably.

In recent years, considerable research has been done on the way in which the public forms price expectations. Equation (21-3) brings together the factors this research suggests are important in determining expectations of future prices.

(21-3)   Price Expectations = f(Current and past prices, expected changes in aggregate demand, and expected changes in production costs)

This equation suggests that the formation of price expectations is both backward and forward looking. Hypothesizing that price expectations depend on the public's experience with prices, as reflected in current and past prices, captures the backward-looking component of price expectations. In macroeconomics, backward-looking expectations formation is typically called **adaptive expectations.** This experience is measured as a weighted average of past values because the recent past (say the last one to two years) is likely to be more influential in forming expectations about the future than prices in the more distant past. Thus, recent years are weighted more heavily than earlier years. For example, if the rate of inflation was 5 percent per year for ten years and in the most recent two years rose 6 percent, then, ceteris paribus, the public will probably expect inflation in the coming year to be closer to 6 percent than to 5 percent.

Other factors that contribute to the formation of price expectations include the effect of expected changes in costs of production and in aggregate demand. Will the price of oil rise or fall? Will policy be expansionary or contractionary? In trying to forecast and anticipate the future, it is unreasonable to believe that the public will take only the past into consideration. To follow up on the preceding illustration, if the public expects a large rise in the price of oil, government expenditures, or bank reserves in the coming year, they may adjust their expectation of inflation to, say, 7 percent. **Rational expectations** is typically the name given to the formation of expectations when both backward- and forward-looking effects are taken into account.

Adaptive Expectations
Expectations formed as a weighted average of past values.

Rational Expectations
Expectations formed by taking past and expected future values into consideration.

2. If firms and households, based on historical experience, expect policy-makers to boost aggregate demand when the economy is in a recession, then the first route, a downward adjustment in price expectations and shift of short-run aggregate supply to the right, will be slow to develop—slower than if firms and households did not expect government intervention. As a result, the economy will stagnate and the pressure on policy-makers to boost aggregate demand will intensify.

Thus, in a very real sense, what firms and households believe policymakers will do has a direct influence on the economy's performance. More specifically, the beliefs of households and firms regarding the response of policy-makers affect how prices and output adjust in the short run as well as the long run. What firms and households believe policymakers will do is, in turn, heavily influenced by what policymakers have done in the past in similar situations. Given the short-run horizons of most policymakers, it should not be surprising that monetary and fiscal policies have, on average, been expansionary for most of the last 35 years.

The experience of the U.S. economy has been characterized by some as a **stop-go policy cycle.** Policy is expansionary, raising aggregate demand perhaps during an election year or otherwise. After a time, the economy expands and, as prices rise, policymakers eventually decide to take some antiinflationary actions such as slowing the growth rate of money and raising real interest rates.[11] These measures are designed to reduce or slow the growth of aggregate demand and initiate the "stop" part of the cycle. As a recession develops, pressure builds on policymakers to stimulate the economy—the "go" part of the cycle—by reversing their antiinflationary, recession-inducing policies.

As the stop-go cycle recurs, firms, workers, and other participants in the economy become increasingly skeptical about what policymakers say about reducing inflation. In effect, the credibility or believability of policymaker pronouncements is reduced. Paying more attention to actions than talk, firms and households are, as a result, slow to adjust price expectations in light of announced plans to fight inflation and even the onset of a recession, believing that policymakers will soon reverse course and boost aggregate demand.

The legacy of this interaction between policymakers and their constituents is that prices have risen more or less continuously over the past 30 years. However, the rate at which prices rise—that is, the inflation rate—has generally decelerated in recessions and accelerated in expansions. The expansion of the early and mid-1990s is an exception; inflation rates remained subdued for many years into the expansion. Nevertheless, the Fed has become increasingly aware of how important expectations are in affecting market outcomes; and because of its commitment to maintaining stable prices, the Fed is extremely concerned with maintaining its credibility. Now would be a good time to look at Exhibit 21-8, which discusses the Phillips Curve that suggests a trade-off between inflation and unemployment, at least some of the time.

So far, we have concentrated on developments that affect aggregate demand. To complete our examination, we need to analyze how developments that affect aggregate supply influence output, employment, and the overall price level in both the short and long run.

Stop-Go Policy Cycle
Policy that switches from expansionary to contractionary and so on.

---

[11] Antiinflationary fiscal policies include cutting government spending and/or raising taxes.

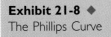

Exhibit 21-8 ◆
The Phillips Curve

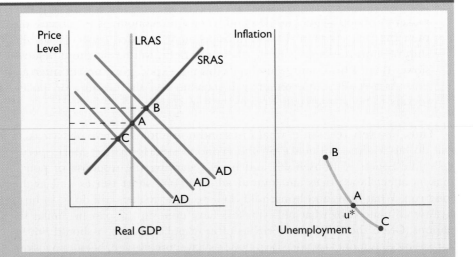

The analysis so far suggests that there may be a trade-off between inflation and unemployment. Such a trade would imply that lower unemployment could be "bought" by the public's willingness to accept higher inflation. In 1957, A.W. Phillips noticed such a trade-off when analyzing British data for the 1861–1957 time period. Actually, Phillips' original work stressed the relationship between increases in rate of growth of wages and changes in the unemployment rate. When the unemployment rate was low, the rate of increases in wages was high. Likewise, when the unemployment rate was high, the rate of increase in wages was low or even negative.

Later economists extended the analysis to suggest an inverse relationship between the rate of price changes (inflation) and changes in the unemployment rate. They could do so because of the strong correlation between wage changes and changes in the overall price level. Thus, a low unemployment rate was associated with high inflation, and vice versa.

RECAP

If firms and households based on historical experience expect policymakers to boost aggregate demand in recessions, then a downward adjustment in price expectations and shift of the short-run aggregate supply curve to the right will take a long time to materialize. The U.S. economy has been characterized by a stop-go policy cycle, which can cause policymakers to lose credibility. In general, inflation accelerates in expansions and decelerates in recessions. An exception is the expansion of the first half of the 1990s, which was not accompanied by an acceleration of inflation.

Changes in Aggregate Supply and Policy

Supply Shock Any event that shifts the short-run aggregate supply curve.

A **supply shock** is any event that shifts the aggregate supply curve. One example of an adverse supply shock is a significant rise in the price of

The concept was immediately embraced by economists and actually served as a springboard for much economic research over the next 20 years. But does a trade-off really exist? And, if so, could policymakers exploit it to achieve their goals?

Actually, we can use the analysis already developed to answer these questions. In the short run, a **Phillips Curve** trade-off does exist. Starting from a point of long-run equilibrium, when there is an unanticipated increase in aggregate demand, the economy moves to a short-run equilibrium where the price level has risen, output increased, and the unemployment rate has fallen (the economy moves from point A to B). The graph on the left is the familiar aggregate demand and aggregate supply model. The graph on the right has the unemployment rate measured on the horizontal axis and the inflation rate measured on the vertical axis. U* is the unemployment rate that is expected when expected inflation is zero. This is the natural rate of unemployment. From the initial long-run equilibrium, if there is an unexpected decrease in aggregate demand, the price level falls and output falls, and the unemployment rate increases (the economy moves from A to C). Thus in the short run, there is a trade-off, but only if the increase or decrease in demand is unexpected. Once expectations about the actual price level have been adjusted, there is no longer a trade-off as relative price adjustments bring the economy back to the natural level of output and the natural level of employment. While a trade-off exists in the short run, in the long run, the Phillips curve is vertical. The implication is again that myopic policymakers can buy "lower unemployment" in the short run by accepting more inflation, but not in the long run. However, as Robert Parry, chief executive officer of the Federal Reserve Bank of San Francisco puts it, "A little inflation may get us more employment, but it would only be a temporary gain. The Fed simply doesn't have the power to push the economy beyond its capacity to produce goods and services for very long."*

> **Phillips Curve** A curve suggesting a trade-off between unanticipated inflation and unemployment in the short run.

*"Fed Official Defends Rise in Rates," *The Orange County Register,* October 9, 1994, p. 5.

oil, a key input widely used in production. Other examples of negative supply shocks would be major crop failures and natural disasters such as earthquakes or major floods. More generally, anything that destroys a significant portion of a nation's productive capacity or reduces the productivity of labor and capital is an adverse supply shock.

As with our analysis of the effects of shifts in aggregate demand, let's begin by assuming the economy is in long-run equilibrium. Now suppose an adverse supply shock occurs. For example, assume the price of refined petroleum increases suddenly and substantially, ceteris paribus. Such was the case in 1974 when the price of refined petroleum increased by more than 70 percent and again in 1980 when the price rose more than 50 percent.

The effects of such a supply shock are felt most immediately and directly by firms. Simply put, input prices rise dramatically relative to what firms had expected. With costs of production higher, firms are unwilling to supply as high a level of output as before. More specifically, in the face of higher production costs, firms will, ceteris paribus, require a higher price level to produce the same level of output. Exhibit 21-9 shows the resulting shift in the short-run aggregate supply curve to the left.

Exhibit 21-9 ◆

An Adverse Supply Shock as a Cause of Cost-Push Inflation

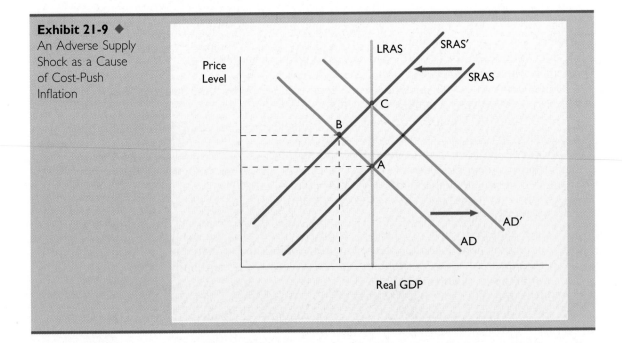

With firms posting higher output prices, ceteris paribus, the quantity of real output demanded falls and firms cut their production and employment. In the short run, the economy moves from point A to point B and experiences rising prices and falling output and employment. Policymakers are on the spot because the economy is experiencing a recession and inflation. Real output has fallen below its natural level and prices have risen. In contrast to demand-pull inflation, the economy has now experienced so called **cost-push inflation** triggered by increases in input prices.[12]

Cost-Push Inflation Sustained increases in the overall price level, triggered by increases in input prices.

The problem from the policymakers' perspective is that monetary and fiscal tools work mainly on the aggregate demand side while the more immediate problem confronting them emanates from the supply side. What can be done? First, policymakers can boost aggregate demand via fiscal or monetary policy. If they do, the economy moves from point B to C in Exhibit 21-9. Assuming this so-called **accommodation** is done quickly, the recession can be shortened in duration and severity, but the inflation problem will be magnified as prices rise further. Second, policymakers can literally do nothing. With the economy at point B and aggregate demand unchanged, the idle plants and unemployment in the economy will eventually put downward pressure on wages and overall prices. As this occurs, the short-run aggregate supply curve will begin to shift to the right toward its initial position. Given enough time, the economy could return to a position close to its initial long-run equilibrium (point A).[13] However, since workers will be reluctant to accept lower wages in the face of higher heating and gasoline prices, the period of adjustment could be quite prolonged. It should not be surprising that policymakers have usually pursued

Accommodation When policymakers increase aggregate demand in response to an adverse supply shock.

---

[12]We should note that a recession is not necessary to have cost-push inflation.

[13]We say "close" because if the price of a major input is permanently higher, then the natural rate of output could presumably be reduced somewhat, but not permanently as alternate inputs are developed or the output mix changes.

an accommodating expansion in aggregate demand in response to an adverse supply shock.

Of course, supply shocks need not always be adverse. In late 1985 the world petroleum market literally collapsed because of slow worldwide economic growth, weak demand, and the tendency for some OPEC members to cheat on their agreed-upon production quotas. With the price of crude petroleum falling from $24.09 in 1985 to $12.51 in 1986, countries such as the United States experienced a beneficial supply shock. The fall in production costs shifted a country's aggregate supply curve to the right resulting in less inflation and more output growth than otherwise would have occurred.

 RECAP

A dverse supply shocks shift the short-run aggregate supply curve to the left. Beneficial shocks shift it to the right. Adverse supply shocks cause rising prices and higher unemployment and are particularly difficult for policymakers to deal with. Given an adverse shock, an accommodating policy will increase employment but aggravate the inflation.

We have considered increases and decreases in aggregate demand and aggregate supply. Whatever the case may be, the goals and policy responses brought together in this chapter suggest ways to achieve full employment and stable prices. The formulation and implementation of policies to achieve these goals are the subjects of the next two chapters.

Summary of Major Points

1. The goal of monetary policy is to influence the overall performance of the economy. The size of the "economic pie" in the long run is influenced by the growth of the labor force and the capital stock, and by increases in the productivity of these inputs. Government policies affect growth through the mix of monetary and fiscal policies and resulting tax and interest rate structures, which affect incentives to invest, work, and save. In addition, to the extent that government policies encourage a stable environment, growth is also affected.

2. In addition to economic growth, full employment, price stability, and a satisfactory external balance are also goals of monetary policy. Over the short run, economic growth depends on the growth of aggregate demand relative to aggregate supply, which determines the resulting fluctuations in output, employment, and prices. An unstable short-run environment is believed to have an adverse effect on long-run growth while a stable short-run environment is believed to have a beneficial effect on long-run growth.

3. Full employment is a goal because if a nation is to reach its full economic potential, individuals must be given an opportunity to become productive members of society. Price stability is a goal because inflation tends to

redistribute income in arbitrary and unpredictable ways, especially if the inflation is unexpected. Inflation also contributes to uncertainty and distortions in decision making. It can have an adverse effect on the nation's international competitiveness. Monetary policy can cause dramatic changes in exchange rates and the balances in the current and capital accounts. Monetary policy must seek to achieve an acceptable external balance compatible with the goals of full employment and stable prices.

4. General guidelines for the macroeconomic goals are contained in the Employment Act of 1946 and the Humphrey–Hawkins Act of 1978. Specific guidelines and the setting of priorities are the result of historical experience, judgments about what is feasible, and the political environment.

5. In the short run, an unexpected increase in aggregate demand produces demand-pull inflation and unsustainable increases in output. If the policymakers do nothing, the economy returns to long-run equilibrium at a higher price level. If the government uses appropriate monetary or fiscal policy, the economy returns to long-run equilibrium at a price level that is lower than what it would be otherwise.

6. In the short run, an unexpected fall in aggregate demand will produce a recession. There are two possible paths to recovery. First, as time goes on, price expectations will be revised downward, inflation will decrease, and the economy will recover as relative prices adjust. Alternatively, if policymakers and their constituents become impatient, demand can be boosted by expansionary monetary and fiscal policy. History shows that the second route has predominated. The resulting stop-go policy cycle has contributed to the tendency for inflation to persist.

7. Supply shocks cause a shift of the short-run aggregate supply curve. Adverse supply shocks pose a real dilemma for policymakers. Real output and employment fall while prices rise. An accommodating policy will moderate the recession but will aggravate the inflation. Cost-push inflation results when the overall price level increases due to increases in the cost of inputs.

Key Terms

Accommodation
Adaptive Expectations
Cost-Push Inflation
Credibility
Employment Act of 1946
Humphrey–Hawkins Full
    Employment and Balanced
    Growth Act of 1978

Natural Rate of Unemployment
Phillips Curve
Rational Expectations
Stagflation
Stop-Go Policy Cycle
Supply Shock

Review Questions

1. What are the goals of monetary policy?

2. How are the goals of full employment and stable prices related to the long-run goal of economic growth? How can policymakers affect long-run growth?

3. Why do policymakers have to be aware of the external balance?

4. Explain why the short-run goal for inflation is not always zero percent.

5. Does the natural level of unemployment ever change? Why?

6. Why do the numerical objectives of policy change? Explain.

7. What is a supply shock? What is the appropriate policy response to a negative supply shock? What determines whether policymakers should act or do nothing in the face of adverse shocks to either aggregate demand or aggregate supply?

8. In the context of monetary policymaking, what is accommodation? What is credibility? If the Fed usually increases the money supply in response to decreases in aggregate demand, how will this affect the adjustment process?

9. Define both cost-push and demand-pull inflation.

10. How is the natural level of real output related to the natural rate of unemployment?

11. What is the difference between rational expectations and adaptive expectations. Consider the impact of a predictable policy action in the context of each.

12. Can the economy experience a demand-pull inflation and a recession?

13. What do economists mean by the stop-go policy cycle? What is the relationship between the stop-go policy cycle and credibility of the policymakers?

14. In the mid-1990s, both Congress and the president are seeking to reduce the federal deficit. What will happen to aggregate demand if they are successful?

15. Can a person be employed but not in the labor force? Can a person be unemployed but not in the labor force?

Analytical Questions

16. Use aggregate supply and aggregate demand curves to analyze a supply shock.

17. Use aggregate supply and aggregate demand curves to illustrate demand-pull and cost-push inflation.

18. Graph a Phillips curve. Explain why the long-run Phillips Curve is vertical. Could there be more than one short-run Phillips Curve? (Hint: Consider a change in price expectations.)

19. The nominal interest rate is 6 percent, expected inflation is 3 percent, and the tax rate is 20 percent. What is the real after-tax return? If the nominal interest rate and the expected inflation rate both decrease by 2 percent, what is the real after-tax return?

20. Draw the long-run aggregate supply curves for successive long-run equilibriums with potential growth rate of real GDP at 2.5 to 3 percent per year. What is the sustainable growth rate of output over time?

21. Graphically demonstrate the appropriate Fed policy in response to a severe unexpected drop in aggregate demand.

22. Graphically demonstrate how changes in aggregate demand cause inflation or deflation (falling prices) in the short run. Explain why only the price level changes in the long run. What happens to the price level over successive long runs?

23. In each of the following cases, explain whether the individual is in the labor force, not in the labor force, employed, or unemployed.

    a. A 14-year-old truant who is looking for work
    b. A person who has started his or her own business
    c. A college student
    d. My retired mother who does volunteer work at a hospital
    e. A discouraged aerospace worker who has given up looking for a job
    f. A recent college graduate who is actively seeking a job

24. Use aggregate demand and aggregate supply curves to show what will happen to output and the price level if government spending is reduced at the same time the Fed takes action to increase the money supply.

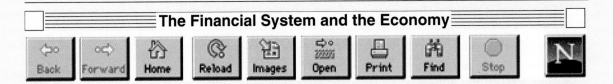

The Financial System and the Economy

1. An extremely interesting article entitled "Formulating A Consistent Approach to Monetary Policy" is obtainable from the world wide web site (http://woodrow.mpls.frb.fed.us/pubs/ar/ar1995.html). Read the introduction and answer the following:

    a. What is the principal long-run goal of monetary policy?
    b. How can monetary policy improve economic performance over the short run?

2. The chapter describes the natural rate of unemployment as the unemployment rate that is consistent with stable prices. Consider the behavior of unemployment, inflation, and the rate of growth of M1 from 1961 to 1971. Provide a "natural rate of unemployment" based explanation for inflation in the late 1960s and the high unemployment rate of the early 1970s. Data on the unemployment rate may be accessed from world wide web site (http://www.stls.frb.org/fred/data/employ/unrate). Data on the money supply growth rate may be found at (http://www.stls.frb.org/fred/data/monetary/m1st). Data on inflation rates may be found at (http://www.stls.frb.org/fred/data/cpi/cpiauesl).

Suggested Readings

During 1994, the Fed raised short-term interest rates numerous times out of concern that the actual unemployment rate was falling below the natural rate and that inflation was just around the corner. For a discussion of inflationary pressures and the natural rate of unemployment during early 1994, see Stuart E. Weiner, "The Natural Rate and Inflationary Pressures," *Economic Review* of the Federal Reserve Bank of Kansas City, third quarter 1994.

For a discussion on whether monetary policy should be used directly to stimulate growth and employment or predominately to stabilize the price level, see Donald T. Brash, "The Role of Monetary Policy: Where Does Unemployment Fit In?" *Economic Review* of the Federal Reserve Bank of Kansas City, first quarter 1995.

In recent years, dramatic changes have occurred in domestic and international financial markets. For a discussion of how these changes affect monetary policy, see Henry Kaufman, "Structural Changes in the Financial Markets: Economic and Policy Significance," *Economic Review* of the Federal Reserve Bank of Kansas City, second quarter 1994.

The above three articles may be viewed and/or ordered on the world wide web at (http://www.kc.frb.org/publicat/pubordfm.htm).

Each year, the March and September issues of the *Federal Reserve Bulletin* contain the Fed's "Monetary Policy Report to the Congress," as mandated by the Humphrey–Hawkins Act of 1978. These reports make for interesting reading regarding monetary policy and the economic outlook. The Monetary Policy Testimony and Report to Congress is available on the world wide web at (http://www.bog.frb.fed.us/BOARDDOCS/HH/TEST9607.htm).

22

The Process of Monetary Policy Formulation

> *Comfort the afflicted and afflict the comfortable.*
> —Finley Peter Dunne—
>
> *You must lose a fly to catch a trout.*
> —George Herbert—

Learning Objectives

After reading this chapter, you should know:

- ◆ The factors that guide the policy process
- ◆ The various lags in the policy process
- ◆ How and why the performance of the economy can differ from policymakers' objectives
- ◆ What intermediate targets are and how they are related to the ultimate policy goals
- ◆ How monetary policy is formulated by the Fed Open Market Committee (FOMC) and the major pitfalls of that process

Setting the Stage

It's the regular mid-month meeting of the Fed Open Market Committee (FOMC). The chairperson orders the huge doors to the Fed's impressive conference room closed and calls the meeting to order. In his opening remarks he suggests that the ensuing discussion focus on policy actions that will raise the inflation rate and increase the cyclical fluctuation of the economy over the next 12 to 18 months.

Hopefully, the last sentence has startled you! Something is wrong. Policymakers and professors consistently tell us that policy actions are directed at reducing the inflation rate and decreasing cyclical fluctuations, that is, stabilizing the economy. But, if this is so, why did the United States experience two recessions at the beginning of the 1980s and a third recession at the beginning of the 1990s? Why does the unemployment rate and/or the inflation rate periodically rise to unacceptable levels? Are maladies that strike the economy avoidable? Are they the result of bad luck or bad policy making? What role do economics and politics play?

In the last chapter we discussed the major goals of monetary policy, which include sustainable economic growth, full employment, stable prices, and satisfactory external balance. The Fed is charged with designing and implementing economic policies that will enhance the health and performance of the U.S. economy and achieve these goals. This chapter provides an overview of the monetary policy process with particular emphasis on what guides the plans of policymakers, how those plans get translated into actions, and how and why, despite good intentions, the performance of the economy can differ from policymakers' objectives. The discussion connects the world of theory to the real world in which policy is made. The approach is also general, leaving the specifics of policy to a subsequent chapter.

The Policy Process

The essential elements of the policy process and the problems surrounding the conduct of monetary policy can be illustrated with the aid of Exhibit 22-1. The policy goals, combined with the expected economic performance, guide policy actions, which then in turn alter spending, saving, borrowing, and lending decisions. Study this exhibit carefully because the rest of the chapter focuses in some detail on the elements and linkages it depicts.

At first glance, the challenges facing policymakers do not seem all that imposing: Compare the expected performance of the economy to the goals. Leave the policy unchanged if the economy's performance is expected to be close to the goals, or, if the economy's performance is expected to fall well short of the goals, alter policy accordingly. The reasoning is so simple and seemingly sensible, one is led to wonder how policy and policymakers can ever go astray. Since any policymaker will tell you that making policy is both difficult and frustrating, laden with a never-ending series of problems and pitfalls, one obviously needs to reflect a bit more deeply about what is depicted in Exhibit 22-1.

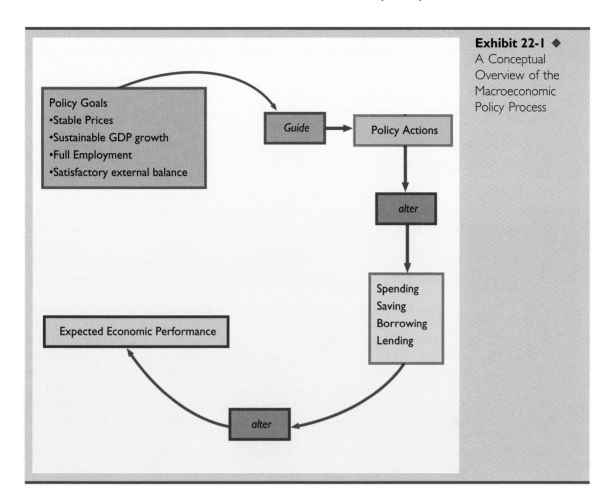

Exhibit 22-1 ◆
A Conceptual Overview of the Macroeconomic Policy Process

The beginning of wisdom about the policy process involves asking and getting answers to specific questions about some basic generalities. How do policymakers figure out what the expected performance of the goal variables is likely to be? How do they decide what to do if they believe action is called for? Once they act, how do they know the actions taken are sufficient?

To begin, let's assume the goals and numerical objectives of policies have already been agreed to, as discussed in Chapter 21. The next step as depicted in Exhibit 22-1 is to develop a view of the likely performance of the economy if policy were to remain unchanged. How do policymakers do this?

The basic approach is to use various statistical methods and models, judgment based on historical experience, and incoming data on the full range of factors comprising and determining aggregate demand and aggregate supply to develop a forecast for the variables of major concern such as real gross domestic product (GDP), inflation, the unemployment rate, and exchange rates. The data that are used include information about retail sales, industrial production, consumer confidence, business capital spending plans, wages, personal income, profits, and the external balance of payments. Assuming it is January, forecasts for key variables would typically cover the first quarter of the year (January to March) and extend over a 12- to 18-month horizon. If the incoming data and the forecasts suggest the economy's performance is deviating significantly from the goals and priorities set by policymakers, then a change in policy will be considered in order to move the economy's likely performance closer to the goals.

Current Conditions Versus Forecasts

In weighing the information contained in forecasts and the incoming data, two factors deserve special note. First, forecasting is an imperfect science. As a result, forecasting errors are fairly large. For example, a Federal Reserve staff study found that during the 1971–1987 period January forecasts of each year tended to estimate incorrectly the yearly growth of real GDP by about 1.75 percentage points and the yearly inflation rate by about 1.5 percentage points.[1] While such forecasting errors may seem small, they are, in fact, fairly large relative to the 3 percent average annual growth of real GDP and 5 percent average annual inflation over this 17-year period. The implication of such proportionately large errors is that the forecasts typically are not given heavy weight in policy discussions.

Second, there is a strong tendency to focus on and thus guide policy with the incoming data. These figures that define "current economic conditions" attract considerable media attention and generate much of the political pressure that periodically bears down on policymakers. For example, if the current data suggest that the economy is growing slowly, there will be considerable pressure on policymakers to stimulate the economy. That is, pressure will be present to boost aggregate demand and economic growth even if forecasts suggest the economy will strengthen in 6–9 months without further policy action. This nearsightedness and impatience, which is partly a reflection of the lack of confidence in the forecasts, is a critical element of the policymaking process and goes a long way toward explaining what policymakers do or fail to do.

Assessing the Economic Situation

Generally, as data reports are published, policymakers are, in effect, asking themselves two simple questions: Are the data consistent with our economic outlook and desires, thus requiring no change in policy? Or, are the data signaling that the economy's performance has deviated markedly from what was expected, thereby requiring that a change in policy be considered? In reality, this filtering and assessing of incoming data (much of which is estimated) is somewhat more difficult than one might imagine. The major reason is that many monthly data releases are quite volatile or *noisy*, possessing a large element of what statisticians call *irregular variance*. The irregular variance or random fluctuations in the data make the data unreliable as policy indicators. As a result of potentially large month-to-month fluctuations, it is often necessary to have 2–3 months of data on hand before the underlying cyclical or trend movements in an individual data series become evident.

Moving from an individual data series (or sector of the economy) to the economy as a whole, the noise in individual series means that a collection of

---

[1] Steven Strongin and Paul Binkley, "A Policymaker's Guide to Economic Forecasts," *Economic Perspectives*, Federal Reserve Bank of Chicago, May/June 1988, pp. 3–10.

different series often transmits conflicting signals on the underlying strength of the economy. For example, the data reported for February might show that retail sales are strong relative to expectations, suggesting that the rate of consumption spending is increasing. At the same time, new orders for capital goods and housing starts are weak, suggesting that the rate of business fixed investment and residential investment spending are slowing. Here again, it is usually the case that if in fact the economy is deviating from its expected track, it will take several months of data releases covering the full spectrum of the economy's performance before the ambiguities in the monthly data are resolved.

In sum, it takes time for policymakers to recognize that a change in the economy's performance has occurred. Economists refer to this as the **recognition lag** in the policy-making process. It refers to the time that elapses from the point when a significant and unexpected change in the economy's performance occurs and when policymakers recognize that such a change has occurred.

> **Recognition Lag** The time it takes policymakers to recognize that a change in the economy's performance has occurred.

From Assessment to Action

As evidence begins to accumulate that the economy is deviating significantly from the desired path, a consensus develops among policymakers that policy needs to be altered. For example, if the economy is strengthening considerably and if inflationary pressures are building, there is a need to reduce the growth of aggregate demand somewhat. At this point, the debate shifts from assessment of the economy and the accompanying need to do something to a debate over what exactly should be done. What policy tools should be used, how large or small should the policy adjustment be, and when should the policy change be enacted?[2]

The net result is that policy actions can be paralyzed for a time and policymakers may do too little too late. In any event, there is a **policy lag** in the policy-making process. It is comprised of the time that elapses from the point when the need for action is recognized and when an adjustment policy is decided upon and set in motion.

> **Policy Lag** The time that elapses from the point when the need for action is recognized and when an adjustment policy is decided upon and set in motion.

From Action to Effect

When policymakers act, is the effect on the economy immediate? In general, the answer is no. The policy action will set in motion a series of adjustments in the economy that will gradually alter the performance of the economy relative to what it would have been in the absence of any new policy actions. To illustrate, suppose the economy has been growing quickly with inflation accelerating, and the Fed decides to pursue a more restrictive monetary policy. To cut the growth in aggregate demand, the Fed takes actions that reduce the supply of funds and interest rates rise. Will firms cut their investment spending right away? Not necessarily. If a new plant is half-completed, capacity utilization in its existing plants is high, and the demand for a firm's products

---

[2]This aspect of the policy-making process, especially in the case of fiscal policy, can be agonizingly slow. It's one thing to decide to cut aggregate demand by reducing government spending and/or raising taxes. It's quite another to decide whose taxes to raise and exactly where spending should be cut. The latter inevitably involves political considerations.

is expected to remain fairly strong for the foreseeable future, then the firm (and other firms like it) will continue spending on investment projects. Gradually, however, as the rise in interest rates and reduction in the availability of funds slows the growth of aggregate demand, sales and capacity utilization will fall and expectations about the future will be modified. At this point, investment spending plans will be reevaluated and possibly postponed or cancelled, leading to a further deceleration in the growth of aggregate demand.

On the aggregate supply side, the slowing of the growth in aggregate demand will be associated with a downward revision in price expectations and an adjustment of wages and other input prices. Here again, historical experience suggests this process will be gradual rather than instantaneous.

Impact Lag The time that elapses between when an action is taken and when that action has a significant impact on economic variables.

The net result is an **impact lag** in monetary policy—that is, the time that elapses between when an action is taken and when that action has a significant impact on prices, employment, and output. How much time you ask? Available research suggests that significant effects generally begin to show up after six months to a year or more and continue accumulating for several years. Exhibit 22-2 brings together the various components of the lags comprising the policy process.

 RECAP

Policy goals, combined with expected economic performance, guide policy actions. Policymakers tend to give greater weight to incoming data about current economic conditions than to forecasts that can be unreliable. The recognition lag is the time that it takes for policymakers to recognize that economic conditions have changed and that a policy change is necessary. The

Exhibit 22-2 ◆
Lags in the Policy Process

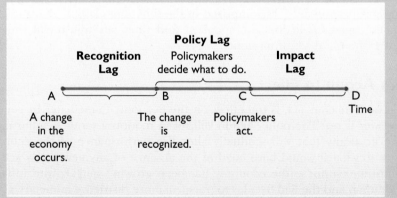

The economy begins to need corrective action at point A, but the need is not recognized until point B which is say, 3 months later. The time which elapses from point A to point B is called the recognition lag. At point B in time, policymakers begin to think about what actions to take and a decision is reached. The time which elapses from point B to point C is called the policy lag. Once action has been taken, it takes time before the economy's performance is materially affected. The distance C through D refers to this impact lag.

policy lag consists of the time that elapses from when the need for action is recognized and when the policy adjustment is enacted. The impact lag is the time from when the policy action is taken until there is significant impact on the economy.

Pitfalls in Policy Making

Despite good intentions, policy does not always produce an economic performance that closely coincides with the nation's economic objectives. There are no simple answers to explain the periodic lack of correspondence between policymakers' plans and economic performance. As in all endeavors, honest mistakes can be made, analysis can be faulty, and unexpected events outside one's control can occur. Against this background, let's briefly examine some of the most prominent problems affecting the successful conduct of policy.

Uncertainty and Lags

Our discussion of the impact lag for policy suggests economic developments today are largely the result of policies pursued over the past several years. Logically then, given such lags, there is little that policymakers can do today to materially affect the current performance of the economy. What policymakers can do is affect the future performance of the economy. However, as we all know, the future cannot be known with certainty. Because economic forecasts, in particular, can be quite wide of the mark, one cannot know for sure what, if anything, should be done today to improve the economy's future performance. To complicate matters further, one cannot know for sure how the economy is currently performing given the large month-to-month fluctuations in published reports on various aspects of economic activity as previously discussed.

The net result is that policymakers are generally quite cautious in adjusting policy. Absent a crisis, they prefer to move gradually rather than precipitously in the general direction suggested by a comparison of the current data on the economy and the policy objectives. As understandable and reasonable as this approach sounds, there are some potentially serious pitfalls lurking here.[3]

To illustrate, imagine yourself in a shower (home, hotel, or dorm) and you turn on the water and begin gradually adjusting the hot water faucet up to attain the desired overall temperature of your shower. The problem, especially in an older structure without a modern plumbing system, is that there is often a lag between when you turn the hot water knob up and when the water temperature in your shower begins to respond. Moreover, the lag can vary depending on how many other showers have been taken in the recent past, how many are currently being taken, and how much hot water is left in the tank. In other words you lack knowledge. That is, you are uncertain about the factors one would need to know to "fine tune" the hot water. As you adjust

---

[3]For instance, the Fed in early 1994 was accused of destabilizing financial markets by making several small increases in interest rates rather than a few larger increases.

ROGER SCHILLERSTROM
Courtesy Crain Communications

the hot water knob up gradually and nothing happens, you grow increasingly impatient and keep turning the knob up. At some point, and with a rush, the water runs scalding hot and you burn yourself. You never intended to burn yourself, but it happened anyway.

So too for policymakers. They don't really intend for example, to raise the inflation rate (and get burnt), but it happens. The economy is performing sluggishly and policymakers want to increase economic growth. They increase aggregate demand (turn up the heat), but nothing seems to happen. They and the nation become increasingly impatient and undertake further demand-increasing policy actions. Eventually, economic growth spurts ahead at an excessive pace causing an unintended acceleration of inflation.

Throughout 1994, rather than facing a lethargic economy with consequential calls for action, the situation was somewhat the reverse. On several occasions throughout the year, strong economic growth prompted the Fed to take action that would raise interest rates to forestall inflation even though little evidence indicated that inflation had indeed accelerated. Such actions drew criticism from observers who thought that the Fed was overreacting. Fed Chairperson Greenspan eloquently explained the Fed's action to Congress:

> Some critics of our latest policy actions have noted that we tightened policy even though inflation had not picked up. That observation is accurate, but it is not relevant to policy decisions. To be successful, we must implement the necessary monetary policy adjustments well in advance of the potential emergence of inflationary pressures, so as to forestall their actual occurrence. Shifts in the stance of monetary policy influence the economy and inflation with a consid-

erable lag, as long as a year or more. The challenge of monetary policy is to interpret current data on the economy and financial markets with an eye to anticipating future inflationary or contractionary forces and to countering them by taking action in advance. Indeed, if we are successful in our current endeavors, there will not be an increase in overall inflation. The trends toward price stability will be extended in the context of sustainable growth in economic activity.[4]

Hopefully, with increased knowledge, economic policymakers will become more precise, like getting a modern plumbing system.

In sum, the existence of lags in an uncertain world complicates policymakers' efforts to act appropriately in a timely fashion regardless of whether contractionary or inflationary forces are building in the economy. More specifically, acting or failing to act today may aggravate inflation and cyclical fluctuations later. The economy may be destabilized rather than stabilized. In the case of recession, the push to do something now to improve the current situation as soon as possible interacts with the difficulties associated with the existence of lags and uncertainty, and may lead to higher inflation later. In the case of inflationary pressures, the pressure not to do something now may, as they say, let the horse out of the barn. When there is pressure "to do something now" or "not to do something now," consistent formulation and implementation of policies conducive to economic growth and stability become even more problematic.

Globalization: A Financially and Economically Integrated World Economy

A new reality is having a profound influence on the conduct and effectiveness of domestic policies. Simply put, a growing interdependence is taking place among the economies of the world. What goes on in Tokyo, London, Hong Kong, Paris, and Frankfurt has an increasingly important effect on economic and financial conditions in the United States. This implies that U.S. policymakers have somewhat less control over the performance of the U.S. economy than in previous eras when the U.S. economy was more isolated with regard to international trade and finance. As Toyoo Gyohten effectively states:

> [In the twenty-first century], the United States, the European Community, and Japan share the role of managing the world economy. . . . In order to fortify our alliance while adapting to the new global environment, both the United States and Japan have urgent tasks to accomplish. The United States must fully recognize that its relationship with Japan is interdependent. It must also accept its share of the burden of correcting its own economic excesses. Japan must open its market in the same way the United States has and recognize that its very survival depends on devising domestic policies that are compatible with those of the rest of the world.[5]

Such observations have given rise to calls for cooperation and coordination among world policymakers. While the difficulties some countries have in

---

[4] *Federal Reserve Bulletin*, August 1994, p. 715.
[5] Paul Volcker and Toyoo Gyohten, *Changing Fortunes*, New York: Times Books, p. xix.

coordinating monetary and fiscal policies within their own country suggest that coordinating policies across countries will never be easy, the fact that globalization exists does highlight the new challenges and complexities facing policymakers. We return to this subject in Chapter 24. For now, we turn to the specifics of how monetary policy is formulated.

RECAP

The existence of lags in an uncertain world complicates policymakers' efforts to act appropriately in a timely fashion. In a recession, the push to do something now to improve the current situation as soon as possible interacts with the difficulties associated with the existence of lags and uncertainty, and may lead to higher inflation later. In the face of inflation, the pressure not to do something now may cause further instability later. Increased globalization suggests the need for greater global monetary policy coordination.

Intermediate Targets

Given the complexities, uncertainties, and time lags, the Fed has long utilized an intermediate target approach to the formulation and implementation of policy rather than focusing on the ultimate goals. The basic idea, illustrated in Exhibit 22-3, is that the Fed selects a variable, such as a monetary aggregate or an interest rate, which is in some sense midway between its policy instruments and the ultimate or final goals or targets of policy.[6] The **intermediate target** is then used to guide day-to-day open market operations. The rationale is that if the Fed hits the intermediate target, it will come reasonably close to achieving its economic objectives.

Intermediate Target The use of a target midway between the policy instruments and the ultimate policy goals.

How does the Fed select a particular intermediate target and a particular range of values for such a variable? For example, the Fed could pick domestic nonfinancial debt (DNFD), the broadest measure of credit, as an intermediate target and choose a growth rate range of 5 to 9 percent. Or, it could use an interest rate as an intermediate target and select some target range, say 5.5 to 6 percent for nominal short-term rates. In any case, the basic criteria for selecting an intermediate target variable fall out of the preceding discussion.

First, the variable should be reliably and thus predictably related to the goal variables. If a variable were not so related, hitting the intermediate target range would not necessarily help to achieve the goals, and selecting a targeted range for the intermediate variable consistent with the economic objectives would be virtually impossible. To illustrate, a sailor traveling between point A and point B will often find it useful to guide his or her ship by initially aiming for a firmly anchored buoy located midway between the two points. However, if such a buoy was not anchored, but instead floated aimlessly, it would not be a useful guide. Second, policymakers should be able to observe the inter-

---

[6] Recall that the basic policy instruments that the Fed uses to manipulate the economy are open market operations, reserve requirements, and the discount rate, and that the major policy goals are full employment, stable prices, economic growth, and external balance.

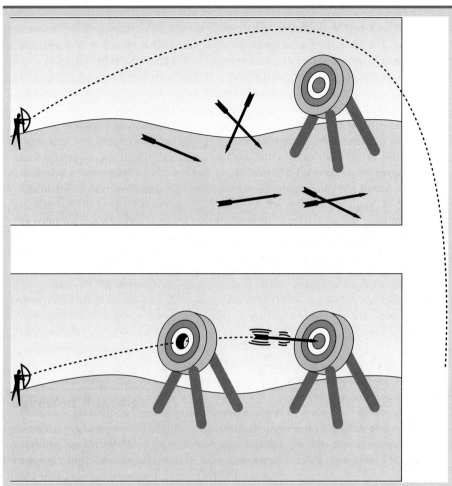

Why an intermediate target? Suppose you were holding a bow and arrow and desired to hit the center of a target that you could barely see way off in the distance. The bow would be your instrument and the target you really wanted to hit would be your final target. Because of the distance and poor visibility you might have great difficulty hitting the final target. One strategy you might consider to accomplish your objective would be to select an intermediate target—a clearly visible target between you and the less visible final target. The idea is to align the intermediate target between you and the final target in such a way that if you hit the center of the intermediate target, your arrow will continue on and strike the final target.

mediate target regularly. That is, the data about the target should be readily available. Third, the Fed should be able to hit the targeted range of the intermediate variable. That is, policymakers should be able to control the intermediate variable with policy instruments with a reasonable degree of precision. As is perhaps obvious, limited ability to observe and control means a particular variable would be of little practical use to policymakers. Our intrepid sailor, for example, would find a navigation buoy of little use without a working compass and good visibility.

Against this background, let's assume the Fed initially decides to adopt and publish the growth rates of more than one monetary aggregate as intermediate targets. But why would it do such a thing? The Fed sets growth target ranges for several aggregates to hedge its bets and to maintain as flexible a position as possible. In recent decades, the relationship between various monetary aggregates and the level of economic activity has also changed and, in some cases, significantly broken down. For instance, up until the early 1980s, M1 was the most closely watched aggregate for the use in policy formulation. However, because of M1's unstable and erratic behavior, the Fed has stopped reporting target ranges for it in an effort to deemphasize its role as an intermediate target. In the mid-1980s, changes in M2 were emphasized more because they seemed to have the strongest correlation with changes in economic

Exhibit 22-4 ◆

The Use of
Intermediate
Targets Since 1970

Monetary aggregates have historically played an important role in the policy process because their behavior has often been related to both the ultimate policy goals and the policy tools that the Fed has available to influence those goals. Until the 1980s, M1 had a stable and predictable relationship with nominal economic activity and therefore was the targeted aggregate. Even though in the short-term control was imprecise, over a longer period, control was reasonably precise and changes in M1 were closely associated with changes in economic activity.

In the 1970s, the Fed sought to exploit the statistical regularity between changes in M1 and economic activity. It targeted the fed funds rate in an attempt to achieve the targeted growth rate range for M1. Under such a regime, if an increase in the demand for credit puts upward pressure on interest rates, including the fed funds rate, then the Fed tends to be accommodating. That is, the Fed supplies reserves to the financial system to keep interest rates in their targeted range. Increases in the demand for credit were accommodated even though it led to an expansion of the money supply and overshooting the M1 target range. If the interest rate target was increased, the increase was usually not enough to choke off the demand for credit and to keep the monetary aggregates in their targeted ranges. Consequently, this method was abandoned in late 1979.

In the early 1980s, the Fed focused on the level of nonborrowed reserves. Nonborrowed reserves were total reserves less those borrowed from the Fed at the discount window. The Fed was convinced that this method would allow them more precision in hitting a monetary aggregate target. By doing so, it was thought that the Fed would have greater direct control over inflation. If the demand for credit went up, the Fed would not increase the supply of nonborrowed reserves. As a result, the fed funds rate would go up. In turn, borrowing reserves at the discount window was relatively cheaper. The result was that borrowing at the discount window increased and borrowing in the fed funds market decreased from what they would have been otherwise.

In the mid-1980s, the relationship between M1 and economic activity stumbled and the Fed began placing greater emphasis on the other aggregates. In the mid-1980s and early 1990s, the Fed targeted the level of reserves borrowed at the discount window. Under this procedure, the Fed

activity. In the early 1990s, DNFD, the broadest measure of credit, seemed to be the monetary aggregate that was most highly related to economic activity. Since history shows us that at times one aggregate may be more closely correlated with the level of economic activity than at other times, it is probably wise for the Fed to monitor more than one aggregate. Exhibit 22-4 discusses the use of intermediate targets since 1970.

But why has the relationship between a given monetary aggregate and economic activity failed to survive over time? Many analysts attribute the breakdown to technological changes in the payments systems and the electronic transfer of funds, and to financial innovation that resulted in the creation of new financial instruments and markets. Some believe that the definitions of the aggregates need to be revised and refined to take account of these

picked a level of borrowed reserves that it believed corresponded to the desired growth range of a monetary aggregate, primarily M2. If the demand for credit increased, pushing up the fed funds rate, then the demand for borrowed reserves at the discount window would increase, as the fed funds rate increased relative to the discount rate. To maintain the target range for borrowed reserves, the Fed would be forced to increase the supply of nonborrowed reserves. Consequently, this regime was more accommodating to increases in credit than the regime that targeted nonborrowed reserves.

In the mid-1990s, the Fed has emphasized the use of the fed funds rate as an operating target. In this case, as already discussed, the targeted rate is lowered to speed up spending and increased to slow down the level of economic activity. At the same time, the Fed has deemphasized the role of monetary aggregate targeting, most likely because of the instability between the monetary and credit aggregates and the level of economic activity.

As Chairperson Greenspan reported to Congress,

> The historical relationships between money and income and between money and the price level have largely broken down, depriving the aggregates of much of their usefulness as guides to policy. At least for the time being, M2 has been downgraded as a reliable indicator of financial conditions in the economy, and no single variable has yet been identified to take its place.[a]

Ann-Marie Meulendyke states,

> While reducing their reliance on the behavior of the monetary aggregates as policy indicators, policymakers placed greater emphasis on measures that might be termed intermediate indicators. These included commodity prices and monthly statistics on employment, production, and trade. Such measures are not directly controllable but, taken together, they ought to suggest at least the direction in which policy instruments should be adjusted to achieve the ultimate policy goals.[b]

[a] *Federal Reserve Bulletin*, September 1994, p. 853.
[b] Ann-Marie Meulendyke, *U.S. Monetary Policy and Financial Markets*, Federal Reserve Bank of New York, 1989, p. 7.

changes. In addition, deregulation is also believed to have weakened the link between some monetary aggregates and economic activity as the share of intermediation that goes through depository institutions decreases.

Regardless of the causes, at times a given aggregate may have a more stable relationship with GDP than at other times. For these reasons, the Fed has monitored M1, M2, M3, or DNFD as intermediate targets believing that growth in at least one or more of these variables may have a reasonably reliable and predictable relationship with real GDP growth and inflation. At the present time, the Fed sets target ranges for M2, M3, and DNFD. Those analysts who believe that the aggregates are good intermediate targets also point to the fact that they are observable and amenable to control, which are also necessary conditions for good intermediate targets. At any rate, if the Fed is using a monetary aggregate or DNFD, the target range is increased to speed up the economy and reduced to slow down the economy, ceteris paribus.

In addition to targeting the growth rate of a monetary aggregate, another possibility is for the Fed to use short-term and long-term interest rates as intermediate targets. Since mid-1993, the Fed has emphasized interest rate targeting even though it still continues to monitor the monetary aggregates. Under such a regime, the Fed increases the interest rate target if it perceives a need to slow down the level of economic activity and lowers the target if it perceives a need to speed things up.

Operating Target A target amenable to control by the policy tools and highly correlated with the intermediate target.

The Fed carries out this procedure by announcing a target for the fed funds rate and using open market operations to hit the target. In this case, the fed funds rate is an **operating target** that is highly responsive to open market operations, the Fed's main policy tool. The Fed adjusts the fed funds rate in line with its intermediate target of other short-term and long-term interest rates. The Fed has more control over the operating target than over the intermediate target. Other short-term and long-term interest rates adjust in response to changes in the fed funds rate.

In the past, the use of interest rates as intermediate targets has been criticized for having either an inflationary or recessionary bias. For example, let's assume that the Fed is targeting an interest rate at a given level and that aggregate demand increases. The increase in demand could emanate from the household, business, government, or foreign sector. In any case, the increase causes the demand for money and credit to increase also as shown in Exhibit 22-5. The demand curve shifts from D to D′, creating upward pressure on the interest rate because the quantity demanded is greater than the quantity supplied at the targeted rate, i_T. To maintain the interest rate target, the Fed would merely accommodate such increases in demand by supplying more reserves, causing money and credit to expand. Down the road, such accommodation could lead to inflation. If inflation does increase, this would put upward pressure on nominal interest rates. To fight this pressure, the Fed must ease even more, creating more pressure and the cycle accelerates.

Likewise, if there is a comparable drop-off in aggregate demand, the Fed would reduce the supply of money to prevent the interest rate from falling. In this case, the drop in demand is exacerbated by the Fed's action and the downturn is greater than what it would be otherwise.

One final point needs to be emphasized. At any time, the Fed can control either an interest rate target or an aggregate target but not both. For example, assume that the Fed has both a monetary aggregate target (M_T) and an interest rate target (i_T) and that the demand for credit suddenly increases as

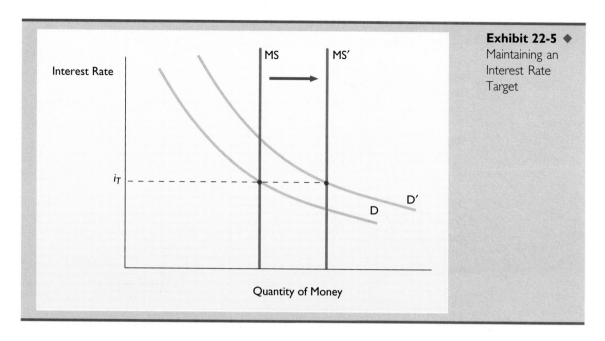

Exhibit 22-5 ◆
Maintaining an
Interest Rate
Target

depicted in Exhibit 22-6. In such a situation, if the Fed is most serious about maintaining the interest rate target in the face of the increased credit demand, then it must use open market operations to increase the supply of reserves. When it does so, credit and hence the monetary aggregates are allowed to expand and the Fed overshoots the monetary aggregate target range as the money supply increases to M'. Serious overshooting of the monetary target can also defeat the interest rate target as inflation sets in. If the Fed is most serious about hitting the monetary aggregate target range, then, in the face of increased demand for credit, it does not increase the supply of reserves. In such a situation, the Fed lets interest rates go up to i' and overshoots the target range. Thus, the Fed cannot have its way with both targets.

Sometimes, an interest rate target has been selected either because the Fed believes that this target rate is most compatible with the ultimate goals for growth, employment, the price level, and external balance or because the relationship between the monetary aggregates and economic activity is no longer stable and predictable. At other times, a monetary aggregate or DNFD has been targeted because the Fed believes that doing so is the easiest way to achieve the ultimate policy goals.

Enough said, let's turn to the specifics of how policy is framed.

 RECAP

The Fed uses intermediate targets to gauge policy. The Fed monitors several monetary aggregates and DNFD, which can be used as intermediate targets. In addition, nominal short-term or long-term interest rates can also be used as intermediate targets. The intermediate target must be highly correlated with the ultimate target and must be amenable to control by the Fed. In recent years, the Fed has emphasized interest rates as intermediate targets and used the fed funds rate as an operating target. They have chosen this

Exhibit 22-6 ◆
Targeting Both an
Interest Rate and
an Aggregate????

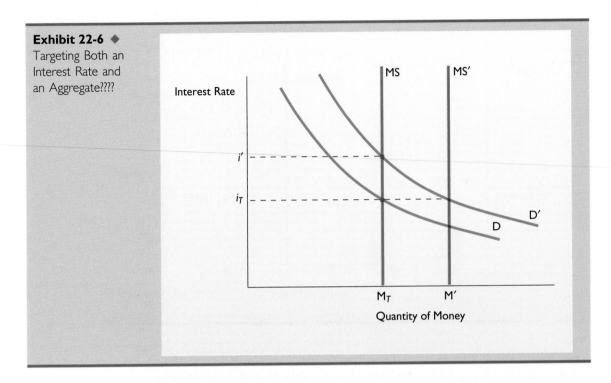

path because of the instability in the relationship of the aggregates and the level of economic activity. The Fed cannot maintain both an interest rate target and an aggregate target at the same time in response to changes in demand.

Fed Open Market Committee Decisions

Regardless of whether the Fed emphasizes a monetary aggregate or an interest rate target, it still sets long-term target growth ranges for the monetary aggregates and DNFD. Congress requires that those ranges be reported to them, and the chairperson of the Board of Governors of the Fed generally appears before Congress during February and July of each year. Exhibit 22-7 gives the forecasts reported to Congress in December 1995.

If an interest rate is being used as the primary intermediate target, the Fed sets broad ranges for the monetary aggregates it believes are consistent with the interest rate target. In this case, deviations of the aggregates from the target ranges are downplayed, and changes in the target ranges may be associated with the unstable behavior of the aggregates rather than with a change in policy. In recent years, the target ranges for the aggregates have been a full 4 percentage points wide. This gives the Fed lots of room to operate and still hit within the target range. This practice is appropriate if the relationship between the aggregates and the level of economic activity is imprecise and if the Fed is focusing more on interest rates. Exhibit 22-8 explains why the monetary aggregates and DNFD have been downplayed in recent years.

Exhibit 22-7 ◆
Longer Term
Policy Goals
December 31,
1995

Target Aggregates	Range of Forecasted Change
M2	1 to 5 percent
M3	2 to 6 percent
DNFD	3 to 7 percent
Nominal GDP	3 3/4 to 5 1/4 percent
Real GDP	1 3/8 to 3 percent
Other Indicators	Forecasted Range
Inflation	3 to 3 1/2 percent
Unemployment Rate	5 1/2 to 6 1/4

As in Exhibit 22-7, the long-term forecasts include target ranges for inflation and unemployment, and growth rates for the monetary aggregates and nominal and real GDP. FOMC members believe that the forecasts are consistent with the long-term policy goals and likely to emerge over the coming year. At the six other FOMC meetings over the course of the year (in addition to the February and July meetings), the long-term goals are reviewed and sometimes revised, but emphasis is on the short-term strategies.

Once the long-term policy stance is set, the focus of the FOMC shifts to the immediate period. Throughout most periods, in addition to looking at one or more monetary aggregates, the fed funds rate itself, as well as other interest rates, are near the center of policy discussions. As noted previously, interest rates have gained center stage as intermediate targets in the mid-1990s, surpassing the monetary aggregates in importance.

At the same time, in the 1990s, policy has been somewhat eclectic and

the process of probing a variety of data to ascertain underlying economic and financial conditions has become even more essential to formulating sound monetary policy.[7]

As a result, the Fed now looks at many indicators. Exhibit 22-9 contains a discussion of an "indicator" that the Fed has been using in recent months.

Given its assessment of current economic conditions and the economic outlook, the FOMC comes up with short-term (usually quarterly) policy goals consistent with the longer-range goals. The policy goals include the short-term growth paths for the monetary aggregates along with the range for the fed funds rate. Higher money growth will require the Fed to engineer a rise in the supply of reserves and money relative to the demand for reserves and money, resulting in a fall in interest rates. Alternatively, lower money growth will require the Fed to engineer a fall in the supply of reserves and money relative to the demand for reserves and money, resulting in a rise in interest rates. The logic is straightforward. The larger the supply of reserves provided through open market operations, the lower is the fed funds rate, given the demand for reserves. The lower the fed funds rate, given the discount rate, the lower borrowing is at the discount facility and the higher borrowing is in the fed funds market. The larger the supply of reserves and the lower the fed

---

[7] *Federal Reserve Bulletin*, September 1993, p. 853.

funds rate, the higher is monetary growth. In addition, as previously discussed, policymakers distrust the forecasts, believing correctly that they are often quite wide of the mark. Operationally, this means the Fed would be unlikely to "tighten" significantly if current data on the economy were weak.

Against this background, the FOMC issues a policy directive that guides the conduct of open market operations until the next FOMC meeting in approximately six weeks.[8]

---

[8] In the next chapter, we shall also see that the Fed, under the leadership of the chairperson, can make an intermeeting adjustment.

Exhibit 22-8 ◆

Targeting the Monetary Aggregates

In recent years, the Fed has reduced their reliance on monetary aggregate targets because the Fed believes the relationship between a monetary aggregate and the growth rate of GDP is often quite unreliable and unpredictable.

The relationship between an aggregate and GDP growth can be summarized by the growth rate of velocity. As in the following equation, the growth rate of the aggregate, $\%\Delta M$, plus the growth rate of velocity, $\%\Delta V$, is equal to the growth rate of GDP, $\%\Delta$GDP.

$$\%\Delta\text{GDP} = \%\Delta V + \%\Delta M$$

Recall that velocity is the number of times that the aggregate turns over per time period, such as a year, to purchase GDP.[a] The often aberrant behavior of velocity is a reflection of ongoing changes in the public's demand for money and other assets. This poses a dilemma for the Fed that has a direct bearing on policy decisions and activity if the Fed is targeting a monetary aggregate. When actual money growth is, say, above targeted money growth range, should the Fed adjust its open market operations so as to lower actual money growth back to the target range? Or, should it do nothing in response? If it does the latter, is it in effect accepting the excess money growth in the belief that velocity is growing more slowly and money demand more quickly than anticipated when the monetary aggregate growth range was adopted? If velocity is in fact growing more slowly, then the monetary aggregate must grow by more than originally thought if the GDP objective is to be achieved. As noted in the "Monetary Report to the Congress,"

> Considerable uncertainty about the behavior of velocity is likely to persist, however, and the Committee will continue to monitor a broad range of financial and economic indicators in addition to the monetary aggregates when determining the appropriate stance of policy.[b]

The issue is, of course, fundamental. Are the monetary aggregates to be targeted and controlled or are they to be used "flexibly" along with other information in guiding the conduct of policy? Suffice to say, the Fed has opted for flexibility, pragmatism, and eclecticism.

---

[a] In this use, velocity is simply GDP divided by the monetary aggregate.
[b] *Federal Reserve Bulletin*, August 1994, p. 683.

In recent years, the Fed has taken a rather eclectic approach to monetary policy. That is, rather than focusing on one intermediate target, they look at many indicators of how well they are meeting the desirable economic goals. One such indicator that has been recently focused on by the Fed is supplier delivery time or the time it takes for manufacturers to get supplies delivered. The thought is that if delivery times are increasing, price increases may be just around the corner. By watching the index, the Fed can get a "heads up" view of potential inflation before it actually arrives. The Fed can start tightening before the actual inflation is upon us and if successful may prevent the upsurge in prices altogether.

The supplier delivery time index is calculated from a survey by the National Association of Purchasing Management. Three hundred purchasing managers from major manufacturing companies are asked if, compared to the previous month, the delivery of supplies was faster, slower, or about the same. The index is calculated by taking the percentage that said delivery time was the same, dividing it by two and adding the percentage that said delivery time was slower. For example, if 85 percent responded that delivery time was the same while 12 percent said it was slower, the index is 54.5. An index above 50 indicates that more managers report slower deliveries than quicker. One problem with the index is that it is based on the manufacturing sector only and doesn't convey any information about prices in the other sectors of the economy.

Still, Fed Chairperson Greenspan explained to a Senate subcommittee why he considers this indicator to be important:

> At some point you do really run into restraints, and the way you know that is that deliveries on materials begin to slow down, shortages begin to pop up, and you have all sorts of collateral indications that the system is running into shortages.*

The following chart shows the index in the first half of the 1990s. Note that the Fed started tightening as the index rose.

*Lucida Harper, "Fed's Key Sign? Supplier Delivery Time," *The Wall Street Journal,* April 6, 1995.

Exhibit 22-9 ◆
Supplier Delivery Time: An Indicator of Inflation?

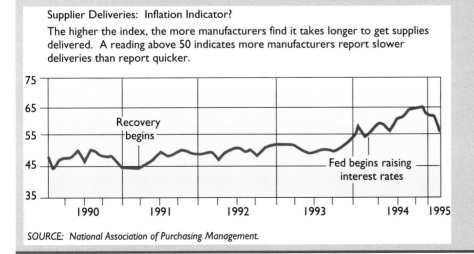

Supplier Deliveries: Inflation Indicator?
The higher the index, the more manufacturers find it takes longer to get supplies delivered. A reading above 50 indicates more manufacturers report slower deliveries than report quicker.

SOURCE: National Association of Purchasing Management.

RECAP

The Fed sets long-term growth ranges for the monetary aggregates and DNFD. The long-term policy goals reflect recent and prospective inflationary and unemployment outlooks. Given the long range goals, the short-term specifications that guide monetary policy between FOMC meetings are set. In recent years, the Fed has looked to interest rates to guide policy and downplayed the use of the aggregates.

In the next chapter, we move on to the specifics of how the directive is implemented.

Summary of Major Points

1. In general, a comparison between the expected performance of the economy and the economic goals guides policy actions. More specifically, given the goals and corresponding numerical objectives, priorities among the goals need to be established, the expected performance of the economy must be developed, and particular policy actions must be implemented. If the economy's performance is expected to be close to the goals, policy is likely to remain unchanged. Conversely, if the economy's performance is expected to deviate markedly from the goals, then policy will be altered.

2. Given the relatively large size of forecasting errors, policymakers tend to focus on incoming data and current conditions in considering policy adjustments.

3. The lags comprising the policy process consist of the recognition lag, the policy lag, and the impact lag. The recognition lag is the length of time it takes for policymakers to recognize that an unexpected and significant change in the economy's performance has occurred. The policy lag in the policy-making process is the time that elapses from the point when the need for action is recognized and when an adjustment policy is decided upon and set in motion. The impact lag is the time that elapses from when an action is taken and when that action has a significant effect on prices, output, and employment.

4. The existence of lags in an uncertain world makes it difficult for policymakers to act appropriately in a timely fashion. Their actions today may increase price and cyclical fluctuations later, which causes them to be quite cautious in adjusting policy.

5. The growing interdependence among economies of the world implies that U.S. policymakers have somewhat less control over the performance of the U.S. economy, thus adding to the challenges and complexities facing policymakers.

6. Because of the complexities and lags involved with monetary policy, the Fed uses intermediate targets such as M2, M3, DNFD, and interest rates to guide policy. The basic idea is that the Fed selects a variable, such as

a monetary aggregate or an interest rate, midway between its policy instruments and the ultimate or final goals or targets of policy. The intermediate target is then used to guide day-to-day open market operations. The rationale is that if the Fed hits the intermediate target, it will come reasonably close to achieving its economic objectives.

7. In the past few decades, at times one aggregate has been more closely related to the level of economic activity than at other times. At the present time, the monetary aggregates have been deemphasized in favor of an interest rate target. The reason for this change is that the relationship between economic activity and the monetary aggregates has become unstable and difficult to predict. The Fed can control either an interest rate target or an aggregate target but not both simultaneously.

8. The FOMC develops long-term policy goals and chooses among short-term policy options to achieve these goals. The major factors influencing the long-term policy decisions at any point in time include: (1) recent and prospective inflationary pressures, (2) the current and prospective pace of economic expansion, especially with reference to the economy's growth potential and degree of capacity utilization, and (3) the recent and prospective movements in the unemployment rate.

9. The major factors influencing the selection of the short-term specifications are current economic and financial conditions such as recent data on inflation, real growth, the monetary aggregates, the exchange rate, and prevailing expectations, including those about policy. Also considered are strains, if any, in the domestic and global financial systems, the political setting and perceptions regarding the reliability and predictability of the relationship between monetary aggregate growth, the interest rate target, and the growth of the economy.

10. The FOMC issues a directive to the Trading Desk of the New York Fed to carry out the alternatives.

Key Terms

Impact Lag	Policy Lag
Intermediate Target	Recognition Lag
Operating Target	

Review Questions

1. What are the ultimate targets of monetary policy?

2. What is an intermediate target? Why does the Fed use intermediate targets instead of focusing on the ultimate targets? What is an operating target?

3. What is the recognition lag? the policy lag? the impact lag?

4. How would the recognition, policy, and impact lags differ with regards to monetary and fiscal policy? What role does uncertainty play?

5. Are current incoming economic data or forecasts more important in guiding monetary policy? Why?

6. When is it most difficult to interpret incoming data? (Hint: Consider the case in which retail sales are weak, but new orders for capital goods are strong, etc.)

7. Why can short-term goals sometimes differ from long-term goals?

8. What is an irregular variance? How does it affect Fed behavior?

9. What are some common intermediate targets that the Fed has used to guide policy in recent years? Give two criteria for intermediate targets.

10. Why can't the Fed target both an interest rate and a monetary aggregate simultaneously?

11. Assume the Fed is targeting the money supply and the demand for money falls. Explain why interest rates will fall.

12. Assume the Fed is targeting an interest rate and the demand for money increases. Explain why the money supply will increase.

13. "The Fed should do everything it can to eliminate inflation." Do you agree? Explain.

14. Can using an interest rate as an intermediate target ever have an inflationary bias? Explain.

Analytical Questions

15. Go to the library and look at recent issues of the *Federal Reserve Bulletin*. Find the minutes of the most recent FOMC meeting. (Since the FOMC meets about every six weeks, minutes appear in eight of the 12 monthly issues of the *Federal Reserve Bulletin*.) Summarize the policy directive.

16. Assume that the Fed is targeting an interest rate and aggregate demand drops. Show graphically why the Fed will have to reduce the supply of money to maintain the interest rate target.

17. Use a graph to explain why the Fed cannot target both an interest rate and a monetary aggregate at the same time assuming that there is a drop in aggregate demand.

The Financial System and the Economy

1. The FOMC meets at the New York Federal Reserve. From the world wide web site access (http://www.ny.frb.org/pihome/fedpoint/fed13.html), find out the unique responsibility of the New York Fed in conducting domestic and international monetary policy.

2. Access the minutes of the most recent January meeting of the FOMC from (http://woodrow.mpls.frb.fed.us/info/policy/fomcmin/961.txt). Go to the end of the report and summarize the long-run policy statement that was approved for inclusion in the domestic policy directive. Summarize the domestic policy directive adopted at the conclusion of the January meeting. In particular, what ranges were estimated for the growth of M2, M3, and DNFD?

Suggested Readings

An easy-to-read and comprehensive book from which much of the material in this chapter is drawn is *U.S. Monetary Policy and Financial Markets,* by Ann-Marie Meulendyke. It can be obtained free for the asking from the Federal Reserve Bank of New York, 33 Liberty Street, New York, NY 10045.

In the 1990s, the monetary aggregates have become less reliable guides for monetary policy and, therefore, alternative intermediate targets have been suggested. Todd Clark, in "Nominal GDP Targeting Rules: Can They Stabilize the Economy?" examines the case for targeting nominal GDP and concludes that using a simple nominal GDP targeting rule would not necessarily improve economic performance. *Economic Review,* Federal Reserve Bank of Kansas City, third quarter, 1994. This publication may be viewed and/or ordered on the world wide web at (http://www.kc.frb.org/publicat/pubordfm.htm).

The minutes of each FOMC meeting, including the Directive, are published in the *Federal Reserve Bulletin* each month immediately after the minutes are released. They make extremely interesting reading. This information is also available on the world wide web site of the Federal Reserve Board at (http://www.bog.frb.fed.US/).

An article that questions how monetary policy should be formulated is Wayne Angell, "A Single Goal for the Fed," *Durell Journal of Money and Banking,* Winter 1994–95.

23

A Field Guide to Fed Watching and Policy Implementation

> *The eyes see only what the mind is prepared to comprehend.*
> —Robertson Davies—

Learning Objectives

After reading this chapter, you should know:

- How to interpret the policy directive of the Fed Open Market Committee
- How open market operations affect the fed funds rate and discount window borrowing
- How the Trading Desk reacts to new information
- The difference between temporary and outright open market transactions
- The major guidelines for Fed watching

A Morning at the New York Fed

Each morning, Peter Fisher goes to work at the New York Fed with a specific job assignment—to implement the monetary policy of the United States. As manager of the Fed's open market account, he interprets and executes the policy directives of the Fed Open Market Committee (FOMC). Under his tutelage, the Fed buys and sells government securities to affect intermediate monetary policy targets and eventually the ultimate policy goals.

Mr. Fisher arrives at the office and immediately meets with his staff and is briefed on the opening level interest rates that morning and any unusual events that occurred over the preceding night that may affect the supply of reserves to depository institutions. After some consultation with the Treasury, securities dealers, and FOMC representatives, he decides the direction, if any, in which he believes interest rates should be nudged to fulfill the FOMC policy directive. He issues buy or sell orders to a room of security dealers who work for the New York Fed.

The traders immediately call the primary security dealers they deal with and advise them that the Fed is either buying or selling. The primary dealers are about 40 or so large banks and securities dealers with whom the Fed deals directly. These dealers respond to the Fed's traders with offers either to sell or buy securities at various prices. After a brief time, the Fed's traders gather in a room and announce their buy or sell offer prices. The manager tells the traders to discharge the transactions that are most profitable up to the amount that the Trading Desk is buying or selling. That is, if the Fed is buying, they execute the purchases up to the amount that the Fed wishes to buy at the lowest possible prices. If the Fed is selling on this day, they execute the transactions up to the amount that the Fed wishes to sell at the highest possible prices.

The deals are consummated and reserves are either supplied or withdrawn from the banking system. In response to this change in reserves, interest rates hopefully move in the desired direction at approximately the desired magnitude. Mr. Fisher goes to lunch and upon his return makes a decision whether additional purchases or sales in the open market are needed. Did interest rates overshoot or undershoot the desired target? In either case, an additional purchase or sale may be required.

You may say what a simple story about an act with complex implications! Don't be fooled. Executing monetary policy is neither simple nor mundane. In a way, it is as much an art as it is a science, and the consequences are astronomical.

In the last chapter, we looked at the difficulties in the policy process, focusing on how the FOMC makes decisions. In this chapter, we look at the intricacies of how those decisions are implemented by the Trading Desk of the New York Fed and how markets respond.

Interpreting the FOMC Directive

As we saw in the last chapter, a directive emerges from the FOMC and is sent to the Trading Desk at the Federal Reserve Bank of New York where day-to-day open market operations are executed. To focus on the nuts and bolts guiding daily Trading Desk activity, it will be helpful to begin by examining a portion of a directive agreed upon at a typical FOMC meeting. Simply put, the directive is the link between the decisions formulating policy and the actions implementing policy. The following synopsis is from the directive of the September 26, 1995, FOMC Meeting:

> . . . The Federal Open Market Committee seeks monetary and financial conditions that will foster price stability and promote sustainable growth in output. In furtherance of these objectives, the Committee at its meeting in July reaffirmed the ranges it had established on January 31–February 1 for growth of M2 of 1 to 5 percent, measured from the fourth quarter of 1994 to the fourth quarter of 1995. The Committee also retained the monitoring range of 3 to 7 percent for the year that it had set for the growth of total domestic nonfinancial debt. The Committee raised the 1995 range for M3 to 2 to 6 percent as a technical adjustment to take account of changing intermediation patterns. For 1996, the Committee established on a tentative basis the same ranges as in 1995 for growth of the monetary aggregates and debt, measured from the fourth quarter of 1995 to the fourth quarter of 1996. The behavior of the monetary aggregates will continue to be evaluated in the light of progress toward price level stability, movements in their velocities, and developments in the economy and financial markets.
>
> In the implementation of policy for the immediate future, the Committee seeks to maintain the existing degree of pressure on reserve positions. In the context of the Committee's long-run objective for price stability and sustainable economic growth, and giving careful consideration to economic, financial, and monetary developments, slightly greater reserve restraint or slightly less reserve restraint would be acceptable in the intermeeting period. The contemplated reserve conditions are expected to be consistent with modest growth in M2 and M3 over coming months.[1]

So what does this mean? The first paragraph of the excerpt from the directive lays out in a general way the financial conditions expected to prevail during 1995 and reaffirms the target growth ranges for M2, M3, and domestic nonfinancial debt (DNFD) that had been established a month earlier. (Note: in July the FOMC had raised the growth range for M3 as part of a technical adjustment.)[2] As noted in Chapter 21, the FOMC establishes its long-run growth rate targets at the February and July FOMC meetings each year. These targets are then reported to Congress in compliance with the Humphrey–Hawkins Act of 1978. At the other FOMC meetings, the committee usually acknowledges the earlier established targets unless a distinct change in circumstances causes them to be revised.

The first sentence of the second paragraph of the directive tells us that no change in policy is in order and that the existing degree of pressure on reserve positions will be maintained. Translated, this means that the fed funds rate should remain at its present level.

---

[1] "Minutes of the Federal Open Market Committee," *Federal Reserve Bulletin*, January 1996, p. 47.
[2] In this case, the technical adjustment was necessary because of balance sheet adjustments of the depository institutions as a result of the strains experienced in the early 1990s.

Symmetrical Directive
An FOMC directive that implies the direction of the next policy move is equally likely to be up or down.

The second sentence of the second paragraph might be called the triggering sentence. It tells us what might induce an additional change in policy between this meeting and the next. The phrase "slightly greater reserve restraint or slightly less reserve restraint" is often referred to as a **symmetrical directive,** usually meaning the FOMC believes there is no immediate need to adjust policy and the direction of the next policy move is just as likely to be an easing as a tightening. In this case, the FOMC was meeting in an environment where no presumption was made about the direction of possible further adjustments in the intermeeting period.

Note that the verb "would be acceptable" is stronger than the often used "might be acceptable" when discussing the future course of monetary policy. This implies a greater possibility the Fed will make further adjustments between now and the next FOMC meeting than if the directive used the terminology "might be acceptable."

Asymmetrical Directive
An FOMC directive that implies the Fed is more prepared to move policy in one direction than in another.

The FOMC can also issue an **asymmetrical directive.** For example, "greater reserve restraint would be acceptable, while somewhat lesser restraint might be acceptable" is an asymmetrical directive implying that the Fed is more prepared to tighten than to ease.

The phrase that precedes the specific directive, "In the context of the Committee's long-run objectives for price stability and sustainable economic growth" gives us an idea of what is currently guiding policy, with the order in which the items appear perhaps providing some information about the priority assigned to each. Perhaps the Fed is most concerned about maintaining price stability at this time rather than sustainable economic growth. Or perhaps the Fed seeks price stability in order to achieve sustainable economic growth.

The expected performance for the next year along with economic projections is also announced in the "Monetary Policy Report to the Congress." In July 1995, nominal gross domestic product (GDP) was expected to grow in the 4.63 to 5.5 percent range in 1996. Note that the lower ranges of the target growth rates for M2 and M3 are less than the expected growth rate of nominal GDP. In the early 1990s, M2 and M3 sometimes declined and sometimes increased, behaving in an aberrant manner with regard to GDP.[3] This was not the case in 1995. The "Monetary Policy Report to the Congress" on July 19, 1995, summarizes the situation as follows:

> The monetary aggregate have been behaving more in line with historical patterns than was the case earlier in the decade. However, financial innovation, technological change, and deregulation have blurred distinctions among various financial instruments that can serve as savings vehicles and sources of credit. As a consequence, considerable uncertainty remains about the future relationship of money and debt to the fundamental objectives of monetary policy; the Committee will thus continue to rely primarily on a wide range of other information in determining the stance of policy.[4]

As already noted, the Fed continues to be cautious in using the monetary aggregates as intermediate targets and to evaluate them in "light of . . . move-

---

[3] In Chapter 17, we noted that Money (M) $\times$ Velocity (V) = Gross Domestic Product (GDP). Therefore, $V = GDP/M$, where V is velocity and M a monetary aggregate. If there is an unstable or unpredictable relationship between changes in GDP and changes in a monetary aggregate, then velocity will fluctuate in an unpredictable manner.

[4] "Monetary Policy Report to the Congress," *Federal Reserve Bulletin*, August 1995, pp. 758–759.

ments in their velocities."[5] No target is announced for M1. Having completed our analysis of the FOMC directive, we now turn to how that directive is executed.

RECAP

The FOMC issues a policy directive reflecting the stance of monetary policy and the degree of pressure on reserve positions. The directive gives growth ranges for M2, M3, and DNFD. The New York Fed uses the policy directive to guide the execution of open market operations. The directive may be either symmetrical or asymmetrical depending on whether an intermeeting change is in more likely to be in one direction than another.

The Reserves Market and Open Market Operations

Recall from Chapter 22 that the supply of reserves has two major components: (1) borrowed reserves, which are reserves borrowed by depository institutions from the Fed's discount facility, and (2) nonborrowed reserves, which are reserves available in the open market. At equilibrium, the quantity demanded will equal the quantity supplied, making the market for reserves like any other market.

But how does this equilibrium come about? Suppose at the present market conditions including the present fed funds rate, the quantity demanded of reserves is greater than the quantity supplied of reserves. What will happen? Simply put, the excess quantity demanded will be evident in the fed funds market where bank reserves are bought and sold among banks. Given the excess of quantity demanded over quantity supplied, the fed funds rate will begin to rise. As it rises relative to the discount rate, depository institutions demanding reserves will be induced to borrow reserves at the relatively cheaper discount window. As Exhibit 23-1 shows, the level of borrowing is closely related to the spread between the fed funds rate and the discount rate. Thus, the excess quantity demanded of reserves will be partially satisfied by an increase in borrowed reserves induced by the rise in the fed funds rate relative to the discount rate.

Against this background, the key variables in terms of policy implementation in recent years have been the level of discount window borrowing and the fed funds rate. More specifically, the fed funds rate and the level of borrowings that we observe are the result of the Trading Desk's operations. In particular, the more generous the Trading Desk is in providing reserves through open market operations, given the demand for reserves, the less the need for borrowed reserves at the discount window and the lower the fed funds rate. Thus, the more generous the Trading Desk is, the smaller the spread between the funds rate and the prevailing discount rate. Note that we are assuming that the fed funds rate is above the discount rate. This has been the usual case in the last 20 years for two reasons. First, fed funds have been

---

[5] "Minutes of the Federal Open Market Committee," *Federal Reserve Bulletin*, January 1996, p. 47.

Exhibit 23-1 ◆

The Spread of the Fed Funds Rate Over the Discount Rate and the Amount of Borrowing at the Discount Window

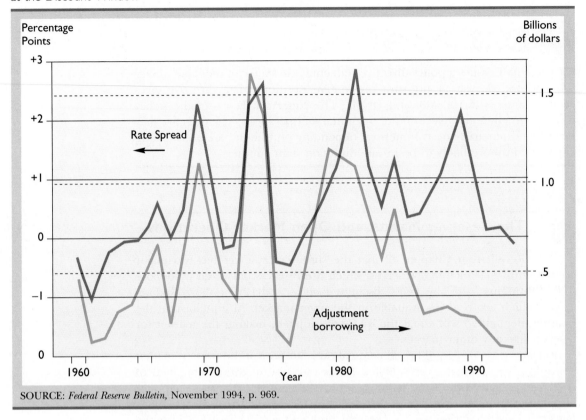

SOURCE: *Federal Reserve Bulletin*, November 1994, p. 969.

used by some large depository institutions as a permanent source of funds. Second, there is some aversion to borrowing at the discount window.[6]

Conversely, given the demand for reserves, the less generous the Trading Desk is in providing reserves, the more upward pressure there will be on the fed funds rate, and thus the spread between the fed funds rate and the discount rate will widen. The resulting higher level of discount window borrowing is, therefore, a direct consequence of the Trading Desk's less generous provision of reserves.

So how does the Trading Desk decide whether to buy or sell securities and whether to be more or less generous in providing reserves? In recent years, the Fed has implemented policy by focusing on the somewhat ambiguous "reserve conditions" and "pressure on reserve positions" mentioned in the directive discussed earlier. In practice, this means the Fed has been guiding its open market operations with an eye toward achieving a particular level of borrowings and fed funds rate. In other words, the Fed has a particular set of reserve conditions in mind as summarized by the values of these variables.

Suppose the Trading Desk begins the period immediately following the FOMC meeting with a directive calling for "maintaining the existing degree

---

[6]As noted in Chapter 5, borrowing is a privilege, not a right and the Fed monitors such borrowing closely.

of pressure on reserve positions'' as in the September 1995 directive. Translated, this means to keep the level of borrowings and the fed funds rate about where they are at the present time. In this case, the Trading Desk derives the **reserve need,** if any, which projections suggest must be met with open market operations in order to maintain the existing level of borrowing and the fed funds rate. Put another way, the Fed makes projections about reserves that will be needed to keep market conditions as they are at the present time. If the Trading Desk supplies more than the reserve need, the fed funds rate will fall, inducing a fall in discount window borrowings. If the Trading Desk supplies less than the reserve need, the funds rate will rise, inducing a rise in discount window borrowings.

> Reserve Need The projected amount of reserves to be supplied or withdrawn by open market operations to maintain or reach the existing levels of borrowings and the fed funds rate prescribed by the policy directive.

If the directive calls for increasing or decreasing the existing degree of pressure on reserves, then the Trading Desk develops the reserve need, if any, which projections suggest must be met to fulfill the directive. In either case, if the Trading Desk supplies more or less than the reserve need, the fed funds rate and discount window borrowings will be different from what was intended in the directive. Note that the reserve need may be negative in that reserves may need to be withdrawn by open market sales to meet the directive.

Operationally, the manager of the Trading Desk begins the initial period following the FOMC meeting with a view that he needs to supply the reserve need on average over the period until the next FOMC meeting through open market operations designed to carry out the policy directive.

In practice, the manager must also consider that other factors are affecting reserves. The overwhelming majority of open market operations are designed to offset unexpected swings in the supply of reserves due to a variety of "other factors," which, if not offset, would induce an undesired change in reserve conditions as measured by the fed funds rate and the level of borrowings. These other factors, discussed in the appendixes of Chapter 16 and this chapter, include changes on the Fed's balance sheet in such things as float, Treasury deposits, gold, and international reserves.

As the period between FOMC meetings progresses, various pieces of data accumulate. Each day, the Fed updates its estimates of the supply of reserves, given yesterday's change, if any, in the Fed's portfolio and new information on the other factors affecting reserves. This continuous updating will lead to revisions in the manager's estimate of the reserves that need to be supplied or absorbed to maintain the desired reserve conditions. Thus, in response to the incoming data, the reserve need may be revised.

New monthly data on economic growth and inflation such as the unemployment rate, retail sales, industrial production, and the consumer and producer price indexes are also released during the intermeeting period. To see how this can affect Trading Desk activity, in particular, and the stance of monetary policy, more generally, we simply quote from the Fed's Record of Policy Actions released with the minutes of the February 1988 FOMC meeting:

> Operationally, the Trading Desk responded to incoming data on the economy during the intermeeting period by increasing its provision of reserves through open market operations so as to "lessen reserve restraint."[7]

---

[7] *Federal Reserve Bulletin,* April 1988.

We are now in a position to look more closely at the mechanics of the Fed's behavior.

 RECAP

The Trading Desk derives the reserve need to fulfill the policy directive. The reserve need is based on the discrepancy between actual reserves and projections of those that will be needed to fulfill the policy directive. The reserve need must be met with open market purchases or sales. In practice, other factors also affect reserves. As new data come in about the monetary aggregates and DNFD or interest rates, the Trading Desk may adjust the reserve need. As new data about the economy come in, the stance of monetary policy may also be changed, which will change the reserve need.

 Trading Desk Market Techniques

Each day the Fed must decide whether to buy or sell securities outright or on a temporary basis. If bought or sold on a temporary basis, the trend is reversed in the next few days. The manager deals with the various factors that affect reserves on a day-to-day basis, attempting to smooth out random factors that affect reserves while overall meeting the guidelines put forth by the FOMC in the policy directive.

Outright Transactions in the Market

Outright Transactions
Open market purchases that supply reserves or open market sales that withdraw reserves.

In general, the manager uses **outright transactions** when he or she wants to provide or absorb reserves over relatively long time spans. More specifically, outright transactions typically are used when projections show a reserve need or reserve excess likely to persist. Such reserve needs may be seasonal, as in the case between Thanksgiving and Christmas, when a rise in currency in circulation drains reserves from the banking system, or more permanent so as to meet the requirements of a growing economy.

Outright purchases in the open market, which supply reserves, occur relatively infrequently and typically account for no more than 10 percent of total Fed transactions.[8] The securities the manager can buy in the secondary market include Treasury bills and federal agency issues. By law, the manager is not allowed to add to the Fed's portfolio by purchasing new securities directly from the Treasury. He may, however, roll over maturing securities in whole or part into new issues. Traditionally, the largest portion of outright transactions is in Treasury bills. The huge size of the secondary market in T-bills and its considerable depth, breadth, and liquidity enable it to absorb large transactions smoothly.

---

[8] Despite that outright purchases usually account for less than 10 percent of total Fed transactions at any time, the Fed's portfolio of securities consist mainly of those bought outright because the temporary purchases wash out over time.

Note that outright sales, even of bills, are relatively infrequent. First, their rarity tends to impart the kind of negative impact on market psychology the Trading Desk prefers to avoid when entering the market. Second, most reserve drains can be dealt with in other less visible ways, including the redemption or runoff of securities held by the Fed when they mature and sales directly to customer accounts as discussed in Exhibit 23-2.

Most outright transactions are technical operations designed to preserve existing reserve conditions against the background of the changing seasonal and secular reserve needs of the economy. However, on rare occasions, the manager uses outright transactions to underscore the thrust of policy and, more specifically, to signal a change in policy.

Temporary Transactions

As we discussed in Chapter 16, the Trading Desk uses temporary transactions when it wants to supply or absorb reserves for relatively short periods, such as a period no longer than a few weeks. Typically, the need to conduct such transactions arises from swings in the various other factors affecting the supply of reserves, such as float and Treasury's balances, among others.

When arranging **repurchase agreements,** the Trading Desk buys securities on a self-reversing, temporary basis. That is, the seller, often a government securities dealer, agrees to buy the securities back from the Trading Desk on or before a specified date. The Fed's use of the term *repurchase agreements* is opposite that of securities dealers' use of the term.[9] The Fed's use of the term refers to the temporary purchase of securities. Usually repurchase agreements are done overnight or for short periods of two to seven days. Since repurchase agreements provide reserves, they can be used to offset a temporary reserve drain arising from one or more of the other factors affecting reserves. If such drains were not fully offset, the supply of reserves would decline relative to the demand, reserve conditions would tighten, and the funds rate would rise. The term **system repurchase agreement** is used by the Fed to describe a repurchase agreement for the purpose of supplying reserves on a temporary basis. The securities that are purchased go into the Fed's system account.

Matched sale-purchase transactions, often referred to in the market as **reverse repurchase agreements** are arranged by the Trading Desk when the manager wants to drain reserves temporarily from the banking system. Technically, when initiating matched sale-purchase transactions, the manager sells securities and simultaneously purchases the same securities for delivery the next day or perhaps several days later. Like their repurchase agreement counterpart, matched sale-purchase transactions are most often used to offset other factors that have changed reserves in order to maintain existing reserve conditions. More specifically, they are usually used to offset temporary reserve excesses arising from the other factors, which, if not offset with matched sale-purchase transactions, would lead to an undesired, albeit temporary, easing in reserve conditions.

Repurchase Agreements When the Trading Desk buys securities on a self-reversing, temporary basis.

System Repurchase Agreement Used by the Fed for the purpose of supplying reserves on a temporary basis.
Matched Sale-Purchase Transactions The Fed's sale of securities and simultaneous purchase of the same securities for delivery the next day or in a few days.
Reverse Repurchase Agreements Another name for matched sale-purchase transactions.

---

[9] In Chapter 6, we saw that dealers use the term *repurchase agreements* to refer to the practice of borrowing money to finance their holdings of securities by selling the securities temporarily with an agreement to repurchase them at a later date.

Exhibit 23-2 ◆
Customer
Transactions

The manager's job of complying with the degree of restraint on reserve positions called for in the directive is complicated somewhat by the fact that various foreign official entities (customers) such as foreign central banks, governments, and international institutions maintain what are, in effect, short-term investment accounts with the New York Fed. Substantial dollar totals, sometimes averaging $500 billion, are held in these accounts with the New York Fed under instructions to keep the bulk of these balances continuously invested in interest-earning assets for the foreign official customer. The manager needs to be careful to integrate movements of funds in and out of these customer accounts with the overall reserve strategy because transactions involving customer accounts can have reserve-absorbing and reserve-supplying effects.

For example, an inflow of funds into a foreign official account will decrease the reserves available to the banking system. This occurs because the funds moving into the Fed are drawn out of the reserve balances of banks. The manager, depending on specific reserve objectives at the time, can offset this reserve absorption. Typically, this is done by executing a repurchase agreement in the market for the account of customers, a **customer repurchase agreement.** Alternatively, the manager can let the reserve absorption occur by selling securities to the foreign customer from the Fed's portfolio.

Customer Repurchase Agreement A repurchase agreement executed by the Fed for the account of a customer.

A customer repurchase agreement has the same reserve-supplying effect when executed in the market as a system repurchase agreement and the same reserve-draining effect when unwound. Although some Fed watchers attach greater importance to system repurchase agreements, the choice usually has little policy significance. In general, customer repurchase agreements, of which the Fed routinely announces the size as they are being arranged, are used for moderate-sized operations; system repurchase agreements, whose size is not announced by the Fed at the time of execution, are used for larger reserve tasks.

Significantly, however, the manager's discretion either to invest customer balances in the market or to invest them internally by selling the customer securities from the system's own portfolio imparts a special character to customer transactions, because Fed watchers are unaware of internally accommodated customer transactions when they are taking place. Only with a time lag, when the Fed's balance sheet is published on Thursday, will the Fed watcher be able to deduce that internal transactions have occurred. By contrast, open market interventions for the Fed's own account are immediately visible, although their size is not announced.

The hidden feature of internally accommodated customer transactions emphasizes the major gaps in the knowledge that outsiders have of the reserve movements being affected at any given time by the manager.

 RECAP

To change reserves, the manager of the Trading Desk may use open market purchases or sales, repurchase agreements, or matched sale-purchase transactions. A repurchase agreement provides reserves until they mature in a few days. They are used to offset a temporary reserve drain. A matched sale-purchase transaction is used to temporarily withdraw reserves from the system. If the change is thought to be permanent, outright purchases or sales are more likely to be used.

Signposts for Fed Watching and Sources of Information

Throughout this text, we have seen how small changes in interest rates can cause large changes in the value of long-term financial assets and can lead to capital gains and losses. We have also seen that monetary policy affects interest rates, securities prices, profits, and the level of economic activity. Thus, investment bankers (market makers) and other financial institutions are keen on trying to understand the basic thrust of Fed policy and detecting any signs that the objectives or goals may be changing. To be able to do so can prevent large financial loses and reap equally large gains. Consequently, many financial firms employ economists as "Fed watchers" to track the activity of the Trading Desk, the FOMC, and the economy. The activity of the Fed watchers helps speed changes in expectations and the rate at which economic activity adjusts to new information.

Since the manager's daily operations involve an ever-changing and subtle blend of purchases and sales, some of which may be in response to changes in other factors, careful Fed watching requires considerable feel for the process and projections of reserve availability and so forth, which mimic to the extent possible the information guiding the manager's operations. In February 1995, the Fed formally adopted the practice of announcing policy changes immediately following the FOMC Meetings. In some ways, this reduced the uncertainty and guesswork about Fed policy and the direction thereof at the time of the FOMC Meetings. It did not eliminate Fed watching during the intermeeting periods to detect subtle changes in policy.[10]

Fed watchers look for certain signposts just as a traveler would look for street signs and landmarks. Even the most experienced voyager sometimes must reassess where he or she is going or acknowledge a missed landmark. It is to the signposts for Fed watching that we now turn. They hopefully will show the way.

By definition, the Fed has much better information on the formulation and implementation of policy than do outsiders. Moreover, the manager exercises discretion in interpreting the implications of the FOMC's directive for day-to-day operations. Taken together, these realities suggest that even the most dedicated and conscientious Fed watchers cannot always be sure that

---

[10]Actually, in 1994, the Fed started announcing policy changes immediately following FOMC meetings. Such a procedure removes the questioning and doubt about changes in policy. The announcements in 1994 occurred after a relatively long period of stable low interest rates. It was anticipated that higher interest rates would catch many market participants off guard, causing the value of their portfolios to decline. (Remember the inverse relationship between the interest rate and bond prices.) In such a situation, market participants would sustain real losses in the value of their portfolios. It seems as if the Fed was attempting to give a "heads up" to market participants by announcing the increases.

"I think the Fed might be loosening up a bit."

© 1996 Arnie Levin from The Cartoon Bank,™ Inc.

they have correctly interpreted Fed intentions. It is possible to lay some basic rules veteran Fed watchers use and to draw on the extensive discussion of policy to list the types of information that should prove useful in unraveling the mystique surrounding monetary policy in the United States. The following list, although far from comprehensive, provides what most Fed watchers consider to be the essentials.

Basic Rules of Fed Watching

1. *Watch the data the Fed watches, not what you think they should watch.* For example, if the Fed is not paying much attention to the monetary aggregates as policy guides, then movements in the aggregates, which you might judge important, will be of little help in anticipating policy actions.
2. *The Fed generally reacts to economic events; it seldom anticipates.* In other words, the Fed gives heavy weight to incoming data and current economic and financial conditions (much of which is estimated) as opposed to forecasts in adjusting its policy stance.
3. *Pay more attention to what the Fed does than what it says.* Though the Fed does not deliberately mislead the market, it is not above waging psychological warfare and engaging in wishful thinking.
4. *The Fed usually prefers to act covertly and to adjust policy gradually rather than abruptly.* Remember that although the Fed is expected to be above politics, it has to operate in a political environment.[11] Accordingly, it sometimes

---

[11] The long terms of the Board of Governors of the Fed supposedly protect them from political pressure.

LOOKING FORWARD

Taylor's Rule for Fed Watchers

Over the past eight years, the Fed, under Chairperson Greenspan's leadership, has opted for eclecticism and pragmatism. Instead of focusing on one variable, it has chosen to focus on a host of variables in judging the direction and stance of monetary policy. In some ways this has made the job of the Fed watcher more difficult. What variables is the Fed looking at and what is to be their next move?

According to *Business Week*, "Some Fed watchers believe they have discovered a monetary crystal ball that could help them anticipate Greenspan's moves."* The panacea is a rule for Fed watching developed by a Stanford economist, John B. Taylor. Dubbed *Taylor's Rule*, the method forecasts when and by how much the Fed will change the fed funds rate by focusing on how much slack there is in the economy.

More specifically, Taylor's Rule looks at the divergence between the actual inflation rate and the Fed's own targeted rate, and how far above or below the economy is from the natural rate of real output. If the economy is operating below its long-run growth potential, then Taylor's Rule would predict how much and when the Fed would lower rates. Likewise, if the economy is growing too fast, the rule would predict how much and when interest rates had to be increased.

The following chart shows how well Taylor's Rule would have forecasted changes in the Fed funds rate in the 1990s. Although far from perfect, the Fed watcher would have gotten a lot of keys to Fed changes by heeding the rule. Will such a rule continue to be of use to Fed watchers in the future? Only the future will tell.

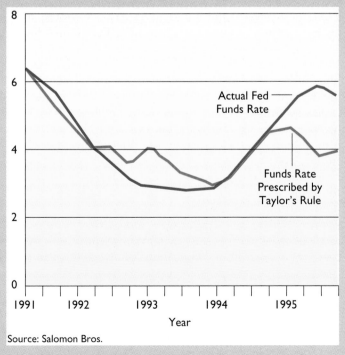

Source: Salomon Bros.

*"How Low Should Rates Be?" *Business Week*, October 9, 1995, pp. 68–70.

tries to distance itself from interest rate increases (if that is possible), and to move cautiously. The belief is that such behavior minimizes market disruptions and reduces the chance of a major policy error.

Armed with these basics, the next step is to pull together the most useful types of information about policy. Many information sources fall directly out of the discussion of the policy process already presented.

1. *Congressional Testimony by Fed Chairperson.* Such appearances, particularly the ones in February and July in compliance with the provisions of the Humphrey–Hawkins Act, typically include a discussion of the FOMC's policy plan, its economic projections, and an evaluation of recent economic and financial developments. The policy plan and projections provide benchmarks against which incoming financial and nonfinancial data can be compared. For example, if the FOMC was expecting real GDP to grow at about 2.5 percent and inflation to be about 3.5 percent, and incoming data suggest both figures are higher, a tightening of policy might well be in the offing. The "Monetary Policy Report to the Congress" and additional testimony by members of the Board of Governors is published in the *Federal Reserve Bulletin.*

2. *Minutes of the Federal Open Market Committee Meetings, Including the Directive.* These summaries of FOMC meetings tell us roughly what the staff forecasts are, how the forecasts and incoming data are being interpreted by policymakers, how much unanimity or disagreement there is within the FOMC, and what specific features are guiding policy actions. To illustrate, considerable uncertainty about the outlook and disagreement within the FOMC typically leads the FOMC to leave policy unchanged for the time being. The minutes of FOMC meetings are published in the *Federal Reserve Bulletin* following their release. As noted in Chapter 5, minutes are released shortly after the next FOMC meeting when they are approved.

3. *Public Statements by Fed Officials.* Speeches and press reports often provide some insight into the thinking of particular policymakers and have on occasion helped Fed watchers detect a swing in sentiment within the FOMC that eventually leads to policy adjustments. Of course, whenever the chairperson speaks all listen because Fed chairpersons have been known to obliquely signal a change in policy in an otherwise unremarkable public appearance. Of course, as previously noted, in 1994 the Fed began announcing the decisions made at the FOMC meetings immediately following the meetings rather than waiting for the decisions to be published with the minutes.

4. *Daily Pattern, Volume, and Type of Open Market Operations.* For changes in monetary policy between FOMC meetings, we must look to daily Fed actions following a meeting for indications of any changes in policy. To the extent possible, market professionals try to mimic the projections by the Fed's staff of the need for the manager to supply or absorb reserves. Armed with such projections, we then try to judge whether the Fed is being more or less generous in its provision of reserves through open market operations. For example, if projections suggest that the Fed needs to supply a large amount of reserves, on average, over the next few weeks, but the Fed appears to be doing little, Fed watchers will be alert to the

Exhibit 23-3 ◆

A Guide to Open Market Operations

Fed Activity	Translation	Implication
I. No Fed buying or selling occurs on this day.	The Fed is not expected to intervene.	A reserve add or intervene drain is not required, or it can be accommodated later when more information is available or market conditions begin to more clearly reflect or indicate the need.
II. The Fed uses matched sales.	Trading Desk sells Treasury securities to primary dealers. Buyers agree to sell them back at a specified time, usually the next day, which temporarily absorbs reserves.	A reserve drain is required, which may mean either (a) the drain is consistent with prevailing Fed policy and necessary to prevent undesired fed funds rate declines, or (b) the Fed has tightened.
III. The Fed engages in system repurchase agreements.	The Trading Desk provides funds (reserves) in exchange for Treasury securities with an agreement that dealers will repurchase them, usually the next day, which temporarily increases reserves.	Reserves must be added, may mean either (a) the increase is consistent with prevailing policy, necessary to prevent undesired fed funds rate increases, or (b) the Fed has eased.
IV. The Fed uses customer repurchase agreements. (Arranged when Fed customer wants to temporarily invest excess funds).	Similar to system repurchase agreements except that the security buyer is a Federal Reserve customer outside the banking system, for example, a foreign central bank.	Reserves must be added. Reserves are injected into the U.S. banking system. May be consistent with prevailing policy or signal that the Fed has eased.
V. The Fed makes outright sales.	Permanent transaction has occurred with no resale agreements. The Fed sells Treasury securities in the open market, absorbing reserves. Bills only are sold.	Reserves are drained out of the banking system. Such a move is usually not associated with a change in policy, but conducted seasonally and occasionally when underscoring a policy move toward restraint.
VI. The Fed makes outright purchases.	Opposite of an outright sale has occurred. The Fed buys securities in the open market with no repurchase agreements on the part of the sellers, injecting reserves permanently.	Reserves are permanently added. The action is usually not associated with policy implications. Conducted seasonally to provide for economic growth. Can occasionally signal policy moves toward easing.

possibility that some tightening in reserve conditions may be underway. To join the preceding discussion of open market techniques to the nuances of Fed watching, Exhibit 23-3 provides a field guide to the Fed's open market operations.

5. *Releases of Nonfinancial Data.* As data are released on retail sales, employment, wages and prices, capital spending, capacity utilization, consumer confidence, the trade balance, and so forth, policymakers ask themselves a simple question: Are the incoming data consistent with, stronger than,

or weaker than the economic projections underlying and guiding the prevailing stance of policy? Generally, no single monthly release, given the considerable "noise" in the data, is viewed as decisive. Rather, it is the pattern across the various pieces of data and the cumulative evidence over several months that are most likely to be persuasive.

6. *Fed Releases of Financial Data.* Data on reserves, the monetary aggregates, the Fed's balance sheet, interest rates, and loan demand at the largest banks are released weekly. In essence, these data give us a snapshot of supply and demand conditions in financial markets. Of particular interest are the Fed's net reserve supplying or absorbing transactions, as reflected in their balance sheet, and the level of borrowing from the Fed through the discount facility.

The Lesson

Fed watching is as much of an art as a science—there are no shortcuts. The complexity of policy procedures, coupled with the political milieu within which policymakers operate and muddle, puts a considerable premium on understanding the relationship among the economic goals the Fed is loosely charged with achieving, the intermediate target approach embraced by the Fed, the economic analysis provided the FOMC, the directive, incoming data, reserve projections, and finally, open market operations. By understanding the process and thus minimizing the risk of misinterpreting Fed actions and statements, market participants should be better positioned to anticipate and deal with Fed policy. This chapter contains one appendix on how required reserves are determined and how the reserve need is estimated. The next chapter is the final chapter on the global implications and linkages of monetary policy.

Summary of Major Points

1. The FOMC issues an operating directive to the Trading Desk of the New York Fed, which deals with how open market policy is to be implemented. The directive may be symmetrical or asymmetrical. A symmetrical directive means that the direction of the next policy move is just as likely to be either an easing or a tightening. An asymmetrical directive means that one alternative is more likely than the other.

2. The staff of the New York Fed estimates the amount of the reserve need to fulfill the policy directive of the FOMC. Given the directive, the manager of the open market Trading Desk then decides whether reserves should be added or removed from the system. The Trading Desk also makes offsetting purchases or sales to neutralize changes in other factors affecting reserves.

3. The manager of the Trading Desk may use outright purchases or sales in the open market to change reserves. The transactions are usually in the secondary market in T-bills. Alternatively, repurchase agreements or matched sale-purchase transactions may be used to change reserves. The seller of the repurchase agreement (usually a government securities

dealer) agrees to buy the securities back from the Trading Desk on or before a specified date. In a matched sale-purchase transaction, the manager of the Trading Desk sells securities and simultaneously purchases them back for delivery on a later date. A repurchase agreement provides reserves until they mature in a few days. They are used to offset a temporary reserve drain. A matched sale-purchase transaction is used to temporarily withdraw reserves from the system. If the change is thought to be permanent, the manager is more likely to use outright purchases than if the need for reserves is thought to be temporary. A more subtle adjustment of reserves can be made if repurchase agreements are purchased for a customer's account rather than the system account.

4. The basic rules for Fed watching include:

   a. Watch the data the Fed watches.
   b. Watch current economic events and incoming data.
   c. Pay more attention to what the Fed does than to what it says.
   d. Expect the Fed to adjust policy gradually rather than abruptly, except in a crisis.

5. The most useful policy information is found in the Congressional testimony by the Fed chairperson, the minutes of the FOMC meetings including the directive, the daily volume and type of open market operations, releases of financial and nonfinancial data, and other statements by Fed officials. The Fed announces policy changes immediately following FOMC Meetings. Fed watching is as much an art as it is a science, and is important in understanding financial market changes.

Key Terms

Asymmetrical Directive
Bank Reserves Equation
Computation Period
Contemporaneous Reserve
   Accounting
Customer Repurchase Agreement
Maintenance Period
Matched Sale-Purchase
   Transactions

Outright Transactions
Repurchase Agreements
Reserve Need
Reverse Repurchase Agreements
Symmetrical Directive
System Repurchase Agreement

Review Questions

1. If the FOMC policy directive states that "slightly more pressure may be acceptable while slightly less pressure would be acceptable," is this an example of a symmetrical or asymmetrical directive? Why? Give an example of a symmetrical and an asymmetrical directive.

2. If the fed funds rate decreases relative to the discount rate, how does this affect the level of borrowing from the discount window?

3. Explain what is meant by the reserve need.

4. Are repurchase agreements and matched sale-purchase transactions more likely to be associated with offsetting open market operations? Are outright purchases and sales more likely to be associated with offsetting open market operations?

5. What is the difference between a system repurchase agreement and a customer repurchase agreement?

6. Which rule of Fed watching do you think is most important? Why?

7. Which information sources do you think are most important? Why?

8. When and why would the Fed "accommodate" a rise in reserve demand by supplying more reserves?

9. What characteristics of Treasury bills make them desirable to be used in outright transactions by the Trading Desk?

10. Float increases unexpectedly. Will the Fed typically respond with outright purchases or temporary purchases?

11. Explain how the bank reserve equation is derived from the Fed's balance sheet. Which items raise bank reserves? Which items lower bank reserves? (Appendix 23-A)

12. Under contemporaneous reserve accounting, how does the computation period correspond with the maintenance period? (Appendix 23-A)

Analytical Questions

13. Assume checkable deposits are $500 billion, desired excess reserves are 1 percent of deposits, the required reserve ratio is 10 percent, and the amount of reserves is $50 billion. What is the reserve need to maintain the existing reserve conditions?

14. Describe the possible actions that the Fed could take to meet the reserve need in question 13. Under what conditions is each most likely?

15. The Fed anticipates a seasonal reserve need of $10 billion over the next month. Is it more likely to use outright purchases or temporary transactions to meet this need? If the Fed supplies $20 billion in reserves, what will happen to the fed funds rate? What will happen to borrowing at the discount window?

16. Explain the following statement: Even though outright purchases account for less than 10 percent of Fed transactions, the Fed's portfolio of securities consists mainly of securities bought outright. (Hint: see Footnote 8.)

17. Assume that the demand for required plus excess reserves is $50 billion, the level of discount borrowing is $100 million, and the actual level of nonborrowed reserves is $49 billion. What is the reserve need if the existing degree of pressure on reserve positions is to be maintained? What will happen if the Fed supplies less reserves than the reserve need?

18. What are the implications of the following Fed activities?
    a. The Fed sells securities using matched sales.
    b. The Fed buys securities using system repurchase agreements.
    c. The Fed makes outright purchases for the system account.
    d. The Fed uses a customer repurchase agreement.

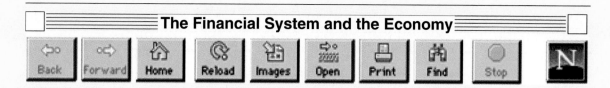

The Financial System and the Economy

1. a. Access the world wide web address (http://www.ny.frb.org/pihome/fedpoint/fed04.html) to explain repurchase and matched-sale transactions.

   b. Access the world wide web address (http://www.ny.frb.org/pihome/fedpoint/fed43.html) to define fedwire.

2. In accordance with the provisions of the Humphrey–Hawkins Full Employment and Balanced Growth Act of 1978, Fed Chairperson Alan Greenspan testified before Congress on February 20, 1996. An executive summary of his testimony can be found at (http://woodrow.mpls.frb.fed.us/info/policy/mpo/mp962.html). Access this address and answer the following:

   a. According to Chairperson Greenspan, what was the overall performance of the U.S. economy in 1995?

   b. What is the economic growth forecast for 1996?

   c. What does the FOMC expect with regard to inflation in 1996?

   d. What is the FOMC's stance on monetary policy for 1996? What recommendations (i.e. policy directives) are made to support this stance?

Suggested Readings

For a comprehensive article on the underlying trends in discount window borrowing in the 1980s and 1990s, see "Recent Developments in Discount Window Policy," *Federal Reserve Bulletin*, November 1994, pp. 965–977.

As mentioned in the body of the text, the monthly *Federal Reserve Bulletin* contains the "Minutes of the FOMC Meetings" and the "Monetary Policy Report to Congress." In addition, the *Bulletin* contains many statements to Congress by the Fed chairperson and other Fed governors. This information may also be accessed on the world wide web site of the Federal Reserve Board at (http://www.bog.frb.fed.US/).

APPENDIX 23-A

How the Demand and Supply of Reserves Are Calculated

Maintenance Period The period in which banks are required to hold reserve assets.

Computation Period The period during which the actual amount of required reserve assets that must be held during the maintenance period is determined.

Banks are required to hold reserve assets during a two-week **maintenance period** that corresponds to the two-week **computation period.** During the computation period, the actual amount of required reserve assets that must be held during the maintenance period is determined. During the two-week maintenance period, the actual average amount of reserves held must at least equal the average required reserves.

The average daily amount of required reserve assets that must be held is equal to the required reserve ratio times the average daily amount of deposits subject to reserve requirements. At the present time, only checkable deposits are subject to reserve requirements. Required reserves against checkable deposits will equal the checkable deposit balances multiplied by the reserve requirement ratio on such deposits. Currently that ratio is 10 percent. By adding an allowance for excess reserves based on recent experience and any seasonal patterns, the staff of the New York Fed produces a path for the demand for total reserves including both required and excess reserves.

For example, if checkable deposits average $600 billion/day during the computation period, then required reserve assets (deposits at the Fed plus vault cash) must average $60 billion/day during the maintenance period ($60 billion = $600 billion × 10 percent reserve requirement). If excess reserves have been averaging 1 percent of deposits, then an additional $6 billion in excess reserves must be included in the path for total reserves that will be demanded ($6 billion = $600 billion × 1 percent excess reserves).

Contemporaneous Reserve Accounting A system of reserve accounting in which the maintenance period more or less corresponds to the computation period.

Since 1984, a system called **contemporaneous reserve accounting** has been used. Under such a system, the maintenance period, when the reserve assets must be held, more or less corresponds to the computation period. The two-week computation period starts two days before the two-week maintenance period. When one computation period ends, another immediately begins. The average daily balance of reserves held during the maintenance period must be equal to the average daily balance of reserves required during the computation period with the exception that average vault cash in a two-week computation period counts as reserves in the maintenance period ending two weeks later.[a] When one maintenance period ends, another immediately begins. Exhibit 23-4 illustrates how the reserve accounting method works in practice.

---

[a]Prior to 1992, the lag in counting vault cash toward required reserves was two weeks longer.

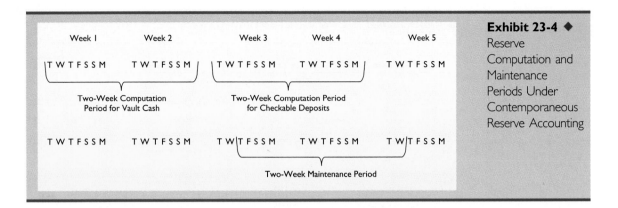

Exhibit 23-4 ◆
Reserve
Computation and
Maintenance
Periods Under
Contemporaneous
Reserve Accounting

The supply of total reserves can be determined by rearranging the Fed's balance sheet, which is displayed in Exhibit 23-5.[b] More specifically, the major items on the Fed's balance sheet can be summarized as follows:

Assets

Government securities held (GS)
Gold and Special Drawing Rights (SDRs)[c] accounts (which reflect) International reserve holdings (IR)
Discount loans (L)
Float (F)
Other assets (OA)

Liabilities

Reserve balances of depository institutions with the Fed (DF)
Currency outside the Fed (C^*)
Treasury deposits (TD) Other liabilities (OL)

Thus, since assets equal liabilities, we know:

(23A-1) $GS + IR + L + F + OA = DF + C^* + TD + OL$

Currency outside the Fed, C^*, is equal to vault cash, VC, plus currency in the hands of the public, C—that is, $C^* = VC + C$. Substituting $VC + C$ for C^* in Equation (23A-1), we arrive at:

(23A-2) $GS + IR + L + F + OA = DF + VC + C + TD + OL$

Since reserves, R, are equal to reserve balances of depository institutions, DF, plus vault cash, VC, we can substitute R for $DF + VC$ in Equation (23A-2). Solving for R yields the so-called **bank reserves equation:**

(23A-3) $DF + VC = R = GS + IR + L + F + OA - C - TD - OL$

Bank Reserves Equation
The equation showing the relationship between reserves and other items on the Fed's balance sheet:
$DF + VC = R = GS + IR + L + F + OA - C - TD - OL$

---

[b] This analysis is similar to the analysis in the appendix of Chapter 16. They differ only in that the Chapter 16 analysis was done in terms of the monetary base. In this chapter, we subtract currency in the hands of the public from the monetary base to arrive at reserves.
[c] Special drawing rights (SDRs) are liabilities of the International Monetary Fund and serve as international reserves.

Exhibit 23-5 ◆
The Fed's Balance
Sheet

1.18   **FEDERAL RESERVE BANKS**   Condition and Federal Reserve Note Statements[1]
Millions of Dollars

Account	Wednesday Jan. 3, 1996	Account	Wednesday Jan. 3, 1996
ASSETS		LIABILITIES	
1 Gold certificate account	11,050	21 Federal Reserve notes	401,236
2 Special drawing rights certificate account	10,168		
3 Coin	412	22 Total deposits	43,525
		23 Depository institutions	38,316
Loans		24 U.S. Treasury—General account	4,787
4 To depository institutions	299	25 Foreign—Official accounts	165
5 Other	0	26 Other	257
6 Acceptances held under repurchase agreements	0		
		27 Deferred credit items	8,137
Federal agency obligations		28 Other liabilities and accrued dividends[5]	4,328
7 Bought outright	2,634		
8 Held under repurchase agreements	1,592	29 Total liabilities	457,225
		CAPITAL ACCOUNTS	
9 Total U.S. Treasury securities	390,494		
10 Bought outright[2]	378,749	30 Capital paid in	3,976
11 Bills	183,667	31 Surplus	3,964
12 Notes	151,013	32 Other capital accounts	192
13 Bonds	44,069		
14 Held under repurchase agreements	11,745	33 Total liabilities and capital accounts	465,357
		MEMO	
15 Total loans and securities	395,019	34 Marketable U.S. Treasury securities held in custody for	
		foreign and international accounts	502.958
16 Items in process of collection	15,725		
17 Bank premises	1,125		
Other assets			
18 Denominated in foreign currencies[3]	21,102		
19 All other[4]	10,756		
20 Total assets	465,357		

1. Some of the data in this table also appear in the Board's H.4.1 (503) weekly statistical release. For ordering address, see inside front cover.
2. Includes securities loaned—fully guaranteed by U.S. Treasury securities pledged with Federal Reserve Banks—and excludes securities sold and scheduled to be bought back under matched sale–purchase transactions.

3. Valued monthly at market exchange rates.
4. Includes special investment account at the Federal Reserve Bank of Chicago in Treasury bills maturing within ninety days.
5. Includes exchange-translation account reflecting the monthly revaluation at market exchange rates of foreign exchange commitments.

SOURCE: *Federal Reserve Bulletin,* January 1996, p. A11.

Increases in any of the items preceded by a plus sign will raise bank reserves while increases in any of the items preceded by a minus sign will lower bank reserves.[d]

To sum up, the demand for reserves is equal to required plus desired excess reserves. The supply of reserves is equal to borrowed plus nonborrowed reserves. Reserves are in turn equal to the Fed's portfolio of securities plus the net amount of other factors affecting reserves in Equation (23A-3).

---

[d] As noted in the appendix of Chapter 16, all the items with a plus sign are from the asset side of the Fed's balance sheet, while the items with minus signs are from the liability side of the Fed's balance sheet.

24

Monetary Policy Under Fixed and Flexible Exchange Rates and the Need for Global Coordination

> *The role of central banks will change as
> financial markets change.*
> —Charles S. Sanford, Jr.
> Chairman, Bankers Trust—
>
> *If countries don't discipline themselves,
> the world market will do it.*
> —Morris Offit, Offitbank—

Learning Objectives

After reading this chapter, you should know:

- ◆ The nature of exchange rate systems in effect since World War II and how they interact with monetary policy
- ◆ The growing influence of international trade and capital flows on monetary policy under either fixed or flexible exchange rates
- ◆ Why monetary policy will most likely require increased global coordination in the future regardless of the exchange rate system

Monetary Policy and the Globalization of Trade and Finance

Throughout this text, we have implied that one of the most important roles of the Fed is to formulate and implement the nation's monetary policy. The Fed attempts to ensure that sufficient money and credit are available to allow the economy to expand in accord with its long-run growth trend with little or no inflation and with minimum fluctuations in output and employment.

Throughout this text, we have also seen that financial markets have experienced ongoing and dramatic change. Driven by technological improvements in computers and telecommunications, the breakdown of barriers to capital flows, and an increasingly globalized environment, the financial system is experiencing a dramatic metamorphosis. This transformation may of necessity change the modus operandi of the Fed despite that its function to execute monetary policy may remain the same.

In this final chapter, we look at the implications of the continuing growth of international trade and finance for monetary policy. We consider the effects of monetary policy under both fixed and flexible exchange rate systems.

Fixed Exchange Rates from 1945 to 1971

The Bretton Woods Accord

Fixed Exchange Rate System When countries agree to buy or sell their currency to maintain fixed exchange rates with other currencies.

Official Reserve Currency The currency by which other countries define the value of their currency; used as international reserves.

Bretton Woods Accord The 1944 accord that established a fixed exchange rate system among the major industrialized countries with the U.S. dollar serving as the official reserve currency.

From the end of World War II until the early 1970s, the major economies of the world participated in a **fixed exchange rate system** with the U.S. dollar functioning as the **official reserve currency.** Other countries defined their currencies in terms of the U.S. dollar and agreed to buy or sell dollars to maintain the agreed-upon exchange rates.[1] The dollar, in turn, was defined in terms of gold. During the post-war period, one ounce of gold was set equal to $35 and the United States agreed to convert any unwanted dollars of foreign central banks into gold.[2]

The **Bretton Woods Accord** that established the system was hammered out by representatives of the major industrialized nations in 1944 at an international monetary conference. The accord got its name from the posh White Mountains resort near the town of Bretton Woods, New Hampshire, where the conference was held.

Under the Bretton Woods Accord, if the trade deficit of a country other than the United States increased, ceteris paribus, there was downward pressure on the exchange rate. That country was essentially flooding the world with its currency in such a case. In order to maintain the agreed-upon exchange rate, the central bank of the foreign country had to purchase the excess supply of its currency using dollars.

---

[1] In this chapter when we use the terms *dollar* or *dollars,* we also mean *dollar-denominated deposits.*

[2] In cases of fundamental imbalances, an orderly procedure was established to make adjustments in exchange rates and thereby avoid the disruptive changes that occurred between World War I and World War II.

An example will help clarify. Assume that the exchange rate between the dollar and the German mark was set at $1 = 2 marks, but supply and demand factors were causing the market value of the two currencies to gravitate to $1 = 3 marks. Perhaps the market value was such because the trade deficit of Germany, ceteris paribus, had increased significantly in recent months causing Germany's balance of payments on current and capital accounts to move into a deficit position.[3] The smaller supply of dollars relative to marks in international markets put upward pressure on the exchange rate of the dollar while the larger relative supply of marks put downward pressure on the value of the mark. In such a case, the Bundesbank, the central bank of Germany, agreed to intervene in the market by buying marks with dollars until the market value of the two currencies converged to the agreed-upon exchange rate. By changing the supply of dollars and marks outstanding, the Bundesbank was able to manipulate the market value of the dollar in terms of the mark. In this manner, the values of the dollar and the mark could be maintained at the agreed-upon exchange rate of $1 = 2 marks.

Such a government transaction in foreign currencies was measured in the **official reserve account** of the balance of payments. We ignored this account in Chapter 9. We can now see that by supplying dollars and demanding marks, the Bundesbank ran a surplus in the official reserve account that just equaled the deficit in the current and capital accounts of the balance of payments. Hence, under fixed exchange rates, it was (and always is) official government transactions in foreign exchange markets that brought the balance of payments into balance at the fixed exchange rate.

Because it was maintaining the fixed exchange rate system by buying marks with dollars, Germany could continue to maintain fixed exchange rates only as long as it had or could acquire the required supplies of dollars to support the value of its currency as needed. If a foreign country, such as Germany, ran a persistent deficit in the current and capital accounts, its central bank would eventually run out of dollars and have to **devalue** or decrease the value of its currency in terms of the dollar in order to reflect the diminished value of the mark. Devaluation occurs when the monetary authorities reduce the value of a country's currency under a fixed exchange rate system. In terms of our analysis, the mark is devalued if the official rate is changed from $1 per 2 marks to $1 per 4 marks. At the original rate, each mark was worth $.50 while at the latter rate, after the devaluation, each mark is worth $.25.[4]

As already noted, in the immediate decades following World War II, the U.S. dollar served as the official reserve currency. Unlike the preceding situation, the United States was eventually in the unique position of being able to run persistent balance of payments deficits on the current and capital accounts.[5] Foreign central banks desired to accumulate stockpiles of dollars to function

Official Reserve Account An account in the balance of payments used by the central bank to make official government transactions in foreign exchange to balance the balance of payments.

Devalue Under fixed exchange rates, when the monetary authorities reduce the value of a currency in relation to the official reserve currency.

---

[3] Recall from Chapter 9 that the current account measures transactions that involve currently produced goods and services (exports and imports) and net transfer payments. The capital account measures the financial flows of funds and securities among countries.

[4] The need to devalue can be accelerated if speculators sense an impending necessity to devalue and increase the supply of marks from what it would be otherwise. The alternative to devaluing would be for Germany to run a severely contractionary policy designed to lower prices in marks and make German goods more desirable to restore the value of the mark to the agreed-upon exchange rate.

[5] Initially after World War II, the United States was running sizable trade surpluses financed by capital outflows under the Marshall Plan. This period was described as a *dollar shortage* as countries were scrambling for dollars not only for reserves but also to rebuild their economies.

as international reserves. Once foreign central banks had acquired sufficient reserves, the ability of the United States to run chronic deficits in the balance of payments on current and capital accounts was also limited. In this case, the dollar, ceteris paribus, would become overvalued in terms of one or more foreign currencies. Under the Bretton Woods Accord, the United States would lose gold as the unwanted dollars were presented for conversion. Foreign central banks would be pressured by the United States to **revalue** or increase the value of their currency in terms of the dollar. Revaluation occurs when the monetary authorities increase the value of a country's currency under a fixed exchange rate system. For example, the mark is revalued if the official rate is changed from $1 equals 2 marks to $1 equals 1 mark. In the original case, each mark was worth $.50 while in the latter case, each mark is worth $1. Ceteris paribus, the revaluation would in time reduce the U.S. balance of payments deficit on current and capital accounts and brake the flow of unwanted dollars abroad. In turn, the gold outflow would diminish. Because revaluation could adversely affect their countries, foreign central banks may be hesitant to revalue.[6] Consequently, they would pressure the United States to correct the imbalance by reducing its deficit on the current and capital account. Note the irony of the situation and the potential for a stalemate to develop when each country is pressuring the other to take action.

Regardless of whether the United States was running a persistent surplus or deficit in its balance of payments on current and capital accounts, the foreign central bank generally changed the value of its currency in terms of the U.S. dollar. This was so under the Bretton Woods Accord because if the United States changed the value of the dollar, the change occurred between the dollar and all other currencies, even though the dollar was out of alignment with only one or a few of the foreign currencies. This, and the fact that other countries demanded dollars for international reserves, resulted in a fortuitous position for U.S. monetary authorities who were able to execute monetary policy relatively independently of international considerations in this period.

A balance of payments deficit on current and capital accounts can also be caused by increases in the capital outflows of a country, ceteris paribus. If a country experienced an increased net capital outflow, this had the same effect as an increase of the same magnitude in the trade deficit. Likewise, if a country experienced an increased net capital inflow, this had the same effect on the balance of payments on current and capital accounts as an increase in the trade surplus. As we have seen, ceteris paribus, such capital flows resulted from changes in domestic interest rates relative to foreign rates.

Revalue Under fixed exchange rates, when the monetary authorities increase the value of a currency in relation to the official reserve currency.

RECAP

The Bretton Woods Accord of 1944 established fixed exchange rates among major world currencies. The U.S. dollar backed by gold served as the official reserve asset, and other countries defined their currencies in terms of the dollar. If a country other than the United States had a deficit in its balance of payments, it used supplies of dollars to purchase its own currency

---

[6] Among other things, revaluation could reduce net exports and have a negative impact on employment in Germany.

to maintain fixed exchange rates. If a country other than the United States had a surplus in its balance of payments, it demanded dollars to maintain the value of its currency.

Monetary Policy Under the Bretton Woods Accord

The Bretton Woods Accord limited the ability of foreign countries to pursue their own monetary policies. Each country had to support its currency if market forces were causing its value to deviate from the agreed-upon exchange rate. If a country wanted to pursue a more expansionary policy, the monetary authorities would increase the supply of reserves available to the banking system. Ceteris paribus, interest rates would fall and the monetary and credit aggregates increase. Such a policy might result in a deficit in the balance of payments on current and capital accounts for two reasons. First, ceteris paribus, net exports (exports minus imports) would decrease due to the rise in domestic income.[7] Second, because of falling interest rates, ceteris paribus, the country would also experience a capital outflow that would further contribute to the deficit in the balance of payments on current and capital accounts. The central bank of the deficit country would have to use supplies of dollars to purchase its own currency to maintain the agreed-upon exchange rate. The act of buying back its own currency would at least partially undo the stimulatory effects of the injection of reserves and would limit the monetary authority's ability to pursue an expansionary policy. When a country ran out of dollars, devaluation would be considered and perhaps, of necessity, be implemented. Such action entails discreet changes in the exchange rate and subsequent destabilization of financial markets and the domestic economy.

If a country wished to pursue contractionary policies relative to the rest of the world, its balance of payments on current and capital accounts would, ceteris paribus, move toward a surplus position. Net exports would increase.[8] The higher interest rate would also lead to a capital inflow. Both factors would put upward pressure on the exchange rate. The ability of the monetary authorities to limit the growth of the money supply would be reduced by the necessity to supply its currency to maintain fixed exchange rates. The supplying of its own currency would at least partially undo the contractionary effects. After a time, if the trade surplus and capital inflow persisted, a revaluation of the currency would have to occur. Again, financial markets and the economy would be destabilized.

Because the U.S. dollar served as the international reserve currency, the foreign country initiated the adjustment in its exchange rate in terms of the dollar when necessary. For many years, this allowed the United States relatively more latitude in pursuing domestic monetary policy. As long as foreign central banks were accumulating dollars to serve as international reserves, the United States could pursue expansionary domestic policies that resulted in balance of payment deficits on current and capital accounts with no need to worry about exchange rate pressures on their own or foreign currencies. Once for-

---

[7] An increase in domestic income causes imports to increase. At the same time, if the expansionary policy causes domestic prices to increase, then exports also decrease.

[8] Imports would fall relative to exports, and if prices also fell due to the contractionary policies, exports would increase as well.

eign countries had acquired sufficient reserves, persistent U.S. deficits on current and capital accounts would result in the need for foreign countries to revalue their currencies. By the same token, persistent U.S. current and capital accounts surpluses would result in the need for foreign countries to devalue. Such a fixed system could be maintained only if countries agreed to and were able to support their currencies and, if needed, to periodically and orderly revalue or devalue them.

The need to periodically revalue or devalue was related to how far the domestic monetary and fiscal policies of the countries that participated in the agreement diverged from one another. Over time, if different countries pursued different policies, then some countries would expand relatively faster than others leading to exchange rate imbalances. For example, either expansionary fiscal or monetary policy could cause a country to grow faster than another. Likewise, contractionary fiscal and monetary policy could cause a country to grow slower.

To the extent that countries experienced different growth rates, inflation rates, and interest rate structures, imbalances in the current and capital accounts would persist. If a country had more expansionary policies than the United States, it would experience chronic deficits in the current and capital accounts and the need to devalue. On the other hand, if a country had more contractionary policies, it would experience persistent surpluses and the need to revalue. If countries refused to make the necessary changes in their exchange rates, the system of fixed exchange rates established at Bretton Woods would break down.

During the 1960s and 1970s, some countries including the United States expanded their economies and their domestic money supplies relatively faster than others such as Japan and Germany. Inflationary pressures in the United States resulted from monetary and fiscal policies associated with the Great Society's war on poverty and the Vietnam War buildup in the second half of the 1960s. The result was that some central banks outside the United States had accumulated more dollars than they wished to hold as reserve assets. Rather than revaluing their currencies, they requested conversion of these unwanted dollars to gold. As more and more central banks chose to do so, it became clear that the United States would not be able to continue to redeem the dollars in gold. It was the suspension of the international conversion of dollars to gold in late 1971 that led to the final collapse of the Bretton Woods Exchange System that had been in place since 1944.

 RECAP

The need to maintain fixed exchange rates limited the ability of a country to pursue its own monetary policy. The United States was in the unique position of being able to run persistent balance of payments deficits as long as foreign central banks were accumulating dollars to serve as international reserves. Once countries had accumulated sufficient reserves, excess dollars would be presented to the United States to be converted to gold. Divergent monetary and fiscal policies led to the ultimate collapse of the system in 1971 as the United States was unable to convert dollars back to gold at the agreed-upon rate.

To correct some of the strains in the old system and to allow markets to adjust to changes on a continuous basis, a flexible exchange rate system was put into place. As we shall see, this system was not without its problems.

Flexible Exchange Rates Since 1971

Under a **flexible exchange rate system,** the value of a nation's currency is determined by market forces. For the U.S. dollar, the exchange rate is determined by the demand for and supply of dollars in international markets. The supply of dollars/month reflects U.S. demand for foreign goods, services, and securities. Ceteris paribus, quantity supplied is a positive function of the exchange rate. The demand for dollars reflects foreign demand for U.S. goods, services, and securities. Ceteris paribus, quantity demanded is a negative function of the exchange rate. Next, consider the case in which the foreign exchange market is initially in equilibrium but that equilibrium is disturbed by a change in one of the following factors: (1) a rise in U.S. income, (2) a rise in U.S. prices relative to the dollar prices of foreign goods, or (3) a rise in foreign interest rates relative to U.S. interest rates. Ceteris paribus, the result will be an increase in U.S. demand for foreign goods, services, and securities, and, thus, an increase in the supply of dollars. The market will gravitate to a new equilibrium at a lower exchange rate that coincides with a depreciation of the dollar.

Likewise, if foreign incomes, foreign inflation, or U.S. interest rates rise, ceteris paribus, there will be an increase in foreign demand for U.S. goods, services, and securities, and thus an increase in the demand for dollars. The market will gravitate to a new equilibrium at a higher exchange rate that corresponds to an appreciation of the dollar.

To summarize, factors such as domestic and foreign income and interest rates affect exchange rates, and "flexible" exchange rates immediately adjust to changing market conditions and expectations. Look at Exhibit 24-1, which reviews the basics of exchange rate determination under flexible exchange rates as first presented in Chapter 9.

With the enactment of a flexible exchange rate system in late 1971, countries in some ways gained greater independence in establishing their own monetary policies. A monetary objective or policy would not be compromised by the need for a country to maintain the agreed-upon exchange rate as under the Bretton Woods Accord. No longer would a country have to support its domestic currency if market forces were causing the currency to depreciate or appreciate. As discussed in Chapter 9, depreciation occurs when the value of a currency falls in terms of another currency under a flexible exchange rate system. Likewise, if the value of a currency rises, the currency is said to have appreciated.

The enactment of flexible exchange rates also added a new element of risk to international trade—the risk that changes in the exchange rate can adversely affect profit. Under fixed exchange rates, the **exchange rate risk** is low and related only to the possibility of devaluation or revaluation. Most trades are executed assuming little or no exchange rate risk. Not so, however, for a flexible exchange rate system. In this case, when an agreement is made to export or import goods and services, prices are set at one point in time, but

Flexible Exchange Rate System An exchange rate system in which the value of a currency is determined by supply and demand.

Exchange Rate Risk The risk that changes in the exchange rate can adversely affect the value of foreign exchange or foreign financial assets.

Exhibit 24-1 ◆
The Market for
Dollars

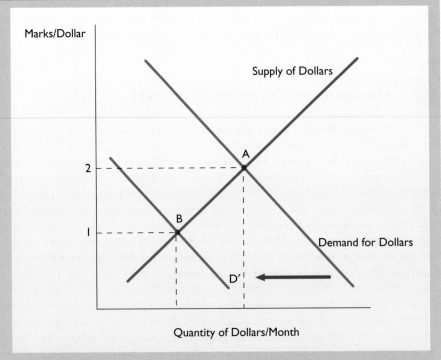

The quantity of dollars is measured on the horizontal axis while the exchange rate (marks per dollar) is measured on the vertical axis. The quantity supplied of dollars/month, reflecting U.S. demand for foreign goods, services, and securities, is, ceteris paribus, a positive function of the exchange rate while the quantity demanded for dollars/month is a negative function of the exchange rate. In this case, quantity demanded is equal to quantity supplied at point A, producing an equilibrium exchange rate of 2 marks. From the initial equilibrium at point A, assume the equilibrium is disturbed by a change in one of the following factors: 1) the mark price of U.S. goods and services rises relative to the mark price of foreign goods and services because of inflation in the United States, 2) foreign interest rates rise relative to U.S. interest rates, or 3) a fall in foreign incomes relative to U.S. incomes. The result will be a reduction in the demand for U.S. goods, services, and financial instruments by foreigners and thus a reduction in

the transaction is usually not completed until a later date. Changes in the exchange rate after the agreement is made and before it is concluded can reduce or even eliminate the profit from the transaction. Such an added risk could greatly reduce the volume of trade.

Along with greater exchange rate risk came new ways of managing risk. As noted in Chapter 9, a foreign exchange futures contract is a standardized contract to deliver a given amount of foreign exchange on a date in the future at a price determined today. Thus, if an exporter knows she will be paid say 1 million Japanese yen in six months, she can enter into a foreign exchange futures contract whereby she can lock in today the number of dollars she will receive in six months for the 1 million yen. In this way, she can effectively reduce or even eliminate the exchange rate risk. The growth in foreign

the demand for dollars—shown as a leftward shift of the demand function above. The new equilibrium at point B results in a depreciation of the dollar from 2 marks to 1 mark.

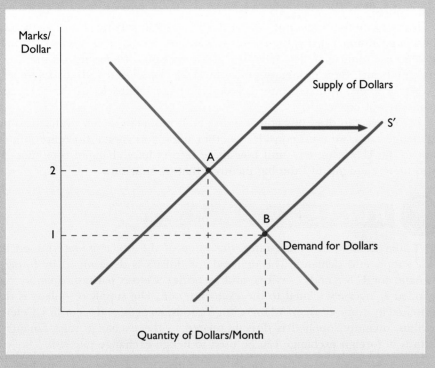

Next, assume that the economy is again at the initial equilibrium exchange rate of $1 to 2 marks. The equilibrium is disturbed by a change in one of the following factors: 1) a rise in U.S. income, 2) a rise in U.S. prices relative to the dollar prices of foreign goods, or 3) a rise in foreign interest rates relative to U.S. interest rates. The result will be an increase in U.S. demand for foreign goods, services, and securities, and thus, an increase in the supply of dollars—shown as a rightward shift of the supply function above. The new equilibrium at point B results in a depreciation of the dollar as the equilibrium exchange rate falls from 2 marks to 1 mark.

exchange futures markets can be attributed to the tremendous growth in trade, the increase in foreign investment, and the increased volatility of exchange rates under flexible exchange rates. These markets, which have greatly expanded since the mid-1970s, allow importers, exporters, and investors in foreign securities to hedge exchange rate risks. Hence, they reduce the negative impact on trade of potentially volatile exchange rates. But, solutions to one problem often illuminate additional challenges and complications. Such is the case with flexible exchange rates, as we shall soon see.

If a country is growing faster than its neighbors, ceteris paribus, the balance of trade can move into a deficit position, with resulting deterioration in its current and capital accounts. Even though the country no longer has to defend its currency to maintain fixed exchange rates, it must consider other international ramifications of its monetary policy. Perhaps the most important effects are capital flows and the conceivable depreciation or appreciation of its currency. Depreciation and appreciation, in turn, can feed back to the domestic economy and cause changes in the growth rate of income through net exports.[9]

If international trade and capital flows are small relative to the aggregate level of economic activity, then monetary authorities may have greater latitude in the execution of policy. However, if international trade and capital flows are significant, then monetary policy must be discharged with an awareness of how it affects foreign countries and what the feedbacks to the domestic economy will be.[10]

Before we can draw any conclusions about monetary policy under flexible exchange rates, we must consider whether trade and capital flows are important to the U.S. economy, and how these factors have changed over time. It is to these elements of "the big picture" that we now turn.

RECAP

Under flexible exchange rates, the value of the dollar is determined by supply and demand. The demand for dollars is determined by foreign demand for U.S. goods, services, and securities. Ceteris paribus, quantity demanded is inversely related to the exchange rate. The supply of dollars is determined by domestic demand for foreign goods, services, and securities. Ceteris paribus, quantity supplied is directly related to the exchange rate. Financial futures in foreign exchange can be used to hedge exchange rate risk.

Monetary Policy and the Growth of International Trade and Finance

The Growth of Trade and Removal of Barriers to Capital Flows

Another international evolution has occurred since Bretton Woods. Nations of the world have become increasingly interdependent because of the growth of world trade. That is, developments abroad and developments in this country have greatly increased the volume and potential of trade. For the United States, in 1995, exports slightly exceeded $804 billion while imports slightly exceeded $906 billion in an economy where gross domestic product (GDP) was just over $7,247 billion. In 1960, exports were roughly $25.3 billion and imports $22.8 billion, while gross national product was $526.6 billion. Thus, in 1960, exports were 4.8 percent of GDP ($25.3/$526.6) while imports were 4.3 percent of GDP ($22.8/$526.6). By 1995, exports had grown to 11.1 per-

---

[9] Remember, net exports are a component of aggregate demand.

[10] In some ways, U.S. monetary authorities have always been aware of how their monetary policies affected interest rates, inflation, and growth in other countries. Only in recent decades has there been an increased awareness of how foreign events can at times influence the U.S. economy and hence, the formulation and effects of policy.

cent of GDP ($804/$7,247) while imports had increased even more to 12.5 percent of GDP ($906/$7,247).

The growth in trade has been partially the result of a concerted effort by developed nations. Based on the recognition of the mutual gains from trade, countries have consistently worked to reduce trade barriers since the end of World War II.[11] The **General Agreement of Tariffs and Trade (GATT)** Treaty, an agreement to reduce tariffs and other trade barriers, was originally signed in 1947 by 23 nations. Under GATT, members meet periodically in extended meetings to negotiate tariff and other trade barrier reductions. The eighth round, which began in 1986, ended successfully in 1994 with substantive trade barrier reductions and the creation of the **World Trade Organization (WTO)** to arbitrate trade disputes and impose sanctions on member nations that violate the GATT.

In addition to GATT, other trade agreements have been consummated including the **North American Free Trade Agreement (NAFTA),** which is a regional trade agreement signed in 1994 by Mexico, the United States, and Canada. NAFTA has and is expected to continue to increase trade among its participants. The **European Union (EU),** another regional trade agreement, has removed most trade barriers among the 15 participating European countries. Many other regions are in various stages of mutually advantageous trade agreements. Trade has occurred in all currencies of the major nations while the U.S. dollar, British pound, German mark, and Japanese yen have come to dominate.[12] Consequently, the United States affects and is affected by what goes on in foreign markets to a much greater extent than during previous eras when trade was less important.

Coincidentally with the growth in trade, a general trend for governments to remove barriers to international capital flows began in the 1970s. The dismantling was virtually completed by the 1980s. In addition, major breakthroughs in telecommunications technologies and the electronic transfer of funds allowed funds to be transferred almost instantaneously anywhere in the world. These two factors have created a worldwide **foreign exchange market** where the buying and selling of different currencies take place and where the "wheels are greased" for international trade and capital flows among nations. In 1995, the foreign exchange market traded more than $1 trillion per day. This amounted to the equivalent of about $200 per day per person in the world, thus making it the largest market in the world. Since enormous sums of funds flow with lightening speed, the ability for funds to find their highest return is greatly increased. From an economic standpoint, economic efficiency is increased when funds flow to the location of their highest return. At the same time, the potential for instability in world financial markets is enormous as was demonstrated by the collapse of the Mexican peso in late 1994. The

General Agreement of Tariffs and Trade (GATT) An agreement among 23 nations originally signed in 1947 to hold meetings that lead to reduced tariffs and other trade barriers.

World Trade Organization (WTO) Created by the eighth round of GATT in 1986 to arbitrate trade disputes and impose sanctions on member nations that violate the GATT.

North American Free Trade Agreement (NAFTA) A regional trade agreement signed in 1994 by Mexico, the United States, and Canada to reduce trade barriers.

European Union (EU) A regional agreement among 15 European nations promoting the removal of all trade barriers and the establishment of a common currency.

Foreign Exchange Market The market for buying and selling the different currencies of the world.

---

[11] Any economics principles text outlines the basic premises of comparative advantage, which support the argument that all trading parties can have more of all goods and services if free trade is allowed.

[12] Since the U.S. dollar served as an international reserve asset up until 1971 and since much of the world's trade between nations was denominated in U.S. dollars, the dollar was the dominant world currency under the Bretton Woods Accord. Under flexible exchange rates, other currencies have gained in importance relative to the dollar. However, the dollar still holds a prominent position in world finance, and as of the early 1990s, still accounted for 60 percent of international reserves. The Japanese yen and German mark account for another 28 percent of international reserves.

peso depreciated more than 40 percent in a two-month period leaving the Mexican economy and financial markets in a severely depressed state.

Capital and Real Flows in Response to a Contractionary Monetary Policy in the United States

Capital flows jeopardize or weaken the intended effects of monetary policy. For example, if the United States engages in contractionary monetary policy to slow the level of economic activity, the result is that, ceteris paribus, capital flows in from abroad and makes attempts to slow the level of economic activity more difficult. Likewise, if a country wishes to speed up economic activity and consequently lowers interest rates, it becomes vulnerable to capital outflows, ceteris paribus, with the resultant depressing effects on the level of economic activity.

Telecommunications advances in a world without barriers to capital flows have hastened the response and adjustment of worldwide capital flows to changes in U.S. policy. If U.S. interest rates move up relative to interest rates abroad, ceteris paribus, the demand for dollars increases and puts upward pressure on the exchange rate. In addition, because of the reduced demand for foreign financial assets, ceteris paribus, there is also a tendency for foreign asset prices to fall and foreign interest rates to rise. On the other hand, if U.S. rates fall relative to foreign rates, ceteris paribus, the movement is towards foreign financial assets and away from dollar-denominated assets, with subsequent downward pressure on the dollar exchange rate. Changes in the supply and demand for financial assets cause capital flows that will bring real interest rates between countries into closer alignment. Given a change in U.S. interest rates, freer capital movements suggest immediate changes in the exchange rate and eventual interest rate adjustments in foreign economies.

Assuming the increase in the domestic interest rate causes the dollar to appreciate, the dollar price of foreign goods falls while the foreign price of U.S. goods rises leading to a decrease in exports and an increase in imports. Thus, net exports will also fall in response to an appreciation of the exchange rate. The latter effect reinforces the contractionary effects of a rise in domestic interest rates.

Two other effects work to increase the growth of net exports in response to contractionary policy. First, the increase in domestic interest rates could cause a reduction in domestic demand as the demand for interest-sensitive expenditures falls[13]. The reduction in aggregate demand decreases the demand for imports. Second, if the slowing of the economy causes domestic prices to fall relative to foreign prices, then ceteris paribus, both foreign and domestic customers have an incentive to switch to domestically produced goods and services. These two effects work to increase net exports and to mitigate the decline in net exports that results from the appreciation of the dollar.

Nevertheless, in most cases, the appreciation of the dollar is believed to cause a larger decrease in net exports than the combined increases in net exports resulting from the two additional factors discussed in the previous paragraph. Hence, the total effect of contractionary monetary policy is to decrease net exports. Despite that it may not always be the case, we usually

---

[13] Recall the analysis from Chapter 20.

The European Union

As we saw in the Looking Out in Chapter 9, 15 countries of Western Europe have been moving in the direction of establishing a single currency unit called the *Euro* by 1999. To establish a common currency, countries must surrender their ability to change their money supply, interest rates, and exchange rates.* Thus, countries have to give up autonomy over their own monetary policy. In addition, countries must meet criteria regarding the government debt relative to GDP and annual government budget deficits. In order to meet these criteria, countries must also surrender control over their fiscal policies. Adopting a common currency, which is the equivalent of perfectly fixed exchange rates, implies the necessity to coordinate monetary and fiscal policies and the loss of macro policy flexibility. Of course, those who support the common currency do so because of the tremendous reductions in the transactions costs of making exchanges with a common currency, which translate to higher economic growth.

*For a description of the specific criteria that must be met for a country in the European Union to participate in a single currency, see the Looking Out section of Chapter 9.

assume that higher U.S. interest rates lead to an appreciation of the domestic currency, capital inflows, a decrease in net exports, and a larger trade deficit (or smaller trade surplus).

The impact of U.S. monetary policy also depends upon the monetary and fiscal policies of other countries. If other central banks are also attempting to slow their economies at the same time that the U.S. monetary authorities are, then what happens to exchange rates depends upon the relative magnitudes of the interest rate changes among the various countries. Thus, we can conclude that interest rates and exchange rates are jointly determined by the monetary and fiscal policies of the various interdependent countries and the resulting market forces.

In summary, the growth of trade and capital flows has occurred in a world that switched from fixed to flexible exchange rates. Given that the central bank is no longer necessarily committed to maintaining the value of its currency, the central bank gains independence in formulating and executing monetary policy. Because of the increased interdependence of economies and the greater ease with which capital flows between borders, if a country chooses to run a monetary policy far different from its neighbors, it is limited to the extent to which it can do so because of the offsetting effect of capital flows. For example, if the U.S. wants to maintain interest rates lower than the rest of the world, it will experience currency depreciation and a capital outflow that will increase its interest rates from what they would be otherwise. Although a country no longer has to maintain a fixed exchange rate, new complications have been added to the execution of monetary policy in that capital flows can occur in response to interest rate differentials. In addition, changes in the exchange rate will effect net exports. External factors are likely to dampen the effects of any action that the Fed takes that results in relative interest rate or income changes. The effects are larger the more important trade is to the domestic economy and the greater ease with which capital flows between nations. In the near term, an increase in U.S. rates relative to foreign rates usually increases the exchange rate of the dollar and capital inflows, ceteris paribus. Using similar reasoning, decreases in U.S. rates relative to foreign rates lead to decreases in the exchange rate of the dollar and capital outflows, ceteris paribus. Exhibit 24–2 shows how investors compare the return on domestic and foreign financial assets.

To conclude, the crux of the dilemma is that under fixed exchange rates, countries are limited in running their own monetary policy because of the need to maintain the value of their currency. Under flexible exchange rates, they can also be limited. If they try to run a policy different from the rest of the world, capital and real flows will occur that will complicate the results and jeopardize that policy. What does all this mean for the future? In a nutshell, it means that in all probability, the future will entail greater monetary policy coordination between nations. It is the specifics to which we now turn.

 ## RECAP

Intersnational trade has increased because of the efforts of developed nations since World War II. Capital flows have increased because of the removal of barriers to capital flows and technological advances in the transfer of funds. Under fixed exchange rates, the need to support the agreed-upon exchange rate limits the ability of a country to pursue its own policies. Under flexible exchange rates, a country can pursue its own policies but if they differ from policies in the rest of the world, changes in net exports and capital flows can mitigate the intended effects of the policy.

 ## The Globalization of Monetary Policy

When considering the future, one must consider a wide range of possibilities. In the broadest sense, major world economies will either remain on a version of the present system of flexible exchange rates or return to a version of fixed exchange rates. In each of these cases, the type of system and road to its adoption varies widely. Indeed tomorrow is uncertain.

With regard to a fixed rate system, such a system can be sustained only if the growth and inflation rates of the participating countries are similar and only if devaluations and revaluations occur in an orderly manner. To achieve such a result for a substantial period of time, both the monetary policies and the fiscal policies of the participating countries must be coordinated. This is so because divergent monetary and fiscal policies lead to different growth rates of income, different inflation rates, and different interest rate structures. If economies grow at different rates, changes in net exports and interest rates cause exchange rate pressures. However, if monetary and fiscal policies are similar, it is possible for large benefits to be reaped from the increased trade and integration that fixed exchange rates could encourage. Not only would increased trade allow countries to enjoy a higher standard of living, but capital

LOOKING FORWARD

Will the Fed Have Less Power to Affect the Economy in the Future?

In the early 1990s, Japan and Mexico struggled to fight the ravages of deflation. The banking systems in both countries experienced near collapse because of falling asset prices. As prices fell, banks owed more to depositors than the value of their assets. Loans to buy property or stocks became worthless as the land and stock prices fell and borrowers defaulted. The ability of the monetary authorities seemed limited to counter the breakdown of the economy as banks became dubious about making new loans. In Japan, reluctant taxpayers were forced to inject taxpayers' funds into the insolvent system. In Mexico, the government, which had privatized the banking system in the early 1990s, was forced to adopt a costly loan purchase program to aid the ailing banks.

The United States experienced no similar collapse in the 1990s. However, the Fed and other central banks would have less control over their domestic economies in such a situation than in the past, because of the following reasons:

1. The banking system is getting a declining share of intermediation.
2. Control over banks is less stringent as banks find new ways to attract deposits that are not subject to reserve requirements.
3. Global forces are more important than ever before.

As a *Wall Street Journal* article puts it,

> An even more pervasive myth is that central bankers have enormous powers to foster economic growth. Paul Volcker (Chairperson of the Fed, 1979–1987) was wryly amused at magazine articles calling him the most powerful man on earth. He knew that global market forces were far more powerful than the Fed. But at least he had stronger controls in the early 1980s over the money supply than the Fed has today.*

George Melloan, "Don't Bank on the Fed to Ease Future Shocks," *The Wall Street Journal,* November 27, 1995, p. A17.

flows would allow for surplus funds to flow to their highest return. The downside is twofold: Countries that value their independence or that have divergent goals with respect to unemployment and inflation would not do well under a fixed exchange rate system. In addition, countries may not have the political discipline to stick with fixed exchange rates if domestic problems become paramount.

Under flexible exchange rate systems, futures markets in foreign exchange can be used to hedge. This will allow participants to achieve most of the gains in trade associated with a fixed rate system. With flexible exchange rates, competitive forces and the price mechanism exert a much greater function in international financial markets, which encourages economic efficiency. In the 1980s, deregulation of financial markets and the growth of market economies around the world had underwritten these effects.

Under flexible exchange rates, since capital flows limit the abilities of countries to execute policies that deviate significantly from the rest of the world,

Exhibit 24-2 ◆
Comparing Returns
in a Globalized
Economy

When comparing financial assets denominated in the same currency, one considers the return, the maturity, and the default risk. If assets are denominated in different currencies, another factor that investors and borrowers must consider is the exchange rate risk. The exchange rate risk is the risk that the exchange rate between two currencies will change and alter the real return of an investment. For example, assume that an investor expects the exchange rate between the dollar and the Mexican peso to remain constant, and the U.S. investor converts dollars to pesos to make an investment denominated in pesos that earns a 10 percent nominal return. If the peso unexpectedly depreciates by 10 percent, the entire 10 percent return is wiped out when the pesos are converted back to dollars. Consequently when evaluating assets denominated in different currencies, an exchange rate risk must also be factored into the decision-making process to capture the possibility that exchange rates will move in a detrimental direction.

In globalized financial markets, financial market players compare expected rates of return on assets denominated in various currencies, including their own. To do so, they must convert all returns to an equivalent return in the domestic currency. The nominal rate of return in a domestic currency on an investment that is denominated in a foreign currency is the nominal foreign interest rate plus the expected change in the exchange rate less an adjustment for risk that results from the uncertainty of the future exchange rate. Equation (24-1) depicts such a situation.

$$(24\text{-}1) \qquad\qquad I_{US} = I_{FOR} + E$$

where I_{US} is the nominal U.S. return on an investment in a foreign asset that earns the nominal foreign interest rate, I_{FOR}, and where E is the expected percent change in the exchange rate plus an exchange rate risk factor.

Lenders compare this nominal U.S. return, I_{US}, with the U.S. interest rate and choose the instrument that offers the highest return, while bor-

incentive exists for nations to coordinate their policies so that a workable policy acceptable to all can be found. Even at this time, there is a great deal of monetary policy coordination between developed countries. Such coordination can be spearheaded by an international organization such as the International Monetary Fund, which was created at the Bretton Woods Conference. In addition, informal groups of major trading partners regularly meet to discuss policy regimes and options, and often communicate and work together to coordinate policies. One such group, called the G-7 nations includes the United States, Britain, France, Germany, Japan, Canada, and Italy.[14]

---

[14]Actually, the G-7 nations resulted from a 1986 expansion of a Group of five (G-5) nations that had consulted since the flexible exchange rate system was put into place in the early 1970s. The G-5 nations included the United States, Britain, France, Japan, and Germany. In a "managed" flexible exchange rate system exchange rates are determined by the forces of supply and demand, with occasional central bank intervention. Since 1971, the central banks of the G-5 or G-7 nations have frequently intervened by buying and selling in currency markets to affect exchange rates.

rowers choose to borrow in the market that offers the lowest rate as expressed in their domestic currencies. Because of market adjustments, if the nominal U.S. return is greater than the nominal foreign return plus the exchange rate adjustment, lenders will supply more funds in the U.S. market and borrowers will borrow more funds in foreign markets. Such adjustments will continue until the U.S. and foreign nominal interest rates are equal except for the expected exchange rate adjustment and risk.

In reality, borrowers and lenders are making decisions based on the expected real return, rather than nominal returns. The real interest rate (return) is the nominal return less expected inflation. At times, we may wish to express returns between nations in terms of real interest rates as opposed to nominal rates. For the United States to do so, we must subtract expected U.S. inflation from each nominal rate in Equation (24-1) as in Equation (24-2). In equilibrium, the real U.S. interest rate, R_{US}, will be:

$$(24\text{-}2) \qquad R_{US} = I_{US} - P_{US} = I_{FOR} + E - P_{US}$$

where P_{US} is the expected U.S. inflation rate. Likewise, we can express the nominal foreign rate, I_{FOR}, in terms of the real foreign rate, R_F, plus the expected foreign inflation, P_F, to arrive at the equilibrium real U.S. interest rate in terms of the foreign real rate, and domestic and foreign expected inflation. The results are summarized in Equation (24-3):

$$(24\text{-}3) \qquad R_{US} = R_F + P_F + E - P_{US}$$

Just as in foreign trade, foreign exchange futures markets can be used to hedge the exchange rate risk when investing in foreign financial assets. This implies that the exchange rate risk—E in Equation (24-3)—can be greatly reduced or eliminated. We can conclude that with greater capital mobility, the real U.S. and foreign interest rates will tend to be equalized after differences in expected inflation have been taken into account.*

*Another fact, which we ignore here for simplicity, is that P_F and E are not independent.

As we look forward to the 21st century, it is difficult to imagine how the Fed will execute monetary policy because the intermediate targets the Fed presently uses may no longer be relevant or effectively related to the level of economic activity in a globalized financial system. In a globalized financial system, the Fed must increasingly be aware of domestic exchange rates, capital flows, and foreign policies. Although the role of the Fed remains the same, new procedures and regulations, including some international regulations, may of necessity evolve. International considerations will play a bigger role. Policies will be designed for a world with increasing trade and with minimal barriers to international capital flows that can occur with great speed.

To conclude we can say that coordination is imperative under fixed exchange rates. In fact, it was the lack of coordination of macroeconomic policies that led to the breakdown of the Bretton Woods Accord. At the same time, experiences in the 1970s, 1980s, and 1990s suggest that policy coordination is still desirable under a flexible exchange rate regime. While flexible exchange rates increase the potential independence of monetary policy, the increasing openness of world trade and finance has elevated the interdependencies among nations. Flexible exchange rates allow the central bank to set its interest rates somewhat independently of other countries. However, capital mobility means that a change in the interest rates relative to other countries is compensated for by changes in exchange rates and capital flows. Thus, central bank freedom to set interest rates is only as great as its acceptance of the foreign exchange rate movements and the capital flows connected with a change in interest rates. Despite this climate of change, one factor seems highly probable: monetary policy in the future will most likely involve more global coordination and cooperation whether it be under fixed or flexible exchange rates.

 RECAP

The future will require countries to coordinate their monetary policies regardless of whether exchange rates are fixed or flexible as countries become more interdependent due to the growth of trade and capital flows.

Summary of Major Points

1. The Bretton Woods Accord of 1944 established fixed exchange rates between the U.S. dollar and other major currencies. Under the accord, foreign countries defined their currencies in terms of the U.S. dollar and agreed to buy or sell dollars, the official reserve asset, to maintain the agreed-upon exchange rates. The dollar, in turn, was defined in terms of gold, and the United States agreed to convert any unwanted dollars of foreign central banks and treasuries into gold.

2. Under fixed exchange rates, if a country other than the United States had a deficit in its balance of payments on current and capital accounts, it used supplies of dollars to purchase its own currency to maintain the exchange value. Likewise if such a country had a surplus in the balance of payments on current and capital accounts, it demanded dollars to maintain or support the value of its currency. Persistent deficits and surpluses resulted in the need by foreign countries to devalue or revalue, respectively. The need to maintain the value of one's currency under fixed exchange rates limited the ability of a country to pursue its own monetary policy independently of other participants in the agreement.

3. The United States was in the unique position of being able to run persistent deficits in the balance of payments on current and capital accounts while foreign central banks were accumulating dollars to serve as international reserves. Once foreign central banks had acquired sufficient reserves, the ability of the United States to run deficits in current and capital accounts was also limited.

4. Because countries had divergent monetary and fiscal policies, exchange rate imbalances persisted. Eventually, the United States was unable to maintain the conversion of dollars into gold and the Bretton Woods Sys-

tem of fixed exchange rates collapsed in 1971. It was replaced by a system of flexible exchange rates.

5. Under flexible exchange rates, the value of the dollar is determined by the demand and supply of dollars. The demand for dollars is determined by foreign demand for U.S. goods, services, and securities. Ceteris paribus, quantity demanded is inversely related to the exchange rate. The supply of dollars is determined by domestic demand for foreign goods, services, and securities. Ceteris paribus, quantity supplied is directly related to the exchange rate. Flexible exchange rates freed countries from the need to support their currencies to maintain fixed exchange rates. Each country in some ways gained greater latitude in adjusting its domestic monetary policy. At the same time, financial futures markets in foreign exchange can be used to mitigate the impact on trade from greater exchange rate risk.

6. Even though countries do not have to support their currencies under flexible exchange rates, they must be aware of the effects that their monetary and fiscal policies have on the exchange rate, capital flows, and net exports. Monetary policy must be executed with an understanding of the international ramifications and the feedbacks to the domestic economy. This is particularly true if net exports are a relatively large component of aggregate demand and if capital flows are unrestricted.

7. Trade has increased because of the concerted efforts of developed nations since World War II. These efforts result from the recognition of the gains from trade to all trading partners. Capital flows have also increased because of the removal of capital barriers and because of technological advances that have increased the speed of such flows. Regardless of whether exchange rates are fixed or flexible, monetary policy in the future will most likely entail greater global coordination as economies grow more interdependent because of the growth in trade and capital flows.

Key Terms

Bretton Woods Accord
Devalue
European Union (EU)
Exchange Rate Risk
Fixed Exchange Rate System
Flexible Exchange Rate System
Foreign Exchange Market
General Agreement of Tariffs and
    Trade (GATT)

North American Free Trade
    Agreement (NAFTA)
Official Reserve Account
Official Reserve Currency
Revalue
World Trade Organization (WTO)

Review Questions

1. Briefly explain the Bretton Woods Exchange Rate System. When was it created? When and why did the system collapse?

2. Under the Bretton Woods System, the U.S. dollar was the official reserve currency. How did this affect the U.S. balance of payments on current

and capital accounts? Could the United States experience large balance of payments deficits on current and capital accounts indefinitely?

3. Assume you work at the central bank of a small country that is considering an expansionary monetary policy to speed up the level of economic activity. Given fixed exchange rates, advise the president of your country what will happen to net exports given the monetary expansion. What action will the central bank have to take to support the agreed-upon exchange rate? How will that affect the expansionary policy?

4. Argue that fixed exchange rates are preferable to flexible exchange rates. Do the opposite.

5. For each of the following situations, tell what will happen to the balance of payments on current and capital accounts in the United States, ceteris paribus.
   a. Domestic income increases.
   b. Domestic interest rates fall.
   c. Foreign income increases.
   d. Foreign interest rates fall.
   e. Domestic inflation increases.
   f. Foreign inflation increases.

6. For each of the situations in question 4, tell what will happen to the exchange rate, assuming flexible exchange rates.

7. Consider the statement and explain whether you agree or disagree: Flexible exchange rates allow nations to pursue their own monetary policies.

8. What is the purpose of foreign exchange futures agreements under fixed exchange rates? under flexible exchange rates?

9. Briefly explain how interest rates on assets of comparable risk and maturity will tend to be equalized in a world without capital barriers.

10. Under a flexible exchange rate system, what effect does contractionary monetary policy have on the exchange rate?

11. Why is a country limited in executing its own monetary policy under a fixed exchange rate system? How is it limited under a flexible exchange rate system?

12. How can monetary policy coordination among countries increase the degree to which monetary policy can be used to pursue macroeconomic goals under fixed exchange rates? under flexible exchange rates?

13. Could high U.S. interest rates affect investment spending in foreign countries? Explain.

Analytical Questions

14. Use graphs to demonstrate what will happen to the value of the dollar in terms of the Japanese yen in each of the following situations:
    a. U.S. income increases.
    b. U.S. interest rates fall.
    c. Japanese income increases.
    d. Japanese interest rates fall.

    e.   U.S. inflation increases.

    f.   Japanese inflation increases.

15.   If the nominal U.S. interest rate is 10 percent and U.S. inflation is 6 percent, what is the real U.S. interest rate. What is the real U.S. rate in terms of foreign interest rates?

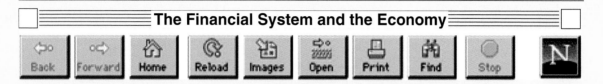

The Financial System and the Economy

1.   The FOMC Meeting Minutes contain the committee's authorization for foreign currency operations. Access the minutes at (http://woodrow.mpls.frb.fed.US/info/policy/fomcmin/961.txt) and arrow down to the Committee's "Authorization for Foreign Currency Operations." According to this directive, which foreign currencies are to be bought and sold by the Fed?

2.   The gopher site listed below has a useful and interesting article, "Strong Dollar, Weak Dollar," that examines how the U.S. dollar's value relates to other currencies and how changes in its value affect international trade and the open economy. Access this at gopher://gopher.great-lakes.net:2200/11/partners/ChicagoFed/genpubs) and answer the following:

    a.   What is meant by a "strong" dollar? Who gains from a strong dollar?

    b.   Where are foreign exchange trades completed?

    c.   During the 1980s, the value of the U.S. dollar was high relative to other currencies. What effect did this have on the economy?

Suggested Readings

For a broad view of critical international financial events since World War II and their effects on U.S. monetary policy, see Paul Volcker and Toyoo Gyohten, *Changing Fortunes*, New York: Times Books, 1992.

In this chapter, we have argued that interest rates are interdependent because of the elimination of barriers to capital flows. For an opposing view, see Adrian W. Troop "International Financial Market Integration and Linkages of National Interest Rates," *Economic Review* of the Federal Reserve Bank of San Francisco, no. 3, 1994. Back issues of the Economic Review may be ordered online from the world wide web site for the San Francisco Fed at (http://www.frb.org/publications@sf.frb.org).

For students interested in a "famous" fixed exchange rate system, the gold standard, see *The Key to the Gold Vault*, published by the New York Fed in 1991. It is free for the asking from the Public Information Department, Federal Reserve Bank of New York, 33 Liberty Street, New York, NY 10045.

APPENDIX A

Financial Information on the Internet
Prepared by Meenakshi Rishi of
Ohio Northern University

 Introduction

The internet or "the net" is rapidly changing the way we visualize and access information. The internet can be an excellent resource for students and teachers alike. However, one needs to understand what the internet consists of before attempting to use it. The internet is comprised of thousands of small networks that connect to a "central backbone network" over which these smaller networks communicate. Users, people such as professors, students, and scientists, manage the internet.

The various ways of accessing information on the internet include such things as FTP (file transfer protocol), Telnet, Gopher, and the World Wide Web (WWW). One can even send electronic mail (e-mail) through the net to anywhere in the world as long as the destination is "hooked up" to the internet. The WWW is the most usable feature of the internet and it may be accessed through any of the popular browsers such as Netscape or Cello.

This appendix is a listing of some Web and Gopher sites that are of particular use to a student of money and banking. You need to be aware of some differences between Gopher and the WWW. Your university most likely has a local Gopher server with several Gopher links. Two particularly useful Gopher search tools are archie and veronica. While veronica can search all possible Gopher links for information on a particular topic, archie enables the user to conduct a search of all possible FTP sites. While Gopher is powerful and useful, it is rather limiting in that information can only be accessed through a hierarchical ordering of inert menus. This constraining feature of Gopher has been eliminated to a great extent by the WWW program.

The WWW, developed in 1989 by CERN in Switzerland, connects all information retrieval systems together so that you use *one* client program to get information from archie, Gopher, and WAIS (Wide Area Information Servers), as well as WWW servers. The WWW enables one to get on the information highway using "hypertext.[1]" Hypertext is a special term referring to an online document that has words or graphics that contain links to other documents; usually, selecting the link area on-screen activates these links. Thus,

---

[1] Recently a new programming language, Java, promises to revolutionize the Internet. Java, developed by Sun Microsystems, is defined as "a simple, object-oriented, distributed, interpreted, robust, secure, architecture-neutral, portable, high-performance, multithreaded, dynamic, buzzword-complaint general purpose program language."

the WWW can help the user to access information without actually leaving the Web document, something that Gopher was unable to provide.

To be able to access the WWW, you must have a direct/indirect connection to the internet and a client program (web browser) running on your computer. In order to establish this connection, you should contact your university about getting your computer network equipped with a popular web browser such as Netscape Navigator. Alternatively, you may "tap" the web by paying a commercial access provider such as America Online. A typical fee is $20/month for 20 hours or so of access time.

Once you are "networked" you may start accessing information by double clicking on your client program. Then go to a specific internet site such as the ones mentioned in this compendium by typing in the exact address. For instance the world wide web site **http://www.cnn.com,** is the location of CNN's home page. The "**http**" is the hypertext protocol communication referred to above. The "**www**" stands for World Wide Web and "**cnn.com**" refers to the "commercial" computer cite at CNN. The suffix "edu" in internet site addresses refers to an educational establishment and "gov" directs you to a location managed by a government agency. An address with a suffix "au" indicates the two-letter country code for Australia. Typing in an address allows you to contact (via modem) a gateway computer which in turn establishes your connection to the web and takes you to web pages from which you may download information, or even send e-mail.

You may end your session by exiting from your client program.

Here again is a summary of the basic steps you need to follow in order to access the "net".

EASY STEPS TO THE INTERNET:

1) Log on, if needed, to your computer.
2) Find your client program, such as Netscape, and double click on it to begin.
3) Begin searching or browsing by entering a specific internet address, like the ones given in this appendix, in the location box at the top of the screen and press enter.
4) You may also use such tools as Webcrawler, Netsearch, or Yahoo by double clicking on any of these and entering your search topic.
5) Continue by double clicking the hypertext of whatever interests you.
6) You can select the Print command to print material on a selected printer. You may also "mail" the document to yourself or your instructor.
7) To exit simply go to the menu under file and select exit.

I. The United States Macroeconomy

A. Statistical Abstract of the United States: http://www.census.gov/ftp/pub/statab/www

The current *Statistical Abstract for the United States* containing over 1400 tables and graphs is a valuable reference for the U.S. economy. The web site is useful for accessing information on population, income, production, price, and trade statistics for the U.S. economy. In addition, fairly detailed state and country information is also available as well as "Monthly Economic Indicators."

Economic Indicators are economic statistics that track the state of the economy. The index of 11 leading indicators enables forecasters to predict economic trends. Other statistics are derived from the measure of domestic product. One way to interpret economic statistics is to classify them as leading, lagging, or coincident indicators. These terms refer to the way these statistics correlate to the pace of economic activity. The first, the **leading** indicator, is so named because it moves down before the economy enters a **recession** and turns up before the **expansion** begins. It is often used to predict where the economy is headed. The opposite of a leading indicator is a **lagging** indicator. A lagging indicator turns down after the recession begins and moves up after the recovery is underway. The final type of indicator is **coincident,** i.e., it neither leads nor does it lag. Instead, it keeps pace with the economy, moving up with expansion and down with recession.

B. Economy at a Glance:
http://stats.bls.gov:80/eag.table.html

This site, maintained by the Bureau of Labor Statistics (BLS), provides a quick overview of current economic conditions in the U.S. economy. Three broad categories of data are reported: data on the labor market, data on earnings and productivity, and data on prices.

Data on the labor market may be accessed, for instance, to gauge the latest unemployment rate in the economy. You may recall that the unemployment rate is the percentage of all people between the ages of sixteen and sixty-five[2] who are able to work and are actively seeking jobs. It is a leading indicator of recessions, lagging for recoveries, and unclassified overall. The unemployment rate is the most widely watched for all economic statistics and is extremely volatile, sometimes fluctuating as much as one or two percentage points.

Data on labor productivity provides a key measure of labor efficiency in the United States. The productivity measures reported describe the relationship between real output and the labor time involved in its production. They show the changes from period to period in the amount of goods and services produced per hour.

Data on prices available at the BLS site reports monthly inflation rates as measured by the Consumer Price Index (CPI) and the Producer Price Index (PPI). The CPI and the PPI are compiled monthly by the BLS.

C. Economic Bulletin Board (EBB)
gopher://una.hh.lib.umich.edu:70/11/ebb/

The **Economic Bulletin Board** at the University of Michigan is an excellent repository of general (current as well as historic) macroeconomic information such as economic indicators, U.S. Treasury auction results, and employment statistics, updated "daily" whenever possible. This is a gopher site at the Uni-

---

[2] It does not include members of the armed forces or those confined to a mental institution or prison.

versity of Michigan which downloads data from the **Economic Bulletin Board** of the U.S. Department of Commerce. General information about this site can be obtained from the "IMPORTANT!! README!!" directory.

D. Other Sites

1. The Economic Report of the President
   gopher://gopher.umsl.edu/11/library/govdocs//erps
2. National Bureau of Economic Research (NBER)
   gopher://nber.harvard.edu:70/77/.macrohist/waistest/index

This is a searchable macroeconomic database maintained by the National Bureau of Economic Research (NBER) at Harvard University.

2) Monetary Aggregates

As we saw in Chapter 2, money is anything that serves as a unit of account, medium of exchange, and store of value. Data on money supply, as well as information on aggregate reserves of depository institutions, is released weekly by the Fed. Money stock data may be accessed from the EBB via the University of Michigan gopher at the following gopher site:
gopher://una.hh.lib.umich.edu/70/11/ebb/monetary

3) Federal Reserve Information

A. The world wide web site of the Federal Reserve Board
http://www.bog.frb.fed.US/

This site of the Board of Governors of the Federal Reserve System contains information about the Fed, the Fed Open Market Committee, statistical data, and speeches and testimony of Fed officials.

B. FRED—Federal Reserve Bank—St. Louis
http://www.stls.frb.org/fred/

FRED refers to Federal Reserve Economic Data. This is a database of historical U.S. economic and financial data maintained at the Federal Reserve Bank of St. Louis. The following Federal Reserve Board Statistical Releases are available here:

G.17 release—Industrial Production and Capacity Utilization
G.19 release—Consumer Installment Credit
G.5 release—Foreign Exchange Rates for the Institutions and the Monetary Base
H.10 release—Foreign Exchange Rates for four weeks
H.15 release—Selected Interest Rates

H.3   release—Aggregate Reserves of Depository Institutions and the Monetary Base

H4.1 release—Factors Affecting Reserve Balances of Depositor Institutions and Condition Statements of Federal Reserve Banks

H.6   release—Money Stock, Liquid Assets, and Debt Measures

H.8   release—Assets and Liabilities of Insured Domestically Chartered and Foreign-Related Banking Institutions

Z.7   release—Flow of Funds Summary

C. WOODROW—Federal Reserve Bank—Minneapolis
http://woodrow.mpls.frb.fed.US/

This site is an excellent resource for general and specific information on the Federal Reserve. A good description of the structure and functions of the Federal Reserve system is available here. A summary of current economic conditions by the Federal Reserve District, the so-called **Beige Book,** is also accessible at this site. The Beige Book published by the Fed summarizes current economic conditions by Federal Reserve District. A national summary also forms a part of the **Beige Book** which may be browsed at the above site.

Woodrow also contains a useful **"Monetary Policy"** link which maintains current information on the Federal Open Market Committee (FOMC) which as you know is primarily responsible for implementing monetary policy through open market operations.

This site may be browsed for FOMC meeting dates, voting members of the FOMC, and the latest available minutes from previous FOMC meetings.

In the realm of monetary policy operations, information on current and archival Treasury auctions i.e. the sales of treasury bills, notes and bonds is also available at the economic bulletin board maintained at the University of Michigan. **gopher://una.hh.lib.umich.edu:70/11/ebb/treasury.**

Another interesting link available at this site tracks the U.S. economy and provides a plethora of economic information. This may be independently accessed at: **http://woodrow.mpls.frb.fed.us/economy/.**

D. Other Federal Reserve Sites

1. The Federal Reserve Bank—Philadelphia
    http://www.libertynet.org/~fedresrv/fedpage.html

    The web page can be used to direct a search of research and statistics published at the Federal Reserve at Philadelphia.

2. The Federal Reserve Bank—Chicago
    gopher://gopher.great-lakes.net:2200/11/partners/ChicagoFed

    This is a good site for background information on the Federal Reserve System with a glossary of "monetary policy terms" that I find particularly useful.

3. Federal Reserve Bank—Atlanta
    http://www.frbatlanta.org

4. Federal Reserve Bank—Cleveland
    http://www.clev.frb.org

5. Federal Reserve Bank—New York
   http://www.ny.frb.org

   The **"pihome"** subdirectory at this site allows the user to browse through several publications that may be ordered "online." The **"Fedpoint"** (searchable) subdirectory is a handy reference guide that explains the structure and functions of the Federal Reserve System.

6. Federal Reserve Bank—Boston
   http://www.std.com/frbbos/

   Currently, this site offers mainly regional information about the northeast.

4. Federal Deposit Insurance Corporation (FDIC): http://www.fdic.gov

The homepage maintained by the FDIC is an excellent source of information on current and historical banking statistics (such as assets and liabilities of insured depository institutions).

Specific data on FDIC-insured institutions is also available at the gopher site maintained by the FDIC: **gopher://gopher.fdic.gov**

The data are updated weekly. Check the 'readme' file under the heading "About the files in this Directory" for more information. These files are also available for anonymous ftp in the **/pub/structure** directory.

5. Financial Markets

A. Financial Market Updates

One of the most quoted measures of stock market performance in the United States is the **Dow Jones Industrial Average (DJIA)**. The Dow Jones Industrial Average is an "unofficial leading indicator of economic activity" listed on the New York Stock Exchange, compiled by Dow Jones and Company, Inc., and available every five minutes during market hours. This average is one of the oldest and most popular measures of U.S. stock market performance. Thirty firms are included in the index. The actual size of the index varies with the fluctuations in the market price of these firms. When the prices of these 30 stocks are down, the DJIA goes down, and it can then be assumed that all stocks are falling in price.

Standard and Poor's 500 (S&P 500) is another popular measure of stock price performance. It is compiled by Standard and Poor's on an hourly basis. It consists of 500 stocks representing four major industry groupings: finance, industrials, public utilities, and transports.

Current market information on stock price performance is available from the Business section of the CNN homepage at the following WWW site:
http://cnnfn.com/markets/

Of particular interest at this site are links to **CNNfn** that lets you check the numbers on any stock, mutual fund or money market fund from your computer.

Another good source of financial market activity is the **"market summary"** link found on the **American Stock Exchange** web site:
http://www.amex.com/

The **Wong and Holt Market** report briefly describes the day's activities in various financial markets. It starts out with a short summary by Martin Wong, then more detailed information is provided by George Holt. The Holt report updates daily activities in various financial markets (NYSE, NASDAQ, AMEX, foreign markets, interest rates, foreign exchange, etc.). This can be found at website:
http://metro.turnpik.net/holt/index.html

B. EDGAR (SEC)
http://www.sec.gov/edgarhp.htm

Edgar is a useful database of corporate information that results from submissions by companies that are legally required to file forms with the U.S. Securities and Exchange Commission (SEC). Public access via internet to Edgar was only made possible in 1994 by the SEC.

C. International Financial Market Information

The Institute of Finance and Banking at the University of Goettingen, Germany **(http://www.wiso.gwdg.de/ifbg/stockl.html)** is an excellent repository of international financial market sites. Most listings at this site are links for stock exchanges and not for financial institutions. Additional country-specific financial information may be obtained by browsing the following sites:

French Finance Ministry's web site:
http://www.tresor.finances.fr/oat

Bank of England's web site:
http://www.coi.gov.uk/coi/depts/GBE/GBE.html

The Madrid Stock Exchange web site:
http://www.bolsamadrid.es

Argentina's Ministry of Economy and Public Works and Services:
http://www.mecon.ar

Africa Stock Exchange Guide:
http://www.africa.com/pages/jse

Amsterdam Stock Exchange:
http://wwwaeb.econ.vu.nl/English/home.html

Bank of Ireland:
http://www.treasury.boi.ie

La Caixa (Caja de Ahorros y Pensiones de Barcelona):
http://lacaixa.datalab.es

Dai-Ichi Kangyo Bank Ltd:
http://www.infoweb.or.jp/dkb/welcom-e.html

Indonesia Business Center Online:
http://indobiz.com/index.htm

LG Securities Co. (Korea):
http://203.248.135.75

Rio de Janeiro Stock Exchange:
http://www.embratel.net.br/infoserv/bvrj

D. Miscellaneous Finance links

1. International Financial Encyclopedia
    http://www.euro.net/innovation/Finance_Base/Fin_encyc.html

    This information base is touted as "the world's only interactive financial encyclopedia." As **euro.net** is located in the Netherlands, you can expect some delays in accessing information. A good feature of this particular site is a **"comment questionnaire"** which allows you to e-mail your feedback to the website managers.

2. Financial Data Finder—Ohio State University
    http://www.cob/ohio-state.edu/dept/fin/osudata.htm

    This searchable database site lists various financial resources available on the internet.

3. Yahoo Directory of Financial Services
    http://www.yahoo.com/Business/corporations/financial_services

6. International Trade & Foreign Exchange

The trade deficit, which is more properly called the *balance on goods and services,* tracks the international flow of goods and services. Since the first quarter of 1976, the U.S. has always imported more than it has exported. For this reason, economists focus on the trade "deficit" rather than on the trade "balance."

The trade deficit is directly related to the national income and product accounts. Initial trade figures are reported in terms of current, constant and seasonally adjusted amounts. These statistics are compiled monthly and quarterly by the **Bureau of the Census.**

The exchange rate is the amount of foreign currency that can be purchased with the dollar. At the moment, there are well over 200 exchange rates all over the world that are compiled weekly and monthly by the Federal Reserve Board of Governors.

For new releases and updated information on foreign trade access **http://www.census.gov/foreign_trade/www/press.html**

For latest exchange rates access **gopher://una.hh.lib.umich.edu:70/11/ebb/foreign** on the internet.

APPENDIX B

Answers to Odd-Numbered Questions

Chapter 1

1. **Economics:** the study of how a society decides what to produce, how to produce, and whom the products are for. In other words, it is the study of making use of limited resources to satisfy unlimited wants

   Finance: the raising and using of money by domestic and foreign individuals, firms, and governments

   Surplus spending units (SSUs): when we spend less on consumption and investment goods than our income, we are called SSUs

   Deficit spending units (DSUs): when we spend more on consumption and investment goods than our income, we are called DSUs

   Direct finance: when SSUs lend their own funds directly to DSUs

   Indirect finance: when SSUs deposit their funds in financial intermediaries and in turn, the financial intermediaries loan the funds to DSUs

   Financial intermediaries: institutions such as banks, savings and loan associations, and credit unions that serve as go-betweens to link up SSUs and DSUs

   Liquidity: how easy or difficult it is to convert a financial claim into cash without loss of value

   Business cycle: short-run fluctuations in the level of economic activity as measured by the output of goods and services in the economy

   Depository institutions: financial intermediaries which offer checkable deposits

   Monetary policy: the Federal Reserve's efforts to promote the overall health and stability of the economy

3. Credit cards are not money. When an individual uses a credit card, he or she is taking out a loan by authorizing the institution that issued the credit card to make a payment with money on his or her behalf. Ultimately, the individual must pay credit card balances with money.

5. Financial intermediaries exist because they help to minimize the transactions costs associated with borrowing and lending. Financial services provided by financial intermediaries include appraising and diversifying risk, offering a menu of financial claims which are relatively safe and liquid, and pooling funds from individual SSUs.

7. The most familiar type and the largest group of financial intermediaries are depository institutions consisting of commercial banks, savings and loan associations, credit unions, and mutual savings banks. Depository institutions are particularly popular with SSUs because the secondary claims purchased by SSUs from depository institutions—that is, the deposits—are often insured and therefore relatively safe.

   Other types of intermediaries offer specialized secondary claims. For example, insurance companies offer financial protection against early death (life companies) or property losses (casualty companies), while pension plans provide financial resources for one's old age.

Checkable deposits are funds that are subject to withdrawal by writing a check. Such deposits are money per se since they can be used in their present form as a means of payment.

9. Views on the appropriate role of policy in the economy—for instance, how "activist" policy-makers should be in trying to manage the economy—have varied over time. Following the relatively poor performance of the economy in the 1970s, there has been a resurgence of the pre-Depression laissez-faire attitude.

11. Laissez faire, or hands-off policy, is when the government does not intervene in the economy. Fiscal policy concerns government spending and taxing decisions. Fiscal policy is determined by congress, while monetary policy is determined by the Fed.

13. a. Direct financing
    b. Direct financing
    c. Indirect financing (assuming the savings and loan lends the money)
    d. Direct financing
    e. Indirect financing

15. The firm is a DSU. It has a deficit of $70,000.

17. 1960s—7.25 percent
    1970s—13.25 percent
    1980s—13.75 percent

Chapter 2

1. **Means of payment:** something which is generally accepted to make payments
Store of value: something which retains its value over time
Unit of account: a standardized accounting unit, such as the dollar, which is the standard measure of value
Barter: trading goods for goods
Monetary Aggregates: the measures of money, including M1, M2, M3, and L, which the Fed keeps track of and monitors
Liquidity: the ease with which a financial claim can be converted to cash without loss of value
Nonfinancial debt: total credit market debt accumulated in the past and present years, including the debt owed by the nonfinancial sector, such as the government, private nonfinancial firms, and households
EFTS (Electronic Funds Transfer System): the transfer of funds to third parties in response to electronic instructions rather than instructions written on paper checks
Risk: the possibility or probability that the value of an asset declines

3. Defining money as that which serves as a store of value is a poor definition. Many items such as diamonds or gold can store value, but they are not generally accepted as means of payment.

5. **M1** = currency in the hands of the public + demand deposits at commercial banks ÷ other checkable deposits + travelers' checks
M2 = M1 + small savings and time deposits (less than $100,000), including money market deposit accounts + individual money market mutual funds

M3 = M2 + large time deposits + term repurchase agreements and term Eurodollars + institutional money market mutual funds

L = M3 + nonbank public holdings of U.S. Savings Bonds and short-term Treasury Securities + commercial paper + bankers' acceptances

DNFD = credit market debt of the U.S. government and state and local governments + corporate bonds + mortgages + consumer credit (including bank loans) + other bank loans + commercial paper + other debt instruments

All of these aggregates are not money. M1 is the aggregate which contains the most liquid assets, and it is also the smallest aggregate. DNFD is the largest aggregate.

7. The reason why DNFD excludes the debt of financial institutions is that including such debt would be double counting. For example, suppose Bank X borrows surplus funds from small passbook savers and relends them to Jack to buy his first home. If the debt of the financial institution is counted, both the mortgage debt of Jack and the debt of Bank X to the passbook saver would be included in the aggregate.

9. The existence of money facilitates trade. The more trade, the more growth there will be in an economy. The existence of money facilitates trade for Zoto and helps it develop rapidly. Zaha, which does not utilize money, relies on barter. It is difficult to conduct trade in a barter system.

11. Both money and other financial assets have the function of store of value. The acceptability of money as a means of payment distinguishes it from other financial assets.

13. a. Gold would not be good "money" because it's too heavy to carry around as a means of payment.

   b. Dirt would not be good "money" because it's not scarce, so it can't serve as a store of value.

   c. Corn would not be good "money" because after a while it rots, so it can't serve as a store of value.

   d. Oil would not be good "money" because it would be inconvenient to carry around as a means of payment.

Chapter 3

1. **Interest rate:** the cost to borrowers of obtaining money and the return (or yield) of money to lenders

   Reserves: assets that are held as either vault cash or reserve deposit accounts with the Fed

   Required reserve ratio: depository institutions must have reserve assets equal to a certain percentage of deposit liabilities; the required reserve ratio is that percentage

   Inflation rate: the rate of change in the consumer price index that measures the growth rate of the average level of prices paid by consumers

3. The demand for money is the entire set of interest rate-quantity combinations as represented by a downward sloping demand curve for money. The quantity demanded of money is the specific amount of money that spending units wish to hold at a specific interest rate (price).

5. The demand for money and income are positively related. The higher the income, the higher the demand for money.

7. Credit comes from depository financial institutions, nondepository financial institutions, and other nonfinancial institutions. The money supply is a stock, while the flow of credit is a flow.

9. The fact that alarm clocks going off and the sun rising are highly correlated does not mean that one causes the other. Correlation and causation are not the same thing.

11.

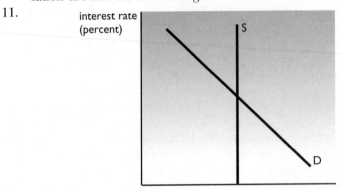

The graph above shows that the interest rate and the demand for money are inversely related. The graph also shows that any given supply of money—as determined by the Fed—is independent of the interest rate. The market is in equilibrium where the supply curve (S) and the demand curves (D) intersect.

13. Graph a illustrates question 12a, where the supply curve shifts from S to S1. Graph b illustrates question 12b, where the demand curve shifts from D to D1. Graph c illustrates question 12c, where the demand curve shifts from D to D1. Graph d illustrates question 12d, where the supply curve shifts from S to S1.

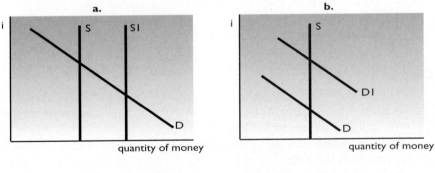

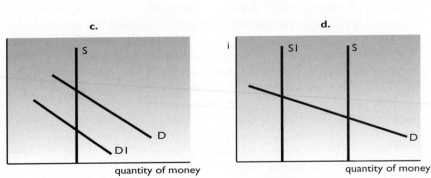

15. Increases or decreases in credit flows lead to the same effects as increases or decreases in the money supply.

17. If there is an increase in credit flows, ceteris paribus, interest rates will decrease, output will increase, and prices will increase. If there is an decrease in credit flows, ceteris paribus, the interest rate will increase, output will decrease, and prices will decrease.

19. If incomes go down, the demand for money decreases (Case I). If reserves go up, the supply of money increases (Case II). The interest rate changes (decreases) in both cases.

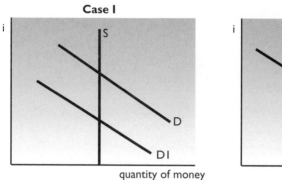

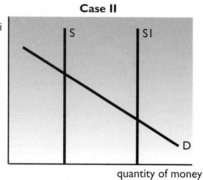

quantity of money   quantity of money

21. The rate of inflation was higher in the second year. If the price index falls from 150 to 145, there is deflation rather than inflation.

Chapter 4

1. In this hypothetical economy, households are SSUs, while business firms are DSUs. DSUs can only invest what is saved by SSUs, therefore, investment in Exhibit 4-3 must be equal to savings.

3. Not all spending units that save are surplus spending units. A spending unit can use saving for a newly constructed house or to lend out to DSUs. Only spending units that have funds left over after consumption and expenditure on newly constructed homes are surplus spending units.

5. The household and business sectors meet in the product market, the factor market, and the financial market. Households demand goods and services, supply labor and other inputs, and in general, supply loanable funds. Businesses supply consumer goods and services, demand investment goods, demand factor inputs, and in general, demand loanable funds. In the circular flow, real flows go in one direction while financial flows go in the opposite.

7. With less funds available for lending, the interest rate will increase, prices will fall, and real GDP will fall.

9. Imagine that John Delaney's main objective is to eat at expensive restaurants every day. Unlike Mr. Delaney, Rosa Moore's main objective is to eat at home so she can save money for her retirement.

  Maximizing his utility subject to his constraints means eating out every day for Mr. Delaney. To achieve this objective, he might have to borrow and therefore become a DSU.

To Ms. Moore, maximizing her utility means saving for her retirement. The fact that she has excess funds after consumption and newly built residential investment makes her a SSU.

11. If households decide to save more, interest rates will fall and investment spending will rise. Higher investment spending will translate to an increase in aggregate demand.

13.

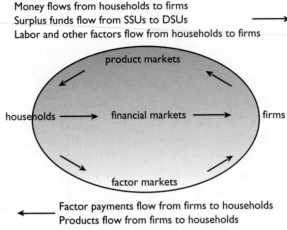

Money flows from households to firms
Surplus funds flow from SSUs to DSUs
Labor and other factors flow from households to firms

product markets

households   financial markets   firms

factor markets

Factor payments flow from firms to households
Products flow from firms to households

15. To undertake a capital investment of $1 million, Tech Corp will have to issue, at minimum, $500,000 worth of bonds. If it pays out $300,000 in dividends, it will have to borrow, at minimum, $800,000.

17.

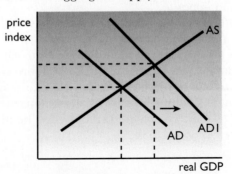

price index

AS

ADI   AD

real GDP

The graph shows that if aggregate demand falls, the aggregate demand curve shifts from AD to AD1. At the new point of equilibrium—where AD1 and AS intersect—the price level and real GDP is lower than at the original equilibrium point (where AS and AD intersect).

19. Aggregate demand and aggregate supply

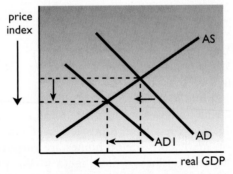

price index

AS

AD   ADI

real GDP

With a higher level of loanable funds, the aggregate demand curve shifts from AD to AD1. At the new equilibrium point (intersection of AD1 and AS curves) aggregate demand is greater than at the original equilibrium point (intersection of AD and AS curves).

The demand and supply of labor

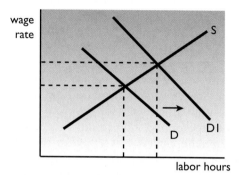

labor hours

With a higher level of loanable funds, the demand curve for labor shifts from D to D1. At the new equilibrium point (intersection of D1 and S curves), the quantity demanded of labor is greater than at the original equilibrium point (intersection of D and S curves).

Chapter 5

1. The primary responsibility of the Fed is the formulation and implementation of the nation's monetary policy. The conduct of monetary policy has two objectives. First, to ensure that sufficient money and credit are available to allow the economy to expand along its long-run potential growth trend under conditions of relatively little or no inflation. Second, in the short run, to minimize the fluctuations—recessions or inflationary booms—around the long-term trend.

   Along with other government agencies, the Fed is responsible for the supervision and regulation of the financial system. In general, supervisory activities are directed at promoting the safety and soundness of depository institutions by making sure that banks are operated prudently and according to standing statutes and regulations.

   The third main responsibility of the Fed is to help maintain an easy-running payments mechanism. The Fed's main activities in this area involve the provision of currency and coin and the clearing of checks.

   The final main responsibility of the Fed is to serve as the fiscal agent for the government. The Fed furnishes banking services to the government in a manner similar to the way private banks furnish banking services to their customers. The Fed also clears Treasury checks, issues and redeems government securities, and provides other financial services.

3. Following the banking crises of 1907, lawmakers were convinced that a central bank was necessary—a kind of bank for banks, which could lend funds to commercial banks during emergencies and thus provide these banks with the funds necessary to avoid insolvency and bankruptcy. Having the Fed should avoid, or at least minimize, financial crises because it is prepared to be a lender of last resort, and it (the Fed) is motivated

by a desire to preserve the public's confidence in the safety and sound-ness of the financial system.

5. The Federal Reserve was established by Congress as an independent agency to give it a certain amount of isolation from the political process. It is allegedly independent because of the way it is structured. Each member of the Board is appointed to a fourteen-year term, so that once appointed, a member of the Board does not have to defend his or her actions to Congress, the President, or the public. Also, the Fed does not need or get an appropriation from Congress. The Fed obtains funds from the interest income it earns on loans to depository institutions and its holding of government securities. Last, the Fed is exempt from many provisions of the Freedom of Information Act and "government in the sunshine" legislation which calls for government policy to be made in meetings open to the public. As a result, Fed policymakers usually meet in secret to formulate policy. Nevertheless, the Fed is not completely outside the government. It is firmly embedded in our political system. In the short run, however, the Fed does not take orders from anyone in the executive or legislative branch of government. Its decisions regarding monetary policy are, in theory, not constrained by the whims of the President or Congress or by any partisan politics. In the long run, however, Congress can pass laws that the Fed must obey. Congress could even abolish the Fed.

7. To promote the overall health of the economy, the Fed can utilize open market operations, the discount rate, and/or change the required reserve ratio.

   Open market operations are the most widely used tool by the Fed. These operations, which are executed by the Federal Reserve Bank of New York, involve the buying or selling of U.S. Government securities by the Fed.

   The discount rate is the interest rate the Fed charges depository institutions that borrow reserves directly from the Fed.

   The Fed requires depository institutions to hold required reserves equal to a proportion of checkable deposit liabilities.

   Unlike the required reserve ratio, open market operations have been the major instrument used to implement monetary policy.

9. Proponents of continuing the Fed's independence argue that politicians are interested in getting elected and reelected, and this means they are short-run maximizers. They (politicians) do not take the long view, which could be disastrous if the long-run impacts of policy are different from the short-run impacts. For instance, to please the electorate, politicians might pursue a stimulative monetary policy resulting in an expansion of economic activity, even though the more long-run impact of the policy might accelerate inflation.

   Proponents for increasing the accountability of the Fed argue that the Reserve Bank presidents represent the interests of the banking community since they are elected by the Reserve Bank directors, two-thirds of whom, in turn, are elected by the member banks. Proponents for more accountability of the Fed also argue that the General Accounting Office should be able to audit all aspects of the Fed and that there should be fuller and more immediate disclosure of FOMC discussions and decisions.

11. The president of the New York Fed is a permanent member of the FOMC because the New York Fed implements monetary policy in accord with the FOMC's instructions. Since New York is the center of the U.S. financial system, it is logical that the president of the New York Fed be a permanent member of the FOMC.

13. a. If the Fed lowered the required reserve ratio, the money supply would increase.

    b. If the Fed lowered the discount rate, the money supply would increase.

    c. If the Fed bought government securities, the money supply would increase.

Chapter 6

1. Primary markets are where new securities, issued to finance current deficits, are bought and sold.

    Secondary markets are where outstanding (issued earlier) securities are bought and sold.

    The money market is where securities with original maturities of one year or less are traded.

    The capital market is where securities with original maturities of more than one year are traded.

3. Market makers disseminate information about market conditions to buyers and sellers, they connect the various markets by buying and selling in the market themselves, and they provide financial services that determine the quality of primary and secondary markets.

    A broker simply arranges trades between buyers and sellers. A dealer, in addition to arranging trades between buyers and sellers, is ready to be a principal in a transaction—that is, they will purchase and hold securities sold by investors.

5. The markets for particular types of financial claims are connected via the buying and selling (trading) of securities by the "participants" in the markets—that is, the substitution among alternative instruments available.

7. **Commercial paper:** a short-term debit instrument issued by domestic and foreign corporations

    Negotiable certificates of deposit (CDs): a debt instrument sold by a depository institution which pays interest payments

    Repurchase agreements: short-term agreements where the seller sells a government security to a buyer with the simultaneous agreement to buy the government security back on a later date

    Bankers' acceptances: a bank draft (a guarantee of payment similar to a check) used for financing international trade, issued by a firm and payable on some future date

    Federal funds: typically, overnight loans to depository institutions of their deposits at the Fed

    Eurodollars: originally considered to be deposits denominated in dollars in a foreign bank. Today, the term Eurodollar has come to mean any deposit in a foreign (host) country where the deposit is denominated in the currency of the country from which it came rather than that of the host country.

The terms defined in this question are all money market instruments. They are different in that some are used more by individuals, while others are used more by corporations.

9. Stocks are equity claims which represent ownership of the net income and assets of a corporation. The income that stockholders receive for their ownership is called dividends.

Preferred stock pays a fixed dividend and, in the event of bankruptcy, the owners of preferred stock are entitled to be paid first after other creditors of the corporation.

Common stock pays a variable dividend which is dependent on the profits that are left over after preferred stockholders have been paid and retained earnings set aside. Owning common stock may result in higher profit rates when the company is growing and electing to pay high dividends.

Corporate bonds are long-term bonds issued by corporations, usually (although not always) with excellent credit ratings. The owner of such receives an interest payment twice a year and the principal at maturity.

11. With bonds, you are bonded to a return agreed on when the bonds were purchased. With stocks, your return on investment can grow as the corporation profits increase. Therefore, if you expect a corporation to earn exceptional profits, it is better to buy stocks.

13. **Fed funds rate:** the rate charged on overnight loans to depository institutions of their deposits at the Fed
Discount rate: the rate charged by the Fed on loans to its member banks
Eurodollar rate: the interest rate on deposits in foreign banks
LIBOR rate: the interbank rate for dollar-denominated deposits in the London market among international banks

The Fed funds rate and the discount rate are manipulated by the Fed. The Eurodollar is not affected by U.S. regulations and not subject to reserve requirements.

15. The following financial instruments are ranked (top to bottom) from most to least liquid or secure.

Liquidity Rank	*Security Rank*
Eurodollars	U.S. T-bills
Large negotiable CDs	Government bonds
U.S. T-bills	Government agency securities
Commercial paper	Large negotiable CDs
Government bonds	Mortgages
Government agency securities	Commercial paper
Mortgages	Eurodollars

17. $72.50

19. 8.33%

Chapter 7

1. Compounding is a method used to find out what the future value of a present value is—that is, what is the future value of money lent (or borrowed) today.

Unlike compounding, which is forward looking, discounting is in effect backward looking. Discounting is the method used to figure out what the present value of money is to be received (or paid) in the future.

3. If the interest rate increases, a bond will sell at a discount from par. If the interest rate decreases, a bond will sell at a premium above par.

5. In financial circles, the interest rate is very important. The fluctuations of interest rates have a direct effect on investments. Any increase or decrease of interest rates can drastically change the values of bonds.

7. In general, nominal interest rates are procyclical and lagging. The real interest rate is acyclical. Prices are procyclical and lagging. The money stock is procyclical and leads the cycle.

9. If the Fed increases the growth rate of the money supply, stock prices will increase.

11. Assuming an interest rate of 5 percent,
   a. $272.31
   b. $1,136.16

13. Coupon rate = 6 percent
    Current yield = 5.45 percent

15. The supply of and demand for funds

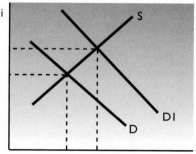

loanable funds

If there is an increase in income, the demand curve for loanable funds shifts from D to D1. At the new equilibrium point (where S and D1 intersect), the interest rate, the demand for loanable funds, and the quantity supplied of loanable funds increase.

The supply of and demand for funds

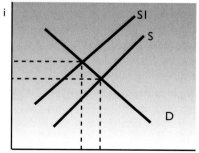

loanable funds

If the Fed orchestrates a decrease in the money supply growth rate, the supply curve will shift from S to S1. At the new equilibrium point (where

D and S1 intersect), the interest rate increases. At the new equilibrium point, the supply of loanable funds and the quantity demanded of loanable funds decrease.

17. At least $311,526 which is the present value of $1,000,000 given a 6 percent interest rate.

19. If the interest rate is 5 percent, Henry and Sheree will have to invest $41,545. If the interest rate is 10 percent, Henry and Sheree will have to invest $17,985.

21. Price of the consol = $2,000
    Interest rate = 5 percent

Chapter 8

1. A yield curve is a graphic representation of the relationship between interest rates (yields) on particular securities and their terms to maturity. This relationship is what determines the shape and level of a yield curve.

    Term to maturity, credit risk, and tax treatment are all determinants of the interest rate on a particular asset. Any or all of these determinants can cause the interest rate on a particular asset to decrease or increase.

3. According to the expectations theory, the long-term interest rate is the geometric average of the current short rate and the future short rates expected to prevail over the term to maturity of the longer-term security. The geometric average is used instead of the simpler arithmetic average to take into account the effects of compounding.

5. Interest rate expectations are determined by the money supply, national income or gross domestic product, and inflationary expectations. Expectations about future prices are not independent of expectations about future money supply growth rate because the larger the supply of money, the more prices will be expected to rise.

7. Yield curves have most often been upward sloping over the past forty-five years because lenders have required a higher return to lend long term rather than short term.

    A yield curve could be upward sloping even if short-term rates were expected to remain constant.

    If interest rates are expected to fall dramatically, the yield curve could still be upward sloping if the liquidity premium is very high.

9. According to the expectations theory, the long-run rate is the geometric average of the current short rate and the future short rates expected to prevail over the term to maturity of the longer-term security. It is reasonable to conclude that short-term rates will vary more than long-term rates because long-term rates are averaged so they don't tend to be scattered as much as short-term rates.

11. If the economy went into a strong expansion, there would be less risk of default, and risk premiums would decrease. If on the other hand the economy went into a deep recession, default risk would increase and so would risk premiums.

13. Expected short-term interest rate = 2.9 percent

15.

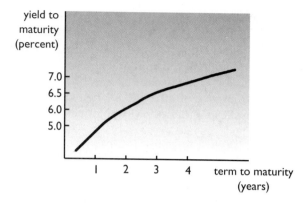

17. If a tax payer's marginal tax rate is 33¹/₃ percent, the after tax yield on a corporate bond that pays 5 percent interest is 3.33 percent interest. If the marginal tax rate of all tax payers is 50 percent, a tax payer with a 33¹/₃ percent marginal tax rate will prefer a corporate security.

19. a.   Decrease
     b.   Increase
     c.   Decrease
     d.   Decrease
     e.   Decrease

21. $9.38

Chapter 9

1. **Exchange rate:** the number of units of foreign currency which can be acquired with one unit of domestic money
    Foreign currency: the supplies of foreign exchange
    Foreign exchange market: the market which trades various currencies

3. All transactions which result in payments by Americans to foreigners are recorded as payments; they are negative or debit items. These payments include U.S. purchases of foreign goods. To purchase these goods, you would need to exchange dollars for the foreign currency. By exchanging dollars for the foreign currency, Americans are in fact adding to the supply of dollars in the foreign exchange market.
    In the balance of payments, all transactions which result in payments by foreigners to Americans are recorded as receipts; they are credit or plus items. These payments include foreign purchases of U.S. goods. For foreigners to obtain these goods, they must exchange their currency for dollars in the foreign exchange market. By exchanging foreign currency for dollars, the foreigners are in fact increasing the demand for dollars.

5. **Trade balance:** the difference between merchandise exports and imports
    Balance of goods and services: net exports of services plus the trade balance
    Balance of payments: the record of transactions between the United States and its trading partners in the rest of the world over a particular period of time

7. If interest rates were lower in the United States than in the rest of the world, the U.S. would most likely experience a capital outflow. Ceretis paribus, the current account would move towards a surplus.

9. If foreigners decided to sell U.S. securities, the exchange rate would decrease.

11. If the yen/dollar exchange rate is 100, the dollar price of the hotel room is $200. If the yen/dollar exchange rate increases to 150, the dollar price of the hotel room decreases to $133.33.

13. After the dollar appreciation, the dollar price of tequila decreases. After the depreciation of the dollar, the dollar price of tequila increases.

15. a.

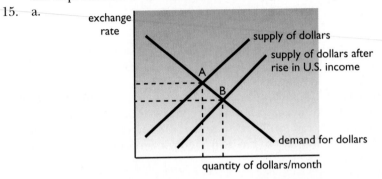

If there is an increase in U.S. income, the supply curve shifts to the right. Also, the quantity demanded of dollars increases. The equilibrium point moves from A to B.

b.

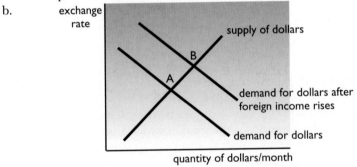

If foreign income rises, the demand for dollars curve shifts to the right. Also, quantity supplied of dollars increases. The equilibrium point shifts from A to B.

c. The effects are similar to graph a.

d.

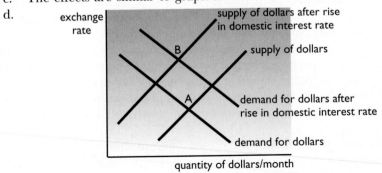

If domestic interest rates rise, the supply curve shifts to the left. The demand curve shifts to the right. The equilibrium point moves from A to B.

17. $100
19. The pound/dollar exchange rate is 11,250.
    The dollar/pound exchange rate is .0000888.
21. If the yen/dollar exchange rate is 125, then $15,000 will be worth 1,875,000 yen. If the exchange rate depreciates to 100, then $15,000 will be worth 1,500,000 yen.

Chapter 10

1. **Financial futures:** contracts between two parties to trade financial assets at a future date and where the terms of the transaction are determined today
   Forward agreements: completing today the terms for a transaction that will occur on a specified date in the future
   Options: standardized contracts which give the buyer the right but not the obligation to buy or sell an asset in the future at a price determined today
   Swaps: agreements which deal with two parties trading interest payment streams to guarantee that the inflows of payments will more closely match outflows
       The instruments above can be used for hedging, but if used for speculation they can cause major financial losses.
       Futures limit both losses and gains, while options limit only losses. However, futures are cheaper than options because of options premiums.
3. As a borrower, Yvette can protect herself from the risk of an increase in the interest rate by utilizing either financial futures or options.
       As a lender, Yvette can protect herself from the risk of an increase in the interest rate by utilizing either financial futures or options.
5. Arbitragers assure that on the day before the delivery date of a futures contract, the futures price is very close to the spot price.
       When there is an opportunity for riskless profit, arbitragers move in and purchase in the spot market (driving up the price of a given asset) and sell in the futures market (driving down the price of the asset) and vice versa. As the time comes closer to the delivery date of the futures contract, the length of time funds are borrowed for reduces. Therefore, the carrying costs are reduced and the futures price approaches the spot price as the delivery date nears.
       Arbitrages continue until the futures price is bid up (down) to the spot price plus carrying cost, and there is convergence.
7. When there is an opportunity for riskless profit, arbitragers move in and purchase in the spot market (driving up the price of a given asset) and sell in the futures market (driving down the price of the asset) and vice versa. As the time comes closer to the delivery date of the futures contract, the length of time funds are borrowed for reduces. Therefore, the carrying costs are reduced and the futures price approaches the spot price as the delivery date nears.
       Arbitrages continue until the futures price is bid up (down) to the spot price plus carrying cost, and there is convergence.
9. Options on futures are options which give the buyer the right but not the obligation to buy or sell a futures contract up to the expiration date on the option.

11. A stock index futures contract give the buyer or seller the right and obligation to purchase or sell a multiple of the value of a stock index at some specific date in the future at a price determined today. By being able to set the price in advance through stock index futures, an investor can hedge the risk of a fall in stock prices.

13. Given the following conditions, the option premium will generally be larger
    1) the more volatile the price of the contract asset is,
    2) the further away the expiration date of the option is, and
    3) the higher the strike price relative to the spot price for put options and the lower the strike price relative to the spot price for call options.

15. IBM loses because the spot price is higher than the futures' agreement price.

17. No

19. If the S&P 500 index is 575, the brokerage house does not make a profit. If the S&P 500 index is 625, the brokerage house does make a profit.

21. To alleviate the fear of interest rates going down, I can hedge with futures and options to minimize possible losses.

Chapter 11

1. FIs provide services which help reduce the risks and costs associated with borrowing, lending, and other financial transactions. FIs also help fulfill the demand for various financial assets and services, including protection against the financial losses associated with various exigencies.
   FIs provide these services because they are profit-seeking firms.

3. Financial intermediation helps reduce the risks associated with lending and borrowing money. Given the relative safety that FIs offer, SSUs don't have to give up as much safety for higher returns, and in turn, the reduction in risks will afford lower rates for DSUs.

5. If an FI has mainly long-term liabilities with few payment uncertainties, it will most likely invest in long-term assets or financial investments. Longer-term instruments generally provide higher yields than shorter-term assets but are not as liquid. Given the nature of FIs with mainly long-term liabilities and few payment uncertainties, holding large portions of liquid assets is not as essential as it is for banks.

7. Banks hold reserve assets because the Fed requires them to hold these assets. Also, banks hold reserve assets to meet their liquidity and safety objectives.

9. Finance-company-type FIs' major sources of funds come from selling commercial paper, issuing long-term bonds, and obtaining bank loans. This type of FI lends funds to households to finance the purchase of automobiles, appliances, and furniture.

11. John can obtain a mortgage loan from commercial banks, savings associations, credit unions, life insurance companies, private pension funds, and finance companies.

13. Casualty companies would hold municipal securities in their portfolio of assets because they are taxed at a full 35 percent corporate rate and municipals are exempt from federal taxation.

Credit unions and life insurance companies would not hold municipal securities in their portfolios. Credit unions and life insurance companies are not taxed as high a percentage as casualty companies.

15. Diversification will help cover the losses of some investments with the profits of other loans and investments.

   In the event of widespread economic collapse, diversification will not always reduce the risk.

17. Depository institutions have deposit insurance.

19. If a bank has assets of $100 million and liabilities of $95 million, its net worth is $5 million. If 60 percent of its assets are loans, 8 percent of its loans could go sour before it loses all of its capital.

21. a. Liquidity risk
    b. Exchange rate risk
    c. Interest rate risk
    d. Liquidity risk
    e. Exchange rate risk
    f. Default risk

Chapter 12

1. The more competitive a market, the greater the risk of failure of an individual firm from the pressure of intense competition. For example, a banking system characterized by many small banks lends itself to greater competition and also greater risk. At the same time, the failure of one small bank does not affect the economy as much as the failure of a large bank.

3. A bank holding company is a corporation that owns several firms, at least one of which is a bank. Most large banks have become bank holding companies to circumvent regulations.

5. By organizing themselves into holding companies, banks could circumvent restrictions on branching and thus seek out sources and uses of funds in other geographic markets.

   IBBEA did nothing more than endorse what banks were already doing under the bank holding company umbrella.

7. The asset-liability committee is responsible for shaping a bank's basic borrowing and lending strategy. It (the asset-liability committee) goes about its day to day business by adjusting its assets and/or liabilities.

   If a bank sustains a large unexpected deposit outflow, it should adjust its liabilities or assets depending on the circumstances.

9. Liquidity risk is not being able to convert assets into cash without the loss of value. Banks deal with this risk by holding highly liquid assets and backup lines of credit. Nondeposit liabilities decrease liquidity risk.

11. Adverse selection is when the least desirable borrowers pursue a loan most diligently.

   Moral hazard is when the borrower has an incentive to use the proceeds of a loan for a more risky venture after the loan is funded.

   To manage the various risks, most banks utilize an asset-liability committee. The committee is responsible for shaping a bank's basic borrowing and lending strategy.

13. The revolutionary change in banking will increase the competitiveness of the industry despite reducing the number of banks. Without regulation, banks will seek every possible opportunity for profit.

15. A credit crunch is when the demand for credit outpaces the supply of credit.

    Higher bank capital requirement imposed by the Fed in response to the many bank failures of the late 1980s contributed to a credit crunch in the early 1990s.

    Unlike large businesses who have a variety of borrowing opportunities, such as issuing commercial paper, small businesses are particularly hurt by a credit crunch.

17. a. the state
    b. the Fed
    c. the FDIC
    d. the Fed

19. In 1992, the smallest 94.6 percent of banks controlled 24.2 percent of bank assets.

    The smallest 50 percent of banks controlled about 4.3 percent of bank assets.

21. Assuming a 35 percent tax rate, the after-tax return on a Treasury security yielding 5 percent is 3.25 percent; this is .25 percentage points higher than a tax-free municipal bond yielding 3 percent.

Chapter 13

1. Because financial claims are fungible and because other incentives have been present, the last thirty years have seen a high level of financial innovation. This has occurred because the benefits of innovating exceed the costs.

    The incentives to innovate include rising interest rates which led to disintermediation, volatile interest rates which increased interest rate risk, technological advances which affected payments technologies, and increased competition.

3. Financial innovation is the adoption of new technologies and products to avoid regulations and to increase profitability. Innovation will always occur to find loopholes in regulations whenever the regulations are binding.

5. Regulation Q set interest rate ceilings on deposits at commercial banks during the Great Depression and phased out after 1980.

    Regulation D prescribed reserve requirements on deposits at commercial banks.

    To get around both regulations, banks innovated their portfolios into nondeposit liabilities and negotiable CDs.

7. Securitization is the process whereby relatively illiquid financial assets are packaged together and sold off to individual investors. By making certain assets more liquid, securitization reduced the interest rate risk. Mortgage loans and small business loans packaged together and sold as a security are an example of securitization.

9. Increased competition and price volatility are two of the primary factors which inspire financial innovation. Technological advances and new as-

sets have been and are being developed to mitigate greater competition and price volatility.

11. As long as there is profit to be gained by utilizing a particular innovation, the innovation will remain, even after the impetus for its development disappears. Eurodollars are an example of such innovations.

13. Financial claims are more fungible today than in the past because of technological advances, and funds are more easily converted and transferred today than in the past.

15. Money market mutual funds pool funds from small investors and acquire money market instruments, such as T-bills, and commercial paper, that would be unavailable to the small saver on her own because of a high minimum denomination. Money market deposit accounts have no interest rate ceiling and permit six third-party payment transactions per month.

   If I had $10,000, I would prefer a money market deposit account because I could obtain as high a return as with a money market mutual fund and the account would be insured up to $100,000.

17. A group of credit card balances could be securitized if a market maker agrees to create a secondary market by buying and selling these pass-through securities, as they have come to be called.

Chapter 14

1. Default risk can be reduced by diversifying or by utilizing experts to evaluate and assess the credit-worthiness of potential borrowers and potential investments.

   Interest rate risk can be reduced through the use of adjustable rate loans or the judicious use of futures, options, swaps, and securitizations.

   In addition to borrowing funds from the Fed, depository institutions can also rely on their ability to borrow nondeposit liabilities to meet liquidity needs.

   Futures and options can be used to hedge exchange rate risk.

3. A financial crises is a critical upset in a financial market that is characterized by sharp declines in asset prices and widespread defaults.

   A general slump in the economy can create a financial crisis. One party defaults because of a downturn in the economy and sets of a chain reaction of defaults. At other times, the causation may flow in the opposite direction. In this case, a financial crisis, such as a dramatic fall in stock prices or a random large bankruptcy causing a chain reaction of defaults, leads to a general slump in business activity or a recession.

5. Interest rate ceilings for S&Ls were higher than for commercial banks. The purpose of this differential was to encourage savers to deposit funds into S&Ls, which then could be used to make mortgage loans, thus encouraging home ownership.

7. "Too big to fail" is the position adopted by FDIC regulators in 1984 whereby the failure of a large bank would be resolved using the purchase and assumption method rather than the payoff method. The costs of such a policy are that the FDIC or whomever the insurer is pays the takeover institution the difference between the assets and the liabilities of the failed institution.

If I had over $100,000 in deposits at a large troubled bank, and the FDIC was going to use the payoff method rather than finding a buyer for the troubled institution, my funds would be safer in a small local bank. With the payoff method, I would lose all funds over $100,000.

9. Moral hazard is the reduction of market discipline experienced by FIs that goes hand-in-hand with deposit insurance.

Deposit insurance inherently involves moral hazard because deposit insurance encourages banks (and other FIs) to make riskier loans. With insurance, depositors do not keep tabs on how banks manage their funds as much as they would if their deposits were not insured.

11. Bad investments in real estate, bad management, several politicians, and the sales of subordinated debt led to the collapse of Lincoln Savings.

The factors contributing to the demise of Continental Illinois bank are easily summarized: (1) Continental is located in Chicago, and Illinois was a unit banking state at the time. No branching was permitted. Without an extensive network of branches, deposits by households and local firms, often viewed as comprising the stable "core" source of bank funds, were relatively small. (2) Given the small source of deposits and a desire to expand loans (earning assets), Continental borrowed large volumes of funds on a short-term basis in domestic and international money markets in the form of large negotiable certificates of deposit, Eurodollar borrowings, and overnight borrowings in the federal funds market. At the time of its collapse, Continental was funding (financing) its assets with about $9 billion of very short-term borrowings. For it to continue to maintain its asset portfolio, it had to be able to regularly reborrow these funds. (3) Remember that the FDIC only insures deposits up to $100,000. Thus, if you are an SSU with a surplus exceeding this figure, you will move your funds out of an FI if you believe the institution is experiencing some difficulty and is in danger of failing. This means the types of funds Continental was relying upon, in contrast to core deposits, were volatile sources of funds.

13. Assuming you know how derivatives work, they can't cause massive losses if they are used only for hedging.

15. 25 percent

Chapter 15

1. The failure of a video rental store will, for the most part, only affect the store owners and their employees. The failure of an FI will affect not just the FI owners and their employees but also people who entrusted their money to that particular FI. Also, the failure of an FI will have numerous and intense reactions throughout the economy.

While an FI might need to be regulated because of the possible effects it might have on numerous parties if it fails, there really is no need to regulate a video rental store.

3. Redlining is the practice of restricting the number or dollar amounts of loans in an area regardless of the credit worthiness of the borrower.

The Community Reinvestment Act attempted to increase the availability of credit to economically disadvantaged areas and to correct alleged redlining practices.

Assessing compliance with the law is difficult since banks are required to practice nondiscriminatory lending while at the same time focusing on safety and soundness.

If my bank fails to lend to businesses located in the deteriorating downtown area, it is my bank which might be violating the law.

5. The Basel Accord is a 1988 agreement between twelve countries, which sets international capital standards for banks.

It's desirable to have uniform international capital standards for banks because all banks that abide by the standards are put on an equal footing.

7. All IBBEA is doing is certifying what banks were already doing, or could have done, through financial innovation. IBBEA will eliminate most restrictions on bank mergers by June 1, 1997.

9. A credit crunch is when the quantity demanded of credit outpaces the quantity supplied of credit. Small borrowers would be affected most by a credit crunch.

11. Since the regulatory structure will continue to change as the financial services industry evolves, innovative regulation for new and existing markets, such as money markets and products may be just around the corner.

The Securities and Exchange Commission regulates securities (stocks and bonds), which are part of the capital market.

13. Risk-based capital standards refer to the amount of capital the Basel Accord requires banks to hold based on risk-based assets. Risk-based insurance premium is the deposit insurance premium that needs to be paid on risk-based assets.

15. Along with being regulated by the SEC and the New York Stock Exchange, security firms are self-regulated by the National Association of Securities Dealers. The National Futures Association is set up by the financial futures industry for self-regulation. The Options Clearing Corporation is set up by the financial options industry for self-regulation.

17. Yes, the bank had adequate capital.

19. Core capital = $17,750,000
Total capital = $25,350,000

Chapter 16

1. The Fed does have precise control over the money supply because the multiplier linking the monetary base and the money supply is not perfectly stable or predictable, especially in the short run.

3. Depository institutions can hold required and excess reserves in the form of vault cash or deposits at the Fed.

Currency outside the Fed can be used for purchases of goods and services or as vault cash where it is part of reserves.

5. Offsetting open market operations are open market purchases or sales to offset changes that arise in the monetary base because of other factors. The Fed would use an offsetting open market purchase when there is an unexpected decrease in reserves. The Fed would use an offsetting open market sale when there is an unexpected increase in reserves.

7. The money supply will be affected because the deposit in the West Coast bank will be credited to the bank before it is debited from the East Coast bank, thereby increasing the money supply.

Federal Reserve Float is the excess in reserves that results from a check being credited to one bank (or other depository institution) before it is debited from another.

9. If the Fed lowers the discount rate, the monetary base will increase. The Fed does not have absolute control over the volume of discount loans.
11. If discount loans increase, the monetary base increases.
13. $200 million
15. The money multiplier is 2.45. If a depository institution's excess reserves increase by $400, it can safely loan $400. Given a 2.45 multiplier, the banking system will create $980.
17. Reserves increase
Monetary base increases
Money supply increases

Fed		*Public*	
Assets	Liabilities	Assets	Liabilities
+$100 (securities)	+$100 (cash)	+$100 (cash)	−$100 (securities)

19. The amount of checkable deposits at the depository institution resulting from new loans based on the excess reserves is $100. This amount is different from the maximum amount of $1,000 in checkable deposits that can be generated by the banking system as a whole because of the money multiplier effect.

21.

Bank of America

Assets	Liabilities
−$1,000 (reserves)	−$1,000 (cash withdrawal)

Bank lending is reduced by $900.
23. M2 multiplier = 8

Chapter 17

1. A real money balance is the quantity of money expressed in real terms (M/P). If the nominal money supply and prices increase by the same percentage, then the demand for and supply of real money balances stays the same.
3. A one-time increase in prices increases prices only one time and is not inflation. Inflation is a sustained overall price increase as measured by a price index. A one-time increase in prices does not affect the demand for real money balances. Expected inflation reduces the demand for real balances.
5. If interest rates on time deposits rise relative to interest rates on checkable deposits, the demand for real balances will fall.
7. The conclusions of Chapter 3 support monetarism, which is the school of thought that emphasizes the importance of changes in the nominal money supply as a cause of fluctuations in prices, employment, and output.

9. The market for real money balances is in equilibrium when the quantity supplied of and quantity demanded of real money balances are equal.

   If the Fed engages in open market sales, the supply of real balances decreases.

11. The benefits of holding real money balances are the interest payments that are earned on checkable deposits plus the stream of services that money balances provide.

   The cost of holding real money balances are the foregone interest payments that holding nonmonetary financial assets would have yielded.

   Households and firms should adjust their holdings of real balances to the point where the marginal benefits of doing so are equal to the marginal costs.

13.

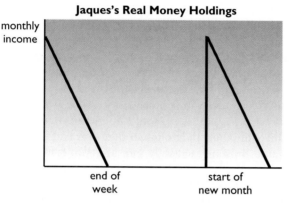

Jaques's Real Money Holdings

15. The equation of exchange is $M \times V = P \times Y = GDP$. If nominal GDP is $6.5 trillion and the money supply is $1 trillion, then velocity must be 6.5.

   If the Fed increases the nominal money supply and velocity is constant, then GDP will (according to the quantity theory of money) increase by a proportional amount. If velocity is not stable, then nominal GDP will not increase by the desired amount.

17. $666

Chapter 18

1. A balance sheet is an accounting statement which measures the value of assets and liabilities held at a particular point in time.

   Due to the availability of credit, assets are not always equal to liabilities for an individual household. In the household sector as a whole, assets are not always equal to liabilities. For the economy as whole, assets are equal to liabilities.

3. Interest rates and income changes will affect spending. To what extent each change affects spending depends on the item or items an individual plans to purchase.

5. a. The household sector will spend and save more, the higher the income.

   b. The more wealth, the more spending and saving by the household sector.

   c. The higher the interest rate, the less spending and more saving by the household sector. Also, the higher the interest rate, the lower investment expenditure by the business sector.

    d.   If capacity utilization increases, so will business spending.

    e.   A change in expectations can increase or decrease household and business spending and saving.

    f.   Depending on the monetary policy, household and business spending and saving can increase or decrease.

7. Money is a financial asset.

9. The stock balance sheet identity is total assets = total liabilities plus net worth. The equation for flows is $\triangle$ total assets = $\triangle$ total liabilities + $\triangle$ net worth.

    Demand for real assets can change if there is a change in household disposable income, household wealth or net worth, the yield or return on real assets, and the market interest rate on financial assets.

11. Most college students do face borrowing constraints. Since college students usually don't make that much money nor do they own real or financial assets, it is hard for them to seem credit worthy.

13. Purchases of nondurable goods don't show up on a balance sheet because nondurable goods are a form of temporary assets. After using up any nondurable good, it ceases to be an asset.

15. Risk-averse investors will acquire risky assets. If these investors were not to acquire risky assets, they would be giving up profit opportunities. Investors diversify their portfolios so that they can acquire risky assets while at the same holding relatively safe assets and retaining a safe financial position.

17. Real assets = \$165,500
Financial assets = \$12,500
Total assets = \$178,000

19. Net revenue = \$12,500

21. 50 percent

Chapter 19

1. The government's decision on whether or not to change government purchases of goods and services should be based on how such changes will affect the stabilization and growth of the economy. Unfortunately, politicians many times based these decisions on political pressure.

3. Government expenditures can be financed either by tax increases or by the issuance of government securities.

5. Yes. Crowding out is bad for the economy.

7. Government securities are typically sold to the Fed or to financial intermediaries, market makers, and individuals. If the securities are sold to the Fed, the government has monetized the deficit. Otherwise, the government has borrowed.

9. If the Treasury increases its borrowing today, an increase of interest rates can be prevented if the Fed purchases the government securities.

11. In what came to be known as the "twin deficits," the record high trade deficit was related by many economists to the record high government deficit. The high government deficit led to very large increases in the demand for loanable funds. Increases in demand pushed up U.S. interest rates above those in the rest of the world. This in turn made U.S. financial assets highly desirable and increased the demand for dollars denom-

inated funds in international financial markets. The exchange rate of the dollar rose, which led to a deficit in the trade balance.

13. If the government's deficit increases, it implies that the combined surpluses of the other sectors must also increase.

15. The government has regularized its borrowing to minimize the disruptions that its financing operations can cause in the market.

17. Case I (Expectations are unaffected by increases in government deficit spending.)

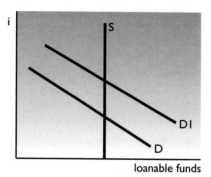

loanable funds

When expectations are unaffected by an increase in government deficit spending, the demand curve shifts from D to D1 and the interest rate rises.

Case II (Increases in government deficit spending cause people to expect higher taxes in the future.)

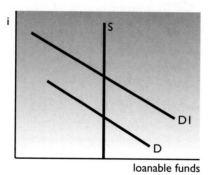

loanable funds

The increase in government spending shifts the demand curve from D to D1, resulting in a higher interest rate. If people expect higher taxes in the future, they might save more and consume less. If the reduction in consumption is equal to the increase in government deficit spending, the demand curve shifts back from D1 to D and the original interest rate is restored.

19.

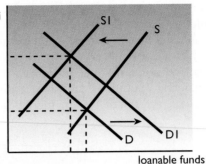

loanable funds

If the Fed decreases the supply of funds, the supply curve shifts from S to S1. If the government deficit increases, the demand curve shifts from D to D1. With the decrease in government funds accompanied by an increase in the government deficit, the interest rate will increase from A to B. The change in the interest rate and the change in the quantity of loanable funds depends on the magnitude of the shift of the supply and demand curves.

Chapter 20

1. Aggregate demand is the quantity of real goods and services that will be demanded at various price levels over a specific time period, whereas the quantity demanded of real goods and services is the amount that consumers plan to buy in a given period of time at a particular price. On an aggregate demand curve, the aggregate demand is shown as the whole curve and the quantity demanded is a point on the demand curve.

3. The major sources of changes in aggregate demand include taxes, government spending, the money supply, interest rates, expected inflation, the economic outlook, and exchange rates.

   The short-run effects of a change or changes in the aggregate demand will result in the disturbance of the equilibrium condition and cause either an increase or decrease in output, the price level, and/or employment.

   The long-run effects of a change in the aggregate demand will be a new set of equilibrium conditions that generally affect prices only.

5. Government transfers are not considered a component of aggregate demand because they only shift purchasing power from one group to another without increasing or decreasing the level of aggregate demand.

7. If prices and wages always change and are expected to always change by the exact same percentage, the short-run aggregate supply curve will be a vertical line.

   The short-run aggregate supply curve is an upward-sloping curve that shows a short-term increase in output is caused by an increase in demand and the lagging of wages and input prices. When the wages and prices are fully adjusted, the short-run aggregate supply curve will move leftward back to the natural level of real output. When full adjustment is completed, only the upward movement of the overall price level will have changed. This upward movement creates a vertical long-run aggregate supply curve. If the price and wages are expected to always change by the exact same percentage, then there will be no lagging in wages and input prices. Thus, there will be no short-run aggregate supply curve.

The real wage is nominal wage divided by the price level.

9. The economy is in equilibrium when the desired aggregate intentions to acquire financial assets equal the desired aggregate intentions to incur financial liabilities. When the equality of the intentions to acquire financial assets and financial liabilities exists, there is no tendency for the economy to change. By definition, equilibrium occurs in a stable state with no tendency to change.

11. Yes, the natural level of real output can change. The natural level of real output is determined by the quantity and productivity of its factors of production. These factors include the economy's capital stock, natural resources, and labor force. Also, it is affected by technology and the economic arrangement of the labor force. When any of these factors change, the natural level of real output will also change. The long-run aggregate supply curve is situated or lies at the natural level of real output.

13. If desired aggregate demand is greater than aggregate supply, the demand for financial assets is greater than the supply.

15. If the aggregate intentions to incur financial liabilities exceed the aggregate intentions to acquire financial assets, the desired aggregate demand is greater than the desired aggregate supply.

17.

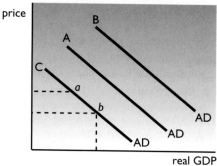

On the graph above, a change in aggregate demand is shown as a shift of the aggregate demand curve, say from A to B or from A to C. A change in the quantity demanded of real GDP is shown as the movement along a curve from a to b.

19. The demand curve for wheat is downward sloping because of the substitution effect.

The aggregate demand curve is downward sloping because of the real-balances effect, the substitution-of-foreign-goods effect, and the constant nominal income effect.

The aggregate demand and the demand curve are downward sloping for different reasons. Whereas the relative price is measured on the vertical axis for the demand for a specific good, a price index is measured on the vertical axis for the aggregate demand curve.

Chapter 21

1. The goals of monetary policy are to design and implement policies that will achieve sustainable economic growth, full employment, stable prices, and satisfactory external balances.

3. Policy makers have to be aware of the external balance because it can affect exchange rates, which in turn can have an affect on domestic employment.

5. Yes, the natural level of unemployment does change; it can change in response to a change in the composition of the labor force, and the changing safety net of benefits available to the unemployed.

7. A supply shock is any event that shifts the short-run aggregate supply curve. The appropriate response to a negative supply shock is to 1) boost aggregate demand via fiscal or monetary policy, or 2) do nothing. The time the economy would take to return to full employment determines whether or not policymakers should act.

9. Cost-push inflation is triggered by increases in input prices.
    Demand-pull inflation occurs when an excessive level of aggregate demand pulls up the overall price level.

11. Rational expectations are formed by taking past and expected future values into consideration. In adaptive expectations, the recent past is weighted more heavily than the distant past. Rational expectations are better suited for predictable policy actions.

13. The stop-go policy cycle is when politicians switch from contractionary to expansionary economic policies. Engaging in such a cycle reduces the credibility of policy makers.

15. No, a person can not be employed and not be in the labor force. A person cannot be unemployed and not in the labor force.

17. Exhibit 21-4 illustrates the effects of demand-pull inflation with no Fed response. Exhibit 21-5 illustrates possible policy makers' responses to demand-pull inflation. Exhibit 21-9 illustrates cost-push inflation.

19. The real after-tax return is 1.8 percent. If the nominal interest rate and the expected inflation rate both decrease by 2 percent, the real after-tax return is 2.2 percent.

21. All of Exhibit 21–6 is the answer to this question.

23. a. Not in the labor force
    b. Employed and part of the labor force
    c. Not part of the labor force if not actively looking for work
    d. Not part of the labor force
    e. Not in the labor force
    f. Unemployed and part of the labor force

Chapter 22

1. The ultimate targets of monetary policy include stable prices, sustainable real gross domestic product growth, full employment, and satisfactory external balances.

3. The recognition lag is the time elapsed between when a change has occurred and when policy makers recognize a change in the economy's performance.

A policy lag is the time elapsed between the recognition of a change in the economy's performance and when an adjustment policy is decided upon and implemented.

An impact lag is the time elapsed between the implementation of an adjustment policy and the significant impact caused by the adjustment policy.

5. Current economic data is more important than forecasts in guiding monetary policy.

The proportionately large forecasting errors and reliance on incoming economic information that receive considerable media attention have created a lack of confidence; hence, policy makers rely more heavily on current economic data than forecasts.

7. Short-term goals can differ from long-term goals when current data on factors such as inflation, real growth, the monetary aggregates, and exchange rates indicate the strong probability of an economic crisis unless the policy is adjusted. The short-term goals depend on how far the economy is from the long-term goals.

9. The Fed has used the M2, M3, and DNFD aggregates as recent common intermediate targets.

The intermediate targets must be reliable, predictable, and observable with controllability.

11. If the Fed is targeting the money supply and the demand for money falls, there will be an excess supply of money available. The interest rate will fall until the quantity supplied and the quantity demanded of money are equal.

13. Without ignoring or jeopardizing other goals, the Fed should do everything it can to eliminate inflation.

17.

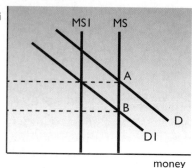

If the Fed targets both an interest rate and a money aggregate, the points of equilibrium in either adjusting the interest rate or money supply are forgone. In a situation where the aggregate demand drops from D to D1, there is an excess supply of money unless the interest rate is lowered from point A to point B or the money supply is decreased from MS to MS1. With no changes in aggregate demand, the interest rate remains at equilibrium point A.

Chapter 23

1. The phrase "slightly more pressure may be acceptable while slightly less pressure would be acceptable" is an example of an asymmetrical direc-

tive. The phrase implies that the Fed is more likely to move policy in one direction than in another.

The phrase "slightly greater reserve restraint or slightly less reserve restraint" is an example of a symmetrical directive.

3. Reserve need is the projected amount of reserves to be supplied or withdrawn by open market operations to maintain or reach the existing levels of borrowings and the fed funds rate prescribed by the policy directive.

5. A system repurchase agreement is used by the Fed for the purpose of supplying reserves on a temporary basis.

A customer repurchase agreement is executed by the Fed for the account of a customer.

7. This answer may vary. Most analysts believe statements made by Fed officials are very important.

9. The huge size of the secondary T-bills market and its considerable depth, breadth, and liquidity enable it to absorb large transactions smoothly.

11. The bank reserve equation is derived from the Fed's balance sheet by rearranging the balance sheet, equating assets to liabilities, and combining items.

Give equation (23–3), $DF + VC = R = GS + IR + L + F + OA - C - TD - OL$, any of the items preceded by a plus sign will raise bank reserves while increases in any of the items preceded by a minus sign will lower bank reserves.

13. $5 billion

15. If the Fed anticipates a seasonal reserve need, it will most likely use outright purchases.

If the Fed supplies $20 billion in reserves, the Fed funds rate will fall, inducing a fall in discount window borrowings.

17. The reserve need is $900 million. If the Fed supplies less reserves, interest rates will rise.

Chapter 24

1. The Bretton Woods Accord of 1944 established fixed exchange rates among major world currencies. The U.S. dollar backed by gold served as the official reserve asset and other countries defined their currencies in terms of the dollar. Divergent monetary and fiscal policies led to the ultimate collapse of the system in 1971 as the United States was no longer able to redeem dollars with gold.

3. A monetary expansion would lead to a rise in domestic income causing imports to increase and net exports to decrease. Also, the monetary expansion would affect interest rates. The decrease in interest rates leads to capital outflows that would further contribute to the deficit in the balance of payments on current and capital accounts. The central bank of the deficit country would have to buy its own currency to maintain the agreed-upon exchange rate.

5. a. Current account moves toward deficit.
    b. Capital account moves toward deficit.
    c. Current account moves toward surplus.
    d. Capital account moves toward surplus.
    e. Current account moves toward deficit.
    f. Current account moves toward surplus.

7. With a flexible exchange rate system, countries in some ways do have more independence in establishing their own monetary policies. A monetary objective or policy would not be compromised by the need for a country to maintain the agreed-upon exchange rate as under the Bretton Woods Accord. Under flexible exchange rates, a country does not have to support its domestic currency if market forces were causing the currency to depreciate or appreciate.

9. With high capital mobility, investors will keep moving funds to where they can obtain the highest return. The back and forth movement of funds will result in interest rates being equalized.

11. A country is limited in executing its own monetary policy under a fixed exchange rate system because it needs to maintain an agreed-upon exchange rate.

    Under a flexible exchange rate system, if a country chooses to run a monetary policy far different from its neighbors, it is limited to the extent to which it can do so because of the offsetting effect of capital flows.

13. High U.S. interest rates could affect investment spending in foreign countries. If interest rates are higher in the United States, there will be capital outflows from other countries into the United States. The capital outflows will result in less available funds for investment spending in foreign countries.

15. The real interest rate is 4 percent. To know the real U.S. rate in terms of foreign interest rates, you need to know the foreign nominal interest rate.

Glossary

Accommodation When policy-makers increase aggregate demand in response to an adverse supply shock.

Adaptive Expectations Expectations formed as a weighted average of past values.

Adjustable (Variable) Rate Loans When the interest rate on a loan is adjusted up or down as the cost of funds rises or falls.

Adverse Selection Problem When the least desirable borrowers pursue a loan most diligently.

Aggregate Demand The total quantity of goods and services that will be demanded at various prices, including consumption, investment, and government purchases of goods and services.

Aggregate Demand Curve A curve showing an inverse relationship between the overall price level and the quantity of real output that will be demanded at various price levels, ceteris paribus.

Aggregate Supply The total quantity of goods and services that will be supplied at various prices.

Aggregate Supply Curve The curve graphically depicting the relationship between the overall price level and the quantity of real GDP that will be supplied at various price levels, ceteris paribus.

Appreciated When a currency has increased in value relative to another currency.

Arbitrageurs Traders who make riskless profits by buying in one market and reselling in another market.

Asked Price The price at which a market maker is willing to sell securities.

Asset-Backed Securities When financial instruments such as mortgages are pooled or bundled together and sold to investors as securities; payments on the securities are backed by the payment streams and worth of the underlying financial instruments.

Asset-Liability Committee The committee that is responsible for shaping a bank's basic borrowing and lending strategy.

Asymmetric Information When a potential borrower knows more about the risks and returns of an investment project than the bank loan officer does.

Asymmetrical Directive An FOMC directive that implies the Fed is more prepared to move policy in one direction than in another.

Automatic Teller Machines (ATMs) Machines that permit a depositor to make deposits and withdrawals to an account even if the financial institution is closed.

Average Daily Holding of Funds A household's demand for real money balances during the month; the amount of each withdrawal divided by two.

Average Marginal Tax Rate The average of the marginal tax rates of all taxpayers.

Balance of Goods and Services Net exports of services plus the trade balance.

Balance of Payments The record of transactions between the United States and its trading partners in the rest of the world over a particular period of time.

Balance on Current Account The balance of goods and services plus net unilateral transfers.

Balance Sheet An accounting statement that presents the monetary value of an economic unit's assets, liabilities, and net worth on a specific date.

Bank Holding Company A corporation that owns several firms, at least one of which is a bank.

Bank Reserves Equation The equation showing the relationship between reserves and other items on the Fed's balance sheet: $DF + VC = R = GS + IR + L + F + OA - C - TD - OL$

Bankers' Acceptances Money market instruments created in the course of international trade to guarantee bank drafts due on a future date.

Banking Reform Acts of 1933 and 1935 Acts passed by Congress in response to the collapse of the banking system between 1930 and 1933, which put in place many banking reforms designed to insure the safety and soundness of the system; also broadened the powers of the Fed.

Barter Trading goods for goods.

Basel Accord An agreement in 1988 between 12 countries, which set international capital standards for banks.

Benefits of Holding Real Money Balances The stream of services that real balances yield defined as the time and distress saved by having money on hand for immediate use.

Bid Price The price at which a market maker is willing to buy securities.

Board of Governors Seven governors of the Fed appointed by the president with Senate approval for 14-year terms.

701

Bonds Financial claims on DSUs; IOUs issued by DSUs.

Borrowing Constraint The impediment to continuous borrowing that may come from the lender's unwillingness to keep lending or the borrower's unwillingness to keep borrowing.

Bretton Woods Accord The 1944 accord that established a fixed exchange rate system among the major industrialized countries with the U.S. dollar serving as the official reserve currency.

Broker A person who arranges trades between buyers and sellers.

Business Cycle Short-run fluctuations in the level of economic activity as measured by the output of goods and services in the economy.

Call Options Options that give the buyer the right but not the obligation to buy a standardized contract of a financial asset at a strike price determined today.

Capital Account The financial flow of funds and securities between the United States and the rest of the world.

Capital Inflows Purchases of U.S. financial securities by foreigners and borrowing from foreign sources by U.S. firms and residents.

Capital Market The market for financial assets with an original maturity of greater than one year.

Capital Outflows Purchases of foreign financial securities by U.S. residents and borrowing by foreigners from U.S. banks and other domestic sources.

Carrying Costs Interest costs for funds used to purchase the security underlying a futures contract plus any transactions costs.

Casualty Companies Intermediaries that provide protection against the effects of unexpected occurrences on property in exchange for premiums.

Chartered Given permission to engage in the business of commer-cial banking; banks must obtain a charter before opening.

Checkable Deposits Deposits that are subject to withdrawal by writing a check.

Circuit Breakers Measures that halt market trading if prices fall by some specified amount.

Circular Flow Diagram A diagram that shows the real and financial flows between households and business firms.

Clearinghouse After the agreement is struck, the part of the exchange that takes on the responsibility of enforcing the contract.

Commercial Banks Depository institutions that issue checkable, time, and savings deposit liabilities and, among other things, make loans to commercial businesses.

Commercial Paper Short-term debt instruments issued by corporations.

Commodity Futures Trading Commission The commission that regulates financial futures.

Community Reinvestment Act Legislation passed by Congress in 1977 to increase the availability of credit to economically disadvantaged areas and to correct alleged discriminatory lending practices.

Compounding A method used to determine the future value of a sum lent today.

Comptroller of the Currency The federal agency that charters national banks.

Computation Period The period during which the actual amount of required reserve assets that must be held during the maintenance period is determined.

Consol A perpetual bond with no maturity date; the issuer is never obliged to repay the principal but makes coupon payments each year forever.

Constant Nominal Income Effect When changes in the price level necessarily cause the quantity demanded to change in the opposite direction to maintain the constant nominal income.

Constrained Maximization The course of action that leads to the highest utility for households or the greatest profits for firms, given the constraints that each faces.

Consumer Price Index (CPI) A price index that measures the cost of a market basket that a typical urban consumer purchases.

Consumption Household spending on goods and services.

Contemporaneous Reserve Accounting A system of reserve accounting in which the maintenance period more or less corresponds to the computation period.

Contingent Claims Claims such as casualty and life insurance benefits that offer the public protection from the often catastrophic financial effects of theft, accidents, natural disasters, and death.

Convergence The phenomenon in which the futures price is bid up or down to the spot price plus carrying costs; the futures price approaches the spot price as the expiration date draws nearer.

Corporate Bonds Long-term debt instruments issued by corporations.

Corporate Financing Gap The increase in a firm's liabilities, which is equal to the increase in assets held minus retained earnings.

Cost-Push Inflation Sustained increases in the overall price level, triggered by increases in input prices.

Costs of Holding Real Money Balances The additional foregone interest that holding nonmonetary financial assets would have yielded.

Coupon Payments The periodic payments made to bondholders, which are equal to the principal times the coupon rate.

Credibility The believability of policymakers' pronouncements.

Credit The flow of money from SSUs or financial intermediaries to DSUs in a given time period, and vice versa; in the balance of payments, any item that results in a payment by foreigners to Americans.

Credit Crunch When the demand for credit outpaces the supply of credit.

Credit Risk The probability of a debtor not paying the principal and/or the interest due on an outstanding debt.

Credit Unions Depository institutions that are cooperative, nonprofit, tax-exempt associations operated for the benefit of members who share a common bond.

Crowding Out The reduction in private borrowing and spending due to higher interest rates that result from government deficit financing.

Current Account Transactions that involve currently produced goods and services, including the balance of goods and services and net unilateral transfers.

Customer Repurchase Agreement A repurchase agreement executed by the Fed for the account of a customer.

Daylight Overdraft An overdraft that results from the Fed crediting a payment in the morning regardless of whether the funds are in the account of the payor.

Dealer A person who arranges trades between buyers and sellers and who stands ready to be a principal in a transaction; a market maker.

Debit In the balance of payments, any transaction that results in a payment of foreigners by Americans.

Default When a borrower fails to repay a financial claim.

Default Risk The risk that the DSU is unwilling or unable to live up to the terms of the liability it has sold.

Deficit Spending Units (DSUs) Spending units such as households and firms where spending exceeds income.

Demand Deposits Noninterest-earning checking accounts issued by banks.

Demand for Loanable Funds The demand for borrowed funds by household, business, government or foreign DSUs.

Demand for Money The entire set of interest rate-quantity demanded combinations as represented by a downward-sloping demand curve for money.

Demand-Pull Inflation Sustained increases in the overall price level due to high levels of demand.

Depository Institutions Financial intermediaries such as commercial banks, savings and loans, credit unions, and mutual savings banks, that issue checkable deposits.

Depository Institutions Deregulation and Monetary Control Act of 1980 (DIDMCA) The act that removed many of the regulations enacted during the Great Depression; phased out Regulation Q and established uniform and universal reserve requirements, increased the assets and liabilities depository institutions could hold, authorized NOW accounts, and suspended usury ceilings.

Depreciated When a currency has decreased in value relative to another currency.

Deregulate The dismantling of existing regulations.

Deregulation The removing or phasing out of existing regulations.

Derivatives Financial contracts whose values are derived from the values of other underlying assets; examples include financial futures and options.

Devaluation Occurs when a country increases the units of currency that equal one ounce of gold under a fixed exchange rate system.

Devalue Under fixed exchange rates, when the monetary authorities reduce the value of a currency in relation to the official reserve currency.

Direct Finance When SSUs lend their funds directly to DSUs.

Discount from Par When a bond sells below its face value because interest rates have increased since the bond was originally issued.

Discount Rate The rate depository institutions are charged to borrow reserves from the Fed.

Discounting A method used to determine the present value of a sum to be received in the future.

Disintermediation The removal of funds from a financial intermediary.

Disposable Personal Income Income available to households to spend on consumption or to save.

Dividends Profits distributed to stockholders.

Domestic Nonfinancial Debt (DNFD) An aggregate that is a measure of total credit market debt owed by the domestic nonfinancial government and private sectors.

Double Coincidence of Wants In barter, when each person involved in a potential exchange has what the other person wants.

Dual Banking System The system whereby banks may have either a national or state charter.

Economics The study of how society decides what gets produced, how it gets produced, and who gets what.

Electronic Funds Transfer System (EFTS) The transfer of funds to third parties in response to electronic instructions rather than instructions written on a paper check.

Employment Act of 1946 The first act that directed policymakers to pursue policies to achieve full employment and noninflationary growth.

Equation of Exchange $M \times V = P \times Y = GDP$

Eurocurrency Market Deposits including Eurodollars and Eurobonds that are denominated in the currency of a country other than the host country where the deposit is placed.

Eurodollars Dollar-denominated deposits held abroad.

European Currency Unit (ECU) A unit of account made up of a weighted basket of currencies of the countries in the European Monetary System.

European Union (EU) A regional agreement among 15 European nations promoting the removal of all trade barriers and the establishment of a common currency.

Excess Reserves Reserves over and above those required by the Fed.

Exchange Rate The number of units of foreign currency that can be acquired with one unit of domestic money.

Exchange Rate Risk The risk that changes in the exchange rate can adversely affect the value of foreign exchange.

Expansion The phase of the business cycle during which economic activity increases and unemployment falls.

Expectations Theory A theory holding that the long-term interest rate is the geometric average of the present short-term rate and the short-term rates expected to prevail over the term to maturity of the long-term security.

External Financing Financing spending that exceeds current receipts by expanding either debt or equity.

Factor Market The market for inputs such as labor, capital, and natural resources.

Fed Open Market Committee (FOMC) The principal policy-making body within the Federal Reserve System; composed of the seven members of the Board of Governors and five Reserve Bank presidents.

Federal Banking Commission A proposed agency that would consolidate the regulatory responsibilities of the Fed, the FDIC, the OTS, and the Office of the Comptroller of the Currency into one agency.

Federal Deposit Insurance Corporation (FDIC) The federal agency that insures the deposits of banks and savings associations.

Federal Deposit Insurance Corporation Improvement Act (FDICIA) Legislation passed by Congress in 1991 to enact regulatory changes to insure the safety and soundness of the banking and thrift industries.

Federal (Fed) Funds Overnight loans of reserves (deposits at the Fed) between depository intermediaries.

Federal Loan Home Bank Board The regulatory body of the S&L industry up until 1989.

Federal Reserve Act The 1913 Congressional act that created the Federal Reserve System.

Federal Reserve Float The excess in reserves that results from a check being credited to one bank (or other depository institution) before it is debited from another.

Federal Reserve (Fed) The central bank of the United States that regulates the banking system and determines monetary policy and that was created in 1913.

Federal Trade Commission (FTC) The commission that regulates finance companies with regard to consumer protection.

Fedwire The communication network that links large bank computers with the Fed and over which payments can be made.

Finance The study of how the financial system coordinates and channels the flow of funds from lenders to borrowers—and vice versa—and how new funds are created by financial intermediaries in the borrowing process.

Finance Companies Intermediaries that lend funds to households to finance consumer purchases and to firms to finance inventories; receive funds to lend by selling commercial paper, issuing long-term bonds, and obtaining bank loans.

Financial Assets Financial instruments such as stocks, bonds, and money, which serve as a store of value or purchasing power.

Financial Crisis A critical upset in a financial market characterized by sharp declines in asset prices and the default of many financial and nonfinancial firms.

Financial Futures Standardized contracts between two parties to trade financial assets at a future date, in which the terms including the price of the transaction are determined today.

Financial Futures Markets Markets in which the terms of a transaction, including price, are agreed upon today for a transaction that will take place on a specified date in the future.

Financial Innovation The creation of new financial instruments, markets, and institutions in the financial services industry; new ways for people to spend, save, and borrow funds; changes in the operation and scope of activity by financial intermediaries.

Financial Institutions Reform, Recovery, and Enforcement Act (FIRREA) of 1989 An act that attempted to resolve the S&L crisis by creating a new regulatory structure, limiting the assets S&Ls could acquire, and requiring S&Ls to maintain adequate capital.

Financial Intermediaries Financial institutions that borrow from SSUs for the purpose of lending to DSUs.

Financial Liabilities Debt incurred through borrowing.

Financial Markets Markets in which spending units trade financial claims.

Fiscal Policy Government spending and taxing decisions to speed up or slow down the level of economic activity.

Fixed Exchange Rate System When countries agree to buy or sell their currency to maintain fixed exchange rates with other currencies.

Flexible Exchange Rate System An exchange rate system in which the value of a currency is determined by supply and demand.

Flow of Funds A social accounting system that divides the economy into a number of sectors and constructs a sources and uses of funds statement for each sector.

Flows Quantities that are measured through time.

Foreign Currency (Money) Supplies of foreign exchange.

Foreign Exchange Supplies of foreign currencies.

Foreign Exchange Market The market for buying and selling the different currencies of the world.

Forward Transactions Transactions in which the terms, including price, are completed today for a transaction that will occur in the future.

Fractional Reserve Banking System A banking system in which individual banks hold reserve assets equal to a fraction of deposit liabilities.

Freedom of Information Act A 1966 law that requires more openness in government and more public access to government documents.

Fungible A characteristic referring to the ease with which a financial instrument can be converted to another.

Futures Contract Standardized agreements in agriculture and commodity markets to trade a fixed amount of the asset on specific dates in the future at a price determined today.

Garn–St. Germain Depository Institutions Act of 1982 An additional deregulation act that authorized money market deposit accounts and Super Now accounts.

GDP Deflator A price index that measures the overall changes in prices of everything in GDP.

General Agreement of Tariffs and Trade (GATT) An agreement among 23 nations originally signed in 1947 to hold meetings that lead to reduced tariffs and other trade barriers.

General Obligation Bonds Bonds that are paid out of the general revenues and backed by the full faith and credit of the issuer.

Geometric Average An average that takes into account the effects of compounding; used to calculate the long-term rate from the short-term rate and the short-term rates expected to prevail over the term to maturity of the long-term security.

Glass–Steagall Act of 1933 Banking legislation enacted in response to the Great Depression, which established Regulation Q ceilings, separated commercial and investment banking, and created the FDIC.

Hedged Reduced risk.

Humphrey–Hawkins Full Employment and Balanced Growth Act of 1978 An act that required policymakers to pursue policies to achieve full employment and noninflationary growth.

Impact Lag The time that elapses between when an action is taken and when that action has a significant impact on economic variables.

Indirect Finance When DSUs borrow from financial intermediaries that have acquired the funds to lend from SSUs.

Inflation Premium The amount of nominal interest added to the real interest rate to compensate the lender for the expected loss in purchasing power that will accompany any inflation.

Inflation Rate The rate of change in the consumer price index that measures the growth rate of the average level of prices paid by consumers.

Insider Trading Trading by those who have access to information before it is made public.

Interest Rate The cost to borrowers of obtaining money and the return (or yield) on money to lenders.

Interest Rate Risk The risk that the interest rate will unexpectedly change so that the costs of an FI's liabilities exceed the earnings on its assets.

Intermediate Target The use of a target midway between the policy instruments and the ultimate policy goals.

Internal Financing The spending of money balances on hand or the liquidation of financial or real assets to finance spending that exceeds current receipts.

Interstate Banking and Branching Efficiency Act (IBBEA) Signed into law in September 1994, an act by Congress that effectively allows unimpeded nationwide branching beginning June 1, 1997, or sooner.

Investment Spending by households on newly constructed houses plus spending by business firms on capital or additions to inventories.

Investment Company Act of 1940 Extended the regulatory responsibilities of the SEC to mutual funds.

Investment Spending For businesses, spending on new equipment and capital or net additions to inventories.

Junk Bonds Bonds rated below investment grade.

Laissez-Faire The view that government should pursue a hands-off policy with regard to the economy.

Lender of Last Resort The responsibility of the Fed to provide an elastic currency by lending to commercial banks during emergencies and thus providing banks with the necessary funds to avoid insolvency.

Leverage Ratio The ratio of debt to equity on a firm's balance sheet.

Life Insurance Companies Intermediaries that offer the public protection against the financial costs associated with events such as death and disability in exchange for premiums.

Liquidity The ease with which a financial claim can be converted to cash without loss of value.

Liquidity Preference The theory of interest rate determination based on the supply and demand for money; it was first developed by Keynes.

Liquidity Preference A theory of the demand for money developed by John Maynard Keynes that results in an inverse relationship between the quantity of money demanded and the interest rate.

Liquidity Premium The extra return required to induce lenders to lend long term rather than short term.

Liquidity Risk The risk that the FI will be required to make a payment when the intermediary has only long-term assets that cannot be converted to funds quickly without a capital loss.

Liquidity Trap When interest rates are very low (bond prices are very high), the demand for money

becomes perfectly horizontal and the economy is in a liquidity trap; the Fed is unable to lower interest rates by increasing the supply of money.

Loaned Up When a bank has no excess reserves left to serve as a basis for lending.

Long-Run Aggregate Supply Curve The vertical curve through the natural rate of output to which the economy will return in the long run regardless of the price level.

Long-Run Equilibrium When all prices (including wages) have fully adjusted to previous shifts in aggregate supply or demand and the flow of spending, saving, borrowing, and lending continues until something else changes.

Macroeconomics The branch of economics that studies the aggregate or total behavior of all households and firms.

Maintenance Period The period in which banks are required to hold reserve assets.

Margin Requirements The amount of funds that must be put down to purchase securities; the amount that brokers must collect from their customers before they purchase or sell any futures contracts.

Marginal Cost The additional cost of selling an additional unit of output.

Marginal Revenue The additional revenue from selling an additional unit of output.

Marginal Tax Rate The tax rate that is paid on the last dollar of income that the taxpayer earns.

Mark-to-Market Accounting A procedure that requires long-term assets and other hard-to-value assets to be properly accounted for on balance sheets.

Market Maker A dealer who links up buyers and sellers of financial securities and sometimes takes positions in the securities.

Matched Sale-Purchase Transactions The Fed's sale of securities and simultaneous purchase of the same securities for delivery the next day or in a few days.

McFadden Act The 1927 act by Congress that outlawed interstate branching and made national banks conform to the intrastate branching laws of the states in which they are located.

Means of Payment (Medium of Exchange) Something that is generally acceptable to make payments.

Merchandise Exports Foreign purchases of U.S. exports.

Merchandise Imports U.S. purchases of foreign goods.

Microeconomics The branch of economics that studies the behavior of individual decision-making units such as households and business firms.

Monetarism The school of thought that emphasizes the importance of changes in the nominal money supply as a cause of fluctuations in prices, employment, and output.

Monetarists Economists who stress the role of money in determining the overall health of the economy.

Monetary Aggregates The measures of money—including **M1, M2, M3,** and **L**—that are monitored and tracked by the Fed.

Monetary Base Reserves plus currency in the hands of the public, denoted as *MB*.

Monetary Policy The attempts by the Fed to stabilize the economy and to ensure sufficient money and credit for an expanding economy.

Monetized When the Fed purchases newly issued Treasury securities, which credits the Treasury's deposit account.

Money Anything that functions as a means of payment (medium of exchange), unit of account, and store of value; something acceptable and generally used as payment for goods and services.

Money Illusion When spending units react to nominal changes caused by changes in prices when real variables such as interest rates have not changed.

Money Market The market for financial assets with an original maturity of less than one year.

Money Market Deposit Accounts (MMDAs) Financial claims, with limited check-writing privileges, offered by banks since 1982, which earn higher interest than fully checkable deposits and require a higher minimum balance.

Money Market Mutual Funds Mutual funds that invest in money market instruments.

Money Multiplier The multiple of the change in the monetary base by which the money supply will change.

Moody's Investors Service One of the major credit-rating agencies that evaluates a borrower's probability of default and assigns the borrower to a particular risk class.

Moral Hazard The reduction of market discipline experienced by FIs that goes hand-in-hand with deposit insurance.

Moral Hazard Problem When the borrower has an incentive to use the proceeds of a loan for a more risky venture after the loan is funded.

Mortgages Loans made to purchase single or multiple family residential housing, land, or other real structures, with the structure or land serving as collateral for the loan.

Multi-Bank Holding Company A holding company that owns more than one bank.

Mutual Funds Investment-type intermediaries that pool the funds of SSUs, purchase the financial claims of DSUs, and return the income received minus a management fee to the SSUs.

Narrow Banking A system that would eliminate fractional reserve banking by requiring 100 percent reserve backing for transactions deposits.

National Association of Securities Dealers The self-regulating agency of security firms.

National Bank A bank that has received a charter from the Comptroller of the Currency.

National Credit Union Administration The regulating agency of federally chartered credit unions.

National Credit Union Share Insurance Fund The insurance company that insures deposits in credit unions up to $100,000.

National Expenditures The sum of the expenditures of each sector.

National Futures Association An association set up by the financial futures industry for self-regulation.

National Income The sum of the earnings of each sector.

Natural Level of Real Output The level of real output that is consistent with long-run equilibrium given the economy's quantity and productivity of the factors of production.

Natural Rate of Unemployment The rate of unemployment consistent with stable prices; believed to be about 5.5 percent.

Near Monies Highly liquid financial assets that can easily be converted to transactions money (M1) without loss of value.

Negotiable Certificates of Deposit (CDs) Certificates of deposit with a minimum maturity of $100,000 that can be traded in a secondary market; first introduced by Citibank in 1961.

Negotiable Orders of Withdrawal (NOW) Accounts Interest-earning checking accounts.

Net Acquisition of Financial Assets The purchasing of financial assets.

Net Capital Inflow Capital inflows minus capital outflows.

Net Financial Deficit When the net incurring of financial liabilities is greater than the net acquisition of financial assets within a given sector.

Net Financial Investment The increase in net financial assets; when the net acquisition of financial assets is greater than the net incurring of financial liabilities within a given sector.

Net Incurring of Financial Liabilities The incurring of debt.

Net Investment Gross investment minus depreciation.

Net Transfer Payments In the current account, the net amount of government aid to foreigners plus private charitable relief.

Net Worth The difference between assets and liabilities at a point in time.

Nominal GDP The quantity of final goods and services produced in an economy during a given time period and valued at today's prices.

Nominal Interest Rate The market interest rate, or the real return plus the rate of inflation expected to prevail over the life of the asset.

Nonbanks Other intermediaries and nonfinancial companies that have taken an increasing share of intermediation.

Nondeposit Liabilities Borrowed funds, such as Eurodollar borrowings, fed funds, and repurchase agreements, that are not deposits and not subject to reserve requirements.

North American Free Trade Agreement (NAFTA) A regional trade agreement signed in 1994 by Mexico, the United States, and Canada to reduce trade barriers.

Off-Balance-Sheet Activities Activities such as standby lines of credit, overdraft protection, unused credit card balances, and other commitments for which the bank is liable but which do not show up on the balance sheet.

Office of Thrift Supervision (OTS) Created by FIRREA to oversee the S&L industry replacing the Federal Home Loan Bank Board.

Official Reserve Account An account in the balance of payments used by the central bank to make official government transactions in foreign exchange to balance the balance of payments.

Official Reserve Currency The currency by which other countries define the value of their currency; used as international reserves.

Offsetting Open Market Operations Open market purchases or sales to offset changes in the monetary base from other factors.

One-Bank Holding Company A holding company that owns one bank.

Open Market Operations (OMOs) The buying and selling of government securities by the Fed to change the reserves of depository institutions.

Operating Target A target amenable to control by the policy tools and highly correlated with the intermediate target.

Opportunity Cost The return one could have earned by using the funds in the next best alternative; for investment spending, the real interest rate.

Option Premium The premium paid by the buyer of the option to compensate the seller for accepting the risk of a loss with no possibility of a gain.

Options Standardized contracts that give the buyer the right but not the obligation to buy or sell an asset in the future at a price determined today.

Options Clearing Corporation An association set up by the financial options industry for self-regulation.

Options on Futures Options that give the buyer the right but not the obligation to buy or sell a futures contract up to the expiration date on the option.

Outright Transactions Open market purchases that supply reserves or open market sales that withdraw reserves.

Par Value The face value printed on a bond; the amount the bond originally sold for.

Pass-Through Securities Securities that result from the process of securitization.

Payments Mechanism The means by which transactions are consummated; that is, how money is transferred in an exchange.

Payoff Method The method of resolving a bank insolvency by paying off the depositors and closing the institution.

Pension Benefit Guaranty Corporation Provides insurance that the pension plan will be able to pay the benefits defined in the pension agreement.

Pension Funds Tax-exempt intermediaries set up to provide participants with income at retirement in exchange for premiums.

Performance Bond A bond required by the exchange of both the buyer and seller of a futures agreement to insure that both parties abide by the agreement.

Pit The trading area on the floor of an exchange where authorized brokers gather to buy and sell for their customers.

Point-of-Sale Terminal Computer terminals that use a debit card to electronically transfer funds from a deposit account to the account of a third party.

Policy Directive Statement of the FOMC that states its policy consensus and sets forth operating instructions regarding monetary policy.

Policy Lag The time that elapses from the point when the need for action is recognized and when an adjustment policy is decided upon and set in motion.

Portfolio The collection of real and financial assets and liabilities.

Precautionary Motive A motive for holding money based on a precaution against unforeseen developments.

Preferred Habitats An expectations theory modification hypothesizing that many borrowers and lenders have preferred maturities, which creates a degree of market segmentation between the short-term and long-term markets.

Premium above Par When a bond sells above its face value because interest rates have decreased since the bond was originally issued.

Present Value The value today of funds to be received or lent on a future date.

Primary Market The market in which a security is initially sold for the first time.

Principal The original amount of funds lent.

Producer Price Index (PPI) A price index that measures the change in the cost of a market basket purchased by the typical producer of goods and services.

Product Market The market for consumption spending by households and investment spending by households and firms.

Program Trading The preprogramming of computers to automatically issue buy and sell orders for stocks as stock prices change.

Public Debt The sum of all past government deficits less past surpluses.

Purchase and Assumption Method The method of resolving a bank insolvency by finding a buyer for the institution.

Put Options Options that give the buyer the right but not the obligation to sell a standardized contract of a financial asset at a strike price determined today.

Quantity Demanded of Money The specific amount of money that spending units wish to hold at a specific interest rate (price).

Quantity Supplied of Money The specific amount of money that will be supplied at a specific interest rate.

Quantity Theory of Money The theory that velocity is stable or fixed and that changes in the money supply lead to proportional changes in GDP.

Rational Expectations Expectations formed by taking past and expected future values into consideration.

Real Assets For households, durable goods and houses.

Real Balances Effect The change in the supply of real balances, which causes an increase or decrease in wealth, when the price level changes for a given supply of nominal money balances.

Real Gross Domestic Product (Real GDP) The real, or inflation-adjusted, quantity of final goods and services produced in an economy in a given time period.

Real Income Nominal income divided by a price index.

Real Interest Rate The interest rate corrected for changes in the purchasing power of money; the nominal interest rate minus the expected rate of inflation.

Real Money Balances The quantity of money expressed in real terms; the nominal money supply, M, divided by overall price level, P, or M/P.

Real Wage The nominal wage divided by the overall price level.

Recession The phase of the business cycle during which economic activity falls and unemployment rises.

Recognition Lag The time it takes policymakers to recognize that a change in the economy's performance has occurred.

Redlining The practice restricting the number of or dollar amounts of loans in an area regardless of the creditworthiness of the borrower.

Refunding The refinancing of past government debt that is maturing.

Regularized The advanced announcements of Treasury intentions to borrow at standard intervals.

Regulation D A regulation that prescribed reserve requirements on some deposits.

Regulation Q Interest rate ceilings on deposits at commercial banks established during the Great Depression and phased out after 1980.

Repurchase Agreements Short-term agreements in which the seller sells a government security to a buyer with the simultaneous agreement to buy it back on a later date at a higher price; when the Trading Desk buys securities on a self-reversing, temporary basis.

Required Reserve Ratio The fraction of deposit liabilities that depository institutions must hold as reserve assets.

Required Reserves The amount of reserve assets that the Fed requires depository institutions to hold against outstanding checkable deposit liabilities.

Re-Regulation The putting on of new regulations in response to innovations that weakened existing regulations.

Reserve Bank One of 12 Federal Reserve Banks located in a large city in the district.

Reserve Need The projected amount of reserves to be supplied or withdrawn by open market operations to maintain or reach the existing levels of borrowings and the fed funds rate prescribed by the policy directive.

Reserves Assets that are held as either vault cash or reserve deposit accounts with the Fed.

Resolution Trust Corporation (RTC) Created by FIRREA to dispose of the properties of the failed S&Ls.

Revalue Under fixed exchange rates, when the monetary authorities increase the value of a currency in relation to the official reserve currency.

Revenue Bonds Bonds used to finance specific projects with proceeds of those projects used to pay off bondholders.

Reverse Repurchase Agreement An arrangement whereby the New York Fed agrees to sell securities to the securities dealers with whom it regularly does business and the Fed agrees to repurchase the securities on a specific day in the near future; another name for matched sale-purchase transactions.

Risk Premium The extra return or interest that a lender is compensated with for accepting more risk.

Rolled Over Borrowing to pay off maturing debt.

Saving Income not spent on consumption.

Savings and Loan Associations (S&Ls) Depository institutions established for the purpose of pooling the savings of local residents to finance the construction and purchase of homes; have offered checkable deposits since 1980.

Savings Associations S&Ls and savings banks.

Savings Banks Depository institutions located mainly on the East Coast set up to help finance the construction and purchase of homes.

Savings Deposits Highly liquid deposits that can usually be withdrawn on demand but not by writing a check.

Secondary Market The market in which previously issued financial securities are sold.

Securities and Exchange Commission (SEC) Established in 1933; regulates stocks and bonds, financial options, and security firms.

Securities Investor Protection Corporation Insures retail customers of securities brokerage firms for up to $500,000 in the event the brokerage firm becomes insolvent.

Securitization The process whereby relatively illiquid financial assets are packaged together and sold off to individual investors.

Short-Run Aggregate Supply Curve A curve showing the direct relationship between the overall price level and the level of real output that will be supplied in response to changes in demand before full adjustment of relative prices has taken place.

Simple Money Multiplier The reciprocal of the required reserve ratio, $1/r_D$.

Sources and Uses of Funds Statement A statement for each sector of the economy, such as the household, firm, government, or foreign sectors, that lists the sources and uses of funds.

Speculation The buying or selling of financial securities in the hopes of profiting from future price changes.

Speculative Demand for Money The theory that individuals will demand to hold money when interest rates are low (bond prices high) to avoid capital losses when interest rates rise and to hold bonds when interest rates are high (bond prices low) to capture capital gains when interest rates fall.

Spot Market Market in which the trading of financial securities takes place instantaneously.

Stagflation A condition of concurrent high unemployment and inflation.

Standard & Poor's Investors Service One of the major credit-rating agencies that evaluates a borrower's probability of default and assigns the borrower to a particular risk class.

Standby Letters of Credit A letter that guarantees that the bank will lend an issuer of commercial paper the funds to pay off creditors on the due date if the issuer cannot.

State and Local Government Bonds (Municipals) Long-term instruments issued by state and local governments to finance expenditures on schools, roads, etc.

Stock Index Futures Contracts that give the buyer or seller the right and obligation to purchase or sell a multiple of the value of a stock index at some specific date in the future at a price determined today.

Stocks Quantities that are measured at a point in time; equity claims that represent ownership of the net assets and income of a corporation.

Stop-Go Policy Cycle Policy that switches from expansionary to contractionary and so on.

Stop Orders Orders to automatically sell if the stock price falls to a certain level.

Store of Value Something that retains its value over time.

Strike Price The agreed-upon price in an options contract.

Subordinated Debt Long-term debt of banks that is paid off after depositors and other creditors if the institution goes under.

Substitution-of-Foreign-Goods Effect When changes in the domestic price level cause consumers to substitute into relatively cheaper foreign goods or out of relatively more expensive foreign goods.

Supply of Loanable Funds The supply of borrowed funds originating from (1) household, business, government, or foreign SSUs, or (2) the Fed in its provision of reserves in the conduct of monetary policy.

Supply of Money The stock of money (M1), which includes currency in the hands of the public plus checkable deposits.

Supply Shock Any event that shifts the short-run aggregate supply curve.

Surplus Spending Units (SSUs) Spending units such as households and firms with income that exceeds spending.

Swaps Agreements in which two parties trade interest payment streams to guarantee that the inflows of payments will more closely match outflows.

Symmetrical Directive An FOMC directive that implies the direction of the next policy move is equally likely to be up or down.

System Repurchase Agreement Used by the Fed for the purpose of supplying reserves on a temporary basis.

Term Structure of Interest Rates The pattern or spread among interest rates determined by the term to maturity, credit risk, and tax treatment.

Term to Maturity The length of time from when a financial security is initially issued until it matures.

Thrifts Depository institutions known as S&Ls, savings banks, and credit unions.

Tiered Deposit Insurance Insurance in which depositors and institutions get to choose the amount of insurance that they want.

Time Deposits Deposits that have a scheduled maturity and a penalty for early withdrawal.

Time Value of Money The terms on which one can trade off present purchasing power for future purchasing power; the interest rate.

"Too Big to Fail" The position adopted by FDIC regulators in 1984 whereby the failure of a large bank would be resolved using the purchase and assumption method rather than the payoff method.

Total Reserves Required reserves plus excess reserves.

Trade Balance The difference between merchandise exports and imports.

Trade Deficit When merchandise imports are greater than exports.

Trade Surplus When merchandise exports are greater than imports.

Transactions Costs The costs associated with borrowing and lending or making exchanges.

Transactions Deposits Deposits that can be exchanged for currency and are used to make payments through writing a check or making an electronic transfer.

Transactions Motive A motive for holding money based on the need to make payments.

Treasury Notes Securities issued by the U.S. government with an original maturity of one to ten years.

Twin Deficits During the 1980s, the high trade deficit and the high government deficit.

Uniform Reserve Requirements The same reserve requirements across all depository institutions would apply to particular types of deposits.

Universal Reserve Requirements Reserve requirements established by the Fed to which all depository institutions would be subject.

Unit of Account A standardized accounting unit such as the dollar that is the consistent measure of value.

U.S. Government Agency Securities Long-term bonds issued by various government agencies including those that support commercial, residential, and farm real estate lending, and student loans.

U.S. Government Securities Long-term debt instruments of the U.S. government with original maturities of 2–30 years.

U.S. Treasury Bills (T-bills) Short-term debt instruments of the U.S. government with typical maturities of 3–12 months.

Usury Ceilings Maximum interest rates that FIs are allowed to charge borrowers on certain types of loans.

Utility The satisfaction that households receive over time from consuming goods and services.

Velocity The number of times the money supply turns over during a year to mediate all the purchases of goods and services comprising GDP.

Wealth Effect The change in the supply of real balances, which causes an increase or decrease in wealth, when the price level changes for a given supply of nominal money balances.

World Trade Organization (WTO) Created by the eighth round of GATT in 1986 to arbitrate trade disputes and impose sanctions on member nations that violate the GATT.

Yield Curve A graphical representation of the relationship between interest rates (yields) on particular securities and their terms to maturity.

Yield to Maturity The return on a bond held to maturity, which includes both the interest return and any capital gain or loss.

Index

Photo Credits

2 Steve Leonard, Tony Stone World Wide; **24** Nick Dolding, Tony Stone World Wide; **44** Win McNamee, Reuters/Corbis-Bettmann; **66** Zigy Kaluzny, Tony Stone Images; **92** R. Visser, Sygma; **96** Ruth Fremson, AP Photo; **97** Brooks/Glogau Studio; **97** Carol T. Powers, AP/Wide World Photos; **97** Doug Mills, AP Wide World Photos; **98** John Duricka, AP Wide World Photos; **120** L. M. Otero, AP/Wide World Photos; **141** Salomon Brothers; **176** Eric Curry, Westlight; **234** Tony Stone Images; **294** David Ake, Corbis-Bettmann; **326** Publishers Depot; **354** Rick Malman, Sygma; **382** Larry Downing, Sygma; **406** Used with permission of the Federal Reserve Bank of New York; **442** Superstock; **474** Rich Iwasaki, Superstock; **504** Superstock; **532** Superstock; **552** Tony Korody, Sygma; **590** Ray Juschkus; **614** Mark Lennihan, AP/Wide World Photos; **638** Mark Harwood, Tony Stone Images.